The Wrong Shaped Balls Tour

By

Dennis Moss

Edited and proof read by Farrah Folami Carrer
and Jonathan Harker
Book Cover / Format by James Gordon
A special thank you to the boys and staff @The Edmund Tylney Weather spoon pub in Leatherhead where this book was written over the last 18 months

Official tour website:-   www.thewrongshapedballs.com
Music website:-   www.soundcloud.com/azboden
ISBN-13: 978-1978074019
Copyright @ 2017 by Dennis Moss
Published by D-Mo Publishing
All rights reserved.

CONTENTS

The Stadiums

Where to next?

Introduction

As soon as I knew I was going to write this book, it was very important to me it was written in my own unique style and not tampered with by any kind of ghost writer, editor or basically altered by anybody else. I wanted to make sure my story was told completely from my own mouth and more importantly, my heart, and solely from the only person who was there and who experienced everything that happened on the tour.....me.

I have never written a book before, so you lot are just gonna have to go easy on me. I've written many songs and most of them have been pretty decent. Well I think so anyway!

I don't know anything about how to put a book together, its structure, grammar, when to stop or start a paragraph, where to put commas, full stops, or any of the other important things (or as I call them...rubbish!) experienced writers use to explain how this writing process works. I'm just winging it as best as I can!

If you do find the odd spelling mistake or error, who cares?, it won't have any bearing on the overall story, I will just blame my eclectic bunch of proof readers!!!

It's not the structure I have tried to focus on, it's the story telling that is important to me and I've done my best to share all the experiences I had in words, as much as I possibly can remember, with the very limited tools I possess.

I have deliberately avoided the normal or usual route of an editor, simply because of the way I want to convey my messages, the swear words I narrate in my own charming way and basically my general use of the English language, which I know is sometimes incorrect. I do not want my words tainted by some person who would file down all of my very rough edges and take away my personality, what I represent and basically who I am.

This is something which is VERY important for me, and vital to the randomness of my crazy story.

I use a lot of my own East London "Cockney" dialect, as I try to explain things in my own mother tongue, but I do put an alternative explanation next to a lot of the slang I use on a daily basis, mainly for my American friends who probably don't have a "Scooby" what on earth I am talking about. (oops, I did it again! Scooby Doo is cockney rhyming slang for I don't have a clue/no idea).

I also emphasise a lot of words in BOLD writing at the end of many of my sentences, purely because I want the reader to try to understand exactly how I was feeling in these intense moments of great elation and joy, as well as huge disappointment and total frustration, usually with swear words, which I have no reason to apologise for. (only if there are children reading my book, and I hope there are...sorry guys, but this is what you will all be doing one day on a regular basis!)

We are all adults and we all curse and swear a lot of the time through both good and bad situations, so I feel these swear words are very important to my story, as they highlight and help demonstrate nicely my emotions in these pivotal moments and these words expressed exactly how I was feeling in those indifferent times.

I believe these words are a very integral part of my storytelling process.

Dedications

I want to dedicate this book to my departed uncle Arthur "Mick" Newman Jr, who in passing, gave me the opportunity to experience this incredible trip of a lifetime with his hard earned cash that he had saved over the years, and in which he left to my mum, his sister and only sibling, who then kindly gave some of it to her number 3 baby, who then had the time of his life.

Thanks Mick, and thanks Mum. XXX

I would also like to dedicate this book to a very special man named Tim "The Captain" Young, a Tampa Bay Buccaneers fan, who connected me to all his amazing "Superfan" buddies across the country, after I had met him in Atlanta on week 8.

To all the wonderful NFL fans who crossed my path all over America, who encouraged and supported me unconditionally on my incredible journey, especially all the truly amazing "Superfans" who went out of their way to help me, connect me, guide me, and most of all, welcome me with open arms into their tailgates, as well as their lives.

Without you guys, my tour would never have been as special as it was. I cannot thank you all enough.

To all my Superfan friends who treated me like a king, I absolutely love you all, you are my friends for life, and it's all your fault that I now support around 20 different NFL teams!!!!!!!

Finally a big thank you to all the fans from the many different NFL fan forums and social media websites who followed me throughout my journey, liked my pictures and videos, as well as making all kinds of good, bad and indifferent comments. You guys really did keep me going. Cheers.

Finding and being D-MO

I've always been a dreamer, a lover of life, a free spirit, a nomad, open to most things, a try anything once kind of boy, but all I ever wanted to be was a rockstar.

Music is without doubt what gives me the most pleasure and has done so throughout my lifetime, but it's also given me a hell of a lot of pain and disappointment over the years in the many bands I formed, managed, financed, and wrote all the songs for.

I learned to play the guitar in my late teens and have been writing songs ever since. Being in a band and playing live to an audience is the best thing I have ever done in my lifetime, without question. Failure at the lack of success I acheived at this, will be with me forever and it's something I simply have to live with and sometimes, it's very hard to.

For 15 years I tried my very best to make it in the world of music, I lived it, breathed it, but sadly for me, I was in bands in which most of the musicians were problematic, unreliable, had no money and basicially were pain in the asses, but all fantastic musicians and singers in their own right. Actually, this is quite normal for most bands.

What hurt me so much, was when these musicians/singers left the band for a myriad of stupid reasons, just when I felt we were making good progress and sounding great, then wallop, the bass player left. So we replaced him, then wallop, the singer's visa expired, so off he goes back to Venezuela, and so on and so forth, so many times.

I was so gutted when our amazing singer Zamir left one of my bands named AZBO, (probably the best band I formed), I've never really recovered from it and what might have been had Zamir stayed, stays within my head full of broken dreams forever.

AZBO did some great gigs, and we had so many potentially excellent new songs that were never written, or half written, or some that were even fully finished, which manifested themselves completely from my extremely unpredictable creative mind, which at the time was like a production line or conveyor belt of exciting new material, sadly never to be heard by the entire planet of music listeners and fans, something which makes my heart bleed like a waterfall.

I was the driving force in all of the bands I have been involved with, I had the complete passion, only matched by my very good buddy, right hand man, partner in crime and brilliant guitar player John Lovell. Together John and I were a great team. I described my songs as skeletons, bare bones, until John brought the skeleton to life by adding muscle to the bones and breathing life into my body of songs.

John had a great ear for sound, production, tone, musical melody and basically everything in between. If anybody ever deserved to be a rockstar, it was and is John.

John always played what I liked in an instant. I loved his guitar playing, style and his brilliant solos. John is a true genius on the guitar, he played lead on my song "Like a Touchdown", the soundtrack song to my tour. I was and will always be John's biggest fan and we were together until the very end of our band AZBO, when everybody else we had in the band deserted us, and basically messed us around, killing my enthusiasm and creative side, which for a while was flowing like a river.

I remember John saying to me at an AZBO rehearsal session, "You're a machine ", after I told him I had a couple more new songs and at that moment in time, I was. I was writing so many songs and good catchy ones at that. This was a time when my creative juices were in full flow. Sadly, most of them songs did not get recorded and will never be heard. A real shame as I honestly thought if we could have stuck together, we could have made a career and possibly a good living from AZBO, touring around this fine planet.

This will haunt me forever. Great times we had gigging around London, usually to one man and his dog. I remember a gig we did at the Bull and Gate in Kentish town, right next to the old Town and Country Club, renamed the Forum. This is a venue where all the famous bands I love played before they hit the bigtime. Everybody from Blur, Oasis, U2 and many many more.

One Sunday night AZBO played at the Bull and Gate to about 10 people, and as we were the so called "headline" band, which incidently does not mean a lot, other than we played last. By this time in the band, I was not only the rhythm guitar player, but now the singer too. So I was getting ready to start the gig and I was probably looking very fed up and disinterested, when the sound engineer came over and said to me "What's up man"? "What's up" I said," there's no fucker here to watch us". "Don't worry " he said, "a couple of years ago on that very stage were three guys from the west country who had even less people here watching them". "Who was that" I asked. "Muse" he replied. "And they played their entire first album that they released later that year". He replied.

That did make me feel better that I was standing and singing in the very same spot as Matt Bellamy of Muse once did. We played our 8 song set to our 10 watchers, including the bar staff, giving them a great 30 minutes!

That weekend Muse played at Wembley Stadium to over 90,000 people. This spurred me on somewhat, but around that time in the band, the best of AZBO was long gone, I knew this, but I did not want to let go or give up the dream, until I had to be honest with myself and John, that I simply was not enjoying it anymore.

The end was immient for AZBO, we had run our course and after around 4 years of making some great music, performing many gigs, times of amazing creativeness for me, intense struggle, frustration, disappointment, but so so rewarding and a whole lot of fun in between, I was absolutely devastated to throw in the towel. I had done my best, but sadly it wasn't good enough and I knew it wasn't meant to be, or it just wasn't my time yet.

Some of the happiest times of my life were in that band and at the time, I was working in the financial area of London, supervising a postroom for an Irish bank, as well as forming a covers band with some members of that bank.

What a great bunch of people I worked with. Anglo culture they called it. We worked hard and partied harder! A very special place indeed, full of very special people, who would eventually lose their jobs and a lot of money in a shares scheme, by the greed and lies of the scumbags who ran the bank.

I lost around 10,000 pounds, but this figure could be quadrupled when the shares were at their height, and some of my friends lost even more. These were the very people who dedicated themselves to build and make that bank an incredible place to work and it really was, only for them to be completely shafted by total mismanagement, malpractice, corruption and most of all greed.

I miss those days and the people I worked with, many who were my very good friends, more than words can say. I must admit, I do live in the past, I can't help it, I simply had the time of my life and I want it back. If only I had a time machine!

I had a very happy childhood in Bethnal Green, East London. I'm back there now living with my mum after moving away from the family home, living with various ex girlfriends and travelling the world over the past 25 years. I'm now back in the old bedroom I had been in since the age of 3. Life has turned a complete full circle!

I loved going to both my schools, St John's C of E and Morpeth Comprehensive. I never really bunked off (stayed away from school) because I was always having so much fun at school. I was a cheeky boy who was always messing about and making people laugh. I was never a fighter, just a fast runner! but I never really needed to run as I had two very good friends who were tough and respected by everyone at the school (Matthew Stewart and Mark Perry) who were my kind of "minders".

From a very early age, I was never a follower, always a leader and always extremely independent. I was in fact a kind of pied piper character and a lot of my friends looked to me for direction and followed me around.

I was also a very clever boy, I was in a small group of the clever kids in my year who were selected to be on a project called "The Yellow Report". I found all the other people in this group to be "boffins", boring and not my kind of kids as they were all interested in learning, or being the teacher's pets! I just wanted to play football, go egging (looking for bird's eggs) go fishing and play out with my mates. I was in the naughty rooms (E06) (W107) a lot for disrupting the classes I was in that I had no interest in. I was even moved to another part of the school across the road, as I could not seem to stop getting into trouble.

The problem was, Matthew, Mark and me were as thick as thieves, little me, and two big boys. We always had a laugh, but it seemed to always be me getting caught by the teachers. I was not a bad kid, far from that, I was just disruptive, easily led, loved a dare, but always very funny and very likeable. A real loveable rogue. I still am!

I hate gutless people. People who whinge and complain, then do nothing, then continue to moan and continue to do nothing. People who would goad me and say " go on Mossy, tell em", and I did, and when I turned around for support, the line had taken a step back. Wimps, the lot of them. So I'm off to the naughty room again! At least if I did moan and I still do quite a bit, I usually did and do something about it until this very day.

I always behaved and paid attention in the classes I actually liked, especially PE, art, history and geography. I always loved looking at maps, I still do. Maybe that was the start of my desire to travel? I also quite liked maths and my marks were always pretty decent.

I've always had an artistic nature, I have loved music with a passion from a very young age, and I loved buying records from my local Music shop "Seddons" in Roman Road. I remember buying songs by ABBA, The Bee Gees, The Carpenters, Smokey, and funny songs like 'Disco Duck' and 'Dancing with the Captain' by Paul Nicholas.

If people wanted a laugh, they knew to follow me, as they would always have a great time in my company. Home life was great with my lovely mum, dad and brothers. We all got on well most of the time. I had a big circle of brilliant friends, always had girls chasing me (sadly not anymore!) most I still see and enjoy the company of. (I mean friends, not the girls!)

I was always a pretty good football/soccer player, an intelligent player, I had a very clever football brain at a young age, I was a good passer of the ball, I could kick with both feet, and I always scored lots of goals, even from midfield. I was like a Bryan Robson or David Platt kind of player, not a good tackler or header of the ball, but I had a knack of knowing where the ball was going and this equalled to lots of goals.

I used to get frustrated very easily as I knew I was better

than most in my teams and when I never got a simple return pass from a greedy player, when I could have easily scored as I was in a better position, or someone could not do something I could have done with my eyes shut, I used to let them know. I never held back my words like most did. I gave them a piece of my mind. It was frustration and something that got worse through my teenage years as a footballer. As I got older, my big mouth, or opinions got me into many problems, as I always felt I should stand up for the "little man" when I thought we had a point.

I remember a game I had played in at the end of my teenage years, when after the game in the dressing room, I screamed at the entire team, pointing my finger and saying, "You're shit, you're shit, you're shit, you're shit" etc etc, and they bloody were! But back in the pub after, I had to apologise to them all, especially the ones who wanted to bash me! But I was right, they were shit, but mainly because I was a good player in a very shit team.

Don't get me wrong, I was never a fighter, but I was cocky on the football pitch, and I gave off the impression I would fight anyone. But this was just bravado, my way of showing people I was not scared or intimidated by them, when in fact, I was, I just made them feel that I wasn't.

I played the last few years of my football career out of position on the wing, basically because I was pretty fast, but I never really enjoyed the last few years of my football career, it was just about spending time with my friends.

My football days ended more or less when I tried to make a clearance from a corner kick in a game, when an opposing player just got to the ball before me, and I kicked the underneath of his football boots on his studs at full power. In an instant, a bump came up on the side of my foot, I still have it to this day. I did play on in pain for probably another season, but the pain was too much, I never told the manager I was struggling, as I wanted to play, but I never really played well again as my pace had gone, as well as my passion for playing, so I was very frustrated with the whole situation and I called time on my football career.

I still get very frustrated a lot on quite a few issues to this day. I simply cannot bear to see people, especially musicians or football players enjoying great careers and getting telephone number salaries who were really no better than me. I know in life it's not what you know, but who you know that is so very important, especially when you are young, it's the worlds best springboard having a friend, or family member in a high place. Sadly, I never did.

It's exactly the same if you are born into money. Unfortunately, I was not. Money gets you anything in the whole world, full stop (period). It jumps any queue, opens any door and gets you any ticket (as you will read later when I was at the Superbowl). Money rules.

I hate to hear stories of great actors or actresses who got their parts as their uncle was the director, or football players got in the team because their dad was the coach or a rock band were signed because their dad was in a previous successful rock band, or pretty Sally got the job in the A+R dept at EMI records because uncle Charlie runs the department. Or vulgar families like the Kardashians or the Osbornes who are basically famous for being nothing but famous, useless and clueless. I fcuking hate this with a passion. It's no level playing field, so what bloody chance have I got?

I like to think I just never got the lucky break I deserved or it was just not meant to be. Maybe I was too laid back, not completely driven, or basically not good enough? Maybe I'm a perfectionist and I have a higher standard of things than some others, but I know I was a good footballer and I can write a damn good tune.

I was also a good swimmer and rounders player (the UK's version of Baseball) I could have played for the Red Sox or Yankees!! I also had a passion for Arsenal FC, where I had a season ticket on and off for about 25 years. Very happy days indeed, until foreign owners flooded the game with dodgy money, cheating is now deemed to be "part of the game" and players who are so overpaid it's ridiculous. They don't give a shit if they win of lose, as long as they are getting their cash. I now despise what football has become. It's not the game I once loved.

My other passions are golf, I'm around a 10 handicap, (some say I'm less!) but I've never been a member of a club, so 10 is about right. I've scored 2 hole in 1's. I love to go fishing, absolutely crazy about gambling, probably do it too much, but I win more than I lose. If I did lose too much, I would simply stop, but I don't and I get a real buzz from it, especially going to Vegas!!

I own a small holding, a hoof! in a syndicate of people who own a very successful racehorse named Vibrato Valtat. He gives me a great amount of joy, especially when we go to watch him run. We have seen him run against some of the best horses in Europe at some of the top racehorse meetings in the country. Sandown, Aintree, Kempton and the world famous Cheltenham festival to name just a few.

VV has won and been placed many times, making us a nice little return thank you very much, I absolutely love that horse. We have rubbed shoulders on a regular basis with so many of racing's royalty, owners, trainers, jockeys, celebrities, TV people and everybody connected to the world of horse racing, which is something that always gives me a huge buzz and a reality check I'm really in fantasy land and so incredibly lucky being in the company of these big hitters or VIP's.

The East End boys mixing with racing's elite megastars and money men, and little old us have beaten them a few times. It's surreal, and absolutely amazing.

Oh, and I also love American Football!!!

I'm a Dallas Cowboys fan, I've been one since Channel 4 started to show a new crazy game called "American Football" back in the mid 80's.

I remember on Saturday mornings watching three new sports I had never seen before, Australian Rules Football, Sumo Wrestling and American Football. I started to enjoy all three, but the Aussie rules faded first, as I think both the Aussie football and the Sumo never lasted longer than a couple of seasons on TV, then disappearing from our screens forever.

I instantly loved American Football, it seemed to me there

was more to the game than just the game itself. It was full of razzamatazz, colour, glamour, entertainment and most importantly, cheerleaders!!! For me it was, and still is, kind of artistic, if you know what I mean?

I know sport is an art and this game appealed to me on a massive scale straightaway. I like the strategy and the fact that all the players on the field are doing something, once the ball is snapped. Not like soccer, as when teams attack, the defenders and the goalkeeper are usually standing still. But this is not the case in NFL games, as everyone is rather blocking, running, chasing or catching, all at once. I find it fascinating.

As I became more interested in this new game, I needed a team to follow to really get into the sport and show some real passion. The Dallas Cowboys were a team I had obviously never heard of and had no affiliation to at all. I chose them not because they were and are "America's Team", far from that, it was purely because around this time in the 80's, I was a massive fan of the TV show "Dallas". That's the truth. I loved that show with a passion and everytime I watched it and it finished, I had to wait a whole week for the next episode and I was totally distraught!

The Ewings and the Barnes's really had me by the balls, parden the pun! A bit like I guess today with people being addicted to "Game of Thrones" or "House of Cards", both which I have never seen. It was not like today with DVD's or Netflix, as back then I would have prayed for that and not have had to wait!

There was another TV show which helped me make my

choice of NFL team. A famous Welsh singer of the 70's and 80's named Max Boyce did a programme where he met and trained with the Dallas Cowboys. The players came across as a really nice bunch of guys. Max had a great time meeting, playing, and joking with the players and I liked that, I really enjoyed the show.

But what totally sealed the deal was the incredible Dallas Cowboys cheerleaders. OMG!! It was babe nation! What gorgeous girls. Of course I had never seen this before and I fell in love over 27 times!! There was Brandi and Candi and Sandi and Mandi and more and more and more stunning girls. That was it, that's my team, after seeing those cheerleaders, I'm a Cowboy. 30 years later, I still am.

Back then in the 80's, Dallas were one of the worse teams in the NFL. I remember my first season, the Cowboys finished something like 2 wins and 13 losses, then 5-10, 7-8, a gradual improvement. Then sadly for me the NFL dissappeared from our screens on the terrestrial TV station Channel 4, to a new satellite TV channel named SKY, which we did not have at our house, so I could not watch the NFL. This lasted about 5 years.

At that time, satellite TV was a very new concept in the UK. We had a satellite dish called a "squarial", a stupid gimmicky name because it was square, which was for a network called BSB, who were the first satellite company in the UK before SKY came along with a round dish, and started buying every TV show on the planet. Ironically SKY eventually bought out BSB. So the moral of this story is, it's not hip to be square! Sorry.....

The American Football eventually went to the channel with the round dish. My parents were not about to break a contract with the square dish network just so I could watch the NFL and rightly so, so I did not see any NFL for about 5-10 years on a regular basis.

Around this time, I was starting to lose interest in the NFL when new teams/franchises came along. When I did start to watch the NFL again a few years later, I did not know who the Carolina Panthers, Jacksonville Jaguars, or the Arizona Cardinals were. The LA Rams became the St Louis Rams (now the LA Rams again), the LA Raiders went back to Oakland, where they were originally from. The Houston Oilers became the Tennessee Titans, then up turned the Houston Texans, another new team. WTF!! Then the teams started wearing these horrible new kits and colours. I did not like the changes, and I made no extra effort to keep up with the game, so I went into a period I called my "lost weekend".

Then Dallas go and win 3 Superbowls in 5 years and I never saw a single play. Now I'm back, Dallas are shit again. What a kick in the nuts! I missed the glory days, the Jimmy Jones era, Troy Aikman, Michael Irvin and many more greats. What a great team and time to be a Cowboys fan. Great?, I missed it all. Now I'm stuck with Tony Romo and Dez Bryant!!! Two great players, but in a very poor team.

I've always been a huge lover of travel and other countries. Most of my girlfriends have been foreign, not on purpose, these were just girls I met who fell for my charms!! French, Australian, half Indian and Czech. I've always found foreign girls much more interesting culturally, as well as having a place to go on holiday to visit their families!, which of course I did many times.

It was also good to hang around with their friends, as there were always things to do, or parties and events going on. Maybe having an English girlfriend, things would not have happened in quite the same way. Great girls they were, and I loved them all very much.

I've travelled to over 70 countries around the world on my last count and there are many more I want to experience before I meet him upstairs, or downstairs! Before this particular tour, 2 years ago I went on an 8 months backpacking adventure, starting in New York, going up to Quebec, back down through the entire US, taking in all 4 major music cities, Nashville, Memphis, New Orleans and Austin, before heading off to Mexico, Guatemala, and Belize, before going down to South America, starting in Peru, then Bolivia, Chile, Argentina, Uruguay and finally Brazil for the 2014 soccer world cup finals.

I've had some amazing experiences in my life, but being inside the fanpark on Copacabana beach with the boys I had met on my travels around South America, watching up to 3 games of football everyday for a month, will always be near the very top of the best things I have ever done in my life. It was simply an incredible time for me.

Imagine laying on the sand, a beer in hand, the sun shining, beautiful women half naked all around, watching world cup football in the country the world cup was being held in? It was absolutely brilliant brilliant brilliant!

I was simply in heaven. I had a fantastic time with my friend Matt Peplow, an English guy I had met on a long coach ride from Northern Chile to Northern Argentina. Matt was the reason I went to the world cup, as I had not given it a thought about going until he offered me a ticket for an England game at face value. Thanks a million Matt, the rest is history and a great history it really was, except England were rubbish and out of the competition by the time we saw the game against Costa Rica in Belo Horizonte. BOLLOCKS!!!

While in Brazil, I came up with a crazy idea, I invented an alterego, a cheeky character for a laugh during the world cup. I was a ficticious English TV reporter on a TV channel called DMTV (Dennis Moss TV). This was a parody of a TV show in the UK called GMTV, Good Morning TV. I did 100's of video's interviewing fans, singing songs with them, on Copacabana and Ipanema beaches, at games, in the fan parks, the nightlife, the bars and basically messing around with my mates all around Rio. It went down brilliantly with all my followers on Facebook and some of the videos I did were so very funny, and mostly done completely spontaneous and in just one single take. I absolutely loved doing these videos (still do) and it was something I would continue to do on my NFL adventure.

The nickname "D-Mo" came from my old workmate, band member and friend Sean Ryman, a name he used to call me in the office. I think he got it from some American TV show, a moniker which gave fame and street cred to Jennifer Jopez, aka J-Lo. So thanks to Sean, (whom I nicknamed "Animal", after the character from Sesame Street, as Sean was a great drummer in our company's band) So D-Mo was born, thanks to an Animal!!

So I digress, what a trip that was, 8 months on the road, across all of the Americas. The music was incredible and I enjoyed my time in all 4 music cities, especially Nashville, as I love country music.

While in Nashville I wrote and recorded 3 of my own songs with some of Nashville's finest session musicians. It really was a dream come true and the results are amazing. Again, I just wish my songs got heard by the right people in the industry, as I am convinced I have many hits in my catalogue of around 30 songs, which I have recorded over the years. Have a listen on www.soundcloud.com/azboden

One of those songs is called "Say you love me". I started to write this song in one of the Nashville honky tonks (bars) after looking across the bar at this gorgeous girl who was with her friends, all good looking trendy younger people. As you do, I tried to catch her eye, but she was not having any of it. So sitting at the bar, on my own, feeling a bit sorry for myself and terribly lonely for some female company and attention, the first line that entered my head was " I can understand the reasons why you haven't noticed me, that's because you're hanging with the "in" crowd".

That kind of meant she was well out of my league and I was basically feeling old, as she was a lot younger than me, just how I like em! The second line "I just want the chance to show you just how much you mean to me, first we could be friends, then maybe lovers?", was basically saying, give me a chance, I'm a nice guy, you'll like me, I promise!

At this time in the Nashville honky tonks/bars, I was hearing the local live bands playing a lot of songs I had never heard before, (obviously because of where I am from) and songs which everybody in the bar was singing along to, except me of course. Artists like Jason Aldean (Dirt Road), Luke Bryan (Drunk on you) and Florida Georgia Line (Cruise), or is it Georgia Florida Line? I can't remember. People must have been thinking, why is this miserable looking guy not singing? Well I wish somebody would have said this to me at the time, as this would have been a great way to have broken the ice and chat to some chicks! Then I could have explained I am from England and that I had never heard these songs before.

So I could not sing along for the first week until I learned the words through hearing these songs 3 or 4 times everynight as I moved from one bar to another. Anyway, one of those songs I heard on a regular basis and fell in love with was a song called "Wagonwheel".

Wagonwheel was sung by a guy called Darius Rucker, who used to be in a band called Hootie and the Blowfish, whom I had heard of, but knew very little about. But then I was told the song was originally written by Bob Dylan, which was a surprise as I never really got Dylan, but he did in my opinion have a few nice songs, but I never liked his rough voice.

So Wagonwheel was stuck in my head when I was writing my song "Say you love me". To be honest, my chorus is a bit of a rip off of Wagonwheel. I don't regret this at all, because it's a great song, which will always remind me of my fantastic first time in Nashville.

Two days later I started recording three of my songs in the studio at the home of a Nashville producer named Jack Irwin. A few days earlier I had by complete chance met a great old guy and bass player by the name of Greg Humphrey, who was playing in one of his many bands in the world famous "Tootsies" honky tonk on the main street of downtown Nashville. Greg was well known and a regular player on the Nashville scene down on the main tourist street named Broadway.

Greg was very well connected in Nashville, so I had hit the jackpot and I was extremely lucky in meeting him, as I was just in the bar watching his band play. The singer in Greg's band was wandering around the bar collecting tips, as the band were taking a break for a beer or a piss, when I got the chance to talk to him. After putting some money into the collection box which was being handed around by the pretty girl singer in his band, who was not only very easy on the eye, she was also a very good singer, this girl planted the seed in my mind regarding recording in Nashville and I thought I could use her to sing on one of my songs?

I explained to her I was a songwriter and I wanted to record a few of my songs while I was in town, she immediately pointed me to the little old guy sitting in the corner with the long grey hair and beard, a cross between father christmas and a garden gnome.......Greg, as he practically knew everybody in Nashville.

Greg and I arranged to meet for a coffee the next day, which we did, and after our chat, Greg organised everything, bless him. All the musicians were his friends and what great musicians they were too. Greg's friend Jack was a producer, so we recorded in his home studio at the end of his garden. What a wonderful experience it was for this boy from the East End of London, to record in the world famous Nashville Tennessee. The sessions over three days went so incredibly well and I'm very happy indeed with the results.

To work and record in Nashville with these fine musicians was yet another massive box ticked and another dream come true for me. I always wanted a famous singer to sing one of my songs, and I thought I may have a chance this could happen in Nashville, especially being from overseas.

Very quickly I learned that Nashville is probably one of the hardest places to break into, or nuts to crack, simply because the level of talent there is so incredibly high, making it yet another shattered dream for me and my music.

Sadly, I heard Greg passed away last year, he was such a lovely old character, a top man and a very talented musician. I loved this old fella so much, he was a real Nashville legend. RIP Greg and thank you for everything you did for me. XX

While recording my three songs in Jack's studio, I had to demo the songs to the session musicians myself by singing and playing the melodies on a guitar, something I have done many times over the years and something I'm very comfortable doing, I love it. On this occasion I had to use one of Jack's guitars, as of course I did not have my own guitar in my rucksack!, so Jack handed me his prized possession, an old relic of a guitar from the wall of his studio and he gave it to me to play.

The vocal booth I was in to sing and play guitar was tiny, I could hardly turn around without hitting the guitar on something. I was sitting on a chair with a microphone in my face, with the guitar over my shoulder.

Then I had one of those heart stopping and embarrassing moments I will never forget for the rest of my days. I leaned across to turn one of the knobs on the amplifier and to my complete horror, the guitar strap broke free from around my neck area and in slow motion the guitar left my shoulder and headed for the floor.

I watched in amazement as the head of the guitar (the top piece where the tuning plugs are) crashed to the ground, and smashed into what seemed like a million pieces. The strings all sprang out in different directions making a funny comedy show sound like "boi yoi yoing". It was like a moment on a film when the picture goes into slow motion and you see the character's face contort, as he tries to grab the tray of plates, or birthday cake, before it hits the deck.

I was in complete shock, numb, mortified, scared. WTF am I gonna say to Jack? This is his prized possession, his baby, his masterpiece. I was as nervous as hell as I walked back into the control room, full of Nashville's finest session musicians who were all Jack's mates and I held Jack's broken baby, smashed into smithereens. I could not apologise enough and I felt terrible and sooooo embarrassed. These lovely people have been so nice to me and I go and smash up his lovely old sentimenal guitar, worth a fcuking fortune!!!

Of course it was a complete accident and at the time Jack

took it quite well, but I could obviously see he really was pissed off. Luckily one of the musicians who played on my record, a guy named Eugene Moles, repairs guitars for a living, and I paid the 200 bucks repair bill it cost to get Jack's baby out of intensive care and back on the wall in his studio.

I will never forget that moment when Jack's guitar fell from my shoulder. I even shudder to this day when I think about it. Oh boy, that was soooooooo embarrassing. HA!

Now I don't claim to be a saint, but I am always polite, I have impeccable manners, can be very funny sometimes, or so I'm told, charming when I have to be and I treat everyone exactly how I would like to be treated myself. I don't mess people about, I am always on time and I'm not afraid to tell people what I think, especially if I believe they are trying to deny me MY rights, what I am entitled to, or especially MY opinion.

I'm extremely loyal and very generous, but only to the people who are generous to me. It's a two way thing with me, and I quickly distance myself from people who are free loaders, scroungers, selfish and tight fisted. Basically, if you are my friend, treat me nice, and show me respect, we will have a great time together and more important, a great friendship. If not, then don't, and keep away from me. It's as simple as that.

I get a great deal of pleasure receiving things, however small they may be. My ex girlfriend used to say receiving was my "love language" and she was right. It makes me feel liked, wanted, appreciated and most importantly, loved. So whenever I do happen to receive an unconditional gift, something out of the blue, say a lift home without asking, a bar of chocolate or even a coffee, it just means a lot to me and I'm just so very grateful.

One massive thing which means the world to me, is when people take an interest in my music. All I want is for people to listen and hopefully enjoy my songs. That's enough and not much to ask for at all I think.

I feel I have given so much to so many over the years, ex girlfriends, friends, work colleagues, bandmates, hangers on, etc, and I've received very little in return from certain people who were in my life and I also feel I have been let down and maybe taken for a bit of a ride, probably just like most of us have.

But then again I have had many people in my life who have been amazing and generous to me too, I just want to get that straight and not feel like a victim, as I'm sure we have all been there. So whoever does kind things for me, I always make sure I return their generosity and love with interest.

I try my best to avoid bullshitters, timewasters and unreliable people. You will read about many of these people in this book. People who offered/promised me things and then basically pulled the rug from under me and not following through with THEIR promises. I never asked them for anything, they OFFERED, and then they go AWOL and even get nasty with me or just ignore my messages of communication. This hurts me more than you will ever know. Raise my hopes then slap my face. This kills me.

I'm a very confident and positive person and try to see the good in people. I have no shame or shyness in talking to anyone of all ages, creeds, colours, sexes, cultures or celebrities, something I needed to be able to do on my tour, as to try to open doors, or just make contacts and friends.

Finally, there is one thing I do hate with a passion, and that's SILENCE. What I mean by this is, say I sent you an email, text message, phone call, a message on messenger or Whats App, asking a question for whatever reason, the word NO never hurts me. "Did you get the ticket you offered me?" "Are you still coming to the game with me?" " Did you give your DJ friend the copy of my CD you said you would give to him so he can play on his show?" " Do you still want to interview me?" NO, lets me know exactly where I stand and I move on. I'm not saying NO does not upset or disappoint me, sometimes it does, but silence, this KILLS me. The not knowing.

I find silence just so rude, and this underlines that you are avoiding a situation we had spoken about and YOU can't deliver. (A bullshitter) There was a lot of this going on from many people on my tour, some of these people I liked a lot, and some were people who offered me things, then never replied to my messages of communication, when I tried my best to makes thing happen or get any wheels in motion.

And women?, blimey, they are the worst. (only my honest opinion girls) These people bloody annoy me and my dislike for their behaviour is massive. This kind of ignorance makes my blood boil. Just answer the fucking message! AARRGGHHHHHH!

People who know me, know that my word is my bond and my words are usually set in stone. I never promise ANYTHING I cannot follow through to the bitter end. I don't mess people around or change my mind. If I say I'm coming on Friday, I'm there 100%, no if's, but's or maybe's. If there are maybe's, I will say maybe, not yes I'm coming and then I don't turn up. It's not difficult is it? This is something I stand by, passionately, always have, and always will. It will be on my gravestone. "I never claimed to be perfect, but I was always true to my word".

I'm not perfect, far from it, but I try my best to be a decent human being. I'm opinionated, sarcastic, synical, hate cheats, especially in sports, EG diving soccer players, I'm sometimes judgemental, I sometimes get people and situations wrong. I think I have a pretty good perception for people I meet and I usually know if I'm going to like someone in 10 seconds of meeting them. I make loads of mistakes, this is how I learn. I should know, as I've made plenty of them over the years and I am still learning everyday.

I have a very busy mind, always have. It's something I cannot control, although I wish I could. Negativity is usually the theme and things most people can do immediately take me a little more time. The analogy for my busy mind is like a constant wheel turning, or a washing machine. My concentration level is extremely poor, as I cannot seem to focus on one thing without thinking of other things in the background of my mind. This is probably why this book has taken me well over a year in the making or writing, as I always seem to find other distractions.

Maybe I have complexes?, but sadly I'm not completely tuned into what they are, but it's quite evident to me they are there. I've been on and off tablets/medication for many years, from pills for depression or anxiety, to things that slow down my overactive mind.

I've tried many kinds of alternative medicines, meditations, massages, treatments, group therapy and even hypnosis. I've really suffered and sometimes still do, and it's all being done totally by myself and my over active mind and sadly, I have to live with this personal torture every single day as soon as I open my eyes in the morning, until I go to bed.

I've been told many times by various people it's depression, but I'm convinced it's not, as I feel it's an easy word these lazy GP's use, just like the word cancer, that is so broad. It's very easy for GP's to guess without knowing the real problem, as the mind is a very powerful thing and cannot be easily diagnosed. I have good days, very good days, and some terribly painful days, as you will read about in the book. I'm much better than I used to be, so that's progress, I'm still taking tablets and they are helping me at the moment. One day at a time.

Actually by this second draft, I have not taken any tablets for over 3 months and I feel fine......thank god. Third draft, it's now 6 months. Most days are good, some days are not and this is sometimes very hard to live with.

I want to give the reader an insight into my background and what makes me function and tick as a person, as I think this will help you understand ME, my actions, reactions, emotions and especially my mental state during the entire tour as you read this book. I want everybody to try to understand exactly how I felt in these times of incredible highs and exciting moments, in comparison to the terrible times of frustration, loneliness, heartbreak and demoralisation.

In this book I will reveal ALL. My hopes, dreams, desires, fears, highs, lows, my personality and my scars. Nothing at all has been left out, I give you my word.

After reading this book, some people may love me, a few will probably not, especially after my revelation of the stories, events and experiences, of the good, the bad and the ugly, in which many people did in fact show their true colours.

The Book

I am a songwriter. Writing a book was never something I ever gave any consideration to as I embarked on my tour, but since so many people I had met along the way asked me if I was writing one, only then was a seed planted in my mind that there may actually be people out there who might be remotely interested in my journey.

It was in fact a journey in many ways as much as an adventure, as I will attempt to open myself up completely for the reader to follow, get to know me, understand what makes me tick and learn what I stand for.

I have tried my best to document my many thoughts and moods, as well as my general state of mind, on my emotional rollercoaster of a ride regarding all the experiences I had on my "The Wrong Shaped Balls Tour".

The book will not just be about the NFL, far from it, as that would be extremely boring, especially for non NFL fans, as this story will consist of a mixture of all the adventures I experienced, including the amazing places I visited, the highest highs, the incredible people I met, to some of the desperate lows and hardships I had to endure.

I include many stories of great kindness, to the complete frustration from so many bullshitters, timewasters and people who promised much and delivered so very little when I needed their help or contacts so badly.

I will try my best to give the reader complete access into my thoughts, state of mind, feelings, happiness, sadness, disappointments, disgust and everything in between that makes a great story of personal challenges, achievements and heartaches.

I'm hoping it will be a compelling read for the NFL community, as well as sports fans, music fans, travellers, especially backpackers, as well as normal men and woman who had, or still have aspirations and unfulfilled dreams, but continue to suffer and struggle to get their projects seen or heard, and who struggle to cope with this frustration on a daily basis.... just like I do.

People who are desperate do desperate things, I can certainly vouch for that, as I did on my tour so many times, like many people do just to be given a chance to show the world they do have a talent, and can be successful. These people will find a connection and a message in my story.Everything you will read in this book really did happen, nothing written is trying to make myself look anything other than what or who I am. I don't portray myself as some kind of modern day hero, champion, or to make any of the people I met along the way look good or bad. In fact, these people made their way into my book and put themselves into these brackets by simply being who THEY were, are, and what they stood for, as well as what they did or did not do for, or to me.

These stories have no exaggerations, dressing up, or especially lies. I am giving the reader a total insight into who I am, what I represent, want, need, expect, fear and resent.

Welcome to the world of D-Mo.

The Concept/Original idea

My The "WSB's" tour was born or inspired from my previous adventure in 2013-14, when I spent 8 months backpacking around all the Americas, starting in New York, and finishing in Rio De Janeiro, at the soccer world cup via Canada, Central America, and 6 South American countries. I had had such an amazing time, especially in Brazil, I did not want it to end.

It never took very long after I arrived back in cold and grey London from that particular adventure, I quickly found myself daydreaming and I felt I had another big adventure waiting for me just around the corner.

So what could I do next that could come anywhere near or match my previous trip of a lifetime? The bar was set extremely high after experiencing the 4 best music cities in the world, (Nashville, Memphis, New Orleans and Austin Texas) as well as the best soccer world cup in probably the first choice destination I would have chosen, had I been given the offer to watch a world cup in any country on the planet.

I thought about what passions I have in my life and how I could incorportate them into a new adventure. Music, Travelling, American Football, Soccer, Golf, Fishing.

Music is my biggest passion, always has been, always will be, but in the past few years, I had given up hope of ever being the rockstar I always so desperately wanted to be, as it's been a terrrible struggle for me to make any headway in the music industry over the past 25 years.

I developed a plan to try to "break America" with my biggest passion, music, using my own material written over the past two decades. But how? I've been trying to be a rockstar since I left school, playing in lots of bands, writing songs, and trying to get them to famous artists, as well as in TV and films, but I've never managed to make THE contact whom I thought would believe in me and my songwriting, and project me into the fantasy world of the successful and beautiful people.

I've had some very minor success, nothing anybody would know, (a song in a film, songs covered by unknown artists) but I never got the lucky big break I so desperately craved.

So I devised the crazy idea to be the first British person to go to watch a game at all 31 NFL stadiums (the two New York teams share a stadium, before someone tries to correct me). What I did not know at the time, was that about 8 years ago, an English guy did in fact do something similar to what I was planning, something which came back to haunt me many times on my trip, as this was the proverbial albatross around my neck.

At this time, I was single, and ready to mingle, unemployed in the winter and not short of a few bucks, so I thought, fcuk it, I'm off. Why not? You only live once is my motto, this life is no dress rehearsal and I'm not saving jack shit for my future, I'm spending it all NOW.

I have always lived for today. Today is the most important day of my life. Tomorrow will be the most important day of my life......tomorrow. This mentality must sound crazy to most, but it works for me, probably as I don't know any other way to live.

My thought process is, I absolutely prefer to be a failure at something I love doing, than be successful in something I hate. So the seed was planted and I started to get excited about the challenge ahead. What I didn't know, was the humongous amount of time, planning, effort and money this crazy adventure was going to cost and take me. There was every chance I had bitten off far more than I could ever chew.

Let's get one thing crystal clear, this was NEVER ever going to be just a holiday, it was ALWAYS about trying to break into a new career, as well as trying to make a pocket full of pictures of George Washington (Dollars), in either of my life's passions, the worlds of music, sport, journalism, TV, radio or travel.

Dennis Moss

The Planning

There was nothing I could do regarding any serious research or planning, until the NFL schedule of games was released in the middle of April, so up until this date, the "WrongShapedBalls" Tour was just a stupid idea in the back of my head.

I could not start organising anything until I knew where the first few games of the season would be, as only then would I be able to attempt a viable route, not only to start in a convenient location within close proximity to the location of the following week, but also the following sixteen weeks of the entire NFL regular season, in a sequence that was not taking me on a zig zagging exercise all across America.

I knew the Superbowl champions from the previous season, the New England Patriots would host the opening game of the season, so Boston was always going to be a potential first port of call, or starting point on my venture across the pond.

Over the next few weeks, I starting to brainstorm about all aspects of the tour, as well as people/organisations to contact, in all sectors in as many of the circles related to the NFL, from players to clubs, different sports stars, music, travel, etc, etc, who may be able to assist me on my tour, maybe open doors for me and people who had a large amount of followers on social media, especially on Twitter, who I could try to tap into in the future.

I did try my best to think outside of the proverbial box and I attempted to make contacts with ANYBODY whom I thought may show an inkling of interest in my adventure and see me, (this little old English NFL fan) as an exciting and unique prospect for say, a possible future TV show, be a guest or a kind of reporter on regular radio shows, giving updates throughout the season, interviews, etc etc etc.... basically anything.

I blitzed and pestered sooooo many categories, sectors, genres, organisations from the worlds of sport, music, celebrity, media and many many more, as I thought surely there was somebody out there in cyberspace, social media, or especially the mass media, who would find this new angle from an English perspective of the NFL, not only fascinating, but fresh, interesting and exciting to follow.

My vision was, that by following an Englishman in an alternative way, or going down a different avenue, seeing the NFL through the eyes of a so called "outsider", would have been compelling viewing for the American audience, not only entertaining, but a refreshing change to the norm of the way Americans perceive their wonderful game.

I honestly thought my tour would interest the American Football watching public in a big way and be a lightheated and an off the wall angle, from being force fed all the usual bullshit by the powers that be in the media, or the usual suspects or puppets on the football panels on TV and radio, having their strings pulled by the devil of all devils, the completely money driven NFL.

Call me a complete idiot, (I heard that!) but I honestly

thought this was going to change my life forever, a fantastic idea, and I was super confident this project was going to be a winner from day one and would make entertaining TV and compelling viewing for my mainly American audience.

I wholeheartedly believed my plan simply could not fail and it was only a matter of time before somebody somewhere, somehow, would hear of my impending incredible journey and they would contact me and run with it.

HOW BLOODY STUPID WAS I THINKING THIS?
Maybe this was the dreamer coming out of me yet again.

I always knew social media was going to be paramount and an extremely important and pivotal vehicle or tool for me to use to convey my message and publicise my tour around the globe. I was very aware this medium is fundamental nowdays in being an integral part of trying to establish a fan base and tapping into a supply line of millions of potential fans, who I wanted to not only follow me on my adventure, but become potential buyers of the songs I have already written and will be writing while on the road in the US. At this stage, the book was light years away.

I started out on Facebook, adding all the NFL clubs as friends, so I had some kind of contact or supply line to the clubs, or so that's what I thought. Next up was Twitter, where I randomly selected hundreds of famous people from all walks of life, from the world of music, the NFL, sport, travel and any number of other celebrity genres who had a large fanbase which I could potentially tap into.

I was basically "dipping my toe into the ocean", or "pissing in the wind", just to see what spray came back at me!! My perception was, if I could get a few celebs following me, the snowball effect would be massive, as one famous face should attract another, and so on and so forth.

This was probably my FIRST big mistake and foolish pipe dream as I never got a single celeb or NFL player to follow me over the entire length of my tour and boy, did I put the hours into doing this. In hindsight, this was such a terrible waste of time, but at the time, I thought it was the right thing to be doing. I just needed that ONE lucky break or connection to start a revolution!

Let's be honest, celebrities are not interested in the general public, FACT. They just use them when they need them for their own benefit. I should know this, I've met many of them in my time, working on a dozen or so of the country's exclusive and prestigious golf courses over the past ten years. In fact I started working as a golf caddie as yet another crazy idea to try to get my songs heard by people in the music industry, people who play at these private courses. That never worked either!!!

I became a golf caddie at the world famous Wentworth Golf Club after being made redundant by an Irish city bank over ten years ago. I took redundancy and did what I do best, I flew off to Asia for three months with my ex girlfriend and lived the dream!

While we were away, we both decided that when we returned home, we would both embark on new career paths, in the fields of something we both have a passion for in our personal lives, not just some shitty new job to pay the bills.

Up until this point in my life, I had been trying to be a rockstar for twenty years or so and I was getting nowhere and things were not exectly going to plan, so I decided to go down the route of my other burning passion, golf.

I put in an application to Wentworth golf club to become a golf ranger, after a guy I knew who worked there got me a form. A golf ranger is a person who just drives a buggy around the golf course making sure players keep up with play and basically make sure everyone is happy and enjoying their games. It was a part time position, a few days a week, very low wages, which did not matter to me at all, as I knew it was something I would enjoy and be stress free and this was far more important to me than any money, as I went back into working mode on both my terms and at own my pace.

It was very easy work, I felt completely contented and it was a way for me to hopefully meet some famous faces from the music industry, who maybe able to open up an avenue, or a door for me, or so I thought and at least keep the dream alive.

It was a new beginning for me and a start of a very lazy lifestyle, which at that time of my life I wanted and something I still have and enjoy to this very day. I do work very hard at making my life very easy!

Thinking I was going to meet THE contact who would help make me a rockstar and tour the planet, was yet another moment of naivety, or yet another massive schoolboy error on my part, and a very long way from being my last. But hey, this is how my mind works, the dreamer in me trying to think outside of the bloody box, but most, if not all of the time, the bloody box is locked!

After a few weeks of working as a course ranger, I was asked if I would be interested in doing some caddying by the caddiemaster at the club, whom I had started to get to know a little from a distance with the occasional bit of chit chat around the clubhouse and the caddyshack.

Looking back now, I have to thank him for giving me the opportunity, and my introduction to the world of caddying, but it didn't take me long at all to see his true colours, the real ogre, bastard and bully, and I grew to loathe this tyrant with a complete passion in no time at all, as this guy had his corrupt fingers in more pies than Mr Kipling. He eventually got his karma, and this always raises a huge smile on my face and I do take great pleasure in knowing that the horrible fat bastard got exactly what he deserved when he got fired. The greedy fcuker eventually got caught, after doing so many dodgy things over the years and he really should have gone to prison. I would have definitely raised my glass to that!

Around this time, I had never given a single thought to becoming a caddie, but the idea interested me as I loved golf and I was at a fantastic golf club with not one, but three amazing golf courses. Not only this, but it was double the money I was earning and half the hours I was doing and there was no future in being a ranger, it was just a stop gap, a bit of fun and pin money and it was certainly not something I would be doing for long, so this new opportunity or direction was a no brainer, so I thought, "he who dares wins".

Once I started as a caddie and became a little more confident in my ability to make people have their best day or experience one can have on a golf course, I totally found my vocation in life. Ten seasons later I am still walking over greens and fairways of some of the best golf courses in the south of England, I really do love it and will probably do it for the rest of my working life, until I become a rockstar of course!!!!!

I love my golf, caddying suits me completely as I like to think I have good people skills, I'm always polite, respectful, and can be very funny and turn on the charm if needed, or if I think my player is up for some cheeky banter or just a good laugh. I'm a good communicator and basically fun to be around. I get good exercise walking around a golf course and having the opportunity to see and be amongst beautiful scenery and nature, is a pleasure to behold, especially when I'm getting paid for the privilege!!

I love meeting nice people, especially celebrities who have the potential to open doors for my musical and golfing talents (but never do), as well as getting some nice tips (I bloody wished, tight as a bulls ass most of these rich fcukers are)!!

The dreamer in me thinks that one day, some celebrity may listen to one of my songs and use his/her influence to get my song sung by Adele or Garth Brooks. This did in fact happen to me with golfer Lee Westwood, who I had dinner with a few years ago when I worked at Anglo Irish Bank. I had won our yearly golf society (not hard for this boy!) and I had been invited with a few of the senior management to meet Lee and his manager Chubby Chandler. They were both very nice guys, great company and I really liked them, still do, and I've met them both again many times at various golf clubs.

Somehow I got Lee to listen to one of my songs on my Ipod, a ballad called 24/7 and he really liked it. He said he would play it to his close friend Ronan Keating, of ex boy band Boyzone, so as you can imagine, I was well chuffed. Sadly I never ever heard from him again and far from not being the first of a million broken promises I will get over the years regarding my music.

So caddie life suits me and not blowing my own trumpet, I'm actually pretty good at it, it suits me like a hand in glove, but sadly the reason I came into this world was to get contacts for my music and songwriting and after ten years of caddying, I have never met a single person in the music industry who gave me the time of day.

I once caddied in a group behind the manager of Iron Maiden, a guy named Robert Stigwood. I was told who he was by the guy I caddied for, who was in his party of friends, but in the next four ball, the group in front.

I said hello to him at the start before he tee'd off and he seemed OK, but I could see he could be a difficult and abrupt man, so I just smiled and said hello, then he played his first tee shot and off his group went.

Iron Maiden are one of my favourite bands and they come from up the road from where I'm from and now live in East London. So by chance we caught up the group in front of us and I bumped into Mr Stigwood at the half way hut and as he walked past me, I said, " Mr Stigwood, What's your favourite Iron Maiden song"? His response shocked the life out of me when he rudely ranted, " Oh come on, it's my day off".

I can kind of understand his answer, but I just thought, you rude old cunt! What was that for? It would have taking just one or two words from him to just throw a song at me, but no, he acted like some real prick, like his shit didn't stink. I did not deserve that kind of response, but this is what you sometimes have to expect from the world of celebrities.

Of course not all of them are like that, but a lot are, some really are out of touch with the real or poor world, but when another celeb turns up, they are a different breed, thick as thieves and as fake as a cake, on the wheel of fortune and forgetting that most of us put them where they are today. I can tell you so many more stories of celebrity retorts or blanks as I call them, as I have had them in abundance over the years.

A real breed these people can be, they love it so much when they get treated like kings and get everything for free, things worth 100's of notes, but when they have to dip into their own pockets for a tip for the caddie who has given so much time, patience and most importantly, help around the golf course, and listened to 5 hours of their bullshit and bragging, not much manifests from their pockets to put a smile on our faces.

As a golf caddie, we rely on tips to make up our wages as our retainer or basic wage from the start is quite basic to say the least. I've only been knocked (not given a tip) once and that was from the ex England cricket captain Michael Vaughan. I spend almost six hours in Michael's company and to be fair, he was a really nice and friendly guy and I liked him a lot. He was a pretty good golfer as you would expect as he was once a great cricketer.

So over the next six hours, Michael informed me he was a director of four companies, worked on the Indian cricket league and was a current contestant on the UK TV show "Strictly Come Dancing". So he was not short of a few bob. Bloody far from it.

The golf day in question was at Wentworth and sponsored by the betting company Betfair, so Michael got the full royal treatment for free, including a £360 round of golf and a caddie (me).

At the end of the game, he said "Thanks Dennis, you have been an excellent caddie and great company. Take this Betfair cap as I'm already sponsored and I cannot be photographed wearing this hat, as my sponsors would go mad". Then he walked off. All the other caddies got tipped and I stood there looking like a fcuking scrounger, or a spare one at a wedding! What a tight fisted bastard, I was so shocked. I never saw that coming in a 1000 years. When I saw him on "Strictly Come Dancing", it made my blood boil and I always wanted him to fall on his bloody tight ass! PRICK.

So April 18th (I think it was), and the day of reckoning came, the 2015-16 NFL schedule of games was released. I was so excited, as the wait was over and this was basically the beginning of the next few months of hours and hours of research and the planning of my NFL tour.

I printed out all seventeen weeks of the schedule from NFL.com and pinned them to my wall. Now I had the labourious task of finding a convenient route around the US without zig zagging all over the place.

If you have the money, flying from one game to the next would be very easy, but for me it was not about that, as that option was no challenge to me at all, as well as being totally out of my budget of course. The initial plan for me was to fly as little as possible, only when it was absolutely necessary, as to cut down the cost of travel and use the cheaper options of Megabus and the dreaded Greyhound buses.

I thought that finding a convenient route around the country was going to be a fairly easy task. OH BOY, how wrong was I? I swear it took me almost two weeks to find a route that was not only accessible, but achievable within the seventeen weeks of the regular season.

New England, or Boston, where the Patriots play their games, was always going to be the number one place for me to start, for three reasons. Firstly, New England were to host the opening game of the season on a Thursday night, as they were the reigning Superbowl winners of the previous season and that's what happens when a team wins a Superbowl.

If I did not attend the first game in New England, I would have to go there at a later date, to a stadium which was the furthest in the northeast and pretty far from a lot of the other stadiums in the north. Secondly was the fact that Thursday games were by far the most important games on my schedule, because Thursday games allowed me the time to move onto the Sunday games, which gave me the choice of fourteen other games at attend, with maybe more than one option and not too far from where I would be on a Thursday.

Monday games were not as important as Thursday ones because most of the time it was not possible to get from a Sunday game to a next day Monday night game unless I was going to fly. Again this was purely down to dollars, as I did look into this, but the flights were always very expensive, probably because the airlines knew there would be fans flying into these cities on game days, so upping their prices.

Thirdly was the weather. This was always going to be a huge factor in my decision making to choose where I was going in certain months. My intention was always to start in the north where the weather was mild in September, as the south is very hot and sticky in the US at this time, and I was advised by a few American people I had spoken to, as to avoid the sweaty and humid south at the beginning of my tour.

This was perfect because I knew by mid October, the north would be starting to get colder and I had already seen a game in New York in December and I knew how freezing bloody cold that was. So I wanted to be in the south before the end of November if possible.

I started to look at the seventeen weeks of schedule on my bedroom wall and I attempted to search for a logical or methodical route around America without too much backtracking. I looked and I looked and I looked and I looked.

I challenge anybody reading this (and I hope there are a few people reading!) to take this years NFL schedule, and try to make a route around the country, that is in some kind of an order. Remember, you need to see a game in all 31 stadiums in the seventeen weeks of the regular season.

It's easy to do if you want to fly from say Miami to Seattle, then Seattle to San Diego, then San Diego to Baltimore etc. But my plan was to go to, say, New York, then Buffalo, then Cleveland, then Cincinnati, etc, all kind of in close proximity to each other, all on buses, no flights unless totally necessary, again because of the dollar effect.

Everytime I got into a nice little route in the planning, I came up against a brick wall, meaning there were no games near where I would be in say week six, or I had already been there, or the Thursday night game was miles away, etc etc. This happened many times for many reasons. Remember teams only play eight home games, so if the team you plan to go to see next are at home (say Chicago), on the same day as the game you are already at, (say Pittsburgh), then that team (Chicago) normally will be in another part of the country on a road/away game the following week, so you have to try to attend another game near Pittsburgh, (say Detroit, but they may also be on a road/away game) and make your way back to the one you could not go to, (Chicago) before you are too far away from this part of the country, making coming back to this area not logical and collating an enormous amount of unnecessary air miles in the process. (Have I lost you yet)? I hope not, it gets better!

So after a couple of hours of staring at the wall, I had to stop and regroup. It was a real mental workout, something I would then go back to and start again and again, and again. I would sometimes get as far as week eleven, then the chain would break again.

I remember my mum poking her head around my bedroom door and saying to me "what are you doing? you're very quiet"? "Well Mum" I replied, "I'm trying to work my way around America"!! It really was a task.

I decided the best course of action for me was to split the country into four sections. Northeast, Southeast, Middle America and the West Coast. The West Coast was in fact a real pain in the back passage!, only four teams, but very far apart in distance, two in the same city, but never playing at their home stadiums in consecutive days on the schedule and sometimes playing at home on the same day. Impossible!

I decided to leave most of the west coast until last, firstly because of the weather and secondly because Superbowl 50 was going to be in San Francisco. My original plan was just to attend all 31 stadiums in the seventeen weeks of the regular season, chill out in LA with my good friend Jorge Gonzalez and his family for a few weeks, then watch the Superbowl with Jorge and his friends at a Superbowl house party, something which we did two years earlier.

As I mentioned there are only 8 home games for each team, this meant that in most cases I had only one chance in the schedule to be in a certain city which benefitted the whole route, because TV dictates the dates of the games and the more successful teams are usually more likely to be selected for the Monday and Thursday night games.

For example, if a team plays a game on a Thursday night, say the New England Patriots and I attend this game, then obviously I will not be seeing another game in New England. So if I go to New England, the next game I want to attend should be relatively close to New England, so I will then look at going to say Buffalo. But then later on in the schedule, Buffalo play at their stadium on a Thursday, but I would have already been to Buffalo, so the chain breaks or then I don't go to a Thursday game and I have to find a place later in the season to fit in another game as I will run out of time trying to get to 31 games into seventeen weeks. Phew.... are you still with me? This is only the beginning.

So basically I have to do 2 games a week for fourteen weeks and three weeks of a single game, including the last week where all 32 teams play on the same day. Confused? welcome to my world.

So what I decided to do next was just get as many blocks of games in a good little route as I could. All three games in Florida worked perfect. Two of the games were to see my Cowboys play on consecutive Sundays, which was important to me as a Cowboys fan to see as many of their games as possible.

Sandwiched in between those two Cowboys games was an invitation from the owner of the Jacksonville Jaguars Mr Shad Khan, to watch a game with him in his private box. So that worked out perfect. I'll be telling you a lot more about this encounter later on.

One team or place, that was always going to be a problem for me was Kansas City. Kansas was a place that never really fit into any of my so called blocks of cities until week 14. But that week I eventually went to Denver because it was after a Monday night game in Phoenix Arizona and onto a Thursday night game in St Louis on week fifteen, a long convenient line through middle America. My only choice for going to Kansas City was on week two at the Thursday night game, but this was going completely out of my way, something I never ever wanted to do, but this time, I simply had no other choice.

Minneapolis was also a problem and I found this location convenient only twice in the entire schedule, where I could get this city to on a respectable route. Week three on Sunday looked very interesting to go to Minneapolis, as on the following day, Monday Night Football, the Green Bay Packers played and they were only up the road so to speak, (seven hours by bus, as I later found!) and this was the only time these two divisional rivals played on consecutive days, giving me the chance to do both teams in succession, before the winter set in and the snow came to this freezing cold part of the US after October.

This got me excited, as now I saw an opportunity to do three games in a week, which gave me a little breathing space of not having to do two games every single week of the seventeen weeks I had, and this gave me a valuable piece of time to play with and do just one game in a week, later on in the schedule. This was something that worked brilliantly for me, so it was definitely worth the effort trying to find these little diamonds or so called lucky local geographical fixtures in the schedule.

I got there in the end and it did indeed take me well over two weeks to finally settle with what I eventually did. The first four weeks would be a bit of a zig zag flying session, actually three flights, but I simply had no choice. Once I got to Houston on week five, I never took a flight for about six weeks, just lots of long bus rides on the lovely Greyhound buses. But at least it would be a lot cheaper and an adventure.

After the middle section of not flying, I only had about twelve games left and I now had to fly to most of them. So after spending around two weeks of staring at my bedroom wall, I had finally worked out a route that would take in all 31 stadiums in the seventeen weeks of the NFL regular season. I'm sure if I tried to do it again for another season, maybe I would manage to find an easier route, but boy was that a workout for my old brain!!

A major factor which influenced the final choice of schedule I eventually settled for, was because I wanted to see as many Cowboys games on the tour as I possible could, as well as a couple of stand out games that were on the calendar and which caught my attention and which I really wanted to see.

Finishing the schedule was a very important stage of the planning process and now it was done, the tour was starting to feel very real for the first time since I dreamed up this crazy adventure and excitement was now growing bigger inside me every day.

The next subject or hurdle of major importance on my very

long to do list, was to apply for and to obtain my US visa. Without this visa, there would be no tour. It would have been easy for me to get a three months visa called an ESTA, as I had already had this 4-5 times before, but I was aware I would have to apply for a visa lasting six months and I would have to go to the US Embassy in London to get it. There was no guarantee at all I would even get this visa, but I set the wheels in motion by applying and filling out a humongous online questionnaire.

A week or so later I received the information/documentation I needed to attend an interview at the US Embassy in London, to inform them of my impending plans while in the US. I had to prove and show the embassy staff I had enough money to support myself and that I was not going to disappear while in the US or going there to work. Oh and to give them my cheque for £175 quid for the visa. Ouch!!

So off I go to the US Embassy at 8am one Monday morning, with all my relevant documents in hand. When I arrived, I was horrified to see a very long queue outside. I had expected a personal interrogation, not a huge long line of people, but it was just security and the first line I was in went through a metal detector, the second into the building, the third into the correct room and so on.

Surprisingly it eventually turned into a very smooth process indeed. For some reason I was a little nervous, I don't know why as I had nothing at all to hide, but I knew this process was the difference as to whether this tour would happen or not. It was just a hurdle I needed to climb over before my tour would become very real.

I was questioned by an officer for a few minutes, I easily answered all the questions he threw at me, even a few googlies (curve balls) to try to trip me up, or basically see if I was a threat to his country. And then BOSH, he gave my documents the stamp of approval and the green light to my application. BINGO!

I left the US Embassy feeling somewhat emotional, as this adventure was now very real indeed, and no longer just a crazy idea or pipe dream. It was now definately going to happen, it was no longer fantasy, it was alive and kicking and very very exciting. I was finally happy I could now proceed to my next step and book my flight to America.

I called Trailfinders, the flight company I normally use,and I booked a flight from London to Boston, arriving on the 8th of September and returning home out of Los Angeles on February the 29th 2016. Little did I know then I would not take the return back from LA, but instead head off to the land of the rising sun...Japan.

The flight was not as expensive as I had expected, less than 600 quid and a flexible flight I could change the return date, if I wanted to, for a small fee. (something I very nearly did, more than once) So I just gave a random return date of the 29th of Feb, knowing I would more than likely change this date to stay away from home longer. Which of course I eventually did.

Now I had my flight booked, over the next 4-6 weeks I was on my computer 7-8 hours a day, sometimes more when I was not working on the golf course. A few hours a day even when I was. I tried my best to network, to touch base, make contact to as many people, companies, teams of all kinds, in all sports, individuals, organisations, institutions, friends, contacts, you name it, I contacted them, mainly by social media. I was so confident and driven I was going to make this tour something very special and life changing for me and I was not gonna fail, no sir.

On Twitter I followed as many people as I was allowed, 2000 was the maximum and I was extremely optimistic at least some, even a fraction of the people I contacted would be interested in my adventure and this could lead me somewhere interesting and off we go.

On Facebook I contacted every NFL club, as well so many of the fan forums, including most of the UK and US based NFL fan clubs on both sides of the pond. I then started on Instagram, a forum I had used on my last trip, but I was not sure how this would benefit me, other than me showing people my pictures. I also heard of a new medium called "Periscope" which I looked into. I thought Periscope may have some mileage for me, so I opened up an account and started playing around with it.

Once I got to America, I did start posting some live videos from a few stadiums on Periscope, but I quickly realised this forum was not going to be as successful as I wanted or had hoped. People seemed more interested in following some bored and foul mouthed dumb young chick, who just whinged at the camera while walking around her home doing practically nothing but chat shit, and was always threatening or promising to get her tits out, if just a few more sad people would increase her viewing figures, which would probably raise her profile, and entice a whole new bunch of perverted followers, in the hope they may see a little piece of her flesh, which incidentally never happened, as I followed her myself a few more times and I never saw a nip or a boob in anger from the bitch!!!

These kind of people posting random rubbish were getting a lot of followers. Some as many as almost 1000 people at a time, but sadly when I posted what I thought were far more interesting videos, I would be getting less than 10 people at most.

So I tried a little trick, call it reverse psychology, while I was in America at the start of my tour. I was inside a stadium, Washington I think it was and I posted a video after the Redskins game against the Dolphins, just explaining what a lovely stadium it was and a little report on how the game went. I titled the clip "Two young naked lesbians having a pillow fight". That clip got more views or people watching live than any other video I did. It only attracted about twenty five people, not a lot, but double my usual amount and for me People turned in to Periscope for all the wrong reasons, so I gave up on that piece of shit before it ever really got off the ground.

It was an extremely laborious task trying to make contacts and gain any kind of interest in any of the areas I attempted. It was actually quite enjoyable in the beginning, but lots and lots and lots of internet research, most of it was hitting a complete brick wall of silence, but I did start to pick up lots of friends and followers, especially from the NFL fan groups, who did support me from the very beginning.

The hardest nut for me to crack without any shadow of a

doubt was the media. Am I really that foolish or stupid to believe maybe just one person from the media on either side of the pond, would take the smallest amount of interest in this crazy Englishman travelling across the Atlantic to watch a NFL game in every stadium in the country in one season?, trying to get his music heard by the masses and played at NFL stadiums and trying to raise money for two prostate cancer charites in the process? I actually thought it would be a story the American media and public would embrace with open arms.

Hindsight is a wonderful thing indeed, and only now can I admit what a silly old fool I had been, and yes I am very very bloody damn stupid to believe I would attract any interest at all from any of the many TV and radio networks.

Maybe that's a little harsh on myself as at the time I was super confident, I had a vision, hope, a dream. Naive is probably a better description, but what I really needed, or prayed for was a big stroke of luck, as after a million messages I sent out to the universe via social media, surely one, JUST ONE would brush, or miraculously find it's way to the right email address, inbox, or wall of somebody's facebook page completely by chance or default and push me in the right direction. PLLEEEAASSSEEEEEEE!

The name "The Wrong Shaped Balls" Tour came from a very flippant and sarcastic remark I made to my good friend Kevin James, who while sitting in the local Costa Coffee shop we used to meet in when I lived in the lovely area of Putney in West London, Kevin dropped the bombshell he had been diagnosed with prostate cancer.

My instant reply to Kevin's terrible news, jokingly was, "You have got the wrong shaped balls mate"! Kevin's immediate response to my flippant remark was, "That would be a fantastic name for your tour". So there you have it, that's where the name "The Wrong Shaped Balls Tour" was born.

Kevin had prostate cancer and I now had the name of my tour, all thanks to my poor friend's misfortune. I'm very happy to tell you Kevin has fully recovered from his cancer and I am over the moon he has, as he really is a lovely man and my good friend.

Kevin also suggested that while I was on my tour, I should try to raise some money for charity. His very words were, "the Americans do love a charity" and he was right, they do.

Charity is a topic I have very mixed feelings and reservations about, as after seeing a TV program a few years ago highlighting the fact that for every pound raised for certain charities, the charities or people/animals/whatever benefitting from these charities, would be lucky to see 3p from every pound generated, so I am very wary and sceptical of this kind of fundraising. This TV program showed how the management of many of these charities were earning big salaries, all coming out of the money which should have been going directly, or so the public thought, to the people or organisations who really needed it. One guy was earning almost 100k per year and his salary was coming out of the donations and this made my blood boil. This is not my idea of charity, it should not be somebody's career.

I fully understand that people need to be paid for their time to make money for their charities, but again on the TV program I watched, some people were drinking champagne in plush hotels and basically spending the charity's money like it was their own and going out of fashion. So I had my reservations about getting involved in charity work, but I thought it would definately be a way of raising my profile, making me good contacts and basically opening a few doors. Yet again, how stupid was I? As I will explain, the charity project I tried to get involved with was doomed even before I left the UK.

One thing I do admit to and I fully hold my hands up for, was that the whole charity thing was without any question of a doubt a way, a springboard, or a vehicle for raising MY OWN profile and to help ME get people interested in my tour. Once I did decide I was going to try to raise money and awareness, I did in fact have every intention of doing my best, in raising money for two prostate cancer charities, one on each side of the Atlantic. But to be honest, always in the back of my mind was any which way, that I could promote MYSELF.

Isn't this what every pop star, sports star or celeb does when any charity event happens for all kinds of reasons?? Are they really interested in the charity itself? REALLY? We all know the answer, it's usually to help promote themselves, their new song, book, movie, or make themselves look kind, caring, human. Bullshit, bullshit, publicity, gravy train etc etc etc.

Of course not all, but just most, anything to keep up with the celebrity bubble or in crowd, and of course, keep the pictures of old Georgie Wash flowing through their bank accounts............off shore of course!

So why don't I join the club?, VIP area, or climb aboard the gravy train? you guys should know by now how much I love trains!! So I tried, and yes, I FAILED, as I never managed to ascertain one single freebie or back stage pass!

An amazing coincidence occurred while I was in the studio working on and recording my new track, the soundtrack song to the tour, called "Like a Touchdown", with my very talented producer friend Felix Macintosh.

I mentioned to Felix I was thinking of trying to raise money for a prostate cancer charity while I was in the US. I'm not certain at this time if I was thinking of doing it for two, one either side of the pond, but Felix mentioned she had a very good friend who was a successful singer back in the day, but she now helped run a prostate cancer charity in Dallas Texas. Wow, Dallas? what a coincidence as, "that's my team", I told Felix. So Felix gave me the email address of her friend, and over the next few days I pinged her an email.

This lady, I won't name her, replied over the next few days with a long and interesting email, after the long and probably less interesting email I had sent to her had somehow hit her in the right spot. Her reply to me seemed very promising and sounded like a great charity to work with. This lady told me she held a pretty prominent position within the organisation and community, she was a very good singer and well connected in the industry, which of course grabbed my attention bigtime, as I thought this would be great for me as I instantly thought of my own music, as well as having a local guide and somewhere to stay while I would be in Dallas.

Anything that benefitted or helped me in the US would be very well received by this boy thank you very much. So contact made, happy days, I was pleased and it was looking like I was off to a good start.

To cut a very boring story very short, over the next few weeks, I emailed this lady a few more times and the replies were taking longer and longer to return to me. So I started to research her and look on the website of the charity she worked for. There was a list of the usual level or position of rank from, CEO, director, manager and so on and so forth, but I could not find this lady anywhere at all on their website. I fully expected her to be near the very top of the food chain after the way she sold herself and her charity to me.

I thought this was a little odd and I smelt the proverbial rat! This lady knew everything about my tour, my basic plans, intentions and efforts to raise money for her charity and yet she made no suggestions or gave me any ideas or guidance about what I should be doing to make this project work for THEM. She basically never gave me any direction at all, in fact, she simply disappeared into computerland.

I decided to leave the last email I sent to her in her corner and surprisingly she has never replied back to me to this very day. It was very strange, as I was trying to help THEM raise money for THEIR charity. This lady was obviously bigging herself up to be more important than she really was. I already had enough on my plate and I had no time chasing shadows or timewasters, so I thought it would be a lot easier to just raise money for one charity and here in the UK.

I did my research online and I found a UK prostate cancer charity named Men United. This looked perfect to me, as it was connected to a lot of famous sports people who were very high profile, which seemed ideal for my fundraising and my own profile.

Then out of the blue I received a random email from a guy, (again I won't name him as to not embarrass him, but he worked for a Prostate Cancer UK charity), and he told he me he had heard about my planned trip to the US and my intention to try to raise some money for charity. How he heard about me, I have absolutely no idea?

His email was interesting, he had some good ideas and I was more than happy to talk to him. He left his number, so I called him the following day. When I called, he did not pick up the phone, so I left him an answerphone message. He returned my call the next day, in fact it went to my answerphone, so I may have been working on the golf course, but his reply was "sorry but I'm up in Scotland on a golf course organising an event and I have a bad signal, so I'll speak to you another time". That was fine by me, I know of many a golf course with a bad signal, so no worries for me there. I understood completely and I awaited his call.

The following day we did speak briefly, as he did indeed have a bad signal and was still at a golf club. He asked me to send him an email regarding my plans and intentions, which is exactly what I did.

I never got a return email for a while as this guy always seemed to be busy on some kind of function, event, party, gathering or jolly up. Being the cynic I am, all I could think was, this guy is just making this very difficult for me, why doesn't he just bloody call me? I simply got fed up with chasing HIM. After all, it was ME who was doing the fundraising for THEM. FFS!!!

I never gave up on this project and we did eventually speak, but I honestly felt these people were making it a lot harder than it needed to be for me to try to raise money for them.

Cancer charities are big business, I'm pretty sure they get big donations from big organisations and I sincerely hope they do, but I felt like a very small fish in a very big ocean and that this organisation had much bigger fish to fry than this little old sardine, and I felt like I was getting no support from them at all and they made me feel like I was just wasting my time.

Now I could be completely wrong, I can only write how I felt at the time, but chasing these people was taking up far too much of my valuable time, time I could and should have been surfing the net on social media trying to contact every man and his dog in the world who had a big bone and a bone I wanted a piece of.

About a week before my departure to the US, I had recently met a fantastic and crazy human being named George Gilbey. I was introduced to George at Chelmsford City racecourse by a friend of mine, Paul Goodwin.

At the time, I had no idea who George was, everybody

around us seemed to, but I honestly never did. So with the whole world hanging around George like flies around horse shit and him revelling in the limelight and loving every minute of it, I basically said hello and no more than a few words or pleasantries to him.

George is in a very famous and successful TV show in the UK called "Gogglebox", a programme where normal people are filmed in their homes, sitting on their sofas watching TV programs and making comments as they watch. It's actually a very good show and I like it, but as I had been out of the UK so much in the past few years, I had never seen this program, until after I met George.

My friend Paul told George of my up and coming plans to tour the US watching the NFL. All of a sudden, George was my new best friend. I told him my plans and he was completely hooked on me and my tour in next to no time. George mentioned that he wanted to come with me and bring a film crew. Wow! I thought, this could be TV gold, as George is a very funny guy and an interesting character. So George informed me he would speak with his agent/PR man and maybe we could do this together? OK, I thought, I'm all ears, let's listen to what these boys have up their sleeves.

I never got overly excited about this idea at first, one because I could see that George was pretty pissed (drunk) and secondly, I did not want to give up all the hard work and preparation I had done in the previous year to let this TV star come in and steal my thunder. But, what an opportunity this could really be for me and one in which I would be a complete fool to let go. Of course I was a little excited, and I wanted to hear what these people could do for me. I have a saying, 50% of something is a lot more than 100% of nothing.

I exchanged numbers with George and we arranged to meet up in the next few days. We spoke on the phone a few times and we eventually agreed to meet in Teddington, on the outskirts of London, a few days later.

By complete coincidence, that was the day I bumped into Sky TV's anchorman for their NFL shows, the ex NFL player Kevin Cadle.(actually he was a very successful basketball coach that was my mistake). I had spotted a random guy standing outside Teddington train station in a Pittsburgh Steelers shirt and I wandered over to him just to say hello, as I was bored waiting for George to arrive.

It turned out to be Kevin and I immediately started to tell him about my impending adventure. That's another story for later.

George picked me up at Teddington station, with his new and lovely girlfriend and off to a local pub we went. We talked a lot about my tour and George was extremely interested, especially in being a part of it. I still wasn't too sure about that, but I thought his idea of joining me at some point in America would be great fun, maybe Nashville as George suggested.

George is a very funny guy indeed and so very likeable and full of charisma, I thought maybe he could attract some interest from the media, which if he came, I knew this would have happened for sure.

As we sat in the pub chatting away and discussing my tour, George told me he was going to ring his agent/ PR man, (again no names for the obvious reasons, so I will call this character Bob), so as I sat next to him in the pub, George made the call and he began to tell Bob about my plans. George eventually handed me the phone and I talked to Bob for the first time myself and I explained to him my basic plan of action.

Bob mentioned almost immediately he normally charges quite a lot of money to represent an artist or client, but he would do it for me for free. My radar went up in an instant, as the first thing that entered my head was, "hold on a minute, WHY would he do that"? he dosen't know me from Adam? "What's in it for him"? But, I was in fact extremely grateful, simply for the interest alone, as Bob seemed very well connected in the showbiz world and this was just what this boy was looking for.

Bob proceeded to bombard me with a barrage of ideas, get rich quick schemes and many things he was going to do, or had planned for me, including releasing my song "Like a touchdown" on his very own record label. Bob was going to get me radio play, contacts in Nashville, TV interviews and Bob even wanted to join me three or four times while I was on my six months of travel around America.

It all sounded amazing to me, too good to be true to be honest, which of course it all was, but at the time, I was caught up in all the hullabaloo and all I was thinking was "where do I sign?"!!

It was very exciting indeed, but I honestly never once felt

like any of this was ever really going to manifest into anything substantial, nothing other than on a very minor scale. It seemed more like hoping rather than happening, like running a marathon without doing any training or preparation.

I got the impression from Bob it was all systems go, as the positivity oozing out of him was contagious. Was this was going to be the start of something special? I wanted to believe him, because he even sold ME to ME better than anyone ever had done in the past. Even I thought I was great!!!!

I've been messed around by so many bullshitters in the music industry over the years, I just could not allow myself to get over excited and feel deflated yet again, as nothing really got off the ground for me in the past and my guard by now was always well and truly up. But I was very open minded and I would do anything Bob wanted me to do, that would help to spread the word or get me some media publicity or airtime regarding my up and coming adventure, which by now, was not far away at all.

A week later, about two weeks until I departed for the US, Bob arranged for me to be interviewed on a TV talk show in Walsall, on the outskirts of Birmingham. The talk show in question was called Cuppa TV. I had never heard of the show, but hey, I was never going to say no was I?

Cuppa TV is a regional TV station, not national. It wasn't exactly the BBC, but I was very grateful to Bob for getting me the interview and giving me the platform to broadcast to the world (well the West Midlands) my exciting plans and adventure to conquer America.

Before I knew it, I was booked in for my first ever live TV talk show and very quickly indeed, in the next few days. RESULT!

I had to be at the studios in Walsall around 11am on Monday morning, so I decided to go up on Sunday afternoon and stay the night in a local bed and breakfast, rather than have to get up at stupid o'clock/very early on Monday, as Walsall was 2 hours away by train, and I hate getting up early and something I only do if it's absolutely necessary, and this time it wasn't.

I got the train up to Walsall around lunchtime, checked into my hotel, and went straight out to find a bar for a few drinks and to watch some football.

Walsall town centre was actually quite nice. I was expecting it to be a real dump, but there was a market, lots of decent looking shops and loads of pubs and bars. As it was Sunday evening, the atmosphere was pretty quiet and laid back, so I found a sports bar, plotted up, ordered a Guinness and watched a game of Italian or Spanish football.

The sports bar was quite big and very much empty, so it had a very sombre feel to it. After a hour or so, I decided to go for a curry in a local curry house fairly close to my hotel. I ordered my meal and a beer and I got stuck in. Then I headed back to my hotel about 10pm and I went to my room, watched a bit of telly in bed and eventually turned it off around midnight.`

That was when the fun started. OMG!!!!! What a terrible

night. A night I will never forget for the rest of my life. I never slept a single second over the whole night and I will do my very best to explain exactly how I felt and what on earth went on in my body and mind, on that bastard of a night.

Now I'm not the kind of person who suffers from nerves. NEVER. When I played live in all my bands, even when I had to sing in front of 700-800 people at one gig, I never felt nerves, excitement, yes. I just loved being on stage.

But something happened to me that night and I wish I knew what the fcuk it was. I started to feel absolutely terrible, no pain, but I developed diahorrea, felt terribly sick and as anxious as I have ever been. It had nothing to do with the meal I had just consumed, I was certain. I felt totally on edge and my mind was running at a pace I had never had in my life. Was it a panic attack? and why? I was not feeling at all nervous about the interview the following day, or was I?

I felt that my heart rate was racing at break neck speed and my nerves were shot to pieces. I seriously considered phoning for an ambulance, as I thought I was going to faint, or even die at any moment, it really was that bad. I decided not to as I thought I would calm down in time. I wanted to cry and cry as hard as I ever have done in my life, in the hope that this would be the release that my body or mind was asking for. But I could not cry. Why? What was happening to me?

All that night I was up and down to the toilet and in a complete and utter mess. My already overactive mind went into overload or meltdown and I simply could not switch it off. I had no idea why on earth this was happening and where it came from. I was sooooo frightened, I just did not know what to do, as I'm very very rarely ill.

I had some tablets to calm me down, I took them but they did nothing. This went on the whole night and I never fell asleep completely, right up until I eventually had to get up, around 8.30am. It was a complete nightmare.

As you can imagine, when I did eventually get up, I felt and probably looked like a zombie, I was totally and utterly exhausted. I had calmed down a little bit, but the tension kept coming back in waves. One moment I felt anxious, then I forgot about it for a few seconds, then it returned, and got worse. It was absolute torture.

I went down to breakfast and tried to eat something as to try to make me feel better. I could hardly eat a thing as I felt physically sick and so terribly ill and extremely anxious. What the fcuk was going on? I was in such a mess.

I left the hotel and headed for the TV studio which was about a 10-15 minute walk away. I have never wanted to go home so much in my life. I was two hours away by train and here I was, going to a TV studio to do an interview. How on earth was I going to get through this?

It would have been the easiest thing in the world for me to just blow out this interview, as my health is so much more important to me than anything else in the world. "Your health is your wealth", my old dear/mum always used to tell me. Good advice mum, and that's probably why I am now potless/skint/broke/bankrupt!!!!!!

I arrived at the studio about 11am for my slot around midday. I met with Bob and he introduced me the lovely lady who was to interview me, Monica Price. After a brief chat with Bob, I had a cup of tea, and waited for my time to be called.

While I waited, I was totally fighting with myself not to faint. I was anxious beyond anything I have ever felt before. I told Bob I was not feeling very well, but he said he put it down to nerves. I knew it wasn't nerves, I was close to mental meltdown without any logical reason. My already overactive mind was torturing me and I simply could not control it, turn it off, or just slow it down. I was really suffering.

After waiting what seemed a lifetime, I went into the studio, met with Monica, and I watched her interview another guy who was also going to be on her show, before it was my turn to make a complete mess of my big moment of car crash TV! Well that's what I was expecting, as I totally felt like shit warmed up!

This guy made me feel even more anxious because he spoke so well, was a very bright young man, articulate, funny and extremely good in front of the camera. B@STARD!!!

I decided I simply had to leave the recording of this interview, as it was torture to watch it, so I went outside for a glass of water and to take a few extremely deep breaths in the bathroom, until it was my turn. Again I told Monica I was not feeling very well and she assured me it was going to be OK and that she would look after me and make sure everything ran smoothly.

We had no rehearsal, no run through and no discussions about what questions Monica was going to ask, so when the time came, I never had any idea what Monica was going to throw at me. Obviously it would be questions regarding my tour, but it could be anything?? How could I think when there was no space left in my mind?, when the wheel in my head was going into overdrive and spinning at over 100 miles a hour and I was feeling sooooo exhausted.

Incredibly, I got through a fifteen minute conversation in one single take. How? god only knows. Everybody at the studio, including Monica said it went great, I spoke well, my answers were good, interesting and sometimes funny.

I watched the clip back online a few weeks later and I'm staggered at how well I came across, but I could see in my eyes and face I was suffering during this interview and I was not in a good place at all. Nobody could tell, but of course I could.

Looking back now, especially after recovering completely, I'm so proud of myself I did so well during that interview, I never gave up and threw in the towel, when that would have been the easiest thing in the world for me to have done.

I put my neck, maybe even my life on the line, literally, because I knew this was my last and only chance to get some media coverage and tell the world (well the West Midlands) about my up and coming plans for my tour, before I left for the US.

This demonstrates just how much I tried to get my story or adventure out into media land, in the hope that someone somewhere, would show any kind of interest in little old D-Mo and his attempt to break America with his music and watch his beloved NFL.

Job done. I said goodbye to Monica and Bob, thanked them for everything, left the studio and got back on the train to London. I felt a little better now all the fun was over, but not much and the journey home was a struggle as my mind was still going mad, but not half as bad. When I eventually got home, I had an early night, I took a sleeping pill and I slept for over ten hours, as my body and mind were so desperate to shut down and restart after a good nights sleep.

I felt like a computer that needed a defrag, or a phone which needed recharging, because at this point, this boy was completely and utterly running on empty.

When I woke up, I did feel better but not a whole lot. So I went straight to my doctor and explained what had happened, and she gave me some pills to calm me down. Yep anti depressants, the easy option. But I didn't care, if they were dog biscuits, horse tablets, or cat food, I would have taken all of them.

Boy did I suffer that night and to this day, I still have no idea why. Little did I know that these demons would return and this was going to happen to me again in a few weeks time, just after I arrived in the US.

I now had less than a week to go before I left home for the US and I felt like complete and utter shit. My mental state organising this tour over the past year or so had been so strong, focused, driven and very good indeed. Now I was reduced to a nervous wreck, but again I never felt nervous, maybe anxious, but what does anxious feel like? I've never had it before now. What was I anxious about?, the tour? I wasn't feeling any anxiety at all about going on my next adventure, I couldn't bloody wait to go. I was so looking forward to having the time of my life. Or was I? I just don't know, but I wish now, I could get an answer from anyone who can tell me what the fcuk was going on with me in these terrible moments and why I suffered so very much?

I was given three months of pills by my GP, that's all I was allowed, but I would be away for 6, what the hell was I going to do when they ran out while I was in the US?

In the middle of all the massive amount of research I did, networking on social media, looking for hostels, tickets, flights, bus timetables, etc, I also had to record the soundtrack song to my tour, "Like a Touchdown".

I had written the words and composed the music about three months earlier, gone into the studio to lay down the guide guitar tracks and riffs, as well as the guide vocals, just as a reference for somebody who can actually sing and make this song sound a whole lot better than I possibly could with my limited range of vocal chords.

The general idea for "Like A Touchdown", was to copy the template, or take influence from the kind of songs I had heard and are usually played inside the NFL stadiums on a regular basis, before, during and at half time at NFL games.

I had been to two NFL games two years earlier, watching my Cowboys in New York and Washington DC and I loved the music that was played between game plays and on time outs.

Songs like "Welcome to the jungle" by Guns N Roses, "Enter Sandman" by Metallica, songs by Nirvana and AC/DC, all bands that I love. The common theme was always an uptempo track, with a catchy guitar riff, big sounds, booming drums and screaming vocals. So my task was to mimic this, use these songs as a guide or, a reference and write my own version. And that's exactly what I did.

The original idea was to write a song completely about American Football, but this quickly changed as it became very cringe worthy and pretty awful to say the least. I invented an idea or analogy which I quite liked, comparing the feeling you get when you are with your loved one, to the feeling you get at the very moment when your team score a goal, home run, or a touchdown. It's about saying to your loved one, "You make me feel euphoric, amazing, excited when we are together, just like the way I feel when a touchdown is scored by my favourite team".

It worked quite well with the lyrics. "Like a touchdown, your love is making me high". Because let's be honest, when our beloved teams score, at that precise moment, the euphoria kicks in and we feel amazing, don't we? All problems are forgotten in that split second and we feel elated, excited and extremely happy. "Like A Touchdown" is a complete feel good song.

I wanted to keep a few NFL references in the bridges of the song. " Heading into overtime, take a time out before crossing the line". I liked it.

For the verses, I had the idea of watching a gorgeous girl on stage dancing, a real babe, and she knew it, she loved the attention and she was using her power and her weapons of mass distraction to her advantage. This idea would be replicated a few months later in New Orleans as I watched a fantastic jazz singer in Preservation Hall. This topic would also be the start of recording another new song, called "You can look but you can't touch", eventually to be recorded in Detroit.

I needed a strong and powerful opening line. "You can break hearts, you can crash cars with your smile", (about the beautiful and confident dancer) I liked that. Then line two with a little piece of sexual innuendo. "Pucker those lips, a flick of those hips and I'm yours". Not bad. So I thought about the power a very beautiful girl has on all of us perverts. "You can stop wars, open up doors with your smile". "A look from those eyes, a thrust of your thighs and you've scored". Now I had the lyrics, the melody and the general idea of where this track was going.

Next up was the task to find a good rock drummer and a bass player. My producer Felix had done a session with a young French Canadian drummer named Pierre. Felix spoke very highly of Pierre, recommended him, so we got him in the studio within a few days.

Pierre was simply incredible, what a player, he nailed the session, did a few takes of the song and it was in the bag. A very easy session for him indeed. Pierre was an absolute brilliant drummer, it was such a pleasure for me just to watch him play and a great privilege to have such a talented guy play on my song.

The bass player, whose name I can't remember did a good job, nothing too flashy, I never really needed anything too difficult, and he did what he had to do, so I was fine with it. Then it was time to get my right hand man, good friend, and superb guitar player John Lovell, to sprinkle his magic over the track.

John came to the studio, plugged his guitar in, played along in his very cool way and own unique style, and immediately improved the track a million per cent, just as he has always done to all my songs he has played on over the years. I just love John's guitar playing, I never really have to tell John what I want, I just ask him to play something, and that something is usually brilliant.

John did about three different versions, all kinds of solos and riffs, shredding, melody, string bending and it all sounded awesome. So I just took sections, or pieces of his ideas, and we eventually came to a conclusion I was over the moon with. Thanks a million Johnny boy. You certainly know how to rock mate!

Finally I needed to find a decent vocalist, obviously not me, but someone who was going to take this song to another level and completely sell this song to the American audience, TV networks, radio stations, advertising agencies etc, I was aiming to attract.

I knew that finding the right vocalist was not going to be easy and I never had much time left to play with and be too over selective or picky, but I was never just gonna take anyone.

I started looking online, as well as asking Felix if she knew anyone decent she had previously worked with, had any mates who can belt out a tune and so on. Felix did have a few people in mind she thought would be interested and good for the track, so I listened to their websites to hear their voices, but none of them really grabbed me, or was the voice I had hearing inside my head, so I continued to look myself.

I put an advert on a music website and I got a few responses, especially after I said I was paying for the session. Again I never really liked what I heard from the people who forwarded to me the demos of their vocals which I requested. Of course I wanted someone special and as yet, I had not heard anything that came close.

The original kind of voice I wanted was like the guy who sang for the 80's band Foreigner. So I went online and searched for Foreigner cover bands, I found a couple, but only one in England, but way up north in Yorkshire. I emailed the guy who was the singer, but he took quite a while responding and I had less than two weeks before I departed for the US, so I had to find somebody else. Shame as I really liked his voice, it was exactly what I had wanted.

Then out of the blue, I got a phone call from a guy who had seen my advert on a website called "Gumtree". He said he was in London and had just arrived from the US, had been in quite a few rock bands, and had done some pretty big gigs over the years.

Nothing ventured, nothing gained I thought, so I decided to give this guy a chance.

I met him later that afternoon at Victoria train station, and his name was Manu. As soon as I saw him, I liked his image, all dressed in black with dyed black hair, a proper rockstar. He looked the part, I just hoped to god the boy could sing.

Manu is from Austria, and I had my doubts immediately from the very first moment I heard him speak, as he quite obviously had an accent, actually quite strong and something I did not want on my song. But as we had a coffee at the train station, I asked Manu if he had anything recorded where I could listen to his voice?

Manu played me a few songs from his Ipod, and it sounded promising, as I could quite obviously hear he could sing and very well too. It was good, powerful and interesting, and I was impressed.

Manu had a very unusual sounding voice, but I liked it, it was very different to my first choice and the vision that I had for the song in my head, but I thought it could work and suit my song. So why not, let's give it a try.

Two days later, we headed off to Felix's studio in North London. Manu didn't start that brilliant to be honest, he struggled a little with the internation of some of the lyrics and his accent was putting me off in the beginning quite a bit. Felix and I talked a lot about whether this was the right guy and I'm pretty certain she thought that he was not.

I was not disagreeing with her completely, but I thought Manu deserved a chance, as well as the fact I had nobody else, especially as I had very little time left to finish the track, before I departed for the US.

There were parts of Manu's vocal I loved, but there were also some sections I didn't like at all, especially the bits where he found it a bit of a problem to pronounce some of the words. Overall I think he did a good job. Felix had reservations the American audience would not "get" the song with Manu's vocal and to be honest, I could see exactly where she was coming from. I fully respect Felix's opinions, especially when they conflict with mine, because she is so very experienced and she is excellent at what she does, so I always take her comments onboard.

But then I thought, maybe they WILL get Manu's vocals, not just because its a little different or unusual, but as he sounded a bit like and could mimic Axl Rose with his high notes and falsetto screams. I thought that being different may actually be of some kind of benefit? Different or unique is usually a good thing in the music world, as the industry constantly strives for new trends and sounds, so I thought the risk was worth taking.

Now the recording of "Like A Touchdown" was finished, the final piece of the jigsaw was my website. www.thewrongshapedballs.com I had to pay a company called GoDaddy for the domain name and to rent a webpage for a year. More bloody money! But this was something I simply had to do.

Now when it comes to computers, I'm far from an expert, light years away in fact. But I do know a man who knows his shit regarding computers, my good friend and Italian brother Fabrizio Lombardo. I contacted Fabrizio, aka "The

Bullshit Man", a name in which he also calls me, (God knows why!) and we chatted about how we can put this website together.

Fabrizio is one of my best friends and a truly lovely man, so we spoke about the website on the phone and Fabrizio suggested a million things, all of which were way over my stupid old head, something which is not very difficult to do at all!

So after various conversations regarding the new website, I decided the best way to get this done properly, was for me to hop on a plane over to Florence where Fabrizio lives and spend time with him building the website. Fabrizio suggested I needed a logo, something people can relate to and has a certain meaning to my tour.

We brainstormed and we came up with a design, mainly Fabrizo's ideas, but I was very happy to follow him and his ideas, as he had built many websites of his own in the past and he was much better at it than I could ever be. After a few days in Florence, the website was done, thanks mainly to the Bullshit Man!

I went online and ordered a t-shirt and a hoodie with the new "WSB's" website logo on, which I thought would be good advertising for me during my tour in the US, especially if I made it onto national TV, or even just to get some free publicity or exposure for the tour while I was wearing it around the country.

Looking back now, I do remember my hoodie getting a lot of looks from the general public, as nobody had any idea what the "Wrong Shaped Balls Tour" was. I did in fact get asked by quite a few NFL fans what it was and when I told people about me going to all 31 NFL stadiums in one season, most of them thought I was totally mad! I eventually wore that hoodie in almost every stadium I attended on the entire tour.

The idea for the logo was always Fabrizio's, but it was my idea to have the image of an American football crushing a soccer ball. Fabrizio designed the layout and had the idea of the flags and the circle. A good partnership of two great creative minds coming together!

Fabrizio is a great designer and for many years I joked with him that when I am rich, he can design my "castle" for me and this castle was going to be financed by the sales of my song "Like a Touchdown" if it could get some radio play in the US. Ha! Sadly the royalties were not even enough to buy me a coffee, let alone a castle!

I remember the first time I encountered Fabrizio's skill of design, which was in the bathroom at his house. It was a seethrough sink and I turned on the tap and jumped out the way, as I thought the water was going to go all over my shoes!!! Great design and something I had never seen before.

Fabrizio was also good at designing websites and what he did in a day, would have taken me over a week, or more. I got giddy watching him click here, click there and more, so fast, as the website started to take shape and I had no input at all, only to watch and try to understand what the hell he was doing.

When Fabrizio finally finished the website, I had the near impossible task of learning how to maintain it on my laptop, updating pages, inputting pictures and text while I was in the US. In the beginning for me, this process was like learning Chinese, I was slow and it took me time to learn, but after I got the general grasp of things, only then did it became second nature and I actually started to enjoy doing it. I was very pleased with myself for this achievement!!

So now the website was finished, everything on my extremely long to do list, had finally been achieved. THANK GOD! All I needed now was for ANY of my plethera or multitude of contacts to come up trumps and start opening ANY kind of doors for me. I had sent out what seemed like 1000's of messages, looking for any kind of help, contacts, assistance, but mainly just support. Little did I know that most, if not all of the doors, would be slammed shut well and truly in my face.

So here we are, tomorrow is d-day, the time has come for me to leave for the US, a day I had been dreaming about and planning for almost a year. I should have been looking forward to this day with a passion and like a kid greeting christmas day, but now the day had finally arrived, a huge part of me was now dreading it, as I was totally exhausted and not in a very good place at all mentally.

This was going to be a massive challenge on a monumental scale, even if I was feeling 100% and firing on all cylinders, but to cross the pond feeling like a nervous wreck, was in fact pretty daunting. Hopefully once I leave home, I will calm down, relax, sleep well and have the time of my life.

Little did I know what torture I was about to experience over the next few days.

The Contacts/Timewasters

Through social media, I attempted to connect with as many celebrities, or people who made the decisions, as I possibly could from all areas or industries, from music, sport, TV, organisations, clubs, etc etc, basically people who had a large amount of followers on their social media websites.

Making any kind of connection was so important for me, and I honestly thought it was simply a matter of time before something would stick, or some kind of friendship with some interested party would soon develop.

I never knew quite where my first break would come from, so I just blitzed the whole damn social media universe and kept my fingers crossed. I call this pissing in the wind, but I knew no different, so he who dares wins I thought, as I had nothing to lose, literally.

I also tried to spread the word as much as I could while I was working and meeting people on the golf courses I worked at, as you just never know what can fall right into your lap, if you chat to the right person.

I was caddying at Wentworth on a Sky TV golf day when I randomly caddied for a guy named Josh. When I told him of my impending tour, he offered to connect me to his workmate and personal friend Charlie, a guy who was one of the decision makers and main men who worked as a producer for the American Football show on Sky Sports. BOSH!!!!

Josh seemed nice and genuine and I honestly believed he

had good intentions from the very beginning, as he filled me with the hope there was a very good chance he could help me to gain access to the NFL people he knew at Sky Sports and through him I could get to these people interested in my tour.

These people were his work colleagues, probably mates and these were the people I very much needed on my side or in my pocket, people who may show an interest in my tour and have the power to make decisions, like getting me an interview on Sky Sports??

I was really excited after meeting Josh, he made me feel like he would make the effort and go the extra yard for me and I honestly thought something interesting was coming my way from our meeting and this connection would be the start of something positive.

Over the next few months, I sent Josh a few messages on Facebook and he always took an age replying to them, even when I could see he was online. When he did reply, it was usually just excuses, "Charlie is on holiday, I will get him to contact you". "Charlie is off today", "Charlie is in a meeting and will contact you soon", kind of thing. This went on, and on, and on.

I never gave up on Josh, even after his silence and ignorance, as I thought this was a connection too important to break, I kept my patience, but it was not easy. I sent Josh at least three more messages over the next few months and he has never got back to me to this very day. Josh had offered to help me, he told me this in person, then decided to completely ignore my messages and slap the very same face he promised to help.

Why on earth do people do this? What a fcuking wanker and bullshitter. That prick raised my hopes and he would not be the last person to do this over the next year or so of the planning of my tour and my quest for friends in high places.

Another guy I met on that golf day at Wentworth, was a guy who works for Sky TV as one of their golf experts and analysts, a man named Simon Holmes. Simon was very interested in the story of my tour and he offered to try to connect me with the guys at the Sky NFL team, as he kind of knew them from a distance.

I kept in touch with Simon via email a few times over the next few months and he did communicate with me, but even though nothing ever came of our conversations, at least he tried and I have no problem with that at all, for this, I will always be grateful to him just for showing an interest.

I still see Simon from time to time at a few golf clubs and he is always nice to me. A nice man indeed is Simon.

Josh would not be the only one from Sky Sports who would give me the proverbial custard pie to the face treatment.

I had met Kevin Cadle (the face of Sky Sports NFL coverage in the UK) at Wembley stadium the day before my Dallas Cowboys played the Jacksonville Jaguars a few years ago. Our chance meeting was not amongst hundreds of other NFL fans, it was almost alone, on the steps of Wembley Park tube station, as I had gone to watch the Cowboys do a public training session, something very rare and where only a few thousand people would get the opportunity to see this, on a first come first serve basis.

I bumped into Kevin as I came out of the underground station, had my picture taken with him and had a little chat. He was really nice. I added him to my friends on Facebook and a few days later he accepted my friend request. Blinding/great contact? or so I thought.

Over the next few months, I sent Kevin the odd message, or replied to something he put on Facebook. I was not exactly his "friend", as in being his mate, but we did exchange a few messages via Facebook. I told him all about my tour, so he knew what I was about to attempt. I clearly remember he wished me a happy birthday on my big day, ironically the 4th of July, his American independence day.

Being in contact with Kevin gave me a lot of confidence and hope that I now had access to a major player within the NFL media world here in the UK. I honestly thought I had my little toenail in the door. WRONG!

Move forward six months and my tour is two weeks away. On this very day in question, I had just finished recording my song "Like a Touchdown", with my friend and producer Felix, and I had just came from the studio with the finished CD in my bag, and I was heading across London to meet with my mate George Gilbey from UK TV show, Gogglebox.

I arranged to meet George in Teddington on the outskirts of London and as I waited for George to pick me up from the train station, I could see a figure in the distance wearing a Pittsburgh Steelers shirt. So I thought I would pop over and just say hello to this random person. "Is that a Pittsburgh Steelers shirt you are wearing mate"? I said. "Yes", the man replied. Straight away I recognised who this fella was. Hello Kevin, I said. "I'm the English guy who is going on a NFL tour to watch a game at all 31 stadiums", I said.

What a chance meeting, especially on the very day I had just finished recording the soundtrack song to my tour. What a coincidence. Or was it? What it fate? Was it my destiny? WAS IT FCUK!

We chatted for a couple of minutes and then to my amazement, along came Kevin's mate, and another ex pro football player who also works for Sky Sports, a guy named named Shaun Gayle, who incidentally is also on the panel at Sky Sports and who I had previously met at the Hippodrome Casino in Central London. Shaun was a very friendly guy, with the added bonus that he had a cracking looking girlfriend. Not that this piece of useless information means anything, I'm just stating a fact!

When I said hello to Shaun, he said he remembered me from our previous meeting at the Hippodrome, as I had told him then about my tour, so that was really nice he remembered.

I thought this was an excellent opportunity for me to get Kevin and Shaun to hear my new song "Like A Touchdown", which was so hot off the press, they would have needed oven gloves to get the CD out of it's case!!!.

The song had been finalised less than just two hours ago and the CD I was holding was the original recording, not a copy. I made the decision to give Kevin my only copy of "Like a

Touchdown", explained what is was about and asked him if he could help me get some publicity for my tour by mentioning me and my tour on his show, maybe play my song, follow me on Facebook, anything that would raise my profile and make the NFL fans in the UK aware of what I was trying to achieve.

Remember at this time, I was also trying to raise money for "Men United" prostate cancer charity, so good publicity on a national level would be massive for both me and the charity.

Kevin said he would do his best to get my CD heard by his bosses, or the people of influence who can make things happen in the NFL world on SKY TV and he would try to help in any way he could. He also told me he would follow me on Facebook and keep in touch while I was on my tour.

Kevin gave me the impression he was very interested in what I was attempting to accomplish (how could he not be?, is this not every NFL fan's dream?) but as soon as Shaun came along, it was a very swift hello, goodbye and they quickly left to catch their train.

At the time, I honestly felt this meeting was not a coincidence, but a sign, or a good omen, a meeting that could be a massive benefit to me and my tour. I was elated, over the moon, a very happy bunny indeed, confident that something good was definitely going to come from this so called chance meeting. It really made my day and gave me a massive massive lift.
YYEEESSSSSSSSSSSSSSSSSSSSSSSSSSSSS! GET IN!!

Sadly, YET AGAIN, I was so totally and utterly wrong. I

trusted, had faith and was absolutely convinced something would materialise from this complete and utter random meeting.

To this very day, Kevin never did return a single Facebook message I sent to him over the 6 months I was away in the US on my tour. I probably made ten or more attempts to touch base with him, I never received a ONE SINGLE RESPONSE. No hello, no sorry I've been busy, no I can't help you, or even kiss my ass. NOTHING, NOTHING, NOTHING. Kevin never liked ONE SINGLE picture I posted on Facebook, out of the thousands I took, neither did he like ONE video of the hundreds I took, and finally, he never made ONE SINGLE COMMENT to the thousands of comments and paragraphs I wrote as I zig zagged across America.

Now call me totally fcuking stupid,

but.............................. **WHY?**

Here is an ex professional football player, he has met me twice, he knows all about my tour, he has got the original copy of my song, he said he would try to help me, then he completely disappears and ignores ALL my attempts to make contact or touch base with him. WHY? Somebody please help me understand, because I'm just not getting it.

How can he NOT be interested? And WHY did he not return a single message on Facebook, even when I sent him a private message as he was online? and even when I knew he was online as his green light was on? "Hi Kev, how are you?" "Hope you are enjoying my posts". NOTHING, Just silence. I AM JUST SO TOTALLY BAFFLED. What on earth did I do to deserve this?

This is the one thing that hurts me more than anything.......SILENCE. I am simply amazed and totally bamboozled as to why Sky Sports showed absolutely no interest in my tour whatsoever. Kevin could have opened so many doors for me, but he decided to completely ignore all my messages. And yet again, all I ask is WHY?

I did bump into Shaun Gayle again at the very end of my tour, outside the Mosconi Media Centre the day before the Superbowl 50 in San Francisco. That's another story for later.

Another media organisation I contacted which I hoped might be interested in my tour was Talksport (talk radio station). I was certain these guys would love my story, as these shows rely on phone ins and especially fan involvement or participation.

Talksport was a channel I used to listen to a lot, especially the morning show as one of the hosts was a guy I used to caddie for at Wentworth, ex England cricketer Ronnie Irani. I used to tweet the show sometimes and Ronnie would mention me live on the show as I laid in bed. It was quite surreal for me to hear Ronnie and Alan Brazil discussing how lazy I was, as I was listening to them while I was still in bed at 9.45am. Very funny. Thanks Ron.

I sent a tweet to a guy named Ian Danter who has a show on the radio station, as I was told he was the NFL guy worth contacting for Talksport and he would maybe offer me a slot on his show with a bit of luck. Ian replied almost immediately and informed me that the guy I needed to contact at the radio station was in fact a guy named Olly Hunter.

Ian gave me Olly's email address, so I dropped Olly an email. I waited a couple of weeks, but sadly I got no reply from Olly. I sent Olly a second email, the same email as the first and I received a reply a few days later, apologising for his slack response and that he had been busy.

Fair enough, I understand that, as I'm sure he is a busy guy. I was just grateful he finally responded and I had made the connection.

Olly was very interested in my email and mentioned to me he will at some point in the season have me on his show. Great! I was well pleased and Olly seemed very nice and genuine. YEAH RIGHT!

I never heard from Olly again throughout the entire tour, until he sent me a very abusive tweet after I responded to a tweet sent by ex Arsenal footballer Ray Parlour.

Funny how Olly could not find the time to like one single tweet I had done all through the five months of the NFL season, but then miraculously found all the time in the world to kick me in the guts about a comment I made to a tweet. Lovely man hey?

Yet another social media contact I thought would have great value to me was channel 4's NFL guy Vernon Kay. He seemed like the perfect guy and a very important contact to try to connect with, as he plays for a UK American Football team. I expected at least some interest from him as he seems a very nice guy.

I've actually met Vernon, as he is a very keen golfer and he sometimes plays golf at one of the clubs I work at, Wentworth. I was already following Vernon on Twitter and one day I was working at Wentworth, where Vernon was playing in a charity event or golf day and he won a nearest to the pin competition and his prize was a very nice and expensive pair of golf shoes.

I tweeted Vernon jokingly and congratulated him on his winning of the shoes. He replied almost straight away with some random funny comment, so I thought great, at least he now knows who I am and I now have access or a supply line to him on Twitter. Mission accomplished.

I tweeted straight back to him about the basic facts of my impending tour, but yet again, to this very fcuking day, the lovely Vernon Kay has NEVER responded to any of the half a dozen messages I sent to him. I know from the tabloid press Vernon had been preoccupied texting a topless model here in the UK, so I knew he had been busy! I just hope those fcuking shoes he won gave him blisters the bastard!!!

Vernon's side kick on the weekly NFL show on Channel 4 was a guy named Nat Coombes, so I contacted him. Nat did in fact respond to a couple of early tweets I had sent to him, but his reply was so yobbish and odd, something I never expected from him at all. I asked him what advice he had to give to me as I was embarking on a tour of all 31 NFL stadiums. I was totally shocked when he replied with pathetic and stupid comments, something along the lines of "Drink loads of beer and bang as many birds as you can". Great advice Nat and I did try! but I was not expecting that kind of a message from him, from one of my close friends, yes, but Nat? What a fcuking idiot.

I just wanted to be taken seriously by all these media guys, but I never made any inroads at all, or even touched base, or had basic dialogue with any of the faces I had seen and associated with the game of American Football on UK TV.

I was just amazed that NONE of these people gave me the time of day. ABSOLUTELY NONE. It was like trying to break into a kind of TV mafia or the freemasons.

Towards the end of my tour, as least I would do a Radio Five Live interview with Nat Coombes and Mike Carlson live from the AFC Championship game in Denver. But these guys never really asked me anything interesting and Mike Carlson just loves the sound of his own voice and talked over me for practically the whole interview. Mike was yet another twitter man who never replied to any of my messages at all.

Then we come to the biggest waste of time and space in the UK NFL world, the legendary Neil Reynolds. I have no idea how this gobshite got the gig for doing these NFL shows in the first place.

I've met Neil a few times at NFL events in London and each time I have, I started to dislike the man even more. Neil simply has no time at all for anybody other than himself, or the NFL big boys he works with or interviews and is usually sucking up to.

I know for a fact Neil is not liked at all by a large section of the NFL fans in the UK, I know this from the people I mix with at the Hippodrome Casino in London where I hang out on most Sunday nights watching the NFL.

This is basically because he has no time for any of the NFL fans and he is always behaving like a prima donna, especially when he is around proper stars. He's aloof and has been rude to me more than once, for no reason. I must have tweeted Neil 5-6 times before I left for my tour, as well as quite a few times while I was away. I never got a single reply.

I finally came face to face with Neil in San Francisco at the media centre the day before the Superbowl. What that asshole said to me I will never forget, as I introduced myself as the Englishman, who HAD BY NOW been to all 31 NFL stadiums, 3 play off games and the Pro Bowl, and had been trying to contact him all season for his guidance, help, etc etc. I will let you know exactly what happened when I get to that section of the book. WANKER!

About a month before I left for America, I had been informed of an English guy who had in fact already done what I was planning to do, go to all 31 NFL stadiums. I cannot remember exactly how I found this about out, but the guy in question is now quite connected in UK NFL circles. His name is Adam Goldstein.

I sent Adam a twitter message and he replied to me pretty quickly. I informed Adam of my intentions and tour and after a few tweeted messages, we arranged to meet up in central London.

A few days later I met with Adam and we had lunch in a restaurant in Soho. Adam seemed like a nice guy and we chatted about his tour, which was mainly about "Tailgating", something I knew absolutely nothing about.

Tailgating for my English friends is basically a party/barbeque before the start of an American football game, usually in the parking lot/car park, in front of the stadiums. Great things they are too and I had many a great tailgate on my tour, I love them.

Adam told me he had written two books on the subject of tailgating and he was pretty well connected in this particular area. The only piece of advice I can remember Adam giving to me was to contact all the NFL teams PR people, which I tried, but to be honest, I could have tried harder, but on their website, it was so hard to find the right people to get to and it tied me up in knots with so much text and reading, I kind of gave up on it as I had so many other leads to follow, on all kinds of fan forums and social media sites across the internet.

Adam said he would help connect and advise me as much as he could while I was in the US. Really Adam? Help me? when? What a complete waste of words, words which came from HIS very own mouth.

Adam was my friend on Twitter and maybe Facebook and he never ONCE liked any of the 1000's of pictures or video's I posted on my entire tour. He also never liked or responded to ONE SINGLE tweet over my 5 months and I did 100's. He never asked ONCE how I was getting on, Why? I have my own views, but only he knows.

So Adam was yet another of a long production line of bullshitters who did NOTHING at all for me, when THEY said THEY would help me.

Now I hate liars, timewasters, bullshitters and fake people. Everything you will read in my book is 100% COMPLETELY AND UTTERLY TRUE. Everything you will read was based on events that really DID happen, nothing has been made up, or been exaggerated, dressed up, call it what you will. I reveal as many of the experiences, incidents and stories I can remember, both good and bad, including the people I met along the way, who were major players within these stories.

I did give Adam a dig near the end of my tour asking why he had not been of any help to me AT ALL and why he did not show any interest in my tour or even send me a single message of good luck or how's it going? His pathetic response was that I "didn't ask". Why would I ask when he had already offered?

I felt so angry towards Adam as this guy had told me to my face when I bought him lunch, he would connect me with people he had met on his NFL Tailgating tour and yet he didn't send me one single damn message of ANY KIND, even when he must have seen me on his computer screen every single day for 6 months, in the millions of pictures I posted on social media, including pictures of many people HE KNEW, people he had ALREADY MET while he was on his trip. Again........WHY?

I remember a time when I was in St Louis with a Rams Superfan, a great guy named Karl, who was nicknamed "RamMan". He told me a story where he set up a situation for Adam to get an interview on the pitch at the Rams stadium the Edward Jones Dome. This story annoyed me as Adam was happy to let people help him on his tour, but he had decided to ignore me completely on mine. Thanks Adam, let's just hope we don't ever meet again, as you maybe on the receiving end of a punt! Yet another bullshitter in the NFL UK world.

That brings me nicely to my final and biggest kick in the bollox.....NFLUK.

NFLUK was THE first and most important name on my list of organisations to contact after the schedule of the up and coming NFL season's fixtures was released. I actually went to their offices in Central London to deliver a letter to them by hand, explaining I was doing this NFL tour and would they be interested in supporting and following me over the next 6 months?

A guy came down to the ground floor reception where I was, as I was not allowed to go up to their floor, so he took my letter and disappeared back into the lift. But just before he went, I asked him if I could arrange a meeting with his people and he gave me the name of the boss, a Mr David Tossell. Great, all good I thought as I headed home, pleased I had done something positive and made a good connection. A nice start, first down!

I did my research into Mr Tossell, later I would call him Mr Tosser, for the obvious reasons, as he was another pointless tosser on a list longer than my mum's monthly shopping list! This list, which had far too many names on it for my liking when it came to fcuking me about, I called my "Tosser list"!

David Tossell had written books with some very successful people in the world of sport, including cricket, horse racing and football, Sir Alex Ferguson amongst a few. I knew David was a top contact to have in the world of the NFL and a person who had the power to connect me BIGTIME, only if he could be persuaded or basically bothered.

At that point, I never gave writing a book a single second thought, It was simply never an option. But now, I wonder if it would be worth me contacting David for his professional help regarding my book? I think I already know the answer to that.

I emailed David, more than once, obviously after getting ignored the first time, then bang! connection is made and an interview was arranged. WALLOP!!

NFLUK are the biggest thing in the UK regarding the NFL, probably only SKY TV have more clout. Now this was a result for me to get the chance to meet with David in person, as NFLUK really have the power to get me connected and open any door in the US for me. This I was totally convinced of, and still am.

This meeting could be massive for me if all goes to plan and NFLUK can use me to THEIR advantage in a huge way, for me to help THEM promote American Football in the UK and show the world how much this amazing game is loved by millions of passionate fans, not only in the UK, but also in other parts of Europe.

It was now around a week before I was departing for the US, so the NFLUK meeting was a very important meeting for me. I met with David Tossell around 10am in the offices of NFLUK in London's West End. I was so excited as I arrived and this grew when I saw lots of NFL memorabilia all around the offices, from statues, mannequins of players in NFL shirts, pictures, posters, flags, banners, footballs and so on. I was like the proverbial kid in a sweet shop/candy store.

We proceeded to go into David's office and we chatted for around 30 minutes. As we started our discussions, I was fully aware I had to sell my story and convey my message to the max, in order to get David interested in my vision, my ideas, my plans, in the very short amount of time I knew I had with him.

In David's hand was the letter I had sent to him, as well as the emails I had also sent, so he knew the score, the whole nine yards and what I was looking to achieve.

I would like to think I have very good people skills, I am a good reader of people, in an instant after meeting them, 10 seconds is normally enough, not every single time, just most of them. Throughout this meeting, I was never quite convinced David was really that interested in my tour, something which was yet again proven so bloody right.

I feel I can gauge a person in a heartbeat and David's

demeanour, body language, wet fish handshake and general interest, just did not feel warm to me and I always felt from day one he was going through the motions and basicially just wanted to know what I was up to rather than show genuine interest in my adventure. Just like an FBI or the CIA agent, monitoring the situation.

I explained to David my objectives, basically all I wanted was their SUPPORT and GUIDANCE within the media. I informed him what I was looking to achieve on a personal level, as well as raising money for charity.

One thing I made crystal clear to David, was that I was offering him MY services for trying to help raise the profile of the NFL in the UK, as the idea of an UK franchise is now becoming very possible. I thought this was an excellent opportunity for NFLUK to use ME as a kind of ambassador, to spread the word and love for THEM, on how popular the NFL has become over here in the UK.

It was in fact amazing how many Americans whom I got to meet on my tour, had no idea how the NFL is perceived in the UK. They were shocked when I explained how popular it has become and how the three games we now have each year in London sell out in hours. They were very surprised. Actually its risen this year to four games.

See one problem (that's probably the wrong word, problem) and no offence meant, but in the US, the general public very rarely get informed of any issues outside of America that does not really have any effect on them and rightly so. The US media do not take much interest or report things like European sports, as they have enough going on in their own country with their many popular sports and these items of news are usually discussed in very fine detail too, in all aspects of the sports, drafts, gossip, problems etc etc and this takes up so much valuable air time on so many channels. So American NFL fans have no idea how popular the NFL is and has grown in the UK and Europe over the past 30 years.

So having this crazy English guy going to all 31 NFL club's stadiums would be very beneficial and great PR for NFLUK and the NFL in Europe, to show an American audience a European perspective and also to demonstrate that the Europeans are indeed very much interested and do follow and love THE AMERICAN'S beloved national game passionately.

I could help highlight the fact a London team is a definite future possibility, especially, as I mentioned to David, I had been invited to watch a game in the private suite of the owner of the Jacksonville Jaguars, Mr Shahid Khan, who is the driving force behind an attempt to get a London franchise, with his Jaguars being firm favourites to secure that position. If that did not interest Mr Tossell, what would?

David informed me that this year, the BBC were taking over NFL TV duties from Channel 4 and showing NFL coverage and highlights on their channel of this coming season. David informed me, one idea he had would be to hook me up with the guys at the BBC while they were covering a particular game on any given week of the season. All I needed to know was which game the BBC would be at and I would do my best to make a beeline for that game.

If I had been offered this gig, I would have flown from say Miami to Seattle if I had to, just to get the BBC behind me. I would have done this in a heartbeat and this would have been a massive break or opportunity for me.

This was just the kind of thing I wanted, access to UK TV, especially the world famous BEEB. To get my face plastered across UK TV talking about my tour and American football in general. AND my song "Like A Touchdown". OH BOY I WAS SOOOOO HAPPY!

David had my schedule, he knew exactly where and when I would be throughout the entire NFL season, so all he had to do was let me know where the BBC boys would be, which week on the schedule and I would walk on broken glass barefooted to get there.

After 30 minutes with David, I left the NFLUK offices feeling totally elated, I was buzzing as I walked down Oxford Street to the tube station going home, very happy I had got my message across as best as I could, to a man who really could make things happen for me......if he wanted to, or could be bothered.

But as I have already said, I was never quite convinced I would get the support and connections David promised, I was simply hoping and praying they would. Yet again, my gut feeling was the meeting was a complete and utter waste of time. And that's exactly what it turned out to be. AGAIN. If I had to beg these guys, I would have, but I felt I didn't need to, as I had an extremely viable product well worth them tapping into and promoting. It was also very much in THEIR best interest, a real no brainer, I was totally and utterly convinced. WHAT A BLOODY FOOL I AM.

I could say more about NFLUK, but I will save it, as they will come up a few more times later in the book, sadly not in a very favourable light at all.

Another crazy, stupid, wacky idea I had in the beginning, was to try to watch a game in every stadium with a celebrity fan of each club. So I Googled NFL celebrity fans and I found a list of celebs and the teams they supported. So George Clooney follows the Cincinnati Bengals, Nelly (the R'N'B singer) the St Louis Rams, Adam Sandler, the New York Jets and so on and so forth.

But the one celebrity who stood out for me was the actor Bradley Cooper. I knew he was an ardent fan of the Philadelphia Eagles and he was on the top of my hit list, or radar, as I was going to be in Philadelphia on week 2 when Bradley's Eagles played my Dallas Cowboys.

I was pretty confident if I somehow managed to get to a message to him, he just might be interested in watching the game with me in Philadelphia, if he was back in town of course on the day of the game. I knew Bradley was performing on stage in London, in a production of "The Elephant Man", at a theatre on Haymarket near Trafalgar Square. I had seen his picture on a billboard as I drove around London on a bus, and seeing his image was what gave me the original idea to contact him.

So I wrote a letter to him explaining the basic outline of my tour and if it would it be possible to watch a game with him when I got to Philadelphia? Well it worked with Shad Khan, so why not Bradley Cooper? I had nothing to lose.

I headed across London to the theatre where Bradley was performing, I went around to the back door and I delivered the letter to a security guard and he informed me that my letter would be handed to Bradley's PA, who would then take it to him. SWEET AS A NUT!

I was pretty confident I would at least get a response from Mr C, as he seems like a pretty normal and decent guy who loves his football. WRONG! Sadly I never got a response from Big Brad and I will never know to this day if he did in fact ever got to read my letter.
GUTTED............TOTALLY.

This is pretty much the same frustration I had in my quest to make contact with any of the many NFL players I tried to connect with via Twitter. I will never know if any of these players ever did read my tweets, or knew whether I did manage to eventually complete my mission. Maybe these celebs have people looking after their accounts on their behalves? I'm pretty sure they do, but again, how can not ONE SINGLE NFL PLAYER show absolutely no interest at all in following me on my tour?

In fact, there were actually only 3 NFL players who I made contact with, who bothered to at least take the time to return a message I had sent to them via social media. The first was the very nice Demario Davis, who played for the New York Jets. I thought this was a nice touch and it meant a lot to me, but sadly he was only one of the many players I tried to contact who even knew I existed.

The other two players who did get back to me, by coincidence both happened to be Cowboys players, Terrence Williams and Joseph Randle. I was really chuffed about this and gutted when Randle was booted out of the Cowboys team, especially at a time when he was playing so well, even after being given the unenvious task of replacing the brilliant Demarco Murray. Joseph was probably one of the better players in this period, at a pretty torrid time for the Cowboys, when Romo was injured. I should know, I saw it at first hand a few times.

But sadly all three of these very brief great new contacts disappeared as quickly as they arrived, into www cyberspace, leaving me as frustrated as ever.

I totally feel that most, not all, NFL players do not give a damn about the fans, I am proof as I was basically ignored by them all, as I was by almost all the celebs I contacted. Again, a massive wall of silence.

Now call me stupid, but I really did expect someone to reply to me, simply because I sent out so many random messages and I really did expect to hit something or someone who may show the smallest amount of interest in my tour. If one player would had just shown some interest, this could have snowballed and led to many others, as these guys are all mates, but sadly it did not and I did feel let down and rejected, especially as the day was almost upon me to leave for the US.

I had put soooooooooo much time and effort into making contacts before I boarded the plane to the US.

After all the ground work, planning, research, pestering, social media, meetings and networking I had done over the past year, the big day finally arrived, D-day (departure day).

This modern day Christopher Columbus is about to embark on his very own voyage of discovery to a new world, a world which was not about to embrace him, anywhere near as much as he had hoped.

The Wrong Shaped Balls Tour Schedule

Week 1 Thursday Sept 10th Pittsburgh Steelers@ New England Patriots

Week 1 Sunday Sept 13th Miami Dolphins@ Washington Redskins

Week 2 Thursday Sept 17th Denver Broncos@ Kansas City Chiefs

Week 2 Sunday Sept 20th Dallas Cowboys@ Philadelphia Eagles

Week 3 Sunday Sept 27th San Diego Chargers@ Minnisota Vikings

Week 3 Monday Sept 28th Kansas City@ Green Bay Packers

Week 4 Thursday Oct 1st Baltimore Ravens@ Pittsburgh Steelers

Week 4 Sunday Oct 4th Oakland Raiders@ Chicago Bears

Week 5 Thursday Oct 8th Indianapolis@ Houston Texans

Week 5 Sunday Oct 11th New England Patriots@ Dallas Cowboys

Week 6 Thursday Oct 15th Atlanta Falcons@ New Orleans

Saints

Week 6 Sunday Oct 18th Miami Dolphins@ Tennessee
Titans

Week 7 Sunday Oct 25th New Orleans Saints@
Indianapolis Colts

Week 8 Sunday Nov 1st Tampa Bay Buccaneers@ Atlanta
Falcons

Week 8 Monday Nov 2nd Indianapolis Colts@ Carolina
Panthers

Week 9 Thursday Nov 5th Cleveland Browns@ Cincinnati
Bengals

Week 9 Sunday Nov 8th Miami Dolphins@ Buffalo Bills

Week 10 Thursday Nov 12th Buffalo Bills@ New York Jets

  Week 11 Sunday Nov 15th Dallas Cowboys@ Tampa Bay
Buccaneers

Week 11 Thursday Nov 19th Tennessee Titans@
Jacksonville Jaguars

Week 11 Sunday Nov 22nd Dallas Cowboys@ Miami
Dolphins

Week 12 Thursday Nov 26th Carolina Panthers@ Dallas
Cowboys

Week 12 Monday 30th Baltimore Ravens@ Cleveland
Browns

Week 13 Thursday Dec 2nd Green Bay Packers@ Detroit Lions

Week 13 Sunday Dec 6th Denver Broncos@ San Diego Chargers

Week 14 Thursday Dec 10th Minnesota Vikings@ Arizona Cardinals

Week 14 Sunday Dec 13th Oakland Raiders@ Denver Broncos

Week 15 Thursday Dec 17th Tampa Bay Buccaneers@ St Louis Rams

Week 15 Sunday Dec 20th Kansas City Chiefs@ Baltimore Ravens

Week 16 Thursday Dec 24th San Diego Chargers@ Oakland Raiders

Week 16 Sunday Dec 27th St Louis Rams@ Seattle Seahawks

Week 17 Sunday Jan 3rd St Louis Rams@ San Francisco 49ers

Let the tour begin

Departure day had finally arrived, after what seemed to have been a lifetime of work and organising, researching, networking, social media, building a website, recording a song and a whole bunch of other things. This intense period of planning had definitely taken its toll on my body and mind, and the excitement I had felt over the previous few months had diminished somewhat, probably lost in all the excitement, struggle, tension, stress and so on.

My emotional state of mind was far from good and I felt tired, very tired, to be honest, I was exhausted, feeling terribly run down and basically burned out. I had not been sleeping that well over the past week before I left home and I needed tablets to help calm down the anxiety I was now feeling.

Finally the day of reckoning had come, it was time to depart. It felt so surreal, I was going on a journey into the unknown and the unexpected and I was not exactly feeling ready and up for this enormous challenge to conquer America, especially without one single decent or reliable contact who could have been my guiding light, safety net, get out of jail card, friend in a high place......................NOBODY!

This adventure was going to stretch me to the absolute limit of human endurance and patience in every which way possible, mentally and physically, and I was travelling solo.

I packed the trusty old backpack which has been with me all

over the world during the past 20 years, since I bought it in Australia, I said a very sad farewell to my best friend, my great old mum and I headed to the local tube/subway station at Bethnal Green, where I live in East London, en route for Heathrow Airport.

I arrived about 90 minutes later, departing on a what would be a crazy 7 months adventure, not knowing from day one what on earth to expect when I get to places like Atlanta, Baltimore, Cincinnati, Kansas City, Detroit, St Louis, Seattle or any of the other places I never thought I would ever visit in my lifetime and an adventure that most normal people of sound body and mind would never attempt in a million years.

But I quite like this thought, as I am far from normal in many ways, a kind of non conformist, and certainly not a follower of the masses and this suits me fine thank you very much.

I advanced through the usual routine at the airport, checking in, going through all the machines and checks, not knowing that by the end of my tour, I would be doing this another 21 times.

It was never my intention to fly so much, but with this kind of trip, you cannot plan too thoroughly as things can, and do change very often indeed, especially last minute.com, for various reasons. Even though I did a hell of a lot of planning, I obviously could not plan everything, because a lot of the things I did and the places I visited, I could only organise once I was there, but I was planning very meticulously a week ahead at all times.

I had a few hours until my flight to Boston, so I did the usual and had my signature dish of a coffee and a cake (funny as I'm having this now as I type away in my local coffee shop!) and I tried to relax and focus on the job in hand, as much as I could.

Thinking of the adventure ahead, of course I was excited, but I was also feeling anxious, extremely anxious, and this was not like me....AT ALL.

Was it going to be possible? Could I get to all 31 stadiums in 17 weeks? My schedule is set, I cannot change that. What if this happens? what if that happens? Am I going to be safe travelling to places like Atlanta, Detroit, St Louis, or Baltimore, on my own?

Most people thought I was totally mad attempting this mission impossible and I know my mum was worried for my safety, and blimey, she had every right to be. But you know what? I was not and never once was I bothered by any kind of potential danger.

Seriously, now I'm far from any kind of tough guy, I don't fight, I can't, but I am a fast runner. I never really ever feel danger or nervousness, if that's a word. Maybe that's a good thing because there were many times I could have been in the wrong place or part of town at the wrong time, but I never once felt under any real threat, in all the 5 months and 40 cities I eventually visited all over America.

Maybe I give the impression that I'm not a weak or easy option and I will fight and stand up for myself and trust me, I would, if I really had to. My bark is very loud and that's probably my biggest weapon or safety net, as my bite is about as hard as an old woman's without her false teeth! But potential intruders don't know this, so please don't tell anybody!!!

As I was about to board the first of many planes, this one to Boston, only then did I fully realise what a monumental challenge was ahead of me. Is this tour going to be successful? Remember, this was not going to be just a holiday, it was a mission, trying to get my music heard in the US, trying to get interest from the NFL and all its connections and media outlets, as well as trying to raise money for Prostate Cancer UK.

I was also trying to manufacture a new career in another area, a new direction in my life and most importantly than anything else, I wanted to be rich.....and famous, mainly from my music. To be honest, what I really wanted was to be successful, with the money being a bonus or a byproduct to this success.

Was I scared? You know what, not really, I felt numb, and more spaced out than feeling any real fear, I just felt kind of like a car in neutral.

Was this going to be too much for me? Was I excited? Of course I was, but I was very tired and all I wanted to do was sleep, for a week, even a year.

My head was completely spinning and I had not even left the country yet.........until now.

Stadium-1
Gillette Stadium
New England Patriots

I landed in Boston, six and a half hours later after a pretty straightforward flight. It was around 2pm in the afternoon, US eastern standard time about five hours behind the UK. I got my luggage without any problems and I made headway to my new fixed abode for the next 4-5 days, a place called the Friend Street Hostel.

I had been to Boston before, the last time in November 2013 on Thanksgiving when it was absolutely freezing cold, so I was not overly excited about being there. I tried to book into a place where I had previously stayed, the "HI" (Hostelling Intenational), as they had nice rooms with really comfortable beds, as well as a big TV screen in a room near the reception area where I could watch a movie or even NFL matches if they were on.

The HI hostel was also near Chinatown, something which is quite important to me as I like Chinese food, as its not quite so heavy like junk food, as well as it being cheap. Well, to be honest, that was the main reason! I wanted to try to keep away from the dreaded McDonalds, Starbucks, and all these kind of places if possible, but I knew from experience that these joints were worth their weight in gold, for two reasons, WIFI, and toilets, both totally necessary when travelling.

Sadly the HI Hostel was full, so my plan B was to book a place online, and I chose the "Friend Street Hostel" basically out of convenience as it was pretty central, close to the basketball stadium where the Boston Celtics play (if there was a game on, or a decend band was in town) and in good proximity to the main train station where I would be catching the "Patriot train" to watch my very first game.

I checked into the hostel, and I realised pretty quickly that the HI was a much better option. I remember in this hostel there were no main public relaxation areas which most other hostels have, like a TV room, lounge or basically a place you can just chill out, rather than being stuck in your dorm all the time. But it was what it was, and there were many more hostels I had and would later stay in that were, and would be far worse in the following months to come.

The dorm itself was not great at all. I was situated right in the middle of about 12 beds, all flimsy metal bunk beds in which I was on the bottom. I had people on both sides of me, so close I could put my arms out and touch them. There was no privacy from anyone at all, not like when you have a wall, a corner, or even your towel dangling, which I usually do to give myself just a glimmer of privacy, which does make all the difference.

I've been in dorms many times before all over the world, and none of this really bothered me. Most people would never stay in these places at any price, but a part me loves hostels and always will, because you meet some truly amazing people, people you would never meet in a hotel. All the hardships I can cope with, no problem at all, until the night comes and the dreaded snoring starts. This is something you simply never get used to, not this boy anyway.

I checked my bags into my new home, and I got out of the hostel as soon as I could and I went for a walk round the area to see what was local things were around me and on my doorstep. This is something I always do, as its very important to know where your local hole in the wall is (ATM machine), places to eat, shops to get emergency provisions and of course, the local bars.

I stumbled across a bar called "Magann's" as there was an English Premier league (EPL) game on that day which I wanted to watch. Sadly Magann's never had the sports channel I needed, but I decided to stay for a couple of beers anyway, something I very rarely do is drink in the afternoon around 4pm. But in my body it was 9pm and I was on UK time, so my body fancied a couple of swift Britney's, (Cockney rhyming slang for beers....Britney Spears). You will get used to my silly dialect!

I got chatting to a nice guy at the bar, whose name I cannot remember, and after the usual general chit chat, I told him why I was in Boston and he was well and truly impressed. I remember the guy, (I think his name was Dave), telling me he had a bet on the Arizona Cardinals to win the Superbowl at 50-1. My instant reaction was that he had no chance, but I never forgot this as the Cardinals at one point were looking very good, getting to the NFC championship game, where they eventually lost to the Carolina Panthers. Unlucky Dave, but you did have a great run for your money.

A part of me wanted the Cards to get to the Superbowl as I

remember this guy telling me he was once a successful man, but was now in fact homeless. That was hard to believe as he was a normal looking, not too badly dressed intelligent guy who had split with his family and was having a few personal problems and mental issues.

Welcome to my world I thought, but seeing and chatting to this poor guy, I realised my problems were nothing compared to his. I hope he is OK and he got round to sorting himself out, wherever he may be today.

After leaving the bar, I went to the main train station (south) to buy my ticket for the "Patriot Train", which is the only mode of transport available, (other than the obvious car), to take fans to the Gillette stadium, which is about a hour outside of Boston in a place called Foxborough.

It was early evening and I was pretty tired, so I went back to my hostel. It was about 6pm, 11pm UK time, so I was ready for bed and absolutely shattered. After pottering around for a bit I finally attempted to sleep on my bed in the middle of the room. You would think I would have dropped off straight away, but after all the excitement, as well as the jetlag, which always knocks me sideways, I struggled to sleep.

All I remember is I could not sleep very well, people came in and out of the room, there were no real issues, but I never got the proper 8 hours of good sleep I so desperately needed.

I had been given the email address of a singer songwriter in Boston by my PR man Bob before I had left home, so we touched base and I was planning to meet him the following day.

David Moore, who I later nicknamed D-Mo, just like me, as we had the same initials, lived about a 45 minute train ride from the centre of Boston, and I arranged to catch the train out to him in a lovely place called Concord. David was waiting for me at the station when I arrived in his open top jeep and I knew immediately we would become good friends as he was a great guy and I instantly liked him very much.

David is a very talented man indeed. He is a singer/songwriter amongst other things and basically a top man, and we got on like a house on fire straightaway.

David gave me a tour of his local area on the way to his house, through the beautiful little town of Concord. It was something I had never seen before, the architecture was so beautiful, huge wooden houses I had seen in the movies and which looked like something from around 300 years ago to me, I loved it. We were driving around in an open top car, the sun was shining and this was my first proper day in America, and we were in a beautiful setting. So it's a great start.

David gave me a great historical tour of a few landmarks that were and are very special events in the history of the American Revolutuion around the time of 1775. First we went to a museum that explained what happened back in this period of time, just so I had some basic knowledge and understanding, which made me enjoy the events and stories a little bit more.

David then took me to a very famous place, the exact location where the very first Englishman was shot, an event which started the whole conflict off. We stood on the bridge where the fighting started, and we saw the gravestone of the first person to be killed in that war. This was the beginning of the famous "Boston Tea Party" and all the other episodes history tells us about, which happened in this area. I was now at a very important place in the history of America, and the beginning of it's independence that was once governed from London. And so it bloody well should be!!!

After my history lesson, we went back to David's beautiful home and I meet his lovely wife and children. What a house David has, probably the biggest house I think I have even been in. The area of my mum's where I live would fit inside David's garage! It was the kind of house that had another room, then another, then another off another, and so on. Massive it was, and very beautiful indeed.

I must admit, I was very envious, as I compared what I have got in my life, to what David has. We are very similar as we are both singers and songwriters, around the same age, although he looks older than me!!! David is also a good looking boy, a bit like me too!

David has a lovely family and lifestyle, and I just felt a bit of a failure as he had all the things in his life I so wanted in mine. But good luck to David as he has worked hard for all he has and he deserves everything he has got. I hope he forfills his musical dreams and gets the world tour if he wants it. The boy has done well and long may it continue.

David got out one of his guitars, and we had an exchange of

a few of our own songs, but by this time I was now feeling very tired and a bit anxious, so singing a few songs was more than a bit of an effort for me.

David offered me a bed for the night, something I had not planned as I had paid for 3 nights in my hostel in the centre of Boston and as far as I was aware, I had just popped over for a day trip. David mentioned to me he was playing football (soccer) that night with a few of his friends, friends were going to the Patriots game the following night and maybe one of them could have a spare ticket? At the time I had yet to buy a ticket for my first game, so I thought this could possibly be a good opportunity for me to purchase a ticket from a true fan rather than a tout/scalper, and get a ticket at face value instead of one at an over inflated price.

Playing a game of football was the last thing I wanted to do. I had not kicked a ball in anger for quite a few years, I was totally unfit, completely knackered and feeling terribly anxious. I really was in pretty bad shape mentally, as my mind was racing like a train, and the strange thing was, I had no idea why. This is something I just can't control and I wish I had an answer as to why this happens to me.

A few days earlier I got some bad news on a NFL level. The big news of the day was that Tom Brady the New England Patriots star quarterback, who had been given a four game ban, had his ban recinded. My dilemma now was not only financial, but whether any tickets would be available. FCUK!!

Brady is god in Boston, even GOAT (greatest of all time) and righly so, as he has been a tremendous player for the

Patriots over the past 10 years or so. His initial ban for allegedly letting air out of some of the balls, an event nicknamed "deflategate", made him unavailable for my first game of the tour, something I was gutted about as I really wanted to see him play. This meant many tickets were still available at pretty decent prices for an opening game to a new NFL season, a game in which the home team are the previous season's Superbowl champions.

Big named players being in or out of their teams line up's was a major factor that worked both in my favour, and against me throughout the course of the season, biting me on the ass more so in later games in my quest to find and buy tickets at decent prices. If you already had a ticket for a fairly important or so called rivals game, the value would increase or drop if a big player got injured, or returned from an injury. This would happen to me in Pittsburgh on week four when quarterback Ben Roethlisburger got injured. I paid for a ticket in advance online, and the price dropped like a stone when big Ben was ruled out through injury.

So my punch in the face, or pocket, happened when NFL commissioner Roger Goddell did a complete u-turn and recinded Tom Brady's ban, making him available for the opening game against the Pittsburgh Steelers the following night. I could have purchased a ticket for about 150 dollars, approximately 100 pounds a few days ago, a price I was more that willing to pay for an opening game of the season, but I thought because Brady was not playing, getting a ticket would be easy. WRONG! But it would have been if Brady did not play.

I never saw this coming at all, and I never even knew there

was a slight chance Brady would return. If I did, I would have been a lot more focused on looking at ticket prices. But as you can imagine, I had been so preoccupied with a million and one other things on my overworked mind, this issue never entered my head for a second. It was probably splashed all over the TV channels, but hey, this English guy had much more important things to do than watch American TV.

The ticket price for the following night's game doubled immediately on the news of Brady's comeback that day, so my stress levels went up, as the thought of me not getting a ticket for my very first game of the tour was simply not an option.

I took the decision to stay at David's house that night for dinner with his family, play football, and hopefully bag myself a ticket for the game the next day. It seemed like the right thing to do, and made perfect sense.

By this time I was starting to feel very unwell, and extremely anxious, something David and his family never knew about as I did a very good job hiding my symptoms. I was suffering from jetlag, lack of sleep, and anxiety on a scale I have only experienced on a very few rare occasions in my life, including the nightmare in Walsall only two weeks earlier before my live TV interview with Monica Price, which incidently, I had not completely recovered from.

As I have mentioned, I don't know why I feel like this, but it really is a horrible feeling and torture on a personal level. My mind just cannot relax or switch off, it's running in all directions. Even when I speak, my mind is thinking about something else and not thinking of what I'm talking about at the time, making it hard for me to concentrate on what I'm actually talking about and draining my body of all is energy.

When I'm in a situation where I have to concentrate, even for a very short period of time, I feel drained afterwards and I need to be alone in peace to recover, some days I don't recover at all, and some days I recover a little. Some days I recover completely and the next few days and weeks I'm feeling reborn, awake, strong and happy to be alive.

When I'm down, and I mean very down, I feel like my only release would be a strong tablet that will make me sleep for 10 hours, recharging my batteries, or simply to die. But things have only been that bad on a very few rare occasions in my life. Thank god!

During my time at David's house, I felt as bad as I had ever been and have ever been since, and there is no explaination I can give you as to why.

We had a lovely dinner cooked by David's wife, a few beers, which I thought would calm me down, and it usually does, but this time it never did, so my anxiety continued to spiral out of control. After dinner I told David I was feeling very tired and I needed a few hours sleep before we eventually went and played football at around 10pm. Remember this was only my second day in the US, so my body was still on UK time, five hours in front.

I went up to the lovely guest bedroom in David's house and I tried my best to fall asleep and give myself a well earned rest from my racing mind. I only had about two hours until David would come upstairs to wake me around 9.30. I needed more like twelve hours, just to get me back on some kind of even keel. I so wanted to fall asleep, to give my exhausted body a rest, but I just could not switch off my mind, it was racing like a train and I started to feel sick, something I had never experienced before. I was in such a state, and David had no idea. I could not bring myself to tell him, as we had only just met, and he and his family were such perfect hosts. I felt terrible I could not spend quality time with them and return the great company and hospitality they were giving to me.

I never slept for a second of the two hours I was upstairs on the bed, and I was dreading the moment David would knock on the door to get me off the bed to go and play football.

When David did knock, I jumped up, got changed into a football shirt and shorts David kindly borrowed to me, and we quickly left for the football pitches where the teams in the league David's team play for, had their games.

There are simply no words in the English language I can use to discribe exactly how I felt that night. I was so exhausted and anxious, I just cannot explain how much. I met some of David's friends who played for his team, and a few of them were in fact going to the Patriots game the following evening, and a spare ticket was possible, so at least the effort was worth all the pain. Well let me tell you........it was'nt.

The football started and I was running on empty, I had not kicked a ball properly in over 10 years and my fitness level for football was not good at all.

Something I was fully aware of whilst running around the pitch like a headless chicken, and this was getting injured. Can you imagine what would have happened if I broke my leg? Something which was actually very possible. So I decided to take it very easy and I never really got much past second gear.

We played against a team of nice guys, mainly of Asian decent, and these guys had more energy than skill, and more energy in their little toes than my whole body, so it was lots of sprinting, something I'm well and truly out of the loop doing. It was roll on roll off subs, which means people walked on and off every couple of minutes, or when they are fucked, just like I was. This suited me down to the ground, so I played at a leisurely level, missed a penalty and basically did as little as possible.

Remember its now 11pm and I'm still on UK time. Who has ever played football at 4am? I bloody well have! I just wanted this game to end, even before it started, and go to bed as quickly as possible.

I was pretty relieved when the final whistle was blown, I survived a broken leg, the tour was still on, now its time for bed, so I thought. Next stop was the pub, and I needed a drink like a fish needed a pair of socks! I could not believe I was now drinking a pint of Guinness at 5am on my body clock and I'm completely feeling like shit warmed up.

We finally returned back to David's house about midnight, 6am to me. I had hardly slept a wink since I left home. I also slept badly the few days before I left home, so my poor body was crying out for a recharge. I felt like I wanted to be plugged into the wall.

You would have thought I would have slept on a bed of nails that night, but my mind would just not shut down, even on a very comfortable bed. That night was the lowest point I would ever go, and I felt like a nervous wreck. I wanted to be sick, I had diarrhea, but most of all, I wanted to cry. But I could not. The stress on my body was enough to make me faint, and I was fighting not to faint, thinking I would die. I was so frightened.

That night I suffered more than words could ever say and I never fell asleep for a single second of the 7-8 hours I tried, up until David knocked on my door around 9am. It was complete and utter torture. I have no idea as to why my mind would not shut down. Was I suffering from a panic attack?

So now you can imagine how tired and anxious I was. David wanted to do something with me that day, I can't remember what, but I was in no fit state to go anywhere. The only way I was going to stop this self inflicted torture was for me to be alone, so I could deal with it in my own way, and not have the pressure of being around people and having to waste what very little energy I had left on talking and trying to disguise my suffering.

After breakfast, the very little that I could eat, I persuaded David to drive me back to Boston. Very kindly, he did, and I suffered all the way back to my hostel.

David was a fantastic host and I feel terrible I could not be myself in the 2 days I spent with him. If David does ever read this book, and I sincerly hope he does, I want to say a massive thank you for the love I felt coming from you, and the kindness you and your lovely family showed me. Little did you know how terrible I felt, but even in the way I did, I hope I came across as a decent guy and not somebody who seemed a little bit vacant and distant at times, which of course, I absolutely was.

David dropped me back at my hostel, I said my goodbyes and thanked him for his amazing hospitality, before I went straight around the corner to a ticket agency I had already been to previously, as I wanted to know how much the tickets prices had increased because of Mr Brady, for the game that evening.

I eventually bought a ticket for 250 dollars without question, normally very unlike me, as I always try to haggle for a price, but at this point I was practically a zombie, I felt so sick and exhausted, I would have paid double. I simply had no fight left in me to haggle or even engage in conversation as I would have to think, and I had no space left in my head for that. I wanted to get the ticket before I attempted to sleep as I did not want the added thought or worry of not getting into my very first NFL game of my tour. If I had this on my mind, it was yet another thing to stress me out even more, if that was possible.

It was now around midday. I dropped a sleeping pill, set the alarm on my phone, and I fell to sleep after a hour or so of tossing and turning, when my broken body finally decided to shut down after about 48 hours of intense torture.

I slept no more than 3-4 hours, as I had to get up, get myself together, and make my way to catch the "Patriot train", which was leaving at around 6pm. So I got up, still feeling stressed, but a little bit better, I showered and I headed for the south train station in Boston.

I arrived early for the train and I wandered around the train station, as I have always had a big love of trains and train stations. The Patriot train is a one and only train taking passengers back and forth to the Gillette Stadium, the home of the New England Patriots on game days. It arrives outside the stadium a hour and a half before the games start and it leaves around 30 minutes after the games end. The "Patriot train" is just one train, but probably the longest train I have ever seen. If you miss it, you don't see the game. If you miss it coming back, it's an expensive cab ride back to Boston. There is no plan B, unless of course you drive. And most do, I didn't.

I sat down in an area of the station where lots of fans were waiting for the train and I closed my heavy eyes about 90 minutes before the train left. I was far too early and if I would have known, I would have certainly stayed in bed.

As I closed my eyes and tried to calm down, I heard an announcement that shook me to my bones. Coming from the loud speakers was the message, "In no uncertain terms were anybody who were going to the game allowed to take a bag onto the Patriot train or into the Gillette Stadium".
Erm....OK, as over my shoulder I had my little backpack, oh well, not a problem I thought, I will just leave it in a locker at the train station until I came back after the game. So I wandered over to a guy at the information desk inside the

station, and I asked him where the lockers were located. "There are no lockers here buddy" he replied abruptly like I had just sworn at him. "So where am I gonna leave my bag" I said. "That's your problem" he bluntly replied. Great, I fcuking needed this in my state of body and mind like a kick in the bollocks. I honestly did not know what the hell I was going to do.

Now I had to think on my feet, and fast, but I really was in no state at all for someone to throw me a curveball. I walked outside the train station, where the weather was miserable and pouring with rain. I was so out of it, I just wandered out into the rain in such a negative state of flux, I just wanted to get the next flight home. Jumping under the nearest bus was an even easier option.

As I walked out of the station like a zombie, I had one of those moments of luck I will never forget. I had had enough, I could not take anymore, fuck the game I thought, this had now become not important at all, I have to get better as I am gonna end up in hospital. I need sleep and as quickly as possible.

At this point I was beaten, and I really was walking home, a long walk, but a walk I was prepared to do in the pouring rain. I was done, my fight had gone, my tanks were empty and I just wanted to cry. Everything that could go wrong, has.

Because it was raining was my lucky break, as I left the train station, I crossed the road, and I found an area about a minute away, which had a small amount of cover or shelter from the rain. I stopped and sat down on a ledge and put my head in my hands, in seclusion. I just wanted to be alone and away from the noise and the crowds inside the train station. I then had a "moment" with myself. I had never wanted to cry as much in all my life, I just needed a release. I came close but the river never quite flowed, the waterfull I so desperately wanted was dry, what remained was just a dripping tap.

In my thoughts were, "how on earth could I possibly fall at the very first hurdle on my tour"? After all the time, money, work and effort I had put into making this tour get off the ground, how could I even consider missing the very first game? I would be letting myself down and look such a fool if I returned home so soon. I was so exhausted, I was now only concerned for my health, and the game and this bloody stupid tour no longer mattered.

I remember thinking I did in fact have a plan B, which was that the Patriots had another Thursday night game on week 7 or 8, so I was thinking of going back to my hostel, cutting my losses, fuck the 250 dollars, just get well, and return to Boston at a later date.

But then something miraculously changed within me, from nowhere I got a second wind after sitting down for 10 minutes. I was determined not to feel sorry for myself and the more I thought of the game, the more I became excited.

So I got up and I headed back inside the train station with a new positive attitude. This is when I got my second lucky break. I approached a random man in a station full of fans, mostly who were wearing Patriots shirts and colours, as this guy had a backpack over his shoulder. I asked the man in question if he had ever been to a Patriots game before. "No", was his answer, "Why do you ask"? he asked me. "Well" I replied, "Did you not hear the announcement that there are no bags allowed onto the Patriot train or inside the stadium"?

The man's wife walked over and asked what was going on, so I repeated my point and she looked at me like she had seen a ghost. "Go and ask the guy at the desk" I said. "He's right", she replied as she returned. "What are we going to do?" she asked her husband. Then came my second lucky break, as the guy casually said to his wife, " No problem honey, see that man over there on that market stall, he looks after people's bags for 10 dollars".

Now I have no idea how this guy knew that piece of amazing info, considering he had never been to a game before, but I saw this as a sign that I simply had to get on that train.

I could have asked an any number of people about the bag thing, and none of them would have known about the market stall holder and his room in the basement he locks up and stores his things overnight until his next day of trading. This was a massive stroke of luck for me and it was exactly the trigger I needed to inspire me to continue.

I left my bag with the man until the following day, gave him the best 10 dollars I had spent since I arrived, then I boarded the Patriot train with a new spring in my step.

The Patriot train was massive, I think it was about 25 coaches long, maybe more. It was also probably the slowest train I had ever been on, but I could'nt care less, as I found a comfortable single seat, pulled my hoodie down over my head, as well as the hood to my body warmer for double comfort, darkness and privacy, plugged into my Ipod, and I fell asleep against the window. A big weight was lifted.

This was an extremely pivotal moment in my return to a complete and full recovery, and I would never feel like that again until this very day, although it did take around another week before I was back to my good old self. THANK GOD FOR THAT!!

I arrived at the Gillette stadium in what seemed like 5 minutes, it was in fact well over a hour, and after my catnap, I did feel a little bit better. But as soon as I saw the lights and the big sign of the Gillette Stadium, adreneline kicked in as I was sooooo excited.

Standing outside the stadium looking at the name in lights was a very special moment for me. I could have cried, (metorphorically of course), as I so very nearly missed this moment, and I knew how devastated I would have been, and how badly I would have regretted it if I had. I took a few selfies of myself holding my ticket next to the Gillette Stadium sign, and I was just so over the moon to be there.

I had seen this stadium on TV many times, and I never thought that one day I would actually be here to see a game in the flesh. The Gillette Stadium, the home of the Superbowl Champions, the New England Patriots, and their hero Tom Brady was back. All this gave me a tremendous lift and for the first time in 3 days I think I actually had a smile on my face, and do you know what, I bloody deserved it for what I had been through.

I was now really excited and looking forward to the game with my new returned passion. I had about a hour to kick off, so I did what I always do and had a good wander around the stadium, just to see what is there and what's going on.

I eventually got to my seat and I had a nice location high up behind one of the endzones, a position I got to like over the next 35 games. I had a couple of empty chairs on both of my sides, maybe because it was raining, and amazingly these seats would be empty until half time, when I moved to another seat.

That's exactly what I did all season, I bought the cheapest seats in the "gods", or what the Americans call the "nosebleeds", and I moved onto the better or more expensive seats in the second half. It just gives you a different perspective of the same game when you move, and I enjoyed this different angle. I really like the nosebleed seats, not just because they are the cheapest, but you get a much better view of the game than the seats on the lower levels, and seats that usually cost a hell of a lot more.

There was a Patriots fan sitting a few seats away from me who was screaming and chanting from the moment I arrived at my seat. He was very noisy, but also very funny and his comments made all the people around him laugh, including me. Raving mad he was, and one of the very many crazy fans I would encounter at almost every stadium I attended over the course of the season.

With gametime approaching and the music blaring out from

some of my favourite bands from Metallica to Guns and Roses, I'm thinking that one day my song "Like a Touchdown" would not be out of place in this environment. I have a dream!

So out came the players to a wall of sound, fireworks, music, cheerleaders, screaming etc. I was soooo excited. I forget all about my tiredness and stress, and it felt amazing.

The players ran out one at a time, with their names being called out, to the delight of the crazy and noisy fans. Once all the players were out, it was time for the national anthem. The national anthem in America is something very powerful. "The Star Spangled Banner" is played in schools, for all occasions, as well as all major sporting events all of the time. Most Americans seem to love it, and sing it, not like us Brits who see "God Save the Queen" as a bit of a pain in the ass to sing to, and very few of us ever bothered to learn the words.

On the last line of the National Anthem, two American fighter planes flew over the field, and this would become a pattern on my tour, and seemed to signify the start of the NFL games. This was to happen at almost every game I was at, and it was something I always looked forward to seeing.

Now it was game time, the ball was kicked and the 2015-16 NFL season officially starts, as does my "The WrongShapedBalls" Tour, when only a few hours earlier, I had so very nearly given up on this moment.

The New England Patriots Vs The Pittsburgh Steelers, two excellent teams and an great first game of the tour to be at.

The game was exciting from the first play, and by half time, the brilliant Patriots quarterback and legend Tom Brady took control. My new mate next to me does not stop shouting and screaming at every play, I don't know how his voice stands up as he really is screaming hard, but he does a great job, especially when slagging off the visiting Pittsburgh Steelers!

Half time comes and I decided to go for a walk and find a new seat, as my new bestie has now become a bit of a pain in the arse, or the ears (an anagram of arse!) and I've been sitting in the rain for over a hour getting cold and soaking wet.

As I wandered around the stadium, I was amazed to see a Patriots fan at one of the bars queuing for a beer, wearing nothing but a pair of shorts, boots and a hat, with no shirt on, yep topless. I was freezing cold and I had a good few layers on, but all he had for warmth was his big fat belly!! Crazy man, I wish I had my picture taken with him.

The Gillette Stadium is a great stadium to walk around as the game is being played. The level I was on was very open, and you had a great view from many of the bars and walkways, where you could easily see most of the pitch. I wandered around for the entire 3rd quarter, but now I was thinking of leaving soon as I was a little concerned that it would be a mission for me to get back to the Patriot train in such a big crowd, and there was no way I was going to miss this only train back to Boston.

I was now feeling tired, but a good tired rather than an anxious tired. After all, I had sleep deprivation over the past few days and it was now 11pm here in Foxboro, 4am UK time and I'm still suffering from the jetlag.

The game continued to be an exciting game, with both the Patriots and the Steelers scoring touchdowns and looking like good teams. The Patriots were leading by 2 touchdowns or more as I very reluctantly left the stadium with about 10 minutes to go. But 10 minutes from the end of any NFL game can take at least 30 minutes with stoppages for time outs, penalties and certain plays that stop the clock.

I wanted to make sure I got a decent seat home on the Patriot train, as if I did not, it would be a difficult and uncomfortable ride home. I boarded the empty Patriot train before the game was even finished, and I found a nice single seat again, just so nobody could not sit next to me. I did leave the stadium far too early, but again I learned from experience and I was quite happy to be in solitude, away from the noise and crowds, and especially the cold and the rain.

I had done it, I managed to make the first game of my tour against amazing odds and many obsticles. I thoroughly enjoyed the game, even through my tiredness and stress. I felt so proud of myself that I never gave up, although it would have been a very easy option to have done so. Good ole D-Mo!

The final score was 28-21 to the New England Patriots, a lot closer than the game suggested at half time. It was a very good opening game for me to attend, and an amazing occasion. Not one of the best games I would see over the next 5 months, but probably in my top ten.

The Patriot train finally pulled out of the Gillette Stadium station about a hour later as I did my best to sleep, and returned to where all the fun started, at south station in Boston about a ninety minutes journey later, where I struggled to get a cab back to my hostel, as there were so many people coming off the train trying to get a cab home themselves, as by this untimely hour the subway was now closed. I finally got back to my hostel at 2am, 7am UK time, which I was still on after only 3 days away from London.

I finally made it to bed, fell asleep quickly, probably with the biggest fcuk off smile in the world on my face. This was the beginning of my complete recovery.

The next day I had a free day in Boston as I was catching a Megabus bus to Washington DC at 7pm. I checked out of my hostel around midday, left my bags with them, and went for a wander around Boston.

I had been to Boston before, so most of the tourist places I had already seen or been to, including Harvard University, the Boston Celtics Stadium, the Cheers Bar from the TV show and a few museums, so I decided to go for something to eat at the famous Quincy market.

Quincy market is great, has loads of food shops, mainly selling the local Boston dishes of clam chowder, crab, and all kinds of other stuff, mainly based around fish. I walked through the inside area of Quincy market, which has a long parade of shops selling lots lovely food.

There are many people handing out samples in Quincy Market, a good way for you to taste an item, to entice you into purchasing these culinary delights. So I walked through the 200 metres of precinct, taking a piece of this, a little bit of that, until I finally had a belly full and got myself a free lunch. Result!!

I did eventually secomb to the enormous temptation and I bought myself a crab roll, as I always like to try the signature dish of the location wherever I happen to be. It was nice, don't get me wrong, but nothing overly amazing the 12 dollars I paid for the bloody thing suggested.

This was a patten or trap I fell into on my travels. Hindsight smacks me on the ass and reminds that I really did waste a lot of money over the six months I spent in America, mainly on food, and a little tiny bit on beer!!

At some stages, I was spending 50 bucks (35-40 quid) on food A DAY. How? Well, if I happen to stay in a hostel that does not provide breakfast, I will go to a cafe, coffee shop, etc. A coffee and a cake is around 8-10 bucks (6-7 quid), a cup of tea and a sandwich 12-15 bucks, (An Ayrton Senna.....tenner) and so on.

What is a pain in the ass for us non Americans, is when the tax is added on top of the price. So when you see a coffee for say, 4 dollars, a cake for the same, its 8 dollars, right? WRONG. Add the tax, usually 5-6%, sometimes more, so for your breakfast, 8 dollars becomes 9. You tight bastard I hear you cry! Well, now I go and buy a meal in a bar, say fish and chips, 14.99 (another tenner) not the end of the world, until you tax it up and the cent short of 15 becomes 16 and a bit. But then comes the Tyson punch to the boat race (face). THE TIP. Ouch!

Tipping, is a subject I could write a whole bloody chapter on. Tipping is mandatory, not customary in the US and 15% is the bare minimum and totally expected, regardless of the quality of service you have received. So when you eat at a bar, resturant or any other place which requires service from a human being, you have to add 15% to your bill, minimum.

So now my lovely cheap fish and chips for 15 bucks, has turned into 17 by the taxman, now manifests into around 20 dollars with the tip. 30 with the one beer that I had, 40 with the desert and coffee! (come on, I'm on holiday!) and so on. The more expensive the meal, the more expensive the tip.

So can you now see how easy it was to spend 50 pictures of George Washington, Abraham Lincoln, or soon to be Donald Trump! (YES HE WON), as I write my second draft! I now realise I should have maybe gone to a supermarket, bought some bread and ham, a tomato and a bag of crisps, but when I see all this incredible food in the bars like pulled pork, brisket, burgers (no cheese thanks, and I will save this subject about the dreaded yellow muk for when I get to Green Bay on week 3), the temptation is too much for me and I want to get stuck in, and I usually did.

I left Quincy market after a nice feed, and I went for a walk in the park in the centre of Boston. I wandered around a bit, looking at a few of the statues and monuments in the park, looked at some nice buildings, then I went on a 2 hour bus tour taking me around the main sites of Boston.

I eventually returned to the hostel on Friend street, picked up my things, and I headed for the bus terminal to catch my overnight bus to Washington DC.

I've never had a problem with travelling long distances on buses, or coaches as we call them in the UK. For me they are a great time to reflect on how things are going, ponder over nice times, people I had met, as well as giving you the time to plan the next week in advance, which is how I rolled. Nightbuses were also a way of saving money on accommodation, which or course, was always a good thing. The buses had wifi most of the time, but on a lot of the Greyhound buses, they did'nt work, and when you were on a long ride, wifi was very much needed to get you through the boredom.

On the buses is where I used the time to write down my notes in my travel journal, post pictures and video's on Facebook, Twitter and Instagram, as well as updating my website www.thewrongshapedballs.com which I did a hell of a lot of times over the six months I was on the road. I also took this time to try to talk, or text (SMS) with as many of my friends around the world as I could.

I remember one time I was having conversations with around 10 people at the same time. From England to Italy to Australia to Canada, America, Slovenia and so on. Technology is so amazing, and it always made me feel closer to home and near my friends and family, something that was very important to me.

I always made sure I planned properly regarding accommodation, and I would never arrive into a city unless I had booked into a hostel or hotel beforehand, especially late at night. The same went for tickets for the NFL games I attended. I was buying some a few days before the games, but mainly last minute.com on my favouite website

Tickpick.

Tickpick were great to me, they gave me 20 dollars off every ticket I bought from them after I informed them of my tour before I left home. I even managed to get a ticket for 1 dollar as it was on sale for 21 bucks. Ha! Mind you, this deal did change later to 20 dollars off tickets I bought which cost over 50 dollars, and 10 dollars off for under.

That 1 buck ticket was in St Louis between the Rams and the Tampa Bay Buccanneers. I also got a ticket for the Arizona Cardinals Vs the Minnesota Vikings game in Phoenix for 5 bucks. On the day of that game, tickets were on Tickpick for 100 dollars. Touch!

The reason these tickets were so cheap was because I had bought them a long way in advance, a few months in fact, and these games were not exactly the biggest or the most attractive games on the NFL schedule, they were normally struggling teams playing in large stadiums.

Of course all the tickets I bought were not this cheap, it did depend on how each team started their seasons, winning or losing. Another factor was the location of the away team as they probably would not have much support, especially if they were from far away, unless you were a fan of the Cowboys, Raiders, Dolphins, Patriots or Packers. These fans were nationwide and tickets for these teams were always a lot higher, purely because of the demand.

My Megabus left Boston right on time, on the 11 hour journey through the night to my next destination, the capital city of the USA, Washington DC. Boston had nearly killed me, but from this point onwards, the only way I was going was up.

One down 30 stadiums to go.

Stadium-2
Fed Ex Field
Washington
Redskins

The bus ride to Washington DC arrived into New York for a 2 hour stop over at around 10pm. So when It did, I do what I always do, explore and have a look round to see what's going on. I knew I could not go too far from the coach station, so I went upstairs and out into the fantastic and busy streets of New York City.

I absolutely love New York, I could live there, it has everything I want, it totally excites me. It was Friday night, so NY was busier than usual. I got myself a hot dog from a street vendor for two dollars, a meal I would have on a regular basis, to keep the dollars from flowing out of my pockets like a river and I wandered around a bit and people watched for an hour or so.

I remember thinking as I stood on the street that I would return here in 10 weeks time, so it felt strange and a little sad that I would not be in this great city for more than 90 minutes, most of those minutes sitting and waiting next to a bus heading for the capital, Washington DC.

Back on board the bus, off we go and it's now midnight, and time to try to get some sleep.

We arrived into Washington DC at 5am, and it's just about getting light and not many people are around when we pulled into the bus terminal. It's also too early to catch the subway to my accommodation, so I have no choice but to get a taxi to my hostel called "Duo Housing".

I arrived at my hostel fully aware I had a small dilemma, as normally you cannot check into your dorm room until anytime between 11am and 3pm, so I expected a pretty rough morning. I was checked in by a really nice friendly Serbian guy named Nino and I sat in the lounge area and closed my eyes, expecting a long wait until I could climb into my bunk. Then to my surprise, I received a lovely gesture from Nino, as he took me to a spare bed in another dorm, so I could sleep until I eventually checked into my own dorm. RESULT! Thanks Nino.

I slept for a few hours, as I was still in a state of vegetation after the past few days, as well as getting hardly any sleep on the overnight bus ride, so when I finally surfaced, I went to my designated dorm bed and organised my things before heading out to see what DC had to offer me.

Hostel Duo Housing was a great choice of a hostel, the dorm rooms were ok, six beds to a room, they had a great TV lounge where I remember watching English football as well as the NFL. There was a great roof terrace, something I always like in a hostel as you can sunbathe, play the guitar if they had one and generally meet and hang out with people. And at night....party. BINGO!

The breakfast at Duo was beautiful. Muhammad the owner, a young African American ex dancer for loads of famous performers, and as camp as christmas, was a really lovely and friendly host. He cooked amazing chocolate chip pancakes for all the guests and we all sat together in the kitchen having our breakfast like one big happy family, which was a nice way to meet other people in the hostel.

I thoroughly enjoyed my time in the three nights I stayed at the Duo and Muhammad made me feel so very welcome.

I had also been to DC two years earlier, so again, as in Boston, it held no real excitement for me. Don't get me wrong, I enjoyed both places, but it had no mystery to me, as I had had a good look around both these places on my previous visit.

The last time I was in DC was on Christmas day of 2014 and the cold weather was brutal, but today the sun was beaming down and I was in shorts and flip flops, so I felt great.

I knew my way around town quite well, so I headed off to Chinatown for some lunch. After stuffing my face, I wandered around a bit and I saw on a billboard that last night Madonna was in town doing a gig at the hockey stadium. I would have loved to have seen her, but I was a day late, GUTTED!!! so I returned to the hostel, watched a bit of telly and I had a much needed early night.

Dorm life is not for everyone, actually it's not for many, but if you are travelling on a budget, it's a necessity. Hostels are a lot cheaper than hotels, especially if you are travelling alone like me. If there are two of you, a hotel can be a better option if you pay the rate by the room and not the person. But you meet so many amazing people as well as some complete wankers in hostels. All good fun and experiences.

I totally love these places and I would not stay anywhere else.

You meet far more nicer people than idiots in hostels and there always seems to be a kind of travellers bond. Making friends is very easy indeed, especially if you are like me and talk to anyone! You normally end up wandering around the streets in groups, looking at the main tourist attractions together, usually ending up going out to bars or dinner, which is much better than spending most of the time being alone, which is what I did quite a bit. I will come to a few lonely times for me later in the book.

A lot of the people I met in hostels, were people travelling for just a few weeks, unlike my six months or more, so lots of these people, who incidently are a lot younger than me, want to party and this does not come cheap. The same goes for eating out. I would absolutely do the same as them if I was away for just two weeks, but eating out, especially drinking, is not cheap in the bars of the US, especially having to tip the bar staff a dollar for simply pouring your every drink. WHAT! yep. I can't imagine how many dollar tips I gave away over six months. Well over 250 dollars I would guess.

There are always the odd random people in hostels who behave the same as they are at home and they don't seem to realise there are other people in the dorm. They can treat the dorm as if it's their own bedrooms and have little regard or respect for the other people who are trying to sleep.

I've had people arrive in the middle of the night, turn the light on at 3-4am, making a noise, coming in drunk, people playing games on their phones, text messages beeping all night, alarms going off, people shagging and basically not giving a shit about the other people trying to sleep. Well that's enough about me!!! But the worse thing ever is ....snoring.

Let's get this straight, most people snore, yep most, but not all, just almost all. I do, so I'm told. Teenagers snore, as do old women, the worse by far are old men. If I saw there was an old man in my dorm and there were, quite a lot of the time, I knew I had to get my head down before him or I knew trouble was coming and a good sleep would be ruined. I wear ear plugs, which are a great help, but not when you have an old man in your dorm who snores like the proverbial pig or somebody revving up their motor bike! I will tell you a story later of a guy who snored so loud in Miami, it was incredible.

I had an incident this night with an Israeli guy who was talking on the phone. He was shouting so loud he never needed the phone, they could have heard him in Tel Aviv without it! But he went on for ages and nobody had the guts to tell him, until I did. He was standing right outside my room but right against the window I was next to and his noisy aggressive harsh tone was giving my ass a headache. So I politely opened the door and kindly asking him to shut the fcuk up. He did and he apologised, as he never realised he was being a pain to others and this is something some people don't realise when they stay at a hostel. But most backpackers are usually very respectful.......most.

That night I think I had my best night sleep since I left home. Not brilliant, but better, which wasn't hard to be honest, as switching off was so painfully difficult up until now. But I was now well and truly on the mend. THANK GOD!!

It was now Sunday and game two on my tour and the kick off time of 1pm was a great time to watch football, so I got up around 8am, had a lovely breakfast of chocolate pancakes and coffee and I headed off to the home of the Washington Redskins, Fed Ex Field.

The visitors were the Miami Dolphins, a team I would see four times on my tour. This was just the way my schedule panned out and I was cheering for the Dolphins as the Redskins are the big rivals to my team, the Dallas Cowboys.

I paid 32 dollars (25 quid) for my ticket from Tickpick, which I found amazing for a team's first home game of the season and I arrived at the stadium a whole lot easier than my eventful adventure on the Patriot train in Boston. I also learned not to carry a bag to anymore NFL games for the entire season!!

I had been to the Redskins stadium two years before, to see my Cowboys win with a last few seconds winning touchdown, so I knew how to get to Fed Ex Field. It took about a hour on the subway and it was a nice and friendly ride with all the Redskins fans in all their colours and funny outfits.

I remember having a few pictures taken with a fan who was wearing a massive belt, the kind worn by a boxing champion. I thought he was mad carrying this thing around all day, as it was so heavy. Crazy, but in a good way. This was just one of the many unusual props NFL fans would wear or carry throughout my tour and it was always hilarious to see some very strange or funny objects associated with their teams.

I so love the NFL fans, they are just such lovely people and I had so many random and funny conversations with fans from practically every single one of the 32 teams on my tour. Some of these brief meetings turned into lucky breaks, like finding tickets, nights out and even long term friendships. Happy times indeed.

After leaving the train, I had a walk of about 20-30 minutes to the stadium from the subway station at the other end. I did not mind this at all as the sun was beaming down, which was much better weather than on my previous visit.

By this time, I had yet to experience a tailgate, as I had arrived at the Gillette Stadium on the "Patriot Train" in Boston quite late and as sick as a pig. Tailgating for those who don't know, is basicially a piss up/BBQ before the game starts, a party before the party!

Tailgates are absolutely amazing and I would attend many a fantastic tailgate later on my tour, with some awesome people who will be my friends for life, all thanks to one amazing man named Tim Young, whom I met in Atlanta. He will arrive in the book seven weeks later.

Outside Fed Ex Field I somehow managed to scrounge a bit of food from some people, after I used one of my biggest weapons.... my English accent. I would say, "Hi, I'm from England, what is that you are eating"? "You wanna try some buddy"? was a normal reply, "Get this man a beer" was another. It was that easy most of the time, but not always, as I did encounter the odd custard pie to the face! Happy days and money saved, as the food and drink prices in the stadiums are so expensive.

After my free meal, I headed into the stadium and I went to find my section. I had a standing ticket high up in the nosebleeds, behind one of the endzones.

Fed Ex Field at one time was the biggest capacity stadium in the NFL and there were a lot of seats in sections of the stadium which were not being used. This probably went back to the days when the Redskins had a bigger following of fans, or when they were a little more successful.

My view was absolutely spectacular and boy I was well pleased paying just 32 bucks, especially as I had paid 250 for my opening game. BOOM!

The weather was gorgeous and I was loving the pre match entertainment as gametime approached. I went and sat in a seat in front of my standing section as the game was about to start because so many of them were empty. And why not?

Out came the two teams to banging rock music and fireworks, the national anthem started, the usual flyover took place, something I always looked forward to seeing, as it could be any kind of aircraft flying over, from a jet to a stealth bomber to a bunch of helicopters, always worth the wait. So a happy bunny is D-Mo.

The game started and a few minutes into the game, a pretty young lady sat right next to me. I apologised to her for sitting in her seat, but she said it wasn't a problem as there were so many empties, so she sat next to me and we chatted away while the game was in progress.

Her name was Christiana, she hated football and was only there because her boyfriend worked at the stadium and got her a free ticket. A part of me was a little bit upset when she mentioned the boyfriend, as she was pretty hot and she did say that she loved my accent!! She was from San Francisco and she followed her boyfriend to Washington DC, because of his job.

We chatted quite a bit and Christiana even opened up and told me about some of her personal issues and previous problems with a drug addiction. This completely made me change my course or action and immediately I switched off my intentions of trying to jump on her bones, to just being an English gentleman.

It's amazing how so many people you meet, tell you personal things when you have only just met them. Maybe its just a kind of release for them to talk to somebody they don't really know, and not be judged? I don't know.

Her boyfriend Tommy eventually came along and I thought he was a very nice guy, especially when he took us both to another area of the stadium where the seats were better and more expensive, so that was good and another piece of luck. Now I was on a roll.

The game itself was not exactly a classic, the Miami Dolphins won 17-10 and I got the result I wanted. There was a great atmosphere inside the stadium, mainly because there were a lot of Dolphins fans inside and all around me.

I had a nice time at this stadium, I liked it a lot. It was big, open and the sun was shining, which always makes things seem a whole lot better. I said goodbye to my American friend Christiana, and I left the impressive Fed Ex Field, to go back to Duo Housing hostel for a BBQ on the roof that evening, provided for free by the lovely Muhammad and to watch the big game that night, my Dallas Cowboys at home to their big divisional rivals the New York Giants.

The BBQ was great, Muhammad did us proud with some delicious food and drinks, all for free, bless him. I went down to the lounge and watched my Dallas Cowboys win in a very exciting game, making a great comeback against our big divisional rivals, the dreaded Giants. The Cowboys had now won their first two games and their next game would be in Philadelphia, just a few hours up the road from here in the capital of the US and I would be there to see them.

But before then, I had the small task of a three hour flight to one of the most difficult places to see a game that I would experience on the entire NFL schedule....Kansas City.

My third and final day in DC, I was a tourist. I had a wander around the centre of the city, took a look at the White House, the Capital Hill building, which sadly was covered by scaffolding and sheets so I could not get the nice pictures I wanted. I went inside the Smithsonian National Museum of America for a few hours, then I saw the Lincoln Memorial, three other ex presidents memorials, the Martin Luther King memorial, all lined up around one big riverside walk, before jumping on the subway to have a look at the grave of John F Kennedy and thousands of others at Arlington cemetery. Arlington cemetery was absolutely massive, there were so many gravestones of fallen American soldiers from the many wars the US have been involved in over the 100 or so years. If there was ever a place to visit for presidents, politicians or leaders of nations thinking of going to war, this was it. Only then will they realise what a complete and utter waste of time and human life war is.

I remember posting a video on facebook highlighting this very fact. Let's be honest, when there are wars, there are never any winners. Did we win the two world wars in Europe, Kuwait, Iraq, or Afghanistan? No, look at the aftermath and repercussions like 9/11, 7/7, Paris, Brussels Etc. If we had never got rid of the likes of Saddam Hussein or Colonel Gaddafi, maybe none of these terrible events would have happened and so many innocent lives lost. The Muslim world would probably not hate us quite as much as they do now?

I wish both the US and the UK would stop trying to police the world and not stick their noses into other country's business, especially the ones run by tyrants, as you can never completely beat these people, no matter how hard you try. The only losers on both sides are the poor people of both countries who simply have to rebuild their shattered lives and mop up the mess left by our stupid governments. We have more than enough problems in our own countries to concentrate on, rather than get drawn into dictatorships, or rogue nation's issues, which have absolutely nothing to do with us and import their third world problems into our more democratic lifestyle and civilised world. Rant over!

Dennis Moss

Stadium-3
Arrowhead
Kansas City Chiefs

I arrived into Kansas City at 4pm, after a three hours flight from Ronald Reagan airport in Washington DC.

When I did my research on Kansas City a few months ago, I found there were no hostels in town, so plan B was Air B'n'B. This is basically where people rent out their properties, or even just a room, usually on a short term basis.

I decided to look into the crazy world of "couchsurfing", which is an option where you can stay in the house of a person who has travelled, and stayed in the home of other travellers in different countries. These people make their homes available to visitors on the Couchsurfing website, and invite you to stay with them in their homes to help you save money.

It sounds a little dodgy, but you have to join the couchsurfing website, input your details and accept to potentially being a host in the future. I did message quite a few people, and after a while I did see an interesting pattern forming, something in which I did in fact experience later on my tour.

I noticed a lot of the hosts were single men living alone, I messaged one, who replied asking me if I had read his advert clearly? I obviously had not, when he asked me if I would be comfortable walking around his flat stark bollock naked! He was claiming to be a naturist couchsurfer, WTF was that? This is one of many weird and wonderful people out there on couchsurfing, and I kind of saw this website as some kind of gay pick up point.

I contacted a guy, and I'm gonna call him Colin, just to protect myself from being sued in the future for defamation of character. (especially as this guy was a lawyer!) Colin replied after a few days and he seemed a little more normal than most of the people I had viewed and emailed from the website.

Colin had travelled a bit, stayed in other people's homes on his travels and he seemed the best of a very bad bunch of people offering their couches in Kansas City. Luckily he welcomed me with open arms, as I was desperate for Colin to put me up as there were no other options available to me in KC, except for expensive hotels.

Colin and I exchanged details and I arranged to meet him in the centre of town at a hotel near the main train station. This is where the fun started over the next 4 nights I stayed with Colin.

I had to get from Kansas International airport to downtown, which was about a hour bus ride away. I arrived into the central bus terminal, where I had to get a number 47 bus to Union Station, which was across the road from the hotel I was meeting Colin.

I arrived into the bus terminal and as I waited for my bus, I quickly noticed I stood out like dogs balls, as I was the only white face around. But this never bothered me as I had experienced this situation quite a lot on my previous trip to America, without any incidents, and I would be in many worse places than Kansas for feeling very much out of place than this.

Luckily I never had any problems, but you always get looks of curiosity, or stares like the way a hungry dog looks at you when you are eating your dinner! but I can live with that. On the very rare occasions where anybody shows me aggression or attitude, I usually end up talking to these people and we tend to get on like a house on fire.

I jumped on the bus and headed for the hotel to meet with Colin. I got there a little early so I relaxed in a bar for a while and I had a coffee.

Half a hour later, Colin turned up in his old car, and out gets this tiny little old man who instantly reminded me of Danny DeVito's character from the Batman films, the Penguin. Colin was very pleased to meet me and he was very welcoming, a really nice and friendly old guy.

Colin is around 65, a lawyer, an atheist, an activist and bisexual, all his own words, which he mentioned to me as he drove me to the airport as I was leaving town 4 days later. Phew! Thank god he never told me this when we first met and before I stayed at his house, as this would have made my very uncomfortable indeed. So off we go to his house, or so I thought. WRONG!

Being some kind of activist, something I was yet to discover, Colin informed me he had a meeting with a group of people regarding a project in Honduras for Amnesty International. People were being persecuted, so Colin and his friends wanted to help raise awareness regarding these issues. I needed going to this meeting like a needle in the eye, but I had no choice but to go with him.

So there I was, in shorts, tee shirt and the trusted trainers I wore every single day at some point on my entire tour of over 7 months, as I had just left Washington DC in glorious sunshine. Kansas in the evening at that time of the year was a bit cooler but OK, so off to the centre of Kansas City we went.

We got to the venue for the group discussion and slide show about Honduras, and I met with the rest of the group, a very eclectic and odd bunch of people indeed. The so called leader of the pack was a very young girl in her early 20's, and she was so passionate about this cause, but I could not quite understand why, in my very own judgemental way.

Good for her for helping these poor people in their struggle with corruption and the hardships imposed on them by their loony government, but should'nt some young chick of this age be out enjoying her own life with her mates? If it was an older woman say, in her 50's, I kind of get that, but this odd looking young girl speaking like she was an elder statesman did not quite correlate with me. But like I say, good for her.

I was in this meeting for about 2 hours, and I was freezing my balls off in the airconditioned room, as well as being bored shitless. I had to look interested as I did not want to seem ungrateful and especially uninterested in front of my new host Colin and his motley crew!! I just wanted to shut off my already overworked mind and go to bed, as I had been travelling for about 10 hours and it was now around 8pm.

The meeting finally ended (thank god) and we headed off back to Colin's house, which was about a 30 minute drive along the freeway.

Not a lot of people know this, but there are in fact two Kansas City's, one in the state of Kansas and the other in the state of Missouri, as KC borders on the state line. The airport is in Missouri, the Kansas City Chiefs stadium is in Kansas, the Amnesty meeting and where Colin worked was in Kansas and Colin's home was in Missouri. Are you with me? Great, lets continue!

The only way for me to get from Kansas City in Missouri, to Kansas City in Kansas, is by car. I think there was a bus, but it was a very infrequent and unreliable service, so I had to rely on Colin to pick me up and drop me off, over all 4 days I was with him. This was a major pain in my ass and a headache for me and my independence, as I hate relying on other people, as I feel I'm a burden, and in this case, I was. Of course I could have taken cabs, but that was a last resort, again because of the cost.

We headed for Colin's place and he suggested we go for something to eat, so we went to an all you can eat buffet he knew, and the food was amazing, as well as fairly cheap. I paid for Colin's as a thank you for letting me stay at his place, something I always did to anyone who let me stay in their homes over the course of my trip. I always paid my way.

After a belly full of the all you can eat buffet, with the usual problem of trying everything on the menu and eating far too much, we proceeded to go to Colin's house.

I had no expectations of Colin's house at all, I never really gave it a thought, but as we pulled into his street, I realised we really were in the middle of nowhere, with no hint of public transport whatsoever.

I had just left the capital city of the USA, with a full public transport system, now I was in the middle of woop woop (nowhere) with no options at all. If DC is the brain of America then Kansas is probably the rectum! (only joking, just my kind of humour)A complete juxtaposition.

This is where the real fun started. (oh boy!) Out of the car we got, and into the house. As soon as Colin opened the door and I walked into his pad, I knew this was going to be my biggest challenge to date, as my sinuses were immediatedy blasted with the strong and pungent aroma of dogshit.

Now I am a dog lover, I really am, and a big one, but dogs have to be trained, and if they mess in the house, love em or not, they will get my boot up their asses, period (full stop), as this is how these little guys learn. You have to be cruel to be kind sometimes as animals do have the knack of walking all over their owners, just like young kids do to their mums.

Colin kept two dogs in a big cage in the corner of his kitchen, and they had obviously messed in their cage as they had been there all day on their own, the poor things, with nobody to let them out. They had also at some point done their business all over the house as there was clear evidence of this by the yellow patches, brown staines and markings they had left all over the entire house.

The smell was just too much for me, that typical pet shop kind of smell that makes you gag after a while. Luckily the room I was staying in was at the other end of the house from the kitchen, and although I could still smell the piss, it was not as bad as the rest of the house. I would close the door and spray the room with my deodorant, which helped a little bit, but not eliminate the smell completely.

I went to the toilet for a pee, and the toilet was absolutely filthy. What the hell was I doing here? I thought, over a million times. If there was a hotel in this area, I swear, I would have left straight away.

Things were about to get a whole lot worse as I returned to my room and one of the lovely little dogs had left me a present (a turd on the carpet next to my bed). I told Colin and he came to pick it up. Then he said something I will never forget for the rest of my life. "Which dog did it?" he asked. "I think it was that one" I replied. "What different does that make? " I said. " Well if it was that one who did it, the other one would have eaten it"!!! I swear, if you could have seen my face, it was a contorted picture of horror. I was mortified, especially as Colin thought this was funny and laughed out load. Sorry, but I did'nt find this funny at all.

On reflection, I can laugh out loud now, and I hope you are

too! but then, especially after the big feed up of all different meats and deserts I had just consumed, I seriously wanted to throw up.

Bedtime came and I actually slept well at Colin's place, christ knows how, but I did, probably because being in the middle of nowhere, it was dead quiet, and dark, plus I could switch off my mind to any distractions that I normally had, eg, the dreaded snoring I had experienced in various dorm rooms I had slept in so far.

My state of mind was now back to normal, I felt no pressure, tension, anger, anxiety or stress. (Thank God) So being in a house that stank of dog piss was a much better place to be than being trapped in my own anxious and stressful world.

I think the initial suffering I had experienced, helped me overcome every obstical or hardship I would encounter over the next 5 months, and boy, there were soooooo many, but as long as I felt strong and healthy, every single problem bounced off me and I coped with these challenges very easily indeed, anything the universe threw into my path, I simply brushed off. I was Superman!!

The next day, Colin was going to work into the centre of Kansas City, as he had to go to court, so of course I was not going to stay at his place all day on my own with his two little smelly rats, so I went with him. He went to work, dropped me off in the centre of town, and I agreed to meet him later for lunch.

I found a nice looking coffee shop downtown, and I got

stuck into the usual coffee, cake and wifi, got online and googled things to do in Kansas City.

As I was on my laptop in the corner of the coffee shop, a guy came over to me, and said. "Excuse me sir, but are you the English guy who is doing the tour of all the NFL stadiums"? "Yes I am, but how do you know this"? was my reply. "I've seen your face online" he said.

I was well chuffed. God knows where he saw me, but this made me feel like some kind of minor celebrity. All publicity is good I thought, it can only raise my profile, and possibly lead to bigger and better things, including my music. BOOM!

Ryan was the guy's name, and he was in the coffee shop to have a meeting with someone regarding his work. We chatted for a few minutes and he asked me if I was going to be at the Chiefs Vs Broncos game the following night. "Of Course" I said. "Well, I'm going to be at a tailgate, why don't you join me and my clients". he offered. "Sweet, count me in" I replied. We exchanged numbers, and in came his colleague and off Ryan went. A really lovely friendly guy Ryan was, or so I thought. But sadly, this would change completely the following day.

Colin picked me up from the coffee shop around lunchtime, so off we went for lunch in a resturant he recommended. Colin said his mate was coming along, which was fine by me, and when he turned up, it did'nt take me very long to realise that he was more than a little odd, just like Colin. But these guys were harmless, and actually quite entertaining in a funny kind of way. Not my usual cup of tea or the company I normally keep, but I could see they had good hearts, and that's normally good enough for me.

We had a nice lunch of Mediterranian food, not my most favouite choice of cuisine in the world, but it was OK. After lunch Colin drove me around and showed me some of the highlights of Kansas City, including the World War one museum, which looked nice from the outside. I saw some funky architecture and many nice modern buildings in the centre of Kansas City, as well as some very beautiful houses, things I never expected to see in Kansas. Maybe I was influenced by the thoughts in my head of the movie "The Wizard of Oz", and I was expecting everything to be made out of wood and a yellow brick road leading all the way to Arrowhead Stadium!!!

Colin also took me to what he called Kansas City's number one tourist attraction, a massive sports shop, or so I thought. Now I had no intention of going to a sports shop as I did not want the temptation of buying some random shit, which I normally do. But this was no ordinary sports shop, it was a huge place full of large stuffed animals and thousands upon thousands of guns and other weapons.

Moose heads, elk, deers, horses, even lions and tigers, as well many other types of large animals were hanging all over the walls, and to me this was quite a scary sight. To a London city boy, this was something I had never seen before. And the guns? I've never seen anything quite like this, rifles of all shapes and sizes, hand guns, big guns, little guns, hunting guns, etc etc. I found it fascinating but also a little bit creepy.

I was in one of the biggest hunting states in America, and something I had never encountered before, so although the experience made me feel a little uncomfortable, it was interesting and quite exciting at the same time. A shop selling death I thought!

See, I'm a big animal lover, and the thought of shooting and killing something scares the shit out of me. I can understand shooting pests, rodents or animals that cause people personal damage, but I get upset to think that people shoot big animals like deers or even bears, but that's what they do in Kansas and I just have to accept it, even though it's not for me. I'm a guest in their town, so whatever goes, goes.

Then there is the topic about having a gun for protection, again normal in many places in America. This is also very strange to me coming from London, as I've never seen a gun in my life that would be used to protect someone or be used to kill something. As a kid, I did in fact have a pellet gun called a "Black Gat", it was so weak that when my friend once shot me with a dart, I laughed!! But sometimes it did hurt if it got you in the right place.

I felt a million miles away from my own world, but I have to admit, it was exciting. I think you had to be there to get what I mean, as Kansas City was without doubt one of the most unlikely places I ever thought I would visit in my lifetime, but seeing this different mentallity and lifestyle was a real eyeopener for me, and I am so glad I had the chance to experience this culture or way of life.

After this interesting experience, we returned to Colin's home, and I was dreading getting back to that rancid smell of stale dog piss. I went straight to my room, basically because there was nothing else for me to do other than post some things on social media and my website. Colin wanted to watch a film together or show me some of his DVD's, but I could not be in that area of the house for more than a moment, as it really did smell so bad. Looking back, I can't imagine what DVD's he wanted to show me!

Thursday arrived, the day of my third game of the tour, and I remember Colin was working from home, so I was stuck in my room trying to avoid the smell for a few hours. I could'nt even go out for a walk as there was nothing local for me to do, or go to without a car.

I was now struggling bigtime at this point staying at Colin's, as I had now been in the house for two nights and I so badly wanted to leave, but I simply had knowhere else to go. I just had to get on with it, which was not easy......at all.

In the afternoon, Colin drove me to the centre of town again as he had to go to court. I had been searching online, and somehow I found a hostel in the centre of downtown Kansas City. God knows how, because I had checked before I arrived into town and there were no hostels on Hostelworld or Hostelbookers, or the other websites I had been using for many years. I emailed the hostel, got a quick reply, so I immediately went to check it out.

When I got to the address of the hostel, it was very difficult to find. It was called the "Loft Hostel", and it was high up in a very large building with no signs or indication as to it's whereabouts or location at all. When I eventually found it, I met the person I had received the email from, and she informed me that this hostel was for women only. FCUK! I have to stay at Colin's for two more nights, was my first thought. Why did this woman not tell me this on the bloody email? The woman in question said she would have a word with the women guests, and see if any of them objected to me staying. If they did not, I was in.

The lady got back to me later that day and she informed me that it was fine for me to stay, so I was well pleased this would be my last night at Colin's pet shop.

I went back to the same coffee shop I usually hung out in, in downtown Kansas, for a few hours of internet, until Colin picked me up and we went to lunch. After lunch we returned to Colin's home for a couple of hours, and again I was stuck in my prison cell.

I was very happy when I received a text message from the lady at the hostel I had visited, saying I could stay at her hostel for the next two nights. This put a big smile on my face, as I was finally going to be let out of prison! I informed Colin I would be moving out the following day into a hostel in the centre, as this made it easy for me to get to the airport when I left town, as I did not want to be a burden to him by asking for a ride to the airport, which was not exactly the real reason for my early departure from his home.

Then came the TYSON PUNCH! a hour or so later, to my complete and utter surprise, I got another text message from the lady at the hostel saying sorry but one of the women guests was not comfortable with me staying at their hostel, so sadly I could not stay. A complete 360 u turn in 60 minutes, fucking great, after telling me by text (SMS) I was welcome. I had the very embarrassing task of backtracking and explaining to Colin and his two mutts I was gonna stay another two nights and they were stuck with me! Colin was absolutely fine I was staying on, but I so badly wanted to leave.

That night was the big game in Kansas, the Chiefs against their divisional and arch rivals the Denver Broncos. Colin had so very kindly offered to drive me to the game, and pick me up after it ended at Arrowhead stadium, which incidently was in the middle of nowhere, and impossible to get to for anybody who never had a car, just like me.

I was very grateful to Colin, it was a lovely gesture as basically I had no other way of getting to the stadium other than a very expensive cab ride there and back. I could'nt thank Colin enough for his awesome gesture.

It took us about a hour from Colin's place as we got stuck in traffic, but we arrived at Arrowhead stadium around 6pm for a 8.30 (2.30am UK time) kick off. It was a just over week after I left home and my body was still more than a little on UK time.

It was a hot and sticky evening as I approached Arrowhead stadium, and I was very excited when I saw the big sign on the stadium. I was in Kansas City, I had never met anybody who had been to Kansas City, so I felt very happy and privilaged to be here at the same time.

My jetlag was still lurking, as you can't change time zones and feel completely as you would do at home in a week, but

I was OK. I was looking to hook up with Ryan (the guy I had met the day before in the coffee shop in downtown Kansas City) at his tailgate, have some food, and a couple of beers. GREAT?............. NO!

I sent Ryan a text message, and I asked him where he was, so I could join up with him and his crowd, have a few beers, and hopefully a bellyfull of some of Kansas City's finest meats. Ryan had already told me he would be at parking lot A area 41, I think it was, so off I go looking for him. After searching for what seemed like ages, I called him, but the signal was not great, so I left a message on his answerphone that I was here and looking for him. I never got any reply for about 30 minutes, so I called again, but again, nothing.

Then I received a text from him saying he had a shitty signal, but he was in another area, something like B26. What happened to A41?? So off I go the try to find B26.

I got to B26 and I called him again, and again he does not answer. Then Ryan texts me and says he is not far away and he will come and get me from right under the big sign of B26. Great, so I find it and I waited for him, I wait, and I wait, but Ryan does not show up.

Fifteen minutes later I text him again. "Where are you"? I asked, and then I was completely gobsmacked when he replied "Oh we are queuing up outside the stadium and we are now going in"."Going in" I said, "I've been bloody wasting my time looking for you for the past 90 fcuking minutes". "I thought you were coming to get me under the sign of B26"? I text. "Sorry, but my clients want to go into the stadium now" he replied. So my next text to him was

"Thanks for wasting my time mate", and this is when the shit hit the fan. Ryan went mad and text me a whole bunch of insults, saying how important his clients were and who the hell do I think I am?

Of course his clients were important, I understood and totally respected that, but HE invited ME. Then HE moved the goalposts, by moving to a different area of the stadium without informing me, then asking me to wait at a new location, then deserting me, leaving me stranded, and it's all MY FAULT? WTF?

Only 30 minutes earlier Ryan had told me to wait under the sign of B26 as he was two minutes away and coming to get me, but he never turned up, left me standing there like a spare one at a wedding, and he has the front to attack me. I was totally shocked, what an asshole. But when I met him the day before, he was the nicest of guys.

I was so disappointed, frustrated and upset. Why do some people do this? I would never dream of doing this kind of thing to anyone. NEVER!

It was now around 7.45pm for a 8.30 start. I had missed my usual walk around the stadium to meet up with this idiot Ryan, and now I had no time left to see what was here. I walked straight to the stadium, had a few pics taken with a few chicks, (as you do), also one with a big bald Chiefs fan with a big bright red bald head, I then got in the queue and went to my seat inside Arrowhead Stadium.

I really did feel totally rejected and disappointed, as I was really looking forward to seeing Ryan, meeting his friends, and have my very first proper tailgate experience ever. But this all disappeared into thin air, and this was no fault of mine at all. I was determined I was not gonna let this upsetting experience spoil the game, which by now, was almost about to start.

The Kansas City Chiefs Vs the Denver Broncos was always going to be an exciting game as these two teams are divisional rivals, and they play each other twice every season. The Chiefs have a reputation of having the noisiest fans in the NFL and I have to say, they probably are, as they never stopped screaming for the entire game, which made the atmosphere electric.

Again I had a great seat high up in the nose bleeds, and Arrowhead was really a beautiful stadium, with a curvy design, unlike the usual bowl shape I was used to seeing. There was a sea of red from all around the stadium, the colours of the Kansas City Chiefs and their extremely passionate fans.

As the national anthem played, a massive American flag was drapped across the entire pitch, and the flyover from two stealth bombers was a very impressive sight.

The game itself was probably one of the worse I would see all season, especially the first half. It was 0-0 after the first quarter, something which is quite rare in a NFL game, and I thought it was going to be 0-0 at half time until a frenzy of scores very late in the second quarter, made it 14-14 at half time. The third quarter was no better, the only scores were both teams exchanging field goals, making the game a close fought battle.

It was 17-17 when I had to leave the stadium at the beginning of the fourth quarter, and I really did not want to leave as I was having a great time, and the game was starting to get very interesting, but I had no choice as I could not get home without Colin, and he was picking me up around 11pm at the place he dropped me off earlier in the evening.

I always knew I would probably miss the ending of this game, and I was so gutted as I very reluctantly left the stadium. Other than my first game at the Patriots Gillette Stadium, this was the only game of my entire tour I left before the end of a game, purely because I was completely stranded without Colin, and his lift home. I hated this, but it was not Colin's fault, it was the public transport system in Kansas, as there simply was none I knew of, and I did look.

I got to the place where Colin was coming to pick me up, I text him to say I was at the meeting point, and he replied that he was on his way, but he would be a little bit late. I was bloody furious as I could have stayed inside the stadium and watched the end of the game FFS!

See this bloody annoys me, as I'm relying on someone to turn up, they are late, and I'm the loser, and missing my game. This is why I don't ever want to rely on people, as sometimes they mess things up for you, even if its not entirely their fault. But I wont be too harsh on Colin as he had been a wonderful host, as well as my cab driver, and without his kindness, I was stuck bigtime. But this still did not mask my huge disappointment.

Colin eventually arrived, and by this time the game was

over, and by all accounts it was a very exciting finish, which the Broncos won 31-24 after making the Chief's star running back Jamaal Charles fumble the ball very close to his own endzone, and return it for a touchdown, with overtime looking very likely. I was pretty pissed off I missed it. So back we go for my 3rd night of 4 at Colin's place.

The next day Colin yet again goes to court and drops me off in the centre of Kansas City. I went to visit the model railway museum inside Union Station, (I do love a train!) as well as the World War I museum, but I didn't have enough time to go inside as Colin would be picking me up in a hour or so, and we would go back to his place as he had to do some work from home. BLOODY GREAT! Back to the prison.

That afternoon I sat in my room for a few hours, probably on the internet, stuck inside the house with nowhere to go. All I was thinking of was how much I was looking forward to leaving Kansas the next day and that I would never put myself in this position ever again. And you know what?, I never did.

Looking back now, I can laugh, but I really did suffer staying at Colin's place, and this was the lowest point I would feel on my tour. Once I left Kansas for Philadelphia, this experience taught me so much, and I learned a lot from it. Trying to save money sometimes comes at a very high cost, and I never sold myself to the devil again........until I got to Denver!!!!!!!

That evening Colin had another guy coming to stay at his house, a fella who had stayed with Colin before and he would be taking over my room once I left the following day. All three of us went out to dinner, sadly I can't remember the guy's name, but we had a nice evening with lots of laughs. It was nice to have new company around and someone else to talk to other than Colin, as by this time, I had practically nothing left to say to Colin, as we were complete polar opposites when it came to our personalities or interests.

Although Colin was not really my cup of tea, he really did his best to make me feel welcome in his home, and for this I will always be grateful to him. I mean absolutely no offense to him when I call his house the pet shop, I am only stating the fact that it really did smell doggy.

The next morning I woke up with much excitement as I was leaving for a new adventure. I always got excited when it was time to move on to a new city, it was like a new beginning, fresh, new people, new accommodation and new surroundings.

Colin drove me to the airport the following morning, and on this journey was the line he hit me with that he is, and in his own words "An atheist, an activist, and bisexual". This was not something I wanted to hear at all, and I'm glad he never told me on the day we met as it would have made my stay with him so much harder to stomach, but I was 10 minutes away from the airport and I was looking forward to my flight to Philadelphia very much indeed.

I want to say a big thank you to Colin, because without him, Kansas City would have been a much bigger struggle for me. If it was'nt for him driving me around, it would have been so much more of a mission for me. I will always be very grateful to him for his hospitality and generosity, as Colin is a really lovely person, a bit strange, but then again, who isn't? I certainly am at times!!!

Kansas City was a very challenging experience for me, totally different to what I am used to, unusual, but fascinating. It did have it's qualities, and yes, I liked it. It was more modern in the centre than I had expected, it had some beautiful buildings and architecture, but it was not one of my favourite places I visited on my trek across America, and not a city I can honestly say I connected with. But trust me, I did try.

Stadium-4
Lincoln Financial Field
Philadelphia Eagles

I flew out of Kansas City extremely relieved to be leaving, after all the hardships I endured over the past 4 days. I had been to Philadelphia before and I knew the hostel where I was staying was very central, right near a subway station, making it easy to get to the Eagles stadium in a few days time, which was a great relief after the location of Arrowhead Stadium in Kansas City and my reliance on Colin.

My flight was going from Kansas City to Philadelphia via Atlanta, which would make my second flight into Philly arrive pretty late. I arrived into Philadelphia around 11pm on Saturday night and I checked into my hostel called "the Green Apple", dropped my bags off, and popped straight around the corner for a few well deserved beers.

I'd stayed in the Green Apple Hostel two years before and I knew it was nice, had good beds, a TV lounge, movie nights with free beers and popcorn, as well as a few nights out and guided walking tours, so I was happy to be there.

Again, as I had already been to Philly a few years ago, I was not overly excited to be there, for no other reason than it was not new to me. I had already been to see the famous Liberty Bell, a few museums, the penitentiary (prison) as well as climb, run up, (humbing the theme tune) and do the little dance with my hands in the air at the top of the Rocky Steps (Sylvester Stallone's hero).

I had also previously been inside the Philadelphia Eagles stadium, but not to see a game, so there were not too many tourist attractions left for me to do this time.

Sunday was game four on my tour, and a very special one for me personally. It was one of the first games I pencilled in when I was trying to organise my route around the country, as it was my Dallas Cowboys against their deadly divisional rivals, the Philadelphia Eagles.

It was the game I honestly thought I had the chance to watch with the famous actor, heartthrob, and massive Eagles fan, Bradley Cooper. I had a crazy idea to try to contact Bradley when I found out he was working at a theatre in London. Why not? I thought, he can only say no. Sadly, big Brad never replied to the letter I had handed in to the back door at the theatre he was performing at in Central London a few weeks before I left for America.

Call me stupid, but I was pretty confident Brad would reply to me, as I know he is a massive NFL fan, and I was convinced he would love my story. Even if he would have, and said " Sorry dude, as you can imagine, I'm pretty busy right now", I would have understood and been well chuffed that he actually repiled. Of course I know he is a busy guy, and yes, I was probably biting off a little more than I could chew.

OK I failed, and not for the first time, and nowhere near my last, but at least I tried, and these stupid attempts to make connections with potential door openers did give me a certain amount of hope, hope that drove me on, and I would continue to try to think outside of the box and touch base with the many random people who entered into my crazy imagination as I possibly could.

After a nice sleep, I got up, had breakfast, and thought about how I was going to buy a ticket for todays game, which was the early evening game, starting around 4.30pm eastern time. I had been keeping an eye on the ticket prices for this game online, and I always knew it was not going to be one of the cheaper games I would attend, by far.

Whenever the Dallas Cowboys come to town, any town, the ticket prices for the game they play in go up, more so than when other teams are in town. I think this is because the Cowboys do have a very large fan base around the whole of the US and the stadiums they play at are usually sold out.

Another reason I think is that the Cowboys are normally hated by all the fans of the other teams, no more so than by the Philadelphia Eagles fans, so everybody wants to be at a game where the Cowboys can be beaten.

I came across a ticket for sale online from a website called "Craig's list". To me Craig's list was a little bit like Gumtree or Ebay which we have in the UK. Tickets were selling for 200-300 dollars, but I found one going for 150 bucks on Craig's List. So I enquired. I touched base with the seller, I asked a few questions, and we agreed to meet at a location up the road in a hour. Happy days, or so I thought.

So up I go to the junction of the main street and the square on the corner near the Liberty Bell. I waited for the guy to turn up, but I hardly had any power left on my phone, so my text messages to and from him I could hardly see in the darkness of my phone and the bright sunlight.
The seller finally turned up, and he seemed like a pretty normal guy, as he seemed friendly, was smiley, quite polite and we chatted for a bit. I told him how grateful I was as I was a big Cowboys fan from England, I passed him 150 bucks (about 100 quid) said thanks, and off he went.
It was only when he walked away, I wondered if something was not quite right about this deal, or to the fact this could

have been a dodgy transaction. I never gave this any thought at all before I met him, and this is sooooo very unlike me, and to this day, I want to kick myself for being so damn stupid.

I think I must have been caught up in the occasion, as I went straight back to the hostel changed into my Cowboys gear, and off I went to the stadium on the Philadelphia subway. An hour later I was standing outside the home of the Philadelphia Eagles, Lincoln Financial Field, and one thing I noticed immediately was the complete absence of Dallas Cowboys fans, as normally you would see them all over the place, at any game, but not this time.

Now, I was never aware of the deep routed hatred coming from the Eagles fans towards the Cowboys. So here I am, in my Cowboys shirt and cap, inside the lions den, and no idea about the rivalry, the history and what kind of welcome was coming my way.

I did notice I was getting quite a few dirty looks from people, but this never really bothered me. Then I found myself right in the heart of the Eagles fans tailgate. I was now the only Cowboys fan on view, and I was right inside the Eagles nest.

The Eagles fans were everywhere, eating and even worse, drinking, so I was fair game for the hecklers. I had people booing me all over the place, even one big fat guy came and booed me right in the face, while his gang of mates laughed at me. I thought that was very brave of him, the fat prick! I saw a guy wearing a tee shirt saying "I hate those Cowboys", when usually the saying goes "How bout those Cowboys". I thought this was funny, so I approached him and asked him if I could have my picture taken with him. He very reluctantly said "OK, but only because you are an

Englishman." I actually thought he was joking, but I could soon see he was deadly serious.

So after all the hostility towards me, I decided it would be better, or safer if I just entered the stadium. It was a little early, but there were other games being played at this time, and I could watch them on the big screens inside.

There were no queues, so I went straight up to the gates, and the guy put his zapper gun to my ticket. I don't know why, but I had a gut feeling before I got to the guy that all was not well, and I was right. "Sorry buddy" said the security guy, "This is a bad ticket" as his zapper made a funny sound. "It's a copy" he said. "Where did you get it?" he asked. "Craig's List" I replied. " Never buy tickets from Craig's List as this website is full of crooks" he said.

My guts dropped to the floor. All I could think about was that I HAD to get in, and this was my only chance to see a game in Philly on my entire tour, as I was not coming back anywhere near Philadelphia when they were playing another game, and I simply had to get in. I asked the guy If there was a ticket office for me to purchase another ticket, and miraculously there was and it was right near where we were standing. WHAT A STROKE OF LUCK.

I went to the small queue and prayed there were general public tickets left for this sell out game. To my complete amazement, I managed to buy a standing ticket for the paltry sum of 55 dollars. I instantly felt like the Cowboys had already won the game, even before it had started. To say I was relieved was the understatement of the century.
I suddenly started to think how bloody stupid I had been, buying this ticket from a guy on a website, and meeting him in the street. I'd like to think that I am pretty streetwise and normally my radar is on. I must have just let down my guard

for a moment of madness, and I paid the full consequences for my stupid actions.

I must admit, I have made many mistakes in my life, but this is how I learn, and I do my best to try not to replicate those same mistakes again. Usually I don't, so this valuable learning curve, or bad experience was a lesson, and I made sure this never happened to me again......... until I got to Oakland!!!

As soon as I got inside the stadium, I completely forgot about the scam, as I was just so relieved, and especially excited to be here in Philadephia to see my Cowboys play against our big rivals, the dreaded Eagles.

On the way up to the my nosebleed seat or standing area, I asked two Eagles fans if I could have a picture with them as they were in their Eagles outfits, and covered in face paint. The two guys had obviously had a few Britney Spears (beers) as they gave me a bit of a hard time, as I was wearing their big rivals colours. But they were two really nice and friendly guys, taunting me with loads of banter, something that I love.

We had a little chat about the rivalry between our two teams and it was only then I really understood the hatred coming from the Eagles fans. I honestly did not know, otherwise I would not have worn any Cowboys colours at all.
The Eagles fans are seen as the baddest set of fans in the NFL, they even have a prison inside their stadium (fact) and they are one of only a few NFL teams with the reputation of causing violence. I did not know this, but to be honest, I wasn't at all bothered....until I left the stadium after the game!

I went upstairs and I found my standing area, and it was packed and the view was not great, and I found myself trying to look over peoples shoulders and past other people's heads. It was far from a great place to watch the game, but I honestly could not care less, I was just so pleased I was in, and my tour was still well and truly on.

The game was about to start and there were many empty seats, which is perfectly normal for a NFL game as people are always turning up late, for a variety of reasons including traffic, tailgating, long queues to get in, and many other issues.

The guard to the section in front of my standing area turned his back on me for a split second, then woouuusshhhhhh, in a flash I was past him and inside the seating section like a ferret down a rabbit hole, and onto a seat in the very front row of the top tier, as far away from the guard as I could get. To my amazement, I was not challenged at all for the entire first half and I watched the game from the most fantastic vantage point or view I could ever have dreamed of, with not a single head in front of me. TOUCHDOWN!!! If this was a boxing match, my elbows would have been on the ring!

After all the usual pre game entertainment, national anthem and flyover, off we go again with the kick off to my fourth game, now I was totally buzzing. To be honest, I thought the Eagles would beat my Cowboys quiet easily, as I had predicted a good season for the Eagles as I thought they were a pretty decent team.

The game started, and it was far from a classic, it was very slow with lots of delays and stoppages, not much real action and my Cowboys took a two field goal 6-0 half time lead. The occasion was much better than the game itself, and I weighted up my good and bad luck over the course of the day, and I came to the conclusion I was definitely winning. I had lost 150 bucks to some scamming bastard, bought another ticket for 55 dollars, and I was now sitting in a seat worth way more than the 200 bucks I had laid out. I took the positive from a negative and I forgot all about the scam, and it never really bothered me again. I just put it down to another kick in the bollocks which I simply brushed off, and at this point I'm now feeling so much stronger mentally and physically, it really did'nt matter, so fcuk it!!

The second half started and off we go again, Dallas scored a touchdown to go 13-0 up and I'm ecstatic to see this in the flesh, in the home of our deadly rivals who totally despise us. Then, BOSH! Our star quarterback Tony Romo gets carried off the field with a bad injury that will keep him out of action for the next 7 games. He will return again for the game I will attend on week 12 in Miami. Little did anyone know the Cowboys would lose all the 7 games that Romo missed.

On a more positive note, it was good to see the ex Cowboys running back DeMarco Murray, now an Eagle, struggling so much with his running game, as I was pretty pissed off when he left a very good Cowboys team, for our big divisional rivals for nothing more than a bigger pay cheque. So on came our back up quarterback Brandon Weedon and to be honest I feared a comeback from the Eagles, and it did in the shape of a field goal. But then to my amazement Weedon connected with wide receiver Terence Williams for a Cowboys touchdown, and victory was more or less ours, unless my Cowboys imploded, which has been know to happen more than a few times before.

As the fourth quarter started, I could not believe it when a woman came to claim the seat I had sat in for the entire game. She was practically legless/drunk, and she probably could not even see the pitch, let alone the ball, as she was totally intoxicated.

So out of the section I went, and as the Cowboys were so far in front, a lot of Eagles fans had already left, so I could practically sit anywhere I wanted.

There was a late rally from the Eagles, but it was too little too late and my Cowboys ran out winners 20-10.

I was so happy as I left the stadium, but I decided to take off my Cowboys hat and put my "TheWrongShapedBalls" hoodie on over my Cowboys tee shirt, as I was a little concerned by wearing my colours on a subway train full of pissed off Eagles fans, I would provoke a lot of people on the way back to my hostel, and most of them had been drinking all day, and I did not want to ruin what had been a very eventful day, and risk getting a smack in the face!

I got back to my hostel around 9pm and I watched a bit of telly in the lounge before I went to bed. Monday I wandered around Philly as a tourist, had a massage and lunch in Chinatown, I went to an place called the "Reading Food Market", where I would be fascinated by the local Amish people in their funny outfits and ever funnier hairstyles and beards.

I returned to my hostel and I decided to go on a "Ghost" walking tour with a crowd of people from my hostel. I met a really nice young Swedish guy named Henning on the tour, and it was a nice evening to walk around downtown Philadelphia and Henning was good company, although none of us saw any ghosts!

The next day I decided to catch a train two hours up the line, to go and check out the New Jersey version of Las Vegas, "Atlantic City". I always wondered how it compared to Vegas, and I knew it was nowhere near as big and glamourous, but I had a spare day and I wanted to see it for myself and maybe have a little gamble.

I got to Atlantic City around lunchtime, and the weather had changed from the beautiful sunshine of the previous day in Philly, to wet and windy conditions on the sea front of New Jersey. I only stayed for the afternoon, played a bit of blackjack and roulette, won 90 dollars, had a bit of lunch, and I jumped back on the train.

I wasn't overly impressed with Atlantic City to be honest, it was very much like Southend on Sea (an Essex beach resort) with casinos.
I got back to my Green Apple hostel just in time for that evening's visual delight... movie night. Tonight's selection was a film called "Pacific Rim", which is right up there with probably one of the worse films I've ever seen. One of those far-fetched disaster movies that are very silly and rediculously and spectaculary over the top. I tried to watch as much of the film as I could, as there was free beer, popcorn and a few other people watching it with me in the main lounge area of the hostel.

It was a nice and relaxing end to my time in Philadelphia, where life was so much easier than my difficult time and experiences in Kansas City.
I headed back to my room, got my bags packed, and got ready for my departure in the morning heading for my next adventure, Minneapolis.

Stadium-5
TCF Bank Stadium
Minnesota Vikings

I was very excited to be heading for Minneapolis, not just because it was one of the first places on my tour I had never been to before (other than Kansas), but a place I knew very little about other than it had been voted one of the best cities to live in, in the whole of the US. I remembered seeing a travel programme about this city, and it looked like a great place, and a city I was looking forward to visiting.
I knew Minneapolis had to be a destination I needed to visit early on my tour, to make sure I took full advantage of the weather, which in the 5 days I spent here, were mostly glorious.

I knew that from November onwards, this part of the US, temperatures can be as cold as I have ever experienced in my life, and this is something I did not want the pleasure of witnessing. Minus 20, 30 , or even 40 degrees is not in my DNA thank you very much!

Another reason I decided to come to Minneapolis on week 3, was the fact that the Minnesota Vikings played here on the Sunday, and the Green Bay Packers would play the following day, up the road in the next state of Wisconsin (7 hours by bus) on the Monday, which was very achievable for me to attend both games in 24 hours.

I wanted to get these two games out of the way early on the tour, and together if possible, not only for the obvious reason of weather, but because they are both a long way from most of the other NFL teams by location and they played one day apart only the one time in the whole of the season. So it was now or never to do these two teams together.

I arrived into Minneapolis and I headed for my hostel, which was way across the other side of town. I was actually staying at the only hostel in Minneapolis, and this would not be the last time I would be staying at the only hostel in a US city.

It would have been nice to have had a few more options for accommodation in a lot of the US cities I visited, purely because a few of the hostels I stayed in were not in the central downtown area's where most of the action is, eg, bars, resturants and mainly the NFL stadiums. I had no choice but stay in these places for the simple reason of the dollars, and these hostels did in fact save me a fortune throughout my tour.

I've always enjoyed staying in hostels over the years, mainly because I have met so many amazing people staying in these places, all over the world, leading to some great nights out, doing touristic stuff together, or just hanging out. On this trip, I even managed to drag a few people I had met in hostels along to some of the tailgates, and games I attended, even getting a few of them free tickets when I had to pay!!! Sad, but bloody true. This was because I had already bought a ticket, and when I was at some tailgates, I was offered free tickets, which I just gave away to the people I had bought along for the ride.....a free ride. Stupid or kind, I will let you decide!!

I took the subway from the airport to the centre of Minneapolis, where I passed right by the unfinished shell of the new Vikings US Bank stadium, finished now and ready for the start of the 2016 season in September. It was an amazing looking stadium with its black tiles and unusual shape. As I write this chapter the Vikings are currently 5-0, but now on my second draft, they are 6-4, my third 8-8. One day I will return and watch a game in their new stadium as it did and does look amazing.

It was around lunchtime and I knew my football (soccer) team Arsenal were playing in a big game and cup tie against our deadly rivals Tottenham. A few years earlier when I was in Boston, I had discovered, completely by chance an organisation called "Arsenal America". AA is a group for Arsenal fans all across the US, and they have branches in around 50 or so cities all over the country.

I looked online at the AA website, and I saw there was a branch here in Minneapolis, so I headed for the designated AA bar in town called "The Local". The Local was right in the centre of town and I had a bit of a trek from the subway station with my very heavy backpack and the sun burning down on me, and I arrived just as the game started. I ordered a well deserved beer and some fish and chips, and for 90 minutes I felt like I was at home, it was brilliant.

Arsenal America bars are fantastic places to watch Arsenal games, I love them and I eventually visited 12 of these bars over the time on my trip. The AA fans are so into Arsenal its incredible, some of them are more passionate towards Arsenal than their very own NFL teams. The AA fans I talked to in the bars I've been to, were always impressed when I informed them I am an Arsenal fan from London. The fans always treated me like a VIP, in all the AA bars I went to, something I will always be so grateful to them for. A lot of the AA fans I met were ex pat Brits of some kind, or are married to or connected to Brits in some way, but not always, as some just love soccer.

In the bars when the Arsenal games are being played, there's lots of singing, chanting, screaming and excitement. It was funny for me to see how passionate the fans in America get, when Arsenal just get a corner or a free kick near the goal, they cheer like a goal. And when a goal is scored, they cheer like we have just won the league! I don't mean to take the piss, I'm just giving you an insight into how passionate these fans are, and I think they are great.

I had many amazing times in these bars and long may they continue, as I met some extremely nice people in these places, and it was my little piece of home or England while I was in America.

Arsenal beat the dreaded enemy Tottentham 2-1, with Flamini scoring both goals, which is about as rare as Leicester City winning the EPL!!! which links nicely to the story of my next visit to the Local bar, three days later when Arsenal were the visitors at Leicester.

After the Tottenham trashing! I left "the Local" for the fifteen minute bus ride to the HI Hostel (Hostelling International) where I was staying.

I arrived at the hostel, which was basically a very large house, and I was pleasantly surprised by the layout of my new adopted home, as I was normally used to being in confined and cramped conditions, sleeping just a few feet away from other people, some above and some below me on bunkbeds. This huge room was different, as it was open plan, there were about 25-30 beds, and it reminded me of a hospital ward!!

This may sound crazy, but I liked it quite a lot, probably because it was different, not like the usual dorm I was used to sleeping in. Plus it had the added attraction of an element in which I have always loved.....space. I mean I felt like I could breathe and spread out a little, and I like that. I took a bed right in the far corner against the wall, and I was really content and comfortable in that corner for the next five nights I spent there.

Out of the thirty or so beds, the most people I saw in this room at any one time on my stay was about ten, possible less. Some of the people I spoke to over my time here were really nice and friendly, but I could see, and some of them even told me, they have had problems with drink and drugs in the past, some still had. So I made sure I was extra vigilant, and my stuff was kept safe and locked, just in case somebody needed a fix or a drink, had no money, and saw this Englishman as the proverbial bank manager, ATM machine or potential cash cow.

In the next bed to me was a guy whom once I introduced myself to, we clicked immediately. His name was Chance, a thirty something African American guy who had his own business in I.T, and was working most of the time here in Minneapolis. Within a few hours of meeting Chance, off we went to the pub, hooked up with a couple of other guys who were staying at the hostel, an Aussie surfer named Jim, and an English guy named Steve, so a new gang was formed in an instant.

When I was in Philadelphia at the Green Apple Hostel, I had overheard a conversation about an English guy named Steve who was staying in a different room to me at that hostel. Steve's name surfaced again after I explained to someone I was going to all thirty one NFL stadiums in the country, and I was informed Steve was in fact doing exactly the same thing as me. WHAT??

My initial thought was horror, as I didn't want anybody else stealing my thunder, I wanted to be the only English guy in history to be doing this!! But I never did meet Steve in

Philadelphia, so I completely forgot he even existed, until I bumped into him in my hospital ward in Minneapolis. Steve was doing a similar tour to me, he had a pretty good city job in London and he was taking a sabbatical. Steve was mainly flying all over America, simply because he could afford it, something I never saw (flying) as a challenge But what did surprise me about Steve, was that he never supported a particular NFL team. I have my Cowboys, but he did not follow anyone, I never quite got this, and I struggled to understand his reasons for going to every NFL stadium in the country, but good luck to him anyway for doing so.

I wondered how, or even if, Steve could have felt or shown any real passion while watching any of these games? At least as a Cowboys fan, every game I watched had meaning. If I was watching a game with, say the Eagles in, as they are in my Cowboys division, I want them to lose. If I'm at a game where the San Francisco 49ers were playing, I want them to lose as they are in my conference. The reason for this is because later in the season, these teams have the potential to knock my Cowboys out of the play offs, maybe getting a "wild card" in front of my team, so I would always support the opposition to the teams who could make an effect on my Cowboys progress, at the games I attended, so every game I was at always had some relevance to me. So off to the pub we all went and we had a lovely meal, a few beers and a good night out.

The next evening I went to my very first baseball game to see the Minnesota Twins play against a team from Cleveland. They had played each other the night before (very strange to me) and I think Minnesota won, but sadly the night I went, they lost. The weather was not great, it was raining, the stadium was probably less than half full and to be honest, after thirty minutes or so, I was extremely bored.

I had only paid ten bucks for the ticket, and I ended up sitting in a completely empty section of the stadium with the only other spectator anywhere near me, and I got chatting to this really nice guy who was a huge baseball fan.

I saw 5 of the 9 innings, and I more than likely would have left earlier if I was sitting on my own. I don't get baseball at all, I didn't know the rules, any players, the history, basically nothing. But as ever, I did my best to embrace the game and try to get into it and enjoy it as much as I could. But all this baseball game did for me was to underline exactly how much I love the NFL. Baseball is not for me I'm afraid, but at least I have ticked the box and I did give it a go.

It was now Friday, and I had two days before my next NFL game, so I did my usual thing and I became a tourist. I wandered around the centre, saw many beautiful Minneapolis buildings, probably hung out in a coffee shop or two (my favourite vocation) and I popped up the train line to look around the twinned town to Minneapolis, a place called St Paul. I checked out a big church/cathedral and had a general look around the main part of town. When I returned back to Minneapolis, I hired a pushbike (the Minneapolis version of the London Boris bike) and I went for a lovely ride around the lakes area of Minneapolis. I saw so many absolutely beautiful and massive houses that line the banks of these lakes. Minneapolis must be a playground for the rich as I did get the feeling that this town is rolling in greenbacks/bucks. I can imagine it must be a very lovely lifestyle here, especially in the summer as it really was beautiful and without doubt one of my favourite places I visited in the US.

One big regret I do have about my time in Minneapolis, was that I always had every intention to pay a visit to "Paisley Park Studio's", owned by the singer Prince. I'm not the biggest fan of Prince, but I am a fan, and I do like a lot of his songs, and as a musician myself, I respect him enormously as an absolutely brilliant musician and performer. Paisley Park was not the easiest of places for me to get to without a car from downtown, as it was about two hours away on two different buses outside of Minneapolis by public transport.

I did my research and I asked quite a few people how I would get there?, is it worth it?, do they do tours of the studios? or even is it actually open to the general public at all?
I received conflicting replies, mainly negative, which clouded my judgement, so I basically decided it was not worth the effort, or risk of going all that way on two different buses, not getting in, and wasting a day in lovely Minneapolis.

The pictures I had seen online of Paisley Park on the outside were not as attractive and inviting as I had expected, but I'm sure it is amazing on the inside. I eventually bailed out, and I never did make it to Paisley Park, and after leaving Minneapolis, I always regretted the decision not to go, a regret which has now escalated a million times over since the terrible news last month (as I write) the very talented purple one has now passed away and gone to the big music festival in the sky. Yet another tragic loss of an absolute genius at a very young age. So sad. RIP Prince.

Saturday the sun was out again and I decided to have a day in the nature at Minnehaha Park to see a waterfall that was there. But before then I was heading back to the Arsenal America bar "The Local", to watch my Arsenal boys play against one of English football's minnows, Leicester City. I had been in touch on social media with an American Arsenal fan named Corey, and I met him at "The Local" bar to watch the game together. As everybody now knows, (or if you did'nt, you do now) Leicester won the Premier League (EPL) which was the shock of the century in English football, and if anybody would have predicted this on the day I was at The Local, I would have laughed them right out of the pub, especially as Arsenal won this incredible game 5-2.

Crazily this would be Leicester's only home defeat of the entire season and it was one of the most open games of football I had ever seen in my life. It was more like a boxing match, you punch, I punch, you attack, I attack, just taking turns of shooting. Arsenal had 41 shots at goal in this game, and they still could have lost. Leicester actually played very well and the game could have quite easily ended at 10-10, a score line probably never seen before at this level anywhere in the world.

As the season progressed, I was supporting Leicester the whole way, right to the very end, even though I am an Arsenal fan. This was simply because I now have an extremely deep hatred for all the cheating, as well as the dirty laundered money coming into the EPL from dodgy foreign owners, where clubs are basically buying the title. Leicester were a team of journeyman and mainly unknown foreign players, mixed in with a few English players who have progressed from the lower leagues. They also have a very eccentric Italian manager named Claudio Ranieri, who I liked a lot. (sadly, now fired by the club, even after performing the ultimate mirace of winning the league) Loyalty, what's that in football?

I'm well pleased Leicester won the title that year, as it was a massive middle finger salute to all the big boys and money men of English soccer, and something I don't expect to see

happen again any time soon, probably not even in my
lifetime, as this was a real story of David and Goliath.
After the game finished, I headed off to Minnehaha Park in
the beautiful Minnesota sunshine, and the waterfall was
quite nice, but a little smaller than I had expected. I had a
lay down in the park for a bit, walked around, then I
returned back to the hostel in the evening, and off I went to
the pub with Chance and a few others for a few non
alcoholic drinks!!!

Sunday was game number five on my tour, the Minnesota
Vikings Vs The San Diego Chargers, and I was really
looking forward to it. It was another beautiful day in
Minneapolis, and I arranged to meet a guy I had been
talking with via Twitter, a nice guy named Ashley.
At the time I was in town, the Minnesota Vikings did not
have their own stadium, so they were using the stadium
which belonged to the University of Minnesota college
team, because the roof to their own stadium had collapsed a
few years ago after some bad weather, and their new
stadium, US Bank was being built and was not yet finished.
I arrived at the TCF Bank stadium about 11pm for the 1pm
kick off. I did the usual lap of the stadium and I got
involved in a few of the festivities that was taking place
around the stadium, mainly for kids. LIKE ME! I remember
taking a shot at trying to kick a field goal through a set of
inflatable field goal posts where lots of people were queuing
up to attempt a kick. I thought it would be easy, but I made
a right pig's ear (fuck up) of my attempt, as I sliced the shot
and missed by a mile, making everybody laugh, including
me.

It was a lovely relaxed atmosphere in the glorious sunshine
and I was really happy to be here amongst a sea of Lilac (the
colours of the Vikings, and one of my favourite colours). I
had lots of pictures taken, including a few with some very

beautiful and lovely Minnesota Vikings cheerleaders, as well as many fans in crazy outfits, face paint, silly hats etc, and it really had a lovely feel of fun, with no stress or the aggression or tension I had felt and experienced at a few of the other games I had previously attended, especially in Philadelphia.

My friend Ashley was stuck in traffic, but when he finally arrived, it was almost game time, so I went into the stadium to our own seats and we agreed to meet up at half time. My philosophy was always to support the home team at the games I attended, unless they played against my Cowboys, or the result could effect my boys later in the season. So today I was a Viking. I have always been a big fan of the colour lilac, (as I've mentioned) so the Vikings have always been a team I kept my eye on from a distance, without really being a fan. The same goes for the Green Bay Packers as my favourite colour has always been green, and I know this is a pathetic reason to like a team, but so many people outside the US support a NFL team for a very strange or silly reason, like their favourite colours or even their favourite TV programme. YEP EVEN ME!
The game started and its a good open game, the Vikings looked a pretty decent team, especially their running back Adrian Peterson. I'm in a tee shirt as the weather is gorgeous and I'm feeling great and enjoying the game. The atmosphere was so nice, and I had decent people around me. I liked everything about the Vikings.

This was my fifth game, and the feel to the game was a little different to the passion I felt coming from the fans on the opening game in New England, obviously as they were Superbowl winners and it was the first game of the season, and on national TV.

Game two in Washington was pretty much similar to here in Minneapolis, game three had more tension because of the divisional rivalry in Kansas between the Chiefs and the Broncos, as was the full on hatred of game four in Philadelphia against my Cowboys.

Minneapolis suited my personality, laid back, passive, non aggressive, warm and civilized. (obviously I'm not always like that, but most of the time I am!) The same goes for San Diego, which incidentally was another place I loved, much later on my tour.

The San Diego fans in my opinion were similar to the Vikings, and there seemed to be no anger or rage towards each other and I like that. Both teams play hard and have the will to win of course, but it didn't seem to be the end of the world if either team won or not. After all, its only a game of football, right?

I moved to another part of the stadium at half time, met with Ashley and sat with him in the second half with the sun beating down on us with no shade, which practically cooked us like a couple of sausages on a BBQ! but it felt so nice to be getting a suntan while watching the game, and I enjoyed being in Ashley's company.
The Vikings eventually won 31-14, which I was very pleased to see, and this was the icing on the cake of a very nice day indeed.

That evening, my final one in Minneapolis, I had to try to organise my travel arrangements to somehow get me from Minneapolis to Green Bay Wisconsin for the game the following night. My biggest problem was not how I was going to get there, but where I was going to stay in Green Bay, as my options were very limited to say the least.

What eventually transpired was my only option, a Greyhound bus which left Minneapolis early the next morning, and this would arrive about three hours before the game started in Green Bay, so I never had a plan B, and if this bus broke down or was majorly delayed, maybe by traffic or bad weather, I was totally up shit creek without a paddle (stranded).

There are no hostels in Green Bay, and the very few hotels located anywhere near the Packers stadium were all sold out or super expensive. Air B'n'B was still a possibility, but I did have a small chance of a very lucky break.
I had made contact with a few people in Green Bay via the Couchsurfing website, and as it panned out, there were only two possibilities of people I had the outside chance of staying with in town, including a guy named Ernesto. My other avenue closed very quickly so Ernesto was basically my last chance saloon, or I was staying overnight in the main Green Bay train station, if one existed. Incidentally, I would have done this if I had no other choice, as there was no way in the world I was missing this game.

Then came yet another complete stroke of luck, (and I did have a bit of the stuff over the six months) the English guy Steve, I had stayed with in my Minneapolis hostel, had beaten me to get the sofa at Ernesto's. Steve was also heading to the game and he was even on the same Greyhound bus as I was to take to Green Bay. I asked Steve if he would mind asking Ernesto if I could stay at his place too, so he did, and to my amazement Ernesto said yes, as long as I did not mind crashing on the floor, as Steve had already booked the couch. I've never been so happy to sleep on somebody's floor, that's how desperate I was for a roof over my head that night.

I love it when a plan comes together!

Stadium-6
Lambeau Field
Green Bay Packers

Steve and I left the HI hostel in Minneapolis and we shared a cab to take us to the Greyhound bus terminal, to catch our 7 hours bus ride to Green Bay. I managed to buy a ticket for the Packers game against the Chiefs online for 100 dollars, something many told me was near impossible, but this is D-Mo here and as I told you, I'm Superman!

If I want something bad enough, there's no stopping me, except if its stupidly expensive, or its not worth the hassle, like Superbowl 50, which I will address later in the book. Luckily we left the terminal in Minneapolis on time, and we headed for Green Bay on the Greyhound bus, and I noticed the weather had already started to change from the beautiful sunshine of Minnesota to the now grey skies of Wisconsin. I was fully aware this little section of northeastern America was a very tricky part of my trip, and it was always a place I knew which could quite easily trip me up, especially doing two games in consecutive days.

Even before I arrived, I knew I would have liked to have had the chance to spend more time in Green Bay, as the Packers have a great history, right back to the beginning of American Football, a landmark stadium in Lambeau Field and a NFL team that are respected all across America. They are also my second favourite team behind my Dallas Cowboys, so I had a vested interest in both this game, and this town.

I didn't know much about Green Bay as a place, other than the fact the Packers dominate life in this town completely. When a game is on, most of the inhabitants of GB are there, and the place is a virtual ghost town on match days.

Green Bay fans are know as "Cheeseheads" something to do with the huge production of cheese in this area of Wisconsin. This is a subject I know absolutely nothing about or care for, due to the fact I have complete and utter contempt for this disgusting yellow gunge! Anybody who knows me, know I hate cheese with a passion, and this substance has caused me all kinds of problems over the years, no more so than here in the US, as they practically smother the bloody stuff on absolutely everything.

Luckily for Steve and I, after seven hours on the road and no drama's whatsoever, our bus arrived on time into Green Bay, and we head straight off for Ernesto's home, which was about a fifteen minutes walk away from the bus stop. Steve takes charge with the navigation, and I follow him down the long main street outside the bus terminal... in the wrong direction. Great map reading, Steve!

My backpack was very heavy, and I needed a long walk the wrong way like an elephant needs a set of golf clubs, but we turned around, and we eventually made it to Ernesto's lovely apartment block overlooking a river. Ernesto was not in, but his mate let us in and welcomed us with open arms. We chatted for about 30 minutes, but we didn't have much time to hang around as the game started in a few hours, so Steve and I left the flat, and we jumped onto a bus to the legendary Lambeau Field, which took about 40 minutes.
Around this time, I had been kindly put in touch with an American guy named Craig Steichen, a guy who has been travelling to all thirty one NFL stadiums for the past few years for his "Warrior Wishes" charity. Warrior Wishes is a

military charity run by Craig that takes a group of people to every NFL game, it could be ex -soldiers, wounded soldiers, family members of soldiers killed in the military and so on. One of my Dallas Cowboys friends on Facebook put me in touch with Craig, so I arranged to meet him at a tailgate outside Lambeau Field. In the beginning, Craig was very difficult to contact, which was quite frustrating for me, probably because he was always very busy and entertaining people at the games he was at, but when I finally did meet Craig, never did I dream that our paths would cross at least eight or nine times at the many different tailgates we were at together, and I really liked him.

I have so much to thank Craig for as it was only through him I ended up such good friends with so many of the Superfans I eventually met, people who spoiled me rotten when I arrived into their towns. Craig was the man who started my domino effect of meeting my brilliant Superfan buddies at tailgates. Top man, Craig, and a huge thanks. Steve and I arrived at Lambeau Field about a hour before kick off, and it was now pouring with rain, and a pretty miserable evening for weather, like a typical English winter evening, cold ,dark, wet and grey.

I had arranged to meet Craig for the first time, so he gave me the location, but we could not find him. Craig gave me a landmark and I went there, but no Craig. So I called him, and I got no answer, then I text him, and I got no reply, but I kept trying.

I gave up after 30 minutes, but then I finally received a text, "Where are you?" from Craig. "Looking for you" I replied. "I'm in the stadium" he stated. Brilliant, here we fcuking go again, I thought, as while I'm breaking my balls looking for Craig in the pissing rain, dragging Steve along for the ride, Craig is inside the stadium after telling me he would be in location A, when in fact, he is in location Z. Oh well, shit happens.

After more texts, confusion and false information, I finally tracked down Craig inside Lambeau Field, and the wild goose chase was over. But it was now practically kick off time, so we said a very quick hello for probably around one minute, and then we parted ways and went to our respective seats and that was it.

Craig told me his next game was in Pittsburgh on Thursday, in three days time, which was where I was heading, and very early in the morning, but I was yet to sort out my ticket for the bus. "Any chance of a lift" I asked. "Maybe" he said, "Keep in touch this evening and I will let you know" he told me. So we said our goodbyes as the game between the Green Bay Packers and the Kansas City Chiefs was now about to start.

Lambeau Field was a place I always knew was special in the NFL world, just as Wembley Stadium is to soccer in England. The hallowed turf, the incredible history, the holy grail, the home of football and all that.

Lambeau was different to many of the stadiums I would visit all around the US, and it was not one of my favourite stadiums to be honest, as it is very old and pretty basic in comparison to some of the more ostentatious and newer stadiums I would attend, like in Dallas and New Orleans, that from the outside both look like a spaceships. All I knew, that it was a real pleasure for me to be in this iconic and historical stadium, even if it was raining and I was getting soaking wet, as sadly for me on this night, Lambeau Field does not have a roof.

There were loads of Packers fans wearing their trademark cheese hats, and I could not resist the temptation of having my picture taken wearing one, especially as I am known for hating the dreaded stuff!

The Packers looked a very good team, and won this game at a canter, a lot easier than the 38-28 scoreline suggests, with Packers main man Aaron Rodgers looking as impressive as he usually does. Little did I know that in the following months to come, I would be at two Packers games where Mr. Rodgers did the almost impossible feat of throwing not one, but two "Hail Mary" passes for touchdowns in the last seconds of both games. I will explain later for those who don't know what a "hail Mary" pass is.

It was the second time I had seen the Kansas City Chiefs play, both times they lost and they looked a pretty poor team to me. I like their running back Jamaal Charles, he was their biggest threat and in my opinion their best player by far. Charles got a bad injury a few games later, that was to put him out for the rest of the season. I was gutted for him, as he really is a good player, and the Chiefs main weapon.

I remember thinking that without Jamaal, the Chiefs were doomed, and they lost their next three games, but then to my complete astonishment, the Chiefs went on an incredible run to win their next ten games on the bounce and even made the play offs. What the hell do I know about the NFL! Towards the end of the game, I went to sit near Steve, so we could go back to Ernesto's flat together. Steve informed me that Ernesto was in fact going to pick us up, which again was a result, so as the game ended, we walked to the pick up point about 20 minutes away from the stadium, met Ernesto and we headed back to his place.

It was around 1am when we got back to Ernesto's, and I was very tired. Yet again, what I needed was a good night sleep to recharge my batteries, but this night I was on the floor, as

Steve had the sofa, and my potential 24 hours of travel by bus to my next destination, which was Pittsburgh, started with a 6.45am bus ride from the Greyhound station I arrived into with Steve only seven hours earlier.

After the game I had sent a message to Craig, asking him how he was getting to Pittsburgh. I asked if he was driving, and was there any chance I could scrounge a lift? This would have been a massive help to me, but again the silence was deafening from Craig and his unreliable cellphone, until about two hours later when I got a message from Craig saying that he was already half way to Pittsburgh. FCUK!!! That would have been a massive help, but it wasn't meant to be.

I must have been laying on the floor for about four uncomfortable hours when I had to get up and rush off to catch my early bus to Pittsburgh via Milwaukee and Chicago. Steve and Ernesto were both fast asleep as I quickly and quietly slipped out of Ernesto's flat at stupid o'clock, trying my best not to wake either of them up. Ernesto had given me the directions to get back to the Greyhound station, he said it was a straight walk along the road where he lived , and only an idiot could get it wrong, and this idiot did!

See, I have a problem. Call it laziness on my part, which of course it is, but whenever I travel alone, I am always in control of my own destiny, aware of what is around me, generally focused, mostly organized and usually completely switched on. But whenever I travel with other people, I tend to switch off. My travel companions from the past few trips and good friends Matt Peplow, Nick Taylor, Rick Walker, TJ and especially my Aussie buddy Luke Host will all tell you that sometimes my powers of listening are terrible. Well they are all completely right. Right boys?

When I have somebody with me and we are going somewhere together, and returning together, I totally switch off, and I rely on being guided by whoever I am with to get back home from wherever we have been. Its probably got something to do with the fact I am so easy going, as I'm normally happy to follow people and do anything they want to do. So if Matt, said "Let's go to the pub", off we go, and I'm with him. He knows the way back, so I press the off button on my head and I follow like a sheep. This happened to me yet again as Steve and I came in on the Greyhound bus from Minneapolis.

But in my defense, this time was not my fault completely. In Green Bay, Greyhound had an old and a new bus terminal, and when we arrived, of course this fact would not come into my thinking at all, why would it? Ernesto drives a car, so he has no need to use a Greyhound bus, and the old Greyhound bus station was about a two or three minutes drive around the corner from the new one, which is no longer in use, although the building is still there.

Obviously, it now makes perfect sense that Ernesto did not know about this new terminal around the corner, so he guided me straight down the road to the old one. I kind of remembered crossing a bridge with Steve on the way to Ernesto's home and we took a right turn, the only turn we took, so it should have not been too difficult to find my way back. WRONG!

I left Ernesto's flat and followed HIS instructions and walked straight, remembering he said I could not miss the bus terminal. What I should have done is to turn left, cross the bridge, and follow the road all the way to the new bus terminal. The terminal Steve and I came into was pretty big, even Stevie Wonder would have found it! but because Steve had taken me the wrong way when we first arrived, we turned around, and I just followed him. I switched off my brain and took no notice of where we were going. What a schoolboy error.

By ths time its now about 6.15am and I have 30 minutes to catch my bus, or the next bus was 3.30pm. I'm now standing outside the shell of the OLD Greyhound station, and I knew this was not the place we came into as I did not recognise it. It was still dark, I was cold and I was lost. Then my guardian angel, crystal ball or huge piece of luck came as my saviour yet again, as I was now definitely surfing the wave of good fortune at this moment in time!!

A taxi drove past me on the other side of the very wide road I was standing at the side of, which I'm guessing would be extremely busy during the daytime. But this was 6am and there was nobody else around at all and not many cars driving past either. The taxi had pulled into a side road about 50 metres across the way from me and I could see the driver looking over at me like I was a potential fare. I quickly crossed the road and made a beeline for him. "Do you know where the Greyhound bus station is?" I asked. "Its just around the corner" was his reply. "Can you take me please?" I begged. "Jump in" he said, and a huge wave of relief came over me.

It only took a few minutes to get to the NEW Greyhound station, but on the way the taxi driver explained the story of the new station and the old station. All I was interested in was that I got to the right station, and I did with about 10 minutes to spare until my bus was due to leave. PHEW, that was far too close for comfort.

I would have loved the chance to have spent a few more days in Green Bay, I would have liked to have done the Lambeau Field stadium tour, and who knows, I may even have gone to a cheese museum if they had one. Errr, maybe not!

I did research Green Bay before I left Minneapolis, but there did not look like there was much to do there other than watch the football, plus I never had much time as I needed to be at my next game, which was on Thursday, in two days time, and it was going to take me 24 hours to get there, so I had a whole full day of travelling ahead of me.
I boarded the bus and I breathed a huge sigh of relief when it pulled away from the new Greyhound station here in Green Bay. I had made it, but only by the skin of my teeth and a bag full of luck.

After all this early morning excitement, I was looking forward to a nice sleep on the bus (which never happened, as it never does, no matter how hard as I try), and I was actually pretty happy to be leaving Green Bay for my next port of call, Pittsburgh.

I never had time to connect with Green Bay, so this gives me a very good reason to return there one day, to see what the place really does have to offer, other than Aaron Rodgers and his pack!

Stadium-7,
Heinz Field
Pittsburgh Steelers

The first of the three buses I took from Green Bay to Pittsburgh on my 24 hours trek was a two and a half hours ride to Milwaukee, a place I knew only from the TV show "Happy Days", the 70's and 80's programme with the Fonz and Richie Cunningham.

It was a smooth and uneventful ride, and I arrived into Milwaukee bus station on time, around 9am.

My next bus to Chicago should have left two hours later, but it ended up more like three, so I was delayed, which did not matter too much as my next bus was a ten hours overnight ride from Chicago to Pittsburgh, scheduled to leave at around 10pm.

I was planning to get out of the bus station in Chicago to find a bar to watch Arsenal play in a Champions League match against Olympiacos of Greece. Sadly, because of the delay in Milwaukee, I was running late, and when I eventually arrived into Chicago, the Arsenal game was almost over.

At this point, I had never seen Arsenal lose a game while watching them in the many Arsenal America bars I had frequented on my two trips to the US, and I did check online to see where the Chicago AA branch was located, in relation to the bus station I was arriving into. I would have gone to the bar if I had made it to Chicago on time, I never did, Arsenal lost 3-2, and my unbeaten record stood for now. As I arrived into Chicago, it was around lunchtime, and my next bus was not leaving until 10pm, and after waiting for a couple of hours, I was bored stiff, especially as this next ride would be my third bus of the day. I did attempt to go outside and have a look around, but the bus terminal is out of the centre of Chicago and it looked like a bit of a sketchy (rough) area, so I decided to return inside to the relative safety of the bus terminal.

You certainly get to meet some very interesting characters when you travel by Greyhound buses. Most of these people are without doubt on the very bottom of the human food chain, and I chatted to quite a lot of them, and it was no real surprise to me that most of them were very nice and interesting people.

I noticed there was an earlier bus leaving for Pittsburgh a few hours before my planned 10pm bus, so I decided to take the 7pm bus and just get out of Chicago, as I had been hanging around the bus terminal for so long, and I was extremely bored. The drawback of catching this earlier bus was that it was to arrive very early in the morning into Pittsburgh, earlier than my couchsurfing host in Pittsburgh wanted me to get to his pad.

Pittsburgh was another US city that did not have a single hostel, so again, I had to use couchsurfing. I was hoping it was not going to be anywhere near as bad as my Kansas City experience, and I had touched base with my host before I left London, and been invited to stay at the house of a guy named Bruce, who happened to be a season ticket holder of the Pittsburgh Steelers.

Bruce was attending the game I was going to against the Baltimore Ravens, which would be very convenient for me to get to the stadium and back home, as Bruce would be driving. This was always such a massive help, as getting back to my accommodation from some night games really was a huge task and sometimes a massive struggle, and a real test of my patience, especially when I was in New York.

I arrived into Pittsburgh very early in the morning, but Bruce had asked me to get to his place around 8am, which was the plan until I got impatient and changed my bus time in Chicago. I got into Pittsburgh around 6.30am, but I still had to get a bus to Bruce's home on the outskirts of Pittsburgh, so that was OK as I had plenty of time on my hands.

As I walked out of the bus terminal, daylight was trying its best to break through, but it was still dark. I had no idea where to get the bus Bruce told me would take me to his house. So I went up to the nearest and basically the only person around and I asked "Excuse me mate, do you know where I catch the P12 bus?" "That way", pointed the black man in his mid 30's.

I had already taken a rough look on Google Maps while I was on the bus and I knew this bloke was pointing me in completely the wrong direction. Giving me a dirty look, the dude then asked me "Hey, what size are your sneakers (trainers)?". "nine and a half", I told him as I quickly walked off, as I smelt a rat, and I instantly knew exactly where this conversation was going, and the consequences it could bring had I stuck around.

My answer must have confused this guy, simply because the sizing system in the US is different from the UK and he probably never had a clue what nine and a half was. If I would have said 44, I think there was a very strong chance this man of the streets would now be walking around Pittsburgh in my lovely Nike's!

Again, I can laugh now, but that could have been a very sticky situation, especially if he was carrying a weapon, which I'm almost certain he probably would have. Who knows, he may even had been packing a gun?? something I will never know.....thank god!

It did'nt take me very long to find my bus stop and I got chatting to a guy at that stop, who was on leave from the military. He informed me that this particular area was not a very nice part of town to be hanging around in on my own, something I now knew, and which made me appreciate the only trainers I had with me a whole lot more, and the ones I would wear every single day on my eight months away from home.

We were getting the same bus and he knew where I was going once I gave him the name of the area, so he kindly told me where to get off, which was a great help, as I was in the middle of nowhere and it was just getting light, but now still only around 7am. I said goodbye to my friend, off the bus I got, and I started to walk towards Bruce's house. I had the phone number of my new host Bruce, I rang him up, got him out of bed, as it was before the 8am time he suggested I arrived, and he came out of his house to collect me, as I was in a long road with a dead end, and I could not find his door number.

The first thing I saw from a distance was Bruce's dog Rudi. My immediate thought was, "Here we fcuking go again"!!! But once I went inside Bruce's lovely house, I realised my judgement was completely wrong, and Rudi was a really lovely and friendly doggy, and Bruce's pad was perfect. Bruce was a fantastic host, and one of the first things he said to me was "The fridge is full, I've bought us lots of food, take whatever you want, anytime you want, and you don't have to ask me first, just take it". What a nice gesture and a top man I thought, and this was the start of a very nice time I had with Bruce.

Bruce headed off to work, left me to sleep for a few hours until lunchtime, and basically said "my home is your home, just relax and do whatever you want", brilliant.
Bruce is an American Football referee in his spare time and he asked me if I wanted to come with him that evening to watch him referee a game between two teams of teenagers around 13-15 years of age. Sure I did, so that evening, that's exactly what we did.

It was very interesting to see Bruce at work on the field and watching these youngsters play football. It was obviously very different to my NFL experiences, but I really enjoyed it, I even ended high up in the stands in a box with the game commentators, scorers and the lady who did all the announcements, including one announcement welcoming me to their stadium all the way from England. What lovely people they were, great company indeed and I really had a fun time with these lovely people.

After the game Bruce took me for dinner at the one restaurant I wanted to try while in town, the world famous Premanti Brothers of Pittsburgh. Premanti's is known for its amazing sandwiches, which have everything but the kitchen sink in them!

I had chicken, beef, salad, onion rings and chips in mine, probably other stuff too, It was lovely, and all washed down with a few local beers in a bar full of NFL memorabilia. What more does this boy want? Not much!
Bruce asked me if I would like to help him at work the next morning delivering meals to pensioners at their homes. Meals on wheels we call this in the UK. "Sure I did" I told him. The next morning I went with Bruce to his place of

work, had a cup of tea, and met his fellow workers, who incidentally are all volunteers, just as Bruce is. What a lovely bunch of people they were. The boss thanked me for my time, and of course it was a real pleasure to help them and especially the people I would visit on their doorsteps. Bruce got the car loaded with the trays of food, he did the driving, and I ran from the car, to the doors to deliver the meals, about 40-50 homes. The job itself was very rewarding and grounding for me, if that makes sense. What I mean is, here I am travelling all over America living the dream, and now I'm meeting many lovely and friendly old people, some with disabilities, most living alone, and I'm bringing them their dinners. It was very touching and extremely sad, especially if you are as sensitive as I am. That morning I met with some very very lovely old people. The look on a lot of their faces when they saw me, "the new boy", was priceless. A lot of them were waiting by their doors as their food came, as they normally receive the food at almost the same time every day.

I felt so sorry for a lot of these people, most of them were in lovely houses, but most lived alone. Where were their families? I thought. Another big fear I was thinking was, is this going to be me in 30 years time? Perish the thought. I enjoyed helping these lovely old folks immensely, I found it personally very rewarding, but it also upset me too, actually quite a bit. My heart strings were well and truly played upon on that day.

Two years later I wonder how many of those lovely old people are still alive, the thought upsets me, and thats why I try to tick as many boxes as I can in my life, as when I get to that point, or old age, I dont want to look back and feel I never gave life my best shot. Even if I failed, at least I tried my very best and followed my dreams.

Tonight was game seven on my tour, the Baltimore Ravens were in town, and at this point they had not won a game so far this season, so it should be an easy win for the Steelers, against their divisional rivals, or so I thought.

I had bought a ticket for this game before I left the UK, simply because I knew it was a close rivals game, and I was thinking it maybe a sell out. WRONG! Especially after the news that big Ben Roethlisberger, the Steelers star quarterback was out injured. The 168 dollars ticket I had paid was now worth about 70. FCUK!

You win some, you lose some, and this night I did lose, bigtime. It got worse after Bruce informed me he had a spare ticket I could have had for a whole lot less than I paid for mine. The plan was to sell my ticket, and whatever I got for it, Bruce could have, and we would sit together. We never did sell my ticket, actually we didn't even try to, but we sat together anyway.

It was very interesting watching a game next to a football referee, as Bruce called all the flags on the plays (penalties) and he never once got one wrong for the entire game.
Heinz Field was a nice stadium, as all the stadiums were on my tour, not one of my favourite stadiums, nothing overly special, but nice. I noticed it was the only stadium I attended on my tour that did not have the name of the home team in both end zones. At one end there were just a few diagonal lines. I had no idea why? But I didn't like that.
I was gutted Roethlisburger was not playing as I wanted to see him in the flesh, but I still expected a very easy night for the Steelers.

After all the usual razzamatazz before the game, the kick off arrived, and I was looking forward to watching it with a guy who was a big Steelers fan.

Pittsburgh always looked in complete control of this game
to me and they raced into a half time lead. The lead could
have been more if the Steelers kicker did not miss a couple
of field goals, something that would later cost his team, and
personally for him, extremely dearly.

The Ravens staged a second half comeback with their own
star quarterback Joe Flacco starting to pull the strings. The
game started to get very interesting and now we had a game
on our hands, and a game which went right down to the wire
as the Ravens kicked a field goal in the last few seconds,
taking this game into my very first game of overtime, extra
time for you lot who don't know what overtime is.

In overtime the Steelers had the chance to kick a winning
field goal, but from a long way out, and as their kicker had
already missed two previous field goal attempts, the Steelers
coach decided this was not a good idea, so he called a
different play, and it backfired terribly on his team. The
Ravens got the ball back, and incredibly they kicked a
winning overtime field goal. I never saw that coming at all.
After the game and this defeat, the Pittsburgh Steelers kicker
took a huge kick up the ass and was fired.

I never did get the chance to see much of Pittsburgh, as I
was only there for three days, and I never even made it to
downtown, mainly because I was mostly with Bruce, and he
made it much easier for me to go with him in his car and
basically just do whatever he was doing. I do kind of regret
this as I always make the effort to see what's in town,
wherever I am.

There was not that much to see or do as a tourist in
Pittsburgh, but I did want to go up to Mount Washington
and see the views over Pittsburgh. I would have gone but
the weather in my time there was very grey and cloudy, and

according to Bruce, I would not have seen much, so I took his advice and I bailed out. On my radar too was the Andy Warhol museum, but again I just never had the time, but at least I had my Premanti sandwich!!!

The next evening I left Bruce and his lovely dog Rudi, as I had decided I was not going back to Chicago by the Greyhound bus, I would take the overnight Amtrak train, my very first Amtrak experience and something I was really looking forward to.

I'm a massive fans of trains, I would travel the whole world on them if I could, but sadly for me, here in the US, they are far from cheap. I could have caught the cheaper option of the Greyhound bus back to Chicago, but I wanted to experience Amtrak at some point on my tour, and why not do it as soon as possible. I hung around the train station like a kid in a sweet shop for a few hours, eventually boarding the train, and off I went.

I enjoyed every minute of the nine hours journey to Chicago, it was a very comfortable ride with even more comfortable seats, a food car and a car with a glass roof and huge windows to see out, which is where I sat for most of the ride. I didn't sleep much on this overnight train, I was just happy to be on board and heading towards my next adventure in another new exciting place I had never been to before, (except the Greyhound bus station) the windy city of......Chicago.

Soldier Field, here I come!

Stadium-8
Soldier Field
Chicago Bears

I arrived into Chicago early the next morning after my
wonderful and virgin Amtrak train ride, and I headed for my
hostel on the other side of town, via the Chicago subway.
I was always looking forward to getting to Chicago on my
tour, as it was one of the very few big US cities I had not
already visited.

I booked into yet another HI Hostel as these places are
always clean, central, and basically do what it says on the
tin. This hostel was in a cracking location, even within
walking distance to my next stadium, the world famous
Soldier Field, the home of the Chicago Bears.

The HI Hostel also had a massive relaxation area, which is
always important to me. There was a pool table, table tennis,
comfortable chairs and sofas to relax on when I am on my
laptop doing my social media stuff, as well as reading my
book. There was also a big screen on the wall next to a
corner sofa, a great place to watch soccer and NFL games,
which of course I did.

My first full day in Chicago I did the usual wandering
around mission, before I jumped on a guided bus tour of all
the main Chicago attractions mainly in the centre of town. I
took a two hour loop on a bus with a tour guide, and he
informed us of some really interesting facts and stories of
old Chicago happenings, characters and landmarks, many
things you would never know about Chicago unless you
were told.

Al Capone had once lived here, and he did this, he did that, all up to no good and getting him in big trouble of course! Elizabeth Taylor stayed there, so did the Queen of England. In a certain building over there, the guide informed us, was the building where Barack Obama met his wife. That apartment building over there is worth five million per household, and so on. Very interesting indeed and something this boy likes very much.

I went past the park where Metallica and Paul McCartney recently played in a big music festival, (I wish I could have seen that!) We drove past many museums, very tall buildings, expensive appartments, the Planetarium, and of course, Soldier Field. I can clearly remember the tour guide call Soldier Field the "ugliest building in Chicago", and to be honest, from the outside, I could not disagree with him! I stopped off for lunch in one of Chicago's famous eating spots, in a lovely funky kind of food hall. I would love to tell you guys the name of it, but I cannot remember. I think it sounded Italian, and the spare ribs I had were yummy. I liked Chicago immediately, I felt very much at home here, just as I do in New York, as I love the amazing high buildings, with many great designs and architecture.

That evening I went out to a local bar called "Hackneys", I chose this bar purely as it has the same name of a place very close to where I live in East London. I had dinner, washed down with a few beers, and I chatted away to the barman and had a nice relaxing evening.

I mentioned to the barman that I was a very lucky mascot for people I had met, and then gone to watch their NFL teams play. I told him I would be a lucky omen for his Chicago Bears and I predicted they would beat the Oakland Raiders the following day and he promised me a few free beers if this came true. Actually it did, but this silly boy did not go back to claim his prize.

Sunday was game day, number eight on my tour and the Oakland Raiders were the guests, two pretty poor and already struggling teams, even after only a few weeks of the season. So I thought it should be a close game, and a close game it certainly was.

I left my hostel around 10am for the thirty minutes or so walk to Soldier Field in the freezing cold and biting wind, which was cutting through me like a knife through butter. Chicago is known for its baking hot summers and freezing cold winters, so my timing for this game was good, as although it was very chilly, it was not half as bad as it would be a month or so later.

I got to the outskirts of Solider Field, and I was in new territory for me, as I never had a ticket for the game, something I had always done was to purchased a ticket before all my seven previous games, including a couple for games before I left London, which in hindsight was a mistake. So by having no ticket for this particular game, I was basically testing the water on how I was going to blag/find one.

I had no doubt at all I would get in to see the game, and I was thinking I would just go straight to the stadium and buy a ticket from one of the booths at the club, just as I did after my scammed experience in Philadelphia.

I walked straight through the first tailgate I came to, which was on the outskirts of Soldier Field, and I looked around and smelt all the lovely food that was on display, and I made myself look blatantly obvious to wanting a piece of the action.

As I approached a bunch of my first potential new best friends, or victims, I decided that my ice breaker of a question to start off a conversation would be, "Hi guys, do you know if its possible for me to buy a ticket for the game at the stadium"?

The very first guy I asked shouted out to his mate " Davie, do you still have the spare ticket"? Davie came over and I hit him with my poor Englishman's tales of woe, mixed in with an added extra amount of bullshit. "Hi Davie, I'm only here a few days, I'm from England and I'm not really that interested in the NFL too much, but I just wanna watch a game while I'm in Chicago and I don't really want to pay too much for a ticket". "Well bud, this ticket is worth 125 dollars, but you can have it for 50", Davie said. "SOLD", I said, in a heartbeat, to the English bullshit man!!! It really was that easy. TOUCHDOWN D-MO!

From that day onwards I never bought a ticket to a game for about the next ten weeks, unless it was dirt cheap on Tickpick. I was now going to wing it at the next few games simply because now the season was into its fourth week, there were a lot of games I attended where certain teams had already started the season badly. This meant that even this early in the season, there was some discontent with the fans, leaving many empty seats. So I took advantage of this, and I picked up cheap tickets pretty easily, everywhere I went. I chatted to Davie and his gang for only a couple of minutes after I bought the ticket from him, as I was hoping they were going to offer me a beer or something to eat, but sadly they never did, so as I stood around in the freezing cold like a lingering fart, I felt like a spare one at a wedding, so I decided to move on and have a wander around the outside of Soldier Field, and maybe then I could find my free lunch! Soldier Field was one of the stadiums I was always looking forward to visiting. Like the Packers Lambeau Field, Soldier

Field has a great history and was one of the older stadiums in the NFL. I remember the great players they had back in the 80's, and I could have easily been a Bears fan as they were one of the dominant teams in the very early days of the NFL on our UK TV screens. I remember the fantastic runningback Walter Peyton, William "The Fridge" Perry, QB Jim McMahon and the great Bears defense which included Mike Singletary. A brilliant team.

Soldier Field, to my surprise was one of the smallest stadiums in the NFL, with only a capacity of just over 60,000. This apparently is the reason why there has never been, and probably never will be a Superbowl played there. I think the weather in the beginning of February in Chicago would also have some influence on that decision. I did a 360 around Soldier Field, took some pictures under the iconic "Soldier Field" sign, and basically took in the atmosphere, as in my mind, I was in a very historic and special place to be a NFL fan.

Soldier Field was opened in 1924, and had been renovated a few years ago to make it bigger, and the only way this could be done, was to place a big bowl inside of the existing exterior that was already there, making it's frame look a little bit of an eyesore. But I must admit, from the inside, I thought it was a lovely stadium, and it reminded me a little bit of Lambeau Field in Green Bay, probably because these two stadiums are two of the oldest, if not the two oldest in the NFL, and probably the two most important stadiums in NFL history.

The game started at 1pm and it was a poor display from both teams from the very start. But this made it a good game for a neutral like me to watch. On this day I was a Bears fan, but they just could not keep possession of the ball at all, they kept giving the ball away to the Raiders, then getting it back, then giving it away again.

The Raiders were in front for most of the game, not by much, and never quite out of touching distance, so the game always looked like it was going all the way down to the wire, which made this game very exciting. It was like watching a game that both teams did not seem to want to win, as both teams quarterback's, Jay Culter of the Bears, and Derek Carr of the Raiders exchanged regular fcuk up's! For this token neutral fan (me), it was very entertaining, but probably quite stressful for passionate fans of both the Bears and the Raiders to endure.

There were a lot of fans of the Oakland Raiders inside Soldier Field, and this was a pattern I saw at another game I attended when the Raiders were the visitors in Denver. Raiders fans are great, and one of my favourite groups of supporters in the whole of the NFL. Firstly, they are bonkers (mad), crazy, wear the most outragous outfits, face paint, all kinds of clothing (gorilla, spaceman, superhero etc) and they always have a huge abundance of attitude. They also make one hell of a noise.

See, I love all this, and it is one of the reasons why I am such a big fan of this game. For me, its not just about the game itself once kick off time comes, that is only a part of the bigger picture, a picture of an experience, not just a game of American Football.

Raiders fans are so funny, mainly aggressive, but trust me, their barks are very loud and they very rarely bite. Its a kind of act, bravado, and I love this. Now I can only give my own personal experience, so for anybody reading this has taken a kicking from another NFL fan, then I'm sorry, but I never experienced anything more than friendly banter from all the

NFL fans I met. Aggression? yes, but I saw so many verbal exchanges during games I was at, that looked and sounded like it was going to kick off (fight). But it never did.
I had experienced exactly this in New York two years ago when watching my Cowboys beat the Giants. The guy next to me had a running battle with a bunch of Giants fans sitting a few rows behind us for about two hours. There was much cursing, swearing, attitude, threats, then at the end, I was gobsmacked, they all shook hands and behaved like friends. Amazing, and brilliant, I love this.

So inside Solder Field at my game, there was a running battle between a small bunch of Raiders fans and the whole of the section of Bears fans I was sitting with. These three or four Raiders fans were like the British Army up against the Zulu's in the battle of Rorke's drift! and these guys really holding their own. The comments and the insults were hilarious, and fantastic entertainment for us all to witness. I was actually enjoying this battle more than the game itself! I was laughing my bollocks off and I was looking forward to hearing the next insult, song, joke etc all the time.

But the best thing of all was when the game ended, these fantastic four who had traded insults with 1000's of people, were hugged and shook hands with the many many people around them, most of whom had been slagging each other off all throughout the entire game. It was a very special moment for me and I was genuinely touched by this brilliant piece of respect between two sets of passionate NFL fans, and this is exactly how all sports fans should be. Cheer your team on completely, slag each others teams off during the game, but when one team wins, shake hands, say well done, go home, and then you can cry or punch the wife!!!! Only joking.

On my NFL adventure, one of my biggest pleasures was my rapport, connection and love for the NFL fans. These people are so passionate about their teams, and most are so respectful to other teams fans, and this is something I love completely.

My "SuperFan" friends, who I had not met as of yet in this section of the book, are a group of "friends" all over America, all supporting different NFL teams. The love and respect they have for each other is very special indeed, completely unique. Whenever they meet up at each other's tailgates, they are welcomed like gods, or family and rightly so, and not just from the hosts themselves, but all the host's friends. Its a very special bond indeed, and I simply love it. In all the stadiums I attended on my tour, I never once felt threatened at any point while at a game, even when I wore my Dallas Cowboys colours in Philadelphia.

Yeah people booed me, and a few times right in my face, but I didn't mind that, in fact I wanted more of it, just so I could give some back!! Many times people would say to me, "be careful when you get to Cleveland", "don't go into the Dawg Pound",or "be careful when you get to Oakland", "don't go into the Black Hole". WHY? So you know what I did when I went to both of these stadiums? I went straight into both of these so called notorious sections, and I had absolutely no problems at all.

How could I not go into these area's being a massive NFL fan? When you go to these stadiums, you have to go inside these areas to experience the atmosphere, rage, anger, excitement, camerarderie. You bloody try stopping me going into them!! Now if I entered both of these sections wearing colours of a rival team, screamed obsenities, behaved like an asshole, then of course someone is gonna smack me, and rightly so. I loved these sections and I wish I could have spent the entire game in them.

Back to my game at Soldier Field and the Bears made a great last quarter comeback and they now had the chance to win the game with a field goal in the last few seconds. I so wanted them to score and win, as the Bears were behind for almost the whole game and I always support the home team at the games I was at, except when against my Cowboys of course.

I was sitting next to a really lovely guy who was a Bears fan, so when the field goal was kicked and scored to win the game, we jumped around cheering and cuddling like old mates. It was so great, and a brilliant end to an exciting game that was full of tension and mistakes, which kept every fan of both teams on the very edge of their freezing cold seats!

I've had yet another great day out, inside another iconic stadium, and at a game in which the home team won. I'm a very happy bunny... again.

After leaving Soldier Field, I returned to my hostel for the later game, my Dallas Cowboys at the New Orleans Saints. The Cowboys had had a good start to the season, but had now lost their star quarterback Tony Romo, who got injured in the game I was at in Philadelphia, and I worried for them as I thought the Dallas Cowboys back up quarterbacks were not looking quite up to the task in hand.....at all.

I watched the game with some lovely people from the hostel, including a top guy named Chris who was a big basketball fan, and in town to watch the Chicago Bulls. The Cowboys game was a tense and very close game, and I will never forget the ending as the Saints had a last second field goal kick to win the game, which they missed as the Lions kicker hits the post..........YEEESSSS!!!!

So the game goes into overtime (extra time), and before it started, I quickly run to the loo, and by the time I returned, the game was over. WHAT? And I only did a number 1! On the second play of overtime, Drew Brees finds his wide receiver and its goodbye Dallas, with only ten seconds off the overtime clock. What a custard pie to the face, as my emotions went up and down like a yoyo in the very short space of a couple of minutes. First great excitement when the Saints kicker hits the post, missing his field goal attempt, and giving us Cowboy fans hope we could break our three game losing streak, then two minutes later a touchdown is scored, the Cowboy get beat, and I'm off to bed with the raving hump! (upset). FCUK!

That night I was invited by my new friend Chris, to go to watch a basketball game with him the following evening. I'd been to see the Boston Celtics and the Los Angeles Lakers play on a previous trip, so I was looking forward to going to see the famous Chicago Bulls. I don't know much about the Bulls, other than Micheal Jordan played for them and that he was a legend.

The game I went to see was a pre season friendly between the Bulls and Milwaukee. Chris had a ticket, I of course never did, but I got to the stadium and I picked one up very cheap in no time. Chris had a good ticket and mine was up in the nose bleeds, just how I like it, but before the game started, Chris was attempting to get a few autographs from the Chicago Bulls players. I wasn't allowed into his section, but this small minor piece of detail was completely irrelevant, as I bunked in anyway...as you do!

So as Chris waited patiently for the pen marks from his heroes, all incidently nobodies to me, but somebodies to everyone else in the room, he politely waited his turn to get a squiggle of the pen on his merchandise.

Now its not because I am impatient, (which of course I am), but waiting in these kind of queues or "shit fights" as I call them, is where I thrive. Its usually survival of the fittest if you want the name on your designated item, something I proved during SB50 in San Fran, when a crowd of peeps/fans wanted a Superbowl golden ticket as a souvenir. (I will come to this later).

If you wait in line for an autograph, some knob (asshole) usually jumps in front of you, (like me!), your hero has signed a couple of programs, books, shirts, breasts etc, then he wants to return to the sanctuary of the locker room for a shower or to get some peace and quiet away from all the crazies and adoring, and usually over enthusiastic fans, so you will generally miss the moment, or the chance to get his autograph or access to his Twitter page.

So Chris was after this one guy, I had no idea at all who he was, or even now is, but he walked past us and I stuck my hand in his face and said "Hello mate, I'm from England, I have no idea who you are, but I just wanna say hello"? He said hi, shook my hand, Chris got his scribble, and everyones a winner, especially the hero, as he met me!!!

I enjoyed the game, but Basketball does bore me a little as I think there is far too much scoring, like every ten seconds, and I find this to be overkill and too much of the same thing. A game usually ends something like 100-96, and that's a lot of baskets. But I do like the last quarter, as this is when the fun starts, and the tension at the very end, if the game is close.

I joined Chris at his better seat in the second half, where he was sitting next to a very pretty girl, and if I would have known this major factor, I would have joined him earlier!! The Bulls won the game, so everyone was happy, even me, although I can't say I really concentrated fully on the game, but I thoroughly enjoyed the company of Chris, a very nice guy indeed and I was pretty sad when he left the hostel to return home to England the next day. I would love to meet up with Chris again one day.

I do get very attached to nice people I meet on my travels, and I always do my very best to stay friends and keep in touch with these lovely people as much as I can. A prime example is my Mexican friend Jorge Gonzalez, whom I met in Berlin in 1992. I was reunited with him in Los Angeles in 2013, after we had kept in touch for over twenty years. You will hear a bit more from Jorge when I get to LA later in the book.

My final day in Chicago I reverted to my usual tourist activities and I ended up in the Chicago Planetarium. I've always had a keen fascination of the planets, the solar system and the stars, and this planetarium was fantastic. I watched a few short films about the universe, space exploration, planets, stars, galaxies, saw models of space ships of all kinds, read lots of interesting things and had a nice relaxing day.

I met my friend Craig Steichen, (the guy who runs the Warrior Wishes charity), as he lives in Chicago, so we had a quick coffee, and off he went to his next game, just as I was the following day. I would bump into Craig the next time in Dallas, the following weekend.

That evening I tried to go to the famous bar of blues guitarist and Chicago legend Buddy Guy, as this bar was a five minutes walk from my hostel. I was told by the staff at my hostel that by being a guest at the HI, got us in the Buddy's gaff/bar for a nice and cheap five bucks, right up my boulevard, or so I thought. When I got to the door, the guy wanted twenty pictures of George Washington, (Bucks), so I decided to abort that particular mission as I'm not the biggest of blues fans and apparently Buddy was not even in the building, so I decided to retreat back to the comfort and peace of my lovely hostel.

I really enjoyed my time in Chicago, I had heard a lot of negative things about the city before I arrived, mainly about gangs, violence and trouble. I had no problems at all as I was in the centre of town, and far away from the bad areas or ghettos. Chicago is definitely "My kind of Town" (sorry about that!) and a place I hope to return to on my next trip to the US.

The next morning after breakfast, I packed my things and I headed for O'Hare International airport on the Chicago subway. I would be taking my last flight for the next six weeks, leaving the freezing cold state of Illinois, for the much warmer climate of the south, next stop.......Houston Texas.

Stadium-9
NRG Stadium
Houston Texans

Leaving Chicago was always going to be a pivotal moment on the planning of my tour. As I've mentioned, I was trying not to fly as much as possible, not just because I was trying to keep hold of as many pictures of George Washington as possible, but because I felt that flying was kind of cheating, and making getting around the US too easy, so I only took a flight when it was absolutely necessary.

I knew that if I flew, I would be missing out on so much adventure, anything from seeing the small towns I love to stop off at, even if its just for a 30 minutes pit stop, a coffee break, or to just stretch my legs. I always felt by flying, I could potentially miss out on something new I have never done or seen before, or lose the chance of meeting potential new friends or different characters of all ages and colours while in these small but interesting places, something I always love to experience while being on the road.

I would also miss out on all the regular kinds of cock ups, breakdowns, delays, hurdles and challenges, which I always saw as a big part of the overall story of my travels. I'm not saying that I completely enjoyed these moments, (some, not at all) as most of them were hardships, but some of these moments of struggle bring great stories, not at the time of course, that's when I wanted to scream, but on reflection, times like these bring a big smile to my face, as some of these times were priceless.

Sometimes I would get lucky and find a flight that was almost as cheap as the bus, but the hidden costs with flights, including having to pay 25-50 bucks for my backpack, was always dead money, and this hurt. One flight I took from Denver to Phoenix, my baggage costs were more expensive than the flight itself.

I had done many long bus rides in the past and I had many more ahead of me, but my benchmark, or maximum length of travel time was always around 24 hours from one city to another, and as Chicago to Houston was quite a bit more than that by the Greyhound bus, I decided to take a very cheap flight, which was actually cheaper than the bus. This flight was going to be my last for around 6 weeks, until I got to New York City, on week 11, a long long way by road, via Texas, Mississippi, Alabama, Louisiana, Georgia and around five or six other states of the US.

Bus rides were not always bad, to be honest I always looked forward to the bus pulling away from a city I was leaving, it signified the start of a new adventure in a new place. No matter how long these bus rides took, I rarely got bored or lost my patience. Around this time, I was having the time of my life and riding on the crest of such a big wave, so all problems, and there were a few, I simply brushed them off, and in a funny kind of way, I enjoyed the excitement and challenge, that some of these problems brought. For me, it was a kind of personal test, and I passed these tests with flying colours..... most of the time.

Delay's in strange places like Montgomery Alabama and Dayton Ohio were interesting to say the least. Changing buses in the middle of the night is no fun at all, especially if its freezing cold and when the driver of the second bus just doesn't bother to turn up, or is in no rush at all to get us back out on the road, can test the patience of a clergyman!

On the many buses I took, all across the country, I got chatting to some very interesting and some very shady characters, something I really liked. People of all ages, sizes, shapes and colours. I met some wonderful people travelling on those buses.

Bus travel did give me another option for saving a few dollars, especially a night bus, as I saved on paying for a night's accomodation. I loved these long night bus rides, as adventure was just waiting to happen on these nights, mainly problematic, but always minor incidents.

Another attraction was that the buses usually dropped me off in the centre of the cities I was going to, saving me time, effort and money to get to my hostels, as most airports in US cities tended to be far away from the centre of the towns where I stayed all of the time.

Most of the people I travelled with on these bus rides were poor, some very poor, this observation was obvious as to why they were on a 24 hours overnight bus, rather than a 90 minute flight.

Now I have been around and in the company of both rich and poor people in my life, usually the poor where I live, and the rich where I work.

In my experience, I have always enjoyed the company of poor people so much more than their much wealthier counterparts, absolutely no question. Poor people are so much more genuine, a million times more honest, and the same amount of percentage less fake. Poor people are soooooo much more generous in giving, even when they have practically fcuk all/nothing, and they are so much more interesting.

It always used to upset me a little when I saw bus loads of families travelling on the Greyhound bus together, a lot of them in clothes looking no better than rags, and with not a pot to piss in/no money. Then I get on a flight and see herds of rude, flashy, noisy, squeaking, usually blonde women (from a bottle), trying to stuff their precious Prada or Louis Vuitton bags into the overhead lockers, with their fake bristols/tits, under their chins and probably with more money than sense, or more likely living off a rich husband.

These money and fashion driven people need to travel on a Greyhound bus to get a dose of the real world, a reality check, a whole new perspective on the true value of what a dollar equates to, and what it must be like to have practically nothing, but still retain the human values of being polite, respectful and have good manners, something which comes completely for free, something money can never buy, and in most cases, including where I currently work, does not exist.

Maybe this is just me and my judgemental opinion as usual, as I have come from a background a lot closer to the Greyhound world, than the business class world, and in my experience, most of the time (not always, just most) you will get a better tip from a poor man than a rich one, and I should know after being a golf caddie for almost 10 years.

I landed in Houston early in the evening and headed for my

latest hostel called the "Morty Rich", ha, not quite the "Filthy Rich"! It was recommended to me by Steve, whom I had met in Minneapolis, he had stayed there a few weeks earlier and said it was a very nice place, and he was right. I always follow a recommendation, as word of mouth from other travellers is usually worth it's weight in gold.

The Morty Rich was a lovely big old wooden house in a nice street, and as soon as I arrived, I knew it was a good choice. Thanks Steve. I dropped my bags at my bed and went straight out for something to eat.

I then had one of those random meetings with a lovely person, something which happened a few times on my tour, sadly most turn into disappointment and a little heartbreak, but they are always good experiences.......at the time.

I walked past a Mexican food truck in the car park of a bar, and I decided to stop and take a look at the menu. As I looked, I got talking to a pretty young girl in her early 20's named Michelle, who had just bought some food from the van. "How's the food", I asked her, "great", she replied, so I ordered a few tacos.

There was a lot of noise coming from the bar we were standing outside, it sounded like some kind of private party to me, as there were lots of laughing and cheering going on. Michelle informed me it was a gathering of a club she was a member of, a poetry club, and they were taking a short break. Michelle asked me if I would like to come inside and watch people from her club recite some poetry. "Sure", I said, as I'm always looking to experience something new, and this seemed like it could be interesting, and as she was quite a cutie, and who knows where this could lead to, my little head was thinking!!

Michelle was a sweetie, quite shy, and very nice to talk to, and she wrote poetry, which is not quite my thing, but I've always been open to it and it does interest me as songwriting and poetry are very closely connected.

The second half of the poetry show began and my gut feeling and character analysis towards Michelle from the second we met was confirmed. Maybe it was the super fashionable nose ring she had, usually worn by cows that starting my personal alarm bells ringing.

The overweight girl on the stage, covered in tattoos and no make up, was screaming out her very own angst and aggressive version of poetry. Yep she was a lesbian, and a very angry one at that too.

Don't get me wrong, I love lesbians, I watch loads of them in my spare time, if you know what I mean!! but I think this poetry club was a way of giving this particular bunch of people a way for them to let off steam, or blow a fuse, because this is exctly what they did. This showcase gave them the platform to vent their spleens, get the anger out of their systems, and basically inform the state of Texas, they were not afraid to be opening the doors and climbing out of their closets, something the Texas bible belt does not empathise to very much...to say the least.

After hearing half a dozen of these aggressive poets ranting and blaming the straight world for all THEIR problems, a pattern was developing and it started to tire and grate the eardrums of this straight boy from East London. The poets and poetry were in fact very good, without question these people were talented, but the message from these angry individuals was always pointing to and aimed at the so called "bigots" of society, people who could not see THEIR point of view, alternative lifestyles and human rights.

These poems of persecution and suffering on a personal level were very powerful and thought provoking messages and I would be lying if I said I was not impressed. I understood the subject matter, got it completely, but I could never fully relate to this angst as I was not a part of this group of people's world. In fact, I was starting to feel persecuted, like I was a part of the problem, the enemy, as I'm a paid up member of the group this angry hate mob were attacking, the straight majority.

I was not really overly offended, as I tried my best to sympathise with their suffering, but some of it was very aggressive indeed against the straight community, and after a while I started to feel a little less comfortable clapping these people, who were making derogatory comments about my hetrosexual lifestyle, and the fact that MY world was to blame.

The poets, mainly women, all in the same box, (I say in my judgemental way again, trying my best not to offend) were mostly overweight, tattooed, wore glasses and no make up, once finished their "five mintues of hetrosexual bashing", they would walk off stage to thunderous applause, and usually into the arms of their waiting partners.

I'm sure this was a very liberating experience for them, but sadly not for me as with every line, sonnet or paragraph expressed, I knew my chances of a sexual liason with the lovely Michelle were dwindling with every vowel or consonant, in the sticky and humid Texan air.

I eventually asked Michelle the "Elephant in the room" question, and she confirmed this was in fact the case. Yep, she drank from the furry cup! FCUK!

We then spoke a little about the subject in which Michelle revealed to me, that her parents had no idea she ("batted for the other side") and that she had just split up with her partner. Michelle showed me the picture of her love, and I tried my best to understand why this very pretty young girl, wearing make up and nice clothes, was attracted to a fattish girl in a baseball cap, without make up and looking like a dude.

See I don't get this, but then I'm not supposed to I guess, as I'm not this way inclined, not yet anyway!! (the thought of getting rejected by men as well as women is simply too much for me to take!)

Michelle read me a poem she had written in which she was too nervous and shy to recite on stage. It was heartfelt, touching and full of personal torture. It was nice, but very sad and I could not only see, but feel her emotions, mainly heartache.

I do feel sorry for the Michelle's and Michael's of this world, as it must be very hard for them, especially in Texas, as they do deserve any lifestyle that they, or god chooses for them. But the hardcore Texan "god squad", will not see it this way, even if THEY are probably breaking every rule that "their" own personal Jesus's have chosen for them. This I guess is called "Religion", and to me its nothing but trouble, dishonest and twisted to suit certain individuals, and always used as a weapon, and a subject I don't have any time for #whatsofcukingever!!

I wish Michelle all the very best in her life, whatever she decides to do as she was a top girl, very nice company and I liked her, probably too much!

On the way back to my hostel, I bumped into two girls who asked me for directions to a bar. When I answered in my English accent, they were temporarily mesmerised, sadly only temporary. The two girls were sisters, one of which told me that her boyfriend was English, so we chatted for a bit at the side of the road, exchanged Facebook names, so we could keep in touch, as they wanted to meet up the following night, something that sounded good to me.

The two sisters were very pretty, and both had the distinctive and latest fad (again) the trademark cow nose ring, (whch I actually find quite sexy) very attractive none the less, and extremely flirtatious, something I never mind at all and encourage as much as humanly possible.

We spoke for about ten minutes, mainly about the English boyfriend, and the time one of the girls visited him in London. YAWN! We exchanged details, and over the next day or so, we tried to arrange to meet up, but In typical fashion, all the plans went out of the window, when the two girls let me down at the bloody last minute as usual, after all the online chats and arrangements I had with them about what we could do or where we could go together. Sadly I never saw them again. Yet another blow out in my quest for the proverbial "leg over"!

I did get a facebook message a year later from one of them asking me for help, "Hiya, I'm coming to London, can you help me find a job". My reply was something along the lines of "Er, let me think about it, no.....fcuk off"!

I retuned to my hostel and got chatting to a guy named Daryl from Canada, and he told me he was going to the game I was going to the following night, to watch the Texans play the Indianapolis Colts, so after pleasantries, we made plans to go together.

Houston is not the kind of city to go to for it's tourism, as there is not too much to see there, IMHO before Houstonians start to correct me. There did'nt seem to be anywhere else for me to visit that interested me, other than the NASA Space Centre which is exactly where I went on my last day. I did go to the centre, or downtown area on the bus, just to have a look around, but like I say, there was not much going on in the way of attractions.

Thursday evening was game number nine on my tour, so Daryl and I left the hostel, and we headed for the NRG stadium, the home of the Houston Texans.

It was a fairly easy ride on first a bus, then a tram, but my old laziness of travelling with a companion and not fully concentrating on where we were going, would later come back to royally bite me, and Daryl on the ass.

We arrived outside the stadium on a beautiful Texan

evening, we wandered through a tailgate area and I did my usual chat up line of "Wow, what's that you are eating?, it looks and smells amazing", in my strongest cockney accent. "Come and join us boys" was the reply, and music to my ears, so Daryl and I got the full Texan hospitality for the next hour or so, until we had to leave for the game.

This was in fact my very first proper taste of tailgating where I was offered the full treatment and tailgate experience on my tour. Up until then, I had not tried too hard to scrounge a meal, or a few freebie beers at a tailgate, as I didn't really take too much notice. But after my first tailgate experience, the lion was unleashed, or maybe the hyena, as I would get stuck into as much of the delicious American cuisine as I could from this day forward, as I was now completely hooked.

I wish I could remember the names of the three nice and extremely generous guys who made Daryl and my good self so welcome. We ate all kinds of their food from brisket to pulled pork, we drank beers, did shots, especially a cracking new drink I discovered and had never heard of before, "Jack Daniels Fire".

I had discovered and fell in love with the similar "rocket fuel", the amazing and mind blowing "Fireball", on my last US visit in Nashville, but this JD Fire was even better, with a bigger kick in the balls!, but a smoother, a more enjoyable kick in the balls, more like a tickle, and everybody love a tickle!!!

I had some pictures taken with a couple of absolutely stunning looking chicks, fans of the Houston Texans, who were walking past our tailgate. What a couple of babes, and dressed just how I like, wearing cowboy boots, ripped jean skirts, tight tops tied into a bow, and cowboy hats. I was completely sold, fell in love, and not for the first or last time I would do so on my tour.

The NRG stadium, the home of the Houston Texans is a cracking stadium, and until then, this stadium was my favourite. A square stadium with a very high retractable roof, with lots of beams that look like scaffolding, making it a nice piece of design and engineering.

The game against the Indianapolis Colts was good, very open, but the Colts looked the better team from the very start. The Colts star quarterback Andrew Luck (who once lived in England) was out injured which pissed me off, as yet again I was denied the pleasure of seeing a star name of the NFL playing in the flesh. The Colts back up QB Hasselback looked pretty impressive and he pulled the strings in the first half.

But I did have the pleasure of seeing the Texans legend JJ Watt, and he did look like some kind of beast, and a very good player in a bad Texans team, but sadly he never had one of his better games.

The very last play before half time was special, because its a play that very few people see in a lifetime of watching NFL games, and a play that does not come off very often, the legendary "Hail Mary" pass.

A "Hail Mary" pass is a very long forward pass in American football, made in desperation with only a small chance of success. During the "Hail Mary"pass attempt, all receivers run straight toward the endzone and the quarterback will make a long desperate pass that is often "up for grabs". The term became widespread after a 1975 NFL playoff game between the Dallas Cowboys and the Minnesota Vikings, when Cowboys quarterback Roger Staubach (a Roman Catholic) said about his game-winning touchdown pass to wide receiver Drew Pearson, "I closed my eyes and said a Hail Mary."

This particular "Hail Mary" pass was caught in the endzone by a Houston Texans receiver, and the first of four "Hail Mary's" I would see on my tour of all 31 stadiums, including two outstanding throws by the Green Bay Packers legend Aaron Rodgers.

This must be some kind of season record, or so I thought, so I have done some research, and I found that in the 2015-16 season, the year of my tour, this season had the most caught Hail Mary passes in NFL history. And I was there. AWESOME!

I'm absolutely over the moon with this stat, but what I find more amazing, is I cannot remember seeing a "Hail Mary" pass that was thrown and not caught or intercepted, on my entire tour. Four thrown, four caught. Incredible hey?

Back to the Texans game, so not only was it great to see this "Hail Mary" pass caught as it was by the home team, but the Texans needed these points to keep this game close, as the Colts were 13-3 ahead before the score. The celebrations were great, and it kept the game alive as the Colts were looking the far better team.

The second half comeback never materialised as the Colts ended up winners 27-20, a scoreline which looks a lot closer game than it really was.

I really did like the NRG stadium, and this stadium was used to host last years Superbowl 51. A very good choice indeed me thinks.

I met with Daryl after the game had ended and we proceeded for the 45 minute ride back to our hostel, or that's what I thought. WRONG!

We got back to the centre of Houston and we jumped off the tram, to catch our bus back to our hostel. But as I had left the hostel with Daryl, I did my usual thing of "switching off", I just followed him, and I never even looked at what tram stop we had got on at, on the way to the NRG stadium, so I had no idea which tram stop to get off at on our return, to catch the connection for our bus.

We both looked at each other for guidance, and I was not at all sure when we got off the tram, we may have got off one stop too early, so we could not find the bus stop, and it was now past midnight in potentially dodgy downtown Houston. FCUK!

We walked to the next tram stop and this still did not look right to me. I remembered an unusually shaped building that I used as a marker, but I was not sure this helped a whole lot.

Anyway we struggled to find our way for about a hour, made a few more wrong moves but eventually thank god, we found our bus stop, and got back to our hostel around

2am. We had made a real pig's of a very easy journey and turned it into an extremely difficult one, and for a while I was a little concerned we could possibly be in the wrong place at the wrong time, as I had been warned more than a few times to be careful in my time in Houston, especially downtown, exactly where we were wandering around lost, and standing out like dogs balls, waiting to be picked off by any number of Houston's night people, nutcases, muggers, loonies or psychos!!

I must admit, it was a bit of a relief once I got back to my dorm and my head hit the pillow that night, but I was mainly disappointed with myself for letting down my guard AGAIN and relying on Daryl to guide me, when unbeknown to me, he did exactly the same as he was relying on me. What a pair of cupid stunts!!!!

The only touristic thing I had on my radar while I was in Houston, other than the game of course, was the NASA space centre, and that's exactly where I went on my last day in town. I mentioned to a young Australian girl named Lauren I had met at breakfast in my hostel, that was where I was heading, and she asked if she could join me.

In Houston, there was a now a regular pattern developing of me bumping into pretty young women, something I liked a lot. So off I go with the young Austrailan Lauren, who informed me she was a model, something I could clearly see, because Lauren was a good looking girl, but she was stick thin, and I remember thinking she could have done with a few decent dinners to put a bit more meat on those protruding bones!!

The NASA Space Center was a two bus and two hours ride from the hostel, but I wanted to go, so it is what it is, and that tiny amount of detail did not deter me at all. Lauren was really lovely, good company, easy on the eye, so all was rosy in the garden.

We arrived at the NASA Space Centre and we went and did the tour. We saw rockets, Apollo crafts, loads of great pictures of early space history, watched films, viewed the main attractions of the Enterprise Space shuttle, as well as a massive Apollo space ship. We also went into the mission control centre and learned about what happened on some amazing and terrible days of space exploration.

I love this kind of stuff and I did enjoy coming to this place a lot, as I felt like I was at the heartbeat of where great things happened in the history of the space race.

Lauren left earlier than me to catch the bus back, but I decided to stay longer as I wanted to see everything. Hindsight tells me I should have left with her as the bus I expected to get back home a hour or so later broke down, and I had to wait almost two hours in the sticky Texan heat to catch the next bus back to my hostel.

The next morning, after breakfast by the swimming pool our hostel had, (that incidently never touched my skin), I packed my backpack, and off again I went to the bus station downtown, as I was catching the Greyhound bus, four hours up the road, to a very special place for me on my tour, the incredible AT+T stadium, the home of my beloved Cowboys....... next stop, Dallas.

Stadium-10
AT+T Stadium
Dallas Cowboys

I arrived into the centre of Dallas in brilliant sunshine around lunchtime, a massive difference from the last time I arrived into town from the beautiful San Antonio in shorts and a tee shirt, when Dallas was on the edge of a terrible front of extremely cold weather that swept across America that year. The locals must have thought I was mad as I changed into warmer clothing at the bus top by the side of the road. I never knew it snowed in Texas?

I headed straight for my new fixed abode, this time an Air B'n'B booking at the home of a guy named James. I basically had no choice as there was only one hostel in Dallas, a hostel I had stayed at on my last visit to the lone star state two years ago, but sadly for me, this time the hostel was full. I think this had something to do with the fact the New England Patriots were in town, and they usually attract a lot of fans to wherever they play, sadly taking up all the cheap beds in town, including mine.

James was another single guy with a dog, the usual drill, with the added mix I knew almost straight away that he was gay as soon as I met him. I had no problem with this at all, and luckily over the course of my stay, James was never a pain in the ass!! (sorry James).

James was a very nice host, very welcoming and friendly, and I liked him. The first night I stayed at James's pad, he already had another guest on his sofa, so I had to sleep on the floor at the end of his bed, being pestered by his bloody dog!!!

Honestly, most people have no idea of the so many hardships I had to endure during my trip. Sleeping rough or uncomfortably was just one of them, and I coped, simply because I had no choice, I had to. I think most people would have jumped on the first available flight home, but not this boy.

So after a rough night on the deck (floor), James kindly gave me a tour around the centre of Dallas. There was not a great deal to see, other than many large and high buildings, and as I had been here before, I did all the tourist things then. I went to a rodeo in Fort Worth, wandered around the grassy knowl and stood on the very spot on Dealey Plaza where John F Kennedy was shot dead, as well as going into the Book Depositary Museum, located in the building from where Lee Harvey Oswald supposedly fired those fateful shots.

I had also previously attended a stadium tour at the AT+ T stadium, the home of my Dallas Cowboys, and to my own very personal mecca, "Southfork Ranch", the home of the famous Ewing family and my favourite ever TV show "Dallas", which is exactly the reason why I started to support the Cowboys in the first place, way back in the mid 80's.

Dallas is not the easiest US city to get around if you don't have a car, especially getting to the Dallas Cowboys stadium which is in a place called Arlington, quite a way from the centre of Dallas. That place has no public transport at all, and I was in exactly the same boat as I was rowing back in Kansas City on week two, so yet again I was relying on the good nature and hospitality of my host, and for the second time, my host did not let me down.

I took James out for an Indian meal, to thank him for his kindness and then we went back to his place for a cuddle of the sofa. No, no, no, I'm joking!!

The next day was game ten and one I had been looking forward to since the schedule came out. At one point this was Tom Brady's comeback game from his ban, but that ban was rescinded the day before the season started, so I think this made it a little easier for me to get a ticket to this game.

I had been talking with quite a few Dallas Cowboys fans on social media, and I had been invited to meet a few of them at their tailgates, one in particular which would include my old mate, the elusive Craig Steichen. I had also been given the contact details of a huge Cowboy's fan, a guy named CY, who according to Jamie Smith at the Dallas Cowboys UK fan club, was a local hero.

So I went to meet them all. CY is a legend in Dallas and a very lovely old guy, who has a clothes line full of underwear on his very colourful tailgate, which looked so funny. I bought a ticket from one of his friends for 125 dollars, about 90 quid, which I was more than happy to pay, as the ticket prices online were a lot higher than that all week. Much higher actually.

I had a bite to eat and a few beers with CY, who welcomed me completely, like I was family. I watched him make one of his famous warrior like speec hes, which was hilarious. I saw a lot of these speeches over my tour and they were always so passionate, heartfelt, loving, sometimes personal and completely full of emotion. I always felt so lucky to be in the company of these tribes of warriors, and more importantly, the wonderful people who absolutely adore their teams.

I experienced this many times, including at the L7 tailgate, in New York with Joe Carlson, Who Dey in Cincinnati, Tim Young in Atlanta, the Buc's Party in Tampa with JayBuc, Woody's Tailgate in Denver, Bolt Pride in San Diego with Josh, Alvarez and their friends, Jay and the boys in Cleveland, Cannonball, Jimbo, Traci and the gang in Seattle, Rick and his crew in Baltimore, Randy in Phoenix, Craig in about 7 different tailgates and many many more with people I had not even met before I turned up. You guys rock, and you are my friends for life. XXXXXXXXX

After chatting to CY for a while, I shot off across the massive tailgate area way across the other side of the huge AT+T stadium, to meet my Cowboys friends I had been chatting to on Facebook, whom I had arranged to hook up with. I arrived at the tailgate of Shelby Kelly, Cowboys Superfan Julio "Prime" Marin, and their friends, and as soon as we met, I felt a big part of the Cowboy fans family straight away. Everybody made me feel very comfortable and these guys are truly a great bunch of people.

After a nice feed and a few more beers in the baking sun, I had to be careful not to be too intoxicated, and watching more than one ball during the game, if you know what I mean?

I said my goodbyes to my new Cowboys family and I headed towards to the stadium like a kid in a sweetshop, after looking at it from a distance for ages from the tailgate, like a car fanatic looks at a Ferrari.

I was so in awe of where I was, what I was looking at, and were I would be going, inside probably my first choice stadium to attend on the entire planet. It was a very surreal feeling and I was bursting with excitement, a dream come true, and a place I never thought I would ever get the chance to visit in my lifetime. I was actually going to watch my team in this magnificent stadium and I felt like I had to pinch myself.

This day was an extra special day for me on my tour, and definitely one of my highlights. Every game day was special to me, I loved every stadium, tailgate, and the passionate fans I met, but this had more meaning than all the others put together, simply because this was my team.

The AT+T stadium in Dallas personifies everything that Texas is, big, brash, and over the top, but in a very nice way. I was looking forward to seeing the massive jumbotron screen that hangs over the playing field, which when it was built, was the biggest in the world.

When I got inside the stadium, I really was swept away by the wow factor, as this stadium is totally incredible. It felt almost twice as big as some of the other stadiums I had already visited, as there were around eight or nine levels of seating, it was absolutely huge. And the jumbotron screen, OMG! I've never seen anything like it.

The question I get asked the most from people regarding my tour is, "What was your favourite stadium"? I always answer, "Its not just because I am a Cowboys fan, but Dallas was the best stadium by far", and it really was. Every NFL fan should try to watch their team play there, you will have the most incredible experience.

I wandered around the stadium for about 30 minutes before the game started, and I went to have a look in the club shop, which was very dangerous territory for me as I would probably buy half the shop! I wanted to see everything this stadium had to offer, and I was not disappointed by any of it at all.

I had the usual nosebleed ticket and I was very happy with my seat. Out came the teams, the usual banging music, national anthem and the fabulous, beautiful and world famous Dallas Cowboys cheerleaders right in my face via the humungous Jumbotron TV screen hanging over the pitch. I was in dreamland.

To see my team, The Dallas Cowboys walk on the field inside their incredible AT+T stadium, really was a highlight in my lifetime. A day I will never forget.

I always knew this was going to be very tough game against the Superbowl champions, the New England Patriots. What made it a whole lot harder was the absence of our main man and Quarterback, Tony Romo. Our back up boys of Brandon Weeden and Matt Cassells are simply not up to his standard, and this game highlighted that fact very clearly.

Brady went to work and the Patriots tore my boys to shreds.

The first half ended 13-3 but the Patriots eventually won this game at a canter 30-6. The one thing I was really wanted to experience in this stadium was to see a Cowboys touchdown in the flesh, but sadly this never materialized and things got even worse on my next visit to a Cowboys game six weeks later in Tampa.

Normally I try to write a little about the games I was at, but to be honest, there was not too much to report on this game as my Cowboys only kicked two field goals, and were basically second best to a very good Patriots team for the whole game. The Pats kicked our butts in our own back yard, with Tom Brady being the main reason why. I hate that guy!! Actually the truth is the complete opposite, Brady is awesome and I'm a massive fan.

Even though my Cowboys got beat, well thrashed to be honest, it was a dream come true just for me to be there, so I tried to savour every moment. My only minor bugbear regarding the awesome stadium was the giant jumbotron screen, which in the beginning was great, mainly for replays, but I found because I was so high up in the stands, the screen was right in my eyeline, which meant that for most of the game, I found myself watching the screen, and not the field, especially when the many close up's of the stunning cheerleaders came on it! But all jokes aside, I wanted to watch the game live, no matter how small the players looked from my seat, and trust me, they did, I was that high up, probably on the seventh or eighth tier.

Obviously I could see a lot more of the action via the screen, but this was kind of defeating the object. Don't get me wrong, the screen is superb, but I'm sure you understand where I am coming from as a fan going to watch a live game. Its the same for me when I attend a horse racing meeting, as I always want to watch the races live on the racetrack, not on a TV screen in the bar area, as what's the point? I may as well be in a betting shop.

After wandering around the stadium for about half an hour after the game, (something I had never done at any other stadium before, as I just did not want to leave) I eventually departed the amazing AT+T in pretty good spirits, even though my Cowboys got their bums well and truly smacked. I had expected it, as we were on a bad run without our main man Romo, but I was buzzing at just being at a Cowboys game in this magnificent arena.

Now the real fun started, as I had to somehow try to meet James who was picking me up in his car, at the spot where he earlier dropped me off. It actually turned out to be not too difficult for James to get to me as I waited for the traffic to die down before I left the stadium. I just found it so hard to say goodbye to the AT+T, if I had a sleeping bag, I would have stayed all night!

That evening James cooked me a lovely Mexican dinner, and my trip to Dallas was almost over.

I never really quite connected to Dallas as a place, or even Houston come to think of it. The reason why was mainly because in Dallas, as in Kansas City, I was relying on my host to drive me around, something I'm not completely comfortable with, as I feel terribly restricted. My independance is so important to me, as I am usually quite spontanious and I want access to everywhere if possible at all times, especially if I hear about something worth seeing in the place I am at, and at short notice I can shoot off to it.

So by me not having my freedom, and not being able to travel into the cities on public transport and being a tourist, I was stuck in a place which was not exactly tourist friendly, and with not a lot for me to do. This actually never happened very often, but when it did, it was very difficult for me to accept.

Texas is not a very user friendly state to be a tourist, unless you had a car. Dallas's public transport system is far from great, especially to get to the Cowboys stadium, and this was a big pain in my ass. But this was a very small price for me to pay, when I think of all the up sides to my fantastic AT+T experience. Go Cowboys!

Now that my biggest game and my Dallas adventure was over, I was happy to be leaving town and excited about my next adventure, to one of the most fascinating, wonderful and exciting cities on the planet. Next stop, the amazing city of jazz, New Orleans.

Stadium 11
Mercedes Benz Superdome
New Orleans Saints

Although I had been to New Orleans on my previous trip two years ago, I was looking forward to returning to this great city, as I had a great time when I was here before and I love this city.

I was fully aware New Orleans had the highest murder rate in the US, so I had to be extra vigilant and on my guard, especially late at night, which of course, I never did!!

On my last visit here, I stayed in a funky party hostel full of youngsters called "India House", but this time I wanted a slightly more quieter location, so I booked into a hostel in the garden district area of New Orleans, appropriately named the "Garden District Hostel", which was a great choice. I met some people straight away, including a nice guy named Mike, and we immediately headed out for an afternoon in the French Quarter, the main part of town.

We wandered around the tourist area of Bourbon Street and had a sushi lunch, followed by a few beers in one of the local bars. I met two girls (lesbians, just my luck!) at my hostel, from Montreal in Canada, and I told them of a fabulous venue I was going to that evening to watch some traditional New Orleans jazz.

Preservation Hall was a place I had found two years earlier, where I had seen the most amazing traditional New Orleans jazz band, all very old black guys who looked like they were from way back in the 30's. They were brilliant, so I wanted to go back to see them again.

We got to Preservation Hall around 7pm for the 8pm show, and it was as cheap as chips, fifteen dollars for the 45 minutes show. The band play three shows every night, and we attended the first one.

This time the band was different to the one I had seen two years prior, including two younger white guys, which I didn't like. It did not have the same power to me as the previous line up, as the previous singer sounded and looked like Louis Armstrong. This new band were still very good, but they were younger than the other band I had seen, and seeing a bunch of very old men singing what I would perceive as traditional New Orleans jazz, was so exciting for me, especially in this tiny and iconic venue.

It was like being in the living room (lounge) of somebody's house, and was very powerful and special. This time it never had the same level of special, but it was still very good and my two Canadian friends loved it, and they thanked me for taking them.

Towards the end of the show, a lady singer got up on stage and sang what was to be the last song of the set. She was quite a big old girl, just what I would expect a typical New Orleans jazz singer to look like, and she was great. As we left the venue, the lady in question was sitting on a chair by the exit, so I sarcastically said to her "Excuse me ma'am, there was only one problem with your performance." "What was that?" she replied, looking at me with great concern. "You only did one song," I smiled, before she let out a huge sigh of relief.

Her name was Shahida and she had a great voice. I asked her if she was local, and she replied she was in fact from Detroit. I chatted to her for about five minutes, and I told her I would be in Detroit in a few months time, as I was on a NFL tour. Immediately Shahida gave me her business card, and she told me to contact her when I got to Detroit, which would be in December, on week twelve of my schedule.

After hearing Shahida's beautiful voice, my songwriting juices were aroused, and I immediately thought it would be a great challenge for me to write and record a jazz song with Shahida singing the vocals. Maybe in Detroit? A big seed was planted in my mind, and as this tour was about music as much as the NFL, this chance meeting was a perfect opportunity to challenge myself in a new genre, way outside my usual rock or pop comfort zone.

We left Preservation Hall for another jazz bar on Bourbon St, named "Fritzel's", which was just a minute walk away. Fritzel's had a different style of jazz, advertised as European, which was still nice, but I enjoyed Preservation Hall much more.

We had a great evening of jazz in two different locations in two different styles, so a good night was had by all. After our fix of jazz was over, we headed back to the hostel on one of New Orleans's iconic and famous trams, which made this particular trainspotter very happy.

The following day was a lazy and domestic day, as I had a ton of washing to do, so off to the local laundrette I went.

While waiting for my socks and undies to wash, I got chatting with a couple of local rednecks about the state of crime and the subject of guns in New Orleans, which was a very interesting conversation indeed.

I always quite looked forward to washdays, why? I hear you ask, well what I mean is, the highlight was once the washing was finished. This was because very frequently I found I had no fresh socks or pants left in my backpack, so I would be in the same socks for up to two or even three days, the same goes for pants. Underpants for my American friends! OUCH!

Remember, a lot of the time I was travelling on overnight bus rides, so having the same underpants on for two days was perfectly normal for me. Sometimes I even went back into my dirty washing bag for a pair of socks or pants that never had too many skid marks on, and they went back on!! I think I have said enough!

Thursday night was game night, so a big crowd of us left the hostel, heading for the Mercedes Benz Superdome, the home of the New Orleans Saints. Craig Steichen was yet again at a tailgate in the same town as me, so I made contact with him to get the location of where he was going to be, so I could hook up with him again.

And what a great tailgate we were at outside the Superdome stadium. I was with Mike and the Canadian girls from the hostel, and we all got stuck into the feast being served on a massive BBQ, everything from steak, burgers, sausages, and all kinds of other tasty treats, as well as loads of booze, and all to a background of banging music. It was fcuking brilliant, and again, all thanks to Craig.

I got the gang from the hostel well and truly looked after, and all completely free, something they were all well pleased and very grateful for. I even got Mike a free ticket, as I was offered one, but I had already paid 60 bucks for mine online. I remember thinking when I gave the ticket to Mike I should have charged him 30 bucks. Why should I pay 60 and he gets in for free off my back? But I decided to let him have a free night out as he was a nice guy and he was totally skint, and heading off after the game to his new life in Austin Texas.

I met with Craig and a few of his guests from his Warrior Wishes charity, one was a guy in a wheelchair who had lost both his legs in conflict, I think it was Iraq, as well as another guy who was very badly burned, practically all over his body and he had lost both of his hands. I always felt so sorry for these people whenever I met them through Craig. These heroes carry on with their lives, and they all seemed very positive, but it must be so very hard for them, and meeting these guys always made me realise how lucky I am. I wish all the military people I met through Craig's Warrior Wishes charity all the very best for their futures.

The Mercedes Benz Superdome was always going to be a highlight for me on my tour. From the outside it looks like a spaceship, or even my perception of what a UFO would look like if one ever did land on earth. A great piece of engineering and a very unique and iconic looking stadium.

This was the stadium that housed thousands of stranded and homeless people after hurricane Katrina hit New Orleans and flooded the entire city a few years ago. I can't imagine what New Orleans must have been like during that time or just after that hurricane. I remember walking down a particular street, and on that very spot during the flooding, I was informed we would now have been under at least ten feet of water when the hurricane hit. A very scary feeling in a place that once had total devastation.

This night, game eleven was a divisional rivals game between the New Orleans Saints and the Atlanta Falcons. The Falcons had started the season on a roll of 5-0, the Saints not so good at 1-4. The only win the Saints had had, was against my Cowboys. Bloody typical!

The Superdome stadium on the inside was very nice indeed, very round, high, and with a roof. Probably a very good reason why it is called a dome! It was a super stadium, and at the time, and even now, it was amongst my favourite stadiums on the tour. I loved it.

Once the game started, I expected an easy win for the Falcons, but in the first half, they were very poor, and they struggled. Their wide receiver Julio Jones, who had been on great form, was non existent. The Falcons did improve a little in the second half, but the Saints played really well, with Quarterback Drew Brees doing what he does best, finding receivers, and in the end the Saints ran out comfortable winners.

I have always found the New Orleans Saints a very difficult team to predict, as they have the capability to beat the best teams in the NFL, and they regularly do. They can also get beat by any NFL team, even the strugglers, but in Drew

Brees they have a special quarterback who has been a great player for the Saints over the years, and sadly for them, he is coming pretty close to the end of his career at the ripe old age of 38 years young!

I met with Mike and the girls after the game, and we all headed back to the hostel in great spirits after watching a good game of football.

I'm not sure a lot of non Americans know what I am going to explain now about NFL kick off times. Maybe they do, but lets try. Game times on Monday and Thursday night football start at 7.30pm eastern time (east coast, New York time zone), so times change depending on which part of the US you are at. So if you are in New Orleans as I obviously was, its one hour behind of eastern time, so kick off time is 6.30pm. What I'm trying to explain is that most of these games finish around 11pm, even midnight, if the game goes into overtime, which for me it did a few times. Getting back from some of these games is no fun......at all. Some stadiums have great public transport available, fairly close to the stadiums, just like New Orleans does, by many don't.

I remember trying to get back to my hostel in Brooklyn from New Jersey after watching a New York Jets game on a Thursday night in November, a 7.30pm start. I had taken the bus rather than a train from Manhattan, and I had to queue up in arctic conditions after midnight, in a queue that moved slower than the pace of a snail.

I must have waited for more than a hour, freezing my bollocks off, until eventually I got back onto the New York subway about 1.30am and into my bed around 2.30.

What I am trying to stress, is that I had many adventures on my trip just trying to get home from the night games, but lucky for me this time was no problem.

Looking back now, I can see the funny side, but I remember at the time, especially when it was freezing cold, I wanted to scream......or even cry!!

I loved New Orleans, it has a great buzz along Bourbon Street, hearing all the different sounds coming from the many bars, in many genres, watching the street people, the connection with voodoo and the characters whom associate themselves and their image with this very dark subject. The trams, the iconic steamboats with their big wheels, the local cajun delicacies, and even the casino, which of course I had to pop in to say hello!

So farewell my darling New Orleans, thanks for everything, especially the great music.

The following day I caught yet another long Greyhound bus journey to my next adventure, and one I was looking forward to just as much as New Orleans, probably even more so, to one of my favourite cities in the US, the fantastic home of country music..... Nashville.

Stadium-12
Nissan Stadium
Tennessee Titans

I left New Orleans in Louisiana heading for Nashville Tennessee on a long bus ride through the middle of the day. This was different for me as I usually did the long bus ride at night, so this must have been because of the bus times, and maybe there were no nightbuses to Nashville during this time, so I spent the next 14 hours relaxing, reading, listening to music and sending emails and social media messages while on the bus.

This was a bus ride I was looking forward to because I was heading through three states of the US that fascinated me, Louisiana, Mississippi and Alabama, basically because I know very little about them and what is there, other than New Orleans.

These southern states were, and are, still integral to a subject that has always interested me, the slave trade. I have been to at least three museums on this subject, as well as the very hotel where Dr. Martin Luther King was murdered, in Memphis Tennessee.

Two years earlier I had stood underneath the balcony of the room where Dr. King was assassinated. There was a plaque in memory of him which was so sad, and I felt I was standing on the spot in a very surreal and important place in US history. It was quite emotional as I read the paragraph explaining what Dr. King represented, his work as a religious man, his positive vision of the future regarding voting and human rights for African Americans, and of course, what happened on that terrible night when Dr. King was shot dead.

Dr King was such an important man for the people from the black community, and I've seen many film clips over the years in the museums I have been to, in which slaves were treated so badly, it was horrifying to see and very upsetting. I cannot imagine what this must feel like for people from the black community to see these images time and time again, and I know these thoughts with remain forever.

I was a big fan of the 70's TV series "Roots", written by Alex Haley, an African American who traced his family tree way back to Africa in the 1700's, where some of his ancestors were taken from and brought to America. So I wanted to see what the south was like with my very own eyes.

The bus went through places I never thought I would ever visit, Jackson Mississippi, Birmingham, Montgomery and Mobile in Alabama, and seeing these places was a real eye opener for me. I knew and had read about all these places, as they were areas where many famous incidents took place during the struggle for civil rights for black people back in the 50's and 60's.

Of course I would not see much as we were passing through on a bus, but I got a small sense of how it was when we stopped off on the occasional stop for lunch. One occasion was when I went to a Mcdonald's in Mobile Alabama, which was opposite the Greyhound bus station we were having a pit stop at.

I remember thinking, this place was the most odd, strange, slow paced and laid back places I had been to in the US. I felt like I was a million miles from home, or modern civilization, in a community of rednecks, or very poor people with very unusual southern drool accents, and probably no idea of what was going on in the world, outside of their neighbourhoods.

I watched some dude talking to himself, actually having a full blow conversation with himself right outside the window I was sitting at having my lunch. He was obviously a sandwich short of a picnic/crazy, but he was not the only strange one or odd ball in town.

I did observe many unusual people coming into the Mcdonalds in the fifteen minutes I was in there on that day, It was an interesting experience, but there were some very subdued, vacant and crazy looking people in that town of Mobile Alabama.

Mobile was a place I did not quite feel overly comfortable in. It felt like I was a stranger in a town where everybody knew each other, or was related to. It was mainly white, but poor white and I could feel a very different kind of vibe than what I had been used to. Hillbillys, roughnecks, hicks and white trash are words I have heard used to describe these folks, and they sounded about right, but these words are my pathetic attempt to try and help you understand how I perceived these different kind of people.

Again, I'm probably completely wrong and being far too

judgemental, as these people were probably as nice as pie, but if somebody pulled out a shotgun and robbed the place right in front of my very eyes while I was stuffing my face with chicken nuggets, I would not have been surprised.

This definitely highlighted to me how divided the black and white communities are, and segregation is still alive and kicking in this part of America, as these groups of people never seemed to mix at all. This town felt like the bottom of the earth's basement, to put it politely, but I always wanted to see and experience a place like this for myself and I'm glad I did, regardless of feeling a little uneasy.

I hopped back on the bus and I eventually arrived into Nashville in the state of Tennessee at 11pm.

I was being picked up by my friend Steffon, who lives in town, a fellow Arsenal fan whom I had met in an Arsenal America bar named "Fleet Street" two years earlier in downtown Nashville. Fleet Street is a London themed pub that sells all kinds of English food, from fish and chips, sausages and mash and lots of other things I am used to eating, which of course was well received by this real Eastender!!

I stayed at Steffon's place for the next two nights on his couch, before I checked into the "Downtown Hostel", which is right on the river and opposite the Tennessee Titans stadium in the Broadway area, which was in the centre of town and the tourist part of Nashville, where all the fantastic country music bars were, and my idea of heaven!!

The following day, Steffon and I watched Arsenal beat

Watford at the Fleet Street bar, then I went off to check out the Musician's Hall of Fame and Museum, which was just around the corner from the Fleet Street bar.

Another place I wanted to sample while I was in Nashville was the famous chicken shack called "Hattie B's"I had heard so much about. I went online, found the location, and off I walked about 30 minutes along a busy main road to get to Hattie's from downtown Nashville. But when I got there, I was horrified to see a massive queue. I stood in line and waited for about fifteen minutes, but in that time I never moved a single footstep, so I decided to bail out and go somewhere else and maybe try again another time.

I was gutted, as I had heard so many great reviews about this place, and I walked all that bloody way for nothing! Plus I was "Hank Marvin".....starving!

Sunday was game number twelve on my The "Wrong Shaped Balls" Tour, the Tennessee Titans Vs The Miami Dolphins. A friend of mine from the UK Nigel Kane, had put me in touch with a guy who was very well connected in Nashville and a season ticket holder of the Titans.

I had spoken to this guy named Colin on the phone, and he seemed like a really nice guy. Colin is an ex pat Brit, now living in Nashville, and one of the owners of the world famous "Grand Ole Opry". I was very grateful to Nigel for hooking me up with Colin, as I thought he would be an amazing contact, especially to help me get my songs played on the radio, in the home of country music.

We chatted a lot about good old blighty (England), and

Colin kindly offered me his season tickets for the game against the Dolphins the following day, as he would be out of town on business and these tickets were going spare. Of course I accepted, but I really wanted to watch the game with him and get to know him. I thought this would be an excellent opportunity for me to pick his brains regarding the country music business in town, and ask him for help with my own country songs I had already recorded in Nashville. Maybe he can connect me with some important people in town? Use his influence?, especially as we are both Brits, as after all, this is how business works....right?

My friend Steffon's mum was also in town from Florida, and they were also going to the game on Sunday, but they also as yet did not have tickets.

Colin kindly gave me four tickets to the game, so I gave one to Steffon, one to his mum and one to Steffon's friend, a guy named Greg. These were grade A top season tickets, 50 yardline, 250 bucks a pop, and we got them all for buckshee (free). OH YES!

To get the tickets from Colin, I had to meet and collect them from his son Sam, as Colin was going out of town. I called Sam, and we arranged to meet up for a coffee or a beer on Saturday afternoon in downtown Nashville.

Sam was yet another person on my ever increasing long list of people, who was very hard to pin down, just like his dad, as I called him more than a few times without an answer, so I left him an answerphone message, and he finally called me and we arranged to meet. Sam eventually showed up and handed me the tickets, but the goalposts were moved yet again as he had to rush off, and I only met him at the side of the road for about two minutes before he sped off in his lovely flashy car.

Sam seemed like a very nice guy, and I sooooo badly wanted to spend some time with him and get to know both him and his dad. This was my big chance to really make something happen with my music, and where better for this to start than in Nashville, the home of the biggest selling genre of music on the planet.

I was invited by Colin to go with him and Sam to watch the Nashville Ice Hockey team called the "Preditors" (now my adopted team) later that week. I accepted immediately of course, not because I wanted to see the Preds, I just wanted to meet and spend some quality time with Colin, as I knew he had the power to open some big doors for me, doors I simply had no chance of opening myself.

Sadly after my many attempts to contact Colin and his son Sam, I never saw or heard from either of them again in the week I spent in Nashville. I was totally gutted, absolutely devastated to be brutally honest, as I thought that in Colin, I had a chance of being introduced to some very important people in the country music industry who I could get to listen to the three country songs I had recorded in Nashville two years earlier. FCUKING HELL!!!!!!

I'm sure Colin is a very busy and probably the nicest guy, but yet again, why offer something to me then simply ignore me like we had never spoken in the first place? This hurts me so bloody much, as I never asked him for a thing. I'm very grateful to him for the Titans tickets, but I really wanted to meet him and have a good old "Eastenders" chat. I think if I had been given the chance to have met with Colin, told him about my country music songs, even got him to listen to them, maybe they would be playing on a Nashville radio station by now, I think he has THAT MUCH power. I'm fully aware in the music business, contacts are so very very important for success, and I felt I had missed out on a very important potential life changing situation for me regarding my music. I have a dream, but it seems to be constantly trampled on.

I had arranged to meet with my friend Steffon, his mate Greg, who like me, was a songwriter, and Steffon's lovely mum Teresa. Off we went to a tailgate to meet a bunch of Steffon's friends before the game. We had a lovely feed of beef brisket with an amazingly delicious home made sauce (with over ten ingredients) made by one of the boys, which was something like a pool party for the taste buds!, and all washed down with some of Tennessee's finest local beer.

With game time approaching, and me feeling a little delicate after one too many beers, off we go to the Titans Stadium.

I had been inside the Titans "Nissan Stadium" before, but not to see a game, as I took a gamble two years earlier on a previous trip, to try to get inside for a look around, on a freezing cold day in midweek. Every time I had left my hostel in downtown Nashville, the first thing in my eyeline was the massive Titans stadium across the river, so of course I wandered across, and I tried to get inside for a look round.

I popped into the club shop and I asked a lady who worked

there if it would be possible for me just to get a picture of myself inside the stadium. I expected to be told it was closed to the public and I would be politely declined, but on the contrary, this lovely lady called one of her colleagues, and this kind man showed me around the stadium. I was well pleased, and these lovely and friendly Titans people were very kind to me.

The man took a few snaps of me inside the stadium, and I was so happy for this opportunity, as it was a bonus to get in when I really did not expect to. This is a prime example of a "never be afraid to ask" situation, as people can only say no, there's not much to lose, but sometimes to your surprise, there are good decent people who will open doors for you, simply because they are nice, and to be honest I was not exactly asking for too much was I?

YES is one of my favourite words in the English language, because If I can help someone, I will always do my best to if I can. So when someone does me a small favor, I am always sooooo grateful, no matter how small it may be to them, because to me, its huge if its something I want to experience.

These moments always mean a lot to me, because trust me, more times than not, I get the door slammed in my face! But it does not stop me asking again. NO SIR!

I wanna say a big thank you to the Titans people who gave me their time, especially the nice lady in the club shop who gave me a free Titan's calendar before I left, what a lovely gesture and I thanked her so very much for their kindness. GO TITANS!!

The Nissan Stadium in Nashville was nice, not one of my favourites, but the sun was shining, which always makes a big difference, and I was as ever looking forward to the game.

The game was against two struggling teams, the Tennessee Titans, and the Miami Dolphins, and this was evident once the game started. What made it a little more exciting for me, was that Steffon and his mum are Dolphins fans, as I was doing my usual thing by cheering for the home team, so we had a little banter going on during the game.

I had seen the Dolphins win in Washington DC, and they were to win this game too, so was I a lucky charm for the Dolphins? Well, we will see, as I would be watching them again in Buffalo on week nine.

I can't remember much about this game to be honest, the combination of sun and booze probably didn't help, but I do remember one thing that happened during the game. Out of the sky, well actually the stand above, something almost hit me on the head, and landed at my feet. It was a pair of glasses which had fallen off the face of an excited Dolphins fan when they had scored a touchdown. I picked them up and looked up into the stand above for their owner, and I noticed a guy who was gesturing to me to throw them back up, but he obviously has never seen my throwing arm!

This was not a very good idea, dangerous for many people if my aim was poor, as well as I did not want to smash this geezer's bins (glasses) if my touchdown pass attempt was incomplete. A man eventually came down from the upper level to collect the glasses from me and he informed me he worked for the Miami Dolphins and that the glasses fell from the face of one of the senior management/owners of the club. He was very grateful to both Steffon and myself, and he preceeded to give us a few Miami Dolphins badges which were a momento of their 50th anniversary. That was a nice gesture Mr. Thank you very much.

I informed the guy in question I was on a tour of all 31 stadiums, I had seen his Dolphins win in Washington DC, and that I would be in Buffalo for their game in a few weeks time. He was very interested in my tour and he gave me his business card and said "Drop me an email, and we can arrange to meet up in Buffalo, and we will take good care of you".

BRRRIIILLLLLIIAAANNTTT!!! I thought, this could be a good opportunity and turn into something interesting and maybe help me get some publicity for my tour.
WRONG..........................AGAIN!!!!

So off goes Mr Miami Dolphins, I sat down with a smile as wide as the football field as my dream of meeting the "special one", who may have the "superpowers", or the key to unlock the catch to the snatch!! (treasure), is back on the menu. YES!!!

The game continued, the Dolphins won, so everyone is a winner, Steffon, his mum, and even the man up in the nose bleeds who probably now has to go and visit his optician for a new set of specs!!

Its difficult for me to write more than a few lines or notes regarding a lot of the games I was at, unless something special happened on the pitch, something worth describing, like a "Hail Mary" pass or a 60 yard field goal to win a game. A lot of the games I attended were fantastic games, which I remember for one reason or another, but the Titans Vs Dolphins game was not one of them, so I don't have much to say or write about this game other than I was happy to be with my friend Steffon, his mum and mate Greg, the sun was shining and we got our tickets for free, right on the 50 yard line. Happy days.

A few days later I emailed the Miami Dolphins man I had met inside the Nissan stadium, but I never got a reply. I tried again a week later and I was directed by his "out of office" email message to a colleague of his at the Dolphins. When I finally did get a response, I was politely informed that the man in question had now left the organisation, so my new friend and yet another potential "friend in a high place" (which he actually was, being above me in the stadium) had been given the push (Fired). FCUKING HELL!

I was so gutted, bloody mortified, as here we fcuking go again, just when I thought I had the slightest of chances something exciting may manifest, it was cruelly snatched away from me before it even started.

Everytime I thought I had met a "somebody", a person who may be able to help me climb the ladder, surf on the wave of success, gain some media attention, a helping hand, a leg up, or kickstart this tour, then BAM!, the door gets slammed right in my boat race (face)....AGAIN! I felt like I was cursed or jinxed, and this bad luck was to continue throughout my entire tour.

A prime example of this is a guy I had met in the Arsenal America Fleet Street bar two years earlier on my first visit to Nashville. Trent was a guy I had met, liked and spent the past two years talking to on social media. Trent introduced me to the amazing drink, or shot called "Fireball". Boy I love that stuff, a very tasty cinnamon whiskey. Don't knock it until you have tried it!!

Trent informed me about a year before my tour was still only a thought in my stupid brain, that he had a great contact for me when I got to Dallas (my team).

"Who's that" I asked. "Jerry Jones", he replied. WWHHAAATTTTTT? JERRY JONES?? This must be a joke, I thought, as Jerry Jones is the owner of the Dallas Cowboys and the only person higher than him in Texas is the good lord himself!

From day one, I thought Trent must be bullshitting me, but he explained that he was linked to Jerry Jones by friends and family marriages. Its something random like, Trent's mum's cousin's son, is married to Jerry Jones's daughter. Trent told me from day one that getting me to meet Jerry Jones was something that WILL HAPPEN 100%. HE PROMISED.

I was soooooo excited, I could have eaten cheese on toast (and everybody knows how much I hate cheese)!! So my destiny was in the hands of Trent's mum, and she had about nine months to get this connection arranged. I kept in touch with Trent fairly regularly over the next six months and I must have asked him over a dozen or so times for an update on whether his mum had yet to plant the seed, that would eventually grow into the tree of friendship between me and the king of the Cowboys, Mr Jones. Trent always replied "don't worry, it will be taken care of, I promise".

Wind forward nine months and I am now on week 12 of the tour, and I am still in regular contact with Trent. According to Trent, Its "still on the cards" as I kept asking him and repeating myself like a parrot, "Has your mum sealed the deal yet?" "Yes," was the reply as always, "She's on the case". FANTASTIC!

So its now just a few days before I will be arriving into Nashville, and still Trent says his mum is on the case. What was she doing? Was this all bullshit the whole time?

By this time I had already spoken to Colin in Nashville on the phone and secured the four tickets to the Titans Dolphins game, and I had originally put one aside for Trent, and I had told him so, an awesome ticket on the 50 yard line, a 250 dollar ticket, and all for nothing, just for you my friend, as a favor for a favor. Of course he was well pleased, as I'm a million per cent sure Trent had never sat in a seat like this in his life. He had probably never even been to a game before??

Once I finally arrived into Nashville, ONLY THEN did Trent say that his mum had tried her best and she could not do anything for me. So much for the 100% PROMISE. I was FCUKING FURIOUS to say the least. This had gone on for almost a year, and my dream of meeting the enigma that is Jerry Jones was dashed by this useless lying piece of shit. I wanted to bloody strangle Trent after all of this family connections bullshit.

This guy had OFFERED this to ME, I never asked, how could I? This redneck had about as much in common with Jerry Jones as I have with Saddam Hussain. This guy was my friend, he said the deal WAS DONE, and now, he casually tells me it's not gonna happen at the eleventh hour, like its nothing important and kind of......oh well.

No fcuking oh well you fuckwit, you messed me about for a year, getting me so damn excited, and now you have killed my dream with your bastard lies. And boy did I tell him. And you know what? He even tried to turn it around on ME, especially when I told him to go fcuk himself regarding the free ticket I got for him for the Titans Dolphins game. Trent said that "I had shown my true colors as a person" after this argument. Yes I bloody well did, as I blasted into this complete tosser with my vocal chords in a major way. What did he expect me to say? THANKS. Why would I take this bullshit man to a game after he had led me up the garden path, let me down so badly after all the promises he made, gave me so my excitement and hope for over a year, then slapped my face at the final hurdle. I was totally and utterly livid to say the least.

I fcuked Trent off completely immediately, and I have never spoken to him since, and never will again. This incident hurt me more than you will ever know, as I was very much taken in by a conman, incognito as my friend, I totally believed him and his shitty story about his family and Jerry Jones's go all the way back to a small town in Arkansas. "Don't worry, the deal is already done"................................REALLY? CUNT!!!!!!!!!

Sunday I had moved out of Steffan's place and into the

hostel in downtown Nashville and I met some nice guys in the games area of the hostel, so I went out with them to a few of the honky tonks (bars). Andy and Chris were good guys and great company, Andy was English, and Chris was from Montreal and yet another person whom I met from that part of Canada who was gay.

Sorry If I sound homophobic, but I really am not, I'm just stating the fact I met quite a few people from Montreal that were mostly gay. I did meet many gay people on my tour and I always had good fun and nights out with them, and we always got on well. Maybe I'm coming out?

We went to a few of the bars which had live bands, most I had been to before on my first visit to Nashville two years earlier, when I lived my dream and recorded three of my own country songs, as well as frequenting all the main tourist bars every night, listening to the great country music. I realised then I was in a very special place. I totally love Nashville, its without doubt one of my favourite places in the US.

This time in Nashville, I felt the vibe to be a little different from before and I was not quite as excited to be here as I was on my first visit. It was now not new to me, no longer fresh, I was not hearing as many of the great new country songs I had embraced on my last visit. I remember how I was bowled over by songs like Darius Rucker's "Wagonwheel", Jason Aldean's "Dirt Road", "Drunk on you" by Luke Bryan, and others, but this time I cannot remember a song touching me in the same way.

Being in these honky tonks, had somehow lost its power.

Don't get me wrong, I still enjoyed being in them a lot, but I never got the same special feeling of excitement in them, in which I had done on my first visit. I think maybe I had just overdosed on them?

A few weeks before I left London on my trip, I had been introduced to a man who was to become my so called "PR man", while I was in America, a guy I have nicknamed "Bob".

Bob arranged an interview for me on a TV show called "Cuppa TV", hosted by a lovely lady named Monica Price, the day after my nightmare from hell in that hotel room in Walsall in Birmingham. I mentioned this in my introduction to the book, and this is something I want to forget completely.

Bob always told me he would come out to the US and see me in about four different locations. Why? I don't know and I didn't ask, I just went along with his random idea's. Great, I thought because Bob was obviously very well connected, extremely enthusiastic, positive and confident, and I really did believe the things he told me and what he said he was going to do for me. So happy days, I thought.

Bob and Monica were in town, so I arranged to meet up with them at their house. I found the location and I jumped on a bus across the other side of Nashville. When I arrived, they were both with a young female country singer who was apparently managed by Bob. I can't remember her name, but she was nice, very pretty, and she had a great voice, as she sang a few songs while I was there, as well as playing the violin. Obviously a very talented girl.

I had already informed Bob of my plans to record a new country song I had written called 4573265 (a girl's phone number) in the next few days, so then Bob did what he usual does and instantly goes into a frenzy of ideas and started making all kinds for plans for its recording, basically telling me what HE was going to do, rather than asking ME what I had in mind.

Bob informed both myself and the girl singer in the room, that she would sing on the track, something I could clearly see immediately from the expression on her face, was simply not going to happen, as it was quite apparent Bob had not even mentioned this minor piece of detail to her. Bob wanted the song to be on the girl's album and so on and so forth. Oh, I almost forgot to mention, and I had to pay for it. GREAT!

So Bob did what he had done when I first spoke to him on the phone back in London a few weeks before I departed for the US, he promised me the world, but delivered nothing. I liked Bob's enthusiasm but it always sounded like bullshit to me from day one. Bob was like a bull in a china shop, or a bus without a driver, and he completely hijacked the plans I had to record my new song with my own contacts.

Bob wanted me to use HIS producer, and I would have done, if only he was not so expensive, more than double to what my guy would have recorded the track for.

I did another Cuppa TV interview with the lovely Monica while I was at the house, and this time I was obviously a lot more relaxed, and we all chatted away for a few hours, incidently very little about ME, mostly about what THEY were doing in Nashville.

I told Bob of the great contact I had made in Nashville with the English guy Colin, and I informed Bob that Colin was a very well connected and powerful man in Nashville, and this was something Bob took a very keen interest in of course, as this could be good for HIM and HIS projects.

I also informed Bob I was going to a party the following night with my friend Steffon, (who incidentally works in the music business, and who eventually recorded my song 4573265 after Bob's involvement evaporated into nothing) and a bunch of his friends, some of who have good contacts in Nashville, and it would definitely be in Bob's best interests to be at this party.

If I could help Bob and Monica in any way, of course I would, and I did try to by inviting them to the party and connect them to potential new friends, ventures, avenues, or associations, exactly what I had wanted Bob to do for me in the capital city of country music. Wishful bloody thinking that was!

One of Steffon's friend's Greg, the guy I got a ticket for, for the Titans game, is in fact by complete coincidence, one of Bob's songwriters and musicians whom he supposedly manages, just as David Moore is whom I met in Boston. I'm not quite sure what Bob has done for either of these guys, but from what I can see, not much at all.

I don't want to speak badly of Bob at all, because he really is a nice, friendly, positive guy, and I really liked him. I was so very grateful to him for just showing an interest in me, making me feel important, talented, positive, and that he was fighting my corner and he believed in me and my music. But I'm only stating the facts here, and what was the eventual outcome of our very brief union.

Bob said to me before I left the UK he would come over and meet up with me on my six month trip across the US around three or four times. Why? only he knows. But after leaving Nashville, I never had any communication from Bob at all. Since I returned from the US, I have had no contact with Bob whatsoever.

Basically, and very sadly, Bob was simply full of hot air, a so called genie in a bottle, but sadly there were no wishes available to me. Bob had so much else going on with all his other probably more important projects, and I was not exactly a money making machine for him, well not yet anyway. But in my opinion he should not have led me up the garden path like he did, leaving me yet again frustrated, dejected, rejected, and totally fed up.

I met with Bob and Monica again a few days later, again the girl country singer was with them, and she informed me she did not want to have her name connected with my song, something which was music to my ears as I never wanted her to be a part of MY SONG anyway.

So after all those broken promises from Bob regarding my new song, I now had a dilemma on my hands, as the producer I had used two years earlier, Jack Irwin, and whom I was planning to use again before Bob got involved, was now unavailable, so now I'm "up shit creek without a paddle/stranded". Luckily I had my friend Steffon, who until then I had never considered asking. But I have a saying "you can't see for looking", meaning sometimes you cannot see what is right in front of you, the blinking obvious.

Steffon took over, did absolutely everything, even after I had left Nashville. Why the hell didn't I just go to Steffon in the first place??? I have no idea.

The end result was amazing, Steffon did an excellent profession job, and I want to say a huge thank you to him and all the musicians who played on my song 4573265, you guys were brilliant and I'm very pleased indeed with the final cut.

If you want to hear this song, please go to www.soundcloud.com/azboden

Thursday was the day I was invited by Colin to go with him to watch the Nashville Predators play at the Bridgestone Arena in the centre of town. I had been trying to contact him for the past few days, as well as his son Sam, and I finally managed to touch base with Sam, but he could not commit to anything and said he had to speak with his dad first. At this point I was starting to wonder if Sam could manage to dress himself in the morning without his dad?

This was the last correspondence I ever had with both Colin and Sam before they both quietly disappeared off into the abyss. It was communication skills at their very worse from both Colin and Sam, a complete combination of dithering and silence.

I eventually gave up on them a few hours before the game would start as my friends Andy and Chris from the hostel were planning to go to the game, and they were waiting for me to inform them of what I was doing, as they knew I was waiting for a call, that sadly eventually never came. FFS!

So off we all went from the hostel to the Bridgestone arena, and we managed to get tickets high up in the nosebleeds for a pretty decent price, and I did my usual second half move down to a better location, eventually ending up in the very front row, as you do!!

The boys eventually followed me down for the second half, or last third, and it was a great view being so close to the players and right up against the barriers, especially when players were crashing into the Perspex plastic right in front of me, it was brilliant.

I liked and enjoyed watching Ice Hockey more than any of the other US sports I tried to embrace while on my tour, not including of course, my beloved NFL.

The Nashville Predators, or my "Preds", the NHL team I now follow, beat the Anaheim Ducks 5-1 and we all had a good time together in yet another lovely sporting arena.

Friday was my last day in Nashville and I had arranged to meet with Steffon to demo my new song 4573265 in his office. I put down a basic guide vocal and played acoustic guitar a few times, we took a basic recording, and the rest was in Steffon's very capable hands once I had left town the following day.

That final day in Nashville I was a tourist, and I went to the Country Music Hall of Fame Museum, the Songwriters Hall of Fame, and a few other country music places of interest.

I loved the Country Music Hall of Fame Museum, it had so many amazing legends from the history of country music in it, from Dolly Parton, Kenny Rodgers, Johnny Cash, Garth Brooks, and so many others, and most of them I had never even heard of, including some bird called Reba??? I spent hours in that fantastic place, I absolutely loved it.

I had a very long day, with so much reading, looking at pictures, watching film clips, music videos, displays, guitars, outfits and all kinds of country music memorabilia, an excellent final day in a truly amazing place on earth.

I love Nashville, its a place every country music fan on the planet should visit one time in their lives. Being in those honky tonks watching live bands with some of the best musicians I have ever seen, was heaven for this boy.

As I left Nashville this time, I was pretty demoralised, as things could have, and should have been so much better for me, but being so badly let down by Trent, not getting the chance to meet Colin, and Bob being here in town and hardly giving me the time of day, I left town with the massive feeling of what might have been.

At this point I was feeling very down and sorry for myself, and I was actually quite glad to be leaving Nashville, until the following week, when I would return for a few days.

Nobody seemed to be hearing my cry, the universe was not on my side, and I was totally fed up with all the false promises from my circle the bullshitters.

That evening I said goodbye to my good friend Steffon, the only one who was true to his word in Nashville and I left town on a Megabus, for another new place I had never been to or knew a single thing about other than the Colts....Indianapolis.

Stadium-13
Lucas Oil Stadium
Indianapolis Colts

I left Nashville on only my second Megabus, the first being my very first bus ride on my tour, from Boston to Washington DC via New York City. What a start, as it eventually turned up two hours late, as my decision to avoid Greyhound bit me royally on the ass!

While I waited, (impatiently I hasten to add, because there was very little information coming from Megabus as to when our chariot was going to bloody turn up), I got talking to a guy in the bus queue who was a history professor, and who specialised on the history of the Native American Indians, something I mentioned earlier which is a subject that interests me.

There is a statue right across the road from the bus stop we were waiting at in downtown Nashville, of one of the early American presidents, a man named Andrew Jackson, who from the state of Tennessee. Jackson was the man responsible for tearing up the treaty which had been agreed by previous governments, allowing the Native American Indians a certain amount of land. Jackson decided to reclaim and basically steal back the land, which legally belonged to the Indians. So the treaty was not worth the paper it was written on and Jackson sent in the cavalry to move the Indians on, to less fertile land towards the great plains in the Midwest of America.

This was the beginning of the "Trail of Tears", where the

Indians were made to march 100's and 100's of miles on foot, in bad weather, little food, and many other hardships, to a new land that was not as prosperous as the land they had stolen from them by Jackson and his boys.

Its a terrible tale of greed, corruption and deception, and a very sad story indeed, as yet again its all about the money. I hate it.

Six hours later I arrived into Indianapolis, a place I was looking forward to visiting, simply because I knew nothing about this place, and I had never known or met anybody whom had been here. I had heard people call it "India no place" as apparently there was not much to do there, but I never get put off by other people's opinions or bullshit, as I always find something that interests me, as I'm usually very easy to please. I would find something to do on the bottom of the ocean, or on the moon, especially if there was wifi connection!!!!

I had to catch a bus to get to my hostel on the other side of town, and we drove along a very long straight street with what seemed like thousands of wooden houses that lined the busy main road. It kind of reminded me of the wooden houses in London, back in the day of the great fire in the 1600's. If there was a fire in the first one, the domino effect could be catastrophic if the wind was blowing in the right direction, and sadly for London, it was.

It was getting dark, and I remember feeling like I was so far away from home, in this quirky, strange and very different city in the middle of America. I checked into the only hostel in town, the "Indy Hostel", which was a great place to stay, and immediately I met a guy in my room named Chris, and within ten minutes we were off to some place he recommended to eat some of the local food.

Chris was a nice guy from New Orleans, he was in town to support the Saints, who were his team, and the team who were playing in Indianapolis that weekend. Chris looked a bit like a homeless guy, probably because of his big scruffy beard, but he was good fun to hangout with.

So off we went to the restaurant he suggested, and I ordered some of the local food, the very reason I thought why Chris wanted to come here. The funny thing was, he never ate anything. So why did he take me to this place? Strange. The food was lovely, we had a few beers, then he went off to find some local "dive bar" in his own words, so I went back to the hostel and mingled with the rest of the guests.

Later that night, a crowd of us went out to a busy and funky area where Indianapolis comes to life called "Broad Ripple". We made a beeline for one of the trendy looking and sounding watering holes, and we were about to enter a lively looking bar, but to my shock horror, I was refused entry, as I never had any I.D on me, even though I was by far the oldest swinger in the group!

This unfortunate incident taught me a lesson from this day forward, to keep my passport with me at all times, something I never do at home.

I tried my best to sweet talk the guys on the door, but they were having none of it. I told the rest of the group to go in, and I would find another spot, or just go back to the hostel, as I was annoyed I had fcuked up the night for the other people. But my new friends were so amazing and loyal, none of them wanted to go in without me, and they all stood by me and we all left. What great people.

So we all came back to the hostel, and I thought this was such a nice touch from the others, especially as I had only just met them, as they could easily have gone in without me, and I did tell them to do so, but they insisted we were all together. All for one, and fcuk the rest! Thank guys. I felt pretty bad about that schoolboy error, so from that day on, I tried to keep my passport with me at all times. IDIOT!

That night we had a good old party in the garden of the hostel, somebody made a big fire (I do love a fire), got loads of beers in, and a guitar came out. I did my usual mini gig of a few of my own songs, as well as a few Pink Floyd and Oasis songs, so I was in my element and everyone enjoyed the sing along.

That night I met some lovely people, including the hostel's staff, who were great fun, and they all joined in with us. It was an excellent night had by all, even after my passport malfunction!

Sunday was game 13, the Indianapolis Colts were entertaining the New Orleans Saints, two very open and attacking teams who both normally score and concede a lot of points. Myself and a nice guy named Ray Wiecha whom I had met at the hostel party the night before, headed off on the bus to the Lucas Oil Stadium, the home of the Colts.

Yet again, I worked the D-Mo magic to blag our way onto a

tailgate, in which I managed to get Ray a very cheap ticket from a bunch of Colts fans. We had beers and food from these top people and very welcoming fans, and we chatted with the group for an hour or so, before heading off to the stadium.

Lucas Oil Stadium up until this day of my tour, became my favourite stadium, apart from my Dallas Cowboys stadium of course, which was in my opinion the best by a mile. Lucas Oil was very similar in design to the NRG stadium in Houston, which until then, was my favourite. It had a very high roof, and a wide open gap at one end of the stadium where you could see right into downtown Indianapolis from inside the stadium. A great design to a very beautiful arena.

I had a nice seat with a perfect view of the entire pitch in the stadium and the sun was shining, so I was well excited and all set for another great game, which it certainly was.

The Saints raced into an incredible half time lead of 20-0, even making it 27-0 in the third quarter, as the Saints looked amazing, even with Colts QB Andrew Luck returning to the team after being injured. "Luck" was something the Colts never had much of in the first half, but they did make a comeback with three late touchdowns to take the game very close at 27-21. The Colts even had the chance to win the game, something which seemed totally impossible in the third quarter, but near the end, the Colts attempted an onside kick which they failed to recover, and the brilliant Saints QB Drew Brees ran down the clock to seal the win. A very entertaining game indeed, and probably the best one I had seen up until then for excitement and tension.

I made a quick dash from the stadium as soon as the game had finished, and I tried to meet up with Ray, but I lost him as he could not find the bus stop I was at, so I rushed back to my local bar near my Indy Hostel as my beloved Dallas Cowboys were playing very soon, and against our big divisional rivals the New York Giants, and of course a game I wanted to watch.

I did, the Cowboys got beat, threw the game away as bloody usual, and I went home with the hump (upset). Our 4th loss in a row since Romo got injured. FCUK!

The next day I had planned to go to the "Indy car museum", not my usual cup of tea, or area of interest, but I had obviously heard of the famous Indy 500 car race, but I never had any real idea what this race was about, its history, or who had ever won the bloody thing, but when in Rome, I thought, or Indianapolis, I had to see their big attractions, like I do wherever I may roam.

It was a quite a long way from town, but this never bothered me at all, actually, what made me bail out of this particular day trip, was the decision to spend some time with a chick I thought was cute at the hostel. BAD DECISION, and a decision which came from my little head.............yet again!

I went for a bike ride around the centre of Indianapolis with the girl in question and we checked out a few of the sights and landmarks of Indianapolis, as well as riding along the canal, even ending up on the grass for a roll in the hay! WALLOP! Sadly, no more than that. I knew I should have gone to that museum!

We had a lovely ice cream on the way home, an ice cream I had never seen made in this way before, as it was with done with nitrogen, apparently the new fashion in ice cream making, and very impressive.

Indianapolis did not seem to have too much to offer for a tourist, hence the nickname "India no place", but I enjoyed my time in this city. It had a slow pace, was relaxing, and different, but in a nice way. This particular part of my schedule meant I only had one game to attend this week, with no Thursday game for me, because this Thursday's game was in New England and I had already been there, so I had a couple more relaxing and lazy days in Indianapolis before I decided to return to one of my favourite places in America, Nashville, but only for a few days before I headed towards my next game.....Atlanta.

Nashville and Chattanooga

I decided to return to Nashville and stop off for just a couple of days, as I had to go through there anyway on way to my next game, which was in Atlanta, and it also broke up yet another very long bus ride.

There was far more for me to do in Nashville than in Indianapolis, or even Atlanta, where I was heading, especially the distraction of the country music that I love, and I was fortunate to be crashing on Steffon's sofa again for the two days I was in town.

It was now a Tuesday and there was a massive Champions League game my Arsenal boys were playing in, against the mighty Bayern Munich from Germany. So Steffon and I went to the Arsenal America bar in Nashville, "Fleet Street" and we watched the game. Everybody had written Arsenal off, including me, as Bayern at this time were seen as the best team in the world. I expected my unbeaten run of watching Arsenal play in the AA bars was coming to an end, but Arsenal won 2-0 with two goals in the last ten minutes, a shock to us all.

After the game Steffon and I went for what was my second attempt to get stuck into the famous Nashville hot chicken shack called "Hattie B's". Lucky for me, this time there was hardly a queue and I finally got my lips into a hot chick, if you know what I mean! It was great, very spicy, and a real ring stinger, or toilet rolls in the fridge experience!

As I had already been to Nashville before this trip, and also on this trip, I did not want to stay here too long and overdo it, or get bored, as most of the main attractions in Nashville like the Johnny Cash Museum, Country Music Hall of Fame, Grand Ole Opry, I had already done. Plus I had been in all the main bars many times and I just felt it was the right thing to do to move on, rather than tear the shit out of this place and do the same things over again.

So I looked at the map to see where I could stop off on my way to Atlanta, and the one place I had heard a lot of good things about was Chattanooga. It was only a couple of hours from Nashville, and a couple more to Atlanta, sounds like a plan I thought, so I caught the greyhound bus the following afternoon and I was in the beautiful little town of Chattanooga the next evening.

I loved Chattanooga immediately. The first thing I saw when I got off the bus was the sign to "The Chattanooga Choo Choo" train museum, right up my alley, or tunnel!

I stayed in the only hostel in town yet again, a lovely place called "The Crash Pad", in a great location just a few minutes walk from the Greyhound bus stop I was dropped off at. I remember this hostel having a lovely comfortable bed, with your very own curtain attached to each bedpost to give you some privacy, something I had never seen before in a hostel. It was great, and this small minor detail made a big different when trying to nod off, read, or be on my laptop. A fantastic idea, and this little masterpiece was worth its weight in gold to me.

The Crash Pad, also had a great bar and restaurant right outside, just a ten seconds walk from the front door of the hostel. Brilliant, so off I went for a nice dinner and a few beers.

One thing I do remember about this bar, was it must have been Halloween, as there were many people in crazy costumes of monsters, mummies, devils and other wacky characters, including girl vampires in very sexy outfits and face paint looking like ghouls. I had a picture taken with some random chick with the most amazing set of tits, probably fake but who cares?, which looked glorious the way they seemed like they were about to explode out of her over worked bra! Oh boy, that girl was truly stunning, and I would have done anything to have played with those incredible fun bags, if only she was not with her boyfriend, who incidentally was fully dressed as some kind of grizzly bear or yeti. I hate that guy!!!

My first day in Chattanooga I had a good wander around, the weather was great, so I checked out a few of the local sights. I crossed the world's longest walking bridge, Walnut Street Bridge, and I read it's history on the many boards that were spread out all across it. It must have taken me over an hour to cross after all the pit stops I took to read the history of this fascination bridge and this pretty little town.

Half way across the bridge I got talking to a group of elderly English people, as I had heard their accents and I stopped for a chat, as this was the first time in a while I had bumped into a group of English people. I stopped off for a lovely lunch at a great stir-fly place called "Genghis Grill", where you select the ingredients, hand it to the chef, and he tosses the wok and works his magic.....nom nom.

After lunch I popped into an IMAX cinema to watch a film about space, the universe, the stars, etc, as I love all that kind of stuff. I almost went into a big aquarium next door to the IMAX cinema, but I've seen more than a few of these places over the years, so I never really had the desire to go in, especially as it was a little bit pricey on the wallet to get in.

Later on I would go to one of the bars right near my hostel called the "Terminal Brewhouse". It's local beer was great, I had yet another lovely meal, this time a steak (and why not, I was flying, and the price was right!) a few bevvies (beers) and I watched the Thursday night game, where as I expected, the New England Patriots thrashed the Miami Dolphins. This game was the first Thursday game I did not attend on my mission impossible, so my days of planning the schedule to my tour, was working out well.........so far.

I must admit, I never went hungry on this trip, and looking back, I can't imagine how much money I spent on meals. I don't think I want to! But whenever I was in a place, I always wanted to try the local culinary delights or cuisine, and especially the local beers, which was something I certainly did to the max, and I enjoyed every mouthful or gulp. Yes sir!

America is known to be the land of fast food, and yes, it is, but they also do have some of the most amazing food I've ever tasted, especially BBQ's, with some of the most tender meats, made even better by the fine sauces these wonderful cook's (and fans at tailgates) create. I tried to indulge in as much as I possibly could, everything from brisket, pulled pork, and stuff I didn't even know the names of. So much delicious grub.

I had done my research and there were a few things I wanted to see and do in Chattanooga, so I had a full day ahead of me the following day. As a lover of trains, I wanted to see the "Chattanooga Incline Railway", which goes up to a lookout called "Point Park". The incline railway was built in 1895, and was a mile in length, all uphill.

I went to the bus stop to catch a bus which would take me to the train, but the buses were not very frequent in this part of the world, so I ended up walking down one long straight road for about an hour, and in this time I never even saw a go bus past me, so it was the right decision to walk.

I arrived at the incline railway, caught the short but very steep ride up, apparently one of the steepest train rides in the world, and I headed into Point Park for a great view of Chattanooga and the Tennessee river.

I knew today was going to be a challenge, as all the places I wanted to visit were only accessible by car. So my only option was to hitch hike, and that's exactly what I did. I got talking to a family in Point Park, found out they were heading to my next destination, and they kindly offered me a lift, which I grabbed with both hands.

My next stop was "Ruby Falls", a system of caves with a 150 feet waterfall deep underground. It was great seeing all the different shapes, sizes, and colours of the rock formations, but a bit scary being so far down, as we had to take a lift deep into the abyss, but I really enjoyed it.

My final stop was "Rock City Gardens", a lookout point

where you can see across seven different US states. This was amazing, with such beautiful views from a very high vantage point as I could see for miles and miles.

I had managed to hitch a ride from outside "Ruby Falls" from three pretty Canadian girls, after waiting ages to be picked up, and even after they had already said no to my request for a ride (pardon the pun!) as they said they were going the other way, but they returned and said that after I mentioned Rock City, they changed their minds and were interested to see it for themselves.

Being at, and on the top of Rock City was one of the many times on my travels I wished I was with a loved one. Rock City was such a romantic and beautiful location, and a setting with stunning views, and being alone here felt like that connection to something very special was missing, and it was.....the power of a loved one.

By this time I had now been away from home for about two months and I had already had many exciting experiences and walked around so many places, seen many beautiful things, and at times, I yearned for the days I had a pretty girl on my arm, whom I could share all these amazing experiences with. I missed this so very much, more than you will ever know.

Rock City is a very romantic place indeed and I do remember feeling a bit down that I had so much beauty in front of me, especially seeing lots of couples in each others arms, taking selfies, sitting together, playing tonsil tennis, and I was by myself. This happened to me quite a lot on my tour, being in some incredible locations, and most of the time on my own, which made these wonderful places, sometimes not quite so wonderful.

I walked around the beautiful little village and gardens of "Rock City" for a couple of hours, but now the time had come for my biggest challenge of the day, getting back to my hostel. I walked down to the car park and I must have asked 20-30 people if they were going back to Chattanooga. Most said they were going the other way or made up some random excuse, but I finally got a ride after about an hour of trying, to my huge relief as it was now getting dark.

Of course I could have paid for a cab, but yet again I was trying not to waste too much money, as it would have been quite a few pics of Georgie. Eventually a lovely couple picked me up and took me back to my hostel, just in time for me to go to the pub for a few local beers before I went off to bed, knackered after another busy and interesting day of walking for what seemed like a hundred miles.

The next day was Saturday, and I was heading for Atlanta in the afternoon, but before then I made yet another beeline for another Arsenal America bar. I had looked online, and I found the Chattanooga AA bar, and off I went on the bus to watch my boys win again....fingers crossed.

When I arrived at my intended destination, I was gutted to be told there were no Arsenal fans organising the watching of the game that day at this particular watering hole, so I had to rush off to find another bar, as my plan B was now needed, and quick. I ended up in an English bar called "The Hair of the Dog", where I got talking to a nice guy at the bar who was an ex pat Brit and a Liverpool fan. We watched

Arsenal beat Swansea 3-1, I had a tasty breakfast, nice company, so everyone was a winner.

I returned to my hostel, gathered up my things and I headed off towards the next city on my very long list, which was Atlanta. I went online to try to find a hostel, but to my despair, there were none. Plan B was usually Air B'n'B, plan C was Couchsurfing, finally the last resort was an expensive hotel.

I eventually booked a night in an Air B'n'B at some random guy's house, as I knew I was only going to be in Atlanta for one night because I was meeting my mucker/mate "Charlton" Dave Kitchener, who was coming to the game in Atlanta with me, and driving us back to his home in Charlotte Carolina for my next game, which was the Monday night game, the very next day.

I almost booked into some random woman's place near the Georgia Dome Stadium, where my next game would be, but many people warned me to be careful in this area of Atlanta, as it was pretty rough, and a big African American area of town, and I would have stood out like a spot on a domino!! So I eventually decided to stay at some guy's house in midtown Atlanta, near Piedmont Park, as this seemed like a much safer option.

See I'm a big fan of open spaces, they are good places to spend time relaxing in when I had a few spare hours, so this attracted me to this particular part of Atlanta. Little did I know what mystery was coming my way over the next 24 hours.

I thoroughly enjoyed my short pit stop in the beautiful Chattanooga, I remember thinking it was the kind of place I could actually live, I loved it.

Just before I was about to leave the hostel, I was on the internet in the main lounge area, and I could hear music being played from the computer of the guy on the front reception desk. I went over and I asked him who it was, as I really liked the very catchy tune. The guy informed me it was a track by a DJ named "Bonobo", I had never heard of him, apparently he is very big in his genre of music, a genre that is not near the top of my list.

The song in question was called "Duals", and this was not normally the kind of music I choose or listen to, but I instantly took a liking to this track. Incredibly a few weeks and months later, a very unusual coincidence occurred regarding me and Mr Bonobo....twice! Keep reading.

Stadium-14
Georgia Dome
Atlanta Falcons

I arrived into the centre of Atlanta on the Megabus after a short trip from the lovely Chattanooga. I had to catch the subway from the coach stop I was dropped off at, to get to my destination, which was about five stops away.

Atlanta was one of the many places on my tour I knew I had to be very careful and street wise while I was there, as it has the reputation of being a rough town, with many dodgy (sketchy) areas. It was not the kind of town to go out exploring, especially in area's away from the centre, so I was careful not to do that.

I knew I was only going to be in Atlanta for 24 hours, because I was heading to Charlotte to see my next game, the Carolina Panthers the following day. A shame really as I did a little research and there were a few things I wanted to see in Atlanta, mainly the Coca Cola museum, but I simply never had the time.

I had arranged to meet my Air B'n'B host John when I arrived into the area where he lived in midtown, and as I left the subway station, I never quite realised I was heading for a bit of a surprise. Actually, a very big one.

I asked a guy who was coming out of the subway station I was at, if he knew where, say, "Smith Street" was. "I'm going that way, follow me and I will show you" he replied, so off we went. We chatted away for the ten minutes walk towards my destination, and I could quite obviously see, and hear a pattern developing from what my new friend was telling me. This pattern was underlined when we approached the main junction of the area we were in, as right in front of me was a big double zebra crossing, painted in the colours of the rainbow. Yep, I was bang in the middle of "Gaytown". YIPPEE!!

Apparently there had been a huge gay pride march and street party recently in this part of town, so I was well and truly on the "Gaydar", especially in my shorts, flip flops and baseball cap, so I blended into my new surroundings like a one of the locals!

I went into a coffee shop, bought a drink, and proceeded to call my host John to let him know I had arrived. I immediately felt like the proverbial "spare one at a wedding", as I noticed couples everywhere, mainly men, some women, but not many, and I basically stood out like dogs balls, and big pink ones!

I had a quick coffee and as I waited for my host John to pick me up, it was only then I started to think "Oh no, what if my host is gay"?

Now I have nothing against gay people at all, but as I am not gay myself, I don't usually mix in these circles of course, and to be honest, its a circle I am not particularly comfortable in, but hey, (chacun à son goût) as they say in France, "each to their own particular taste".

My phone beeped, and John was waiting for me outside in

his car. Here we go I thought, into the stallions den. He who dares wins and all that!!

The moment I saw John, I knew immediately this was going to be an enormous challenge for me and a real test of my resolve and patience. John jumped out of the car, tall, skinny, black, and as camp as Christmas!! He instantly reminded me of Leee John of the UK 80's band "Imagination". Leee is also as gay as a box of frocks, and speaks with a very gay voice, as did John. HEEEEELLLLLLOOOOOOOOOOOOOOO!!

John was dressed in a vest, lycra shorts and flip flops, so basically we looked like the perfect typical gay couple, as I was wearing a similar outfit! (Minus the lycra I must add!) Oh well, things can't get any worse, or so I thought. WRONG!

As I climbed into John's car, I noticed immediately it was absolutely filthy, as there were empty cans, coffee cups, food wrappers, containers, stuff strewn all over the back seat in a right old mess. But the worst thing were the stains all over the seats, it looked like coffee had been sprayed all over the insides of the car, and it smelled pretty musty. I tried to block out of my mind some of the other antics Johnny boy probably had got up to on the back seat of his passion wagon......oh god, perish the thought.

It was blatantly obvious to me that John and I were coming from different worlds completely, total polar opposites, but I had to try my best to get through this enormous challenge and life experience as much as I could. Once we arrived at John's flat, this is where things got a whole lot worse.

John lived down an alleyway off a long street in a very nice area of Atlanta, and when we arrived at his main entrance, John had one of those kind of prison cell gate things covering the front door, and bars on every window, probably to stop him being robbed on a daily basis. Maybe these were to keep people in?? Who knows!

As John opened the front door, a dear old friend returned, one I had completely eradicated from my life, disowned, wiped from my memory banks and thought never to be so lucky as to experience ever again, and something which slapped me full in the face, the beautiful fragrant aroma of a smell I simply could never get used to.......DOG SHIT!!

I had experienced this rancid smell in my time in Kansas at Colin's pet shop, but this was a whole lot worse......much worse.

I turned to John and I said, "My god, what's that smell". His shocked response was that his boiler had recently leaked and flooded his whole house in hot water, and the smell was from the damp the water left behind. Maybe so I thought?, but I knew the smell was more likely coming from the poor dog that was stuck in a cage in the corner of the room. OH NO, NOT AGAIN!!

What is it about people in the US having pets?, when they go to work all day and leave the poor animals in cages for hours on end, whom obviously mess in the cages, tread in it, then walk it all around the house when the owner finally returns home. This is soooooo damn selfish and cruel. Those poor dogs, it must be bloody torture for them.

Then John showed me to my room, in which there were four flimsy metal framed bunk beds, it totally resembled a prison cell, no wallpaper that I can remember, filthy carpet, dirty net curtains, a real proper shit hole.

As I was only there for one night, I just bit my lip and took it on the chin...pardon the pun!

Almost the last straw for me was when I saw a cockroach run up the wall next to the bed I had chosen. But as it was early evening, I had no plan B, so I was stranded, and I had to make do with the situation I had firmly put myself in, or the bed I had made, which I now had to lay in.

This really was the bottom of the food chain when it came to accommodation and I remember thinking that once I left this dump, I would report John to Air B'n'B because for 25 bucks a night, this was not anywhere near up to standard. Nobody should be paying any amount of money to stay in a place like this in such awful conditions, even stay here at all. I wonder if Air B'n'B check these places before they allow hosts to accept guests? I think I already know the answer to this very stupid question.

It was around 5pm, so I decided to go out and spend as little time as I had to at this disgusting place, and as I left, little did I know I would never see John again, as I came in late, and left early in the morning, and this suited me down to the ground.

I went out and I headed to Piedmont Park, right through the centre of "Gaytown". I took a great picture of a couple of women on the rainbow crossing in the road, dressed as

Batman and Robin, pushing a baby in a pram. I felt more like I was in Old Compton Street in London, Castro in San Francisco, or Kings Cross in Sydney Australia, rather than midtown Atlanta.

Now I know what you are thinking, this boy seems to know a lot about these areas.....stop it!!!

As I got inside Piedmont Park I got the feeling I was in a place where many of the local boys hung out, and were looking for a piece of the action, and as I was walking along, I glanced across to the lake next to me, and I could see a guy looking over at me. Then to my amazement I recognised the face, it was Steve, the English guy I left on the sofa in Green Bay who was doing the same NFL tour as me. Blimey, what a shock!

I always had my suspicions, or an inkling Steve "prefered the back door", and when I saw him in the park, he did look a little like he was looking for his "George Michael experience" or dangerous liason. We were probably both as shocked to see each other in the same place, but we quickly overcame this, and we had a wander around the lovely park hand in hand!!!

It was Saturday night, and that evening we decided to go for a drink in a more funkier part of Central Atlanta and we found a nice sporty pub and plotted up at the bar.

As we walked to this area of town, somehow I got talking to a girl who was jogging past us, and who had stopped next to me at a set of traffic lights. I asked her if she could please point us in the right direction as to where we were heading, and she kindly sacrificed her run, to walk with us and show us the way to the party area. She was really nice and friendly and even mentioned she may join us later in the evening with a few of her friends. RESULT! Sounded like a great plan as she was quite a beauty. I had given her my digits, but as so bloody usual, and sadly for me, she never turned up, never phoned, never text. Another potential one bites the dust!

Steve and I plotted up at the bar, and we met a lovely couple, a guy named Scott and his German wife Angela. Scott was wearing an orange football shirt from a team which until that day, I had never heard of, an American college team named "Clemson", who had a big game coming up that weekend. We had a nice evening talking about American Football, my tour, and my experience with "camp Johnny", which he and his wife found hilarious.

At the end of the night, Steve headed off to his nice hotel, and Scott gave me a lift back to John's place as he didn't want me walking the streets of Atlanta after midnight alone, and it was pissing down with rain, so I was very grateful indeed to Scott for the lift.

We searched for John's place for what seemed like ages, as I could not remember exactly where his place was, as I had arrived there in his car, and I had made the quickest exit of all time once I arrived there, and bolted off without really taking too much notice of the location...AGAIN!

Scott did me a huge favour as I would have got soaked, probably lost, maybe even abducted, but we eventually found it, and I opened the metal bars and I went into my horrible and smelly little prison cell.

I deliberately had a good drink that night as I wanted to block out all the bad things about staying at John's. I never slept very well as you can imagine, but just enough to get the night out of the way ASAP. I must have attempted to fall asleep around 2am, and I woke up around 7ish to go to the toilet, an area I had not yet even seen as I rushed out of the place as quickly as I could when I had first arrived.

OMG! That's it, I'm off. The toilet and shower was the last straw. ABSOLUTELY FILTHY. I packed my things as quickly as I could and I left immediately. I never showered or even brushed my teeth, as I just could not spend another minute in this disgusting shit hole. I won't elaborate anymore, I will just leave this part to your vivid imaginations.

By 7.30am I was back in my favourite gay coffee shop, the one right next to the big rainbow coloured double crossing and waiting for my friend Dave Kitchener to come and get me, as he was on his way from his home in Charlotte Carolina, as we were going to the game together in Atlanta later that afternoon.

Dave arrived about a hour later, so my terrible nightmare was over. PHEW! If I would have been in Atlanta any longer, there is no question at all I would have moved out of John's, even into an expensive hotel, as I could not have spent another minute in that disgusting place. I am totally baffled as to how people can live like this in these horrific conditions. I even felt sorry for the dog.

Dave turned up bang on time, and I was so happy to see, and meet him in the flesh for the very first time, after chatting online with him for the past few weeks. I was put in touch with Dave by my friend George Gibbs, whom I had met in Guatamala two years earlier, and whom I would be meeting in Buffalo in a couple of weeks' time. Dave and I clicked immediately, he is an ex pat from London, and my only disappointment was that I wished I had more time to have spent with him as I was only in town for 24 hours, because I had a very long bus ride already booked for my next stop, which was in Cincinnati for my next game in three days time.

We arrived outside the impressive Georgia Dome, the home of the Atlanta Falcons which incidentally was being knocked down after the following NFL season, before being replaced by a brand new super futuristic looking stadium right next door to the Georgia Dome, which at the time I was there, was being built. On this final draft of the book, it is now finished and ready for action this coming season, and it looks like an incredible stadium.

I took Dave under my wing and we headed off to meet my "Warrior Wishes" pal Craig yet again, at another tailgate. There was a great buzz at this particular tailgate, mainly coming from the brilliant fans of the Tampa Bay Buccaneers. The music was loud, the food was great, the drinks were flowing and the company was awesome, all thanks to my old mate Craig Steichen and his "Operation Warrior Wishes" charity.

On this day, I encountered a very lucky and extremely pivotal moment, probably the most important day for me so far on my tour, as I had a chance meeting with a very special and remarkable human being by the name of Tim Young. Tim is a Tampa Bay Buccaneers fanatic, and he is in an amazing group of very dedicated NFL fans called "Superfans", who have been inducted into a very special club called the "Pro Football Hall of Fame", not for players, but for fans, in Canton Ohio. A truly amazing bunch of people whose dedication to their teams is remarkable.

Tim, or as he is known "The Captain", (probably because he is dressed as a pirate! which is the Tampa Bay Bucs logo), I clicked with immediately. I was so happy and extremely grateful to Tim when he showed interest and was impressed with what I was doing and trying to achieve on my mission of attending a game at all 31 NFL stadiums in one season.

I already had a ticket for this game which I paid just 30 bucks for, but Tim gave me AND Dave two tickets for free, and good seats too, much better than my cheap seats. What a lovely gesture from a guy I had only just met.

My tour really did take off after meeting Tim, I owe him bigtime and I cannot thank him enough for his kindness and friendship. I sometimes wonder what direction I would have taken, or what would I have done if I never met Tim? Of course I will never know, but what I do know, is that Tim opened so many doors for me over the next ten weeks, and he is the reason why I met so many amazing and interesting people, who to this day I can call my very good friends, all over America. Thanks a million, Captain. I love you bro. XXXXX

Tim started a domino effect by contacting all of his

Superfan friends at every other NFL club I had not already been to, telling them I was coming, what I was doing, and to look after me, right up to the very end of my tour. And you know what? THEY ALL DID. Boy, I wish I had met Tim on the first week!!

After the brilliant and very noisy tailgate, Dave and I staggered into the Georgia Dome for game fourteen on my tour, The Atlanta Falcons Vs The Tampa Bay Buccaneers.

I had seen Atlanta lose their unbeaten run in New Orleans a few weeks earlier, but I expected them to beat the struggling Buccaneers quite easily. WRONG! Yet again.

The Bucs started like champions and raced into a half time lead of 13-3 in the beautiful Georgia Dome stadium. I liked this stadium very much and did not quite understand why it was being knocked down, but I recently saw the pictures of the new Falcons stadium and it really does look amazing, and is well and truly on my radar.

Because of Tim, Dave and I were sitting with a great bunch of Buccaneers fans, which gave us a very good reason to be Bucs for the day. Remember, I always supported the home team, out of respect for being in THEIR stadiums, but after meeting Tim and the rest of the gang, I broke from my usual tradition and I was now supporting their Bucs.

This was also my introduction to yet another top man who became my friend that day, Jamal "Jay Buc" Sanders. Jay Buc, like Tim, was completely dressed as a pirate, including a great half face mask, which I think looked fantastic.

The second half started and to my surprise the Bucs went

even further ahead, and my new friends around me were going crazy. It was so amazing and exciting for me to be a part of their group, to be amongst these lovely people and very passionate Buccaneers fans.

But as the 4th quarter started, the Falcons comeback started too, making this a very nail biting, tense and nerve racking time for my new Bucs friends. I was feeling the tension too as the Bucs lead was diminishing as the clock ran down, and to our horror, the Falcons came back and eventually sent the game into overtime with the score tied at 20-20. It was great drama for me, but not for my new mates, it must have been torture!!

Tampa Bay kicked a field goal in overtime, but the new ruling meant the opposing team gets the ball back. If then a field goal is scored to tie the game again, then the next score wins. If a touchdown is scored, the team also wins.

So the Falcons got the ball back, so now it was squeaky bum time for all of us, and if Atlanta score a touchdown, the Bucs lose.

The final play of the game was electric with excitement, but incredibly tense at the same time, as the Falcons had a 4th down and a lot of yards, and if they don't get the first down, the Bucs would win the game. The ball is snapped, the Falcons QB Matt Ryan attempts to pass to one of his receivers, but the ball incompletes and hits the ground. GAME OVER. Victory goes to the Buccaneers. YYYEEEEEESSSSSSSSSSSSSSSSSSSSS!

My new friends and Bucs fans were ecstatic. There were

many tears, hugging, relief and great joy, I was so pleased for them, especially my friend Jay Buc who was crying his eyes out. Some of these fans had never seen their beloved Bucs win a game on the road (an away game) before, and I was absolutely delighted for them. Well done to the Bucs.

Dave and I left the stadium and we continued to party back at the tailgate with our new good friends. I eventually said my goodbyes and huge thanks to Tim, Jay Buc, Craig and many others, before Dave and I proceeded to drive the four hours to Dave's place in Charlotte Carolina for my next game the following night.

I remember during the drive to Dave's place, we heard a song on the radio called "Werewolves of London" by the crazy Warren Zevon, Dave and I laughed all the way home after hearing the first line of the song which is, "I saw a werewolf with a Chinese menu in his hand". Boy, did we laugh....all the way across the border into North Carolina.

Stadium-15
Bank of America Stadium
Carolina Panthers

Dave and I arrived into Charlotte, Carolina about nine in the evening and we dived straight into Dave's local pub for a couple of sneaky drinks before bedtime.

The next morning, I got up quite early as my horse Vibrato Valtat was running in a big race at Exeter in the UK. My head was in Charlotte, but my heart was at Exeter, as I was gutted to be missing this big race for my boy. My heart was racing faster than the horses as I watched the race at 7am Carolina time on my laptop, VV ran like a true champion and I was screaming Dave's house down as VV cruised to the front, and won the race at a canter, winning me 800 notes in the process. RESULT! I was so over the moon, I almost cried as my baby crossed the winning line. YYEESSSSSSSSSSSSSSSSSSS!!!! GET IN YOU BEAUTY!!

Dave made me a lovely breakfast in bed, well actually on his sofa, and he even did my laundry for me, good boy he is!, and after a few lazy hours, we took off for lunch, before we headed off to the Carolina Panthers stadium.

I had made contact with a local Carolina TV station via Twitter, and they wanted to interview me outside the Panthers "Bank of America Stadium" before the game.

I was well pleased and very excited, as this was the first time I had the chance to speak to the American media. I thought this would be a great chance to publicise my tour and inform the people of America, well Carolina at least, what I was up to.

The weather that evening was absolutely chucking it down with rain, and I mean the entire evening. So Dave and I went off to meet the film crew for my interview. I was also meeting with a Superfan from Carolina named Jeff Pintea, or as he's called in the Superfan world, "Pantherman", so I had to juggle between these two meetings as the film crew were running late.

After numerous texts and calls, the two man TV crew finally arrived outside the Bank of America stadium, and we proceeded to start our interview....in the torrential rain. The interview actually went very well, I spoke confidently, and I got my message across in a pretty interesting way, but a few times during the interview, the cameraman mentioned that his battery was running out of power, so we stopped and restarted, did it again, restarted again, until the interviewer said we had enough material or footage, to cut and paste a decent piece of TV air time. BINGO!

I was well pleased I had finally made it onto the TV screens of America, after all the hard work I had put in trying to make this happen, by contacting the media and a million other people, teams, players, companies etc etc, especially after being completely ignored. I honestly thought this was the beginning of something special. HOW BLOODY WRONG AGAIN WAS THIS IDIOT?

During the following week, I tried a few times to touch base with the guy who interviewed me, and when he FINALLY returned my messages, he totally apologised to me for wasting my time, as he then informed me that his stupid cameraman had in fact messed up bigtime and wiped the entire tape clean of our interview. I was so gutted I could have cried, and to be honest, I nearly did.

These two idiots were like the "Keystone Cops", a couple of bumbling buffoons who probably could not even tie their own shoelaces, and they made a real mess of my big TV moment and interview. The opportuntity for me to get some publicity or interest in my tour was gone, and I never did get the chance to do another TV interview on the entire tour. And boy did I try. I WAS DEVASTATED.

This was a very low moment for me as I honestly thought it would be very easy to get the American media interested in the story of a crazy Englishman, who was going to every stadium in the NFL. How stupid was I? The US media completely and utterly ignored all my attempts to get any publicity for my tour, and that hurt me so much, and still does to this day. I would just love to know WHY?

Dave and I rushed off in the monsoon rain to find "Pantherman Jeff" at his tailgate. When we did, Jeff gave us a few beers and a bite to eat, but it was getting very close to kick off time after those two idiots from US TV had turned up so late, leaving me with little time to get to know Jeff. But in the very short amount of time I spent with Pantherman, I knew he was a top man.

I managed to get Dave a cheap ticket off some guy we bumped into at the side of the stadium, I already had paid only thirty bucks for mine, so off we finally went, into the home of the Carolina Panthers.

I liked the Bank of America stadium, it was a big round football arena, but sadly for us, there was no roof to cover us from the pouring rain. Dave and I had flimsy plastic macs on, and we really did look like a couple of wallies/funny, but without them, we would have been even wetter. In fact we were totally and utterly soaked, even with these stupid outfits on!!

The visitors on this Monday night to Carolina were the very unpredictable Indianapolis Colts, a team who on their day, can beat anyone, but they can also lose to anyone, a team who are very hard to predict.

The Panthers were on an unbeaten run of 7-0 at the time, and I wanted to see that continue. It started well for them as they raced into a first quarter lead of 10-0. Dave and I were in and out of our seats, running for the cover of the stands as the rain was constant lashing down on us, and we were soggy and cold, but we were having a great laugh together.

The Colts kicked a couple of field goals to make it a 10-6 lead to the Panthers at half time, which made this game a lot closer than I had expected. The Panthers increased their lead as the fourth quarter started and Cam Newton the Panthers QB was looking pretty impressive, throwing three touchdown passes, giving the Panthers what looked like a very easy win.

But then came the comeback from 23-6 down as the inconsistent Colts got two quick touchdowns and making the Panthers unbeaten record look a little shaky. The Colts kicker kicked a field goal with three seconds to go, to take this game into overtime, my second in 24 hours.

To be honest I never wanted overtime, I'm sure Dave didn't either as we were both like drowned rats, and soaked to the bone, but it was an exciting game, so I didn't mind too much.

Both teams scored field goals in overtime, then the Panthers turned the ball over (got the ball back) and their kicker made a 52 yard kick to win the game. It was a very exciting end to a very long and terribly wet evening, and I was well pleased to see the Panthers winning run continue.

Dave and I left the Bank of America stadium, had a quick beer with Pantherman Jeff, and we headed off to the car to go back to Dave's pad as it was now well past midnight and I was soaked right through to my underpants! Thank god it was finally over, especially after Dave and I must have been in that persistent rain for around six hours in total.

The next morning, Dave kindly drove me to the Greyhound bus station a few miles away as I had to catch another extremely long and overnight Greyhound bus to my next destination, Cincinnati.

I would have liked to have spent a few more days in Charlotte with Dave, as he is a diamond geezer from my manor (my part of the world), we did have a lot in common and we did nothing but laugh all the time we were together.

Sadly, I did not have the time to see or experience anything of Charlotte, but I will return one day, mainly to spend more time with my good mate and top man, Charlton Dave.

My next game was on Thursday and I never had much time to play with, as Cincinnati was a long long way from Charlotte Carolina by bus. I had to go on a massive detour through a lot of states to get to Ohio (around five I think it was?), as there was a huge natural obstacle in the way, something called the Appalachian Mountains.

Stadium-16
Paul Brown Stadium
Cincinnati Bengals

I left Charlotte and my mucker Dave, after a very short but sweet stop and off I headed towards Cincinnati on yet another long overnight ride on the Greyhound bus. This time it was a twenty hours cross country trek.

I did consider flying from Charlotte to Cinci as it was a very short flight of about a hour, but again Mr Greenback was bullying, and telling me the bus was a far cheaper option. This particular ride was a pain in the ass, simply because there is no direct way to get from A to B, or as the crow flies, and I blame this on the Appalachian Mountains, I mean, who bloody put them there?!!

I recently watched a program about these mountains, and apparently these are the oldest mountain range in America. NICE! At least I got the chance to see North Carolina, West Virginia, Virginia, Kentucky and Ohio along the way, so that was good.

Call me mad, but I was never put off at all by these extremely long bus rides, I loved them. It was a peaceful and laid back time for me to reflect and plan, after rushing around a city, watching a game, being a tourist as much as I could, and trying to tick as many boxes as possible, as I usually did.

I always made the effort to see anything of any importance or interest in all the places I visited. I knew most of the cities I would be visiting, would be a one off visit, never to return, so I made every effort to see as many of the historical landmarks, museums, sporting events, arena's, or points of interest as I possibly could.

I eventually arrived into Cincinnati early in the morning, and as Cinci has no hostels, well not according to Hosteworld or Hostelbookers, I returned to the dreaded couchsurfing website for the third time.

Before I had left London, I had arranged to stay with a guy named Billy. His profile looked far more normal than some of the weirdo's I had contacted on this website, so I thought "He who dares wins"..........again!

Billy was young and he likes soccer, so we got on well from day one. Billy is an Everton fan, so he does not know too much about soccer I think!!!

I met Billy at the Greyhound bus terminal in downtown, and straight away he offered to take me on a tour around the centre of Cincinnati, showing me a few points of interest, including the 2nd tallest building in town, which we went to the top of, and checking out the incredible views all over Cincinnati and Kentucky. I could see the beautiful river, lovely bridges, and three stadiums, the "Paul Brown Stadium", the home of the Cincinnat Bengals where I would watch my next NFL game the following day, the Cincinnatti Reds stadium (my new team), and I'm sure there was a third, (the Ice Hockey team?) but I may be wrong. Anyway, the views were amazing.

Cincinnati is a very modern city, lots of lovely buildings, all the big named stores are there, all different cuisines, and basically everything I needed, I liked it.

Billy took me to a local sports bar for lunch called "Molly Malones", where the owner was an ex pat Englishman (or was he Irish?) and a West Ham fan, so I felt quite at home in this pub. That day Arsenal were playing the second leg of their Champions League game against Bayern Munich, and I wanted to watch it in the designated Arsenal America bar in town. I looked online to see where the Cinci AA bar was, found it, so off we went to the bar called "The Rhinehaus".

We got to the Rhinehaus just before kick off, and to my massive disappointment, there were no Arsenal fans in the bar other than one guy in an Arsenal shirt with his mate. Where were everybody? this was a massive game. Granted, it was the afternoon and people were probably at work, but I had been in AA bars in other towns on afternoon game times and there were always a hardcore amount of noisy fans. Not this time.

That was not in the manual, nor was the fact Arsenal got their bums smacked 5-1, and are now out of the Champions League, and my unbeaten run in AA bars had come to an end with an enormous thump. Or did it?

As I re write this chapter, Arsenal have just been drawn in the knockout stage of the Champion league against.......Bayern Munich. That's us fcuked!!!! Ha! On my third re write, Arsenal got beat yet again 5-1.....BLOODY TWICE!!

I made an executive decision, and I decided this AA disaster was not going to ruin my unbeaten run in AA bars, because there were no Arsenal fans, no atmosphere, no singing, cheering etc etc, so this was not an Arsenal America experience, so in my eyes this game did not count. Null and void me thinks because it was not the Arsenal America occasion I had been used to. I just wish I could null and void the 5-1 scoreline! All three of them!

After the game Billy took me to the Cincinnati Reds baseball stadium, and we popped into the stadium shop. I was instantly attracted to the team as they are called "The Reds", the colour of my Arsenal, and although I'm not a fan of baseball, I decided to adopt this team, as I liked Cincinnati and the colour of the Reds kit. I celebrated my new union with my "Reds" and I christened my new team by buying a pair of Cincinnatti Reds socks, and these socks are still in good working order, even after two years of walking around the streets of London and various golf courses of Surrey and Berkshire to this very day. On my third draft, they are now totally knackered and are long gone, thrown in the bin. But they were a great servant...............up the Reds!

Thursday night was game fifteen on my tour, a divisional rivalry between two Ohio state teams, the Cincinnati Bengals and the Cleveland Browns.

The Paul Brown Stadium in Cincinnati looked great from the outside, glowing in the dark. I was a little confused as to why the stadium was called the "Paul Brown", when the Browns were the big rivals, but when I was told this guy was a legend back in the day for the Bengals, it all made perfect sense.

My good friend Tim "The Captain" Young had put me in touch with the Bengals Superfan, a guy named Shawn Moore, aka "Who Dey". I had been in contact with Shawn on Facebook and I was looking forward to meeting him and his friends at his tailgate outside the stadium.

As soon as I met Shawn, I knew we would be friends forever, as he made me and Billy feel so welcome, and so did all his friends, both Bengals and Browns fans. I'm sure I've already written this somewhere, but I love the way these fans invite the opposition fans to each others tailgates and they all get on like a house on fire and its one big party. The banter is always great, there are opinions exchanged, sometimes heated of course, but always in the nicest possible way with total respect shown from both sides, its fantastic, I love it.

The atmosphere at the tailgates is always brilliant and its the perfect way to get you pumped up before the games. I had so much fun at so many tailgates, and many times had to be careful not to eat and drink too much before the games, which of course, I always did!

After experiencing these tailgates, I could not imagine going to a NFL game in the US again, without attending a tailgate. It would just not be the same, and something massive would be missing, and some of the time, the shitty games get in the way of a brilliant tailgate. Honest, its true.

I'm so glad my amazing friends helped me experience these tailgates, I absolutely loved every single one of the many I was fortunate enough to be invited to. All your bloody fault Tim Young!!!

I met some great people at Shawn's tailgate, including many from Cleveland, including Mike "Facepaint" Bonnell, who I would meet up with when I got to Cleveland a few weeks later.

My old tailgate mate Craig Steichen was there, incredible that our schedules were clashing yet again, and it was always good to see Craig as he introduced me to some very interesting and nice people.

I got talking to a lovely lady named Rachel at this tailgate. Sadly Rachel had lost her son, who was a soldier in the military, and he was killed in action in the conflict in Afghanistan. Rachel was a guest for the evening of Craig and his Warrior Wishes charity, a charity which invites and entertains people connected to the military to watch NFL games.

Rachel was lovely and I was attracted to her immediately, she was pretty, funny, bubbly, great company, as well as she had all the lumps and bumps in the right places! I fancied her straight away. Rachel kindly helped me get a ticket for the game and she even offered to pay for it, which of course I turned down. But a lovely gesture indeed, from a very lovely person.

So after a good feed, a few drinks and a few shots, we all walked to the stadium together like one big happy family.

I was sitting on the other side of the stadium from Rachel and her sister, with my new friend and Bengals Superfan Shawn "Who Dey" Moore, but I joined the girls in the second half high up in the nose bleeds and we chatted away and flirted all through the second half. To be honest, I was more interested in Rachel than the game itself!!

It was great to stand with Shawn and meet his crazy bunch of Bengals fans, including one guy who looked and dressed as Jesus Christ. Shawn was singing and screaming all game, god knows how he does it, but it was great entertainment for me to see how passionate he and his friends were to their team. I liked the Bengals song "Who dey, who dey, who dey think gonna beat those Bengals, who dey, who dey". This is where I guess Shawn got his nickname from.

I was looking forward to seeing the controvertial Cleveland QB Johnny "Football" Manziel playing for the Browns, and he started quite well by throwing a touchdown pass. But Bengals QB Andy Dalton had a very rare good game on national or prime time TV, something he has been known to choke on more than a few times in the past. This night, Dalton upped him game, and he eventually managed to secured an easy win for his Bengals in the end.

The Bengals eventually beat the Browns 31-10 to continue their unbeaten run, the second unbeaten run I had witnessed on the tour. I was'nt bothered at all about the result, as by now I was far more preoccupied with a certain sexy lady who was well and truly on my radar.

After the game we all headed off to a bar in the centre of town and all I had on my mind was the lovely Rachel. Sadly not a lot happened with Rachel that night, but I could see and feel something would definately have happened if only I never had to catch a very early bus to Buffalo the next morning around 7am.

Oh boy, I wanted something to happen, but Rachel lived such a long way from where I was staying with Billy, and there was no way I could go back to her place, then get back to Billy's to collect my things, before getting the early bus. FCUK!!!

This was when a seed was planted in my head that maybe I could return to Cincinnati if the Bengals made the play off's?? The chances of this happening was extremely high as the Bengals were 8-0 after half of the regular season, and leading their division by a mile. Sounds like a plan I thought, all coming of course from my little head!!

Billy and I left Rachel, her sister, and Craig at the bar around 1am. It took all the willpower in the world for me to decline the invitation to go home with Rachel. The only option I really had, was to abort my 7am bus, and go the next day to meet my mate George in Buffalo, but I had already told George I was coming on a certain day, and I didn't want to mess him about. In hindsight, I should have let the bus go and banged Rachel into next week and left the following day.......or month!

From the very first idea about doing this tour, I had never once thought I would continue into the play off's. My feeling was that after 17 weeks of zig zagging across America I would have had enough, but the longer this tour went on, the more I loved it, mainly because of the amazing people I met along the way who were making my adventure so much fun. I was totally living the dream, and I never wanted it to end.

So goodbye Rachel........for now, I will return. (but only if your Bengals make the play off's with home field advantage). My fingers were well and truly crossed. GO BENGALS!!!!!!!!

Billy was a great host, he restored my faith in Couchsurfing after a few bad experiences, as Billy really looked after me. Without him, it would have been yet another struggle to get around a city, a city with no hostels. Thanks a million Bill.

Billy kindly drove me to catch my bus, which left the Greyhound bus station in Cinci around 7am, for yet another long ten hours ride, this time heading north to my next destination, and into the freezing cold of New York state, and the home of the Bills...........Buffalo.

Stadium-17
Ralph Wilson Stadium
Buffalo Bills

Buffalo was always a place I was looking forward to visiting, mainly as I wanted to see my old mate George Gibbs, whom I had met on my previous tour of the Americas in Guatemala two years ago. Our introduction was me playing the guitar and both of us singing "Wish you were here" by Pink Floyd in a coffee shop.

George is a great fun guy, always upbeat, loves to sing, have a beer and a laugh, he's right up my street and we had been talking on Facebook about meeting up for over a year.

George used to be a professional footballer in the UK, playing mainly in the lower leagues at Bristol City (I think it was), but George went off to play in the North American Soccer League in it's heyday of the late 70's when all the great players around the world were playing there, including George Best and Pele. This impressed me very much. Amazing George, good work mate.

After another long ride and a sore bottom, I arrived into a place near Buffalo called Batavia, where George lived. This particular Greyhound stop was very different to what I had been used to as it was more or less a petrol station that had no shelter, ticket office, waiting rooms or anywhere for people to wait to welcome you.

George arrived with his wife Lesley about ten minutes after my bus dropped me off, and we went to grab some dinner together at a local restaurant. Many months before I arrived into the US, I had numerous conversations via Facebook with George regarding my time in Buffalo, and George mentioned he had some very good contacts at the Buffalo Bills, as well as the local radio station in Buffalo, and it would not be a problem getting my songs played on this particular radio station. Obviously I was over the moon and very excited George was going to help me with things in Buffalo, especially my music.

George mentioned a guy who was his relation, a fella named Lou, who would make sure I was taken good care of in my time at the Buffalo Bills. I hooked up with Lou on Facebook, and again, I was very excited, especially when George mentioned that he and Lou were going to organise a stretch limo to take us all to the game when I got to Buffalo. This sounded insane, and something I was looking forward to so very much. A game in a limo? YES PLEASE.

But as the time got closer for me to arrive in Buffalo, I smelt the proverbial rat, as by now, the promises I had been offered by George, were now all starting to fall down one by one like skittles. First, the limo was not going to happen, something that annoyed me considerably, as I was so looking forward to this. Don't forget, I've already been offered so much by so many, and received so little from many bullshitters along the way on this tour so far. I do get so FCUKED OFF, when people don't follow through with their promises, especially when they OFFERED in the first place.

The next kick in the nuts came when the man at the radio station who was going to play my songs on his show never did, then he preceded to disappeared up his own turntable, and so on, and so on......

After a nice dinner, off we went back to George's lovely house, we had a few drinks and a chat, before callling it a night and going to bed.

The following day was a Saturday, so we took it easy and had a lazy day of watching soccer on the telly (TV). We watched a game between Manchester United and Chelsea and then an Arsenal game, so I had a nice relaxing day posting lots of pics and vids on social media, as well as updating my website, which incidentally took up a huge amount of my time on a regular basis while I was on the road. I loved doing those social media posts and my website, especially making the videos as I always had a good laugh while doing them. I still do!!

George has a lovely house in the countryside in Batavia, quite secluded and peaceful, I loved it, especially having a room to myself with a lovely comfortable bed, and no sounds, especially snoring. The sound of silence was fantastic.

While in Buffalo, I was expecting snow, and a lot of the stuff, and George informed me many times how lucky I was because snow should have been on the ground by now at this time of the year. A week after I left, I saw incredible blizzards on TV in this area of New York state, so I know how very lucky I had been while I was in Buffalo. The previous year at this time, Buffalo was under three feet of snow, so I was in fact very lucky indeed.

In London, especially when I was younger, we had snow almost every year, and as a kid of course I loved it, but London snow and Buffalo snow are two completely different animals, as London usually gets a sprinkle, where Buffalo gets more like a deluge, or an avalanche, something London has only experienced on a few very rare occasions.

When I arrived into Buffalo, George informed me he had a few great nights out lined up for us, as well as a nice surprise for me. Great! I love surprises, and to be honest Georgie Boy never let me down on this one.

Saturday night, George and a bunch of his lovely friends took me to Batavia Downs racetrack. OH YES, right up my sidewalk!! so as a lover of the races, I was chomping at the bit (pardon the pun!) with excitement. As a racehorse owner (part of a syndicate) in the UK, I always try to go racing when I travel, as much as I can. This was slightly different as it was the "Trotts", which is where jockeys are being pulled along on kind of chariots. Not my usual choice of racing to be honest, well actually we don't have this kind of horse racing in the UK, but it is what it is, and I was just very happy to be there.

George informed me that at the racetrack, there was a casino and we were going to it after the races. YEEESSSSSSSSSSSS!!!!!!!!!, horses, blackjack and roulette all under one roof?, this is what my idea of heaven is!

Before the real fun started, we had a feast of a buffet dinner, and what a buffet it was, as we had everything from fine meats to massive crabs, and delicious desserts. Beautiful, it was.

As we tucked into the feast, what happened next I will remember for the rest of my life, and this was a truly touching moment for me, and bought tears to my eyes. George had arranged with his friend Chuck to sponsor one of the races that night and they named it "The Welcome Dennis Moss from England" race. It was written in the race card, my name was flashing on a big board in the centre of the racetrack, and they even announced my name over the tannoy system.

I felt so humbled and special to have a race named after me, I felt extremely emotional. I remember taking a video for Facebook and I blubbered my way at the end as I felt so tearful. It was a lovely gesture by George and Chuck and something I will treasure and remember forever. Thank you so much, guys.

That evening I had a couple of winners at the racetrack, but overall I lost a few bucks, nothing much, but I thoroughly enjoyed myself. Once the racing had finished, we headed off to the casino, but unbeknown to me, disaster was waiting around the corner and getting ready to creep up on me yet again.

Included in the price of the entrance fee to the racetrack and dinner, we were given ten dollars of free plays on a fruit machine (slots) at the casino, but I'm not into that so I went hunting for the blackjack tables or roulette wheels. This is where the fun stopped, as sadly there were not any, and only then was I informed this was no real casino, just some kind of bingo hall and bar. AARRGGGGHHHH! I was soooooo gutted, another minor custard pie to my face, (not exactly a major one this time!) as I was well and truly up for a good old gamble.

I quickly lost my free ten dollars on the slots and rapidly realised there was nothing of real interest here for me, so I went to find the rest of the gang and I bought a drink and got chatting to a very nice old guy at the bar who worked at the casino. (that place should not be called a casino, that is defamation of character!)

At this point I was pretty chilled, enjoying being the centre of attention, relaxed, happy, half Brahms and Lizst (drunk), so all was going swimmingly at this point, until, BANG! emergency stop.

George mentioned that his wife Lesley was not feeling very well and she was tired and wanted to go home. As this was my first night out in Buffalo, as well as being Saturday night, I was buzzing and I did not want to go home as it was only just after 10pm. So I had a dilemma, I either went home with George in his relation's car with him and Lesley or stay with George's friends and go home with them or get a cab. I was having a great time, and I never wanted to leave, but I also wanted my mucker George to stay with me as I love him to death and he is such great company, I just wanted to spend some quality time with him, especially away from his miserable wife Lesley.

She who wore the trousers got her way, George left, and I stayed, and this would not be the last time Lesley would ruin a good night out with her games or sudden "bad turns" by taking George away from me or any of the parties or get togethers we had.

A lovely couple I had met encouraged me to stay, so I did, had a few beers with George's friends, and I had a nice evening with them. I eventually got back to George's place a couple of hours later, and he kindly left the door open for me, and I finally hit the sack about 2ish. I had had a great evening.

Sunday was game day and I was looking forward to experiencing watching a game with George. Then BAM!! George dropped yet another bombshell on my head, or hit me with another Tyson punch, telling me he was not coming to the game with me. Instead, he would drop me off outside the stadium while he and Lesley visited their daughter, who lived somewhere not too far from the stadium. Yet another skittle from George, (definitely instigated by Lesley).

This really fcuking infuriated me so bloody much, as I wanted to spend some quality time with George, away from his wife Lesley's constant nagging, frequent interuptions, attention seeking and non stop moaning, as I could quite obviously see an extremely regular pattern emerging.

I felt uncomfortable around Lesley the very first moment we met and I was pretty certain she did not like me at all. Why? Only she knows, but it would have been nice if she would have made the effort to try to get to know me. George was the complete opposite, he was so great, funny, positive, happy, friendly and the perfect host, other than saying we were doing things together, which then never materialised, mainly because of Lesley's Oscar winning performances of being tired or feeling unwell.

I honestly think Lesley was jealous of my relationship, or

the friendship I had with George, because every time George and I would engage in some mischief, laughter, sing, or just be mates, Lesley made every effort to spoil or ruin the moment. She would butt in or distract and drag George away or even just kill the mood in her own very special negative way. I felt Lesley did not like the fact George and I were having so much fun together, laughing all the time, and getting on so well. We had so much in common and she obviously hated seeing this, and how we had bonded so much, and she felt threatened I was taking George's attention away from her which, of course, I was, which was'nt hard as this woman was so damn miserable.

George drove me to the Ralph Wilson Stadium, the home of the Buffalo Bills, which was about forty five minutes away from Batavia where George lived. He dropped me off, and he and Cruella DeVille zoomed away in a puff of smoke to see their daughter, taking all the promises and plans I had in Buffalo with them.

As the car pulled away, I was very much fcuked off that here I was, in Buffalo, on my own yet again, no George, no Lou, no limo, and basically all of the promises these timewasters had offered to me were now just shattered dreams.

I had the choice of two tailgates to find at two different areas of the Buffalo Bills Stadium. My old mate Craig Steichen yet again set me up with one of these, but he was busy and already inside the stadium and on the pitch with his "Warrior Wishes" people and ex Bills QB Jim Kelly when I arrived at the stadium, so I never got the chance to see Craig this time.

It was a beautiful sunny day on gameday seventeen, but
with a chilly wind that went right through to my skinny
bones, especially when the sun went behind the clouds, as
then it was bitterly cold. I did my usual wander around the
stadium, taking pictures and videos, then I tried to find the
Buffalo Bills Superfan I was supposed to meet up with,
whom my mate "Who Dey" from Cinci had put me in touch
with.

I looked for ages, but I eventully found the first tailgate, and
I'm sorry to say I cannot remember the name of the guy I
met that day, a big tall man with a funky wagon with a big
"Bills Van" sign on it. He was a nice guy and he looked
pleased to meet me, but as I stood around chit chatting to a
few people at this tailgate, I did not feel totally comfortable
as I did not know anybody there, something which never
stopped me before, but my Bills friend and host was busy
most of the time with his own friends, and I was standing
alone feeling a little awkward, like a spare one at a wedding!
So I decided to abort this mission and head for the other
tailgate Craig had told me about.

The second tailgate was a long walk, way across the parking
lot on the other side of the stadium and the game time clock
was ticking down, and at this point I still never had a ticket
for the game. Again I looked for ages, and by the time I
arrived at the 2nd tailgate, the people were packing their
things away as it was now getting very close to game time.

I did meet the host of the second tailgate, I wish I could
remember his name as he was super friendly and a great
guy, and he had a friend with him who was a Bills fan and
he was an Englishman. I remember this English guy was

wearing a very funky suit with a big Union Jack all over it, it looked great.

The host very generously passed me a beer and told me to eat whatever was left of his food. A lovely gesture as I had just arrived at the tailgate, scoffed a few things and then I had to quickly rush off to the game. Thanks, buddy.

The reason I never had a ticket for the game was because I was waiting on George's relation Lou to contact me, as he mentioned he may be able to get me into a private box. I had been in contact with Lou for probably the last six months, and Lou always took ages to reply to my messages, and now was no different.

I had tried to touch base with Lou in the few days before the game, right up to a hour before kick off, but sadly again, I got the usual silent treatment from this useless communicator.

Buffalo was starting to look like the city of broken promises, which by now had quickly turned into the place of total letdowns. It seemed to me that the Buffalo gold or treasure I had dangled right in front of my face, was quickly turning into sand between my fingers, and it was starting to wear me down BIGTIME. And this would continue, right through to the very last hour of my time in Buffalo.

With around thirty minutes to game time, I bought a ticket from a fan for 60 bucks, after doing the usual shout out "Anybody got a spare ticket to sell?", routine that never fails with this cockney accent, and I headed into the Ralph Wilson stadium in the glorious sunshine. Again I got lucky as I purchased a great seat for half price, face value was 120 bucks, as I asked the guy who sat next to me what these tickets usually cost. This fella was a really friendly and nice guy and I enjoyed watching the first quarter with him in this section of the stadium.

Then completely out of the blue my phone rang, it was Lou. "Where are you?" Lou asked. "I'm in block 107" I replied. "Do you wanna join us in a private box in section 117?" "Sure", I smiled from ear to ear! If only Lou would have got back to me a hour earlier, I would have saved 60 dollars, but hey, I'm not complaining.

A big part of me wanted to stay with my new friend at my seat in section 107, as I liked this man a lot, and we were having a great time chatting away about football and watching the game together like a couple of mates. To me, HE was a real fan, and its people like him I wanted to be around as much as possible on my tour as he was showing a great deal of passion for the game and his team, not like most of the people I met in the private area, as these people are mainly corporate and only there for the free ride, or to network, and most (not all) of these people couldn't give a damn about the game, and most of the ones I met here in the private box, had their backs to the field of play for pretty much most of the time.

I said goodbye to my friend in section 107 and I kind of felt like I was selling out on him by leaving him behind and moving on to a so called "better place", and I had only just met him. I liked this guy very much, and I'm very sad to say I cannot even remember his name, so he is gone into the universe forever. This friendly stranger meant more to me than all the people I would meet in the next three hours combined. Coming up in the rest of this chapter you will fully understand exactly why.

The visitors that day were the Miami Dolphins, a team I have always had a little affection for, mainly because I used to like their legendary QB Dan Marino. Also because of an old workmate named Mike Jewell, as I used to be his wide receiver who tried to catch his "bomb" passes outside the back door where we used to work as teenagers in Central London at Keith Johnson Photographic. Mike was a huge Dolphins fan and together we had a love for the NFL, when NFL fans in London were an extremely rare breed indeed.

I had seen the Dolphins play in both Washington DC and Nashville and they had won both times, so maybe I was their lucky mascot?

I found my way into the box where Lou was hosting his guests in, and there was food and drinks all over the place, but sadly I had just filled my belly at the second tailgate I had attended. Damn! But this greedy boy picked away at a few bits and bobs, as you do when you are on a free ride!

I met Lou inside the box and I liked him immediately, he made me feel very welcome and he introduced me to many of his friends, colleagues and clients, some of whom seemed quite important and connected in the world of the Buffalo Bills, and other area's in general.

Lou's boss was in his party, and Lou introduced her to me, a lovely lady named Debbie. We chatted away for ages as we watched the game from the open window of the private box we were in and she was very impressed and expressed an interest in my tour. Debbie informed me she was very well connected in the world of the NFL, especially the media. This was EXACTLY what I was looking for, a help in hand from an insider, or a friendly face in a high place. BINGO!

Debbie told me to make contact with her through Lou, then we could keep in touch and she would make sure I would get looked after or taken care of at a few of the NFL stadiums I had not yet visited.

I was just so happy, this lady was going to try to help me raise my profile, connect me with some influential people and more..........YYEEEESSSSS!!! I honestly felt that something positive was going to come from this chance meeting. WRONG AGAIN!

I wish I would have got Debbie's contact details directly rather than rely on Lou as the middle man, because then it would have been in my own hands, my own destiny, which could have made all the difference, and help avoid what massive heartache was to follow. What a complete schoolboy error, I was furious, I so wanted to kick myself, as yet again I trusted another fcuker of a bullshit man who simply disappeared into cyberspace and left me with a head full of what might have been's.

I was introduced to another very enthusiastic lady who apparently was a very well connected PR person. Again, she was very interested in what I was doing and she informed me she could possibly be able to connect me in the media. She said she could do this, do that, she knew this contact, that contact, etc. She seemed like she knew what she was doing, she talked the talk, and again, exactly what I was looking for. That's two great contacts. COME ON. Bring on the third down!

This particular woman told a great story, or spun a beautiful yarn in front of the other guests listening around us, and she had this sucker (me) convinced I was to be the next Justin Bieber or Sylvestor Stallone! I was hanging onto every single word that came out of this lying bitch's very big and annoying mouth, like a monkey on a tree. So now I'm flying, and I'm not even watching the game anymore as I'm networking!!

I took the lady in question's business card and she asked me to contact her in a few days' time, as it was busy and noisy in the box, and we were also all trying to watch a game of football. Things were looking up, or so I thought? I was beaming with exciting thoughts of my amazing future.

The 2nd half started and I felt on top of the world. Here I was, in a private box, a fantastic view of the pitch, the sun was burning down on me, I had a beer in my hand, and I'm in a room full of people who think I am Superman (and I'm feeling like I am), and they also think what I am doing on this tour was incredible. To top it all off, the Buffalo Bills were winning, so everything in the garden was rosy and everybody was happy, no one more so than my good self. I was absolutely buzzing.

As you can understand, I was slightly preoccupied with the game, I did watch as much of it as I could with the stunning view I had from a private box with the big windows wide open and me hanging out of them, with no heads in the way or people screaming in my ears, and the glorious sunshine beating down. I can get used to this I was thinking. I loved it. Pass me another beer!!

The game ended, the Bills won, my Dolphins winning streak was over and I said a massive thank you to Lou, his boss Debbie, who said she was looking forward to keeping in touch with me, and the other PR lady (Annabelle, I think her name was) as well as a few of the other very nice people I had met in the private box that afternoon. I left the Bills stadium on a high, with more than a spring in my step, probably more like the feeling one would get after snorting the fattest line of coke known to mankind!!

The sun was going down and it was starting to feel very cold, especially in the shade. Now I had to find my way back to the point where George earlier dropped me off. I did eventually find the spot, but only after asking half a dozen people for directions as sometimes my map reading or general sense of direction is usually pretty terrible to say the least, as you all very well know by now!

George very kindly picked me up and we went back to his home to freshen up and get ready for a big boozy night at his neighbour Chuck's house, something George had mentioned was planned for me. Excellent! or so I thought.

Chuck like me is a Dallas Cowboys fan, and that night we were going to Chuck's place, which is about 300 yards from George's house, a three minutes walk along George's driveway, to watch our Dallas Cowboys play their dreaded divisional rivals the Philadelphia Eagles in the Sunday night game.

I absolutely loved Chuck instantly, he was such a lovely, funny, generous guy, and George is very lucky to have a friend like Chuck. Everybody should have a Chuck in their lives, boy I wish I did, as he was constantly laughing and is a huge bundle of fun and just the nicest man. Chuck reminded me of the big fat character in "Family Guy", and I'm not the only person who thought this!!

George informed me that on this night, we would be having a right old knees up (party) getting the guitar out, singing a few songs and basically have a great evening with lots of laughs. Brilliant, I was very much looking forward to it.

We arrived at Chuck's and the food his wife Debbie laid on the table for us all was impressive to say the least. The hospitality at Chuck's was as warm as a bonfire, and the drinks flowed like a river. Sorry for all the similes, but it was true!

George and I did a few Pink Floyd songs early on, then we stopped for some lovely food and had a few drinks in Chuck's beautiful home. The Cowboys game started and as most of the guests stayed in the kitchen, I watched the game with Chuck and his son in the lounge. Not long into the game, it was probably around 9pm, George informed me Lesley wanted to go home, AGAIN. My immediate thought was great, let her go home on her own, as she only lives next door and we can all have a right old party after the game finished. George will then come out of his shell and be the great company I know he is, when Lesley is not doing her utmost to drag him down to her pathetic level.

Sadly, George played his "keep the peace card" again, and

he went home with Lesley, meaning the party was over
before it started. Yet again Lesley pulled rank on George,
got her own way, and killed any chance of me spending any
quality time with my mate, singing and playing more Pink
Floyd and Beatles songs. I was so fcuking annoyed Lesley
ruined this night for me. MY NIGHT.

I remember having a rant to Chuck and Debbie, as I got to
the end of my tether with Lesley's selfish spoiling tactics,
childish behaviour and the acting she was clearly doing on
purpose for some reason to keep me from having a good
time with George. George and I got on so well when we
were together, all we did was laugh, constantly. But it was
so obvious to me from the moment I met Lesley that she felt
threatened by this. I was having such great fun in the very
small amount of time I actually spent with George, and she
was probably jealous. It was crazy, but this really happened.
Lesley tried to sabotage everything I did with George, and
her wicked game plan worked a treat.

After chatting all evening with Chuck, he mentioned it was
in fact HIS friend who worked at the Buffalo radio station
George had mentioned to me months before. Chuck said it
should not be too difficult for him to get my song "Like a
Touchdown" played on the Buffalo radio station. Obviously
I was on cloud nine, as Chuck seemed to me to be a man of
his word, and a million miles from the bullshit man that
sadly George turned out to be. HOW WRONG AGAIN
WAS I?

I knew I only had one copy of the CD for my song "Like A
Touchdown", the original copy in fact, and this was in my
bag at George's house. I can't actually remember if I gave

that copy to Chuck or I sent it to him on an email, but I know I did give it to him somehow, and I waited with anticipation for him to use his influence, and return with some news.

Chuck like me loves to gamble, and I told Chuck and his wife Debbie I had planned to meet my good friend Mike McCarron in Las Vegas in February, after my NFL tour was over. Chuck and Debbie seemed very interested in making a journey to Vegas and it would have been nice to see them again and spend some quality time with them in Vegas. It was not exactly booked with them, but the offer was there and I kept in touch with Chuck on Facebook after I eventually left Buffalo.

Sadly Chuck ignored all my attempts to contact him regarding my music and getting my song played on the radio station his friend was a DJ on. I was also very disappointed I got no response at all from my attempts to ask Chuck if he wanted to meet me in Vegas.

I am completely baffled to this day as to why this lovely man ended our friendship, or broke our union or connection, as we had so much fun and laughter together and we got on so well. I honestly don't understand this, and this hurts me to this very day. The Buffalo curse continued and I could only think Lesley must have had something to do with this. Why else would these lovely human beings turn into complete assholes and abandon me?? I really liked these people, and that's why I am so very sad about this particular episode. If I had no feelings for them, it would not bother me at all, but I did.

The last thing I ever want to do is upset my friend George, I love this guy to bits. So George, if you ever do get round to reading my book, please don't hate me for telling my side of the story regarding Lesley, because everything I have written really did happen, and YOU know this, because you were denied access to spending time with me, and you saw at first hand, all of the nonsense and the games Lesley played with your very own eyes.

Leslie spoilt our time together with her constant nagging at George and that's the truth. It was a terrible shame I spent so very little quality time with George in the four days I was in Buffalo, because Lesley was such a killjoy and a nagger to George when he was close to me or showed me affection. I wish George would have been stronger to tell his wife to let him breathe, and give him the space to spend a little time with his fellow English buddy, whom he will almost certainly never see again.

I honestly cannot remember a single moment I would spend alone with George without Lesley performing her spoiling tactics, other than when we watched football on TV on Saturday afternoon, or when Lesley went to the toilet. It really was that bad.

Lesley was like a wasp, always buzzing around like a fcuking pest, butting in our conversations, despertely trying to change the course of brief moments of fun and laughter that George and I were having. I gradually grew to loathe this woman with a passion, as she totally ruined everything for me in Buffalo, and I know this vindictive woman would have enjoyed every minute doing so, in which she spoilt for me.

George showed me a scrapbook of his time in the NASL (North American Soccer League) and I was soooooo impressed with his pictures and newspaper clippings of him playing on the same pitches with some of the most famous and talented football players of all time, including George Best, Franz Beckenbauer, Pele, Bobby Moore, Johan Cryuff and many many more.

Good for you George, what a tremendous achievement, I thought that was very special indeed, as not too many people on this planet can say they achieved this. Amazing.

The next morning I was leaving Buffalo on the Megabus, and the night before I left, Chuck had kindly offered me breakfast, then a lift to the bus stop to catch my coach. Plan A before Chuck's offer was Lesley. DOH!

I never had any intention of going with Lesley, as my patience with her by this point, had gone completely, and I just wanted to get away from her as quickly as possible.

George had asked Lesley to take me, as he could not because he had to go to work, but Lesley made every excuse under the sun not to take me as she claimed to be busy, (busy doing what? as this woman doesn't ever do anything, she certainly doesn't go to work, so only she knows what she was doing, maybe she was tired again?) But then she said she could take me at a certain time, a time which was only convenient to her, not me, as her time was far too early and I would have been waiting in the cold for my bus for well over an hour.

I told Lesley, Chuck had offered me a lift and I was going

with him, so I was relieved (and I'm sure she was too) when I finally said my awkward goodbyes and I walked up the path to Chuck's place for breakfast before he took me to the bus stop. WRONG!!!

I knocked on Chuck's door and there was no answer, I tried again, and again, and again, as the thought of me back tracking down to Lesley was something I could'nt bare thinking of.

Chuck had OFFERED me a lift and breakfast at a certain time, then when I turned up, he was not even home, or probably fast asleep as Lesley informed me, because I knocked so damn hard many times to no avail, as I never wanted to go back and suck eggs at Lesley, which of course, I now had to.

I then had to take a humongous deep breath, put my proverbial tail between my legs and make the "walk of shame" back to Lesley and grovel for a ride. That really hurt, and I felt so embarrassed to even ask.

I liked Chuck so much, I won't and can't say a single bad word about him as he was simply amazing company, he really made me laugh and his kindness to me was so much appreciated. I have no idea why he let me down, I just have to give this lovely guy the benefit of the doubt, but at the time, I was pretty upset he disappeared on me.

I hope all is well with Chuck as I never got the chance to say goodbye to this "diamond geezer"/special man. George is so very lucky to have Chuck as a close friend and neighbour, and to say I am envious of this kind of friendship, is a very large understatement indeed, as Chuck is the kind of friend everybody should have, and a true legend.

Lesley (probably reluctantly) dropped me off at the Megabus stop bound for New York City, and it was a very uncomfortable ride for me, and I guess it was for her too, from the woman who tried, and basically succeeded, in spoiling the whole four days I had wanted to spend with my friend and very lovely man, George.

I'm certain the feeling from her was mutual, and Lesley was probably as glad to see the back of me as I was to see the back of her, and now her mundane life would be back to normal......poor old George. This guy really needs to grow some balls.

As I left Buffalo on the ten hours ride to New York City, I really was down in the dumps, alone and feeling sorry for myself. I was expecting so much in Buffalo with all the promises I received before I had arrived in town, a kind of lift off time for me and my tour, my music, publicity, media, radio station, a limo to the game with my friends George and Lou.

George even had a bird (woman) lined up for me, which turned into another almighty slap in the boat race (face). I had been texting this woman over the previous week, I did the groundwork, we flirted, and things were looking good for a rendezvous, until we had a big arguement on the phone over something totally pathetic, and this woman turned into a big problem in no time.

Anyway, as I left town, we were supposed to meet up, and

yet again I was totally messed around and she never returned my calls, even after we spoke like old friends on on the phone the very previous night.

So on the long ride through the middle of New York state, I'm feeling very demoralised, wounded, and totally unloved. I'm jinxed, I thought, nobody is interested in this Englishman and his crazy adventure, and I simply could not understand WHY they were not, and WHY everybody seemed to be against me and deliberately doing their very best to mess me about. I felt like the universe was not my friend, as I was trying so hard, and I was getting no help at all.

Buffalo was a terribly disappointing and very frustrating time on my tour for me, and as I left, I was extremely low in spirit, and totally deflated. It had promised so much, and delivered so very little.

I never did hear from the lovely Debbie (Lou's boss), even after she offered me assistance and contacts when we met in the private box at the Ralph Wilson Stadium. Lou disappeared yet again into social media la la land like a genie in a bottle, eventually surfacing by sending me a stroppy message via messenger claiming HE had asked Debbie to contact ME three times, and SHE had never replied to HIM, which incidentally HE never informed ME HE had even tried to do, as yet again HE ignored the THREE messages I had sent to HIM over a few weeks, asking HIM if HE had in fact asked Debbie if SHE would contact me. PHEW! Did you get that? Thanks a million for fcuk all Louie!

I really was gutted as I was so confident good things were on the horizon with Debbie, especially after hearing these words of wisdom roll off her very own tongue. Why on earth would she backtrack? She seemed so nice, and so genuine. Yet another massive disappointment and yet another kick in the nuts.

I called the PR lady Annabelle whom I had met in the private box at the stadium a few days earlier, who had offered me her "hand of god", or the hope of potential good rock solid connections, and who was soooooo interested in getting me media coverage, well at least that's what she said when we were in the company of a bunch of VIP's. But when I called her, she didn't even know who I was, and almost immediately told me there was nothing she could do, even after informing me when we had met that she loved my story and it would not be a problem to get me media attention.

Yet again I was crushed, but I was more than used to these disappointments by now, as I simply had had so many. I tried my best to continue to be positive, as I knew better times were ahead of me, well at least I hoped they were, well they could not be any worse, could they?

I did try my best to stay positive, focused, and driven, but I won't lie to you, sometimes it was not easy.....not easy at all.

As I left town, I remember thinking about the lovely Buffalo Bills fan I had deserted at section 107 inside the Ralph Wilson Stadium, to go inside a different world, a fantasy world, a private box world with my head full of aspirations of meeting "the one", the important person who maybe had the power, or the key to unlock the door to my dreams.

Looking back now, I enjoyed the thirty minutes I had spent in the company of this very real and passionate football fan, a million times more than the three hours I spent trying to make a connection and converse with this bunch of vultures, fake social climbers and promisers of everything and delivers of nothing, who are so far up their own arses its incredible. Of course not all of them, just most.

It took me all of five minutes with most of these people to realise I am not like them, and thank god I am not. This was a vile club, full of fake members at its very worst, completely money driven of course, very short on morals, manners, standards and communication, a world I don't want to be associated with AT ALL. Nice to your face, not to your laptop, cell phone or email address.

I would like to wish all of the people who slapped my face, in my time in Buffalo all the very best, as I do believe karma will come round one day and kick their asses, well at last I hope so. Then you will know exactly how it feels to be so badly let down.

This bus ride was a long and slow one to New York City. I was feeling pretty sorry for myself, upset that after over two months on the road, I still had not made any solid contacts or inroads in the media world, as well as not having a single play of my song "Like a Touchdown", on any radio station.

I felt convinced that I was cursed, because after ten weeks of trying, and with so many broken promises under my belt, I had made absolutely no progress at all in my quest for fame and fortune.

At least I was heading for one of my favourite cities in the world, and I was looking forward to meeting up with a new friend, a guy who had given me great support on my tour so far, ever since I left home. His name is Joe Carlson, a great guy who runs a tailgate outside the Metlife Stadium named "L7".

I was looking forward to finally meeting Joe and his buddies at the L7 tailgate, as well as saying hello again to many of the sights and sounds of a place I love very much.

New York City, here I come.

Stadium-18
Metlife Stadium
New York Jets

I arrived into one of my favoutite cities in the world, in the darkness of the evening and I had to get from the Megabus stop at the Port Authority Bus Terminal to my hostel in Brooklyn, way across the other side of New York City.

I know my way around New York quite well as I had been there a few times before and I always loved to ride around the New York subway. and two subway trains later I arrived at my fixed abode, the Brooklyn loft hostel.

As I arrived into the hostel, I could hear the sound of music coming from an area below, so it took me all of two minutes to drop off my backpack into my dorm room, and have a beer in my hand, (a Brooklyn Beer of course) as there was a jazz club in the basement of my hostel. I watched a great live band for an hour or so, had a couple of beers and went to my dorm as it was now close to midnight.

Wednesday I had a long and interesting day ahead of me as a tourist. I started by going to one of my favourite places in New York, Greenwich Village. The history here for music is amazing, with people like Bob Dylan, Jimi Hendrix, Bruce Springsteen, The Velvet Underground, and many more, who used to gig and hang out in this area of NYC.

I had a look around at a few music bars and clubs, including the iconic "Cafe Wha" where Jimi Hendrix was discovered by an English musician named Chas Chandler, who was a member of the 60's UK band "The Animals". Cafe Wha was the place where many famous performers and bands played back in the day before they were famous.

I had experienced these kind of music venues myself in London with the various bands I have played in. I have in fact played on the same stages as many of the world's greatest bands, from U2, to Blur, Oasis and Muse, long before they were famous, and playing to the proverbial one man and his dog. Been there, done that, and even bought the same bloody dog food!! But don't worry, there's still hope for me yet.

I had a coffee in what was advertised as the very first coffee shop in New York, or maybe even America. It was a lovely venue with a great busy vibe, I loved it. After my cappuccino, I wandered around a bit before going around the corner to check out "Electric Lady Land Studios", which was once owned by Jimi Hendrix and where he recorded his many big hits like Purple Haze, Hey Joe and Voodoo Chile.

I went for a wander through Little Italy and Chinatown, where I stopped off for lunch and a 90 minute massage by a big fat Chinaman. He was very good and strong, and he gave me a right going over, just what I needed after all those airmiles!!

Later that afternoon I went to the top of the Freedom Tower at Ground Zero, on the location that was once the Twin Towers. While at the top of the tower, I remember thinking what it must have been like to be inside these towers when they were hit by the two planes on September 11th. I was so high up, and with a head full of frightening thoughts, I could feel I was at a very infamous place in history and a spot where terrible devastation was caused and 3000 lives lost. And for what? A complete and utter waste, with nothing achieved at all. A very moving and somber place.

As you can imagine, the views across New York City were very impressive, as you can see almost all the many landmark tourist spots across town, everything from the Empire State Building, the Statue of Liberty, and all of the iconic NY bridges, from the Brooklyn to the Williamsburg. But I could not stop thinking about what had happened here on that fateful day in 2001.

It was now evening and I wanted to go to see the new James Bond film, which had been released that week. I Googled a cinema and off I went to watch "Spectre". What a brilliant film, I love Daniel Craig as Bond, so what a great end to a lovely day in one of my favourite places on the planet.

I left the cinema around midnight and I had to cross to the other side of Manhattan to get back to my hostel in Brooklyn, again on my beloved NY subway. I always thought of my favourite film "The Warriors" when I was on the New York subway, as a lot of that movie was filmed on these subway trains.

I wish I had the chance to have experienced New York back in the 70's. I loved the music from that period, the early rap from Grandmaster Flash and Afrika Bambaataa, 70's rock, and especially the disco sounds of Earth Wind and Fire and Chic. I would have loved to have gone to Studio 54, also to CBGB's to have watched Blondie or Talking Heads.

New York must have been great then, but I also hear it was a very dangerous place too, full of crime, drugs and violence, something that always fascinates and interests me hugely.

I am also a big fan of 70's US TV cop shows, as a kid, I loved Starsky and Hutch, Cannon, Columbo, Kojak, Charlie's Angels, the Streets of San Francisco and the Rockford Files. I love these programmes and to this day on the retro TV channels, I still watch some of them.

Thursday was game eighteen on my tour, and as the game was not until the evening, I had a lazy morning and lie in. When I finally surfaced, I chatted away over breakfast in the hostel with a few of the other guests. I got talking to an Australian guy who was a decent fella, so I invited him to have a wander around town with me. He politely declined as he said today was his "washing day" for his laundry, and then he was getting ready to go to a gig in the evening.

"Who are you going to see" I asked. "A DJ named Bonobo" he replied. WOW!, I thought, what a coincidence, as Bonobo was the name of the guy whose song I had heard and liked at the "Crash Pad" hostel I stayed at in Chattanooga.

Bonobo was doing a gig that night about a mile away from my hostel and I said to myself I just had to go to see him. I even sent him a message on Facebook, to see if I could get myself a ticket as it was a sellout. As usual I got no response, something I never really expected, as I'm sure he had a lot on his plate getting ready for his show.

But I now had a dilemma, as tonight I was going to see the New York Jets play against their big divisional rivals, the Buffalo Bills. The game starts at 7.30, would last around three hours, and it would take me at least an hour and a half to get back to Brooklyn. So realistically, I was going to miss Mr. Bonobo. Damn shame, but I would try my best to get back for the gig if I possibly could.

I left my hostel around lunchtime and headed towards the Port Authority bus terminal where I had to get the bus to the Metlife Stadium, which is in New Jersey, not New York City, and over an hour away from the Big A. I arrived far too early at the bus terminal and had to wait quite a while for the first bus out, which headed to the Metlife Stadium around 3.30pm, and this bus would only leave once it was full with supporters like me.

I arrived at the bus terminal before 3pm and there were not many people waiting, so I just wandered around the bus station for a while and looked in a few shops, just to kill some time.

I wanted to get to the stadium around five as I was meeting a guy I had made contact with many months ago on a random New York Jets fans forum. Joe Carlson was the very first person who showed any kind of interest in my tour, and this was at the time the tour was just a figment of my crazy imagination. Nothing was booked, the schedule was not even out and it was all fantasy at this point in time.

Joe invited me to his L7 tailgate long before I even knew what a tailgate was, and I always remembered his kindness, which meant a lot to me. Joe and I kept in touch all through my tour, so I was really looking forward to meeting him in person, as well as his fellow Jets fans at his beloved L7 tailgate.

I arrived at the L7 tailgate on a miserable cold and damp November evening, but this was instantly forgotten by the incredibly warm welcome I got from my new good buddy Joe and his gang at the L7 tailgate. I was very much welcomed and received like a long lost friend by the entire group, and I was made to feel very much at home by everybody straight away. A truly great bunch of people.

Its moments like this that gave me a huge lift on my tour. I had been on a bit of a downer after Buffalo, and I get so touched, and extremely grateful when people treat me nice and look after me, like the L7 gang did. I really felt a strong bond with Joe and his friends, just as I had with "Who Dey" in Cincinnati, as well as Tim "The Captain" Young and "Jay Buc", with their awesome Bucs fans in Atlanta.

I've mentioned before, my "love language" according to my ex- girlfriend is receiving, and she is totally right. I don't mean gifts or money (but that always helps!), what I like to receive more than anything is other people's interest in ME and what I am doing, or trying to achieve. I got this from all of my Superfan friends, and this is exactly why these people are so special to me, and they always will be. They showed me unconditional friendship.

I have so much to thank my Superfan friends for, as those guys really kept me going, especially in times of intense frustration when going home would have been a very easy option indeed. Something I found amazing was that all the

Superfans I have mentioned so far, and the ones coming up in the next half of the season, practically all knew each other, and some are long time great buddies, even though they are all spread out across the whole country. I feel very honoured and lucky I am associated with or connected to a special group of wonderful people, crazy characters and very passionate football fans and I am very proud to call these people my friends.

I am usually very easily pleased, I don't generally ask people for anything, I mostly go with the flow, I don't really make any real demands and I never throw tantrums (well, only the odd one if I'm pushed too far, which is rare). I'm extremely laid back, too much for one ex girlfriend as she used this reason to dump me!

But I can only be what and who I am, so when people take an interest in my ventures or adventures, especially my music, or my tour, it gives me a huge lift, and I feel I'm doing something worthwhile. So being interested in ME means the world to me, and these Superfans were.

This trip was about me trying to establish a new career in music, it had nothing to do with generating a fist full of dollars, although that comes with success, and would be kindly accepted if this ever materialised. All I have ever wanted is a "chance" to show the world I can write a nice song, and this tour was a vehicle for me to travel around the US and try to get ANY kind of breakthrough, especially in the worlds of rock or country music.

Back to the Metlife Stadium, and a very entertaining and funny moment for me was watching Joe do his "war cry" speech to his L7 congregation before the game. This lovely placid man turned into some kind of Viking Warrior with his beard and his booming voice screaming out to his fellow soldiers, rallying them to cheer on their heroes. This was the first time I had seen this since CY had done the same thing at his tailgate in Dallas and it was brilliant to experience.

It was a call to arms, to beat the opposition, the dreaded local New York state rivals the Buffalo Bills, where I had just been, and this was a pretty important game in the season for the Jets fans. After Joe's amazing performance, a round of shots were sunk, and we started to get ready for the game.

I got introduced by Joe to a guy named Tyson, who did a regular podcast on a local internet radio station. Tyson loved the idea of my tour, so we did an interview in the car park right next to the L7 tailgate. It was great, spontaneous and for a moment I felt like things were looking up for a change ?????

Game time was coming and I never had a ticket, but then my guardian angel surfaced yet again at a tailgate, as Joe had kindly offered me a ticket sitting next to him, and he even gave it to me for free. What a lovely thing to do, and I always get touched by people's generosity to me. Thanks a million Joe.

Joe and I sat high up in the nose bleeds in the magnificent Metlife stadium, just where I love to sit. I had been to the Metlife stadium two years before to watch my Dallas Cowboys beat arch rivals the New York Giants with the last kick of the game. That game was also in November, but on that occasion, it was a whole lot colder than it was on this night, thank god!

As ever I was looking forward to the game, I knew it was going to be hard for the Jets, and I so wanted the Jets to win, for the sake of Joe and his L7 tailgaters.

On this occasion the two teams changed the way they normally wore there outfits/kits, which was different for me to visualise, as they were all one colour. I'm sure it symbolised something, I can't think what?, but it looked very strange to me, and this was something I would see again when I got to the game in St Louis, a game in which I described as watching the teams dress as " Mustard Vs Ketchup"!! This game looked more like "Broccoli Vs Tomato!!

Both teams had had an inconsistent start to the season and this was always going to be a tough and very difficult game to call. Another huge reason for the Jets fans to want to win this game was because of the return of their old head coach Rex Ryan, now the coach of the opposing Bills, which added an extra incentive for both teams to win this massive rivals game.

It wasn't the best of games, as the Bills took an early lead after a fumble by the Jets, and the game ended 12-3 at half time. It was great sitting with Joe, watching him run every play, catch every ball and scream at every decision. Joe showed great passion and this was something I always loved to see.

The second half got gradually worse for Joe and his Jets, as the Bills extended their lead to 22-3, as the Jets could not seem to keep hold of the ball. But then came the comeback. The Jets scored two touchdowns in quick succession, and as the game clock approached the last seven minutes, the score was now 22-17, so it was game on.

The atmosphere was electric, Joe was going mad, and so was I, especially when the Jets got the ball back for what looked like their last chance saloon, late on in the final quarter. If the Jets scored, they would take the lead for the very first time in the game.

The Jets got within five yards of the end zone and they now had a crucial 4th down. It was so exciting and we were screaming the Jets on at the top of our voices as we were witnessing a magnificent comeback, and this would have been a great ending to a brilliant night at the Metlife if only the Jets could make this vital match clinching play.

OH NO! Sadly the Jets just came up short with the 4th down as the Bills defense held out. FCUK! I was so gutted, but as you can imagine, not half as much as Joe. I really felt for him as I could see how much it meant for his beloved Jets to beat their rivals the Bills, and to be honest, they should have.

This was a massive game and a critical loss for the Jets at this stage of the season, as they eventually missed out on the plays off by just one game, this bloody one, and I was there to see it! Sorry Joe.

After meeting Joe, a small part of me became a Jets fan, as it did with about another fifteen teams after meeting all their Superfans, so I now have a small holding or interest in almost twenty different NFL teams in total!!!!

I said goodbye and a big thank you to Joe, and I attempted to make a quick exit, with the outside chance of getting back to Brooklyn to watch the Bonobo gig. This plan was immediately quashed when I saw the massive queue for the bus back to NYC. BOLLOCKS!!

I did want to go to see Bonobo but I always knew I never really stood much of a chance, as I was just too far away from Brooklyn being at the Metlife stadium in New Jersey, well over a hour away.

I eventually found the end of the queue, and boy was it a long one. It was now around midnight and there were hundreds of people in front of me, and the queue was moving at a snail's pace, probably slower. I must have waited for more than an hour until I got on the bus, and I was absolutely freezing my nuts off! It was November, after midnight and I was going nowhere fast, not quite the best combination to be in.

I finally boarded the bus, after what seemed a lifetime of waiting in arctic conditions, and as expected, we got stuck in a bit of traffic and I eventually arrived back in NYC about 1.30am. This was before I had to ride on two subway trains to Brooklyn, so I must have got to bed around 2.30am.

My final day in New York I decided to go to a museum I had read about which was showing an exhibition about Superheroes, something I like and wanted to see. I got all the way across Manhattan near Central Park, only for the museum to be closed for a private function. SHIT! I was totally gutted as I really wanted to see it, and this was my only chance to before I left town.

It was raining this day, so walking around was not much of an option, so I went inside a big museum whose name I cannot remember, but I walked in and sat down just to keep out of the rain.

There was another museum that caught my attention, and this was the "Tenement" museum. This museum tells the story about the poor immigrants who came to New York back in the day of the "Gangs of New York" period, and it was something that interested me and I wanted to know more about.

Again I caught the subway across Manhattan to the Lower East Side of town and I went into the Tenement museum. I was horrified to learn that the entrance fee was twenty five dollars, plus tax. FCUK THAT! twenty quid to go to a museum? bloody hell. So I bailed out of that one and went for a coffee and looked online to see if I could find anything interesting I can do for a few less bucks.

I finally ended up in the "National Museum of the American Indian", near Battery Park, the park on the southern tip of Manhattan Island which has the view of the statue of Liberty in the distance.

I've always been interested in knowing more about what happened to the Native American Indians, and I did learn a bit from a previous visit to a museum in Washington DC and the chat I had with my friend at the bus stop in Nashville regarding President Jackson and his contribution to the terrible "Trail of Tears".

This particular museum was massive and there was so much to read. I spent a few hours looking around, and I never knew there were so many different American Indian tribes. It was very interesting and sad at the same time as these poor people really had hard times, back in the day.

When I was a kid, I always thought the Cowboys were our saviours from the dreaded horrible nasty tomahawk wielding Indians. The Cowboys were always perceived as the good boys, gun slinging heroes to the villains the Indians were portrayed as, especially with their war paint, wobbling war cries, amazing head dresses and bow and arrows. How wrong was that?, thanks Hollywood.

These poor people were robbed of their land, cheated and lied to by many people of power and basically treated worse than dirt, just like the African slaves were. It was painful to read and it was a truly terrible time in American history.

I wandered around a bit more of New York, but only seeing stuff I had already seen, so I headed back to my hostel on the subway and got ready for my first flight in over six weeks the following day, as my adventure was taking me south to the much warmer climate of Florida.

My Cowboys were up next and looking to stop their terrible losing run of five consecutive games without their star man Tony Romo. I was heading to Tampa, the home of the Buccaneers. Surely my Cowboys can beat the Bucs????

Stadium-19
Raymond James Stadium
Tampa Bay Buccaneers

I landed into Tampa and headed across town to yet again, the only hostel in town, a hostel called "Gram's Place". I jumped on a bus which took about an hour, and I arrived into East Tampa and headed to the hostel. As I got off the bus, as usual at the wrong stop, it was now dark, so I had a look at Google maps on my phone, and I had about a fifteen minutes walk to the hostel.

I was fully aware I was not in exactly the best part of town, and walking around with a big backpack over my shoulders down a long dark street with nobody around, I stood out like dogs balls and I was asking for trouble, so I trotted off to find my new fixed abode with my radar well and truly up.

"Gram's Place" had a very bohemian vibe, as well as a musical theme after the musician Gram Parsons. It was a very quirky hostel and I loved it the moment I arrived. The layout was quite unusual for a hostel as it was basically a huge converted house, and it reminded me of a kind of tree house on the ground, if that makes sense, all wooden and a little bit like a scrap yard, with clutter everywhere. The best thing for me was that Gram's Place had a very small but sweet jacuzzi (spa bath), and a tiny roof terrace, just enough space for a few people to sit, read and sunbathe.

As soon as I arrived, I met the owner and I checked into my six bed dorm. My bed was on the bottom bunk, practically on the floor, but I didn't mind as I had stayed in far worse places than this. I dropped off my things in my dorm and I went straight to the communal area and started to chat with a few of the other guests, and to see if anybody was up for a night on the town.

It was a Friday night, I had been travelling all day, and I wanted a few beers, and it took me all of five minutes to pull a crowd of us together, we all got changed and out we went to the main drag in Tampa where all the action was.

I met an English guy named Steve, and in his own words, he was an entrepreneur, (of what?, only he knew), and apparently according to him he was very successful, or so he bragged. Good for him I thought, as I like to hear people are doing well.

Steve said he was coming out, then he wasn't, then he was, then he wasn't, so I gave him a very quick ultimatum, "Listen Steve, I leave in ten minutes, with or without you, so make up your bloody mind and stop fcuking me about". He got the message and he eventually came, especially after he heard that a couple of the pretty girls were coming.

A very kind old lady, who was a guest at the hostel, offered to give us a lift to where all the action was. A lovely gesture, so off we went.

Steve, who was about 45 and bald as a coot, made it pretty obvious to me straight away he was completely full of hot air, but he seemed like he would be a good laugh on a night out, so I decided to give him a chance to prove it, or the benefit of the doubt.

We were meeting a few of the other guests from the hostel

at a bar/club they had somehow managed to get free tickets for, in the funky street we got dropped off at by our new bestie and Uber cab driver, the old girl from the hostel.

I didn't want to jump straight into the club we were meeting the rest of the group in because I wanted to see what else was on offer in this area of action before we plotted up, so Steve and I walked up and down the long street full of bars, restaurants, fast food joints, strip clubs, gay bars and cafe's until we decided to go into the club where the other people from the hostel were.

I can't remember the name of the bar we went into, but I could hear the banging dance music, something in which is usually my biggest nightmare and enough to make me go somewhere else, as we were in the queue outside the door. But he who dares wins I thought, so a few deep breaths and ten bucks lighter, in we go.

I offered Steve a drink, a beer I expected, but he ordered some fancy concoction with an umbrella and a set of golf clubs hanging from it!, which cost me another ten bucks. Fuck this, I thought, I don't even know this dude and I already thought he was taking the piss, something which he underlined perfectly when he returned to the bar to get round two, as by now his sophisticated palate changed dramatically from his "penis colada" to the same cheap beer as I was pouring down my throat, when it was his time to flash the cash.

See, I have morals and respect, I don't do shit like this. Steve kept going on about how well he is doing, but he was a tight as a bulls ass, so I dumped this fcukwit as quickly as I met him.

The best thing about this bar were the fantastic and very sexy dancers, not quite the strippers I had wished for, which would have been nice, but gorgeous pole dancers, very easy on the eye indeed while cutting their shapes up on the tables.

By this time I was now struggling with what was becoming a real pain in the ears (anagram of arse again!), the very loud constant remix beat. That very annoying metronomic drumming sound that drives me round the bend! Actually, some of the music was eventually not that bad, as I don't mind the odd bit of drum and base or trance music, so I lasted a couple of hours. I even had a little dance, so I must have been well pissed!!!!!

The next day I was attempting to go to check out the local beach, but it was about a hour away, and very hard to get to on public transport. As luck had it, there were a few people from the hostel going there for a sunbathe and a swim in the sea, but sadly for me there was not enough room in the car, so I could not go with them. Doh! As the weather was pretty overcast, I was not overly concerned, so I stayed at the hostel and had a lazy day on my laptop updating my website.

I quite enjoyed these lazy days, as I was usually rushing around like a nutter, doing all kinds of weird and wonderful things, whichever town I was in, as I always had the curiosity to visit as many of the places of interest as I could and I did not want to miss a thing or an experience in the very limited time I had in many of these cities.

I actually did miss something in Tampa, a major tourist attraction I cannot believe I missed, Busch Gardens. If this idiot would have know this place even existed, I would have been over there like a bullit out of a gun. I always googled "Things to do" in all the places I visited. This one must have slipped through my usual very tight net. GUTTED! On reflection, I would have loved to have gone there. I will return.

Sunday was gameday and my Dallas Cowboys were in town. As I've said many times before, I always enjoyed all the games I attended, but watching my Cowboys always gave me that extra level of excitement. I put my Jason Witten 82 shirt on, and my Cowboys cap, so off I went to the bus stop to go to my nineteenth game of the tour.

As I waited at the bus stop for my ride, its amazing how much abuse I took from passing cars, beeping their horns, insults screamed, (which I loved), hand signals etc. etc, obviously as I was wearing my Cowboys colours and they were playing the local team, the Tampa Bay Buccaneers.

Before I came to America, I had no idea how disliked the Cowboys are by the other NFL team's fans. It was something I had to endure quite a lot, especially when I had my colours on, but this never bothered me too much as sometimes the banter was great fun, but sometimes it was far from that.

I was meeting my friend, massive Bucs fan and truly nice guy "Jay Buc", whom I had met in Atlanta, and he invited me to his tailgate named "Buc Party". I took two buses from my hostel to get to the Raymond James Stadium, the home of the Bucs and I eventually found my way to Jay Buc's tailgate.

I arrived at the tailgate and it was great to see so many familiar faces. My Cowboys friends Julio "Prime" Marin, Shelby Kelly (I think) and a few more guys and girls who names I cannot remember were there, and Jay Buc welcomed me with open arms, as did all of his amazing Buccaneers friends.

Attending these tailgates was one of the most special things I experienced on my entire tour. Here is this stranger of an English guy, dressed as a Dallas Cowboys tight end, at a tailgate party mainly full of opposition fans, and they treat me like one of the family. Its amazing, and something I've never seen anything like before over the many years I have attended games at English soccer matches.

Jay Buc's tailgate was brilliant, the food was amazing, drinks everywhere, banging music, and a pirate ship in the middle. The vibe was brilliant and I was loving it.

One of Jay Buc's buddies climbed aboard the ship and started a performance of one of his amazing raps, with the audience participating in the chorus. It was awesome and the atmosphere was electric, and this rap was something I expected to hear inside the stadium as it was brilliant. But when I spoke to the rapper afterwards, I found that he was sailing on exactly the same boat (another coincidental pun) as me in trying to get his songs heard by the right people in the music industry. As we talked, I could see how badly he wanted to succeed with his music, and I really felt for him as he was great, and I realised we were both singing from the same hymn sheet and nobody was hearing our hymms. Amen!

I loved Jay Buc's tailgate, he was the perfect host and he even helped me to get a ticket for the game. Thanks Jay. So off we went in the beautiful Florida sunshine, but very humid conditions to the stadium.

The Raymond James stadium is quite different to a lot of the NFL stadiums I attended over the season. Not one of my favourites to be fair, more like an English soccer stadium, square with open corners. I had been used to big round stadiums, dome's with very high ceilings, so this was a little different, but I still liked it, especially the pirate ship at the opposite end of the field.

My seat for this game was very low down near the end zone, not my favourite place to park my bum, but this was a 140 dollars ticket I got for 70, so I ain't complaining. I much prefer the nosebleeds (top tier), as the view is so much better of the whole field. Its amazing for me to hear most fans prefer to be close to the pitch, but I personally don't like watching too much on the screens, as I can do this in a bar for free.

Before the game started, loads of tee shirts were fired or projected from plastic guns by gorgeous looking Bucs girl into the crowd, and I was incredibly lucky enough to catch one with my old wide receiver hands, pushing away three kids and two women in the process!! (only joking!) When I returned to my hostel that night, I gave it to the owner, and as he was a Bucs fan, he was well pleased.

The Cowboys were still without their injured first choice Quarterback Tony Romo, and they had lost every game in his absence since I saw the Cowboys win in Philadephia on week two, the very game Romo got injured.

No disrespect to the Bucs, but this was a game I expected my Cowboys to win, with or without Romo. Surely we had more in the tank than this one man? WRONG! What a game, for all the wrong reasons, and this would be by far the worse game I had seen up to then, and it would be for the rest of the season.

I won't bore you with any details, as this game doesn't deserve any time wasted on it, and even if I wanted to, there are basically no words for me to write as it was that bad. Half time was 6-3 to Dallas, with all the points coming from field goals. The second half was no better, as I mentioned, I sat low down and close to the end zone and I can clearly remember Dallas did not get any closer than 30 yards to my end zone, FOR THE ENTIRE GAME.

It was a terrible performance from my Boys, and with a minute to go on the clock and both teams looking rubbish, the Bucs ran in the only touchdown to win the game 13-6. I was so disappointed, not because we had lost our 7th game on the spin, but we looked like a team without a leader, a ship without a captain, a car without petrol, a one trick pony. Without Romo, this team is doomed.

I struggle to understand how a franchise as huge as the Dallas Cowboys seems to have all its eggs in one basket, or it's whole future on one player. Surely a back up quarterback can be found who is a better option than the ones we currently have? Come on Jerry, liven up!

I returned to Jay Buc's tailgate after the game to drown my sorrows and all the Bucs fans were obviously over the moon, screaming, cheering, dancing and celebrating their win over my Boys. I was honestly happy for them as they are my friends, and as the Bucs don't win very often, well not that particular season anyway, so good luck to the Bucs, especially their amazing loyal fans who really are amazing.

I met a guy named Lowell Moore at the tailgate who runs an organisation called "What a Fan", which looks into the lives of fanatical and passionate sports fans all over the world. Lowell loved my story, so we arranged to meet in Orlando a few days later and chat about a plan to try to get me some publicity in the media. I was so grateful to Lowell, again just for showing his interest in me and my adventure.

Lowell was amazing, as he never promised me anything he could not deliver. But what he did say he would try to do, he did, and for this I will always be so very grateful to him.

After the tailgate, I said goodbye to my friends Jay Buc and Prime and I headed back to my hostel across the other side of town.

I had met a guy when I first arrived at my hostel in Tampa, and he mentioned a potential fishing trip, maybe on Monday, so as I was leaving for Jacksonville on Tuesday, I was well and truly up for going sea fishing, something I have never done before, mainly because I don't exactly have the best sea legs, or belly for the boat ride!!

Sadly I could not find the guy in question, so my plans to go fishing evaporated before I even got my worm out!! Then I found out how expensive it was to hire a boat, and we needed five other people, and I did have three or four people interested, but it never got off the ground or dry land. GUTTED!

Monday was a beautiful sunny day and I went on a bike ride with a nice girl named Phillipa who was working at the hostel. We cycled along a river and into the centre of Tampa for the afternoon and we had a general look around.

That evening was my last night in Tampa and a bunch of us sat around chatting, and we all ended up in the tiny spa/jacuzzi, about six of us.

One of the girls who got in was a French Canadian girl who I thought was absolutely gorgeous. Lovely long dark hair and a body of a mermaid, with the best pair of weapons of mass distraction I'd seen in a long time! What a beauty and what a pair of mods and rockers (knockers). If she was my daughter, I would still be bathing her!!!!

We had a good laugh and a great time that evening and I was now getting ready to leave Tampa for my next stop, which was Jacksonville, but before then I was stopping off to meet up with Lowell Moore in Orlando, to discuss a way to get me some publicity for my tour.

I never quite connected with Tampa, it was not one of my faviuites places I visited, maybe because it is not exactly a place with that much history, or tourist attractions which were within my interests. I would have loved to have gone to Busch Gardens.

I had had a great time at the game with the amazing Bucs and Cowboys fans, but there was not too much else for me to do in the four days I spent here, mainly as I never had a car as usual. But this was fine, as it was a time of relaxation, and I needed this to try to recharge my batteries.

But now I was happy and ready to be moving onto a new adventure in a new city in the stick heat of Florida. The Jags were up next, and a huge highlight of my tour was on the horizon, a personal meeting by invitation only from the king of Jacksonville!

Stadium-20
Everbank Stadium
Jacksonville Jaguars

I left Tampa on the afternoon bus, heading for Orlando to meet with my new friend Lowell. Orlando was two hours from Tampa and three hours from Jacksonville, so it broke up my journey.

Again sadly for me, Orlando had no hostels so I was on the lookout for a cheap motel. Most people go to Orlando for the theme parks, and I did consider going to one, but I never had much time and they are also quite expensive, and I was now spending money like it was going out of fashion! I found a cheap motel online, checked in, and a few hours later Lowell came to pick me up, and we went for a coffee.

Lowell is a top man, who has a lovely wife whom I also met in Tampa at Jay Buc's tailgate. Lowell is very driven and ambitious about his "What a Fan" project, and I'm sure he will make this a resounding success, at least I hope so. Lowell is very well connected to a lot of the fans from many NFL teams, and he informed me he would speak to some of his contacts within his circle, and try to get me some media coverage.

Lowell was one of a very rare few people who promised to try to help me, and actually followed through with his promise by getting an article written on me and my tour in an Orlando newspaper. I was well truly pleased and I will always be very grateful to Lowell as he was true to his word, unlike so many other bullshitters, and this was something that is so very important to me. So many people promised me things that simply dissolved into thin air which upset me immensely. Thank you Lowell, you are a good man, you are my brother and friend for life. I wish you every success with your amazing "What a Fan" project.

Orlando was going to be a very short pit stop, as I was only going to meet Lowell, and I'm very glad I did because I now have another great friend.

I did my research on how I was getting to Jacksonville, and I saw there was an Amtrak train station in Orlando not far from my motel. I'm all over that thank you very much, I thought, so I jumped in a cab to the Amtrak station and I caught my favourite mode of transport to Jacksonville.

Jacksonville was always going to be a special place for me to visit, and I had been looking forward to getting here since I left home. Why? I hear you cry. Well, in the very early days of my planning, one of the first things I did was to try to make contacts at most of the NFL clubs, fan clubs, celebrity NFL fans, eg "Vernon Kaye, Nat Coombes, Neil Reynolds, Kevin Cadle" and many stupid outside of the thinking box random other people I stupidly thought maybe interested in what I was looking to do.

All I needed was to make contact with any one of these people, and maybe a door of opportunity or two could be opened for me, and the snowball effect would elevate me to a new stratosphere. WRONG AGAIN, well not completely.

Sadly for me, none of these people replied to any of my

twitter messages over the next few months, and boy did I try. I spent hours, and days, and even months blitzing social media, with absolutely no response from any of these so called NFL celebrities in the UK.

I could not think of a single reason why any of these "friends in high places" would not be interested in my crazy plans, which at this stage, were still only pipe dreams. I know people are busy and all that, but all I wanted was a response. Is that asking too much? Well, yes it was and to this day, these guys have NEVER got in touch with me, and I'm totally certain they all know exactly who I am, and what I achieved.

I used to live in Putney, a part of West London, a lovely area on the banks of the Thames, so one day as I walked along the river, I gazed across at Fulham Football Club, and yet another crazy or stupid idea came into my head.

The guy who owns Fulham FC, is also the owner of the NFL team in Jacksonville, the Jaguars, so when I got home, I sent a cheeky email to Fulham, and I informed them of my plans to go to all 31 NFL stadiums in one season, and would it be possible to watch a game with the owner of the club, Mr. Shahid Khan, when I got to Jacksonville??

It took about a week or so for Fulham to get back to me and they suggested I contact the Jacksonville Jaguars directly, as they are a completely different entity than Fulham FC, other than the fact they are owned by the same man.

I got that, but it sounded like another blind alley or dead end I was attempting to walk up, but I forwarded the same email

I had sent to Fulham FC to the Jacksonville Jags, and I expected the standard rejection letter I had been slapped around the face with what seemed like ten million times.

It must have been around a month later, when my cellphone beeped in my pocket, and as I looked at the message I had just received on messenger, I could see it was from the Jacksonville Jaguars. Oh, I thought, maybe they are going to send me a tee shirt or some random souvenir. I opened the message and it read " We have sent you an email". That's all it said, and I thought this sounds interesting. I opened the email and read "Hi Dennis, Mr. Khan has invited you to watch a game with him in his private suite and he would be very pleased to meet you when you come to Jacksonville. We have eight home games, which one did you want to attend"? WWOOOWWWWWW!!!!!!

After all my hard work of what I call "pissing in the wind" or random messaging on social media, one email hit the bullseye and boom! I was completely over the moon.

I always thought, if these random emails would somehow make it through the filtration system of managers, management, secretaries, PA's, clubs, etc, and got read by my intended individual, I would have got sooooooo many more offers like this.................I am completely certain. Although I will never know, I assume.

The schedule had just come out, and I now had to find a game which would fit into my route. One game stood out for me, and this was the Thursday night game against divisional rivals the Tennessee Titans on week eleven, not the best game to watch in the world, but I had a few reasons why this had to be the game.

The weekend before this Thursday night game, my Dallas Cowboys would be in Tampa, just up the road from Jacksonville, and on the following weekend my Cowboys were playing in Miami, again just up the road, (well not exactly as it took me nine hours on the train), but all these three games were in Florida and it worked out perfect.

Another reason I chose this particular game, was because I thought the Jaguars had a very good chance of beating the Titans, as both teams are not exactly the best two teams in the league and I wanted the chance to be next to Mr. Khan when his Jaguars won.

When I was working out my schedule, this section of the route was set first, week ten Tampa, week eleven Jacksonville and Miami, then I scheduled the rest around this. I was always going to start in New England as it was the first game of the season and on a Thursday night, and I always wanted to see my Cowboys play in Philadelphia, and I was praying Bradley Cooper was going to contact me after I left him a letter at the back door when he played the Elephant Man in London. I was hoping he would reply to me before the game as I wanted to watch it with him, as I know he is a big Eagles fan and it would have been a great laugh. Call me stupid. Yep, but it worked with Mr Khan, why not Bradley? Sadly, I never did hear from the Elephant man!

The Amtrak train from Orlando arrived into Jacksonville about three hours later and I now had to take two more buses to get to my cheap motel across the other side of

Jacksonville. Yet again, Jacksonville had no hostels, so I rocked up at a cheap and cheerful motel called Super 8.

I took the first bus from the Amtrak station in Jacksonville to downtown, and I noticed immediately from looking out the window I must have been in the poor or bad side of town, from the state of the houses. Rows and rows of grey looking wooden shacks, looking more like a shanty town or ghetto, certainly a place to stay as far away from as possible. It reminded me of the shacks that slaves once lived in, which I had seen in all the films.

I changed buses downtown, and I caught the second bus south across the river and near to my new home for the next four days, the wonderful Super 8 motel.

The Super 8 was very similar to the motel I had stayed in while I was in Orlando, and it looked like the kind of motel you see in the movies where villains who had just robbed a bank stay, or pimps and prostitutes hang out. But I didn't mind, I had been in far worse places than this.

I checked in, then went straight out to get something to eat, some local food in a nice restaurant I was recommended. It was quite a long walk along a dangerous motorway and it also looked like a sketchy area, a place I would not have walked around at night.

I had a nice room at the Super 8, basic but comfortable, a nice big bed, a telly (TV), and nobody else to keep me awake with their snoring. I was content, as it was a nice break from the noise and crowds of the many people I had shared with in my many dorm rooms, which to be honest, I had been getting very used to.

That evening I ordered a take away Chinese meal, got it delivered to my room and watched telly in bed, lovely. The next morning, I got up after a good night sleep and went for a wander around downtown Jacksonville.

That day I had arranged an interview on a US podcast, with a guy who's name I wished I could remember, and when he called me, I was sitting in a lovely coffee shop in the centre of Jacksonville. We chatted away for about half a hour, and the man asked me many interesting questions about me and my tour. He actually asked me all the questions I wanted him to ask, about my planning of the tour, my objectives, my music, my favourite stadium and city so far, best game, and so on.

It was a brilliant interview, just like talking to one of my good friends, we laughed a lot and I was very so happy as to how it went, I absolutely loved it. It was such a contrast and incomparable to the four live radio interviews I did with Talksport and Radio 5 live from the UK. I will come to them later.

While I was in the coffee shop, I overheard two guys talking with English accents, so I asked them where they were from and what they were doing in Jacksonville. They told me they were both journalists and they worked for the BBC, so I mentioned my tour and they were very interested, so we arranged to meet up the next day.

I was thinking maybe the BBC connection could be of help, but as usual, I was barking up the wrong tree and I never saw the guys again.

Jacksonville is not exactly the kind of city people visit to be a tourist, I'm sure there are interesting things there, but not quite as many tourist attractions as most other cities, so I never really got up to much in my time in Jacksonville, other than watch the game.

I hear there are some amazing beaches in this part of northern Florida, but sadly in my time in Jacksonville, the weather was more favourable to ducks than to sun worshippers.

The following morning, my run of good luck changed and disaster struck from absolutely nowhere. I was sitting down in my motel room and on my laptop doing my social media and website, and as I attempted to stand up and stretch, something went "ping" in my lower back. I've suffered a little bit over the years with a lower back problem, but nothing too major, but as I slowly attempted to rise from leaning over my laptop for a few hours, crash bang wallop.........................pain!

I knew in an instant I was in trouble, big trouble, as my back simply locked like a bank's vault and I could not even open my legs to walk. It felt like my brain and legs were not connected and on a different wavelength, and my legs were not getting the signal to move. All I could do was pigeon steps, a couple of inches at a time, this wasn't good at all and I was in a huge pickle/situation, especially with my big game coming up TONIGHT.

I spent the next few hours face down on my bed, scared to

death, and pondering over how on earth am I going to attend a game with Mr. Khan and his friends in his private suite, as I felt like I was paralysed from the waist down. What great timing.

At this point, I had absolutely no chance at all of going to this game, it was a major struggle just to get dressed, especially trying to put on my socks. I really was in trouble and worried bigtime, as my legs were completely stubborn and they made the decision we were going nowhere.

What the fcuk have I done?? I struggled to a local pharmacy and I got some pain killers and something to rub into my back. Actually standing upright was not too bad, but walking was, bending was impossible and very painful and scary.

This was always my biggest nightmare on my many travels over the years, being ill or crocked while being away from home. Luckily I have not experienced much of it, but this was different, I really was suffering. I've had food poisoning a few times, and felt terrible, but that usually only lasted a painful day or night, but this was different.

After taking the tablets, having a hot shower, and rubbing my back in, I did get some well deserved relief from the previous 4-5 hours of agony. How did this bloody happen? I was just sitting down, it wasn't as if I had just been tackled by JJ Watt or Clay Matthews!

I left the motel around 4pm for the 7.30 kick off and I jumped on the bus to downtown Jacksonville in what was like a typical English winters evening, dark, grey with that very fine rain where you don't know you are soaked, until you are soaked. And I got soaked, even in my waterproofs.

As I walked to the Everbank stadium in the gloomy conditions, I was in a kind of negative state of flux mentally. Of course I was looking forward to meeting Mr. Khan and watching the game in luxury, but my back was totally fcuked and I was worried it would give up on me at any moment.

I entered the stadium and I was taken to the VIP's area where I waited to be forwarded to Mr. Khan's private suite where we would watch the game. There were about four or five huge private suites, and I was lucky to be in the one Mr. Khan would be in for most of the time during the game.

My first impression was disappointment as my understanding of a private box was 8-10 people, not the 100 or so who were in this area. But I got over this minor detail immediately after I was introduced to Mr. Khan, and I was given a lovely golden name tag badge with my name on and The WrongShapedBalls Tour.

Mr. Khan is a very powerful man indeed in Jacksonville, he has come from a very modest background and upbringing, originally from Pakistan, and is extremely wealthy after building up his empire by hard work. A self made billionaire, and good luck to him.

Mr. Khan made me feel very welcome from the moment we met, and we chatted away quite a bit before the start of the game. I noticed a lot of business people were in the suite and it looked to me like most of them were a little bit intimidated by Mr. Khan, and were a little apprehensive to approach him. But not this boy, we chatted away like old mates, about the NFL, bringing his beloved Jags to my home town, as well as his soccer/football team Fulham.

At this time, Fulham, Mr Khan's London soccer team, had just fired their manager and I asked him who the new boss would be. If he told me, I was going to call my brother Paul and tell him to go and put as much money on the name Mr. Khan had given me ASAP!

Mr. Khan said he was flying to London in the morning for a meeting with the Fulham board to discuss the new candidates, so he never gave me a name. Steve Clarke was hot favourite in the betting, and I asked Mr. Khan about him. Mr. Khan made it clear Steve Clarke was not getting the job, and he never did.

I said to Mr. Khan, "Can I make a suggestion"? "Of course" he replied. "In my opinion, employ an English manager, don't employ a foreigner as they are just there for the money and they don't show as much passion for the team as a local Englishman who has history or a connection to Fulham FC would". "OK" he said, I will take that on board. A month later Fulham employed a Serbian named Slovisa Jokanovic who almost took Fulham down to the 3rd tier of English football. I was ignored and Fulham are now in a right old mess, even more so than when the Serbian arrived. What do I know?

I really liked Mr Khan, he was very nice and friendly towards me. The food in the suite was incredible, I could have anything I wanted, and any drink, the full royal treatment.

The game started and I had the most amazing view from the private suite, right on the 50 yard line, and right in the centre of the pitch. I stood with Mr. Khan for a fair bit of the game, and he was totally focused, concentrating and playing every play. He really is passionate about his team and it was wonderful for me to see this at first hand.

Both teams were wearing the all same coloured outfits in which I'm not much of a fan of, so today it was sky blue against gold. Come on the golds!!!

The game started, and as expected it was far from a classic against two struggling teams, and it showed as four field goals were the only score in the game and it was 6-6 at half time.

As I was stuffing my face with as much of the delicious food as I could, I recognised a guy who was standing near me, a familiar face which was confirmed when I saw the name on his golden name badge, as it was the American professional golfer Brandt Snedeker. I introduced myself as an English caddie who was going to all 31 NFL stadiums, he seemed impressed and he was really friendly. He told me he was playing in a tournament a few hours away and he was here at the game to hit some shots from the roof of one of the stands, to a target in the middle of the pitch at half time.

At the time of me writing this section, Snedeker is playing in the Masters at Augusta, and I have had a two quid bet on him. Go Sneds!!! On my final draft, I can report that Sneds came nowhere, and was last seen working on a driving range somewhere in Oklahoma!!

I decided to go for a walk around the stadium at half time as I wanted to see the two famous swimming pools at one end of the Everbank Stadium. I found them and they were amazing, and so were the chicks with hardly anything on standing in the pools! There was more silicone and botox in those pools than in a Harley Street surgery!

I soooo wanted to go into the pools and have a few pictures taken with these stunning birds, (which of course I did, the pics I mean) but as I never had any swimming trunks on, and something which normally would not have stopped me, I almost went in in my underpants. I eventually decided not to go in, basically because I never had a towel, and I would have looked stupid in my white pants, which incidentally, show off far too much once they are wet!

I had an access all area's pass so I could go anywhere in the stadium I wanted to, and of course, I did. I even had a massive argument with some asshole fan, a season ticket holder who screamed at me to get out of his section. All I did was to look over his balcony onto the field, nothing more and he aggressively told me to get out of HIS area. I eventually did, but only after telling this ignorant pig to go and fcuk himself! What a rude bastard.

I watched my new friend Mr Snedeker and a few other pro golfers hit balls into the centre of the pitch for some kind of charity, and then I continued my walk round the Everbank Stadium.

The swimming pool area was a bit too much for me to see at a NFL game. It was a novelty which probably brings in a lot of money for the club, and a great idea to generate an extra income by Mr. Khan, but I thought this section was a cross between a spa and a nightclub, and belonged to the "beautiful people". Obviously these people had far too much money, paid for almost certainly by daddy, and mainly frequented by fake football fans, more like high society boyz and galz, and whom most of the time were not even watching the game.

But good luck to them, they are not my kind of people and I could not imagine being in this section at all, I would much rather be with my Superfan buddies, real fans who show incredible passion for the games and their teams, people like "Who Dey, Cannonball, Josh and the Bolt Boys, Jay Buc, Burnt River Bob, the Cleveland gang and many more amazing fans, not people who are at the stadium to swim or party, especially when the game is in progress, I find this totally disrespectful.

I returned to Mr. Khan and his private suite as the second half started, and in the third quarter the first touchdown was scored......by the Titans. AARRRGGHHH!!

I watched Mr. Khan grimace at every missed tackle, block and attempted pass, he really was fully involved in the game, he was practically playing in it!

The fourth quarter started and the game was 13-9 to the Titans, so the game was still very much on. The Jags had the ball and they made a great play, when one of the running backs broke through and run almost the entire field to the five yard line from the Jags own twenty yard line. Mr. Khan was going mad, jumping up and down like a real fan, just like the rest of us.

Then the Jags scored what turned out to be the winning touchdown, with a throw from Quarterback Bortles and Mr. Khan turned to me and hit me with probably the greatest high five I would ever receive in my life. My decision to choose this game worked out perfectly, and I was so happy I was standing next to Mr Khan when his team had won. It was a surreal and very special moment for me and one of the highlights of my incredible tour.

After the game ended, I left Mr. Khan alone to give him the chance to talk to some of the other people in the room, as I had almost had him to myself for most of the game, so I thought I better at least share him with the other hundred or so people in the private suite who never got near him during the game!!!

One person I got talking to was a big noisy American guy named Don Dovey. We clicked immediately and he constantly took the piss out of my English accent.

Don used to play for the Jacksonville Jaguars and he was recognised by most of the people in the room, but not me, I had no idea who he was. Maybe he liked that because he very quickly became my new bestie. Don kept punching me on the arm, and quite hard too, and I clearly remember saying to him, "Don, seriously, If you were not so big, strong and good looking, I would smack you right in the fcuking face"!! He laughed out loud.

Don and I really did get on well in the few hours we spent together, the banter was brilliant and sometimes full on, from both sides. The C word was used a lot, mostly from him, but only in the nicest possible way, if there is one! Don even gave me a lift home back to my Super 8 motel.

I remember Don telling me in the car that he is very well known in Jacksonville and if the cops stopped him, they would recognise him straight away, and as he had been drinking maybe more than he should have to be driving, he could be in big trouble, and at this point, we were going around in circles in downtown Jacksonville trying to find my poxy motel.

Don even offered me a bed for the night in his house on the beach, even though he was leaving early in the morning for a flight out of town. "Don't worry" he said, "My wife and daughter will look after you". What a legend.

I really liked Don, I would love to see him again, as we really did have a great laugh in the very brief time we were together.

Don mentioned he would be at the Superbowl in Santa Clara and I did try to stay in touch with him on Facebook, and for a while we did, but like a lot of my other contacts, he faded into the background. Nevertheless, a top top man.

I said goodbye to Mr. Khan and his PA, who had helped set up my meeting, and I thanked them so very much for an incredible experience, something I would never forget in a million lifetimes.

Don finally dropped me off, and I was relieved to be back at my motel, as my back was absolutely killing me. I was so pleased I had managed to make it through this fantastic evening, when earlier in the day, I thought I had absolutely no chance at all.

The next morning I was planning to leave Jacksonville for Miami, but I had not yet booked a ticket. As I woke up, and tried to get out of bed, I knew straight away it was going to be impossible for me to carry my heavy backpack, as my back had locked up again and was fcuked.

I managed to stagger to the reception desk to inform the guy I would be staying for another day, and a day I would spend most of facedown on my bed. I just couldn't move, as my back had gone into spasm and seized up completely, and I must admit, I was more than a little concerned. How long was this going to continue?

This was one of the lowest times on my trip, as there's nothing worse than being unwell when you are away from home, and for a couple of days, I really did suffer.

But then completely out of the blue, a miracle happened and my luck changed. I could hardly move, and just rolling over on the bed was a major task, let alone getting up to go to the toilet, which was impossible and probably extremely funny to witness, especially when I had to attempt to wipe my bum!

I remember leaning across the bed to try to grab something, probably my phone, or the TV controls, and as I twisted, I felt and heard a beautiful loud crack, or crunch. I say beautiful, because my back was locked rigid and after this crack, my stiffened back simply let go and released. Oh boy, the relief, or release, it was like the most amazing orgasm!! This wonderful crack was exactly what I was waiting for and immediately my movement was a whole lot better, not completely, but a vast improvement on feeling like the tin man from the Wizard of Oz!

I did eventually manage to leave Jacksonville the next day, and I was so pleased to get out of that bedroom at the Super 8 motel, which felt more like a prison cell or hospital bed after three days of hell.

I took the two buses back to the Amtrak train station, passing the ghetto I had witnessed on my way into Jacksonville, and I boarded the train for the nine hours ride to Fort Lauderdale, for my next game at the Sunlife Stadium, the Miami Dolphins Vs the best team in the NFL, my Dallas Cowboys, and guess who was back for the first time in seven weeks????

Dennis Moss

Stadium-21
Sunlife Stadium
Miami Dolphins

As you know, I do love a train and this was my 3rd ride on the Amtrak and I was as excited on this ride as I was on my first.

I boarded the train and I went to my lovely comfortable seat, and as I sat down, a young American guy in his mid 20's came over to me. "Excuse me, but are you D-Mo"? he asked. "Yes" I replied. "I thought so" he said, "I've been following you on your tour on Facebook". Wow, someone has recognised me. AWESOME!

I was well pleased, as this was what I had wanted from day one, to be followed by the masses, or the NFL fan community from all over the world, and for people to interact with me as I zig zagged across America.

One of my plethora of ideas was to get fans who were following me on social media to ask me all kinds of questions regarding my tour, as I moved from place to place. Asking me things about all the kinds of experiences I was having, not just about the NFL or the games and stadiums I attended, but the cities I visited and their general vibes, other sporting events I watched, what the local people were like, food, weather, nightlife, etc. etc. etc. Then I could paint an overall picture of the whole of the US, from the perspective of an English backpacker. A kind of travel program, and my dream job.

I felt the tiniest piece of fame as I met this fella, again something I have always wanted, and this guy looked very happy to meet me, just like I was in fact a celebrity. (an extremely minor one of course!)

Before the train departed, we both made our way to our seats, but we arranged to meet up for a chat once the train pulled away from Jacksonville, which is exactly what we did.

This guy (sadly, I cannot remember his name), was a big Jaguars fan, and we had a great conversation, mainly about the NFL and my tour, for at least a few hours in the food carriage. This guy was a top man, and I always loved talking to fans about the NFL, as a lot of them were fascinated as to how much this Englishman really does know about their wonderful game. I was probably just as happy, if not more, to meet this guy on the train as he was to meet me. Again, simply because he was just interested in my tour and he told me how much he admired me for what I was doing.

I remember him saying to me I was "living every true NFL football fans dream", and millions of fans around the world would absolutely love to be in my shoes. It was not the first, or last time I would hear this, and it did make me feel extremely humbled, and so very lucky at the same time. But I did inform my friend it was not all "champagne and skittles", or "all rosy in the garden", as most of my posts he saw on social media were the good and happy times, which incidentally hugely outweighed the down sides and times of intense frustration. But these hardships were.........to put it bluntly HARD, and a massive challenge to anybody's patience and human endurance, but these times of struggle are an extremely important part of the whole bigger picture of what makes a great story. I think so anyway!!

It actually would have been very boring if everything had gone to plan all of the time, and most of the time it did, but a few spanners thrown into the works always magnified the great times to another level of greatness, if you know what I mean?!

I did try my best to be super positive at all times on the tour, even in the face of adversity, and I always tried to highlight this in the thousands of social media postings I made, and not over reporting or complaining too much about the hardships. I always saw the hardships as challenges or hurdles to jump, and most of them turned out to be very funny experiences.

I'm not a fan at all of people using social media to whinge about their problems, especially relationships and personal misfortunes. When I go on Facebook, I want to see my friend's good times, smiling faces, positive sides, happy moments and situations or holiday pictures, not people whining about feeling ill, being bored, gossip or negativity. I go on Facebook for entertainment, to make me laugh, see positive things, and I always try to post things people would perceive as being positive or entertaining. Unless it's about politics, which I have to admit, I sometimes do just to annoy the super liberal brigade!

Sitting next to me on the Amtrak train was a lovely old guy who arrived at his seat on crutches, and I could quite obviously see he was not very well at all. We had a nice time chatting together on the 5-6 hours until he left the train the stop before I did.

I noticed he was reading a book called "The book of Mormon". Now this totally non religious Englishman honestly doesn't know what a Mormon really is, believes in, or represents, so I asked him the elephant in the room question. What does a Mormon believe in?

I don't ever judge any person I meet who is religious by their religion, so please don't judge me when I say I am not religious at all, because I think its ALL bullshit. I respect people who have THEIR faith, as long as they don't preach THEIR faith onto me, or tell the world that THEIR faith is the only one which should be followed, and all the other religions are rubbish and THEIR god is the best and the only one, etc. etc., blah, blah, blah bollocks.

To me ALL gods are the same, pointless. They all eventually arrive at the same conclusion, TROUBLE. All gods are invisible, all invented or fabricated, their messages of peace constantly change on a daily basis, words are twisted, manipulated, molded and modified to fit into a convenient situation for its believer and sit nicely with the thoughts of many a so called nutcase, fruitcake, fundamentalist, attention seeker, and a way to brainwash a nation of idiots who need to be led because they have no minds of their own to function normally without some random "know all" who has a "personal agenda", informing his flock of "sheep" that HIS god or "book of horse shit", that incidentally has no cast iron evidence at all any of its subject matter was said, done, exists or existed. This subject is the main contributor to genocide and wars all over the planet, all over the course of time, from the very first moment when mankind formed on this floating chunk of rock, then discovered and developed the talent of using his vocal chords. FACT!

Religion equals to control, power, money and nothing but aggression and complete lies to brainwash uneducated fuckwits (many, not all) who have nothing else in their lives. Most of the religious arguments as to why these warring factions are fighting, causing total devastation in theirs and other countries, some for thousands of years, is so laughably stupid and ridiculous. It's simply incredible to me how any human being that owns a head with just one single braincell cannot see right through this complete nonsense and follow this absolute rubbish. Just my opinion.

Gods are in people's hearts and minds, something I respect completely, and some people need guidance and faith, I get this too, (I think I'm doing alright on my own at the moment thank you very much), but this is something I have no interest in at all because all religion does in my eyes is cause trouble when all religion should represent is peace, and we all know this is not true.

So my new friend and travel buddy on the train attempted to explain to me what the difference between what a Mormon believes in, and what a Christian believes in is. OMG!!! WHAT A PILE OF SHIT!

I remember from school who Brigham Young was, the leader of the Mormons, but I never knew much about him or what he did or represents. But from what I was told by the old boy next to me, was that a guy named Joseph Smith had a vision (yep a vision or a dream) that Jesus Christ walked on the soil of North America. OK, but any normal educated individual would know this simply could not be possible, especially 2000 years ago. How would JC get here from Israel? Maybe he flew over on a giant stork?, or came in a tardis? OK I'm being flippant now, but we all know Jesus never set foot in America, but Mormon people still believe to this very day the vision Mr. Smith had. MADNESS. What a load of complete rubbish.

This kind of thing simply baffles me, especially when so many extremely educated people can be so damn stoopid! But that's religion folks, and this cancer or virus continues to spawn a monster, spreads and moves in many mysterious ways, all over our fcuked up planet.

I decided to get off the train at Fort Lauderdale rather than Miami, as Fort Lauderdale was closer to the Miami Dolphin's Sunlife stadium, where my next game would be.

I had booked into "The Chocolate Hostel" which was one of only four choices I had in Fort Lauderdale, and I knew as soon as I arrived I had made a huge mistake. The hostel reminded me of a prison block, and there were many people hanging around the balconies, smoking, drinking and some probably taking hard drugs, or that's how it felt and seemed, as the smell of ganja (marijuana) was a dead give away.

I checked into my room and I met a young Swedish guy who warned me straight away about another guy in our dorm, who actually lived at the hostel This guy made the other people in the room feel like they were in HIS house, so it wasn't long before I met the guy in question and he seemed alright to me, but a little territorial, as he had lived in this room for about two years.

Why people do this I will never know. Why doesn't he get a flat?, it would probably be cheaper. I did eventually feel the wrath of my new roommate later that night when I attempted to turn off the noisy fan which was right next to my bed, as he quickly jumped out of bed and shouted, "We have the fan on in this room". "Fair enough" I said. So he got his way.

The Swedish guy I had met informed me that a lot of the people at the hostel were in Fort Lauderdale to find work on the expensive and flashy private boats which were docked in the harbour, owned by the multi millionaire community.

That night I was staying up late as I had my first of what would be three live interviews with UK radio station Talksport, and because of the time difference, it would take place well after midnight, so I popped out for a meal at Denny's fast food joint where the grub was very greasy and fattening, and of pretty poor quality, but of course, it was fairly cheap, so I suppose you get what you pay for.

Midnight came, and so did the call I was waiting for, I think it was the Hawksby and Jacobs afternoon show, and I was really looking forward to getting some exposure in the UK for my tour and at the time, my fundraising.

The interview must have lasted no longer than five minutes, and I could have talked for five hours. When it ended, I was so disappointed with most of the boring or pointless questions I was asked, and it was over almost before it started.

I was so pissed off I had stayed up so late and given up a night out, for a second rate interview where I hardly had a chance to get my story, opinion or vision across, or to comment on one of the many great experiences or funny stories I had waiting to share with my UK audience. One good thing came from it, I got over 250 hits in one day on my www.thewrongshapeballs.com website after that interview. A record which stands until this day.

After a shitty night sleep with snoring and a noisy fan getting on my tits, I had arranged to meet my friend Steffon from Nashville, who was arriving into Fort Lauderdale that day, as he was coming with me to the next game, his Dolphins against my Cowboys.

Steffon was staying in a lovely hotel a ten minutes drive up the road from me. When he arrived, I told him what a dump I was staying in, and Steffon immediately told me he had a room with two beds in, and he invited me to stay with him.

I was out of that place faster than Usain Bolt, I packed my stuff away in a frenzy and off we went to Steffon's plush hotel. When we got to the hotel and we unloaded the car, I nearly had a heart attack, as I could not find my small backpack full of all my valuables. I realised immediately I had left it back in the hostel room I had just left, at least I hoped I did, and I did not trust those people with my bag for a second. It would be a great find for some random chancer or a lucky day for a person with little or no money, who would have thought Christmas had come early if they found my little bag of goodies.

Steffon kindly drove me straight back to the shit hole of a hostel, and I nervously knocked on the door of my dorm mate, Mr. Grumpy. If he said my bag was not here, I had no idea what I would have done next. To my intense relief, bringing a massive smile to my face, and a PHEW from my mouth, I was reunited with my bag. I had left it on the sofa as I was rushing around so much to get out of this bloody place asap.

Boy was I relieved. What a plonker (idiot!) I cannot imagine what I would have done if I had lost my bag, as I had everything in it, my laptop, passport, ipod, and my debit cards. Saying I was relieved was an understatement.

I couldn't thank Steffon enough for his patience and for taking me immediately back to the hostel to retrieve my bag, as well as letting me stay in his lovely room, so I paid for all his drinks that night, which was the least I could do for the kindness he had shown to me.

Sunday was game and stadium number twenty, the Sunlife Stadium, the home of the Miami Dolphins. So off we go, in the beautiful Florida sunshine. Steffon and I managed to latch onto a tailgate, and all I can remember about this particular tailgate was meeting a Cowboys fan who is now my Facebook friend, a guy named Lloyd Wheeler, who was with his son. I also met a lovely lady dressed as some kind of fairy or superhero, who was one of the Miami Dolphins Superfans, a very colourful little lady.

Steffon and I managed to get a couple of good tickets for

seventy bucks a piece, a pretty good deal as tickets online were way over a hundred dollars a pop. So off we go to the Sunlife Stadium, and the timing was impeccable.

As soon as we arrived into the stadium the heavens opened and we were hit with a violent rainstorm, as the weather had changed from beautiful sunshine to monsoon conditions in minutes. The funny thing was, a hour earlier as we let Steffon's car, Steffon offered me a poncho to keep us dry, but as we were then in complete sunshine, with not a cloud in the sky, I declined, basically because I did not want to carry it. What a schoolboy error that was!!

Around thirty minutes before the game started, Steffon and I were standing under the cover inside the stadium near to where the food sellers were, watching an incredible thunderstorm heading completely in our direction and which eventually went right over our heads and into the stadium. For me it was great to watch, but now I was freezing cold and soggy, amazing as a hour earlier it was an absolutely glorious day.

The game was now about to start so we headed for our seats, and as the game kicked off, the rain was torrential and we got completely soaked to the bone in minutes.

The good news for me and my fellow Cowboys fans was our hero and main man Tony Romo finally returned to action after missing the past seven weeks through injury, a period in which the Cowboys had lost every game Romo was absent.

The Cowboys looked like a different team with their leader

back, it was a massive boost, and the level of confidence was evident from the very start. But after the first quarter, which was played in terrible gale force windy conditions, making playing the game near on impossible, the scoreline at the end of this period was almost as bad as the weather at 0-0.

Incredibly, as the second quarter started, the sun came out. Hallelujah! Long gone was the driving rain and strong winds, replaced by a beautiful blue sky which stayed with us for the rest of the game. We had now going from soaking to cooking, as the weather turned completely from terrible to glorious.

The sunshine must have given my Cowboys the proverbial "kick up the ass" because they scored two quick touchdowns to take a 14-0 lead. The Dolphins responded with a touchdown of their own, right on the stroke of half time. Oh no!! So it was a 14-7 half time lead for my boys.

Over the many games I attended on my tour, there were sometimes the odd token "assholes" sitting near or next to me in some of the stadiums. I never had a problem with passionate fans, I'm one myself, and most of the "crazies" I have met had been great entertainment and mostly extremely funny. At every stadium I attended, many fans had been tailgating before the games, then enter the stadiums "Brahm's and Lizst/drunk as a skunk", and continue to drink the "devil's water" inside the stadiums, turning "priests into beasts!" and when their teams are winning, these fans are great entertainment, but when their teams are losing, they can be a problem, and a big one. But hey, that comes with the territory and like I say, its usually for the better far more than the worse.

On this occasion, I had an "asshole" sitting right in front of me, obviously totally intoxicated and he kept standing up, only him. Every time he stood up, I could not see, and if I stood up, the fans behind me would not be able to see, so I had a dilemma.

People behind me kept shouting at him to sit down, and this of course made him stand up even more. So I was stuck between a rock and a hard place, and this guy had really been giving my ass a headache. So at half time, Steffon and I decided to move to another area of the stadium, because it was only a matter of time before my already overworked patience finally gave up, and things could have got nasty.

The second half commenced and the Cowboys slowly started to take control, and with Romo back, the Cowboys actually looked like a team, unlike in his absence, which was a shambles. The Cowboys eventually ran out easy winners 24-14 and the seven game losing streak was over. YES! Thank god for that.

As we left the Sunlife Stadium, I was well and truly pleased, especially after the rubbish I had witnessed in Tampa the previous week when the Cowboys had lost and played terribly.

That night Steffon and I went for dinner, had a few drinks, and we watched the Sunday night game at the poolside bar. My Cowboys had beaten Steffon's Dolphins, so I was a pretty happy bunny, but I'm sure Steffon was probably was not on my particular cloud!!

The next day Steffon was leaving, to return to his family home of Orlando and he very kindly gave me a lift down to Miami, about 40 minutes away from Fort Lauderdale. We had a nice breakfast on the beach front, the sun was shining and life was feeling pretty damn good, especially as my Cowboys had stopped the rot, until the next game!

Steffon dropped me off in the South Beach area of Miami, and as I had plenty of time, I wandered around looking for some cheap accommodation and I eventually decided to stay at a hostel called "Bed and Drinks", as it was in a good location and the price was ok, about 25 bucks a night including the bog standard breakfast.

By this time, I had been on the road for over two months, so I decided I needed a break from all the constant travelling, and where better place to chill out than in Miami. WRONG!

When most people think of Florida, and especially Miami, you would normally expect amazing weather, but when I arrived into Miami I noticed as soon as I stepped out of Steffon's car it was extremely windy, I don't mean a slight breeze, I mean a wind strong enough to blow your hat off your head, and it did this to me many times, and chasing that fcuker down the street or into the road with a big backpack on my back and a smaller one on my front was a challenge to say the least, and probably very funny to see for a passing bystander!

I booked into the "Bed and Drinks" hostel for the bog standard two nights, something I always did because if I booked for more than a few days and the room was bad, or maybe the bed was uncomfortable, had shit pillows, people snoring, etc. etc., I would suffer, so this plan always gave me a kind of bailout clause, and a chance to move onto more suitable accommodation if I was staying in town for longer, and in Miami I was here for five nights. As it happened, for reasons I will be telling you shortly, I did in fact move out of this particular hostel after two nights.

My plan while in Miami was to hang out on the beach, relax by the pool, watch sport on TV in the bars, and basically recharge my batteries, so I checked into my room, dropped off my bags and I headed straight for South Beach to hang out with the beautiful people. I wished!

I knew as soon as I walked out of the hostel this was a complete waste of time, as when I got to South Beach it was practically empty. It was soooo windy, the sand was being blow all over the place, making it impossible to sunbathe. FCUK! So off I went for the usual wander around to see if I could find anything of interest.

That evening I plotted up at an Irish bar, had dinner, and watched the New England Patriots beat the Buffalo Bills on the Monday night game. I returned to my hostel and I got chatting to a few of the other guests, a great Nigerian guy named Victor, and a Serbian guy named Abs, so off all three of us went for a wander around the area, and we had a nice evening together.

The following day was a champions league day of soccer, and my Arsenal were playing Dynamo Zagrab from Croatia, so I checked on the Arsenal America website and I found the AA bar in Miami. Victor and Abs were both keen on watching the game too, so we all jumped in a cab, and we crossed the bridge from Miami Beach to downtown Miami and a bar called "Elwoods gastro pub". Arsenal won easily 3-0, so happy days. I had a nice afternoon watching soccer, had a bit of lunch, and enjoyed the company of my two new friends.

On the way back to Miami Beach in the cab, I saw a few signposts indicating there was a casino in town. I mentioned it to Abs, and he was well up for going, so that night, that's exactly what we did, but it wasn't easy finding the bloody thing, a real mission to be honest.

We took a cab to the location we thought the casino was at, and after a 20-30 min drive, we arrived, but in a pretty sketchy looking part of town. We went inside, only to find they had no blackjack or roulette tables, not even a poker room, which was what Abs wanted. All there was were slot machines. SHIT! This was a brand spanking new casino and it wasn't even ready for it's grand opening. So why the fcuk was it open?

Plan B was to go right across the other side of Miami to a different casino, which is what we did. I played some blackjack and roulette, winning just a few bucks, while Abs went and won a few hundred dollars in the poker room, so a good night was had, and it eventually turned out to be worth all the hassle.

Abs and I were staying in the same dorm room at the hostel, which we were sharing with six other people. The second night I was at this particular hostel, I got talking to a guy in the bed opposite me, as there was a fan in the room and it was right next to my bed and just a few feet from my head on the wall beside my bunk, and as it turned, it was making a bit of an annoying noise. So I asked the guy in the next bed if it was OK with him for me to turn the fan off, as it was right next to my face. "No problem" was his reply, "but I must warn you, I snore", he informed me. "Most people do" I mentioned, "so don't worry" I said. "No", he insisted, "I really do snore". OH NO! I thought, here we go again.

I turned off the fan and we all attempted to go to sleep, and this is when the fun started. It didn't take very long at all for my new friend to start snoring in a way I had never experienced before. OMG! I have never heard anything like it, it sounded like a cross between a motorbike being revved up and a lawn mower, it was absolutely incredible, and the loudest I have ever heard by far. FCUKING HELL!

Before going to sleep, the guy had told me he had a condition, or an illness called sleep apnea. Now this is not snoring, it is completely another level on the decibel level of sound, or another notch on the Richter scale compared to the usual bog standard snorer. I wanted the whole world to hear this incredible wall of sound, so I filmed it and put it on Facebook, because no matter how much I tried to explain or prove how loud this snoring was, I could never do this terrible sound any justice just by telling this story, it really was that loud, and torture to be around while trying to sleep.

It never took me very long to get out of bed, I just could'nt stand it, so I went down to the reception to see if I could get a move, and luckily, I got it. Thank God I did, as there was no way it was possible I would have slept a wink with this incredibly offensive noise.

In my opinion, this guy should have got a private room, especially as he knows he has this problem and he would be keeping the whole room awake every single night, while he made his horrendous racket. Very selfish.

Abs and I did have a laugh about this the next morning, as Abs said he only slept because he was so drunk. He must have been bloody legless to sleep through that!

I decided to look for another hostel as I had had enough of "Bed and Drinks". I looked on the Hostelworld website and I found another hostel called "Freehand", which looked much better than the hostel I was at. It was about ten blocks to the north of south beach, but it had a swimming pool, so I decided this was my next home for the following few days.

I took a cab because the weather outside was absolutely terrible, with gale force winds and torrential rain, and honestly, I have never seen rain like it, as my street almost turned into a river and even after just a few seconds of just getting out of the cab and into the hostel, I was soaked. Thirty minutes later, the sky was clear blue and not a cloud in sight, amazing.

But it was still very very windy, and somebody eventually informed me the reason why we were having these extreme winds, was because there was a tropical storm off the coast of Florida, and it was not moving on or going anywhere, just sitting there, probably waiting for me to fcuk off out of Miami before it did!!

During the last few days of my stay in Miami the winds dropped a little, but not much, and this totally ruined what should have been five days of relaxing, sunbathing, frolicking on the beach, looking at all the Miami Beach babes parading up and down in their bikinis and thongs, with all their crown jewels on display. But no, it was'nt meant to be, and I was sooooo disappointed.

Whenever I am in a city, I usually try my best to go to watch a major sporting event if there is one. I had already seen the Chicago Bulls play earlier in my tour in Chicago, and I had seen the Boston Celtics and the LA Lakers on my previous trip to the US, so I thought going to see Miami Heat would make up a perfect set of the big four US basketball teams.

I arrived into Miami on the 23rd of November, and that night the Miami Heat were playing at home, but at the time I had no idea, so a few days later when I looked at their schedule, I saw the next two Heat games were being played away from Miami, and their next home game was on the 30th of November, the day after I left Miami. GUTTED!

I would have loved to have gone to that game, and it was against the Boston Celtics, who actually won the game 105-95, so I was a little annoyed, as I felt like I had missed out on another great experience. FCUK!

I checked into the "Freehand" hostel and I went to my dorm room around 3pm, and as soon as I opened the door, I could not have been greeted by a more annoying sound than the noise of some fat old bloke snoring like a bloody pig. You couldn't make this up, I was fuming. Out of the frying pan, into another frying pan?

Then I just snapped, my patience went in an instant and I

shook the fat guy to stop him snoring, and I had only been in the room for seconds. I simply had enough of this fcuking horrible sound, and it was 3pm in the afternoon, and now I was gonna have to deal with this yet again later tonight.

I went for a wander around the hostel and the "Freehand" really was a step up from "Bed and Drinks", as there was a lovely pool, a nice lounge area to hang out and relax in, a bar by the pool, and a lovely looking restaurant, so I felt I had made a very good move, and I wished I had came straight to this lovely hostel in the first place..

I went back to Bed and Drinks, met up with Victor and Abs, and an English girl they were with, and we all went off to dinner, then onto a very trendy bar on South Beach for a few drinks. We went to a great place with some amazing pole dancers with incredible figures and everything hanging out, in a bar frequented by the "beautiful people" of Miami, and Victor started to do what he does best, hit on the ladies.

We got talking to two Russian girls, and I could instantly see and feel they were not in the slightest interested in us, so I gave up far before Victor did, as I recognised the blatantly obvious signs, but Victor has much more persistent than me, but he eventually rejoined me at the bar around five minutes later!!

We headed off to another bar on the super trendy South Beach to meet up with a few of the other people from our hostel, where I remember getting a bottle of beer for ten bucks (7-8 quid) thinking that was probably the going rate on South Beach for a beer, which I thought was fair enough.

I got talking to a pretty nice girl in our group and I offered to get her a beer, so I went up to the bar and I ordered two pints on draft. The waitress pulled the beers and turned to me with a big beautiful smile and said "that's 42 dollars please". "WHAT?" I nearly choked. "I ain't paying that" I said rudely. I turned and looked at the embarrassed girl I was buying the drink for, and we both laughed, then I just left the barmaid standing with two beers in her hand and we walked away. The barmaid looked me right in the face as she poured the two drinks into the sink with a combination of disgust and arrogance. That was about seventeen pounds a pint. FCUK THAT.

I got back to my hostel around midnight, and as soon as I got into the room, the fat man was snoring. He was laying on his back like a beached whale, and blowing bubbles into the air. I simply had enough and I snapped, so I pushed him really hard and he instinctively grabbed my arm and shouted at me, "What are you doing"? "Stop fcuking snoring" I shouted, "I've had enough" I said. I didn't care who I woke up, I had had a few drinks and I was ready to kick his snoring fat ass!

The next day, a young guy who was sleeping above the snoring fat man thanked me for stopping the snoring the previous night, as this guy had kept the youngster awake for the past few nights. "Why did you not just tell him"? I said. Clearly the young man was shy and probably scared to say anything to the fat git. So I moved rooms yet again, as I was not putting up with this anymore.

Thursday came, and it was the US holiday called "Thanksgiving", and this means NFL. Oh yes! There is a tradition with a couple of the NFL teams, as they always play games on thanksgiving day. Why? I have no idea, but I'm sure there is a logical explanation as to why the Detroit Lions and my Dallas Cowboys, the two teams in question who always play on this day.

My Boys were playing the high flying and yet unbeaten Carolina Panthers, so I was looking forward to watching this afternoon game in a bar, right on the iconic South Beach area of Miami. I spent the morning with Victor and the English girl walking along the beach, as they were both working out with all the muscle men, and I was watching!! Sad? Yes. True? yes! I got out of breath just watching this shit!

I did partake briefly by doing two or three pull ups on a bar, a few stomach crunches on my one pack, and then I did what I do best, I gave up!

I left them on the beach as I felt like a spare one at a wedding when I was in their company, as the chick in question clearly wanted a bit more from Victor than he wanted from her.

By now, my confidence of getting stuck into the American chicks or backpackers was at an all time low. Of course I tried, but not with any real conviction as I really couldn't be bothered to put any real time and effort into trying to get laid, as usually the outcome was disappointment, and a very empty wallet!

Some guys will go from one rejection to the next, and the next, and so on until one door eventully opens, even after twenty or more were slammed in their faces, but I usually give up after one door hits me square on the jaw. Some guys use the old adage of blitzing the forest to find the truffle, or chatting to anything that has a pulse, but me, I need my Wonderwoman served up on a plate, to come and sit on my lap, to basically throw herself at me. This is probably why I am single, I just can't be assed anymore with all that shit, but I still continued to try, but not with any real conviction.

I walked along the still very windy South Beach to find a good bar with a big screen and a decent menu, and I caught the end of the Lions thrashing of my divisional rivals the Eagles, before my Cowboys game started.

I was quietly confident my Cowboys had every chance to win this game, as don't forget we were on a one game winning streak! and I honestly felt it was only a matter of time before the high flying Panthers would finally get beat. How bloody wrong was I? AGAIN!

The game started and I was looking forward to an exciting game as Dallas started with possession of the ball. That was the beginning of the end and at 0-0, the closest my Cowboys got to winning this game. Within the first minute, our returning hero Mr. Romo, (Tony Homo to all other NFL fans), never let anybody down, and he did what he is very good at, he threw an interception which was returned for a touchdown, something which in the trade, is called a "pick six". FCUK!

14.20 on the clock in the first quarter and already we are 7-0 down, 40 bloody seconds. Then incredibly Romo did exactly the same again with his next attempt, and even worse, in the second quarter, another pick six.

I could not believe it, it was a total catastrophe from the Cowboys, which would continue for the rest of the game, and at half time the game was practically already over at 23-3.

I like the Carolina Panthers, especially their quarterback, Cam Newton, as he is a new breed of quarterback who is very exciting to watch. He runs, he has a great arm, is very unpredictable and he is a showman, even doing the odd somersault. But sometimes he is very erratic, and when he is, he really is, so I honestly thought it was only a matter of time before he had a so called "off day", and as the season progressed, Newton proved me wrong week after week after week, as the Panthers continued their unbeaten run, which finally ended in Atlanta on week 16, but they eventually made it all the way to Superbowl 50. What the hell do I know?

The second half was not quite as bad for my Cowboys, but no better either as Romo threw yet another interception, but this didn't matter as the game was already long over. It finished 33-14, and Romo even left the field injured, so he had a day he will want to forget, and to be honest...so did I.

As a passionate Cowboys fan, of course I feel disappointed when my team lose, but it just seems to me that the Cowboys more than any other team in the NFL always do their very best to beat themselves. Is this just me? or does every NFL football fan think the same about their teams? Probably.

I have a love hate relationship with my Cowboys, or course I love them, and I have done for over 30 years, but they do drive me mad with their so many shitty performances. Like I say, the Cowboys seem to beat themselves, far more than the opposition teams do by being better on the day. The amount of times the Cowboys have thrown away good leading situations in games to miss out on the play off's is a joke. As for that Dez Bryant catch against the Packers a few years back, boy that hurt, but it seems the luck is out in Dallas at the moment, or a referee conspiracy is against them!

Another game I saw Dallas capitulate in was back in season 2013-14, I was travelling around America again (I was actually in Toronto) and I remember a game where the Cowboys were leading 26-3 at half time. The game should have been over, but 34 second half points saw Green Bay (my 2nd team) beat the Cowboys (my 1st team) 37-36, even without the brilliant Aaron Rodgers. The Packers did not win that game, well they did, but what I mean is, Romo handed it to them on a plate yet again, and that particular loss meant the Cowboys missed out on the play offs that year. Typical.

The following day I was moving on from the sunshine and violent winds of Miami, back to the cold of the north, Cleveland, and I was ready to continue and return back into my NFL world.

I never quite connected with Miami, even though I knew what to expect, as I had been there a few years before with an ex chick. The weather was definitely the major factor, I blame the humid sticky heat combined with the horrendous wind, and sometimes monsoon rain, as it was supposed to be a time for relaxation on the beach and catching some rays, something which was simply not possible, and not a time to be stuck indoors, or wasting copious amounts of money drinking in bars.

Miami to me was like being in South America, especially as most people were and spoke Hispanic. I remember going into many cafes and bars, and I was instantly spoken to in Spanish. "No entiendo Espanol, soy Inglese (I don't understand, I am English)" was my response, as I was always mistake for being Spanish. But I'm used to this as I always get mistaken for a foreigner wherever I travel around the world, and this never bothered me as it gave me the chance to used the very limited language skills or one liners that I have tucked away under my belt!

Friday morning came, and I got ready to leave my lovely "Freehand" Hostel as my flight was departing around 10am, so I had to get up fairly early to catch a cab to the airport. I had been using Uber cabs in the US, which as a tourist, work very well for me, mainly as they are a lot cheaper than the normal taxis.

Uber has caused carnage for the traditional London "black taxi" drivers, as these guys have studied the streets of London for over four years before they get their official licences. Uber drivers just get sat navs and basically have no idea where the hell they are going, and they have muscled in on the very lucrative London cab market that has been around for well over 100 years.

That morning I had a problem with my cell phone, as my

monthly contract had expired the day before, and I had no signal or connection to use my phone. I asked a guy in my hostel reception if he had the "Uber app" on his phone, as practically all backpackers have it, luckily he did, so the nice man in question kindly ordered me an Uber cab for me from his phone. Great, or so I thought.

When the cab arrived, I was a little on the clock (running late) for my flight, so when Mr. Uber arrived and I sat in the front seat, he informed me that this particular job had now been cancelled. "How"? I asked with more than a little bit of attitude. The driver informed me that my original booking and thirty bucks Uber fare was now not on the menu, and he had to revert to the normal sixty bucks fare a normal cab would charge.

I instantly told him to shove the fare up his cheating ass, and I attempted to play the game and get out of the cab, which was a pretty stupid idea as I had no phone to call another cab, it was pissing down with rain, and I was late in catching my flight.

I managed to knock the conman down to forty bucks, so off we went to the airport in Fort Lauderdale, about a forty minutes ride away.

It was a very uncomfortable ride for me as I was fuming, as I hate being ripped off BIGTIME, and I only found out after this event, that this was in fact a typical Uber driver scam. When we arrived at the airport and I got out of the cab and I had full possession my bags, I gave the driver a massive piece of my mind. I told him he was a conman and I looked at his number plate and I told him I was going to report him to Uber. We had a pretty good argument and I certainly didn't hold back, or reduce the volume of my voice, which was witnessed by a lot of other people outside the departure area of the airport, and Mr Uber looked terribly embarrassed in front of an audience and he quickly returned to his cab and disappeared forever. BASTARD!

I never did report Mr Conman to Uber, as I was lazy and I basically could'nt be bothered, you win some, you lose some I believe, and this time I lost, buy hey, that's life, at least I live to fight another day, as you simply can't win 'em all.

I did lose quite a lot of times on my trip, but I always won far more than I lost. I met a lot of idiots, bullshitters and timewasters on my trip, but I met far more great people who looked after me, treated me like a god, and most importantly showed me their kindness.

Miami was nowhere near the top of the list of my favourite places I had or would visit on my tour, and unknown to me at the time, my next destination would be very high up on that list. Next stop....Cleveland Ohio.

Stadium-22
First Energy Stadium
Cleveland Browns

I landed into Cleveland after a three hours flight and made my way to yet again, the only hostel in town, appropriated named "The Cleveland Hostel". I caught the subway from the airport to a place named Ohio City, which was just up the road from downtown Cleveland, where my hostel was located.

My friend from Minneapolis, Chance, was flying in to meet me the following day, as he mentioned he wanted to experience a game with me somewhere on my tour, something I was looking forward to, as we had a great time together when we had met in Minneapolis.

I had been talking to Chance on a regular basis on Facebook, all the usual FB rubbish, but one thing did make my day, and this was when he informed me he was writing a book and he based the main character on me. WOW! what a honor, and I can't wait to read it, as I'm sure this character must be handsome, brave, charming, charismatic, or basically all the things I am not!!!

Chance was arriving in the early hours of the morning, coming in from somewhere in the south, and I was really looking forward to seeing him again, but he was having problems with his flight, and sadly that night he never arrived, even though I thought he had done so, as there were a few people asleep in my room when I arrived home late, but I learned by the next morning he was not one of them.

The sunshine of Florida was replaced by a very gloomy grey sky here in Cleveland, but I didn't mind this at all, I was just happy to be in Cleveland as there was absolutely no wind, which was a refreshing change, and worth its weight in gold, as Miami's weather really did piss me off bigtime.

My hostel was in a very nice location, on a long road full of bars, coffee shops, a massive indoor food market, and a lovely ice cream parlour. I had a little wander around the area, looked inside the food market, and I ended up having a sample of a few of the local micro brewery beers, which at some point, I tried practically all of them, as you do!

My friend and Cleveland Browns Superfan, "Facepaint Mike Bonnell", was coming to pick me up the next morning from my hostel and take me to the "Pro Football Hall of Fame Museum" in a place called Canton, about 45 minutes drive from Cleveland. I had met Mike in Cincinnati at Shawn "Who Dey" Moore's tailgate, and we bonded in no time. Mike arrived bang on time, and off we went to Canton.

The "Pro Football Hall of Fame" is a NFL fan's dream of a museum, I absolutely loved it. The history of this great game is fascinating, looking at the early days with leather helmets, no pads, terrible playing fields etc. etc. I did so much reading while in this museum, watching TV clips, looking at the shirts and the outits of the "Hall of Famers", and so much more.

I learned about all aspects of the NFL, right back to the very start, long before the NFC and AFC was formed, as well as so many other interesting things that I simply had no idea about. It was great to see how the game has developed over the years, with so many changes to what is the game we all know and love to this day.

I was totally engrossed and completely fascinated by this great experience, and a NFL fans dream of a museum which every fan should go and see if possible.

Mike wanted to watch his college team's game which was being played that afternoon at his local sports bar, and Mike was extremely patient with me as I ran well over our planned amount of time in the museum. I just couldn't help it! but Mike could see how happy I was to be there, and he never rushed me at all.

Mike introduced me to a nice bunch of his friends in his local club, all screaming for their college team Ohio State. We arrived around half time, with Mike's team winning, so the atmosphere was great and full of very happy bunnies. This continued to the end, as Ohio State held on to win, in what I was told was an upset, as the opposition were the favourites to win that day. I wish I could remember who they were!!!

We went back to Mike's house and I recognised immediately his home is his very own Cleveland Browns shrine, with memorabilia everywhere, covering all four walls. Mike like me is a musician, and his instrument is the trumpet, which I saw next to a stand with sheet music, so he gave me a little tune, or blast. The first thing I thought was "thank god I am not his neighbour"!!!!

That afternoon we went out to visit a place where a few of Mike's music friends were auditioning for a part in a national brass band competition. We went to a school, or college, and this building was absolutely huge. We went downstairs and walked around a massive area of rehearsal rooms, waiting rooms, long queues of people, all with their instruments waiting to be assessed and tested.

I love being around musicians, especially being one myself, which always makes me want to have a jam session, talk music, or just watch others perform. I love seeing people play different instruments to my guitar, and this brass experience was something I had never really witnessed before, especially on this level, with so many extremely talented young people in one place.

Later that evening Mike was going to a party with his friends, and I was invited, but I decided to return to my hostel, as I had had a long day, and I wanted to sleep in my own bed rather than on Mike's sofa and recharge my batteries properly, if possible.

Mike kindly dropped me back at my hostel, I had dinner and a few beers in one of the many local micro breweries before heading back to my place where I played a guitar which was in the lounge area, before I headed to bed.

The following day a new guest arrived into my hostel dorm room, well nothing new there, as new guests were arriving every day, and they usually turn into new friends, but this was totally different. I was walking out of the room for a moment as a new guy came walking in, and the first thing I noticed was this horrible overpowering smell coming from him, as he smelt like a homeless person.

I mentioned this to another guy in the room, and he agreed (well, it was impossible not to), so I went down to mention this to the guy on reception, and when we came back upstairs, the guy in question had gone for a shower, but the room absolutely stank, so bad it was making me gag. YUK!

When the guy from reception eventually entered the room, he immediately screwed up his face, as he could clearly smell what we could. When "smelly man" came out of the shower, the guy from reception informed him he had made a mistake and put him in the wrong room, so luckily he got moved out of ours. THANK GOD! as that smell really was unbearable and something I could never had been able to put up with for any more than a few seconds. It really was that putrid.

I could still smell that man long after he left the room and I have no idea what that disgusting smell was, I can only imagine he must have been living on the streets, and for a very long time, but he actually looked totally normal, no sign of tatty clothing, just normal. But all I knew was I could not stay in the same room as him.

Sunday was normally game day for me, but not this day, as my game this week was the Monday night game, and would be the only Sunday I did not attend a game throughout the entire tour, so on this particular day I was a tourist, so I had a wander around downtown Cleveland.

The "Rock and Roll Hall of Fame Museum" was well and truly on my radar, this time for music, and my second "Hall of Fame" museum in consecutive days in and around Cleveland. The "Pro Football Hall of Fame" in Canton, as I've mentioned was brilliant, but as music really is my first love, so this place was on another level, absolutely superb. Most of my heroes are inducted into this incredible museum, everybody from The Beatles, Pink Floyd, Queen, U2, Jimi Hendrix, The Doors, David Bowie, Michael Jackson and many many more. I stayed in this museum for over six hours, and the only reason I left was because they were closing.

I can honestly say the "Rock and Roll Hall of Fame Museum" is the best museum bar none I have ever visited. I could easily have spent a week in there, as there was so much to see, and it just got better and better and better with each corner I turned or floor I visited.

I watched so many film clips, saw hundreds of iconic outfits worn by all kinds of legends over the years in so many classic moments in music history, from the Beatles, Michael Jackson, Madonna, Pink Floyd, Elvis, Johnny Cash, Led Zeppelin, Genesis, the Police, Stevie Wonder, many many country artists and so many more. I really was in heaven.

Although I was sooooo happy to be in this brilliant museum, I remember feeling so jealous, or envious of all the success these guys had, and continue to have, and something in which I worked so hard for, and so badly strived for in the time I spent in the bands I had formed, after writing what I thought were great songs.

I actually could have cried, as all these guys, my heroes, made it to the big time, and I never did. TOTALLY

GUTTED. This is something that haunts and hurts me very deeply every day of my life, and always will, and who knows, maybe I still can do the AZBO world tour we always talked about? I still have a dream.

The "Rock and Roll Hall of Fame Museum" is located next door to the home of the Cleveland Browns, the "First Energy Stadium", where I would be attending my next game, and hopefully witnessing a Browns victory against their divisional rivals the Baltimore Ravens the following evening.

I wandered around the outside of the stadium for a look and took a few pictures, then onto downtown Cleveland to find a bar to watch the late Sunday game, as I had missed all the afternoon games by spending far more time than I expected in the "R and R Hall of Fame Museum".

After watching the NFL in a bar for a few hours, I arrived back to my hostel quite late, and when I woke the next day, I expected my friend Chance to be there, but sadly again Chance never did show up as he said he could not manage to get a flight, but he did say he would see me when I got to Phoenix Arizona, the following month. Oh well, these things happen.

Monday was game day, but not until the evening, so I decided to walk across the bridge over the Cuyahoga River into downtown, had a look at the baseball and basketball stadiums, and I wandered around looking for a decent coffee shop to hang out in, and got on my laptop updating my website, social media, and all the usual stuff I had to do on a regular basis.

This social media stuff was always very time consuming, so I had to be very disciplined all throughout my tour, because if I was lazy or slack, it would take me many hours of catching up because of the huge backlog if I never kept on top of it. Once I had finished this, I somehow eventually found myself inside the Horseshoe Casino, as you do!!

I was meeting Facepaint Mike and his friends at their tailgate near the "First Energy Stadium" on a cold and miserable night in Cleveland. When I eventually found them, after looking for ages, at the edge of one of the massive parking lots across the road from the stadium, I was welcomed like a long lost family member by a great bunch of people including Browns Superfan Bob "Burnt River" Hostutler, his son Justin, Shawn (Sasquatch), Karen, and the very funny host of the tailgate Jay Negin.

I remember getting on a Cleveland Browns bus, drinking beer and doing shots with Bob, a great guy whom I clicked with immediately, as he was brilliant company.

The Cleveland "gang" as I call them are truly wonderful people, they welcomed me so much and they instantly made me feel like I was with long term friends as they made such a fuss of me, and so they should!!! They were the perfect hosts and I will never forget their kindness to me. They did Cleveland proud. Thanks guys.

The atmosphere at the tailgate was a little less crazy than usual, but I was told this was because it was a Monday game, and that the Sunday tailgates were usually busier and a little more boisterous. But I did'nt mind, as the food at Jay's tailgate was beautiful and as usual I probably ate far too more than I should have.

As ever, I had a very cheap ticket. I had bought it from my favourite website Tickpick.com for five dollars, Yep, five bucks, but Bob and his son Justin had a spare ticket in a much better seat, which they offered to me, so I decided to sit with them.

The Cleveland Browns Vs the Baltimore Ravens was not the most glamorous game on my schedule, as both of these teams were struggling to get anywhere near the playoff picture. I was looking forward to seeing Browns QB and bad boy Johnny "Football" Manziel for the second time, but sadly he was dropped from the starting line up, for yet again being a naughty boy.

The Ravens started the game the stronger team and they returned a punt for an 80 yard touchdown in the first quarter. But the game was always in the balance throughout, as the lead changed hands a few times, especially in the second half. It was a quite a good game for a neutral like me to watch, and of course I was cheering for the Browns because I was in their home, and of course because of my new friends, and especially as I was sitting with two Browns fans in Bob and Justin.

Half time came and I decided to take a wander around the stadium, as I wanted to go inside the Browns famous or infamous section of the stadium nicknamed the "Dawg Pound". I had seen this section on TV and heard of it's tough reputation, and I really wanted to experience it and sit in there for a bit while the game was in progress. Indeed I did, but not for very long as I did not want to disrespect my new friends, and be away from my hosts for more than a few minutes.

The game was now getting interesting as we approached the two minute warning/two minutes to go, with the score at 24-20 to the Ravens. The Browns quarterback, who incidentally was their current back up to first choice QB to Johnny Manziel, got injured, and he had to leave the field, only to be replaced by the Browns 3rd string QB, and not Manziel. This was a massive slap to the face to "Johnny Football", who was benched as he had gone on one of his famous lost weekends and broken the clubs rules......again.

The Browns 3rd string QB then amazingly threw what we all thought was a winning town down pass to make the game 27-24, but with a minute left, the Ravens managed to make their way down the field and tie the game with a field goal. But even bigger drama was to come, when the Browns somehow managed to get into field goal range themselves to attempt to kick a winning score, with just a few seconds left on the clock, and almost certainly the very last play of the game.

If the Browns missed the field goal attempt, the game would then go into overtime, so it wasn't exactly the end of the world for them, but of course we wanted the Browns to score and win the game. What came next, was a combination of total horror and intense laughter as complete disaster struck on this final play of the game. The ball was snapped, the Browns kicker's attempt of glory was blocked by the outstretched hand of one of the Ravens defense, the ball bounced and was gathered up by a Ravens defender, who then incredibly ran along the outside of the entire length of the field with the ball, 65 yards back into the Browns end zone to win the game.

The crowd went silent and were in complete shock. I turned to Bob and Justin and they looked totally mortified, like they had just seen a ghost. What an ending, nobody expected or could have called that play before the ball was snapped. I didn't know whether to laugh, shit or cry!! and because of this incredible finale, this game was one of the many games on my tour I will never forget, as I was so lucky over the season I was at so many classic games, many more good ones than bad, and this was a very good one, well at least the second half, and especially the ending.

I was totally gutted for Bob, Justin and all the other Browns fans, as their team were struggling bigtime in this particular season, and we all thought this game was over on the very last play. But if you were a Ravens fan that evening, you would have been jumping for joy in a huge way, but this night I was a Browns fan, and I was pretty disappointed, so Bob and the gang must have been totally devastated, and the look on Bob and Justin's faces as this happened in real time, was priceless!

The first thing that came out of Bob's mouth as this happened was "only the Cleveland Browns can do that"!! Sorry guys, but I did want to laugh, as I couldn't believe what we had just witnessed, but I remember something similar happening to my Cowboys earlier in the season, and that time, it was me who was not laughing, so I knew exactly how the guys felt, so they had my sympathy.

We left the stadium as quiet as mice, and Bob, Justin and

myself returned to Jay's tailgate, and the mood was as expected, very somber indeed. I felt really sorry for my lovely hosts as their Cleveland Browns were not having a good season at all, even worse than my Dallas Cowboys, so the party atmosphere which we had before the game at the tailgate was gone, and this was now replaced by something which resembled more like a funeral wake.

Before I left to return to my hostel, Browns Superfan "Burnt River" Bob kindly gave me a bag full of Browns souvenirs, including a tee shirt, a hat, badges, stickers, towels, bottle openers, and other goodies all Cleveland Browns. It was a very nice touch from a very nice man, and a good ending to an excellent night with great new friends. Thanks Bob, you are my friend for life.

I had a quick drink and a chat with the guys, most who actually were still in great form in spite of this cruel defeat, I thanked them all so much for their generous hospitality, and I jumped on the Cleveland subway, back to my hostel in Ohio City, as the time by now was past or coming up to midnight.

I really had a cracking time in Cleveland, probably up there with one of the best places I visited for overall experiences, or the bigger picture on my entire tour. This may amaze most people, but I thoroughly enjoyed my time here, mainly because I met amazing people, went to two of the best museums I've ever been to, as well as spending time in the local bars, consuming the very tasty local beers.

Cleveland is real football country, a lot of history is here, maybe a while back, but I hope it returns to this part of

America soon, as these fans deserve it, and I hope they get it in the very near future.

Not too many people I had met said anything good about Cleveland, but I thoroughly enjoyed it, and so much more than windy Miami. But not just because of the freak weather conditions, I liked the people, they were more real, normal and not fake like "the beautiful people" of Miami.

Thanks Cleveland, for an amazing experience, I will defend you always. So a message to all you people who are maybe thinking of visiting this lovely city, please don't judge this fine place until you have experienced it for yourselves. I did, I loved it and I am now a big fan of this great city.

Stadium-23
Ford Field.
Detroit Lions

I left Cleveland via the usual route, the Greyhound bus, and it was only a short hop of three and a half hours to Detroit, much better than the last Greyhound bus ride I took from Charlotte to Cincinnati, which was a bum breaking twenty hours slog.

Detroit was always a place I knew I had to be extra vigilant in, and on my guard, as I had heard a lot of bad stories and given many warnings on how rough and dangerous parts of this town were.

I arrived into Detroit and I noticed immediately the Greyhound bus station was not in exactly the best part of town to be walking around on my own with a big backpack over my shoulders. I headed off looking for the bus stop to catch my ride to my hostel on the west side of the city. I remember standing at the bus stop thinking this area looked pretty sketchy/rough, and it wasn't long before it would be dark, so my radar was well and truly on.

I was happy once my bus arrived, and a twenty minutes ride later, I checked into yet again the only hostel in town, the aptly named " Hostel Detroit". This must have been the 5th or 6th time I would be staying in the only hostel in town.

"Hostel Detroit" was a very nice and quirky place, with not many guests as it was in fact a bit out of the way, and

Detroit was not exactly one of main tourist spots on the US map for backpackers. I was well pleased when I was given the keys to a dorm room which I had all to myself on the first night I spent in Detroit. RESULT. No snoring......YES!!

I was pretty hungry as I arrived, so I went straight out to a bar restaurant in a nice funky street across the motorway about ten minutes walk from the hostel. I was told by a member of the staff that the area the hostel was in, was once a very dodgy/sketchy part of town, but it was now on the up, and a pretty safe area, but somebody was recently robbed right outside the hostel. OH BRILLIANT! Thanks for that info.

It did look pretty rough to me, and as I walked home from the pub in the dark, I was fully aware this was not a city to fcuk with, and I was sensible..... most of the time.

The one subject I knew of and which I wanted to indulge in, and a subject which grabbed my full attention while in my time in Detroit was the music of Motown, so I headed over to the "Motown Museum" on the morning of my first day in Detroit.

Somebody told me I had to call them to book myself on a guided tour, and lucky I did as these tours were held at certain times of the day, or I could have been waiting for hours at a time. I jumped on the bus to the museum, which was about twenty minutes from my hostel.

Standing outside the "Motown Museum", I could feel the amazing energy of a very special place indeed in the history of music, a place where so many talented and iconic singers and musicians made some of the best music of all time, in this very humble looking building on the outskirts of Detroit. I felt exactly the same as I felt when I stood outside Abbey Road Studios in London, made famous of course by the best band of all time, the Beatles. Two world famous studios a million miles apart, but they have absolutely everything in common......major success on a monumental and universal scale.

The tour started at 10am, and we were guided around what was basically a house with a basement. The tour started with a short film about how Motown was born, and how the founder Berry Gordy ran the show. It was soooooooo interesting.

It was amazing to see so many great photo's, gold discs, memorabilia, Michael Jackson's glove from his legendary moonwalk at the Grammy's, and so much more. Some of the best artists of all time recorded here, everyone from Stevie Wonder, The Jackson 5, Marvin Gaye, Smokey Robinson, Diana Ross and The Supremes, The Commodores and so many many more.

We went down to the basement and we saw where practically every one of the Motown hits were recorded in the tiny studio and control room. I was standing in one of the most special places of all time in music history, and I loved every minute of it. Our tour group even sang our own pathetic rendition of The Temptations "My Girl", which was pretty embarrassing for us all!!

The tour only lasted a hour, it went so quick, and I was gutted when it was over as I would have liked longer to have looked around a bit more and read a few of the many newspaper cuttings, articles and pictures that were all over the walls.

I had ticked yet another amazing box in the world of music history, and I knew I had been in a very special place indeed. Again as I saw all these successful people, I just couldn't help but be sad, as I so wanted to have a long and successful music career like these amazing artists. I always felt jealous, but never in a bad way, but basically feeling sorry for myself as my songs have not been heard by too many people outside of my bedroom.

I'm not saying for a second that I or any of the bands I formed could have matched these incredible artists and performers, but I just wish I could have maybe got a lucky break from within the industry, from somebody who believed in me, which would have been the ultimate challenge of my talent as a songwriter and guitar player to sustain a career in which I would have needed to churn out a high level standard of material, just to keep up with the rest of the talent of that time, and keep me out of the bargain bucket or the pound shop!

Eventually I very reluctantly dragged myself out from the "Motown Museum", and I was standing outside taking a few pictures of the house, and I was chatting with the tour guide who had showed me around the museum, and I could see from a distance my bus approaching my bus stop. The guy said to me "You better grab that bus man as they don't come along this road very often". "That's ok", I said, I will catch the next one as I have no small change to get on the bus with.

"Get your ass on that bus", my new friend demanded, handing me a couple of bucks, probably from the tips we had given him for his excellent tour guiding inside the museum. Normally I would have stood my ground and declined his kind offer, but I never had time to think about it, as this guy made it perfectly clear to me I was in for a very long wait if I decided to let this particular bus pass.

What a top man, and a lovely gesture of human kindness, as he didn't have to do that, but he did, and I was very grateful to him. Thanks Mr Motown.

I love nice people, its great to know that they are out there somewhere.

I asked one of the workers at my hostel to recommend a few things I should check out whilst in my time in Detroit, as there were not that many stand out things for me to do other than Motown or the NFL game I was attending. This girl mentioned a place or thing called "The Heidelberg Project", which was way across the other side of town on the east side, so I thought he who dares usually wins......Mmmmm.

It was apparently a very artistic thing to see, and as I like artistic things, I jumped on a bus heading east, to check out this unique collection, or if you like, street exhibition. When I got on the bus heading to my destination, I asked the driver if I was going into a safe part of town, she replied it should be OK during the day, but I should not be in that neighbourhood late at night. Point taken and noted.

I had about a 10-15 minute walk from the bus stop I departed the bus at, along a long straight road to get to where this "Heidelberg Project" was. From what I saw and I could feel this was not exactly a great part of town to be wandering around in, especially as I was the only white guy in the whole area. But to be honest, yet again this never bothered me at all.

I eventually arrived at the "Heidelberg Project", and my first thought was "What the f..k is all this"? It was a few streets, or a block full of old wooden derelict houses, with loads of trees with all kinds of signs hanging and painted on them, in all different funky colours. There was a square in the middle, which was full of piles of old kids toys and other random basic rubbish, all salvaged from the streets of Detroit over the years.

This exhibition was started by some guy after he returned from the Vietnam War in the 70's, then people from all over the world started to send him random things, and the project grew and grew. Don't get me wrong, it was nice, but not exactly my kind of thing to be totally frank, and I felt I had come a long way on a recommendation which was a little bit over dressed or exaggerated for my particular kind of taste. But at least I gave it a go.

As I looked around in the middle of the square, I was wandering around looking at the three or four different kinds of tree houses that were there, and I was completely alone, except for a squirrel that ran across the square right in front of me. The squirrel was very unusual to me, as it was jet black, something I had never seen before as I had only seen, knew and was used to squirrels which were either grey or red, and even the red ones were extremely rare in London.

Around this moment I was recording a video of the project and on my commentary I stated, I was "the only honky in town, and even the squirrels were black in this neighbourhood!", which was in fact very true. I posted this on Facebook, as I did not see a reason why this would cause offence to anybody, as everybody knows Detroit has a very large African American community, and certain neighbourhoods were very densely populated by black people.

If I did think this video would be in any way offensive or racist to black people, of course I would not have posted it. I was only stating a fact, but I think my friend Chance from Minneapolis must have taken offence at my comments, because after I posted that video, he never responded to any of the ten or so messages I must have sent to him after that video.

It did make sense because I remember Chance making more than a few comments of being the "poor black man" in a "white man's world". These were HIS words, and I was a little sad to hear him state this and the stories he told me of his struggle to be taken seriously as a black man with his own company.

I really liked Chance, we had a great time together in Minneapolis and I was really looking forward to seeing him and spending time with him in Cleveland, but he never showed up, and he also ignored all my messages to contact him when I got near to and eventually arrived into Phoenix, the city he said he would meet me in, but never did.

If I did offend Chance, I wish he would have told me,

because I would have apologised to him immediately as I never wanted to insult or offend him in any shape of form at all, as he was my friend and I liked him very much. A real shame, as to this very day, I've never heard from Chance since, and a friendship has been lost. Maybe he continues to follow me from a distance, but only he knows why he decided to completely sever our ties, especially as he surposedly used "my character" as his lead man in his book. Shame as I would have loved to have read that.

On the way back from the "Heidleberg Project", I stopped off at the Eastern Markets, an area of Detroit where there were lots of nice bars and restaurants, and a place where I would tailgate with the Detroit Lions and Green Bay Packers fans the following evening.

A few weeks before I arrived into Detroit, I touched base with the singer I had met at "Preservation Hall" in New Orleans a few months before, a lady named Shahida. She lived in Detroit and she invited me to call her once I arrived and we would meet for dinner. I did exactly that, and I met with Shahida on my way back from the Eastern Markets that evening.

Before I met Shahida, I went to have a look at "Ford Field", the home of the Detroit Lions, where I would attend my 23rd game the following evening. I walked into the ticket office area to ask if I could buy a ticket, just to test the water and to see how much they would cost, and to my horror they were very expensive, and at this point, I was yet to have a ticket for tomorrow night's game.

I got talking to a security guard at the back entrance next to the ticket office, who amazingly like me was actually a Cowboys fan. It was incredible how many people I had met in random places who were Cowboys fans across America. I remember a bus driver in Jacksonville, a second bus driver, this time a woman in another city, (St Louis I think?) as well as a few more people in odd situations or places who were also fans of my C-boys.

I asked the security guard if I could have a look inside the stadium, but he said "sorry, I cannot let you in". "Oh well no problem" I replied, but then I hit him with my little trick line, "Would it be possible for me to look inside the club shop"? "Yes you can, but you cannot look at the pitch or take any photo's" he informed me. "OK" I said.

I knew the club shop was inside the stadium, so if I could go to that, which incidently was right next to the field, what was I gonna do, close my eyes? or look away?

I had to laugh, as I knew I was going to do absolutely everything the guard was going to tell me not to, and of course.......I did.

The security guard told me to walk along the long corridor beside the playing field, and the club shop was on the left. He also mentioned I could get out of the main exit at the other end of the long walk, so I would not have to come back past him again, perfect. "Thanks very much", I said, and off I went, but not before giving him one of my business cards, as he loved the idea of my tour and he wanted to take a look at my website, which he did, I know this because he made a few nice comments on my webpage. Good boy!

I walked along the corridor beside the pitch, and when I got to the area where the shop was, I was so far away from the security guard, he had no chance of seeing me. I went inside the shop and had a look around for ten minutes or so, and when I came out, I was right next to the pitch, with all the exits open, so off I go into the stands and I had a good look around "Ford Field", and I did everything the security guard told me not to do!!

Nobody stopped me, I walked confidently past many people like I owned the joint and I had free reign of the huge empty stadium. I took loads of pictures and videos as per usual, and I enjoyed yet another beautiful stadium, this time before all the crazy people came in. RESULT!

I really do love stadiums, I'm so lucky as I managed to get into so many without being stopped. Maybe its just my don't give a shit attitude, or just being brave enough to take the chance, and most of the time I succeeded. A few times I must have got turned down, but not many, actually hardly any at all I can remember.

I left Ford Field, and I went to meet Shahida for dinner. I met her outside a popular bar called the "Hockeytown Cafe", opposite the Baseball stadium "Comerica Park", which is right next door to "Ford Field". Shahida picked me up, but as I jumped into her car, she had temporarily blocked the road and somebody tooted their horn at her. This must have hit a raw nerve with Shahida, as she let go of a torrent of abuse at the driver behind, and I was very surprised and taken aback that this little old lady had more than a lot of steam to let off, if pushed.

So off we went to meet a few of Shahida's friends who owned an art gallery somewhere in Detroit. The lady who owned the art gallery was a really lovely old girl, she had owned this particular art gallery for many years, and there were many nice things in this gallery, but mainly not to my particular taste.

You see art is a very odd subject for me, especially modern art where your so called "perception" comes into the equation or enters the affray. This is something I struggle with as I find a lot of this so called "perception" a load of old rubbish. Just like most of the things in the "Tate Modern Gallery" in London. I don't get a lot of that stuff, but then again, I'm not supposed to?? That's modern art I guess??

Shahida took me to a restaurant she recommended, and we had a nice evening talking mainly about music, as she was an amazing jazz singer.

I had written a song especially for Shahida to sing called "You can look but you can't touch", which was completely inspired by her, when I saw her sing on stage at "Preservation Hall" in New Orleans a few months earlier.

I had a bass line idea stuck in my head, which was a bit of a rip off of the song "The Stray Cat Strut" by The Stray Cats, mixed in with the bass line of the White Stripes song "Seven Nation Army". It would be a very sexy and sensual song with a jazzy swing, something that was very new to me, and outside the normal genre of music I was used to writing.

It was very exciting, and a huge challenge for me to write a song for this fabulous singer, so I worked and developed the song over a few weeks, on various guitars at some of the hostels I had stayed in, before I started playing around with the lyrics. I had the idea of a madame at a strip club or burlesque show, and she was saying things to the audience like, keep your hands to yourself boys, you can look, but under no circumstances are you allowed to touch the goods on display. No sir.

I thought about what a madame would say to an audience at the start of a show. The first line was "Settle down gentlemen, welcome to the show. I'm madame sin and I'm the boss and your host for the evening". "Please be on your best behaviour and keep your hands to yourselves, otherwise you will be in biggggg trouble, you got me?". And so on.

The vibe was a smoky and seedy nightclub frequented by dodgy people, corrupt officials, mafia types and people of good standing in the community who really should not be in these places, but of course....they are. One of the lines in the song I like a lot is "Influential people, they're here somewhere, they hide in the shadows, Politicians Policemen, they work all day, at night time they play". Which of course is very true.

Shahida agreed to do the song, but she was not available on the date I had booked the studio for, so I had a dilemma, shall I record the music first? Try to get the studio on another day as to accommodate Shahida? Or abort the project completely, as it was going to cost me about 1500 dollars?

The funny thing was, before I arrived into Detroit, I had been in contact with Shahida for a few weeks, and I had sent her emails asking if she would be happy to sing on the song, as well as a few other issues regarding the recording sessions and costs. When she finally responded, as Shahida was not the best of communicators, she said yes, so I asked her if she could arrange the studio with any of her friends or contacts in which she may be able to get us a good deal?

I had also informed Shahida I would pay her and all other parties who played on the track the going rate of a session, and would she be able to get me a price for the whole project and recommend me other musicians?

Shadida eventually came back to me with a ridiculous figure of over 2000 dollars for the session, something I thought was excessive and way over my budget, and much more than my vision, or what I would usually pay for a song I had recorded many times in many different studios.

I decided to decline her offer, and I contacted the studio directly, the exact one she had recommended to me in Detroit, and almost straight away the producer laughed when I told him Shahida's ballpark figure.

Was Shahida trying to rip me off? Was she trying to price me out of the market and scare me off? Did she in fact want to even sing on the track? Keep reading and all will be revealed.

After a nice dinner, Shahida dropped me off at my hostel and we tried to arranged to get her in the studio by the time I left Detroit, a city which I was only in for three days, so my schedule was extremely tight to say the least.

I had touched base with a top bloke named Dave from the

recording studio Shahida put me in touch with on the outskirts of Detroit, a studio named "Tempermill". Dave was really friendly and extremely patient with me, especially as I simply could not pin down Shahida to a definite time and date, as she was very slow at returning my emails or phone calls, hence I could not confirm any concrete date or times with the studio until Shahida made herself available to me.

This I found extremely frustrating indeed, and very quickly I was losing patience with Shahida as her silence was deafening, and I had to move quickly and make a decision, now or never?

I was caught between the proverbial rock and a hard place, as the studio wanted to know when we were coming, I tried to contact Shahida, she ignored my messages for days at a time, long before I even arrived in Detroit, so I always knew this was going to be an enormous challenge, stressful and extremely frustrating, but also very enjoyable and rewarding at the same time, and if I managed to pull this off, I would be a very happy bunny indeed.

I wanted to do this BIGTIME, I was driving this bus, not bloody Shahida and I decided I was not going to be messed around by this timewaster anymore. I was fed up with her constant excuses and waiting for her replies, as I was determined not to let her sabotage MY project, so I went head first and took the plunge, with or without a singer. I decided to book the studio time, I hired a drummer, a double bass and trumpet players, and I would play the guitar and sing the guide vocals.

The day of reckoning came, and Dave the producer was an absolute dream to work with, as were the three musicians who eventually played on my song. Great guys they were, excellent company, very friendly and most importantly, very very talented musicians indeed.

The drummer, bass player and me played the song through three times, and that was it, they nailed it. The trumpet player did his bit afterwards, and again nailed it in a few takes. I did a reasonable guide vocal and guitar, and we had the music in the bag in a few hours.

I loved every minute of that session, these guys were sooooo proffessional and they did everything I asked of them with complete ease, without any disagreements, opinions, ego's or problems whatsoever.

I have recorded with producers before who want to change things just to put their mark on the track, and this was something Dave never did in the slightest. Dave just did what he was brilliant at, I followed his guidance, and it worked out like a dream.

These guys gave me yet another amazing box ticking life experience, and it was a pleasure for me to "Jam" with them, because that was exactly what we did, and this vibe was perfect for me and my song.

All it finally needed was Shahida to come in and do the vocals, and hey presto, the song would be finished. But I always knew this was going to be the difficult part.

After the session was complete, I was really pleased with the results, I said goodbye to Dave, thanked him and the other guys enormously, and I paid everyone. I explained to Dave what I expected and wanted from Shahida, and I even left the money to pay her for when she came in to do her vocal session, whenever that would be?

I never had much time in the studio, probably around four hours in total, because I knew my timing was tight, as later that night was the next game on my tour, the Detroit Lions against my second team and divisional rivals of the Lions, the Green Bay Packers.

I ordered a cab, left Dave at Tempermill Studios and I proceeded to return to my hostel to pick up some things before heading off to watch my 23rd game of the tour.

Back at my hostel, I met and got talking to an Aussie guy, and he told me he liked the NFL, so within an hour of meeting him, both of us were off to the NFL game together on the bus. I wish I could remember the guy's name as I really enjoyed my very very short time with him that evening.

"Ford Field" in Detroit was our destination for the visit of divisional rivals, the Green Bay Packers. Before the game, my Aussie friend and I had a couple of beers in the "Hockeytown Bar" I had met Shahida outside a few nights before. "The Hockeytown Bar" was full of flashy motorbikes and sporting memorabilia, exactly my kind of bar.

I was invited to the tailgate of the legendary Detroit Lions Superfan Ron Crachiola "Who loves ya baby" Crackman, to have a few beers and a feed with Ron and his Detroit Lions mates. The tailgate was at the Eastern Markets, which I had been to the day before, so I knew where these guys would roughly be, which is great because usually it was a huge task to find some of these tailgates as some of them are so big, its impossible to find your friends unless you know exactly where they are located. I spent many a time wandering around looking for my Superfan friends at quite a few tailgates, luckily, not this time.

My Aussie friend and I managed to find our tailgate without any problems, but Ron was not there when we arrived, but he was on his way soon. I met a bunch of Crackman's Lions friends, and as usual they were all very welcoming and friendly. I met the Packers Superfan Steve Tate, a great guy, all dressed up in his Packers uniform with traditional cheese head hat. Cheese.........yuk!

Ron eventually arrived, and when he did, I could see immediately he was a great character and a much loved part of the tailgating community in Detroit. I had been told about a certain tailgate in Detroit which had a jacuzzi, I think it was on the back of a big van, and I heard it was usually full of Detroit Lions babes, so count me in I thought, and I really was up for it, even though it was a freezing cold December night in Detroit and I had no towel or anything to put on. (This has never stopped me in the past), and it would not stop me this time either.

So me and my Aussie friend went off looking for the jacuzzi full of pretty lionesses, but sadly we were told by someone that the jacuzzi man with the hot tub only tailgated at the Sunday games, and as this was Thursday night football he wasn't at the game that night. Oh, what a kick in the nuts! I really wanted to get into that baby, and I would of for sure. Yes it was cold, and I'm sure shrinkage would have been on the menu, but hey, that small minor detail would not have stopped this boy from getting his kit off!

After a few hours chatting to Ron, Steve Tate and the gang, off we all went to the stadium. My Aussie friend and I managed to get a pair of tickets together for a very good price, yet again under face value, which is always nice, and to be honest, not that difficult to find.

You see, at NFL games, the tickets usually sell out way before the day of the games, but there are ALWAYS so many tickets flying round outside the stadiums, and at tailgates before the games start, for a myriad of reasons as to why people do not turn up for the games. And believe me, they don't, leaving people like me to pick up the scraps.

What usually happens is sellers tend to panic with a few hours left before the games start, thinking they will be left holding the baby or the tickets and get nothing, so they will sell them at much reduced prices, just to get back something, or just make a small loss on their investments. This is where I usually benefitted from. KERCHING!

Little did I know what would be ahead of me on this crazy night of football, probably one of the best games I would see on my tour was coming up tonight. My Aussie friend and I made it to our seats high up in the nose bleeds behind one of the end zones, yet another great seat, and yet another great stadium, this time a dome with a closed roof, and thank god it was, as is was freezing cold outside, but inside it was lovely and warm.

The game started after all the usual pre match routine and the Lions started like a bullet out of a gun, and they raced into a half time lead of 17-0. The Lions were so dominate it was one way traffic, with the Packers being so extremely poor, and very unlike them, as they got nowhere near the Lions end zone at all in the whole of the first half.

The Lions increased their lead to 20-0 in the third quarter and to be honest, by this time, this game was well and truly over. WRONG!. Again, what do I know?

The Packers scored two touchdowns in the third quarter and this game was very quickly transformed, and now the game was at last a competition at 20-14 going into the final quarter. I thought the game was over when the Lions kicked a field goal to make it 23-14 with just a few minutes left on the clock, but this is where the fun started.

The Packers scored a touchdown with three minutes to go in the game, making the score 23-19, unrecognisable from the first half dominance of the Lions, but the Packers needed to score a touchdown, as a field goal was not enough, and the Lions had possession of the ball.

Incredibly the Lions fumbled the ball and gave it back to the Packers, but the Packers could not get close to the Lions end zone as the clock ticked down to the last few seconds, and the very last play of the game. It was sooooo exciting, as there were many Packers fans all around us in our block in the stadium, which obviously was dominated by Lions fans. The atmosphere this night was incredible.

Aaron Rodgers took the snap of the final play of the game,

and he passed the ball sideways to his running back, who then threw the ball to a team mate, who then threw the ball back to Rodgers, a bit like a rugby game. Rodgers then got sacked (jumped on) and the game was over. A win for the Detroit Lions. OR WAS IT?

I remember recording that play, and in my commentary, I said, "so there you have it folks, the Detroit Lions surprisingly beat their divisional rivals The Green Bay Packers, no wait, hang on, there's been a flag for a facemask offense on Packers QB Aaron Rodgers, so there will be one more play with the time on the clock at 0.00". Incredible drama, a second chance for Green Bay.

Everybody in the stadium was in shock, as we all thought the game was over, and I think by this time a lot of the Lions fans had left the stadium, not knowing the game was in fact still in play. The excitement was electric and must have been incredible for the fans of both teams. It was for me and I was a kind of neutral. (Well, I do like the Packers!)

We all knew what was coming next, the amazing and exciting "Hail Mary" pass. A "Hail Mary" pass for you guys who have no idea what it is, is a last chance saloon attempt to score a touchdown, with the very last play of the game, with no time left on the clock. It's usually a complete shot in the dark play, a long throw into the abyss, or end zone, and if caught by the offensive team, the game is won, but if not, and this is something which usually happens I would guess at 99% of the time, the game is lost.

The phrase "Hail Mary" was devised or invented by a player named Knute Rockne in the 1920's who on a late play of a game, got down on his knees and prayed a "Hail Mary" with his teammates. The play scored a touchdown and a phrase was born.

Back to the game, so Rodgers takes the snap, and launches his 60 yard "Hail Mary" rocket of a pass into the Lions end zone, and incredibly it's caught by another Rodgers, Packers tight end, Richard, who stood alone up against six Lions defenders, and unbelievably came away with the ball. What a play, and I was there to see it!

This pass will go down in NFL history, and what a pleasure for me to say I was there on that famous night in Detroit to see that amazing pass with my very own eyes. Incredibly, unknown to me at the time, I would have another date with Aaron Rodgers and destiny later in the season, at the play offs in Phoenix, where he would repeat this amazing play, probably even better than this one, if that was physically possible?? And it was.

The Lions players and fans must have been totally distraught, the Packers completely elated. I later learned that the 60 yard pass was the longest "Hail Mary" pass ever recorded in the history of the NFL, and I was there to see it. Fantastic. What an end to a brilliant game.

This was the second "Hail Mary" pass I had seen on my tour so far, and a play many fans have never seen in years of following the game, and little did I know, I would see two more before my trip would end, at Super Bowl 50, three months later.

Me and my Aussie friend left the stadium and I was buzzing

as we went to a few bars, had a few drinks, let the crowds and traffic empty, and we jumped in a Uber cab back to "Hostel Detroit".

I said farewell to my Aussie friend as I went to my room, because I was leaving Detroit early the next morning for my flight out of town. I wish I could remember his name, as the 7-8 hours we spent together was very enjoyable, very nice man indeed and great company. Good luck to him wherever he may be.

I really enjoyed my time in Detroit, even after all the warnings about the problems this town has or may bring me, but I never once felt in any real danger, but then again, I don't feel it, maybe this is stupid on my part, but if I want to do something, danger never enters my mind at all, unless I am told not to go somewhere or do something which has a high chance of putting me in a bad situation, then of course I listen........... sometimes.

I was only in Detroit for three nights, but it was a very busy time trying to fit everything in, especially the elusive and unreliable Shahida.

Sadly for me, Shahida did what I totally expected and she disappeared completely and went AWOL after I left Detroit. She ignored all of my attempts to contact her, to try get her to commit to a date in the studio to record the vocals for my song.

Finally after weeks of silence, Shahida hit me with the Tyson punch, or bite to the ear, when she finally surfaced out of nowhere, saying she could not do the vocals to my

song with the most pathetic piss poor excuse as to why.
FUCKING GREAT!

I was so pissed off with this woman as we had been
speaking about this project for a couple of months at least,
and she was always so positive and up for it, and now, after
weeks of me practically begging her to do it, she pulled out,
and with no real rhyme or reason.

My plan B was to record the song with another singer, but I
so wanted Shahida to do it, especially after seeing her sing
in New Orleans, and even more so as this song was
completely inspired by her. I was so annoyed with Shahida
for pulling out, after all the hard work I had put into this
project, and putting everything on a plate for her, she only
had to turn up, and she could not even do that. Thanks for
messing me about Shahida.

I asked Dave at "Tempermill Studio's" if he knew of any
singers in the same style of Shahida, and he came back to
me with a women who apparently is quite big on the Detroit
jazz scene, but she wanted 500 bucks to do the song.
WHAT! I was only paying Shahida 100, which was the
going rate for a session. Dave informed me the singer he had
in mind was great and I managed to knock her down to 300,
and a week later, the song was complete and she did a very
good job. But I always wanted Shahida to do it, mainly on a
personal level as she totally inspired me to write this track,
and it basically had her name written all over it. A real
shame.

The women in question who eventually sang on the track, I
won't name her, but we exchanged a few emails as I needed

to convey the message and the vision I had, regarding the vocal style I wanted for the song. Emails were exchanged and replies were very swift, so all hunky dory (great) I thought.

After the session was finished, I emailed the lady in question to ask her if she would be interested in singing this song at any of the gigs she performs at on a regular basis. I waited in anticipation for her reply, or her thoughts, as this would be great publicity for my song, and who knows, it could maybe even end up a hit, not just for me, but for her?

Sadly the reply never ever came, so two weeks later I resent the same email, and yet again I was met with a wall of silence. I tried for the third and final time a few weeks later to touch base with this lady, and it was only until then I realised I was wasting my time and I gave up. Three strikes and I was out.

At the time, I was fcuking furious, and to be honest, I still am upset with this woman to this very day, as I have never got a response from her. But what makes it worse for me, was that I always got responses from this person IN AN INSTANT, before she recorded my track, especially when we were discussing her fee for the job. But then as soon as she had the money in her hand, she decided to completely ignore all my attempts to contact her. Why did she not just say no? yes, I would have been disappointed, but I can live with that. But not responding at all? this is just a shitty thing to do and this hurts me so very very much. This lady has shown me her true colours, actually both singers did this, and to do this kind of thing tells me a lot about what both these human beings represent, and are really like. Thanks very much you horrible bitches!!

That morning I booked a shuttle bus from my hostel to Wayne County Airport and I departed Detroit for what would be my longest flight so far on my adventure, from the freezing cold northwest, to the beautiful sunshine of southern California and one of my favourite cities in the US, the beautiful San Diego.

Stadium-24
Qualcomm Stadium
San Diego Chargers

I landed at San Diego international airport after my seven hours flight from Detroit in typical and beautiful southern Californian sunshine. Off came my jacket for the first time since windy and sweaty Miami, so I was happy to be back in nice weather after a week or so of grey skies and cold.

San Diego has the most amazing climate in the whole of the US, the heat is dry, not sticky like Florida or Texas, and the temperatures don't really go much higher than 90 degrees, unlike the 110 you can get in many other parts of the US. It also does not get very cold, like an English winter, or the east coast of America, especially not the north east or north west, so San Diego is definately my kind of town.

I had been to San Diego two years before on my previous trip, so I knew my way around and I jumped on the airport bus that took me into the downtown area and the Gaslamp district of town, where all the action is.

I booked into the "HI Hostel" across the street from the corner of the Gaslamp district, a fantastic location, all of twenty seconds walk away from the first bar. The Gaslamp district is an area full of bars, resturants, fast food chains, cinema's, hotels and practically everything else inbetween anybody would need.

I dropped my bag off to my new home, and as it was

lunchtime, I headed out for something to eat. I decided to go into a nice looking Indian resturant I found and it was a great choice as the food was delicious.

My good friend Charles Zizzo lives in San Diego, so I contacted him and we planned to meet up on Saturday morning as yet again I wanted to watch my Arsenal boys play in an Arsenal America bar. I found the AA bar in town named the "Bluefoot Bar", and Charles picked me up in the morning, and off we went.

I met Charles about 7-8 years ago in Halong Bay, Vietnam and we got on well immediately, so we kept in touch via social madia, and I visited Charles a few years earlier and I always love being in his company as he really is a great guy.

So off we went to the Arsenal America bar, Arsenal beat Sunderland 3-1, so everyone was happy, including great bunch of lads I had met at the bar.

Charles headed back home to his family and I arranged to meet him at the big Chargers game the following day.

I had been chatting to a guy who was a San Diego Chargers Superfan named Josh Casillas on Facebook, as I must have been intoduced to him by Tim Young or Shawn "Who Dey" Moore, and I arranged to meet him for a drink the following day in downtown SD. Josh picked me up the next afternoon with one of his friends and off we went for a few beers and a chat about all things NFL and his beloved San Diego Chargers.

Josh invited me to go with him to watch his college football team play that Saturday evening, and as I had never been to a college game before, I jumped at the chance, as this was my opportunity to tick yet another box.

After a quick pitstop to grab a few beers on the way, we arrived for the college game at the "Qualcomm Stadium", which is the home of the San Diego Chargers, where I would also be on Sunday afternoon for the game against their divisional rivals the Denver Broncos. But tonight, it was San Diego State against a team from the military.

I can remember there was quite a lot of military related action going on before this game started, as there were quite a few soldiers and sailors in the crowd, creating a pretty good atmosphere.

It was a very close game, with the lead changing hands quite a few times, making it a very exciting game. San Diego eventually ran out winners 27-24, but I must admit, I was not really that much into the game or focusing as much as I usually would for a NFL game, as I was just warming up for the big game the following day.

That night Josh took me out to dinner with a few of his friends, and I had a great a time with him and his friends in one of San Diego's funky bars in the Gaslamp district.

Sunday morning I jumped on the San Diego subway, and I made my way to Josh's "Bolt Pride" tailgate outside the "Qualcomm Stadium". I was met by one of Josh's friends, a great guy named Dave Alvarez as I arrived into the "Bolt Pride" tailgate, and he instantly made me feel like a member of the royal family had turned up, as his welcome to me was amazing.

I liked Josh very much from the moment we met, it was like I had known him my whole life, a wonderful warm man. I could really feel the friendship coming from him, and all his friends at "Bolt Pride", yet another bunch of amazing people, whom yet again we will be friends for life.

All of these great people whom I am now friends with, all across America, have all materialised from meeting one very special man, Tim "The Captain" Young, who I met in Atlanta. This chance meeting with Tim has "created a monster!!" of friends, through the links of his "Superfan Family", in which I am so proud to say I am now a part of.

All these guys are so very special to me, and all basically for the same reasons, because they all showed me immense kindness, respect and love, and making me feel at home immediately when I was in their company, and in the company of their super friends at all of their tailgates I attended.

It was unconditional friendship from day one, and these guys really did help to keep my spirit up with their continued support, because when I was around these guys, they made it a lot easier for me to cope with the much loneliness I felt over the 6 months I was on the road. This will be with me forever as these guys are a truly special group of very kind and fine human beings, incidently, who have a burning passion for their NFL teams, and a following which is second to none.

My good friend Charles Zizzo arrived at the "Bolt Pride" tailgate looking like a Superfan, in his Chargers outfit, hat, white sunglasses and his long beard, I felt extremely underdressed! The tailgate was absoluely brilliant, loud banging music, great food, and lots of beers.

I remember there was a guy driving around the tailgate area in a very flashy car, and somebody told me the guy in question was a famous MMA fighter, which to me meant absolutely nothing, as I don't follow this sport in any way, as it's too violent for this soft boy!

I met another nice guy named Scott Ditcham from Australia, he was a Broncos fan, and he told me he is trying to get a petition together to get a NFL game played over in Australia. I wish him all the best with that, he's gonna need it!

What a star Josh was, as he somehow managed to get me a free ticket for the game, and an even bigger bonus was that I was sitting next to his lovely and very beautiful younger sister Marina. OH YES! Cheers Josh.

Of course I can't complain as I got a free ticket, but Marina and I sat in the very second row at the side of the end zone, a place I don't really like to be as you tend to watch too much of the game on the big screens. The other bonus was that the San Diego Chargers cheerleaders were performing their dance routines right in front of me. RESULT! But to be honest, my eyes were firmly fixed on just on thing......Marina, and far more so than the actually game itself!!

At this part of the season, there were rumours this could possibly be the last season for the San Diego Chargers to be playing here in San Diego. There was a very strong rumour the Chargers would be moving to Los Angeles the following season, and my Chargers friends were praying their team would remain in SD. Luckily for them, they did, and I was well pleased for Josh and his friends at "Bolt Pride" they stayed, but boy it was close for a while.

BUT! As I write my second draft of the San Diego section of the book, I'm gutted to write this stay of execution only lasted another season, and now the San Diego Chargers are gone from SD, and are now the second LA team, the Los Angeles Chargers.

I simply cannot imagine how painful this must be for my good friend Josh, all his friends at their "Bolt Pride" tailgate, and basically all the Chargers fans in San Diego. Losing your beloved team must be a devastating blow for loyal fans, and a huge gap in their lives, especially on game days, for the people who tailgated and met with their buddies at each home game over the years.

I'm no fan at all of teams moving to other cities, or new teams being created purely off the back of the American dollar. I understand money does make the world go around, but these teams are people's whole lives. What about their history?, sadly to the greedy fcukers at the NFL, this matters not one bit. A terrible shame in my opinion, and it's something like the break up of a family to me.

I noticed inside the Qualcomm Stadium there were probably more fans of the visiting Denver Broncos than the home team, as there seemed to be a sea of orange all around the stadium.

The game itself was far from being a classic and was extremely poor, probably up there with the terrible game I witnessed in Tampa on week ten, when the Buccaneers beat my Cowgirls 13-6.

Philip Rivers the Chargers QB threw a pick six (a returned score for a touchdown against his own team) and the Broncos ran it into the end zone which was right near where I was sitting.

I was a bit gutted the Broncos main man Peyton Manning was not playing, as he was dropped to the bench, which was even worse for me to stomach than if he was injured, as I wanted to see him in action, but his back up Osweiler was not doing too bad as he threw a touchdown pass to make the game 14-0, and it was still only the first quarter.

The sun was shining and I was in the company of a very lovely girl in Marina, not only was Marina beautiful, she was single (god knows how) she was intelligent, very smiley, very nice company and she loved football. This girl is definately wife material I thought, and I must admit, I fancied the pants off her.

Marina was in her 30's, just the age I'm looking for, but lets be realistic, would she be interested in an almost 50 year old (who looks 35 by the way) who would be leaving San Diego in two days time? Would she? Please say yes!!!!

The game ended 17-3 to the Broncos, and incredibly in the second half there was no score at all. Has there ever been a 0-0 second half in NFL history before? I don't know, but I bloody witnessed one!

We all returned to the "Bolt Pride" tailgate after the game ended for a short while, before I departed and said a massive thank you to Josh, Alvarez, and all the guys who made my day at "Bolt Pride" so special. Charles and I caught the subway train back to the Gaslamp district, where I departed the train to return to my hostel, and he stayed on, heading for home.

Monday I had a free day so I decided to go to the beach, even though the weather was not great, but off to "Mission Beach" I went, just to get away from the centre of yet another busy city. It certainly was not sunbathing weather as it was quite windy, and I was definately not going into the sea, as the waves were very high and the sea looked extremely violent, something that usually scares the shit out of me.

I walked along the beach, gazed at lots of the beautiful house's which lined the sand, (daydreamed about buying one of these baby's when somebody sign's up one of my songs!!) had a bit of lunch, then I plotted up at a coffee shop right on the beachfront.

I got talking to a lovely local lady for a hour or so, an ex pat English woman now living in San Diego. I also got talking to a guy who was sitting on a bench with his pet parrot, which was quite funny to see. He told me he has much more interesting conversations with the parrot than he does with his wife!

I was leaving that night on the overnight Greyhound bus to Phoenix Arizona, and my bus left late, around 11pm, so I had time to visit my friend Charles in his home and watch the second half of the Monday night game, my Dallas Cowboys against their biggest rivals the Washington Redskins.

My Cowboys simply had to win this game if they had any chance of making the play offs, and without our star man and QB Tony Romo we usually lose, so I expected this to continue. The game was the usual Cowboys rubbish I was now getting very used to watching, and after three pathetic quarters, the score was only 6-6, two field goals each, exactly what I had witnessed in Tampa, and yet another extremely dreadful game of football from my boys.

Absolutely nobody could have expected what was to come in the final quarter, the game simply exploded into life out of nowhere. Both team scored touchdowns, had fumbles, scored field goals and both teams were leading at some point, but it seemed like both teams did not want to win the game, but it was now totally compelling viewing.

The Redskins amazingly fumbled a play with very little time left on the clock, to hand the ball back to the Cowboys, and with seconds to go the Cowboys brilliant and super reliable kicker Dan Bailey kicked a 54 yard field goal to win the game. YEESSSSSSS!!

I was so pleased as it kept my Cowboys season alive for another week, giving me a huge amount of false hope. But sadly, what I did'nt know then, was that my Cowboys would lose their final four games of the regular season and easily miss out on the play offs. WANKERS!

Charles kindly walked with me to the Greyhound bus station

which was just a few blocks up the road from his house. We said our goodbyes, and I went into the bus station to catch my ride out of San Diego.

I handed my ticket and ID to the guy behind the desk to check in, and I nearly had a heart attack when the man behind the counter said "Sir, your ticket is not valid until tomorrow night, you are a day early". FCUK! What a stupid fcuker I am, a massive schoolboy error on my part, AGAIN! I had somehow mixed my days up. Don't you learn?................no I bloody don't!

The man informed me there was a bus at 11pm I could catch and there was space on it, but it would cost me twenty dollars to change the ticket. PHEW. When I usually departed from a city, I was always mentally prepared and ready to move on, and looking forward to the next adventure. Some places I would liked to have stayed at a little longer, but when I knew I was leaving a city, I accepted it, and I was ready to go, including this time, so the twenty dollars I wasted was a very small price to pay.

There was no way I was going back into downtown and back to my hostel, my only intention was to move on.

I paid up, got on board the bus, and I tried to get my head down for the nine hours overnight ride through the Arizona desert to Phoenix.

Stadium-25
University of Phoenix Stadium
Arizona Cardinals

I arrived into Phoenix at 7.30am after another night bus where I hardly slept a wink, and yet again I had booked a room at the only hostel in town, so I jumped in a cab and headed off to the "HI Hostel" in the downtown area of Phoenix.

The "HI Hostel" was run by an ex pat Englishman named Keith, a crazy and very funny guy who talked for England! (never stopped) A bit like me!!

I could'nt check in my dorm room until the afternoon, so I went out for a wander around downtown Phoenix, looking at the usual baseball and basketball stadiums, as you do. I watched a game of Champions League (European soccer) in a bar while having lunch and I eventually ended up in a beautiful Japanese garden, looking at and feeding a load of koi carp.

After feeding the fish, I decide to feed myself, so I visited the usual pit stop, a local coffee shop, and later I returned to my hostel, and I checked into my room.

I really liked this hostel, I eventually stayed here three times on my tour, as it had such a laid back vibe, including a nice relaxing area with a hammock, a TV room, guitars to play and lovely pancakes for breakfast. I also met a lot of nice people in the times I stayed at this hostel.

The first night I stayed here, there was a film being shown about the many hardships and problems of being an artist in Cuba. A group of people who were connected to a charity were putting on the film in the front garden of the hostel, and I noticed after a short period of time, some extremely strange looking characters sitting around me and watching the programme. I also noticed there were quite a lot of girls in pairs. Hmmm...

The penny finally dropped when I was told this group of people were a club where most of it's members were lesbians or people of transgender. No problem, but when I saw a gorgeous chick I fancied sitting alone, I was disappointed when her partner turned up and they held hands while we all watched the film. DOH!

The film was actually really interesting and I was thoroughly enjoying it, but I was very tired and I could not keep my eyes open, so I missed the ending as I had not slept much the night before on the bus, so I aborted the mission and I went off to hit the sack/bed.

After a lovely long night sleep, which I so needed to recharge my batteries, I jumped on the local train to a place on the outskirts of Phoenix named "Tempe", as I was heading for the Phoenix branch of Arsenal America, to watch my boys. Arsenal were playing against Greek side Olympiacos, and they needed to win by two clear goals or they were out of the champions league, so I knew it should be a very interesting game.

"Tempe" has a university in the area, probably the reason why so many young people were here, and it was a lovely place, full of very modern bars, resturants, coffee shops, ice cream parlours, and all the other things that usually attract students and young people. Apparently the night life is amazing, especially if you are young, so that counts me out!

The "Yucca Tap Room" was the AA bar in Phoenix, and the football was being shown in the dark and dingy back room of the pub. There were probably about 25-30 Arsenal fans watching the game and the atmosphere was great with lots of singing and shouting, just what I love and am used to back home.

I met some great guys in the "Yucca Tap Room" bar, very passionate Arsenal fans. It's amazing how crazy these guys are for Arsenal Football club when they get together to watch the games. I always met great Arsenal fans in all the AA bars I attended, all across America, and this one in particular.

Arsenal managed to get out of jail and won the game 3-0, so everyone in the bar went home happy. One of the guys I had met kindly offered me a lift to the train station, and I caught the train back to downtown Phoenix. Little was I to know, I would see the same guy a month later, back in the same AA bar, when I returned to Phoenix for the NFL play offs.

A bloke named Josh who worked at my "HI Phoenix" hostel, recommended to me a great and cheap place to have lunch, just a short ten minute walk straight along the busy highway. So off I go to find the cheap Indian resturant in question, but ten minutes quickly turned into forty as I asked loads of people for help or directions, as I seemed to be walking round in circles. I finally arrived at my destination, almost a hour later, it was so hidden away, none of the local people I had asked for directions knew this place existed, even the workers in the local bank!

When I returned to my hostel I told Josh of my incredible journey and how long it took me to get there. "Ten minutes, my ass" I said to him. Then he dropped the bombshell telling me he had gone on his bike, "What was it, a fcuking motorbike!!" I laughed" "If I would have known it was that far, I would not have gone" I told him. I did'nt mind, as Josh was a great guy, I liked him a lot and we always laughed when we were together.

The following day was Thursday night football and my 25th game of the tour, at the University of Phoenix Stadium, the home of the Arizona Cardinals. I did my research on how I was getting to the stadium, and I discovered the Cardinals stadium was in a place called Glendale, about ninety minutes away from my hostel by two different buses. I had expected the stadium to be in the centre of town near the baseball, basketball and hockey stadiums, but sadly for me, it was not...far from it.

It did not look too far away from where I was staying on the map, but that was deceiving, especially the road I had to take on the second bus, which would eventually take over a hour on that one long and straight freeway. This road was only just over two inches long on the map!!!!

I got on my first bus easily enough as there were a few options of different buses for me to take, to get me to the second bus stop, which took me around twenty minutes, but I had to wait ages for bus number two, because I was waiting for one particular numbered bus, and they were not exactly frequent. In fact, I almost grew a full beard waiting for the fcuking thing!!

When the bus finally arrived, it took a hour to get to the stadium along one long straight road (I've already said that!) I thought the public transport system to get to this stadium was very poor, and not very regular, just like in Dallas, but I guess this is America, and the car does usually rule the roost. There was a great train line in downtown Phoenix, but sadly this never went anywhere near Glendale, where the stadium was located.

I finally arrived at the University of Phoenix stadium with a few hours to spare before the game started, as yet again I was tailgating, this time with an Arizona Cardinals Superfan, a guy named Randy Earick. It took me bloody ages of wandering around a huge area of fields full of tailgates outside the stadium to find Randy, as this tailgate area seemed like the biggest one I had been to so far. Randy's tailgate was tucked away in a field quite far away from the stadium, so it took a few text messages between us for me to eventually find, and finally hook up with him and his gang of Cardinals fans.

The visitors to Phoenix for this game were the Minnesota Vikings, a team I have always had a tiny affection for, simply because I like the lilac colour of their shirts, (I know this is sad, but it's very true!) and on this day at Randy's tailgate, I was very happy to meet a real Vikings character and a great guy named Syd Davy. Syd is a Vikings

Superfan, and he was in full Superfan regalia, completely as a Viking, and totally covered in facepaint. I thought he looked great, and I remember thinking it must have taken him ages to get ready for action.

Syd told me he has not missed a Vikings game in 29 years, and he lives in Canada. How amazing is that? Unbelievable dedication to his team. I just hope he gets some kind of recognition from the Minnesota Vikings, as I think he should be given a free season ticket in recognition for his incredible support over the years, especially as the Vikings are not exactly one of the better NFL teams in the league. Now that's dedication, following a team who to my knowledge have never been anywhere near a Superbowl since 1980??? Great work Syd.

Randy's tailgate was great as usual, especially the food, followed by a load of beers and great company from Randy, his Cardinals friends, Syd the Viking, and a bunch of other Vikings fans who had made the long journey from Minneapolis.

The University of Phoenix Stadium as the sun went down looked amazing from the outside, like a massive spaceship, but it was even more impressive when I got inside.

This stadium held the previous year's Superbowl, and I think it was in my top five stadiums out of the thirty two I would eventually attend, including the one I went to in Hawaii for the Pro Bowl.

The University of Phoenix Stadium was a new stadium and in an area surrounded by funky bars, resturants and cinema's, a kind of village if you like, and I liked the vibe very much.

I still cannot believe how much I paid for the ticket to this game. On my life!, I swear I paid five dollars from my favourite website Tickpick.com, simply because I bought the ticket over two months in advance. Definately my kind of price!

Did I mention earlier in the book, (I'm sure I did, as I'm known for repeating myself) after spending far too much money than I would have liked to have spent on tickets for a few of the earlier games on the tour, I had an idea. I discovered that if I went forward and worked my way backwards on my schedule, I could see how much tickets cost for future games towards to end of the regular season on my favourite website Tickpick.com.

This gave me a general idea as to which tickets to buy in advance, and what tickets to wait on. Ticket prices would depend on how teams were performing around this time, and this indicated to me if teams were struggling, and unlikely to make the play offs, tickets would be available in abundance and I will simply pick up the pieces, as cheap as chips. And this is exactly what I did for the rest of the regular season, saving me a kings ransom or a fist full of dollars.

Tickpick were great, they supported me from day one, after I informed them of my tour. I asked them if they could give me a discount if I purchased many tickets from them over the course of the season. Tickpick offered me twenty bucks off all tickets I would purchase from them, and I found two games where the tickets were so cheap, I would get them for practically nothing.

This game in Phoenix, Vs the Minnesota Vikings was twenty five bucks, so I got the ticket for five. The game in St Louis against the Tampa Bay Buccaneers was twenty one bucks, so I got it for one. OH YES!

Most other games were of course a little more expensive than this, but some were not much more, say 30-50 dollars, but for me this was always a lot cheaper than I ever expected to pay. Over the entire season, I would hazard a guess I would have paid on average around 50-70 bucks a ticket. The most I paid was 250 for the opening game of the season at the Patriots "Gillette Stadium" in Foxboro, the cheapest a dollar in St Louis, I got into four games for free because of the kindness shown to me by my good friends Joe Carlson in New York, and Josh Casillas in San Diego, Colin in Nashville, and Shad Khan in Jacksonville. And then there was Oakland......that's coming up.

I also bought the odd ticket before the game started from fans who had a spare, and I always got the ticket for less than face value. This happened to me in Tampa, Buffalo, San Fransisco, Seattle and Miami.

Whenever I speak to anybody online from the various NFL fan or team websites I follow, who ask me what they should do when attempting to buy tickets, I always say do not buy them off websites like Stub Hub or Razorgator, as they are very expensive. Go to Tickpick.com as they do not charge any commission. I'm sure there is some commission charge factored into the price you pay, but it must be minimal, and even tickpick are expensive sometimes, so it all depends on the game.

Another major factor which influences the price of tickets, is when a big name player misses the game through injury, or returns from injury, or for any other reason like being dropped or suspended. This happened to me more than once, as when Tom Brady got his four game ban recinded, the ticket price almost doubled in minutes. When Ben Rothlisburger, the Pittsburgh Steelers QB got injured, the few days before the game I attended in Pittsburgh Vs the Baltimore Ravens, my 168 dollars ticket was worth about 60. You do win some, and lose some, but overall I think I came out on top.

I always bought the cheapest ticket and moved around the stadium once the game started. Sometimes I had a nose bleed seat and I stayed in it for the whole game, as I just love being high up with a view across the whole field.

Tickpick eventually moved the goalposts a little by saying they would give me twenty dollars off every ticket I bought over fifty bucks, and ten dollars off everything under. I understood why, as they had to make some profit from a ticket and they had been pretty damn good to me, so I didn't want to take the piss too much, and I accepted the new T's and C's.

This particular seat in Phoenix was a real cracker, especially for five bucks, and I sat next to a couple who were Cardinals fans, the husband was an ex pat Englishman who had been living in Arizona for many years, his wife was a local girl, and they were Cardinals season ticket holders. Two lovely people indeed and great company throughout the game.

This game, I was to change from my normal affilliation for supporting the home team, as I was chearing for the visiting Minnesota Vikings. The reason for this was because I had such a lovely time in Minneapolis when I watched the Vikings game while there, I loved the city, and they were a team on the up, I liked their runningback Adrian Peterson, and oh, I love the colour of their lilac shirts!

Around this time, I was pondering over an idea, (a very stupid one) something which will SHOCK genuine football fans all across the globe, and make me public enemy number one, especially in the Cowboys fraternity. I was seriously considering changing teams. YEP. I can almost feel the disgust coming through my computer screen!!!!!

I was getting fed up with my Cowboys being so shit, a one man team in Romo, and sometimes even HE is rubbish, well most of the time actually. Letting Demarco Murray go I thought was massive, Dez Bryant holding the club to ransom, and the Jerry Jones circus was just getting on my tits. (only Joking Jerry, if you are reading this, I'm very sorry, oh and by the way, I would love to watch a game with you in your private suite!)

The Minnesota Vikings would be moving into a brand new stadium the following season, so this will be a new beginning or era for this team, so maybe this could be a new beginning for me? I thought.

So am I gonna change? Well I've calmed down a little bit since then, but it's still something I will consider as the new season gets nearer. Watch this space!

On the second draft of my book, I have calmed down completely, and to this day, and probably to my last, I will always be a Cowboys fan. PHEW, but I must admit, it was a close call not to become a Viking.

The game started, and in typical D-Mo fashion, a complete jinx to my temporary new Vikings, as they were two scores and ten points down in no time. But the brilliant Adrian Peterson, who was outstanding all evening, made the half time score level at 10-10.

The second half came and Carson Palmer, the Cards QB was having a pretty good night, and the Cardinals took the lead again. But back came the Vikings yet again, so it was a very exciting game, and it was pretty clear this game was going right down to the wire.

The Vikings did themselves no favours at all by fumbling the ball three times, giving the ball back to the Cards, then getting it back, then losing it again. It was very exciting and frustrating at the same time.

With about five minutes left on the clock, which is probably about thirty minutes in real time with all the time outs and other stoppages, I decided to leave the stadium as I had the long bus ride back to my hostel, well two buses actually, and with the extra traffic, I was knew I going to get home well after midnight.

The game was 20-20 when I left, and to be honest I was gutted to be leaving as it really was on a knife's edge and an end to end game which I was enjoying very much.

I said goodbye to my new friends whom I had sat with, and

I begrudgingly departed off to my bus stop. Lucky I did, as when I got to the bus stop, which was about a 15-20 minutes walk from the stadium, a guy who was working for the bus company, was standing by the bus stop listening to the game on his radio. This guy informed me that the next bus, approaching soon, was in fact the last bus of the evening. I was amazed, as not only was there a big game on, it was only 9.00pm. What the fcuk? this is a major city in America, not a small town in middle England.

As I waited for the bus, I listened to the game with the man and a few other fans who were like me, waiting for their ride home. There were now about two minutes to go, and the game was still very close. The Cardinals had kicked another field goal after I had left, but the game continued to be alive for the Vikings who were only trailing 23-20, but they had posssion of the ball.

With seconds remaining, the Vikings were 48 yards away from the endzone. A field goal could have been attempted, and if successful, the game would then go into overtime. I had very mixed feelings about this, because if the field goal was kicked, I would loved to have been there to see it and watch the drama of overtime.

Also, if the field goal was successfully kicked, there would be less people coming out of the stadium, meaning the roads would be empty for me to get home without sitting in the gridlocked traffic for hours on end.

The Vikings head coach made the call, or the decision to take one final play, to try to gain some extra yardage, to have a shorter field goal attempt. Teddy Bridgewater, the

Vikings Quarterback took the snap, and fumbled the ball with only seven seconds left on the clock. FCUK!

That was it, the Cards recovered the ball and the game was over. Oh boy, what a way to lose a game that was so close for the entire three hours. I was gutted for the Vikings fans, especially my Superfan friend Syd. What a stupid decision by the Vikings coaching staff??

Typically my bus was late, and heavy traffic started to form, but eventually the bus turned up, and off we went. But I knew I was on the clock to get to my second bus stop before that last bus left, but it looked like I was ok for time. WRONG!

I got off the first bus at my stop about a hour later, and I had been looking on my phone, and I knew that my next and last bus was at 10pm. The time now was about 9.56, so me and a young guy who had been working at the University of Phoenix stadium, and was also on my first bus, ran to the next bus stop about one hundred yards across a busy intersection.

As 10pm approached, my phone indicated the next bus was arriving in seven minutes. PHEW, I thought, at least it's coming and we had not missed it. HA! five minutes later I looked again, and it said the next bus was at 5.45am the next day. Brilliant, so our bus simply disappeared from the radar, and we were now stranded at the side of the road in a pretty dark and seedy looking area of Phoenix.

Plan B was an Uber cab, so I got on the app, and I ordered a cab for me and my new friend, who incidently explained that he had no money on him. I was never going to leave this guy stranded, so I told him the ride was on me, and he looked pretty relieved. The cab arrived ten minutes later and off we go to my hostel. Or so I thought.

Downtown Phoenix Arizona takes a little time to get your bearings, as there are numbered streets as well as numbered avenues. On the way home I made ANOTHER typical Dennis Moss schoolboy error, as I usually take a landmark near to where I stay, as to explain where I am staying to bus drivers or cabbies. This time my landmark was a supermarket/gas station around the corner from my hostel called "Circle K".

The cab ride was a long straight road and after about fifteen minutes, I knew we were close to my hostel as I saw the "Circle K". I decided I would jump out and buy the usual two dollars hot dogs which I ate on a regular basis, so I jumped out, and off the cab goes, taking my new mate home just a few more blocks up the road.

I looked around as I stood outside "Circle K" and I noticed immediately I did not recognise where the bloody hell I was. I opened up Google Maps, put in my location, and I realised I was still a twenty five minutes walk from my hostel. How the fcuk has this happened? Well. What I did was, I got out on 7th street, when in fact I wanted 7th avenue. What a cupid stunt!

Honestly, I never cease to amaze myself sometimes how stupid I can be. I can laugh about it now, but this was not the first, or the last time I would do something idiotic like this. I already told you about my bus trip from San Diego to

Phoenix when I arrived at the bus terminal a day early, but did I tell you the story about the same cheap flight I booked twice? The same bloody flight. Yep, stoopid hey? Well that's me!

I ordered another Uber cab as I was not going to walk in this very dark and dingy part of town at this time of night, and I eventually got to bed around 1am. What a nightmare journey to get home that was, and you wait for my next time in Phoenix in the play off's, it gets even worse than this!

I woke up the next morning, had breakfast, chatted with a few of the guests, and I thought about what I would do that day. I felt like a hike, and I heard a couple of the girls who worked at the hostel mention they were going on a horse ride into the desert. That sounds interesting I thought, and I was well up for that.

I asked the two girls, Caila, from California and Alexa from Finland, if I could tag along. They said yes, so I made a call to the people who rent out the horses, to book myself a nag, and I was gutted to be told there were no more horses available. FCUK! I was so up for going and bloody damn disappointed.

I went along anyway, just in case there was a no show, and somehow I always normally blagged my way in everywhere I go. Not this time buddy! But to be honest, when I got to the area for the trekking, it was so beautiful, I was happy to spend a hour or so wandering around the desert looking at all the cachtus (cachti?) and climbing up a big chunk of rock with a big hole in the middle, with fantastic views all across Phoenix.

I got talking to a lovely lady from California on top of the rock, we took a few pictures for each other and sat chatting for a while in the amazing and tranquil setting in a part of the Arizona desert. The view reminded me of something you see in the old red Indian movies, lots of reddish coloured rocks and dust, cachti, blue skies, and mountains in the distance, it was beautiful.

When the girls came back from their horse ride, or actually, horse walk, I could see from their faces I had not missed too much. So we all headed off for a walk for a hour or so and we enjoyed the scenery.

Arizona is the warmest state in the winter, across the entire US, and it was lovely to be in the sunshine and the heat, and nice dry heat, unlike Florida where it is very humid and you sweat like a pig in minutes. This kind of heat is so much more enjoyable and comfortable to be in for me.

Tonight was my final night in Phoenix, and the hostel owner Keith recommended me a local bar to have a couple of bevvies (drinks) in. I was told by the younger crowd, the bar was not that great, and they were heading off to a more funkier bar to play pool, listen to banging modern music, and had to pay to get in, all of my biggest nightmares rolled into one.

I said I would go, but on the way I was told by one of the gang it was a 20-30 minutes walk, so as I approached the locar bar Keith recommended, I bailed out of the plan to go to the noisy bar, as I knew I would not last long in that place and I never wanted the long walk back, especially if I got as pissed as a newt!! so I went into my first choice bar.

It was a cool little bar, with a good selection of beers, and live music. A great jazzy/bluesy band played, with a brilliant guitarist and singer, so I plotted up at a table and listened to the music.

Going out into bars alone was something I was very used to, and sometimes I really enjoyed being alone, just me, my phone and my social media buddies from all over the globe having a chat. Technology really is an amazing thing and I would be lost with out it, especially on these kind of adventures. I like the thought of being just a click of a button away from talking to friends and family, when being far away from home, even seeing them on the screen while talking, and all for free if you are on wifi. But when the wifi is slow, or does not work. AARRRGGGGHHHHHHH! Its sooooo frustrating.

After watching the band play for a hour of so, I returned to my hostel to get my bag ready for my flight to Denver the next afternoon.

Right outside my dorm room in the hostel was a small TV room that nobody ever seemed to used. As it was Friday night, most people were out, and the hostel was very quiet, so I turned the telly on, and I saw that the hostel had Netflix, so I could watch practically any film I wanted. RESULT!

I had hardly seen any TV so far on this trip, only NFL games, English soccer, and the odd film when I was at a film night in a hostel, or the very rare occasion I took a motel room.

I decided to watch one of my favourite films of all time,

"The Warriors", a movie about American street gangs in New York back in the 70's. A brilliant film.

I was so content watching this film, laying on the sofa with peace and quiet all around me, and for those two hours, I felt like I was in my bedroom at home, it was absolute bliss, and a great ending to a lovely time in a very nice hostel in beautiful Phoenix Arizona, a place I would return to a month later.

Stadium-26
Mile High Stadium
Denver Broncos

I flew out of Phoenix on a very cheap afternoon flight to my next destination, Denver Colorado. Actually, my flight was cheaper than the fifty bucks I had to pay to get my bag on board, so the money I saved on the flight, was lost on the bag.

I have always been used to booking a flight, and the bags are a part of that deal or included in the price, but not here in America, no sir, and this system has now reached the UK with all the cheap airlines moving the goalposts. So just when I thought I had found myself a nice cheap flight at a convenient time to fly, then BOSH! twenty five dollars on top for the bag. If you didn't book your bag in advance, it could go up to fifty bucks, and on this occasion for me, it bloody did!

I would'nt have minded this if I only took one flight, but I ended up taking twenty one. What a complete waste of money, but something I simply could not avoid.

Denver was one of many US cities I never thought I would ever get the chance or reason to visit. I had a similar feeling at many of the other US cities I arrived into, and this always gave me a little buzz, and made me feel excited to be there.

I had met a nice couple in China a few years earlier who lived in Denver, and according to them, it was a lovely city, so I was looking forward to seeing it for myself.

I had the choice of three hostels in Denver which were advertised on the Hostelworld website. One was in the centre of town called "Hostel Fish", a great location, but very expensive for a hostel, fifty bucks a night, compared with around the bog standard 25-30 I was paying on a regular basis across the country. The other two options were cheaper, so of course this major factor attracted me more, and something which always had some baring on my final choice.

I must admit, like most things, you do get what you pay for in the price of a hostel, but yet again, I was away for eight months, and if I kept going to plush accomodations, I was defeating the object, and wasting a fistfull of dollars, which incidently I was doing anyway, practically everyday on some random items of food, drink, snacks, merchandise or any form of entertainment I was experiencing.

I eventually decided to stay at a place called "The Funkhaus", as it was half the price of "Hostel Fish" and the location was great and easy for me to get to the Denver Broncos "Mile High Stadium" on Sunday, as well as the downtown area of Denver, just a few stops away on the subway. There was a train station just a five minutes walk from the "Funkhaus Hostel", which was the icing on the cake, which I soon found out to be a from another planet...................a space cake!

I had heard Colorado was one of only a few US state's in which marijuana was legal and available in abundance. This meant absolutely nothing to me as a passionate non smoker who had never smoked dope before, but I would have a go at anything that was offered to me, usually doing it once, and never again, well sometimes, so I was not bothered or concerned either way about the copious amonts of drugs that were freely available to me at the "Funkhaus".

I had left the warm climate of Phoenix, for the much obvious colder weather of Denver, which was evident by the melting snow I saw all around me from the bus window I took from the international airport to the subway station, heading to my new fixed abode.

I arrived at the "Funkhaus", and as soon as I opened the door, I was immediately hit by the overpowering pungent aroma of skunk, pot, dope, marijuana, call it what you will. I have always liked the smell of marijuana, even though I don't smoke it, but this was different, as it smelt like I was entering a poppy field.

The hostel was run by a fantastic and very friendly host named Mark, friendly probably as he was always as high as a kite, even at 9.30 in the morning! I checked into my room and I met a few of the people staying at the hostel.

I went up to the TV area where around seven or eight people were sitting on bean bags, all smoking their funny fags, and all completely off their tits on another planet. Mark was passing around the peace pipe (bong) and he offered it to me, so I had a couple of goes or sucks, but it just made me cough, probably as this novice was doing it wrong, and I felt no different at all for this experience. When in Rome and all that!

I have to admit, I loved my three days in this hostel, Mark ran this place brilliantly, and everybody had his complete respect, as well as his stash!! All the guests were very nice people and behaved themselves all of the time. Mark was a great host indeed to his guests, and very generous, always offering food and drinks, as well as phoning up for take away deliveries of pizza and other things, and handing out the goodies for free when they arrived. I really liked Mark.

Now let me stand on my soapbox for a moment. I've never been a user of smoking dope, and I had no problem at all with all the stuff that was being smoked around me at the "Funkhaus" hostel, as I personally have great willpower for things I don't want or particularly need, even when they are full in my face. I was offered all kinds of drugs constantly and I could have had as much as I wanted, if that was my thing, but it's not. (yes on a very rare occasion). People were smoking it around me practically all of the time I was at the "Funkhaus", day and night, and I never battered an eyelid, and this never bothered me in the slightest.

This smoking of dope never caused any problems EVER, as everybody was happy, laughing, chilled, relaxed, spaced out, call it what you will. It made for a good atmosphere, nice conversation, and a nice smell around the place, if you like that kind of thing. There were people staying here from all across America, mostly from states where "Mary Jane" (dope) was illegal, and they were enjoying it to the max.

I can never understand why this is deemed to be a dangerous drug, as it never makes people crazy, aggressive or angry, everything that alcohol does, and I'm a regular consumer of the devil's water. This amazes me, as alcohol, a substance that turns lovely people into psychopaths, and creates more problems, fights, arrests, and so much more, is allowed to be sold free and easy everywhere, and yet marijuana, a substance that calms people down and never creates a crime at all, is seen to be a bad drug, and something extremely illegal. This simply baffles me, and always will. Money is probably something to do with this fact as per usual.

I would not go on a march and say drugs should be legalised and wave flags all over the place, but it does seem crazy to me how two different so called "past times" are perceived in two very different ways, when they are both coming from natural herbs, plants or crops, both grown from our very same earth. I don't get it.

And let's be honest, most of our law makers are law breakers, and these people who say it's illegal, are probably all smoking themselves stupid behind their closed doors . OK, rant over.

That night I popped out to look around the area to see what was in my neighbourhood, and there were lots of nice bars, resturants, fast food joints and shops. I ended up having a lovely sushi meal, again stupid on my part, as I spent about fifty dollars, when I could have had a cheap fast food meal for much less than ten.

I know this was wasted money, and I did this so many times over my eight months away from home, but I was always interested in trying new things, especially the local foods, and even more so, the local beers. This is something in me that will never change.

I returned to my hostel, which by now I had nicknamed "The drugs den"! and I sat around with a bunch of people, and the bong was being passed around as usual.

There was a nice mix of people in this hostel, mainly young, pretty girls, nice lads, some looked a bit damaged or oddballs, and to me, it seemed like they were smoking themselves in their own oblivions, probably trying to temporarily forget their not so happy real worlds?? Maybe I'm wrong and they just loved being high??

A pretty attractive woman, who incidently caught my eye immediately, arrived into the group and she made herself comfortable and quickly snuggled up next to Mark, the owner of the hostel, so I assumed she was in fact Mark's girlfriend. This happened again the following afternoon and evening, and I basically took no notice as they looked like a pretty nice couple.

But as I am quite an observant and perceptive kind of guy, something looked a little odd to me. The woman in question named Ashley, who by the way was around 6ft tall, blonde, in her early 40's, an ex lingerie model with a body like a mermaid, with incredible and massive knockers. Basically, she was a babe.

Ashley looked much more interested in Mark, than he was into her, as Mark was totally ignoring all of Ashley's advances and flirtatious ways, as he was far more interested in sucking on his bong and getting high, than the cuddles Ashley was obviously wanting in return from him.
Erm.......... I could quite obviously see something was amiss. It was like they had had a massive argument or something??

Mark was simply not interested.

The next evening I was walking along the main street in our area called "Santa Fe Drive", which was the street with most of the bars, resturants and the fast food places that most of us from the hostel were getting our dinners from, and as I was wandering along in my own little world, I looked into a shop window, and I saw Ashley coming out of this one particular shop.

"Hi Ashley", I said. "What you up to". "I'm working" she said "I'm trying to get some business from this shop as I work as a sales person". "You got time for a coffee" I asked. "OK, I've got about thirty minutes" Ashley replied.

Ashley was hot, red hot, and she had a ten out of ten body. So hot, I would have needed oven gloves to grab hold of those great and huge fun bags! She was wearing a very short skirt. long socks up to her knees and a very tight top with those great tits bursting to get out of the jumper she was wearing.

As we walked to the coffee shop, we chatted, and I asked Ashley, "So how long have you been with Mark"? "WHAT"? she gasped. "Mark's not my boyfriend", I just hang out with him at the Funkhaus", she said, to my complete delight. "I've been hanging around with Mark for about three months, and we have not even kissed". "WHHAATTTTT"!! I said. "Yep" she said.

I found out Mark was in fact Ashley's landlord, and she was obviously trying to keep him sweet and on side, as she was probably getting a very good deal out of him. Ashley was a single mum and had two young kids, and from what she told me, she wanted to move out, but she was struggling financially, so she had to keep Mark where she wanted him.

We went into a local coffee shop/cafe, and immediately, and I mean instantly, probably within a minute after we sat down in the cafe, I went straight for the proverbial jugular, (the jugs would come later!) We sat across from each other, and I was flirting outragiously with her, and getting back from her just as much as I was giving."Ashley, you are amazing, and you have a better body than a Ferrari, I'm sooooooo attracted to you it's incredible". I told her.

Ashley told me she absolutely adored my accent and she really liked me as I was just her type. BINGO! After she said this, I leaned forward and kissed her right on the lips, she was a little surprised, as it had taken me all of five minutes since she came out of the shop I had seen her in and told me she was single, but she loved it, and boy, so did I.

We talked a little more, especially about meeting up later that evening, to continue what we had started, but Ashley had a meeting to attend and was going to finish late, but she could come over to the hostel around 11pm. "Fcuk the hostel" I said, "Mark will be there, come and pick me up and we will go for a drive and have some fun in the car". "OK, she said, but I need to get my friend to baby sit for me" Ashley said, "So no promises", she told me.

I walked Ashley back to her car, we had a quick snog up an alleyway and I managed a quick grope of those glorious cannons of her's, and we arranged to see each other later that night to continue what we had started. Or so I thought.

WRONG! FCUK FCUK FCUK!

I waited in complete anticipation and much excitement in the hostel for the messages I had sent to Ashley, to be returned by her, confirming the gig was on, as I had some amazing plans for her that night, I bloody swear I did!

I never heard anything from Ashley for ages, and the waiting was pure torture for me, but when she finally did respond, she said she was waiting for her friend to finish work, and she would ask her to pop round to look after her kids, who were in bed. So I waited, and waited, and waited....nothing. I called Ashley's phone and I was completely ignored for over two hours. I was fcuking livid!

That night I layed in my bed staring at the ceiling, absolutely fuming with Ashley until about 1am, when I finally gave up on the idea, or the dreams of my very own interpretation of the "Karma Sutra", or the marathon session I had planned with Ashley, I totally lost my patience with her.

You know by now I absolutely fcuking hate silence, if she was not coming, why did she not just tell me? not bloody leave me hanging around like a fcuking horny dog in season!

When I finally got through to Ashley the next day, she very casually said to me "Oh, I fell asleep with the kids around 10pm, and my phone was on silent". Yeah fcuking right you did, I thought. I wanted to give her the "hairdryer treatment", but as I was in Denver for two more days, I did not want to ruin the small chance I thought I had, of getting

Ashley's lovely long legs high into the air and pointing towards the moon!!

See its this kind of bullshit I hate more than any words I could possibly type. As I approach the grand old age of fifty this year, I simply will not put up with this kind of behaviour from a woman ever again, and I will drop a useless timewaster like Ashley after the first letdown every time now. Why do people not return messages? I don't mean in 5-10 minutes, or even a hour, I mean full stop, period, never, total silence. I hate it.

Sunday was game day, and an afternoon game between the Denver Broncos and their divisional rivals the Oakland Raiders. I like the Oakland Raiders, especially their crazy fans, who always dress up to the max, which could be anything from a "Darth Vader" look alike, a gorilla (which there is, a fruitcake/madman fan named "Gorillaman"), all kinds of gory looking scary monsters, and so much more. They are great, the best fans in the NFL in my opinion.

I had been given the contact details to my next new Superfan friend, from the usual sources of my Superfan family of Tim "The Captain" Young, "Who Dey" from Cinci and Josh from "Bolt Pride" in San Diego, and I touched base with Robert "Woody" Woodworth, the Denver Broncos Superfan on Facebook before I arrived into Denver.

Woody's tailgate was just in front of the main entrance to legendary "Mile High Stadium", and I found him very easily from his directions, as I just followed the beautiful aroma of his incredible food! I always looked forward to these tailgates as I knew the food was going to be delicious, and

Woody's food was up there with the best of what I had at any tailgate.

As soon as I arrived and I met Woody, I knew I had yet another friend for life, and within a minute I was holding a cold beer, and within two, I was tucking into an amazing hamburger that Woody's friend and chef had just cooked on the BBQ. What a fantastic welcome.

It was a lot colder in Denver than it was in Phoenix, so I was wearing all my cold weather clothing, as there was a bit of snow on the ground, but the sun was shining, the skies were blue, the party was in full swing, and another brilliant experience and the start of another great day at another iconic NFL stadium.

Yet again the weather was being kind to me, as usually this time of the year the weather in Denver was normally a lot colder than it was on this day, and it was usually covered in a lot more snow than which was currently on the ground. I was very lucky in my time in Denver with the weather, as the sun was shining most of the time, as I was told it does for around 300 out of the 365 days of the year.

I actually like it when the weather is cold and the sun is shining, as it has a very fresh feel to it as it's dry, not like the damp and bleak conditions a London winter has. I was fortunate to miss the bad weather in my time in Denver, but not quite, as I will write at the end of this section of my adventure.

The "Mile High Stadium", the home of the Denver Broncos was one of the stadiums I was always looking forward to visiting. The Broncos were a good team when I first started watching the NFL on our TV screens back in the 80's, and I was a big fan of their golden boy and quarterback John Elway, and Denver were always a very strong team at home and they did not lose at their home stadium very often.

I remember a few of the Broncos games I watched over the years, that were played in terrible blizzards of snow, which I thought looked great from my warm and comfortable armchair at home in London! and I have always wanted to watch a game in a blizzard and the freezing cold, just for the experience. When I did in fact see games in horrible conditions, this novalty wore off very very quickly indeed, as being soaked by monsoon rains, or freezing your nuts off in the extreme cold is no fun at all, I can assure you.

The "Mile High Stadium" always seemed like a very special stadium to me, as it was what it says on the tin, a mile above sea level, obvious really! To me this sounded crazy, but when I was there, it felt no different than being in any other stadium, as for some reason I thought the air might be thinner, so it could be an unfair advantage against the visiting teams who were not used to this. I wanted to experience how this would feel to me, but to be honest, I felt there was no difference at all. But then again, I wasn't exactly running around was I!

I was buzzing as I walked into the iconic "Mile High Stadium", so now I'm officially a member of the "Mile High Club"!!! I wished!

The visitors on this day were divisional rivals The Oakland Raiders, a struggling team who I saw lose to another struggling team, the Bears in Chicago. I have huge respect and a love for the Oakland Raiders fans, as they are in my opinion, more crazy than all the other crazy fans in the NFL, of course in a very nice way.

The Raiders fans get a bit of a bad rep (reputation), but I always found them to be noisy, passionate and crazy in the nicest possible way. There were always a big following of Raiders fans in all the games I attended, when they played away from their Californian home, and they really supported their teams to the max, even when they were losing, which in this season, was quite often.

This is why I expected an easy win for the Broncos, and if they did, it almost certainly booked their place in the play off's, and ended the Raiders yet again poor season.

I had a great seat for this game, right near the very top of my usual nose bleed section. I remember sitting next to two big fat ladies, the one next to me was so large, she was hanging all over me, which I didn't mind too much, because when the sun down went behind the stadium, it was quite cold, so her body heat gave me a little extra warmth and insulation!

After the usual pre game entertainment, including a grey horse racing around the field looking like a raindeer with a silly hat on, (which reminded me of my horse Vibrato Valtat) the game eventually started.

I was pretty upset yet again on seeing the Broncos play without their legend and normally first choice QB Peyton Manning, who was on the bench, as of late he had not been playing to his usual very high standard, and back up QB

Brock Osweiler was playing very well and unbeaten in his three starts for the team.

I expected a high scoring game, but as usual, what do I know?, and as half time approached, the Broncos were winning 12-0 from four successfully kicked field goals. Both teams could not get anywhere near the end zones and yet again this game reminded me of the terrible game I had witnessed in Tampa when my Cowboys and the Bucs could not score a touchdown, until the Bucs finally did in the last minute.

The Raiders had not scored a point in the first half, but little did I know the Broncos would do exactly the same in the second. The Raiders scored the only touchdown of the game in the third quarter, so now at 12-7, it was game on and a lot more exciting.

At half time I decided to go for my usual wander around the stadium, and get away from the fat bird squashing the life out of me in my seat. The sun had now gone down behind the stand I was sitting in, and it was now very cold indeed, so I went high up into another section where the sun was still shining into that area of the stadium. It was a very good move as I felt so much warmer, and the view from the very top of this stand was amazing. I was feeling so great to be in this stadium, a real dream come true. I'm in the famous and iconic "Mile High Stadium", and I was soooooo happy to be here.

The second half was a marked improvement to the dull first, and the Raiders started to look like a pretty decent team, especially a guy named "Khalil Mack", who sacked (tackled) the Broncos quarterback five times, including in the end zone for a safety. (a two point score). I was very disappointed with the Broncos wide receivers, as they dropped about five very easy catches, which if caught, would have easily won them this game.

Field goal attempts were missed by both teams, which made the final quarter very exciting, as this game would be remembered as a game of mistakes. Raiders QB Derek Carr threw a touchdown, but then he missed out with an incomplete pass to try for the two point conversion, rather than kick the extra point.

I could not understand why the Raiders went for the two points and not just kick the field goal, because after missing this two point attempt, a Broncos field goal would tie the game, when the extra point would have given the Raiders a four point lead, with the Broncos needing a touchdown to win. Maybe this call was made because the pressure of needing a touchdown, would make the Broncos more cavellier, chase the game and take more risks, making a bigger chance of turning the ball over, giving it back to the Raiders, and the game would be over???

Listen to me, I sound like I know what I'm talking about!! but how can this stupid Englishman tell these so called American experts how to play their beautiful game? But sometimes, some of these stupid play calls made by the coaches simply baffled me.

The Raiders defence held tight for the entire fourth quarter, and they went on to win a very tight game 15-12. I really enjoyed the second half, but I was a little sad the Broncos lost as I wanted them to make the play off's, and especially gain home field advantage back in Denver. Not because I was a fan, but because I wanted to return to Denver and bang the lovely Ashley into next week, more than once!!!

I left the very impressive "Mile High Stadium" and I headed back to my drugs den of a hostel, which was a very short two stops and five minutes hop on the subway. Thank god for that as most of the time it took me ages to get home after games, sometimes over two hours, including night games, as it did in New England, New York, Phoenix and San Francisco.

One thing I was soooooooo gutted to hear, was that the "Mile High Stadium" I had just left and enjoyed so much, was not the original "Mile High Stadium" I thought was the one I used to watch on TV back in the 80's where Elway dominated. In fact, this was a new "Mile High Stadium", now named "Sports Authority Field", built right next door to where the old "Mile High" used to be, the very one I thought I was actually in. It was like being in the new "Wembley Stadium", but not the original one with the famous twin towers.

Don't get me wrong, the new "Mile High" was for sure one of my favourite stadiums on my tour, but sadly not THE original. I'm sure most NFL fans knew this minor detail, but this dopey Englishman had no idea at all, and was not a happy bunny when realising this.

I returned to my hostel and I sat with the drug squad (as I called them) all smoking dope and sucking on bongs, and I watched my Dallas Cowboys get thrashed yet again, this time by The Green Bay Packers, my second team. This effectively finished off the Cowboys season, and now my Boys had no chance of making the play off's, so this pissed me off, as I would have travelled anywhere in the country to see my Cowboys if they had made it into the play off's. The Cowboys would lose their final three games anyway, so this Packers defeat made no difference at all.

The next day I was offered the chance to have a relaxing day at a spa named "Idaho Pools", with Mark from the hostel and another guest named Jen. This was on the grounds of a very old natural spring, which was once used by the Native American Indians many years ago. "Idaho Pools" was in a lovely little quiet town in the rocky mountains and I absolutely loved it. I felt like I was a million miles from home, which incidently, I actually was.

We spent a hour or so bathing in these theraputic and very relaxing hot springs, as I love this kind of stuff. I really liked Mark, and I felt a little bit of a wanker for snogging his bird the day before, but then again, she was not really his bird as Ashley told me they had not even kissed, (god knows why Mark??) and she gave me the green light to play on her bongo's, and have tonsil tennis with her, so my conscience was fairly clear, but still not totally, as Mark was really a nice guy to me.

But if Mark had any idea I was trying to jump on his so called chick, then this would have been a very awkward situation indeed for me, or even both or us.

I tried my best again to meet with Ashley that evening, which was my last night in Denver and I knew if she really wanted to see me, or she wanted a good servicing, she would have made every effort to have got to me. Again the bloody silence was deafening, as she never communicated with me at all, and boy did I try. Ashley messed me about yet again, and to cut to the chase of a very short boring story, I never saw that prick teaser again.

I can't begin to tell you how totally fcuking gutted I was, this body of a goddess, which was mine for the taking, was dangled right in front of my face (literally), and yet I could'nt touch the bastard. I was livid, gutted and so very frustrated, as I wanted my hands on those fcuking weapons of mass distraction, or her very only personal "rocky mountains" more than anybody will ever know.

I had tried so hard on my tour to get some action with the American chicks, or even birds staying in my hostels. I had soooooo many women say to me, "I luuuuurrrvvvve your English accent", something I was told would open more doors for me than a concierge at a five star hotel, but sadly I seemed to be jinxed in this department, as all liasons eventually led up the garden path to nowhere fast, and boy, did this boy try.

But what was funny (I don't mean ha ha funny, I mean bloody typical), was as soon as I left Denver, Ashley started communicating like I would expect a normal decent human being to do. She would return a text message straight away, or answer her phone. Why could she have not done this while I was in Denver for fuck sake?

Later that afternoon I decided to go downtown to see what Denver had to offer. 16th Street is where most of the action takes place, and where all the nice bars, coffee shops, resturants and everything else are. It's Denver's version of Oxford Street in London, and I liked it a lot.

I had a bite to eat, then I went to look around the "Colorado State Capital Building" and I ended up in Union Station, the Denver main train station where the Amtrak train comes in and goes out of town. Sadly for me I could not take this train from Phoenix, or to my next destination of St Louis, mainly because there was a small obsticle in the way called the Rocky Mountains!

I really liked Denver, it was clean, laid back, the sun was always shining, even when it was freezing cold, and it had everything I needed in one long street. Oh and it also had great trams which I could ride on for free, which of course, this boy did. Perfecto.

It also had as much dope as a person could consume, without the threat of the "hand on the shoulder treatment" from the boys in blue (cops), if that was your particular thing. No wonder Denver is so laid back, everybody was permanently stoned!

I was leaving early the next day and I had been informed bad weather was forecast in Denver over the next few days, so I thought I would be lucky and get out of Denver just in time. WRONG!

I had a good night sleep, my bags were packed and I was ready to embark on my next adventure. I said my goodbyes to all the lovely guests I had met in the "Funkhaus Hostel", and as I opened the main door to depart for the airport, I nearly had a heart attack as I walked out of the hostel, Denver was under a foot of snow.

My immediate thought was, "fcuk, my flight will be cancelled". It was Tuesday and my next game in St Louis was on Thursday evening, so If I missed this flight, my mission of completing all 31 NFL stadiums will be doomed to failure, as there was no place left on my schedule to get back to St Louis if I missed this game. And there was absolutely no chance of St Louis making the play off's and gaining home field advantage. OH NO, and I only have five more stadiums to go.
NNNOOOOOOOOOOOOOOOOOOOOOO!

I headed to the subway station, which was only a five minutes walk away, but it took me more like fifteen, as I was walking knee deep in snow, carrying a heavy backpack and thinking the very worse about my flight.

I eventually made it to the station, and I was bloody exhausted, as the snow really was that deep, I felt like Scott of the Antarctic!

I boarded the train, and I got the subway five stops to downtown, and I caught the shuttle bus to the airport in complete Colorado blizzard conditions.

I remember filming myself and putting it on Facebook, walking to the subway in the blizzard, getting wet feet in snow up to my knees and laughing like a little boy on christmas day. Crazy, but I look back on it now with a huge smile, as this could have been a time of potential big trouble indeed.

It's funny because even though at the time I was more than slightly concerned regarding my flight, well majorly actually, It was so exciting. I was walking in arctic conditions, probably minus ten or more, snow all over me like Frosty the Snowman and my plane was probably going to be cancelled, but this was another exciting adventure I was on and these struggles really challenged me, and I loved it.

I was always up for these challenges whenever they arose, and boy did they over the six months I was on the road in the US, but I managed to overcome these obsticles or setbacks as I always seemed to get there in the end, sometimes with an enormous amount of struggle, or hardships.

I needed the patience of a saint so many times on this trip, and patience is something I don't normally have in abundance, but I simply had to adapt, and I did. For this, I am so proud of myself, as most people would have thrown in the towel, given up, and gone home, so many many times. For me, this was NEVER EVER an option.

I was so focused and driven on these times of adversity, I was now feeling as strong as an ox, having the time of my life and I wasn't stopping for anything. As I write these words today, I reflect on all those challenging situations I experienced and I'm completely staggered as to how on earth I made this journey right through to the very end, after all the obsticals the universe put in front of me.

Seriously folks, I was Superman, I just had to be.

Stadium-27
Edward Jones Dome
St Louis Rams

I arrived at the airport in Denver not knowing whether my flight had been cancelled, delayed or if I was still leaving today. As I glanced at the departure boards, all I could see were rows and rows of cancellations, probably 75% of all flights were cancelled. Incredibly, amongst all those cancellations, a few random flights were still flying, including mine. TOUCH!

I went through the usual airport security, made it all the way to my boarding gate, and I was trying my best to ignore the negativity in the back of my mind of the prospect we were going nowhere. To my amazement, all went as smooth as silk, when many flights, mainly the long haul ones, grounded to a halt. I knew I had been very very lucky indeed, especially as more snow was forecast, and if I didn't get away now, I could be stuck here in Denver for a while, and this would be a complete disaster, as I had no plan B whatsoever.

I could only relax completely once the plane finally took off, and incredibly we did, in terrible snowy conditions and just a little behind schedule. I knew for a while it was touch and go whether we would in fact get off the ground, so the NFL gods were yet again on my side and making sure my adventure was still on course, and not doomed to failure, which was sooooooo close to happening.

St Louis was a place that was very high on my list of major cities in the US which I knew very little, or practically nothing about. The only thing I did know of, was the iconic "Gateway Arch", the monument which looks like half the Macdonald's logo! I knew the R'n'B star "Nelly" was from here and he was a big fan of the Rams, as I had sent him a message on Twitter to try to watch a game with him. Of course I never got a response, maybe it was too "Hot in Herrre" for him. SORRY!

I had also heard the Baseball team in St Louis were called the "Cardinals", just like the NFL team were back in the day, but the baseball team had quite a bit more success than the NFL team.

I booked into yet again the only hostel in town, named the "Hucklebury Finn", and it was now up to at least five US cities I had visited where I was staying at the only hostel in town. The "Huck Finn" hostel was in an area called "McKinley Heights", a hour on the subway from the airport, and a short bus ride from downtown St Louis.

There were many nice bars in the area I was staying, one right across the road from my hostel, which was great and very convenient as I did not want to be too far away from my hostel late at night. Yet again I had been warned by a few people to be extremely careful while in St Louis, as there are some very rough areas.

The hostel reminded me of a homeless shelter, and the dorm I was in accommodated about twenty people, but luckily for me there were only three of us in there on my first night. The dorm was open plan, which I liked as I felt like I had more room to move around than in a room full of the usual rows of bunk beds, and no space at all. This was different, and reminded me of the nice hostel I had stayed at in Minneapolis, so I was pretty comfortable here.

I signed into the hostel, dropped my bags off and I headed straight out for a bite to eat. I went into the bar opposite the hostel and looked at the menu, it was OK, so in I went. I ordered a beer and some food, and got chatting to a local guy named Jeff, who by complete chance owned another bar just around the corner. Jeff informed me there was a "quiz night" in his bar later that evening, so I ate my meal, and off to Jeff's bar I went. I do love a good old quiz.

Jeff's bar was a lovely place with a good selection of local beers, which I'm always looking to sample rather than the bog standard beers I usually drink at home, so I got stuck in, and had a good slerp/gargle at a few of the local delights.

I met and sat with a lovely bunch of local and regular people to this bar, young, old, men and women, and we formed a team for the quiz night, and I named us "The Cupid Stunts". When I explained to my new friends what the name meant, (I'm sure you can work it out!) they all laughed out loud and loved it, especially when the quiz's compare called out our name after each round, everybody looked at me and roared with laughter. It was a very enjoyable evening with a lovely bunch of people. Believe it or not, we actually won the quiz night, and I really enjoyed the company of my new friends in the couple of hours I spent with them.

I was informed there was an open mike night on Thursday evening and I did say I would try to attend, but I would be at my next game on Thursday night, so I would do my best to get back in time for a sing song and a few of my own songs, which I usually perform if a guitar becomes available.

Wednesday was a free day, so I did my research online as usual, to see what things of interest St Louis had to offer me. The obvious attraction was the "Gateway Arch", so I walked along the river to get to this beautiful monument, which is the number one tourist attraction in St Louis.

I passed yet another baseball stadium, the "St Louis Cardinals" I guess it was, and I did think about doing the stadium tour, but my timing was not great, as the last tour of the day was sold out, which was a shame as I would have done it as there really was not that much else for me to do in town.

I arrived at the "Gateway Arch", and I never quite realised how big this arch was until I stood underneath it. I also did not know you can go inside it, including right up to the very top. Even though I am not a lover of heights, I could handle this, so off I went to get a ticket, which incidentally was in the building I had just left, about a ten minutes walk away. Typical.

I returned to the ticket office, and I was informed the next ticket available to go up the arch was in a hour or so. This was fine, as it gave me a chance to look around the building I was in, which happened to be a museum.

The main subject of this particular museum was local history, as well as the history of slavery in St Louis going back to when slavery was alive and kicking in this part of the US. As I've mentioned before, I have always had a big interest in the story of slavery, especially after seeing the brilliant Alex Haley series in the 70's called "Roots".

It always touched and upset me when I read about the many horrific things that happened to these poor people back in these terrible times in our history. I was watching a short film about a woman slave named "Harriot Tubman" who was a pioneer in her time, to help slaves escape to the north via what was called "The Underground Railroad".

As I watched this film, an old African American couple sat next to me and we watched the film together. I must admit, I felt very awkward, especially when the film clip showed graphic scenes of terrible torture and treatment of the slaves, as well as stories of many horrific things the slaves had to endure.

I cannot imagine how these two people next to me must have felt when they saw those shocking things that happened to their ancestors. In fact, this helps me try to understand how painful it must be for the whole African American community regarding this very dark period in our history. I don't think us white people will ever understand fully how much this subject is still prevalent in black people's lives, even in today's society and how deep this is and always will be.

I felt like I wanted to apologise to the two old people sitting next to me, as I'm sure they had seen many horrific things, even in their lifetimes being black in the south of the US. This film upset me, and like I said, I cannot imagine how painful this must have been for those two old African

Americans, and I left that museum feeling pretty sad and even guilty, for just being white.

The "Gateway Arch" has an amazing view across St Louis, and the state of Missouri. It's only when you are inside this monument you realise how high it really is, and looking out of the small windows from the top took me a little time to get used to, and to get over my fear of heights, but once I did, it was a spectacular view. I could see across the whole of downtown, the baseball stadium, the river, and the Edward Jones Stadium, where I would be the following evening for my 27th game. I even saw a casino!!

After leaving the "Gateway Arch", I wandered around downtown St Louis for the rest of the afternoon, and as it's not exactly a tourist town, I ended up in a coffee shop for a while, before jumping on a bus back to the hostel, or so I thought, as I took the right bus in the wrong direction, of course in typical dopey D-Mo fashion, ending up in a shady part of town, in the dark, and not knowing where the fcuk I was. GREAT!

I was looking out of the bus window thinking, "Where the fcuk am I going?", as nothing looked familiar to me, so I asked the driver, and he quickly informed me I was actually going away from the area I had wanted, the wrong bloody way. The driver told me to get off the bus, cross over to a stop he pointed at, and he informed me a bus was coming in around five minutes. Ok, no harm done there, shit happens I thought?

I crossed over the road and I stood at the bus stop alone, probably as there were no other stupid people who used the bus system in this dodgy looking area. There was a huge and beautiful looking church right beside the bus stop, which to me looked very out of place in this run down part of town, and if it was daytime, I probably would have gone into it and had a look round.

I waited for what seemed like ages for the bus in the darkness and freezing cold, and I was listening out for or anticipating the sound of a gun going off at any moment, before my bus finally arrived about thirty minutes later. I was bloody relieved to say the least, not because I was scared, as I could quite obviously see I was the only white face in this area, I was relieved purely because I was freezing my balls off!

I had tried to call an Uber cab, but there were no cars anywhere near the area I was in to give me a ride, which highlighted the fact most sensible drivers will stick to downtown, and not mess about in dodgy areas like the one I was standing in.

I jumped on the bus, and half an hour later I was safely back at my hostel, or homeless shelter!

I met another Jeff in St Louis, a quiet old guy who was staying in my dorm room at the hostel. Jeff told me he was a farmer, and I remember a time where Jeff and I helped a girl who lived next door to the hostel to lift a mattress onto her bed, which was high up a ladder in a kind of loft area of her apartment. So like two knights in shining armour, we went into the property of this pretty girl, to give her a helping hand.

It only took us a few minutes, but mattresses are very heavy and there was no way this young lady could have done this on her own. Jeff went back to the hostel next door, and I got chatting away to the pretty girl as she mentioned to me she has been to London.

The D-Mo "radar" goes up as usual when an opportunity arises to talk to a babe, as this girl in question was very easy on the eye, but sadly for me this is quickly dashed when the lovely young lady's partner comes in from another room, another chick. This girl was quite plump, plain and as gay as a box of frocks! As soon as the other girl came in, it was obvious to me they were a couple, so another one bites the dust!

I met quite a few lesbian couples on my travels, and I always got on very well with them. This probably has something to do with the fact I'm a closet lesbian myself!!

Jeff told me he was going to a place called the "Budweiser Brewery and Museum" the next morning, as it was only a five minutes walk up the road, and he asked me if I would like to join him. Sweet, especially as I had no idea the place even existed, so off we went on a Budweiser tour.

I've done wine tours in Argentina, and a beer tour somewhere else before, and they are usually as dull as dishwater in my opinion, but this gave me a fascinating insight into the interesting subject of how beer is actually made, and I expected a few samples to be thrown in for good measure.

After my time at the "Budweiser Brewery", and learning a

few things about my favourite tipple, I would love to know who discovered the way of making beer, as it really is a complicated process. My assumption is that most of these processes must have been made by complete chance back in the day, because who the hell thought of boiling the liquid before cooling it down, before the best part comes of actually getting it down your neck? It does amaze me, but whoever did discover this, I would like to buy them a pint!

Jeff and I got talking to two American guys on the "Budweiser tour" or "booze cruise", who were in town for the game that night I was attending. The two guys were cops, and two nice blokes, so after the tour, I went for lunch with them, dropping Jeff off first, as he wanted to go to some random museum about agriculture. Yawn!, well that was his area I guess.

We went to a lovely restaurant called "Pappy's Smokehouse" a place the guys had recommended, and this place was a BBQ restaurant, so I was well up for that. The food was great, the company was great too, I liked these guys and I arranged to meet them later that evening and we would connect by SMS before the game started and try to meet up.

I had arranged to meet my latest new Superfan friend, a guy nicknamed "Ram Man", whom I had been talking to on Facebook, and I was meeting him and his friends in a bar in downtown St Louis early that evening. As soon as I met "Ram Man" (Karl Sides), and his lovely friends, (yet again my SuperFan family never let me down), I was welcomed with open arms and much warmth immediately.

"Ram Man" is regarded as a hero to the fans in St Louis, I remember walking to the stadium with him, chatting away like old friends, and he was kitted out from head to toe in his awesome St Louis Rams uniform, complete with his ram head hat, getting a lot of attention from fellow Rams fans, some shouting out to him from their cars as we got near the stadium, and many coming up to him and shaking his hand as we wandered along. I felt as though I was in the company of a celebrity, and I kind of was, but in all the time I was with him, he was simply Karl, a lovely man, where "Ram Man" was a character he was playing but he never lost contact with Karl, and he made me feel special just being with him. That meant a lot to me and this is something I will always remember about Karl, a very nice man, and someone I will always call my friend. Thanks Karl.

We entered the "Edward Jones Dome" in downtown St Louis and I hung around with "Ram Man" and his lovely friends, including a top Mexican guy named "Fernando Flores" who was in town for the game, who lived in Mexico City, and he was a huge fan of the Rams.

I always get on like a house on fire with Mexican people, to me they are a very friendly bunch of happy go lucky people, and always fun to be around. Some of my best friends around the world are from Mexico or from Mexican decent including "Jorge Gonzalez", whom I met twenty five years ago in Berlin on my very first backpacking adventure, and a guy whom I met up with twenty three years later at his home in LA, and who is one of my best friends, a truly lovely man, and someone I would return to see later on this trip when I got to LA.

"Daniel Nieto", who I met through Jorge, and who I stayed with in my time in Mexico City, his relations "Pavel Perez and Eddie Nieto" who I also met in Mexico City, are all my very good friends, wonderful people and great company.

"Carman Garcia", who I met in Guatamala two years earlier, "Josh Casillas", my San Diego SuperFan buddy, all my Mariachi brothers who I keep in touch with on Facebook, and now my new Mexican friend "Fernando", I met here in St Louis. Great people indeed who always make a huge fuss over me, which of course I love, and whose hospitality towards me has been truly amazing.

Game twenty seven between the St Louis Rams and the Tampa Bay Buccaneers, on paper was not the most attractive game on my schedule. This was the game I thought I had paid one dollar for the ticket, it was in fact twenty one bucks, as Tickpick recinded their offer of twenty bucks off each ticket, as they decided to cancel this discount for tickets under fifty dollars. I understood this completely and I was not gonna be greedy, as Tickpick had been very generous to me.

I labelled this game "Ketchup Vs Mustard" after seeing both teams wearing the same head to toe coloured outfits. What I mean by this is, normally, say my Dallas Cowboys have white shirts, and silver pants, (shorts, trousers, whatever you call the garments covering the legs), but this evening, as I'd seen on a few previous occasions, the teams wore the same colours for their shirts, pants and socks. The Rams wore gold, and the Bucs wore red, hence the Ketchup Vs Mustard comment.

I wasn't and I am not a fan of these outfits as I think they look horrible, just as I am not a fan of the occasional retro jerseys (shirts) the Packers and the Steelers wear one or two times a season, to indicate the good old days. I'm sure there is an obvious reason for this, and I'm sure many NFL fans know why, but I don't, I just know I am not a fan of these wardrobe malfunctions, as to me they are an eyesore.

Around this time of the season, as in San Diego the previous month, there were rumours of a move to another city by the Rams franchise. The Rams were in LA when I first started following the NFL back in the 80's. I remember some great LA Rams players from that era including quarterback "Jim Everett", and one of the best running back's of all time, the brilliant "Eric Dickerson". I even remember his funny goggles as apparently he was as blind as a bat!

In those days, St Louis had the Cardinals, in both football and baseball, so when in a period of around five years I had a break from the game (mainly because of pay TV nicking the game from my terrestrial and free TV station), it got very confusing for me when the Houston Oilers became the Tennessee Titans, the LA Raiders went back to Oakland, along came the Carolina Panthers, the Jacksonville Jaguars, and a new Houston team called the "Texans" arrived, after the Oilers left town. Confused? Well I was, and after my five years hiatus or "lost weekend" I gave up following the NFL, and what a humungous schoolboy error that was, because this was when my Cowboys were having their glory days of three Super Bowl wins. I missed THE WHOLE BLOODY LOT OF IT! What a complete slap in the face.

So now the Cardinals are in Arizona, and the Rams were in

St Louis. PHEW! Now it's looking like the Rams were leaving yet again, but where to? who knows. Well we know now, as on my second draft of this book, the St Louis Rams are now the LA Rams.

I felt at the time what a shame it was for all the great Rams fans like "Ram Man" Karl and his friends, who worship their team, and I could see how upset they were at the prospect they may be losing their beloved St Louis Rams forever.

Sadly, they did, as this was in fact the last home game the St Louis Rams would ever play. I'm far from proud to say I was there on that fateful last Rams home game, and I can't imagine how this must have rocked the Ram's fan's worlds and left a huge gaping hole in their lives, just as it has now done in San Diego and soon to be Oakland.

One thing which was very evident to me in the stadium, were the many empty seats inside the Edward Jones Dome for this game. I know it was a Thursday night game and it was being shown on national TV, but I had been to many games on a Thursday night, and most of the stadiums I had attended were practically full. This was far from full, half empty to be honest, which was real a shame, and it did feel to me like a franchise coming to it's very own natural end in the city of St Louis.

The game itself was complete one way traffic in the first half with the Rams star man Tevon Austin running wild. Little would I know that on my next stop in Baltimore, I would get a taxi to the airport, driven by the cousin of Tevon Austin. Small world, hey?

The Rams obviously wanted to end an era on a winning result, and it was 21-3 at half time. The Bucs were pretty poor in the first three quarters, especially quarterback Jameis Winston, who only came to life in the final quarter, but the Bucs were too far behind to make this a victory for them and the game ended 31-23 to the Rams, a lot closer than the game really was.

At the start of the game I wanted the Bucs to win, only for my Bucs Super Fan friends "Tim Young" and "Jay Buc", but by the end of the game, I was happy for "Ram Man" and his friends their team won, especially on the very last time they would see their beloved Rams play in St Louis. It was quite a sad occasion at the end as the move to LA looked imminent at the time. Sadly for the Rams fans, imminent is now permanent, and a real shame.

The game ended, I said a big thank you to "Ram Man", "Fernando" and the rest of the people I had met that evening, as it was now close to midnight as I headed back to my hostel, which was a subway and a bus ride away. The subway station was very close to the stadium, and I took the train around five stops to the location of where the bus stop was I had to catch my bus which took me back to my hostel.

As I stood waiting for the bus after midnight, for probably the very first time on my tour, I felt a little bit uncomfortable, and I was thinking maybe I could have been in an area I really should not be in, especially this late at night. In my experience as a traveller over many years, I always knew train stations are a magnet for dodgy people, everything from beggars, thieves, pickpockets, homeless people, drunks, crazies and so on, and on this occasion as I stood at the bus stop, I noticed again I was the only white guy around.

Before I am accused of being a racist, like as in Detroit, I am only stating a FACT, and obviously I stood out like dogs balls. My perception of the people who were around me were mostly very poor, as they were not exactly wearing Prada or Gucci, more like rags, or charity shop clothes.

I never actually felt threatened, but there seemed like there was a lot of activity going on around me, maybe I was just being paranoid as I was guessing I may be in an area where a lot of dodgy things went on, so my radar was well and truly up.

Standing at the bus stop hearing these people not just talking to each other, but shouting in their funny Missouri accents, was quite entertaining for me, and in a strange way, exciting, but when two teenagers walked past me, I heard one of them make a comment to the other in their own street talk and staring at me, only then I was hoping the bus would arrive, and asap.

Maybe I was wrong and these two kids were just talking to each other, and I started to feel a little uneasy, but this quickly diminished as my big silver chariot arrived and I was now homeward bound on the bus.

I wanted to check out the bar I went to on Tuesday for the quiz night, to see if the open mic night was still on. I'm always up for a song or two if a guitar is on offer, but it was almost 1am and I was thinking it would be empty or closed. I was pleasantly surprised the bar was still going strong when I arrived, so I ordered a beer and sat with a few people I had met on my previous visit to the bar, and I listened to a few performers.

To be honest the standard was not exactly X Factor stuff, well actually it could have been, because a few of the artist were so bad it was actually entertaining! More like X rated!

I hate to be too judgmental on these people, as these wannabees were having fun, and good luck to them, as they did in fact entertain everyone. I decided not to get up and sing any of my songs, which is very unlike me, as I was feeling tired after a long day and I didn't think I would fit into the vibe of the current performers this late in the evening.

There was a lovely girl who worked behind the bar whom I had met at the quiz night on the Tuesday, and she was working again on this night. She was very heavily pregnant, and she told me she knew the baby was going to be a boy, and I think she had already named him. This girl was a big fan of the Rams, and at the game I had just returned from on this night, I had collected a piece of memorabilia which was being given away at the stadium, and to be completely honest, I cannot even remember exactly what it was. It must have been something like a kids toy or a baby's bib, so I thought, who better to give it to than my new little mate who hasn't even popped his head out yet!

His mum was really touched when I said "Please give this to your little man when he turns up"! She was really pleased, and so very grateful, and I could see the tears forming in her eyes, bless her. I hope this little man and his mum are keeping well.

I had another beer, listened to a wonderful ear shattering rendition of Whitney Houston's "I will always love you", waiting in anticipation for the extremely high notes in the chorus, which always brings a smile to the faces of a crowd, as nobody hits those high notes quite like Whitney does, before I retreated back to my homeless shelter of a hostel at the ungodly hour of around 2am.

Overall I enjoyed my stay at the "Huckleberry Finn Hostel", probably because there were not many people staying in the big room full of bunkbeds. This dorm was spacious and basically just another big old house converted into a hostel, but I'm sure if there would have been a full house in this dorm, I think it would have been a complete nightmare as none of the guests I saw looked anything like backpackers, they were more the kind of people who were here for work, down on their luck, or basically with no other particular place to go.

I left the "Hucklebury Finn" on Friday morning and I caught the bus to the dodgy area I was at the night before, just to connect to the subway, to catch the train to the airport for my next stop, Baltimore, and yet another US city I knew very little about.

Stadium-28
M+T Bank Stadium
Baltimore Ravens

I arrived into Baltimore on the short flight from St Louis, and I took the subway from the airport to the centre of town, where I had to catch a bus to my hostel, which was only about a mile up the road.

It was so cold in Baltimore, now December and in the middle of winter, and after looking at the bus timetable, I could see the buses were not that frequent, so I started to walk, as according to Google maps, it was only about a twenty minutes stroll to my hostel. The walk would normally have been easy, but with my backpack now weighing a ton, with all the shit I keep picking up, this walk was like climbing Mount Everest, and I was well pleased and pretty knackered once I arrived at my new home for the next 3-4 days.

The "Hi Hostel" in Baltimore was in a nice and convenient part of town, and I liked this place as soon as I arrived. The chick on the reception desk, a beautiful African American girl by the very unusual name of Miracle, was probably to blame for this!

I checked into my room and I came back down to the lounge area, where a bunch of people were watching a movie. Miracle had told me on my arrival that she and a few other guests from the hostel were going out to a few bars that evening, especially as it was the start of the weekend and would I like to come? "Erm, let me think about it", I said to the Whitney Houston look alike, "OK", I replied as quick as a flash after about two nano seconds!! so we arranged to leave in a few hours.

A hour later, Miracle asked me if I was still going, "Of course" I replied, "Why do you ask?" I said. "Because nobody else is going". "Really?, Why?, Whatever?" I mentioned casually, thinking the night had been cancelled. "But you and I can still go if you want?", she said. "OK", I replied, and a hour later, off we went. What idiot would turn down the chance to go out with a right sort (babe)? Not this idiot.

I should have smelt a rat immediately, especially as Miracle kept me waiting, but my little head was now in charge and doing the thinking at this time, not the more sensible or logical big head, which my normal level of judgement usually relies on.

We left the hostel, and I must admit, Miracle was looking red hot, so off we go, and she took me to a bar a short walk from the hostel. It was a very modern and funky place, with loads of bars lined up next to each other, all under one big roof, something very unusual or new to me.

Miracle mentioned she would be meeting a bunch of her mates later at another trendy bar, and this sounded good to me, as who knows? this could lead to something interesting, my little head was thinking........praying actually!

I bought Miracle a drink, and we got chatting about the

usual rubbish, before the topic somehow moved onto the subject of sex, which is very unlike me!!! Miracle informed me immediately that she likes girls almost as much as she loves boys. OH BOY! I LOVE THIS GIRL!! This always gets the boys going, well especially this one! So as you can imagine, I wanna be all over this bird like a cheap bar of soap. "Waiter, get this girl another drink, and make it a big one", I was now thinking!

Well my friends, that's as good as it got. BOLLOCKS!!

Miracle then looks over and spots a guy who is staying at the hostel in the bar we were at. The guy see's her, and he heads over to where we are sitting. The guy is young and good looking, and I'm thinking straight away, "Oh please fcuk off"!

I was feeling as protective as a Kardashian to a Louis Vuitton handbag, as this was my bloody gig mate, so get lost!!

The guy in question was called Marts, and he later informed me he was a mixed martial arts fighter, so I was not gonna mess with him! Marts was not a big guy, and he looked young, around 23, and he told me he had won over 30 fights, he had no marks at all on his face, but he did show me a gruesome video on "YouTube" of him in one of his fights, which definately underlined to me that hitting this guy would be a huge mistake indeed!!!

Marts was actually a really nice guy, I liked him, but conversing with him was extremely difficult as Marts was dumb. I'm not saying he was stupid, what I mean is he could not talk. Honest, no joke.

Marts told me, well demonstrated through hand signals and nodding, he had a very bad stammer, so bad it killed his confidence and made him too embarrassed to even try to talk. I felt really sorry for him, and I told him not to be shy around me, and try to talk to me, as I was not going to laugh or ridicule him in any way shape or form. But he would not do it, so the questions I asked him were mainly answered with a nod or a wink. Sounds like a Monty Python sketch does'nt it? Where do I find these bloody people?

As soon as Marts came over to where we were sitting, I could see by the way Miracle looked at him, that my new union with this Babe from Baltimore was in major jeopardy and I knew in an instant there was history between them. I realised straight away Miracle had totally used me to get her ass to this particular bar as she knew Marts would be there. BITCH!

We had another drink, which I made damn sure Mirace bought for me, (as normally getting a pretty bird you have just met in a bar to buy YOU a drink is usually a fcuking Miracle!) before going off to the bar where Miracle said she was meeting her mates. It was quite a long walk to this next bar, and once we arrived, as soon as I walked in, I knew I was going to hate this place immediately........and I was right, I did.

It was a salsa bar, and there were couples performing all kinds of exotic moves, or erotic shapes, which actually looked pretty amazing. We entered the bar and Miracle proceeded to disappear straight onto the dance floor and left me in a nano second, like we had never even met, which by this time, I had her card well and truly marked, which to be honest suited me fine.

Marts joined her immediately on the dancefloor, and now it is clearly obvious to me these two people have in fact been here before together, and I was now the proverbial spare one at a wedding, or the third wheel, which was now quite evident to me this was always in Miracle's plan, and this boy, ME was the clown.

I was now sooooo annoyed with myself, feeling like some old fool chasing a young ass, I felt totally used by Miracle, and yet again I was being a total idiot, thinking I had even a fraction of a chance with this pretty young thing, again following the stirrings in my little old boy/head, chasing after young piece of skirt, trying yet again to get laid, and yet again, getting used in the process.

But at least I had not given up on trying, and even this incident would not deter me, as I would continue to chase the ladies right up until I finally left America, actually even after when I got to Japan amd Korea, but sadly for me, always with the same result or end product. SPLATT!!

I watched the two lovebirds or dynamic duo dance their provocative salsa for about five agonising minutes, as my boiling blood would only allow that amount of time before I spontaniously self combusted on my bar stool, as I wanted to give Marts a Bruce Lee style kung fu kick, and a karate chop to his fcuking MMA neck!! Actually I wanted to do it more so to that bloody user bitch Miracle, and it would have been a bloody Miracle if I could even get my leg up as high a Marts neck at the ripe old age of 48!!!!

I drank my beer and I left without telling the happy couple I was off, as they would not have noticed anyway, given a shit or exactly begged me to stay would they? unless Miracle wanted me to buy her a drink of course. I wanted to give Marts a couple of hand signals, and you can probably guess what kind of hand signals I'm talking about!!!

I basically ignored Miracle for the rest of the time I was staying at the hostel, especially after Marts told me (well he pulled a few faces and made a few dolphin clicks) the next day that he banged Miracle into next week that night, and a few nights before, so I was right about them two having some history. B@STARDS!

That episode did not exactly do my already shattered confidence around chicks any favours at all, as my track record by this time was about as bad as the England football team at a world cup! I've now even lost out to a bloke who can't even talk!!

But Marts seemed like he was a nice guy, young, good looking and a mixed martial arts fighter, at least two of the things which I am definately not, and I won't lie, I actually quite liked him.

I took an Uber cab back to my hostel, and I watched a bit of telly before going to bed, feeling frustrated, stupid and very very old.

The next morning I had a nice breakfast in the hostel, and I spent a few hours updating my website, and posting stuff on social media, something I did almost every day, sometimes for many hours at a time.

I spent quite a lot of time in the lounge area on my laptop over the 3-4 days I was in Baltimore, and I got to sit with an old Italian guy on a regulr basis who was always watching football of the telly. Of course I tried to speak my useless form of schoolboy Italian to my new old friend, but this usually turns into English after twenty seconds of ciao, come stai, and me chiamo Dennis sono Inglese!! (Hello, how are you, my name is Dennis and I am from England), for all you non Italian speaking people.

Lunchtime came, and I went out for a wander to the harbour area, about twenty minutes walk from my hostel. I did'nt get very far, as just around the corner from my hostel was an Indian restaurant, with a cheap lunchtime menu, and it would have been extremely rude for me to have walked right past!

It was December the 20th and Baltimore was freezing cold, especially as I walked around the harbour area where all the action in Baltimore is. The wind off the sea was going right through my four layers of clothing and straight to my bones, it really was bitterly cold.

I stopped off at the harbour area to watch a huge group of people performing christmas hymns on their tuba's, all 380 of them. It sounded really beautiful, and touched me in a deep and long forgotten place inside of me, which made me feel nostalgic, making me feel quite emotional, as it reminded me of the times when I was little boy and I used to love singing these hymns at school. Now I was here in Baltimore, on this festive holiday, a very long way from home, far way from my family and my friends, and this made me feel very lonely indeed.

All 380 tuba players were being watched by a big crowd, probably being supported by their family members and loved ones, and at this moment I watched and listened to the hymns feeling very tearful indeed. I wondered what the fcuk was I doing with my life, travelling all across America watching bloody American Football, when I could be at my beautiful home with my hypothetical beautiful wife, kids and dog in my lovely hypothetical house, getting ready for christmas with them.

This was a very sombre and difficult moment for me, a kind of reality check which underlined all was, and is not well in my world. I pondered over all the miles I had covered on the previous three months, as well as the next 8-9 places I still had left to visit, I thought about the many cities I had been to, experiences, hardships, great times etc, and I remember thinking I would have given all of this up in a heartbeat, to be at home with my hypothetical family.

"Silent Night" and "We Three Kings" were like sharp knives slicing away at my emotions, they sounded so beautiful, tranquil, serene, peaceful, and this completely underlined to me the fact christmas was coming, and I would be completely alone. I have always loved christmas, but this year it would be a very sad time for me.

I wandered around that afternoon a little bit like a zombie, or a car in neutral, as I watched families having fun ice skating, before I tried my best to snap out of my momentary state of vegetation and depression, as I looked around at a few ships that were docked in the harbour.

I decided to go and have a wander around to see what "Little Italy" had to offer, other than a pasta dish or a cuppaccino, and this area was about a fifteen minutes walk away from the harbour.

When I got there, I was very disappointed in "Little Italy", maybe I was asking too much after going to the version in New York, which is huge and full of bars and resturants. But then again, Baltimore is not exactly New York, nevertheless I liked it, even though it was absolutely freezing cold.

I found myself by complete chance walking past a big hotel on the harbour named the "Marriott Waterfront". I saw a few guys wandering around in Kansas City Chiefs outfits, and I immediatly presumed these guys must be Chiefs fans in town for tomorrows game with the Ravens. Being the inquisitive type, well nosey actually, I did a lap around the hotel to the main entrance, and I was pleasantly surprised when I realised that the guys in the Chiefs outfits were not fans, but Kansas City Chiefs players.

I said hello to a group of about five players, who were massive in size, and wide with it. I told a few of the players I was from England, and about my tour, and they seemed quite impressed. I chatted to the number 97, a guy who I did not know named Allan Bailey, and I proceeded to offer him one of my "The WrongShapedBalls Tour", business cards so he could take a look at my website, or even follow me on Twitter or Facebook. But as I went to my pocket, I searched, then to my horror, realised I had none left in my wallet.

Yet another MASSIVE schoolboy error on my part as he seemed interested in my adventure, and this was, and could have been THE MOMENT I had been waiting for on my entire tour to get my message to any NFL players, teams, media, bloody ANYBODY. If I could have got Allan to have followed me on social media, then maybe more players would have followed suit through his spreading the word, and this would or could have esculated, then helped me get some publicity for my tour, and my song "Like a Touchdown", and so on, and so on and so forth. FCUK FCUK FCUKING HELL!!!

I was so so so so so annoyed with myself, what terrible terrible luck again, as I ALWAYS had business cards on me wherever I was, all over the country, but not at this vital or crucial moment. Who knows? this could have been a humongous turning point for me and my tour.

Today as I write these words, I can only feel total dejection, and I just want to slap my stupid self in the face, as I reminisce what might or could have been? FCUK.

I left the Kansas Chiefs players with the raving hump (upset), as yet again I felt like a huge potential opportunity had been missed.

Now I don't really believe in the old addage or bullshit that everything happens for a reason, maybe sometimes it does?, but I do subscribe to the thought process that you make your own luck in this life, and sometimes I simply don't help myself by making too many basic and stupid cock up's.

Evening was coming and it was now getting really cold, so I

decided to go up to the top of the tallest building in Baltimore, which was a museum looking over the harbour area with amazing views, and which luckily was indoors and in the warm. There were pictures all around the top floor of the building, showing many of Baltimore's famous people from the past and the present, most of them of course, I had no idea at all who they were.

Baltimore was yet another US city I knew practically nothing about, the only things I did know a fraction about were the Baltimore Ravens and their ex player Ray Lewis. I knew absolutely nothing about any of the tourist attractions, monuments, landmarks, or any points of interest in town, and for this reason, it made it fresh and exciting for me to investigate.

I had heard in the past, people mention there was a very good American Cop show called "The Wire", and this was filmed in Baltimore. Of course I had never seen or heard of it, as I'm well out of fashion when it comes to cool new TV shows, I'm too busy watching old US cop shows like Starskey and Hutch and Columbo. Typical D-Mo, always behind the times and living in the past.

I spent Saturday evening in a nice bar just around the corner from my hostel, and I watched my Cowboys season end with a whimper with yet another defeat and shitty performance, this time against the New York Jets. I did not mind too much, as my good friend Joe Carlson whom I met when I was in New York, is a massive Jets fan, and I was kind of cheering for his Jets to get to the play off's, as I wanted to go to a play off game with him the following month.

Sadly even after beating my Cowgirls, the Jets blew their big chance of making the play off's on the very last game of the season, by losing to their dreaded divisional rivals the Buffalo Bills, who coincidently I saw with Joe when I was in New York on week 10.

I was so gutted for Joe, and for me too, as I knew if we would have gone to watch a Jets play off game together, we would have had an amazing time.

Sunday came, and it was game 28 on my tour, the Baltimore Ravens Vs The Kansas City Chiefs. Baltimore, like Kansas, was a place on my tour that was a tricky little piece of the overal jigsaw puzzle. I remember getting so close to my final schedule route, and Baltimore was the only place where it was difficult for me to fit in. It would have been nice if I could have squeezed Baltimore in just before or after Washington DC or maybe Philadelphia, as these three cities are located very close to each other, but it was not quite as simple as that. I wished it was, but there were many factors as to why this was not possible.

After Baltimore, my next stop would be Oakland in California, practically next door to San Francisco, and this would be the longest flight (about 6 hours) I would take on my entire tour. I know it seems crazy as to why I scheduled Oakland just after Baltimore, but I will do my best to explain as to why.

After pondering over the schedule on my bedroom wall for about two weeks, I finally found a route I was happy with, but I had to take a few detours, as it was more or less impossible to do every game in some kind of a logical geographical order or sequence, as some teams which are near each other in location, play at home on the same day, then they can both be on the road (away) the following week, or have a rest week, and so on.

So after getting a few clusters or groups of games conveniently located in close proximity together that worked well, I then had to find a way of connecting the remaining games. So after I arrived in Detroit, I had almost attended all of the eastern side of the country's games except for a just a few places. It actually worked out very well after I flew from Detroit to San Diego, because the schedule then allowed me to go in one long line, or continuous direction from the west coast to the east coast of America, to my next destination of Phoenix Arizona, which is not that far from San Diego, and the same goes from Phoenix to Denver, then Denver to St Louis and finally St Louis to Baltimore.

It was a lot of travelling and a long overall distance, but it was something I simply had to do, as after Baltimore I only had three west coast teams left to complete the set.

In the very early days of my planning, as I have already mentioned, the play off's were never in my plans at all, as I thought that after 31 stadiums, I would have had enough. Well that eventually changed completely and the play off's became well and truly in my plans, as I was having such a great time, I never wanted this tour to end, not now anyway.

Another massive factor was the weather, I always intended on finishing in California because my good friend Jorge Gonzalez lives in LA, and I wanted to visit him, chill out in the Californian sun for a month, probably go to Vegas, then return to LA and watch the Superbowl with Jorge and his friends at a house party, just as I did two years earlier.

Another integral part of the planning was Seattle, as this city is so isolated, and far away from all the other cities I attended in the US, I never had many chances in the schedule to go to Seattle and combine this visit with Oakland or San Francisco, which are also on the west coast. I needed to get lucky with convenient times in the schedule for me to do all of these three stadiums together, rather than taking very long flights in and out of Seattle, back to middle or maybe even eastern America, taking up far too much time.

Boy I hope this makes sense as its giving me a headache just trying to explain my schedule, can you understand now how it gave me a "headfuck" at the time of planning it?

Game day had arrived and I had another tailgate to attend, this time I had been invited by the Baltimore Ravens Superfan Rick Bowlus after chatting to him on Facebook. I met Rick at his tailgate and again immediately I was made to feel a part of the Ravens fans furniture.

Rick is such a lovely man, yet another friend for life, as he made such a fuss of me and he really was a fantastic host, as were all his fellow Ravens fans at the tailgate, including his friend Chip, who kindly gave me a ticket to the game for free. I can't thank these guys enough for their hospitality.

After another great feed and a belly full of beer, I headed to the M+T Bank Stadium, the home of the Baltimore Ravens, with Rick and Chip.

My ticket was in the third row from the very front and almost on the playing field, with Rick and Chip two rows in front of me in the very front row itself, and as you know by now, not my kind of seat, but again I was not complaining as I got the ticket buckshee (for free), and the Baltimore Ravens cheerleaders tits and asses were practically right in my face!! SWEET!

I did my usual wander around the stadium on this beautiful sunny but cold day, and I also did my usual second half move to the nose bleeds, just to get a better view and to take some pictures for my website.

The visitors on this day, the Kansas City Chiefs, I had seen on two previous occasions, and they had lost both times, and I was hoping their bad run in my fine company would continue, so Rick's Ravens would end their own poor run of losses to win this game, making everyone happy.

I last saw the Chiefs play in Green Bay on week three, which now seemed a lifetime ago, as it was now week 15, and I thought they looked a very poor team that day. The Chiefs had lost their main man Jamaal Charles through injury, and I thought at the time they would endure a huge struggle for the rest of the season, but amazingly they went unbeaten for their next 10 games, and incredibly the Chiefs would continue their amazing winning streak well into the play off's. What a complete turnaround, and definately not a one man team, as they well and truly proved me totally wrong.

The Chiefs were hot favourites for this game, and it did not take them long to go into the lead. The Ravens really did look like a poor team, it was men against boys and I felt sorry for my new Ravens friends as yet another defeat was staring them in the face, and we were still only in the second quarter.

With four seconds left until half time, the Ravens attempted the exciting "Hail Mary" pass, a play I had already witnesssed twice in two previous games, and both attempts had been caught. Surely it could not happen again??

The ball was snapped, launched skywards, a crowd of players from both teams jostled for their positions in the endzone, then....BOOM. Can you believe it, I witnessed "Hail Mary" completed pass number three, caught by the Ravens number 11. UNBELIEVEABLE.

Little did I know there would be yet another "Hail Mary" coming my way, and probably the best one yet I would see, in one of the play off games I would attend a few weeks later, back in Phoenix.

What I do find amazing, is I cannot remember seeing a "Hail Mary" pass being thrown which was not caught, in all the games I attended on my tour. Four out of four passes thrown and caught is simply unheard of, and I feel incredible blessed to have seen and experienced them all.

So what a finish to a half, the stadium erupted, and this lifeline gave the Ravens fans new hope of a second half comeback. Sadly for my friends and the other Ravens fans, this comeback never quite materialised, as the Chiefs stepped up their game, and won convincingly 34-14.

I returned to Rick and Chip's tailgate for a chat for a hour or so after the game, and we all stood around a heater as it was in fact fcuking freezzzzzing, especially as we were drinking cold beer. HA!

After saying goodbye and thanking everybody I had met, especially Rick, I returned to my hostel and I watched the later game between the Denver Broncos and the Pittsburgh Steelers. I was cheering for Denver because I was desperate for them to make the play off's and gain home field advantage, as my intention was to go back to Denver, and you know exactly why!

In typical fashion, Denver lost, which was yet another blow to my non existant sex life, so I went up to bed, sad in the fact that Ashley's lovely hot air balloons were floating away from me right up into oblivion!

Amazingly Denver did eventually make the play off's, and they did in fact gain the home field advantage I had prayed for. I did make it back to Denver, but the elusive Ashley became even more slippery than an eel, and as reliable as an English summer. My patience had gone with this bloody timewaster, and this boy can only be taken for a mug/fool for so long, and in my opinion, it had already been for far longer than my liking.

That night when I went to bed, there was a guy in my dorm who was snoring the house down. Snoring is such an irritating sound, and a noise I never get used to or can block out, even though I always wear ear plugs. I've got so many stories I could tell regarding snoring, and looking back, I suffered so many times by this horrendous punishing and annoying sound.

Monday was a free day for me, so I became the usual tourist, so I jumped on a tour bus and I did a loop of Baltimore, to take in the sights. I spent some time in a museum, looked at a few monuments, did a small walking tour, basically killing time, as after 15 weeks on the road, the days in between games were becoming a little bit harder to fill with things to do, but I always tried my best to see the most interesting or iconic things that were available to me, in all the US cities I went to.

That evening, I watched the first half of the late NFL game, then retreated to my dorm room to pack my bags, as I had an early flight to San Francisco the next morning.

I called an Uber cab around 5am as I was on my way to the international airport, far too early for my liking. The cab driver was a great guy named "Chuck". When I told him about my tour, he mentioned he had a cousin who played for the St Louis Rams. Chuck's cousin was the brilliant Rams receiver Tavon Austin. I told Chuck that I saw him play a great game last week in St Louis.

I also told Chuck I had tried to contact Tavon on Twitter, as I did with many other NFL players, and I gave one of my business cards to Chuck and I asked him to get Tavon to follow me on Twitter as I would see Tavon's Rams play their last two games of the season, in Seattle and San Francisco.

Whenever I gave out my business cards, I always thought, or dreamed, this could be "THE ONE" or the lucky break I needed to gain support or publicity for my tour, or to generally open a door which would connect me to a person with influence or power within the industries of the NFL or music. It felt like I was always one business card away from hitting the bulleye, or making the great connection I was so desperately craving for, even after giving out over 500 of my business cards in the 20 weeks I was away.

I never did find my genie who would open the bottle, or the hen which layed my golden egg, as sadly for me, all I was left with I'm afraid was egg on my face or chicken shit, and boy I tried every avenue I thought was humanly possible.

I never did hear from Tavon Austin of the Rams, so yet again, the feeling of hope I had temporarily gained when I gave my card to Chuck, was just another pipe dream, that sadly for me, only got flushed straight down the toilet.

Dennis Moss

Stadium-29
Oakland Alameda Coliseum
Oakland Raiders

Six hours after leaving Baltimore, I finally landed at Oakland Metropolitan airport. I had looked on Hostelworld for a place to stay, and all the hostels were in San Francisco, a short subway ride across the bay from Oakland, and a much more interesting place to hang out.

I never realised how close Oakland was to San Francisco. I did know they were not very far apart, but I did'nt know they were practically joined at the hip. This was great as there was so much more to see and do in San Fran, so it was the obvious thing to do to stay there.

I booked into one of three "Hi Hostels" that are in San Francisco, my one being in Ellis Street, which was in a pretty central location. The hostel itself was really nice, as most HI hostels are. They are always clean, have a nice breakfast area, and generally well behaved guests, unlike a lot of the party hostels I have stayed at where most people party through the night getting up to all kinds of debauchery, as well as making all kinds of noise.

Don't get me wrong, I love to party as much as the next man, but sometimes you just wanna get a good night sleep, and with up to a dozen other bodies in the dorm room (my record is 36), falling asleep is not easy at the best of times.

This is why I spent so much time in the bars, for the sleeping pills (booze)!!!!

San Francisco has a massive homeless problem, much more than any other US city I visited, and Ellis Street where I was staying, probably had the most homeless people, beggars, odd balls, crazies and people openly taking drugs I would see in all of San Fran.

I walked past lots of these people many times a day, and they were regulary shouting and screaming at each other, probably high on drink and drugs, and craving for their next fix, and sometimes it was even quite entertaining. I had never seen such a large motley crew of people or dodgy characters before in one street, and a place where I was constantly asked for money and offered drugs, but I never once felt threatened by these people, or in any danger whatsoever, and even though many of these people hung out in groups, it didn't bother me in the slightest, where most people would have been scared shitless.

Maybe because I was just so used to wandering around rough/sketchy area's, I got to recognise the signs of danger, and I never saw these people as danger, I just saw them as pests. There were just so many people living on the streets in San Fran, and there were so many interesting characters I saw at least a few times a day, every day I was here. These people even got a verse in a song I wrote a few days later. I will come to that in a minute.

The following day I went on a walking tour of San Francisco which started in Union Square. I met a great bunch of people including Dominic from Germany, and

Adrian from Spain. We wandered around the sights of downtown San Fran, including Chinatown, the financial district, Little France, Little Italy, and little everything else.

San Francisco has a great history including the gold rush, and I always like doing these walking tours as you learn so much about a city, you would never know unless you are told by the locals or guides.

After the tour, Dom, Adrian and myself went to have a look at the Golden Gate Bridge, in which we walked about a quarter of the way across it. I've been under the bridge before on a boat a few years ago, but never on it, and its only when you are on it, you realise how big, high up from the sea and long the bridge really is. It's an incredible piece of engineering across a very wide bay, and the views in the distance of the city of San Fran are amazing, including a small chunk of rock all by itself in the middle of the sea, the world famous or infamous and iconic island of Alcatraz.

Dom and Adrian were staying at a different hostel to me called "Hostel Adelaide", and I would meet up with them very early the next day, as we had arranged to go on a day trip to Yosemite National Park, about a three hours drive away.

Later that evening I met up with a guy whom I had been in touch with on Facebook who was coming over to Oakland from England, to watch his beloved Oakland Raiders. I met Lee Matthews in a bar called the Golden Gate Tap Room, which had a fantastic selection of beers from all around the world.

I liked Lee immediately, he was a funny bastard and he had a real passion for his Raiders. Lee made me realise I knew very little about the NFL, compared to him, as he was very knowledgable about many things in the NFL, things I never had a clue about. Lee was great company and it was good to be with somebody I felt comfortable around, it was like we were old friends from home.

Now I can only write what I experienced and felt at the time, and I have always told the truth of EVERYTHING I experienced throughout this tour. Let me make this perfectly crystal clear, ALL of these stories happened, NOTHING AT ALL is fiction, its all based on FACTS COMPLETELY.

I just want to highlight this, because its been well over a year since I returned home, and just a few weeks ago, as I re write this section of the book, I was informed by a complete stranger on Facebook that Lee Matthews has just been sentenced to seven years in prison for being a paedophile.

I had tried to contact Lee about six months ago, but he never replied, which was unusual for him, as he always replied to me immediately. So with the new season starting in a few weeks time, I tried again to touch base with him, as my Cowboys will be playing his Raiders this season, and I was asking him if he was going back to Oakland this year, and again I was met with the silent treatment.

To be honest I was a little worried about him, as we did indeed text each other quite a lot while I was on my tour.

This is when I received the out of the blue and shock message on Facebook from some random woman who used to work with him. I had sent Lee a message just saying "Where are you?", when she replied, "You will not be seeing him for a while". I thought he was maybe ill and in hospital, but then she dropped the atom bomb.

To say I was shocked is an understatement, simply because I would be lying if I said I had not enjoyed the company of this strange, odd, unusual but funny and likeable man. Our connection was the NFL, and of course I would have had no idea of what this guy got up to in his sordid personal life.

This makes me feel very uncomfortable, as I did indeed spend quite some time with Lee, and this horrific news saddens me as I would be lying if I said I never liked this guy.

The next morning me and the boys were on our way to Yosemite National Park, and by the time we got there, it was snowing and very cold, so much I didn't really want to get out of the warm car!

We saw some of the famous peaks including "El Capitan", something Dom was absolutely over the moon (excited) to see, as I think he had a big interest in climbing. I must admit it was nice to be here, but it was a long way to come to look around for a couple of hours, then return to San Fran, another three hours back. But hey, another box ticked I guess.

I had been staying in the HI Hostel for the past two nights, and I decided a change of scenery was needed, so I moved into the Adelaide Hostel where my friends were staying, which was a bit cheaper, and nearer to the main and more central area of downtown SF. There were also a lot less beggars in this street than on Ellis.

Thursday night was game number 29, and Christmas Eve, and I met up with Lee at his hotel just around the corner from my hostel. My German friend Dom had never been to a NFL game before, so I invited him to join us, so off the three of us went, heading for the Oakland Coliseum on the San Francisco subway.

This night I was spoilt for choice as I had been invited to two tailgates. I had met a Raiders SuperFan, a guy named "Kurt" in Denver, and he informed me that his tailgate was one of the biggest Raiders tailgates in Oakland. Kurt was known to be a fantastic cook, so I went looking for him and his tailgate.

Lee had his own friends to meet, so Dom and I left him at his tailgate, and we headed for one of the two of ours I was trying to locate.

It took absolutely ages to find the Kurt's tailgate, as he was tucked away far in a corner of one of the massive parking lots, hidden behind many other tailgates, and I dragged poor Dom all round the stadium, and back, until we finally found our man.

When I got to the tailgate, I met some fantastic Raiders fans, including an English guy who is nicknamed "Raider Crusaider", and who is also a Leyton Orient season ticket holder. (a lower league English soccer team) Poor guy!!!

I also met a guy whom I had heard so much about from my all my SuperFan friends around the country. "Raider Ron" was one of the original SuperFans, and he was held in such high regard and very much loved by all of the people I was now calling my friends.

I was informed Raider Ron had not been very well, and he was in a wheelchair when I was introduced to him. Ron was incredibly friendly to me straight away, and even though he was not well, he was always smiling and I could see immediately why everybody loved him.

Ron had an aura about him, and he had the complete respect of everybody who was at the tailgate, and probably in the whole of Oakland. I honestly felt like I was in the presence of a very special man, a legend.

As I write this book, I'm gutted to hear the sad news that Raider Ron "The General", has passed away. He had a lovely send off from his beloved friends and SuperFan family, I know this as I saw some pictures of his funeral on Facebook.

I'm very happy to have met Ron, because I had heard so many nice things about him from so many of my new friends, I really wanted to meet him and see for myself. Ron was such a lovely guy and an inspiration to many other SuperFans. RIP Raider Ron, you will never be forgotten.

The second tailgate Dom and I went to, was organized by another Oakland Raiders SuperFan I had met in Denver, a lovely lady named Pam, or "Black Barbie" as she is know as, in her circle of football friends.

Dom and I met a nice bunch of people as usual at the tailgate, we had a nice belly full of lovely food, a few beers, and we chatted away with our new friends, before we had to head off to the stadium for the game.

I never had a ticket for this game, as I thought being Christmas Eve, most people would be at home wrapping up their presents, cooking their turkey's and spending time with their loved ones, just normal things, normal people do. Who goes to watch football on christmas eve? I do!!

I did the usual wander around to see where most of the scalpers/ticket touts where hanging around, and I kept reassuring my friend Dom, that I am the master of getting cheap tickets, as I do it all the time, and I have had plenty of experience. REALLY?

After the experience of being scammed in Philadelphia, my plan when buying tickets off these extremely dodgy individuals was, asking them the blatantly obvious question of "is this ticket bona fide"?.

"Of course it is", would be my expected response, so my reply would then be, "Well in that case, you will have no problem if I take a picture of you on my cellphone, which I will delete as soon as I get into the stadium if the ticket is OK. If it's a fake, I will take your mug shot to the old bill/police and you will be arrested".

That was the plan, BUT, Oakland has a reputation of being quite rough/sketchy, well very rough actlly, gangs are all over the place, guns are as common as Ipod's and you simply don't fcuk with Raiders fans. So when I saw this big dude was waiving two tickets in the air at 25 bucks each, this cupid stunt grabbed them with both hands. The master of tickets? YEAH RIGHT!

I had a bad feeling about these tickets as soon as the guy who took the 50 dollar bill I handed to him, as he was gone like a bullet out of a gun. I have never seen such a fat git move so fast, but I never said anything to Dom, as I did'nt want him to get stressed while we queued up, and this was his very first NFL experience.

We got talking to two girls in the queue, and I showed her the tickets I had bought. She compared them to her's, they looked exactly the same, and she said, "All good, these babies are real". Maybe she was talking about her boobies, because as we got closer to the guy with the ticket checker, I had a gut feeling I had been a very silly boy, for the second time.

The queue was quite busy, game time was approaching fast and my ticket was up next. As soon as I heard the sound of the ticket man's ticket reader, my balls felt like they had hit the floor. FCUK!!

"Sorry Dude, you have a bad ticket" the guy said, in his stroppy tone, with more than a little attitude. I acted like a lost tourist, puppy dog eyes, innocent and completely stupid. Dom was a few people behind me, and his face was a picture of horror as I told him our tickets were fake.

I felt such an idiot, as I like to think I am streetwise, and can spot a scam a mile away. Normally I think, if something seems too good to be true, it usually is. I should have bloody known this, and I was sooooo angry with myself I let this happen, especially when I was telling Dom I was so damn good at getting cheap tickets.

As I tried my best to get sympathy from the guy checking the ticket, telling him I was a tourist, had never seen a NFL game before, practically begging him to let us in, the large crowd behind us were shouting "hurry up", and "come on, let them in, its Christmas". But the guy did not budge, and in all the commotion, his supervisor saw the kurfuffle, came over and he was even more adamant we were not coming in, and even less sympathetic than his colleague.

The first guy with the ticket checker gun was so engrossed in beeping the big queue of tickets, he simply ignored my plea's for mercy, and he turned his back on us completely, just like we were not even there. Dom's face was a picture of massive disappointment, and it was all my fault. SHIT, what am I going to do?? I just have to get in, missing this game is simply not an option.

As my mind raced at 100 miles an hour, pondering over my next move, I found myself standing next to a large metal door, probably an exit door, something which is usually closed as people go into the stadium, and of course, is wide open as people leave. Inside this door stood a man with his young daughter of around 10 years of age. They had obviously heard the commotion regarding my dodgy ticket, as they were only about 10 feet away from the man with the ticket gun, but inside the stadium and behind the metal barriers which separated us from them, and they must have felt very sorry for us.

The little girl looked at me, then very slowly and deliberatly she pushed the big metal door slightly with her foot, indicating to me the door was in fact open. What a girl!

The guy in front of me with the ticket gun was concentrating so much on his job, bless him, he had no clue as to whether we were still there or not. But the problem for us was not him, but his supervisor who was inside the turnstyles, and he was standing not that far away from this door.

I had to think fast, and I did. I turned to Dom and I said, "Get ready, stay close to me". I looked at the little princess, she pushed the door with her little foot and I noticed the supervisor guy inside had wandered away from his spot for a split second, and he was looking the other way. "Dom, go", I said, and I was gone instantly, but as I turned around, Dom was routed to the spot and still standing like a frozen statue outside the door, FCUK! on instinct, I turned back, grabbed him by the arm, pulled him through the door and we disappeared into the crowd as quick as a flash, and as far away from that area of the stadium as we could.

My heart was absolutely pounding and my adrenaline pumping at full speed, as I knew we could be in serious trouble if we got caught, and maybe even spend Christmas Day in the local nick/prison. Maybe even Alcatraz!!!! Now that would have been an experience!!

Dom looked as scared as a puppy dog to a baseball bat, after doing a shit on it's owners new carpet! but I thought it was exciting, especially after being scammed, we had done it, we made it into the game. PHEW!

I would like to say a huge thank you to the little girl and her dad, who brought to my attention that door was open. If it was not for them, I would have had to find myself, and Dom another ticket for the game. This little girl was my guardian angel that day, and I hope she and her dad had a Merry Christmas.

We quickly hurried along, high up into the nose bleeds/top tier, and we lost ourselves in the crowd, as far away from the entrance we came into, just in case they were looking for us.

After all the usual pre game activities had ended, the game began, and I started to calm down a bit, but not completely. I'm fully aware of the technology these days at stadiums, mainly for security or to catch hooligans, so I kept thinking maybe CCTV had seen us run in, and we still could be traced. I certainly did not want to spend christmas day in the local jail, giving Mr Big his Christmas present, access to my lovely unopened back pipe!

I don't remember too much about the first half of this game to be honest, I was still bloody annoyed I had been so stupid again with the tickets, and a little nervous we still may get caught by the long arm of the law. And then.............OMG!

This was my 29th game, and I could never remember seeing any police officers inside any of the previous 28 stadiums I had attended, so my heart was racing ten to the dozen/incredibly fast, when I saw two LAPD officers looking up into the section of the stands we were sitting in. Were they looking for us?

I never said anything to Dom, as I think he had already practically soiled his underwear!, but I must admit, when I saw these cops looking around, I feared the worse. They were on their radio's, and looking up in our direction. Did CCTV follow us? I must admit, at this point I was a little more than concerned, I was in fact very worried.

The police eventually moved on, thank god, and as the second quarter started, I told Dom we should move, and we went right across to the other side of the stadium. It was only then in the second half we could both laugh about what had happened, but it was a very close call and a very stressful situation to be in, especially when we should both have been enjoying the game, as well as it also being only about three hours away from christmas day, the season of joy!!!!

The San Diego Chargers were the visiting team, divisional rivals to the Oakland Raiders, and two struggling teams from California, who were basically playing for local pride and bragging rights.

By now I had calmed down and I did my best to relax and try to enjoy the rest of the game, which to be honest, wasn't easy. I usually learn from my mistakes, and I'm almost sure this will never happen to me again. Until next time!

Half time came and I wanted to go to check out the famous Raiders section of the crowd called the "Black Hole". Again I had been told to be careful as Raiders fans are crazy, and sometimes can be violent, but this piece of minor detail never detered me, and as I'm not going to cause any trouble, so why would anybody give me any shit?

The Raiders fans are no different to any other NFL club's

fans. Anyone can find trouble, if you go looking for it. Raiders fans are great, probably my favourite fans in the NFL, as they get totally immersed in the whole NFL experience.

As in Cleveland's "Dawg Pound", the "Black Hole" was a great experience for me to sit in. I felt privaliged to be there, as I never thought I would ever be in this stadium in my lifetime. It felt great, and another massive box ticket and experience for me.

The game itself was in fact quite exciting, with the Chargers leading 17-10 at half time. This game was very special for the Raiders legend Charles Woodson, as it was his very last as an Oakland Raider, after many years. He got an amazing send off from the Raiders fans, and they will miss him badly, as he has been a great servant to the club.

The game swung from Chargers to Raiders and back, and it was great viewing as the game entered the fourth quarter at 17-12 to the Chargers. It wasn't the Chargers lucky day, as they had what looked like a perfect touchdown pass deemed incomplete, then they missed a field goal attempt, which kept this game in the balance and a one score game.

The Raiders then quickly raced down field, which had been quite rare during this very tight and tense game, and to the noisy crowd's delight, scored a touchdown. Then the big gamble came as the Raiders attempted the two point conversion, and if scored, would go three points ahead. The atmosphere was so exciting as QB Carr took the snap, threw the ball, and made the play to score the two points. YESSS!!

The Chargers were now only three points, or a field goal behind, and somehow with hardly any time left on the clock, they made a few good plays and gained a lot of yardage quickly, to get them within field goal range for a last chance kick to take this game into overtime.

The Chargers kicker put the kick through the posts, even after the Raiders fans made as much noise as they could to put him off, to take this game into overtime. This was my 4th game that went into overtime I would see so far on my tour.

Its incredible how often NFL games can be so different in the final quarter, from the game it had been in the previous three, as it was in this game. This final quarter was so exciting, with both teams playing their parts, as the previous three quarters had been very tight, close, cagey, boring, call it what you will, but in the fourth quarter the game exploded into life, and something I had seen so many times.

The Raiders won the toss, gained possession, and kicked the first field goal in overtime, meaning if the Chargers did not reply with a touchdown on their possession, the Raiders would be victors, but if the Chargers scored a field goal, then the game would continue.

The Chargers had a fourth down and the tension was electric, so after four hours of football, the last play of the game was coming, as the Chargers quarterback Philip Rivers took the snap, shuffled backwards, threw a bad pass, and as soon as the ball hit the ground, victory belonged to the Raiders. YEESSSS!

I was well pleased because I was supporting the Raiders as the home team, and I was well chuffed for the brilliant Raiders fans, as their boys still had an outside chance of making the play offs.

Our evening of excitement and interesting experiences was almost over, and I went home very happy, as well as relieved that Dom and I were free to fight another day, or at least free to have a good drink on Christmas Eve!

We left the stadium and returned to our hostel in downtown San Francisco, where the beers we bought tasted amazing. What an evening, for all different reasons, and something I will not forget in a hurry. A turbulent rollercoaster ride of emotions, and a great workout for my blood pressure, nervous system and my ass hole!

Friday was christmas day, the sun was shining, but it was a bit chilly, especially around Fisherman's Wharf where I went for a walk and a bite to eat.

A friend of mine from my horse Vibrato Valtat's racing syndicate, a lovely man named Ian Thurgood, had sent me an email a few days before, wishing me a merry christmas, and asking how my trip was going. Ian made a suggestion for me to write a song about my trip or maybe even a christmas song.

My first thoughts were "fcuk that, it's far too corny", especially a christmas song. Usually when I get an idea, mainly a stupid one, I try to think outside of the box, so I thought about writing a christmas song with a difference, a song which had all the things that a christmas song is not.

The usual format for a christmas song is a ballad, has bells, is sweet, soft, romantic, pathetic lyrics of opening presents, raindeers and snow, and all the usual bullshit. OK, there's a start. So what is a christmas song not? I thought.

I started to hum along as I wandered around Fisherman's Wharf, looking across to Alcatraz and the Golden Gate Bridge, and I started to laugh as an idea formed, which developed fairly quickly into the basis of the song "I don't wanna be alone this christmas".

The initial idea I had, was an uptempo punk rock song coming from the prospective of an English yobbo/hooligan, who was on his own in San Francisco on Christmas Day. The first two lines I settled for were "Its no fun, being here, on my own in San Francisco, all the shops, they are closed, so are all the bars and disco's.

I was thinking alone the lines of the punk band "The Buzzcocks", and this helped me find the direction I wanted. Then came the chorus, "I don't wanna be, I don't wanna be, I don't wanna be alone this christmas. I just wanna be, I just wanna be, I just wanna be at home this christmas".

Of course this song was all about me, I did make up the lyrics, but as usual in my songs, there are words, experiences, heartaches or truth's that sum up my thoughts and feelings at any particular moment in time.

I continued to write verse after verse in my head, and the lyrics got funnier and funnier. Like I've said, the song is about a yob, a typical rude slob, a chauvanist pig, which of course, I'm nothing of the kind!

Verse two. "All the guests, they've gone out, walking round and being tourists, I'll stay here, drink some beer, then I'm gonna watch some football!" "I don't wanna be, I don't wanna be......

Verse three. My best mate, he went out, to see Star Wars at the pictures, I had a feed, smoked some weed, now I'm gonna bonk his sister!

Verse three. "Walking down Ellis Street, seeing all the homeless people, they ask me, for money, to continue their addictions. I don't wanna be.....

Verse four. "All my friends, are at home, eating turkey with their loved ones, oh not me, just coffee, I spent lots of time in Starbucks. I don't wanna be.....

Some of these things I was actually doing, other than the bonking!, especially Starbucks as this was useful to keep out of the cold and use their wifi.

When I got back to the hostel, there was a guitar in the lounge area, so I played around a bit on it, and I found the melody for my funny new punk rock christmas song.

I met a very talented and pretty young Greek girl who was staying in my hostel Adelaide. She sang and played guitar very nicely, and on that night we sang a few songs together, including my new christmas song. She absoluetly loved it and she could not stop laughing, as she sang in harmony with me on the chorus's and it sounded great.

Maybe I will record this song one day, it has the chance to be a hit, and remember you guys read about it here first, long before anybody will ever get to hear it.

I mentioned earlier San Francisco has a massive homeless problem, more than any American city I had been to, so I wanted to do something for them on Christmas Day.

On the corner of the street where my hostel was located, there was a homeless charity where lots of the street people hung around, got fed, and were probably even given prescription drugs?

I went inside and I offered my services of help to the people on the reception desk and I was very surprised not to get the welcome I had expected. I thought these people would grab me and my offer of assistance with both hands, but I was told by some random guy, who looked totally bored and never really gave me the time of day, to call a certain telephone number and speak to them as to whether they wanted people to help them. When I did, I was made to feel like I was asking THEM for something, and not offering them MY services.

The people who were working for the homeless shelter made it so very difficult for me to help them, and basically put me off from offering my services on Christmas Day. I thought I could just turn up, roll up my sleeves, and give these guys some food, or just generally help out. Maybe this only happens in Hollywood movies?

This made me sad, as I really wanted to do something worthwhile and helpful on this day rather than just wander around the "Streets of San Francisco" (I used to love that show!) doing my best and killing time.

I did feel pretty lonely on Christmas Day to be honest, seeing families with their loved ones together underlined the fact that yet again I was on my own, single and feeling a little sorry for myself.

But when I realised how lucky I was to be in the beautiful city of San Francisco on Christmas Day, I thought "fcuk this negative mood, I'm off for my Christmas dinner". So in the beautiful but freezing cold Californian sunshine, in the tourist area of Fisherman's Wharf, overlooking Alcatraz and the Golden Gate Bridge, I had my Christmas dinner of fish and chips, right next to around 100 noisy sea lions on pier 39. Now things did not feel quite so sad after all. Merry Christmas D-Mo!!!

I love San Francisco, its a very beautiful and interesting city with so much to do. I knew I would be coming back here two more times before my tour was over, so I deliberately left out a few touristy things for when I would return the following week, as tomorrow I would be leaving for my next adventure, to a place I have always wanted to go, mainly because of one of my favourite bands of all time, Nirvana. Next stop.......... Seattle.

Stadium-30
CenturyLink Field
Seattle Seahawks

I flew into Seattle after a nice and easy two hours flight from San Francisco, and by this time, I had now taken around a dozen or so flights, far more than I ever had planned.

Flying in American is so easy, everything about it is so straightforward, unlike a long haul flight from London, where constant waiting and queuing for all different reasons is a massive pain in the ass. In the US checking in is usually quick, sometimes I was the only person checking in, so I had no queue's at all. The only thing I didn't like, was having to pay extra for baggage, something our cheap and so called "bucket airlines" have slapped our faces with in the last few years.

I knew this would be a very short pitstop in Seattle, a shame really because there were quite a few things I wanted to see, but I knew I would not have the time, as I was heading up into Vancouver Canada to visit my good friend Bruce Kagetsu and his lovely family for the new year.

I always did a lot of research on the upcoming cities I was travelling to, and this was done mainly on the long bus rides I had taken. Of course my tour was mainly about American Football, but I have such an inquisitive mind, and a broad interest in many other things, meaning basically I will go and take a look at anything I felt would be interesting in any city I visited.

I always Googled "10 things to do in, say Seattle". If anything interested me I would most times go and check it out, if not, then I would leave it.

Seattle was always a place I was so looking forward to visiting, especially as I'm a massive fan of Nirvana. I also like Pearl Jam and the music of the late 80's which was spawned from Seattle, and I knew there was a big museum dedicated to the grunge scene, something I was not going to miss. I also wanted to see the gravestone of Kurt Cobain, the singer and guitarist of Nirvana, who are probably in my favourite five bands of all time.

I actually had a ticket to see Nirvana play in London in 1994, before the concert was cancelled due to the fact Kurt blew his brains out. I was so gutted at the time as I loved that band, still do. That curse was repeated a few years later when I had tickets to see another one of my heroes, the fantastic Michael Jackson.

Seattle is also the birthplace of another one of my guitar heroes, the brilliant Jimi Hendrix, who incidently died in my home town of London. Both Jimi and Kurt are members of the infamous 27 club, a group of very successful musicians who sadly all died at the very young age of 27, far too early. Other members of the club include Jim Morrison of The Doors, Janis Joplin, Brian Jones of the Rolling Stones, and the latest inductee, Amy Winehouse. What a terrible waste of amazing and talented people.

I took the subway from the airport and I headed for downtown and I booked into my next hostel, called the "Green Tortoise". It was in a great location, right next to the big fish and meat market on the corner of 3rd street.

I checked into my room, and went straight out for a wander around, as it was Saturday night. I walked along the river, saw a big wheel lit up like a christmas decoration, and as usual I ended up in a bar watching American Football, as it was pretty cold up here on the Pacific Northwest.

I liked Seattle as soon as I arrived, as it seemed to me like a great place to live, even though the weather reminded me very much of London.

Sunday was game 30 and my penultimate game of the regular season. I had made contact with Seahawks SuperFan Bradley William "Cannonball" Carter, after yet another hook up from my SuperFan family via Facebook.

I met Cannonball in the bar where he hangs out with his fellow Seahawks fans, not far from the Seahawks stadium. The beer was already flowing, the music pumping, and it was only 10am.

The moment I met Cannonball, I knew he was a special guy, a true gentle giant in full Seahawks regalia, with blue paint all over his face and bald head. He made me feel a part of his family in a second as he introduced me to his lovely wife and his great friends.

Cannonball, like all my other NFL SuperFan friends, has such a passion for his team, and this dedication these guys have for their beloved teams, I feel should be much more recognised by the clubs they idolise. Sadly, is it not.....at all.

So many of my SuperFan friends must spend so much time putting on their "Warpaint", the facepaint some of them wear to every game they attend. Its funny as my good friend in Cincinnati, Shawn "Who Dey" Moore, who I had met and stood with at two games, I had never seen him without his make up on, so when there were pictures of him on Facebook, I never recognised him! A very handsome man is Shawn without his warpaint , a bit like myself! but he looks much better with his warpaint on!!!

Then there's Keith "Big Nasty" Kunzig who I met in Tampa with Jay Buc and Chris Elmore, Ram Man in St Louis, and now Cannonball in Seattle. I actually think these guys are bonkers/crazy, but hey, I admire them completely as their passion for their teams is a million per cent and second to none. This is why I would love to see the clubs recognise these amazing dedicated fans and take good care of these wonderful people, maybe giving them a few free tickets??

Cannonball took me for a walk to meet one of his friends, who had a spare ticket for the game to sell, so we walked around the outside of the stunning "Centurylink Field", the home of the Seattle Seahawks, and everywhere we went, Cannonball was treated like the local hero by the fans, which of course, he is.

Just as I had experienced in St Louis, when I walked along the street with Ram Man, I felt important in Cannonball's company, simply because I was with a very important person in the eyes of the Seahawks fans.

Cannonball was always polite and extrememly friendly to the fans, as was Ram Man in St Louis, and these guys were seen as legends by their fellow fans. It was so nice for me to experience this.

We arrived at the tailgate of Cannonball's friend, the lovely Traci Williams. Traci was an ex military girl who helped to defend her country all over the world over many years. Traci was so nice to me, another friend for life, as was the brilliant and very funny Jimmy Sabado and his lovely wife, whom I would meet again in San Francisco at Superbowl 50.

The concept of the Seahawks fans, who are called "the 12th man", is to support their team and get behind them as much as they can, and be as loud as possible in the process, and inside the stadium, boy they certainly were. I really liked the Seahawks fans, yes they were noisy fcukers, but in such a nice way that you can only love them!

I had a couple of beers with Traci, Jimmy and Cannonball at their tailgate, but it was now getting close to game time, so we headed to Centurylink Field Stadium for the game against the Seahawks divisional rivals, the very unpredictable St Louis Rams.

As always, I was looking forward to this game very much, especially as I had not seen the Seahawks play at any of the previous 29 games on my tour. The only other team I had not seen, and would eventully not see, was the New York Giants.

Centurylink Field is an amazing piece of design, unlike any

of the other NFL stadiums I had attended. Along both sides or lengths of the field are two long stands, which look like kind of arches, very unlike the usual dome or square stadiums I had been used to.

Then there was the iconic "Hawks Nest". I was so excited to see this stand in the flesh, I was absolutely buzzing, especially after seeing it on TV so many times. I simply had to go and stand in it, just like I did in the "Black Hole" of Oakland and the "Dawg Pound" in Cleveland.

Traci and I had seats very low down, again not my favourite place, but it was a great view, especially of the Hawks Nest stand opposite, which I could see right through the goalposts and end zone. Centurylink field was, and is definately in my top three stadiums I visited out of the 32 stadiums I eventually attended, (including Hawaii for the Pro Bowl, before somebody pipes up about my figures!).

It had been raining for most of the morning, just like the very fine London rain I am used to, the kind of rain in which you don't know you are getting soaked, until you are totally soaked, and in the first quarter, Traci and I bloody were!!

Traci then, bless her, played her "trump card". "Do you fancy watching the game inside the club lounge"? Traci asked. "Let me think about it, yes please" I said in a nano second. So off we went to the warm and dry club lounge.

Traci is pretty well connected at Centurylink Field, as she told me she used to work there, and I must admit, her friends did look after me. I sat in a seat under the covers right on the 50 yard line. I felt like I had the best seat in the house, and probably one of the most expensive, all thanks to the lovely Traci. What a girl!!! Thanks T.

The Seattle Seahawks are a team I've always liked from afar. My brother Paul followed them back in the 80's when they were as rubbish as my Dallas Cowboys, and I never did understand why my brother chose the Seahawks, probably a stupid reason, as in mine to follow the Cowboys, my choice only because I loved the 80's TV show Dallas!

I did recently mention this to my brother, and when I asked him why the Seahawks?, he said "for no reason at all"!! Ha, what an answer!!!

The Seahawks had had a very up and down season so far, and at one stage a few weeks earlier, it looked like they could possibly miss out on the play offs. But in the past two weeks, the Seahawks had thrashed their opponents by big margins, so I expected a very easy win indeed for them on this day against the Rams.

Yet again, what do I know, and as I have mentioned, the (unpredictable) Rams raced into a 14-0 lead, and to be honest, it could have been more than that, as the Seahawks, and the usually impressive QB Russell Wilson in particular looked very sluggish indeed.

Half time came, and now this was my moment of real pleasure, as I made a beeline for the section of the stadium called the "Hawks Nest". This stand is in the shape of a triangle, with the top tier becoming a point, obviously! I eventually went and stood right at the very top of the Hawks Nest, I was sooooooo excited and honoured to be there, I felt like a kid in a sweet shop, or on top of the world, just like Kate Winslet and Leonardo Di Caprio were on the Titanic!! It was a lot higher than I had expected, but I overcame and ignored my vertigo, and I watched the 3rd quarter inside this iconic section in NFL football.

I got talking to a family of season ticket holders of the Seattle Sounders, the soccer team who also play their home games at Centurylink Field. We had a good chat about soccer, and it was unusual to hear from some American fans who loved a different kind of football to their beloved NFL.

I could have stayed in the Hawks Nest until the end of the game, probably even until the end of the week! but I thought I had better get back inside the private area of the club lounge to see Traci, and also get out of the still pouring rain.

I expected a second half comeback from the Seahawks, they tried, and did get better, but so did the St Louis Rams, and amazingly to me, the Rams ended up winning the game 23-17.

I left the stadium with Traci, said my thanks and goodbyes, and I headed back to the bar where Cannonball would be with his friends. The Seahawks loss on this day eventually made no difference, as they thrashed their divisional rivals the Arizona Cardinals 36-6 in the final game of the season, to take their place in the play offs in two weeks time.

After a few beers back at the pub, I said goodbye to my new friend Cannonball and and I headed back to my hostel downtown, as that night there was free food for all the guests. RESULT!

The following day I was heading off to visit my good friend Bruce Kagestu, who lives in Vancouver Canada, a short bus ride across the border from Seattle. Bruce had invited me to stay with him and his family for a few days over the new year period, so I organised my ticket on the Greyhound bus, and up into Canada I went.

I met Bruce over twenty five years ago at a ski resort in Switzerland, and we have always kept in touch. Now we had planned to ski in Whistler, something I was really looking forward to.

My bus was leaving later that afternoon, so I had a few hours to see at least some of Seattle. The first, and most important thing on my to do list was the EMP Museum. This museum had an exhibition about one of my favourite bands, Nirvana. For a Nirvana fan like me, this was heaven, a great exhibition, and very interesting to learn so much about the band, especially their early days here in Seattle.

After seeing and reading all things Nirvana, it made me very upset to think as to how much brilliant material we would never get the chance to hear from Nirvana, after Kurt took his life far far too young. The same goes for Jimi Hendrix, the Doors, Michael Jackson, and now David Bowie, and Prince. A real shame indeed, and a terrible waste of talented people. There would have been so many more songs to have enjoyed if these heroes would have lived longer.

The EMP Museum also had sections on Jimi Hendrix, the grunge movement, including another band I like, Pearl Jam. The museum also had a horror movie section, sci-fi, and a part dedicated to the Seattle Seahawks 12th man, the fans.

I loved this museum, I wish I had more time to spend in it, but I was on the clock, so I only did about three hours before I had to leave, I could have done another ten. I also wanted to go up the Seattle "Space Needle", a tall thin monument looking over Seattle. I had already been up a few of these buildings, in Toronto, Sydney, and Auckland, and this one was a bit expensive, so I just stood underneath it and took a few pictures.

It was a real shame I was only in Seattle for less than forty eight hours in total. This gives me a very good reason to return to this lovely city on my next adventure, if there ever is one.

So sadly I had to nip this fine city in the bud and move on, as my time had come to head for the bus station on my next chapter, and a break from the NFL over the next four days, by relaxing and skiing in the beautiful Vancouver in Canada.

Vancouver Canada

I met Bruce over 25 years ago while skiing in Leysin
Switzerland, he is a great guy, always happy, smiling, funny
and great company. Bruce is also a great hockey player, a
brilliant skier, a New England Patriots and a Manchester
United fan, so we always have a lot to argue over!

We have met up a few times since we met all those years
ago, both in London and Vancouver and we always have a
good time together. Bruce had invited me to his home for
the new year holidays, and I thought it would be great to
spend some time with him and his family over this period,
especially after being alone on Christmas Day, it would be
nice to have a few days relaxing with friends in a nice home.
I organised to meet Bruce that evening to watch the late
NFL game with him and his friends in their local sports bar.
It was a game I wanted to watch as I had a vested interest in
the result. The Denver Broncos were hosting the Cincinnati
Bengals and I was cheering for the Bengals, because I
wanted them to get home field advantage for the play offs,
as I had unfinished female business to attend to in Cinci,
and by this time, I was now thinking of continuing my
adventure way past the regular season, and all the way to the
Superbowl.

The four hours bus ride from Seattle turned into five, thanks
to an arrogant young American emo lesbian psychobitch
chick, who never had the correct documentation to cross the
border into Canada. She didn't mind delaying the thirty or so
other passengers sitting idol on the bus getting bored and
very impatient, especially this one, who wanted to watch a
very important NFL game, which incidently could be the
difference between getting some female attention and
action, or continuing my world record barren run of no fun

and frollocks and carry on with the monk like existance I was living.

This rude girl never even apologised to any of us when she eventually got back on the bus, in fact she just laughed out loud with her fat girlfriend, as they openly kissed, talked loud, and had no regard for the other passengers on board whatsoever.

Now I have nothing against lesbians, I have said this before, I love them, but not the ones with attitude who look like boys. I love the pretty ones who wear make up, not the ones who make a personal stance and behave like activists, freedom fighters or minority rules types, which these two reminded me of as they nibbled on each others ears and spoke so overly loud on the seats right in front of me.

I finally arrived into downtown Vancouver, jumped on the subway across town, and met with Bruce, just as the game between the Denver Broncos and the Cincinnati Bengals ended in overtime. What wonderful timing.

The Bengals lost, but luckily for me this had no bearing on my return trip to Cinci, as the Bengals did eventually gain home field advantage in the play offs, and my booty call was still on the cards........by the skin of my Bengals!

Bruce and I had a few beers with his friends in the sports bar, before returning to his home, where I would meet his lovely wife and son.

The next morning we were up at stupid o'clock (very early) as we were heading off to ski at to the amazing resort of Whistler in the rocky mountains. I had been to Whistler about fifteen years before with Bruce, but on that fateful day the weather for skiing was terrible, very foggy and extremely dangerous to ski in, so as you can imagine, I was looking forward to returning to one of the world's premier ski resorts in the beautiful early morning sunshine.

I had to be careful when skiing as I had had a bad crash on my last ski trip a few years ago, fracturing my shoulder,

which incidently is something I have to live with every day,
as I still get pain whenever I hold out my arm.

We were picked up by Bruce's friend John, and off we went
to Whistler. I rented skis and boots, got my ski pass, and up
the mountain we went.

The first half a hour was a complete disaster, as my shitty
rental ski boots were rubbing on my shins and absolutely
torturing me. These boots looked quite worn and shabby,
like they had been rented out a million times, and I was in
constant pain as I tried to ski in them. Bruce and John could
see I was in agony, so I decided to ski back down to the hire
shop and change them. Thank god I did, as once I returned
with the new boots, my smile returned and my day of skiing
begun.

Whistler is one of the best places to ski in the world, and I
was loving being in this truly amazing place, as the sun was
shining but the temperature was way below freezing. I
remember taking a few pictures on my phone from the top
of the mountain, and it took all of five seconds for my hands
to tell me to get my gloves back on asap. It really was
incredibly cold, and I could not remember ever feeling this
cold before in my lifetime.

It was great conditions while skiing, but as soon as we got
on a chairlift to go back up to the top of the mountain, that
5-10 minutes ride really was complete torture, which was
forgotten once you got off, until you got back on it and did
it all over again.

We had a great day skiing in Whistler, but as it was the
holiday period, so it was quite busy on the slopes, but this
was a very small downside to all the upsides of skiing on
amazing long pistes. I loved every minute of it.

The next few days were lazy days, wandering around
downtown Vancouver, the harbour area, Harbour Park and
the Gastown area, having nice lunches, looking at a few
sights in Vancouver, and spending time in coffee shops and
general shopping areas.

New years eve was spent at a house party at one of Bruce's wife's friends lovely home, a nice bunch of people, including an old boy who came long with his guitar. He played quite a few songs, but most of them sounded the same. So of course when the people heard from Bruce I played and sang, I was asked to perform a few of my own songs, and a selection of covers, which I'm always happy to do. This was well received by the people, but not by the guy whose guitar it was, as I had clearly stolen his thunder. Whoops!

New years day came and Bruce took me and his son to an open practice session by his beloved hockey team the "Vancouver Cannucks". Apparetly this is a very rare occasion as the Cannucks never practice to an audience, so I was very lucky to be there.
To be honest, I'm not much of a fan of hockey, and this was boring to me after a hour or so, but I did enjoy the experience, and as Bruce and his boy were having a great time, that was good enough for me.
We departed to have lunch in a sports bar, and we watched a Premier league game (EPL) while we had our grub (food). That night was my final night in Vancouver, as I was flying back down to San Francisco the next morning for my final regular season game of the tour. I went to bed around midnight, and I had one of those tossing and turning sessions where I could not nod off (sleep), that you get once in a while.

After a hour of so, I felt this quick jolt, or a kind of shudder on my bed. To me it felt like a small dog, or cat had jumped up onto my bed. This scared the shit out of me, as I had no idea what this was, as I knew that Bruce did not have any pets. I thought it could have been anykind of animal that somehow got inside the house, especially as I was on the ground floor, maybe I could have been a rat? That thought made me get up straight away.

I got up to go to the toilet, and I was met in the kitchen by Bruce's wife Laura. "Did you feel that"? Laura asked. "What was it"? I asked. "That was an earthquake" she replied. So that's what I had felt from the bed, which actually made me quite happy and relieved to discover, as I could now go back to my room knowing there was not a huge rat underneath my bed!!

Laura turned on the TV and we watched the local news channel, where they were already talking about a 4.6 earthquake on the richer scale in the Vancouver area. Luckily 4.6 is not a big one, but it is big enough to make a mess, and thankfully this time, no lives were lost.

I must admit, I was slightly concerned as I know very little about earthquakes as we never get them in London, so I had no idea if this was the calm before the storm, or a warning an even bigger one was coming next. Luckily nothing else came, but this was the big news the following day on all the TV networks.

It was a nice and relaxing four days break for me with Bruce in Vancouver, and a change from the constant rushing around I had now been doing for now over three months. I needed this small break to recharge my batteries, which I did, and now I was ready to return to the next section of my tour.

The following morning, Bruce gave me a lift to the airport, I said my goodbyes to him, jumped on my flight, and I headed back down to San Francisco for my 31st and final NFL stadium on my tour. But this tour was now going into overtime, and I would continue my adventure all the way to Superbowl 50.

Stadium-31
Levi Stadium
San Francisco

I flew back into San Francisco and I headed back to the Adelaide hostel I had stayed in the previous week. I liked this hostel a lot, the staff were nice, the guests were too, it had a nice quiet lounge area, where I used to do my social media and website. The breakfast was good, and they showed movies in the evening, so a lovely comfortable hostel indeed. Oh and the beds were great too, which included a curtain for extra privacy, which always helped.

Adelaide Hostel was in a very nice location and close to everything I needed, so happy days. I felt very much at home in San Francisco, I walked everywhere, never feeling threatened at all, even by the massive presence of homeless people, drug dealers and all kinds of crazies on almost every street corner. I quite enjoyed all that, I found it interesting and exciting.

It was now Saturday, and my soccer team Arsenal were playing against Newcastle in the Premier League, so I did the usual internet surf, found the address of the local AA bar, then off I went to find the San Francisco branch of Arsenal America, the bar in town where I can watch the game with the local Arsenal fans.

I walked across town to "Maggie McGarry's" which was just past San Francisco's Chinatown. If you didn't already know this, San Francisco is very hilly indeed, hence why that have the iconic trams, and I had to walk up one of these very steep streets to get to the pub I was going to watch the Arsenal game in, and this was no fun at all at 8am in the morning, with last night's beer and burger hinting to me they were thinking of reapperaring out of the same hole they went down!

I eventually arrived at the Maggie McGarry's bar, which was a longer walk than I expected, but I soon got talking to a nice bunch of Arsenal fans, including a top man and fellow Gooner named Bobby Beer, an ex pat from the UK, now living in San Fran.

The game ended in a 1-0 victory for Arsenal, which kept them in with an outside chance of the title behind eventual winners Leicester, incidently the team I wanted to win the title as they were massive underdogs at the start of the season and given a snowballs chance in hell of winning the Premier League by the so called experts, including me. Well done Leicester.

I was introduced to a pretty little Russian chick named Irene, whom I was told was a member of a "Moscow Arsenal" fan club. Wow! I was surprised enough to find Arsenal America, even more so to find an Arsenal Russia. Could this be my next challenge? to visit all the Arsenal Russia bars? Probably not!

Irene adored Arsenal, and she was very knowledgable about the team, which I must admit impressed me a lot. We chatted about football for a while, and I asked her if she wanted to come with me for some breakfast or a coffee, as the game was over and it was now only 10am.

I had noticed Irene was on the radar of another Arsenal fan, a weird looking guy who simply would not fcuk off and leave us alone. When he did leave us briefly, I asked Irene if this guy was her friend? She said she had just met him, could not get rid of him, and she thought he was creepy. Irene probably told him the same about me!!

I suggested we dump him and go for breakfast alone and she agreed, but then he returned and suggested we all go to a very popular Chinese cafe together for a local delicacy, some kind of Chinese cake.

So off we went, but Irene made it quite obvious to me she wanted to shake off this leech. We went to the Chinese place with our new friend which he suggested, but it did not quite meet with our expectations, so I told him we were going somewhere else, and basically three was a crowd. He got the message pretty sharpish and off he went, leaving me with "red" Irene all to myself, so we headed off for breakfast.

Irene was not exactly my cup of tea, as she was no real looker, but she supported Arsenal, and she was very nice company, so I thought it would be nice to spend the day with her. After almost four months on the road with no female company at all, Irene started to look a lot better than she actually was, as yet again my little head had dodgy intentions lined up for Irene the Arsenal fan, if only I got the chance. At this stage for me, any hole was a glorious goal!!!

After breakfast we headed off to have a look at a few sights of San Francisco. We went to the Japanese Garden in Golden Gate Park, the very eye opening gay district of "Castro" and the amazing area of San Francisco called

"Haight Ashbury".

I loved Haight Ashbury, a very artistic and bohemian place which is known for it's hippie movement and the 1968 "Summer of Love" marches and concerts. It had a cool and funky vibe, as well as a great history for music from a very special era.

The Beatles had been here, Jimi Hendrix, the Grateful Dead, the Mama and Papa's, and many more groundbreakers from that period. Haight Ashbury is a beautiful neighbourhood, clean, happy and full of life. I'm sure this area is a great place to live and hang out.

I had been with Irene for most of the day, and I did enjoy her company, as we got on very well, and I felt maybe there could be something to come later that night, as we did have some interesting chats about boys and girls, and the birds and the bee's.

I was reading the signs throughout the course of the day, and I thought they were extremely positive, so I attempted to kiss Irene towards the end of the evening, and this went down like a french kiss at a funeral, and as usual, I played Russian roulette and this wanker found the fcuking bullet!

That monumental mistake was the beginning of the end of my new friendship, well it actually killed it stone dead to be brutally honest, and we went our own ways a hour or so later. We did arrange to meet up later in the evening, which incidently never happened, as Irene made up some random pathetic excuse she was staying in for a few vodka's with her aunt who she was staying with. I knew this was complete horse shit, and I never saw my new Russian bride, er... I mean friend....again! so another one bites the dust, and I took yet another very firm kick in the roubles!

I wasn't overly concerned, as I never really fancied Irene, but I was thinking, "any port in a storm"!, but for me the storm had turned into a bloody hurricane and there was no chance of docking my canoe whatsoever!

Sunday was my final regular season game, and this was held in the stadium that would be hosting Superbowl 50, a month or so later. The "Levi Stadium" was not actually in San Francisco as I already knew, but a two hour and two train journey south of SF in a place called "Santa Clara". As usual I did my research and I worked out the easiest way for me to get down to Santa Clara for the 1pm start time.

The trains heading south down to Santa Clara are not very frequent at all, even on game days, which surprised me, as I always thought the Americans were so organised. I got to the main SF train station around 8am to catch my train, but if I missed it, the next train was around 90 minutes later. I thought this was madness, and I expected the train I eventually took to be absolutely packed, but luckily for me, it was not.

The San Francisco 49ers are currently a team in disarray, once a very good team from back in the 80's, in the era of Joe Montana and Jerry Rice, but now a very average team with ex first choice quarterback and superstar Colin Kaepernick being totally ignored after behaving like a spoilt brat and showing a complete lack of respect to the American flag.

I rate Kaepernick, I think if he gets the chance he will do well for another team, but I couldn't see why he had had such a bad season, in the season I saw him play.

This would be the last game in a very poor season for the 49ers, and this was probably why the stadium would be far from full, as was my train to Santa Clara.

The train ticketing system was so complicated and I remember struggling to get my ticket from the machine, as it did not like my debit card and it was a far from a straightforward process as I had to get on two different trains, and they were different companies, so I had to get a special ticket. I can't quite remember what the issue was, but I do remember it being so complicated and taking ages for me just to buy a damn train ticket.

When the train eventually left the station, I was happy and very content as I was upstairs on a lovely double decker train in a very comfortable seat on my own. I do love a train. (you already know this!)

The first train I boarded took just over a hour, and during this ride I just caught a glimse of a stadium we went past, I had no idea who or what is was, but I later found out was the football field to Stanford University, yet another iconic name on the US map.

The college game is something I have never given any time to, mainly because I have enough on my plate with the NFL, and a few other passions of mine, but I completely get why most Americans I meet love this side of football more than the NFL, especially when they went to these particular colleges to do their studying, as this is their own personal connection to their beloved college football teams.

After changing from a huge train, and catching what looked a little like a subway train for around a dozen stops, I eventually arrived at the station for Levi Stadium.

The first thing I thought of as I arrived at this stadium, was that this was a very poor choice for a Superbowl venue. Not because it was a bad stadium, far from it, but because it was so very difficult to get to from downtown San Francisco, for the thousands of fans coming to the game.

Well, not exactly difficult, but a pain in the ass, unlike most of the stadiums I attended which were quite straight forward to get to from the downtown areas I was staying in.

I came to this game without a ticket, and very unusually, without a tailgate to attend. The reason for this was because the San Francisco 49ers do not have a SuperFan, so my SuperFan family had nobody to hook me up with. I think this is the only NFL team that does not have a Superfan?, or maybe there was one other team without one? but I know the 49ers definately do not, otherwise I would have been at their tailgate.

Strange really, as a lot of the other clubs have many, especially next door in Oakland, who must have at least 5 to 10, including Kirk, Black Barbie, Gorilla Man, as well as the Legend who started all this craziness off, Raider Ron. RIP.

Something didn't quite feel right to me about the Levi Stadium, I knew it was only a few years old, and had

replaced the iconic "Candlestick Park" (a stadium I would
have loved to have visited), but to me it lacked soul,
atmosphere and the extreme passion I had been very much
accustomed to experiencing at practically every game I
attended. But I put this down to the fact the 49ers had had a
poor season, and this was the last painful game for the fans
to endure for another year.

There was not much of a tailgate area too, compared to what
I had been used to, but I wandered around the small area,
looking for a new friend, or a victim I could maybe
scrounge a beer and some food from, as by this time I was
getting pretty good at this, especially as my confidence at
this point was now sky high.

I found my target or my new best friend as I spotted a guy in
a Dallas Cowboys shirt, standing on a tailgate with a beer in
his hand. Very strange as the visitors to the Levi stadium on
this day were the St Louis Rams.

I introduced myself to Mr Cowboy in the usual way with the
usual line. "Hi, I'm Dennis from London England, and I'm a
Cowboys fan". Before I knew it, a beer was in one hand, and
a local delicacy in the other. BOOM!

Fair play to all the tailgaters I had met all across America,
most are now my friends, some I don't know, never knew,
and will almost certainly never see again. I cannot thank all
these people enough for the kindness and generosity they
showed, to not only me, but the many people I dragged
along with me to their tailgates, from the many hostels I
stayed at. We were always treated like VIP's and instantly
made to feel a part of their group, posse, gang, call it what

you will. THANK YOU SO MUCH.

I've tried to remember as much as I can as I write this book, obviously I will forget some things, but from the very first tailgate I attended by complete chance in Houston, where I got chatting to a great bunch of Texans tailgaters, these wonderful tailgaters all across America are some of the nicest people you could ever possibly meet.

NFL fans are simply amazing people, it does not matter which team you follow (except the Cowboys or the Patriots!), the opposing fans don't seem to have any real malice towards the other teams fans, especially at tailgates. I'm sure you get the usual bad boys and trouble makers, but I have witnessed so many acts of kindness by not only my new friends all across the country, but people I have never met, and withing a minute or two, they are helping me in any which way they can. These people to me are very very special indeed, and a huge part of my overal story.

Of course there are many fans who dislike other teams, for example say San Diego Chargers and the Oakland Raiders, (as they are in the same state, as well as divisional rivals), but when Oakland Raiders SuperFan Kirk Bronsord goes down to the Bolt Pride tailgate in San Diego, Chargers SuperFan Josh will make sure Kirk gets the royal treatment as they are great friends, just like all the SuperFans are across the whole country. I think that's amazing camaraderie and complete respect for each others teams. I like this a lot. These guys all meet up once a year for a huge party in Canton Ohio in August, and I plan to get there myself one year and join them.

Mr Dallas Cowboy and his friends were so very welcoming and kind to me at the tailgate, again lovely people, but I could not stay long as I needed to get a ticket for the game. There are always tickets flying around outside stadiums or at tailgates, no matter what the game was, mainly from fans who have friends who decided at the last minute not to come, or have committments, or season ticket holders who cannot make it, as well as lots of other reasons.

Many tickets are basically given away if you are in the right place at the right time, and sometimes I was, especially at tailgates with my new friends. Sometimes I missed out by minutes as people would tell me they had just given a ticket away for free. NOOOOOOOOOOO!!

On this day I had to work for my ticket, mainly because I had no help from a Superfan friend, so it was in my own hands. There were tickets on sale at the ticket office, but a nose bleed (high up) was 75 bucks, and much more than I wanted to pay. At least I knew if I had to pay that, then so be it, this was my safety net just to get me in and complete my set of all 31 NFL stadiums. Nothing was going to stop me getting into this final stadium, whatever the cost, because today was now or never, and never was simply never an option.

I wandered around the tailgate, asking people if any of them had a spare ticket to sell, and it did take a lot longer than I had expected to get one in my hand.

I never ever got worried or concerned at any stadium I attended in finding a ticket, I simply saw this as a challenge, and I actually got a buzz from this, crazy I know, but the adreneline this gave me was a kind of high, and I was surfing this wave, as I knew I would get one eventually, as my English accent was such a valuable weapon, and I used this vital tool on my tour to the max. Just a shame it never worked as much as I would have liked with the chicks!!!

I always had a price range in my mind for tickets, I would look on Tickpick.com and see what the going rate was, then settle for a price range around what was currently available online. As this was a totally dead game, and with no real interest other than diehard fans, both teams could not make the play offs, so I thought 75 bucks was far too high, and no value at all, as I expected to get a ticket for practically nothing, just as I had done at some of the previous lesser games I had attended.

The problem at the Levi Stadium was that there were hardly any scalpers (ticket touts), which was unusual for a NFL game because normally they were all over the place like flies around shit! So my plan B was to stand near the entrance to where the constant flow of fans coming into the car park were congregating into a small area like salmon down a narrow river. I stood by this barrier and I just repeated in my loudest cockney accent "Has anybody got a spare ticket to sell?".

I had done this a few times at previous stadiums, and it has NEVER let me down. At first I was a little bit tentative and embarrassed to do this, but after experiencing so many situations at most of the 30 NFL stadiums I had already attended, and with so much knowledge gained as how to get my hands on a cheap ticket, I now had the confidence of an Olympic 100 metres gold medal winner running against a man with one leg! of finding a ticket at the price I wanted to pay.

It took less than five minutes before a lady walking amongst the crowd came over to me and said "hey dude, my girlfriend is not coming, and I have a spare ticket".

The woman explained to me the ticket was in a great location and was worth over 120 bucks face value, but I could have it for fifty, and I would be sitting next to her. I was thinking the game would be starting in around thirty minutes, so time was not exactly on my side. It was in fact a great deal, so I accepted the offer pretty sharpish/quickly, so off we both went, inside the Levi Stadium. It really was as easy as that. BINGO!

If I would have had more time to have hustled or ducked and dived around the stadium area in finding a ticket, I would have, remember this was an exciting game to me, and I was thinking fifty bucks for this nothing game was still far too high to pay in my opinion, something I knew from experience, as don't forget I had paid just five dollars, and twenty dollars a few times for previous tickets for much better games than this.

But at the time, fifty bucks was a steal, especially as 75 was the cheapest I could have bought from the club, and most importantly of all, because this was my final stadium of the tour and I was going in regardless of the price.

Once I arrived inside the Levi Stadium, it was worth every single cent, just for the incredible feeling of achievement I got for completing the set of all 31 NFL stadiums in one season.

The seat was quite low down, again not to my particular liking, but a very good seat indeed. I could see there were so many empty seats around the stadium, especially high up in my favourite area of the stadium, the nose bleeds, and I could have gone and sat anywhere, which is exactly what I did in the second quarter.

The game itself between divisional rivals the San Francisco 49ers and the St Louis (soon to be the Los Angeles) Rams, was not one of the best I had seen on my tour, in fact far from it. There was no real atmosphere inside the stadium, not like most of the other games I was at, which were normally extremely noisy, passionate and tense, as in this game there was nothing for either team to play for.

I spent the first quarter in the company of my new friend, who was a season ticket holder and a big 49ers fan. We talked about how bad her beloved team had become, especially after having so many past glory days in the Joe Montana and Jerry Rice era. The 49ers are definately a team living in the past, and this was evident as I watched this very average last game of the regular season.

I liked sitting next to random fans of the teams I was watching, it was always entertaining and great fun to be next to a person who showed passion for their teams by screaming out support, advice, insults to the opposition, and normally some very funny comments.

I left my seat low down after the first quarter, after telling my friend I wanted to go up high and take some pictures of the stadium, and I thanked her very much for the great ticket. I wandered around the stadium for a while taking a few snaps from a few different vantage points, and as half time approached, I plotted up high in the top tier in a section of seats in the beautiful Californian sunshine.

Half time came, and it felt very surreal as I sat high up in the nose bleeds, in a whole block of seats completely to myself, as I pondered in silence over my journey and adventure, as I reminisced about the previous three and a half months I had been on the road.

I had a little moment to myself, and I felt tears forming, for many reasons, joy, relief, sadness, disappointment, frustration, loneliness and intense happiness all mixed in together.

It was such an amazing personal achievement, especially after such a torturous start with being so ill, jet lagged, stressed and as tired as I had ever been in my life. Now I felt the complete opposite, I felt strong, driven, and totally ready to continue all the way to Superbowl 50.

I filmed a video around the Levi Stadium and posted it on Facebook. "I did it", I said happily, "I've done all 31 NFL stadiums in one season".

It was never my intention to go all the way to the Superbowl when I had the initial idea to come to America. (Have I already said this? probably more than once!) I had overcome so many obsticals on my way zig zaging across America, I now felt that doing another four more games would be easy, even though they would be very far apart in distance, but I didn't care, and at that moment, I decided I would not be stopping here, I'm now going to continue right through the play off's, and back here to San Francisco for Superbowl 50.

Half time came, and I got talking to a San Francisco cop, who was standing at the very top of the nose bleed section I was in. I have no idea why he was guarding this particular section, as nobody else but me was sitting in it. The cop was a nice guy and he took a few pictures for me on my phone of me at the very top of the Levi Stadium.

I told the cop of my story, and he was very impressed indeed, as he was also a big NFL fan. He told me he and his colleagues would be working on the Superbowl next month at this very stadium, so I decided to keep in touch with him as maybe he could help me get inside the stadium?, maybe through the back door if I bunged him enough cash??

The cop asked me for my home address, as he wanted to send me some Superbowl memorabilia only the San Francisco police department were given as a thank you for working on the Superbowl.

He said he would be sending me a special superbowl pen that the general public could not buy, which I thought was a very nice gesture from a very nice man. Sadly as I write this chapter a year later, I'm still waiting for the pen, or maybe it was nicked by my postman? To this day I never received it, a shame really as that would have been a nice souvenir from SB50.

The second half of the game was as dull as the first, and I found myself sitting alone, high up in the stands, and pondering over my incredible journey. My emotions were all over the place, and of course I was happy, but I was also quite sad as I had come to the end of the road I had been planning for well over a year.

Most of all, I was so very proud of myself for what had been and incredible journey and adventure I had had up until then. I could have so easily have given up sooooooo many times, I wanted to give myself the biggest pat on the back the world has ever seen, as I totally deserved it.

Looking back now, I realise just how so very difficult my journey had been. I wonder how many miles I had travelled? how many cities I had been to? different beds I had slept in? hours I had been on buses? and many more statistics which were way beyond my comprehension.

It was only at this moment at my last regular season game inside the Levi Stadium, I fully realised what an enormous travelling experience I had completed. I always knew it was going to be extremely tough from the very first seed I planted in my mind regarding this crazy tour, a tour every NFL fan in the world would have loved to do, but I never thought it would have been quite as hard as it eventually was.

You have to have an extremely thick skin to go on a six months adventure like this, as well as enormous patience, incredible drive and focus, as well a never give up attitude, which has to be completely open to all kinds of situations, challenges, problems, fcuk up's, delays, cancellations, break downs, terrible accommodation, bad weather, broken promises and many other random situations that fully test your resolve and character as a person, and most of all your patience, to the absolute limit.

You have to be able to handle many dodgy situations, sometimes well outside of your usual comfort zone, like sleeping in complete strangers houses at short notice, on sofa's, even floors, next to new friends, eg.....pets.

Planning was so very very important along the way, I cannot stress this enough, as finding the right accommodation in the nicer or safer parts of these cities was essential, as were booking buses, flights and tickets to games. The timing for organising all of the above was so important, simply to get all these things at the right price, but if the timing was wrong, trouble could be waiting around the corner.

A few examples of this were that the only night bus on a particular night maybe full, a convenient timed day bus maybe full, a NFL game was a sell out, the best hostels in town for location had no beds available, flights were more expensive the day before or after my planned day of flying, so if on my chosen day of travel there were no seats left, the cost would double for a different day, and some days there were even no flights available, etc etc, so it was extremely important for me to be completely organised a week in advance AT ALL TIMES, and I was.

Looking back, I made no real major cock up's, a few minor ones along the way, but that's always going to happen on such a massive trip, and when I look back and think about the few cock up's I did make, it does make me laugh, but these were small and nothing major as to cause me too much grief.

What I'm trying to say is, no matter how many people would want to do an adventure like this, the reality is very few would see this right through to the bitter end, unless you had the money to do this trip in style, which would cost an absolute fortune.

My opinion is you would have had to have been a regular backpacker/traveller, who has endured tough times, and slept in many dodgy places, good and bad beds, mostly in dorms with many other people, mainly great, sometimes terrible, have the ability to block out a lot of the bad things that come along like snoring, other noises, rude and disrespectful guests in your room talking, playing with their phones, laptops, games, turning on lights and so so so much more. I experienced all of these things more than once on my travels.

Back inside the Levi Stadium, the game was now just in the background as my mind wandered and I daydreamed about the next section of my tour, the play off's. This game eventually went into overtime, my 5th or 6th overtime game, but I decided to leave just before the end of normal time, because I knew if I missed the next train, I would have a pretty long wait on a very overcrowded platform at the train station, and get back to San Francisco later than I wanted, so I decided to avoid overtime.

The San Francisco 49ers eventually won this game, but by this time, I was back on the first of two trains to San Francisco as my challenge had been completed.

I had done it, challenge complete, 31 boxes ticked, D-Mo is the king of the NFL, and yet I had nobody waiting for me at the finishing line with a gold medal, no tickertape parade, no big cake, not even someone to just congratulate me and say well done.

This made me feel very sad and down in the dumps, as I so desperately wanted recognition by anyone connected to the world of the NFL for my achievements, especially as I was from the UK, did it alone, and completely on public transport except for Charlton Dave's lift from Atlanta to Charlotte Carolina on week eight.

I had left home on September the 8th, totally confident in my ability to follow my dreams of breaking America with my music, getting as much media coverage as possible, try to raise my profile in the music world, as well as raising as much money for my Prostate Charity as I could, while travelling around the country watching my beloved NFL.

I thought at the time, and I still think to this day, this is wonderful story of human endurance, an incredible adventure of an Englishman who has a real love of travel, music and the NFL, who combined his three passions to create a trip of a lifetime, and something which makes a compelling read.

This is why I have decided to write this book, I want to give as many NFL fans as I can, an insight into what I had to endure during my trip, and share these experiences, ALL OF THEM, both good and bad, to let everybody into the crazy life and world of D-Mo, over the six months I travelled to all 31 NFL stadiums, as well as experiencing so many other exciting adventures in so many different places.

I never did plan to write this book, but I had been asked so many times by fans I met along the way, as well as on social media, if I was writing a book about my journey. I always replied I never had any intention of doing so. But a few months after I arrived home, I thought it was a great way for me to remember my incredible journey, and have this in print for myself, and if a few other people read it and like it, then that would be a bonus.

Now I knew the play offs were on my radar, my blood started to pump at full speed and my excitement level was as high as it had ever been. A new chapter was on the horizon, and a very unexpected one at that, now I was returning to Cincinnati to see my good buddy Shawn "Who Dey" Moore, I'm also on a promise with the lovely Rachel, whom I've got more than a few tricks stored up my sleeve with!!! Maybe this is where I will end my barren run with the ladies, and retire forever from being a monk?? Please pray for me!

So.... now the adrenaline was pumping as my "TheWrongShapedBalls Tour" of all 31 NFL stadiums has entered overtime, and this boy was heading back to four of the cities and stadiums I had already attended.

My mind was full of plans and adventure, going back to Cinci felt great, (except for the six hours flight) and the not knowing where I would go after that was sooooooo exciting for me. Would it be Pittsburgh? Would it be New England? Would it be Phoenix? Would it be Denver? I bloody hoped it was Denver at some point, as I had another chick waiting on the nest for me there, and this boy was going to do his best to score a touchdown!!!

All I knew is, I was now 100 million per cent committed to going anywhere in the US on this incredible adventure, and I would return all the way back here in San Francisco California, to my final destination, Superbowl 50.

Play Off Game 1
Paul Brown Stadium
Pittsburgh Steelers @ Cincinnati Bengals

I had been in regular contact with my friend Rachel in Cincinnati ever since I left Cinci for Buffalo on week ten of my tour. We text messaged each other quite a lot, and chatted a few times about the fun we were going to have when I returned to Cincinnati for the play offs, if the Bengals made it.

I had been praying to the NFL gods most nights before bedtime to make this mission possible, as by this point I was like a drug addict that needed a score! Thank you god, you never let me down, well not yet anyway!

I was over the moon when the Bengals made the play offs with home field advantage, not just because of Rachel, but because it gave me the chance to go back and see my good friend Shawn "Who Dey" Moore, the Cincinnati Bengals SuperFan who had helped hook me up with so many great people on the rest of my tour.

I was so happy for "Who Dey", that his Bengals got into the play offs, as Shawn is such a nice guy and a massive fan, he deserves to see his beloved Bengals do well, as it has been a very long time since they did.

I organised my flight to Cinci, and as it was now the play offs, I had the wonderful luxury of time, OH YES!, a rest from the constant booking of all kinds of things was an absolute relief and a godsend. No more two day stops in cities, then rushing off to another, as these play off games were only weekend games, so I had plenty of down time to relax and explore during the week and this suited me just fine. Now I would be travelling at a pace I was much more comfortable with.

The flight to Cincinnati from San Francisco was about five and a half hours, and my accommodation would be free, as I was staying at the home of my friend Rachel, well that was the plan we had been discussing for the past two months, so I told her I would see her in a few days, and all things in the garden seemed to be blossoming nicely. Or so I thought!

The day before the flight I sent a text message to Rachel, but she never replied, which for her was very unusual, because she normally returned my messages quite promply in the past. I didn't read much into this, but when I text her again the next day to give her my flight details, I became a little concerned when again I got no reply. This was very unlike her and to be honest I was a little worried about her and by now I was just hoping she was OK.

As I boarded the flight to Cincinnati, I was now more than a little concerned by this point, as this flight would arrive into the Cinci airport, which was across the Ohio state line in Northern Kentucky at 9pm and I was expecting Rachel to pick me up from the airport as planned. Things got even worse once I had landed, as I still had no reply or had any news from Rachel at all.

Now I was very concerned for Rachel as she was normally so reliable, so now I was pretty worried about her, and the usual thoughts entered my mind that something could be terribly wrong. I guess this is only normal and a very common human reaction?, and in this moment, I temporarily forgot I was now "up shit creek without a paddle" and totally stranded.

In times like these, and trust me, there were a few over the six months I was on the road, I'm very proud of the way I handled these situations, I never panicked, there was no point and in a funny way, I enjoyed these moments of turmoil. What I mean is, I found these situations a real challenge and of course I was always the winner.

See I love change in my life, and these moments of last minute.com let downs, always pushed me into a new direction or situation, which gave birth to new adventures, or chance meetings with wonderful people whom I would have never met, if these cock ups never happened.

So here I was, at the airport in Kentucky in the middle of nowhere, nowhere to stay and Rachel had gone awol. I knew from my previous visit to Cinci there were no hostels, so I had to couchsurf at the home of my now friend Billy, but now my only choice was to book into a local hotel a short drive from the airport.

Anybody who is a seasoned traveller, especially backpackers, know there is always a list of local hotels on a wall at all airports across the planet and it didn't take me long to find this, which had around a dozen or so fairly local hotels in and around Cincinnati. I eventually chose to stay at the "Quality Inn", simply because it was the cheapest, even at eighty bloody bucks a night. I needed this extra payout like a fish needed a baseball bat. FCUK! Nice one Rachel.

I called the hotel and fortunately for me, they had a service whereby their driver picked people up from the airport, so within ten minutes, I was picked up by the hotel's driver, and off to the "Quality Inn" I went.

The Quality Inn was in fact quite a nice place to stay, but it really was in the middle of the woop woop/nowhere, and without a car, I was pretty much housebound. My first day there I hardly left my room as it rained for practically the entire day, so I took advantage of this to chill out, sleep well, do my social media stuff, and watch telly.

I continued to try to contact Rachel, but yet again, all I got in return was the dreaded wall of silence, and to be honest, I was absolutely fcuking fuming with her. But I was also very worried about her too, as she is a lovely lady, and I knew something must have been very wrong for her to ignore all my messages for the past three days.

I was BLOODY RIGHT! When Rachel finally surfaced and sent me a text message, she dropped me the A Bomb of a bombshell.

Rachel had been separated from her estranged husband for a while, I knew all this, as we had spoken about it when we met. If Rachel would have told me she was happily married, I would probably have continued to be friends with her, but I would not have tried to take it to the next level, as I'm not into cheating or breaking up couples or families. No sir.

I knew the full story, that Rachel and her husband were finished and she never wanted him back at all. But he wanted HER back and she gave him the message loud and clear that she wanted shot of him for good, but he was not getting the message and still hung around her like a bad smell.

So, the reason Rachel had ignored all my messages, was because her estranged husband had turned up at her house unannounced, which incidently he owned and was still paying for, even though he had moved out a long time ago. Rachel claimed she could not return any of my messages as this guy was now staying for a few days. WHAT A PATHETIC EXCUSE!

To say I was fuming was the understatement of the century, not because her husband had turned up, but because Rachel could not find TEN FCUKING SECONDS to text me to let me know she was OK.

The first thing I flippantly asked Rachel on a text massage was , "Have you been to the toilet over the past three days"? "Why do you ask this stupid question" Rachel replied. " "Because while you were having a piss or a shit, you could have at least replied to any of the dozen text messages I had sent to you"!!! I wrote furiously.

I was fcuking livid with her to say the least. Rachel told me so many times in the chats we had on the phone over the past two months how much she hated this guy with an absolute passion, something I now totally dispute, because over the next four days I spent in Cincinnati, Rachel would not leave her house while he was there. WHY?, only she knows.

I told her so many times that I had a nice hotel room and to pack your things and come and stay with me until he leaves, but she always said she could not. "WHY", I screamed, "Especially when you say you hate this guy"?

I could say a lot more about the situation with Rachel, I learned a lot of things about her in her private life I would like to write more about, but I won't, just out of respect for her, as she may read this and I don't want the world to know her personal stuff and I don't want to offend her in any way, as I really liked her.

But I am going to tell MY story, and the events which took place, because this book is about MY whole experience, whether Rachel likes it or not, because all of the things I will write, really did happen.

I met Rachel at my friend Shawn "Who Dey" Moore's tailgate, as she was a guest of the Warrior Wishes charity run by Craig Steichen, a charity who take family members of bereaved soldiers, as well as ex military personnel who have bad injuries caused by war, to watch NFL games. I had met Craig in Atlanta, before I coincidently bumped into him at many other NFL tailgates around the country. Craig is a top man and does a great job in raising money for his Warrior Wishes charity.

Rachel lost her son, who was killed in action in Afghanistan, so she was a guest of Craig's at this particular game I was attending.

After exchanging a few text messages, I eventually spoke to Rachel on the phone the following day, although very briefly as she seemed terrified of getting caught talking to me, so the conversation was brief to say the bloody least. Nevertheless we arranged to meet up the following day, Saturday.

It was Friday night and I had no intention at all of sitting in my hotel room brooding or feeling sorry for myself, fcuk that! I heading off to the local horse racing track called "Turfway", and I did my best to try to persuade Rachel to come with me, but she told me could not leave her beloved husband in the house alone, even though she insisted she hated this man's guts. I started to smell a big rat at this point, or a big fat whopping lie.

I don't know what bullshit Rachel was feeding me, but I had the impression or vision they were both sitting in the same room, in opposite corners watching bullshit TV like Judge Judy, and not speaking a word to each other. This perception came from what I had been constantly told by Rachel. But for all I knew, they could have been in bed, breaking the fcuking headboard, and by this time, to be honest, my patience had long gone and I couldn't give a shit, as I was going horse racing and this minor blip was not going to ruin my night out.

Turfway was far from the greatest track I have been to, certainly not anywhere near the amazing "Churchill Downs", the venue of the Kentucky Derby and a track I had visited on my previous trip to the state of Kentucky two years earlier, but I always enjoy going racing in a new venue and especially in a foreign country.

The beer was cheap, two bucks a pop, but it tasted like it too, weak and cheap. You do get what you pay for in a good beer and I did! I had a few winners at the racetrack, but I lost money overall, but not much and I quite enjoyed my time at the races that evening.

Yet again I was lucky enough to be dropped off and picked up at Turfway by the same driver from my hotel who had picked me up at the airport, who incident informed me of Turfway racetrack when we first met. I say lucky as this race track really was in the middle of nowhere in Kentucky, where all I could see were open fields and land for miles and miles, so I would never have known it was there unless I was told.

The following day, HALLELUJAH! I finally met up with Rachel, three days later than I had anticipated. She tried her best to apologise about the awkward situation regarding her estranged husband and she told me he was leaving the next day, so of course I was absolutely delighted.

The next day came and Rachel dropped the "Atomic Bomb" yet again, informing me that he was now not leaving today (which was now Sunday), but now he was going on Monday, the next day, which of course he never did.

I never did make it to Rachel's house, something I will regret forever, as the chemistry between us was amazing, especially of the sexual nature and we certainly would have had a whole lotta fun. I was sooooo gutted.

Saturday afternoon came and Rachel managed to prise herself away from her new best friend (sadly, not me) and we had lunch in a resturant not far from my hotel. I remember a very interesting conversation we had while we ate. I asked Rachel "Where is your husband now", she told me "He has gone to the shooting range". "How is he getting there"? I asked. "By car" she replied. "So how did he get to your house from where he lives"? I mentioned. "He drove" she informed me. "But he lives three states away", I trembled. "Well he drove all the way". she said. "How far is the shooting range from here", I said, "Just up the road", she told me. Can you see where I am going with this folks? "Is there any chance he could have followed you when you left home?". I asked, like a bunny rabbit to a hungry fox. " It's possible, but I doubt it", she laughed.

OK, so lets put this pathetic and dangerous liaison totally into perspective, here I am, having lunch with the wife of an extremely jealous and crazy stalker of a husband, who desperately wants her back, he has guns in his car and he could so very easily had followed her to our destination or potential booty call location, or maybe even spot her car in the parking lot outside the restaurant we are eating in by complete chance, on his way back from his adreneline infested shooting session at potential cardboard cut outs of ME!!!

I had this vision of a man walking through the restaurant door with a double barrelled shotgun in his hand, blowing the pair of us into kingdom come, before turning the gun on himself and splattering all the people dining and eating their deserts with his very own tomato sauce/blood!

This was an extremely pivotal moment for me in the very uncertain relationship I had with Rachel and this was MY trigger point (ha!) in calling off what was obviously a farce of a potential future union between two very desperate human beings who simply wanted to get laid.

Maybe this could be the big break in the media I had been working so bloody hard on? I can almost see the headlines in the New York Times or the UK's Daily Mail. "ENGLISHMAN ON NFL TOUR SHOT DEAD IN CINCINNATI RESTAURANT"!

I decided at this moment Rachel was not worth the hassle of being blow into smithereens, as I was enjoying this trip immensly, as well as my life, thank you very much and don't forget, I still had the play offs to look forward to!!

This whole Rachel situation pissed me off probably more than anything else I encountered over my entire trip, as this woman royally messed me about, after promising me so much, especially her crown jewels.

We finished our food, had a little cuddle in the car, I tried to get Rachel back to my hotel, but no, she had to go home to be with the bastard she claimed she despised so much, leaving behind someone who only had good intentions and affection for her. Honestly, I don't understand this and this sorry story makes me think that Rachel had been totally lying to me from day one.

But I will always remember Rachel with much fondness, this poor lady has not been dealt with the best hand of cards in her life, and I wish her nothing but happiness for the rest of her days. If this lady enjoys being treated like a doormat, then a doormat she will always be, until she finally sees the light, and I sincerly hope she does.

Later that day I decided to move out of the Quality Inn, into downtown Cinci to somewhere more convenient and of course cheaper. I had gone well over my budget and had paid more than treble the price for the hotel room than I was used to paying in a hostel, this was all thanks to Rachel and I may as well have flushed 250 dollars down the toilet. What a bloody waste of time and effort, as well as the bucks.

As there were no hostels at all in Cincinnati, my next option was "Air BnB", so I started my online search. I stumbled across a place which was in a great location in central Cinci, and I headed for it in the downtown area of town.

Again I had a stoke of luck and by complete chance this place turned out to be a real gem of a place to stay, as it was in fact a "Hostel". How? But there were no hostels in Cincinnati, I had checked more than once. Well this place used to be, before it was officially closed down a few years earlier and now it was the home of a lovely lady named Susan.

I liked Susan straight away, she was tall and blonde, and around 55-60 years of age. I was thinking immediately what a cracker she would have been in her younger days, right up my street.

I stayed in a lovely old private room, but there was a small minor problem, as there was a man in a room next to me, which he could only access by walking through mine. Oh well, it was a small price to pay for what I was getting and I didn't really mind.

The weather in Cincinnati by this time was bitterly cold, with it now being January and the middle of winter in the state of Ohio, snow was on the ground, unlike the sunshine I had just left in San Francisco.

You should have seen my face when Susan gave me the amazing news she had her very own steam room in the house, YIPPEE! wow, that was a great addition to this boy's plans, and what a pleasure this was to come home to jump in that after walking around in the snow and freezing cold temperatures all day. BLISS.

Today was the day of the huge play off game between the Cincinnati Bengals and the Pittsburgh Steelers. These two teams are divisional rivals, and absolutely hate each other with a passion, as they have a lot of bad history together over the years. The Bengals had not beaten the Steelers in a play off game for a very long time, so a win for them and their suffering fans was very long overdue.

I met with my good friend Shawn "Who Dey" Moore at his tailgate, and I had my face painted like a Bengal Tiger by one of Who Dey's mates, as of course I was supporting his beloved Bengals on this day.

The atmosphere at the tailgate was electric, as you can imagine for this "rivals" game, and after the usual few beers and lovely food, I found myself a ticket thanks to "Who Dey", and off we all went to the Paul Brown Stadium for play off game number one.

This was well and truly a massive game for both teams and both sets of supporters, I felt so lucky to be back here in Cincinnati to witness it, as the crowd were going wild, even before the game started.

I started the game in my usual nose bleed seat, incidently in a section full of noisy Steelers fans and this boy was wearing a face full of Bengals warpaint. GREAT! This never really bothered me, and as the game kicked off, I enjoyed the banter which was going on all around me and the atmosphere which was very heated indeed.

So after all the usual pre game festivities, the game started in what I can only describe as terrible monsoon rain conditions.

The first half was probably the worse game of football I had seen on my tour so far, (other than my Cowboys game in Tampa) with the half time score being 6-0 to the Steelers, with two field goals converted. I put this down to the fact that the game was obviously so important, and had so much local pride at stake, both teams were being super careful and of course did not want to lose, so no real risks were being taken.

I eventually moved down from the top tier/nose bleeds and I joined my friend Who Dey and his friends for the second half, as I wanted to watch this massive game with Who Dey as the atmosphere around him is always full on and a great thing to experience during the game. This would multiply ten fold after what was about to happen in the second half to Who Dey's beloved Bengals.

If it was possible, the game was even less of a spectacle in the third quarter, and it ended 15-0 to the Steelers. The Bengals were simply not in the game at all, and this game was as dull as dishwater and a total disappointment. But what came next, I will never forget.

Nobody in the stadium, fans watching at home on prime time TV, or anyone on the planet would ever have predicted what was to come in the final quarter of this game. I think this could be possibly the best, or tensest final quarter to a game in the history of the play offs, especially after what preceded this, which was probably three of the worst quarters in the NFL play offs.

The Bengals finally came to life at long last, and they had to, as they had been dreadful all night, especially back up QB McCarron, who just could not land a pass, and was only playing after the Bengals main man and first choice QB Andy Dalton was ruled out through injury.

The Bengals finally ran in a touchdown to make it 15-7, then stopped the next Steelers drive, getting the ball back and kicking a field goal to make it 15-10. This game was now on, had turned completely on its head and was now a one possession/score game.

The torrential rain had not stopped pouring all game, so WhoDey and me were completely soaking wet and our face paint was smudging and running right down our faces, but this didn't matter as we were now having a brilliant time as the Bengals were making an incredible comeback.

The Bengals got the ball back yet again, so this was now their big chance to take the lead, and the Paul Brown Stadium totally erupted when Bengals QB McCarron found wide receiver AJ Green for a touchdown to make the score 16-15 to the Bengals, the first time in the whole game the Bengals were in front. YYEEESSSSSSSSSSSSSSSSSSS!!!

The Bengals failed in an attempt to make the two point conversion, but this didn't matter, because with just 1.36 left on the clock, the Bengals intercepted a pass from the Steelers back up quarterback, (after first choice QB Roethlisburger had been carried off on a stretcher a few plays earlier) and gain fantastic field position to run down the clock and seal this win with a truly fantastic comeback.

The crowd went wild, the Bengals had done it after all these years, beating their dreaded enemy the Pittsburgh Steelers. My buddy Who Dey was looking to the sky saying thank you to the big man, as he has been waiting his entire life to witness this special night. It was absolutely brilliant for me to be next to Who Dey watching him scream, suffer, and now cry with joy, and right inside the eye of the Bengals fans tornado in the Paul Brown Stadium, this intense relief and excitement for the thousands of long suffering Bengals fans was a real pleasure to witness.

Finally the jinx was gone, the curse was lifted, the thirty years of hurt and wait was over. THEN CAME THE TYSON PUNCH!

The Bengals had the ball on the Steelers ten yards line, and they just had to run the clock down, and the game was over.

Then on the very next play, disaster happened, the Bengals runningback fumbled the ball and gave possission back to the Steelers. OH NO.... The atmosphere in the stadium changed from total celebration to absolute horror in a flash, and the Bengals fans were now in complete shock and the silence was deafening.

I looked at Who Dey standing next to me and I could see immediately his massive smile was now completely gone and replaced by the look of the face of a man on death row on his last day.

Then to everybody's surprise and the Bengals fans absolute biggest nightmare, the Steelers main man, QB Ben Roethlisburger returned to the field. HOW? We all thought by now he must be in the bath and he was gone for the night? This was not a good sign for the Bengals at all, because if anybody could pull this out of the fire for the Steelers, Ben was THE man.

Here we fcuking go I thought. My nervous system was starting to let me know all was not well and dandy in this body, especially after it only just told me to relax and tell me this game was well and truly over. What a rollercoaster ride we were all on.

A few plays later, and with the clock running down to just 22 seconds, Roethlisburger attempted a pass to his wide receiver Antonio Brown. The ball was incomplete, and a huge play for the Bengals, but an extremely late hit by one of the players from the Bengals defence brought a penalty flag and incredibly gave the Steelers a field goal chance. What a terrible mistake of monumental importance this was by the Bengals, absolute bloody madness and a massive schoolboy error of all errors.

Then all hell breaks loose, fighting starts on the pitch and the Bengals lost their discipline completely and another penalty is given against them, thirty yards in total, which now put the Steelers in field goal range. The silence in this stadium is now deafening.

The Steelers kicked the field goal with 18 seconds left to unbelievably win the game, and I only believed this really happened because I saw it with my very own eyes. The Bengals fans were in total and utter shock, especially my friend Who Dey, who was completely mortified and inconsolable.

The Bengals completely capitulated and imploded, and through terrible play calls by the coaches, combined with total indiscipline by the defense, they simply threw this game away to their deadly and hated rivals. This game will NEVER be forgotten by both sets of supporters for the rest of their lives and probably even longer.

For me, I was just so lucky to be there to witness such an amazing last quarter and an incredible end to a game of NFL football, in my opinion for drama and tension, probably one of the best final quarters of all time, that I could think of.

My boy Who Dey was totally distraught and speechless, I really felt for him, as this game with 1 minute 23 seconds to go was well and truly over.

I was soooooo angry with the Bengals coaches stupid play calls at the end of this game. I can't remember how many time outs the Steelers had left, it was two or three, but I will never understand why the Bengals QB did not get the instructions to make the play to go down on one knee and take 30 seconds off the clock at least three times, then kick a practically unmissable short field goal for a four points lead, leaving the Steelers needing a touchdown with less than 30 seconds to go with no time outs. This which would have been almost impossible for them to do.

Why the Bengals played the riskier running play, with a wet ball, only the play callers know. It was such a terrible mistake at a crucial time in the game, even this stupid Englishman knew this.

We all left the Paul Brown Stadium like we were leaving a funeral, it was heartbreaking for the Bengals fans and there were tears all over the place.

I finally said goodbye to my good friend Who Dey as he was in no mood to talk, so I just gave him a big cuddle, and I told him "My friend, you are my brother, I love you very much, and you are a very special man to me, thank you so much for everything".

I slowly walked back to Susan's place feeling pretty down, about thirty minutes away from the stadium. It was now around midnight and I was in no mood to party as I was absolutely gutted for the Bengals fans.

The following day was spent in a bar watching English soccer, then a play off game between the Seattle Seahawks and the Minnesota Vikings, which ended 10-9 to the Seahawks, after the Vikings kicker missed what was probably the shortest field goal attempt in the history of the play offs, which would have won them the game, but in missing it, lost them the game. That kicker must have been totally gutted, as I'm sure the Vikings fans were, as their beloved team, just like Cincinnati, had not seen much play off success for many years.

I had a bit of a wander around downtown Cinci, only really seeing what I had already seen on my previous visit a few months earlier. I ended up in the local casino which was only a ten minutes walk from my hostel, as I had to be inside somewhere as it was so cold outside. I eventually returned to my lovely hostel, and I jumped straight into the steam room and I had an early night, as this was my last night in Cincinnati.

The next day I was trying to get out of town to my next destination, which I now knew would be back to Phoenix Arizona. The direct flights were so expensive, so I looked at all kinds of options, permutations and alternatives to get from the freezing cold of Cincinnati, to the beautiful sunshine of Phoenix. It was way too far to go by bus, which I probably would have attempted, but the rocky mountains put pay to that idea, so I had no choice other than to fly.

After looking for what seemed like ages, I eventually found a cheaper option, but this would include a massive detour, an incredible journey, but at a third of the price. I didn't mind the extra travelling, as I now had time on my side for a change, so I decided to take the Megabus on a nine hour diversion northwest to Chicago, then a four hour flight to Phoenix.

I had also looked into taking my favourite mode of transport, the Amtrak train, but this only departed in the middle of the night, which I would have done, but again dollars dictated everything and this option was far more expensive than the plane.

My lovely landlady Susan offered to take me to the

Megabus pick up point on the edge of Cincinnati the following morning, and oh boy, I'm so grateful to her she did, as when we woke up that morning, we were faced with what was an absolute blizzard of a snowstorm.

Luckily for me Susan knew exactly where to take me, because before she had offered, I did look on Google Maps to see for myself where the Megabus bus stop in town was situated and I was actually thinking of walking to this spot, which in those conditions, would have been absolute madness and putting my life at risk.....bigtime.

We made it to the Megabus pick up point and there was nowhere at all for me to wait. I had expected the normal terminal or waiting area I had been used to before catching my buses, the usual check in desk, baggage desk, cafe bar to have a coffee and a cake and so on, at least somewhere inside and warm to wait. Nope, none of that at all.

Again I am so lucky Susan gave me a lift as it was incredibly cold outside, the snow was getting worse and now over a foot deep on the ground and if I had got out of Susan's car, I would have died of hyperthermia for sure, it really was that cold and there was nowhere at all for me to have sheltered from this.

The Megabus was over a hour late arriving into Cincinnati, making my connection and flight out of Chicago heading for Phoenix, extremely tight for time and now making me a little uneasy as I knew time would be now not be my friend, especially in these conditions.

Susan was great and in no hurry, so we grabbed a coffee at

the local gas station and we chatted in her lovely warm car until the bus arrived. When the Megabus finally came, it was music to my eyes, if you know what I mean, and I could not thank Susan enough for waiting with me, she really did save my life.

The thirty seconds I spent in the fresh air and driving snow, between getting out of Susan's car and boarding the Megabus, was as bitterly cold as I can ever remember experiencing. (up there with my skiing in Whistler) If I had been waiting outside in that snow and those temperatures and wind, for say, thirty minutes to a hour, I would have been in big trouble for certain, as the weather really was that cold. Thanks Susan, you really did save my skin. X

Because of the now intense snow, the Megabus was delayed for even longer and I knew by now I was in serious danger of missing my flight in Chicago. The bus journey was now not going to be a relaxing or enjoyable one, as I was now fully aware l was seriously on the clock.

Once we finally arrived into the Megabus station in Chicago, I had another obstacle or hurdle to jump over, the Chicago subway, which I needed to take to get me to the airport and it was now going to be a very close call indeed if I was going to catch my flight. I was nervous to say the least and running from the bus station to the subway with a backpack as heavy as a five year old, I feared the worse.

I got to Chicago's O'Hare airport around forty minutes before my flight was due to leave, knowing normally by now the check in would be closed. I was quite stressed as I stood in a long queue, so I chanced my arm by asking one of the airport's female assistants if I could possibly jump the queue as my flight was just thirty minutes away from leaving? Lady luck shined on me again as she informed me of the fast track check in system which was just outside the door of the terminal, near to where we were queuing.

I rushed over to this area where nobody else was waiting, obviously as they were already at the departure gate, I handed over my bag, they quickly took it and in seconds I was checked in, it really was as simple as that. No checks, no hold ups, no nothing, it was like I was dreaming and I was so relieved I had made it. I quickly went through the usual airport process, walking straight onto the plane without waiting a second, and off I went.

Incredibly against all odds, I had made it to my flight for my next destination, back to the lovely warm weather of Phoenix Arizona. RESULT.............PHEW that was close!

Play Off Game 2
University of Phoenix Stadium
Green Bay Packers @ Arizona Cardinals

I arrived into Phoenix absolutely knackered, after a long journey from Cincinnati via Chicago. That journey was a bit like travelling from London to Paris via Dubai, or New York to Chicago via Miami, but it was less than half the price than flying direct and as I was spending money like it was going out of fashion, I didn't have a lot of choice, so I had to take one for the team.

As I had been to Phoenix before, I knew my way around a lot better than when I arrived last time. Back then, I took an Uber cab from the airport to my hostel in downtown Phoenix as it was the easy option, but this time I took the subway to the only hostel in Phoenix, the "HI", where I had stayed on my previous visit.

As in Cincinnati, the previous city and my first play off game, I had a lot more time to spare than on my regular season visit to Phoenix, when I was on a strict schedule and I usually only had around three days before I had to move on to the next game. This time I had a week and I wanted to use this time constructively, rather than waste it being over lazy, and getting bored walking up and down the old same streets.

The weather in Phoenix was great again, as Arizona is the warmest state in the winter in America, much warmer than Chicago and Cincinnati where I had just left, which were under huge amounts of snow.

It was great to see a few friendly faces again, whom I had met a few months ago on my last visit. Keith the English ex pat owner was always good for a laugh, as was Josh and a few of the girls who worked at the hostel.

I checked in, unpacked my things, and got chatting to a few of the guests. I met a nice girl from Montreal Canada, who apparently was one of the youngest politicans in her country before she quit. She told me some incredible stories of how corrupt politics really is, (as if we didn't already know) although we can assume, we only know the tip of the iceberg, regarding some of the dodgy stuff going on and this came from my politician friend, not my own personal opinion.

Almost everybody I had already met from Montreal were gay, except for the stunning goddess I was in a hostel with in Tampa. I have no problem with this, I'm just stating a fact and I think this girl was another lesbian. She was very nice, and we went for a walk to check out the night market which was in downtown Phoenix.

The markets were a little disappointing, mainly due to the fact we were too early and most stalls were not even open, so we went for a coffee, before heading back to the hostel.

On the walk back, we passed a small and quirky looking cinema, so we popped our heads in. I love going to the pictures when I'm travelling, so I asked what movies they were showing.

A new film had just started with Matt Damon called "The Martian" and it was only fifteen minutes in. The guy who owned the cinema was really friendly, and he asked me if I wanted to see the film, I could go in for free as I had missed the beginning. Top Man.

My Canadian friend did not fancy it, but I did, so in I went and I left her to go back to the hostel. It was a shame I missed the beginning, as I really enjoyed the film.

The following day I returned to the Arsenal America bar in Tempe, just outside of downtown Phoenix, as there was a big Premier League game against Liverpool I wanted to watch. I had met a few people on my previous visit to this bar a month or so earlier and the same people were in the bar again for this game, so I watched the game with them and what a game it was, finishing 3-3, with Liverpool getting a last minute equaliser. FCUK! But it was a fair result as both teams played really well.

On the way home from the Arsenal America bar, I got an unlikely text message from the unpredictable and now forgotten Rachel, the woman who ignored my messages in Cincinnati, and the very same woman who told me her estranged husband would be leaving town on Sunday, then Monday, then she never contacted me again, until now. I thought she could go and fcuk herself, so I ignored her message. I also ignored the second message a few hours later.

The following day, I received a third, and this time an abusive message from the lovely Rachel, saying something along the lines as "Yeah, you go and ignore me, why don't you answer me"?, something along those lines of horse shit. Coming from Rachel, this was rich with her pathetic communication skills and considering the silent treatment she had given to me over the course of the week I was in Cincinnati. I was just given her a taste of her own medicine and she didn't like the taste at all, but it was OK for her to do this to me, right Rach???

When I finally replied, with something along the lines of "How does it feel being ignored Rachel?, hurts doesn't it?", of course this hit a raw nerve, and she gave me a mouthful, well a text full to be more accurate.

I really wanted to go for her jugular by telling her a few home truths, as this woman totally fcuked me about BIGTIME and now she was pissed off at me for giving her a piece of her own medicine and useless communication skills. Nothing worse than a woman scorned me thinks.

Anyway, I gave her a piece of my mind and then I just deleted her number and she was gone from my life. SEE YA!

I'm not gonna lie, I was really upset with this situation when we never hooked up, especially as we had arranged to get together for months and when I finally made it across the whole country, she dropped me deeply into the brown stuff the moment I arrived in Cincinnati. A shame really, as Rachel really was a lovely lady, as well as being very good on the eye.

See this is why it hurt so much, as Rachel was so nice when we met, and so lovely when we talked on the phone, which was quite a lot. I never expected her to fcuk me about like this in a million years, but she did, and she had her reasons which only she knows.

But I do have to thank Rachel for one thing. If it was not for her, I would definitly not have continued my tour right through to the play offs, as my original plan was to head to Los Angeles, to see my good friend Jorge Gonzalez, then hop over to Las Vegas for a week, after I left San Francisco on the last regular season game of my tour.

This booty call was a massive attraction for me, for the obvious reasons, but there were other factors involved as to why the play offs were a great idea, including seeing my friend Shawn "Who Dey" Moore again. After all, it was only another four games and as I had already done 31, this would be easy and to be honest......it was.

As soon as I had decided to continue all the way to Superbowl 50, I was as excited as I was at the very beginning of my tour, probably more actually, as now I was feeling great and as tough as an old pair of boots!

I returned to my HI Hostel and I received the bad news there was not a bed for me the following night as the hostel was fully booked, and this was the only hostel in town. FCUK!

One of my guardian angels from my Superfan family (I think it was Tim Young yet again), had told me he had a friend who lived just a few miles from the University of Arizona stadium, the home of The Arizona Cardinals, (where my next play off game was in two days time), and he would call her and ask her if she would be so kind as to give me a bed for a few nights, which is exactly what happened.

I made contact with the lovely Karen, got her address and I

headed across Phoenix to a place called "Glendale" on the west side of town. As I left my hostel heading to Karen's place, little did I know what a terrible journey I was about to have.

I attempted the same route I had used to get to Glendale for the previous Cardinals game I attended in the regular season, as I knew this way by taking two buses. But as I got to the first bus stop, I was horrified to see a massive queue of people waiting, but as it was a Friday night, I thought it was just rush hour and people going home from work. WRONG! There was a bloody bus strike and I was informed by a woman at the bus stop that the bus I wanted had not turned up for over a hour and even if it did, I would never get on it with my massive backpack and all these people in front of me.

I simply had no choice but to catch a cab, as it was a long way to Karen's house, so it was gonna cost me a fistful of dollars. SHIT! I called for an Uber cab and he turned up about fifteen minutes later and picked me up at the side of the jam packed bus stop.

The cab driver was a really friendly nice man and very helpful too, so as we got to the long road that goes all the way to Glendale, I was shocked to see the second bus I was due to catch was in front of us in the traffic, as I was told this bus was on strike and it was not running, this was obviously bullshit as we had just driven past it.

The cabbie suggested we drive to the next bus stop and he would drop me off in front of it, so I could catch the bus. What a nice guy. I paid the fare of twenty five bucks and I jumped out of the cab and onto the bus. This probably saved me about thirty bucks, and I was now pleased this difficult ride to Karen's place was almost at an end.

I was meeting Karen on the corner of a main junction on the freeway, not far from her house. It was now around 10.30pm, very humid and extremely dark where I was waiting to be picked up by her. It was also totally deserted, not exactly the best combination or scenario to be in, so I was quite relieved when Karen finally came along in her car to pick me up, before I got mugged, robbed or kidnapped!

Karen is a lovely lady and she was also a great host, she lived alone in a lovely big beautiful house, she made me a nice dinner and I stayed in a room which was nothing short of five star luxury, a whole lot better than I had been used to over the previous four months.

The next day, I accompanied Karen to another property she owned, just a few minutes drive up the road from her main house, as she had a guy coming over to show her some samples of carpets Karen was buying for her somewhat smaller place.

As I listened to the salesman's bullshit, I felt he was doing what most salesmen do and trying to fleece Karen for as much money for his commission as he possibly could. Most of the time I waited outside and at one point I got chatting to a neighbour but upon my return, I showed a little more interest in his salesmanship or gamesmanship and I started to ask him a few basic questions.

I wanted to help Karen, but as it was none of my business, I did not poke my nose in too much. I mentioned a few points to the guy and I could instantly feel he was a little intimidated by me, as he probably saw me as less of a pushover than Karen.

See I'm used to haggling for a price on most of the things I buy. I certainly have no shame in asking, as these people can only say no. So when I asked the guy about a discount for cash, he became a little bit uneasy.

Never be afraid to ask for a deal, because you will be very surprised sometimes when you get your way, I've done this so many times. So after the salesman left, I told Karen when the guy calls back, tell him you have another salesman coming over and if he offers his product at a few bucks less than he did, then you may as well go for that. This way you have a little more bargaining power and usually you can get a little movement on price.

I never did know what happened regarding the carpet, but I hope Karen did not pay the over the top first price the salesman offered to her and that and she managed to knock him down a few bucks, so both parties were happy with the deal.

We left the mobile home park and headed for a local bar restaurant for a few drinks and some lunch, before Karen dropped me off at the University of Phoenix Stadium for my second play off game between the Arizona Cardinals and the Green Bay Packers.

I was meeting my friend and Cardinals SuperFan Randy Earick again at his tailgate, so I headed straight over to him and his friends. It was a whole lot easier to find him than it was on my previous visit and before I knew it, I had a beer in hand and a mouthful of Randy's delicious cuisine. Beautiful.

It was a beautiful evening in Phoenix, the sun was going down, the sky was red, and it was a nice warm temperature, perfect conditions for watching a game of football. I entered the University of Phoenix stadium for the second time as I was looking forward to a great game, and what a great game it turned out to be. Never in my dreams would I believe what I was about to witness.

The University of Phoenix Stadium was probably in my top five stadiums that I visited in the NFL, it has a beautiful design, a great section called "The Red Zone", and I thoroughly enjoyed myself on the both occasions I attended a game in this lovely stadium.

As I entered the stadium, I picked up an Arizona Cardinals towel which was being given away for free and as the game started, there were thousands of these towels being held up high and swung around in circles by The Cardinals fans. It looked like thousands of tiny helicopters all around the stadium, it was a great visual spectacle to see.

This game I was supporting my second team The Packers, but it was The Cardinals who started the game better and they took the lead with a touchdown in the first quarter.

It could have been worse as The Packers star quarterback Aaron Rodgers threw two interceptions before half time, but The Packers did score two field goals to make it a very close game and the first half ended 7-6 to The Cardinals.

During the game, I had received a text message from Karen, (the lady whose house I was staying at), that she had fallen ill and she was now in hospital. She had had stomach pains, which at the time, was thought to be gallstones.

The first thing I thought was "Fcuk, how am I going to get back to her place tonight as she was supposed to be picking me up?". I know it sounds terribly selfish (which it was), but where the f..k would I go if she stays in hospital tonight? I would be completely stranded.

The second half of the game started and my mood changed as I was not only concerned for Karen, but for myself, as I had to think of a way to get back to Karen's house after the game and with all those thousands of other fans in their cars blocking the traffic. Karen gave me her home address on a text message and she informed me she had left a key for me under the doormat. PHEW!!!!

What a legend Karen is, even through all her pain and in the hospital, she still made the effort to make sure I could get back into her house. Good girl. Thanks a million Karen. X

The Cardinals kicked a field goal, then The Packers scored a touchdown, to take the game into the final quarter with The Packers now leading 13-10. Both teams were making so many mistakes, it made for a tense and a very exciting game.

The Cardinals scored a touchdown to take the lead 17-13 and they were very lucky that a pass from Arizona's QB Carson Palmer got deflected right into the arms of a

Cardinals wide receiver in the endzone. The atmosphere was electric and the crowd were going wild with their spinning white towels everywhere, it was brilliant.

The Cardinals scored another field goal to make the game 20-13 with less than two minutes left on the clock, so now The Packers needed a touchdown to take the game into overtime.

The Packers were in big trouble with a 4th down and 20 with less than a minute left on the clock. The next play could possibly be the last play of the game and The Cardinals would win if this 4th down was not converted.

Enter the fantastic Aaron Rodgers. Never underestimate this legend, as the brilliant Packers quarterback had other ideas when he dodged his way out of a hole to throw a 61 yard pass to one of his wide receivers to keep the game alive. What a great throw, and even better was to come.

The final play of the game was to be the super exciting "Hail Mary" pass. I had already seen three of these passes caught, and one from Aaron Rodgers back in December in Detroit. Surely he could not do it again.......could he?

The ball got snapped, Rodgers stepped back, ducked and dived in the pocket (his small area) and avoided a few attempted tackles, then he launches his"Hail Mary" high into the Arizona sky of the University of Phoenix stadium.

Incredibly, amongst three Arizona Cardinals defenders, Packers wide receiver Jeff Janis, (the receiver who caught the pass on the previous play, a 61 yard catch to keep the game alive, and who incidently was only on the pitch because two of his teammates were injured), jumped high, outfought the Cardinal defence and caught the pass to take this game into overtime.

It was just truly incredible and my fourth "Hail Mary" completed pass of my tour. I was absolutely in dreamland......again, but this one was the best by far.

Only Aaron Rodgers can do this, the guy is amazing and simply never gives up until the clock says 0.00 and sometimes even then, the game is not over, as it was in Detroit.

The silence in the stadium was deafening, as the Cardinals fans were in complete shock, and to be honest, so was I! It was incredible drama and again, as in the previous play off game in Cincinnati, I was so lucky to be here to watch yet another unforgettable game of NFL football.

The game now entered overtime, my 6th of the tour and the atmosphere was now off the richter scale, the noise was as loud as any stadium I had attended so far, I was honestly in NFL heaven.

The Cardinals started overtime with the ball and what happened next, was probably right up there with one of the best plays I have ever seen.

The Cardinals QB Carson Palmer took the snap, manoeuvered his way away from a few Packers defenders and he managed to riggle out of the pocket, bumping into one of his own players, then he threw a cross field pass to the Cardinals wide receiver and legend Larry Fitzgerald, who was wide open.

Fitzgerald caught the ball around his own 35 yard line and he proceeded to run for the end zone. He evaded tackle after tackle as the entire Packers defence chased him, it was one man against the world and Fitzgerald was winning the battle. The crowd were going absolutely ballistic as Fitzgerald kept going and going and going, bobbing and weaving all over the field, passing Packer after Packer defender. Fitzgerald was finally tackled and brought down on the 4 yard line, and to be honest, I was gutted he never ran in the winning touchdown, even though I was supporting the Packers!! What an amazing run.

The stadium erupted and the Cards fans were going absolutely crazy. The ball is now on the 4 yard line and on the next play Cardinals QB Palmer flicks the ball to Larry Fitzgerald again and this time he runs the ball into the end zone to win the game for the Arizona Cardinals. What a game, what a player, and very fitting for Fitzgerald to get the winning score. What an end to an amazing game of football, the crowd were going absolutely wild, and I think I had just witnessed the best game of my tour by a mile. What a incredible evening.

I was so happy Fitzgerald won the game for the Cards, after his 75 yard run on the previous play, he deserved to get all the headlines, as he has been a great servant for the Cardinals for many years.

I stayed behind after the final whistle inside the stadium to watch all the after game celebrations, and in all the furore I temporary forgot for a while I was totally stranded as Karen was now in hospital and on the verge of an emergency operation to remove her gallstones or something similar.

We had been texting each other for most of the evening and we joked it must have been the poison I had put into her food we had together at lunchtime!!

It must have been around 11pm, probably later, as I eventually left the University of Phoenix Stadium, as I attempted to head back towards the area in which Karen lived. I had her address, so that was a result, otherwise I was totally and utterly screwed.

As I walked back through the area full of bars and resturants outside the stadium, the place was banging, with parties going on all over the place. At this point I wished I had some mates with me so we could all have joined in with the celebrations, but all I had on my mind was the thought of getting a cab back to Karen's place, but I knew this was not possible at that moment as the traffic was at a gridlock, with thousands of fans honking their horns everywhere as happy as can be. I knew that finding a cab in all of this was not going to be easy.

The atmosphere after the game around the stadium was amazing, but all I had on my mind was getting back to Karen's place and I even considered walking, as I thought it was not that far (it actually was very far), but my biggest problem was that I had absolutely no idea where the hell Karen lived.

My only choice was to plot up in a bar, (well, there's far more worse places to plot up in I guess!!) and I waited for the traffic to calm down a bit, before I ordered an Uber cab. I walked to a place as far away from the stadium as I could, as I thought this would be an easier place to get picked up from, rather than outside a stadium with thousands of fans and cars everywhere.

I ordered a beer, sat down for half an hour, then got on the phone to try to order an Uber cab. Easy? No.

Uber cabs are absolutely hated in London by the traditional black cab drivers, but here in the US, they are well worth using as they are so much cheaper than the usual local cabs. BUT, Uber have a system whereby when an area or a time in the evening is busy on their circuit, like tonight after the game, the price trebles. So my 10-15 dollar fare would now be almost 50, fcuk that! and I only want to go a couple of miles up the road.

I had a few beers, waited a while for the price to drop a little and I eventually got my ride home back to Karen's house. I think I eventually paid around 30 bucks, double the usual price.

The door key as planned was waiting for me under the mat and as I let myself in, I felt a terrible sense of guilt indeed to be in Karen's lovely home, while she was lying in a hospital bed in complete agony.

I went straight to bed because I had to be up early the next day, as I had my next adventure already booked. I had a week until my next game in either Denver or Pittsburgh and as I had been to Phoenix before, I wanted to get out of town and go to see one of the wonders of the world, the Grand Canyon, which was a few hours north in the state of Arizona.

I took an Uber Cab all the way to the Greyhound bus station

on Sunday morning. The driver was a lovely girl, there was practically no traffic, as most people would have had a very late night after the Cardinals win and after half an hour we arrived at the Greyhound bus station on the way to my next destination, Flagstaff.

I never did see Karen again, but we did keep in touch and I'm very happy to inform you she made a complete recovery. Thank god for that.

Thanks for looking after me Karen and letting me stay at your lovely home, it was a real shame we only had 24 hours together as you are a lovely lady and I really enjoyed your company in the very short time we had. XX

Flagstaff Arizona

I had done my research and had looked online to see what I could do, or where I could go in the week before my next game, which would now be in Denver. I was well pleased with this destination, as I would now try to rekindle the very weak flame I had left with that pain in the ass and terrible communicator, but amazing figure that was the lovely Ashley.

The Grand Canyon was something which was well and truly on my radar, so I headed north to a small but very interesting place called "Flagstaff".

I knew very little, well practically nothing about Flagstaff, but I had read that the famous route 66 runs right through it, and Flagstaff was a good place to base myself to get to the Grand Canyon.

The bus ride to Flagstaff was about four hours north from Phoenix, and I had arranged my second live phone interview with Talksport, the biggest talk radio station in the UK. The expected call came, but sadly for me, and the listeners!, I was going through the Arizona desert at the time of the arranged call, and my signal was very bad. I spoke briefly to the guy on the phone, but I was breaking up badly. We decided to reschedule for the following week, and at the time, I was fcuking annoyed and gutted again I had missed another opportunity to get some publicity for my tour, and also the opportunity to get more people following me on my websites and social media pages. Again I thought I was cursed in this area of publicity.

I really enjoyed doing these live interviews on the radio, but they were always so short, and practically over before they got interesting. What annoyed me most, was the fact that the person interviewing me, would constantly speak over me, and ask me some stupid and pathetic questions, when I wanted much more interesting dialogue. I had soooooo much to say, I could have talked for hours, and I'm pretty good at that!!!

I had done a few previous podcasts, one with a guy named Mark Teese on his UK podcast and we had a few great chats at length. Mark is a passionate follower of the New York Jets, his podcasts are excellent and he was genuinely interested in my tour way before anybody else gave me the time of day.

I enjoyed the conversations I had with Mark, as he actually listened to what I had to say and he showed enormous interest, but the Talksport interviews seemed rushed, unprepared and not taken very serious at all and I felt like a dancing monkey.

The worst interview I did was with Colin Murray, this guy loves the sound of his own voice, and I basically never had a chance to get a word in. He asked me stupid questions, when he could have asked me things much more interesting than "what is the Levi Stadium in San Francisco named after"?, I flippantly replied "Jeans", as I had no bloody idea where this comment was leading, he was probably lining me up for one of his very unfunny jokes. He then replied in a deadpan voice "Yes".

This went down like a very unfunny gag a live comedian would tell and nobody laughed, and was followed by five seconds of embarrassed silence.

I was thinking what kind of fcuking question is that you prick? Ask me about my experience with Shad Khan, or any of the 31 stadiums I had attended, or the 32 teams I had watched, the fans, the weather, the tailgating, my accommodation, travel stories, cock ups, any fcuking thing, but why they named the Levi stadium? what a bloody waste of time.

Before I knew it, the interview was over and yet again, disappointment and frustration kicked in. I was fcuk.....ing fuming, as yet again another wasted opportunity on national radio.

I did another live interview the following week from inside the Mile High Stadium in Denver with Radio Five live, this time with Nat Coombes, another integral player in the UK NFL media who decided to ignore my every attempt to get him on my side. I could not even get a Twitter reply from him while I was in America, but he did return a truly pathetic response to one of my tweets before I left home. I had asked him for some basic advice for when I got to the NFL games, just to try to get him interested in my tour. I was totally gobsmacked by his reply of "Drink lots of beers and look out for the tits". WHAT?

OK listen up, this boy likes beer and loves tits as much as any human being with a heartbeat on this planet, and if this tweet came back from one of my mates, I would have laughed my bollox off. But from Nat Coombes? Mr NFL on UK TV. I wanted him to follow me, help me raise my profile, support me, encourage me on my humongous adventure, and all he could say was "drink beer and look at tits". What a fcuking wanker. This is no joke Mr, I'm taking this tour very bloody serious. I know he was probably joking, but then why did he ingore all my other attempts to touch bass with him as he never replied to me ever again?

So when Nat Coombes interviewed me for Radio 5 live, I wondered if he knew he was actually talking to me? Probably not. On the interview I spoke to Mike Carlson, the American NFL pundit who I love to watch on TV, and I was really excited and honored to talk to Mike as I like this guy a lot, but Mike really does have verbal diahorrea and he completely spoke over me for much of the interview.

I so wanted a platform to inform all the NFL fans around the entire planet of my (and probably every other NFL fans) dream adventure, or the top wish on the bucket list for all passionate American Football fans, and a forum to share my stories and experiences, but I never got that chance when these interviews arose. I had just a few moments to try to convey my messages, amongst some truly random questions which ate into the very precious seconds of airtime I had to project my story as much as I could.

During this particular interview inside the extremely noisy Mile High Stadium in Denver, about five minutes before the teams came out onto the field in this AFC championship game, (semi final for people who don't understand what a AFC championship game is) the crowd were in such a frenzy in anticipation for this massive game, I could hardly hear what Matt Coombes and Mike Carlsson were asking me.

I can clearly remember finding a corner tucked away near a kitchen, with its door open just outside my nose bleed block, that I snuggled up behind to try to get some kind of a screen or cover as to help block out the noise being generated by crazy fans everywhere. These fans must have wondered what on earth I was doing bending over with my head more or less between my legs, trying to cover my ears, just to hear what these guys were asking me on the phone. Complete full on concentration was needed and squinting my eyes to the max, just to hear these questions I was being asked, as I thought his was my moment and I was not going to mess up this time, not for anything.

But at least these guys did actually ask me some serious questions regarding the NFL game I was at, which was the massive game between the Denver Broncos and the New England Patriots.

I thought this particular interview went very well, and I even cheekily managed to squeeze in the name and my website's address out onto the airwaves at the very end of the interview, which proved to be a big success. I got the most amount of hits on my website in one day that I ever received, which was over 250 views, which for me was massive.

Brilliant! what I now wanted was this virus to spread all over social media and project me into a new NFL stratosphere, but sadly this momentum quickly hit a brick wall and the dripping tap did not turn into the waterfall I so desperated craved, and within a few days I was yet again back in the bargain bucket bracket and like yesterday's newspaper at the local chip shop.

Before I did these live interviews I always tried to inform my friends on social media I was going to be on the radio and to tune in if you can, and listen to me speaking live, miles away from home in America. The feedback I would normally get back from my friends was that I sounded great, spoke well and I was very good and well received. This positive feedback always gave me a huge boost.

I absolutely loved doing these interviews, I just wished I could have done more, and boy did I make the effort and put the time in on social media contacting soooo many people in the worlds of music and the NFL, to very very little response indeed, which was so damn frustrating.

I arrived into Flagstaff to a bit of a shock, as Flagstaff was under snow. I was warned by some of the local people Flagstaff would not be anywhere near the same temperature as the beautiful sunshine of Phoenix, as it would be colder, but I never expected snow. I thought I left that back in Cincinnati!

I had booked into a nice hostel in Flagstaff aptly named the "Grand Canyon Hostel", and I walked the twenty minutes or so journey with my very heavy backpack and on very slippery pavements/sidewalks from the Greyhound bus station to my hostel, in the snow. I must have looked like Bambi on ice!!!

As soon as I walked into the hostel, I knew it was going to be a nice place to stay as the staff and the guests were great from the first minute I arrived. I watched a movie with a guy named Colt, whom I would spend quite a bit of time with, as he was a really friendly and nice guy. But everytime I was with Colt, he informed me he was just about to leave the hostel, as it was time for him to move on. So it was very strange and funny when I said goodbye to him, then I said hello to him again the next day, as by now Colt had made more comebacks than Fleetwood Mac!!!

I got talking to a really nice Irish guy named Brendan, we clicked immediately and soon the conversation evolved onto the subject of the Grand Canyon, which was the main reason most people, including us, were in hostels in Flagstaff, as the GC was a couple of hours drive away and Flagstaff is the obvious place to crash when visiting the canyon. Brendan mentioned to me he was driving there tomorrow and would I like to join him. RESULT! Of course I did.

We arranged to meet at stupid o'clock the next morning, my least favourite time of the day, and we left our hostel around 5am for the 2/3 hours ride to get to the Grand Canyon for sunrise. As it was winter, the sun was coming up around 8am, so we had enough time to make it to the canyon to see the sunrise. We left the hostel in complete darkness and freezing cold, then we headed north for the Grand Canyon.

We made it into the Grand Canyon National Park, had a Macdonalds breakfast just before we entered, as you do, and it was bloody freezing cold with snow everywhere as we got out of the car, which did make it feel a little more special, as the snow made everything look very pretty to me.

We stood in an area with around a dozen or so other people, then we waited for the sun to come up. As the sun broke through, the views were truly breathtaking right across the amazing Grand Canyon. You will never realize how big this place is until you witness this with your very own mince pies/eyes, as it's absolutely huge.

Our timing was perfect and I got some brilliant pictures of the beautiful sunrise. I was so happy to be here in a place I have always wanted to see, and what is commonly known as one of the eight wonders of the world.

The sun eventually came up, which was extremely well received and totally needed, which warmed us up a little, as it really was cold as we went for a walk for a few hours along a trail around the top of one side of the canyon.

We plotted up to defrost for around thirty minutes in the Grand Canyon museum, or lookout point, where the views were simply amazing, more than I could have ever imagined.

We wandered a bit further to a little tourist souvenir shop on the edge of the canyon which sold coffee and momentoes of the canyon, and we bumped into some people who were actually staying at our hostel. We sat there for a while chatting, got some great pictures, and relaxed watching the condors flying around on the termals inside the canyon in the beautiful sunshine.

It really was spectacular, and it was at this point I realised I was in a very special place on planet earth, and I was enjoying every single minute, other than the fact it was absolutely freezing when the sun went behind the clouds, as the temperature gauge would drop like a stone.

Brendan and I got some brilliant pictures of each other standing on the edge of the canyon, some a bit riskier than we should have taken as we were standing on snow and ice, and if we slipped, well it could have been goodnight Vienna. But we survived and the pics were fab.

Brendan and I had been talking about going to another beautiful place just outside of Flagstaff called "Sedona". Sedona was once voted the most beautiful small town in the whole of America. I had seen the pictures, and this was definitely a place I wanted to visit. Brendan wanted to go too, so off we went to Sedona. Three hours later we arrived, and straight away we knew we had made a great decision.

As you drive into Sedona, straight away you are mesmerized by the beautiful views and coloured rock formations of mountains, hanging high above this tiny and simply stunning little town. Brendan and I had a coffee, then we proceeded to go for what was supposed to be a short hike into the rocks, hills, mountains or whatever you want to call them.

It's amazing how you meet people and become friends completely at random. This was something that happened to Brendan and I as we started to hike into the hills of Sedona. A guy on his own walked past us and I asked him if he knew where he was going, as there were two trails and we did not know which one to take, as we obviously did not want to get lost or be too far away from the car.

"Nevada Backwards" was the man in questions name, well that's his Facebook name, but he also had a native American Indian name, "Lonewolf", as that was his background or ancestory.

Lonewolf was a musician, so we had a lot in common, and all three of us clicked immediately. But three quickly became four, as Lonewolf was with his friend and fellow bandmate, who had been taking pictures of the amazing rock formations during the time Brendan and I had met Lonewolf.

All four of us headed off into the rocks for a short hike, which eventually turned into a massive climb, which was absolutely awesome, but also very dangerous, especially as I was climbing in the trainers I had been wearing for every one of my 120 or so days I had been on the road up to now, and these trainers had about as much grip as a bald tyre to an ice skating rink!

Also the three months insurance policy I had taken out before I left home, had run out, so if I hit the deck and got hurt, I could be paying off the air ambulance bill for the rest of my life!!

These guys were great company, as we hiked high up onto the rocks to get some incredible views of the soon to go down sunset, which would be around another hour away. So we climbed very high indeed, probably a lot higher than we, (especially me) should have, and along some scary sections of rocks, which was bloody dangerous, but so exciting, as I was having a such a great time with these lovely guys.

We eventually made it to the spot we wanted, then the sun started to go down behind the beautiful surroundings of Sedona. I knew I was in a very special place with a really lovely bunch of new friends, I felt as free as a bird and so very content and lucky to be here and experience this wonderful place.

It was times like these I soooo missed not having a loved one in my arms, someone special to share this incredible moment in my lifetime, including these breathtaking views. I wanted this more than anything in the world, but my three new friends were a very good substitute for these sad feelings indeed.

We got some great group pictures together and I felt so happy to be with these nice guys. Brendan started to sing out loud an old Irish folk song, then Lonewolf from nowhere pulled out a harmonica which he played very well. It was a special moment and so amazing to hear the boys perform beautiful spontanous music together, I just wished I had my guitar. It was the perfect place to hear this unique sound and it fitted the surroundings like a hand in glove, in a place of such incredible beauty.

Brendans voice was great, very Irish in sound, and Lonewolfs harmonica complemented the vocals nicely, it really was a special moment between new friends, a kinship, a kind of mystical, spiritual, organic and very very natural connection on the same wavelength.

I remember looking across the vast plains and mountains thinking I was in the perfect place to see a UFO land, that's the best analogy or the picture I can paint, as I was looking at what was probably the best view I had ever seen, with nothing at all moving, in complete tranquility and peace. It was just perfect.

It was now getting dark and cold as the sun disappeared behind the rocks, and as we were so high up, I knew it would be a challenge to get down before we were in complete darkness. It eventually took us around a hour to get down, and it was great fun to slide down rocks, zig zag massive boulders, through bushes, across a river and around the winding road, back to the carpark, and most of this was done in the dark. It was a fantastic hike and I loved every minute of it. Cheers boys.

When we got back to Brendan's car, we said goodbye to Lonewolf and his friend, who I think was called Tony, (sorry my friend, I can't remember) and I arranged to meet them in San Francisco in a few weeks time, as we would both be there at the same time, for Superbowl 50.

We arrived back at the hostel around 10pm and we were both pretty tired as we had been up since 4.30am, so it was not long before we both went to bed.

Brendan informed me he would be leaving Flagstaff for another national park in the north, very early the next morning, as he was heading towards New York in persuit of a new career and driving the whole way. Wow, that was a long ride I thought, all the way from here in Arizona?

I only knew Brendan for 24 hours, I really liked him and I would have loved to have spent more time with him if possible, but he had his own agenda, so I thanked him for a brilliant day, and I wished him all the very best for his future and a safe journey to New York. Thanks a million Brendan, you're a top man.

The next few days I spent in Flagstaff were very relaxing, I spent a lot of time in various coffee shops doing research, booking flights and tickets, as well as the usual mountains of social media I was used to doing, and of course, my website.

While in Flagstaff I went to see the latest Star Wars film at this time. I don't profess to be the biggest Star Wars fan, not like my nutty friend Lee Matthews, the Raiders fanatic whom I met in San Francisco. Lee went on Christmas day in San Francisco to see the film I would watch here in Flagstaff. I've only seen the first and second films from way back in the day, and now this one, which I thought was alright, nothing special in my eyes, but overall I quite enjoyed it.

I had a funny night out the following evening when I went for a few beers and to play table tennis with a few of the hostel's staff members and my new friend and "comeback kid" Colt, the guest who kept leaving and resurrected more times than Jesus Christ himself!

We got to the bar which had the table tennis table and we played a game of doubles. Colt was totally hilarious, I honestly don't think he had ever played table tennis before in his life, as he was absolutely terrible and he would have probably got beaten by a five year old, as he could hardly hold the bat properly. It was soooo funny, we were all laughing hysterically. Poor guy, he was such great fun to be around, he made that night, especially with his amazing technique!

I don't mean to poke fun or take the piss out of Colt, as I really liked him, I'm just stating the facts, but it really was a great night out in his company, a laugh a minute.

I only found out the day I left Flagstaff that Colt was in fact homeless. I had no idea and I was a bit shocked, as he was not too shabbily dressed, and he just looked like a normal guest. But I heard he was down on his luck, out of work and sleeping in the TV room at the hostel, which was where I saw him most of the time. Apparently he was not paying to stay, and the staff were onto him about him staying overnight in the TV room, and he was on the verge of being kicked out. It was so freezing cold at night here in Northern Arizona, he would have died of hypothermia if he had to sleep rough on the streets, and it would not have surprised me if he actually did this and survived.

I liked Colt and I was pretty sad I never did get the chance to say a final goodbye to him, which made no real difference really, as I had already said goodbye to him three times before. Actually, I would have liked the chance to have said a final goodbye to him, especially after I heard about his bad luck stories. I hope he is OK and things picked up for him, as he was a very nice and funny guy.

I had plans for my final day in Flagstaff, as I wanted to get out of town to go for a hike in the snow and hills of "Buffalo Park", a short bus ride outside of Flagstaff. The sun was shining in a beautiful blue sky as the bus driver dropped me off, AT THE WRONG STOP! after I specifically asked him to tell me when to get off the bus for the stop for Buffalo Park. Doh! He did apologise and was a little embarrassed, but I said no worries as he was a friendly guy, so I walked back the few stops, about a fifteen minutes walk to the entrance to Buffalo Park.

There was snow everywhere and very few people around as I walked into the park. I decided I was going to climb up the hills for a few hours and be in complete solitude and isolation for a few hours at least.

I walked into the unknown for a hour or so and it was great being on my own, seeing the odd person every half an hour or so. It was so quiet, I could have heard a pin drop, and it was lovely, peaceful, and relaxing.

I got to a point where I had the chance to climb up a rock formation and look out over the entire park, something which was in my plans as I entered the front gates. I thought I would go up, but not too high, take a few pictures and not be as greedy as I had done in Sedona, because I was very concerned about the state of my trainers/sneakers as they were looking pretty knackered by now, plus there was snow all over the big rocks and boulders I was attempting to climb.

The voice of reason in my head won the day and told me I was punching far above my weight, as If I did slip, and I got hurt, I was in the middle of nowhere, with nobody else around to help me. Another reason was because I had no signal on my phone, so not exactly a good mix of ingredients to make a decent cake I thought, and for the first time in ages, I took the logical way out and I decided to abort that particular mission impossible.

I slowly wandered back the hour or so to the entrance of Buffalo Park in the snow and sunshine, talking to myself, singing stupidly out load, and thinking about what I would be doing on my next adventure, which I now knew would be back in Denver Colorado, as their Broncos had just beaten the Pittsburgh Steelers in the play offs, the night I arrived into Flagstaff.

I was quite pleased that I was going back to Denver, as it was much closer to my only other option of Charlotte Carolina, where the NFC Championship game was taking place between the Carolina Panthers and the Arizona Cardinals, (incidently a game I would have loved to have seen, as these were two excellent teams, as well as revisiting my old mucker "Charlton" Dave Kitchener). But Denver was a lot easier to get to from Flagstaff as well as being on the way to the west coast where Superbowl 50 would take place, in San Francisco.

Another reason Denver was on my radar, was that I wanted to try to resurrect my fling with the lovely but very unreliable Ashley, the bird with the great set of Bristols/tits!!

On my final night in the lovely Flagstaff, I went to see a film/documentary made by the BBC, as I had noticed on the many occasions I passed the local cinema/theatre, they were showing a documentary this evening about an expedition by a group of people who had retraced the route along the Colorado river, made by an explorer named "John Wesley Powell" way back in 1869, who travelled through the Grand

Canyon for the very first time.

A guy named Dan Snow, who makes great historical documentaries on UK TV, was a part of this team, so I wanted to go and check this out. The film started around 7.30 and I got to the cinema about 6.45 as I expected to walk straight on in. WRONG!

Christ! It looked like the whole of Flagstaff were there queuing up to see this, and there were only a few hundred tickets, but I was now here, so I was gonna give it a try. I went to the back of the queue, but it was a very long one and I thought my chances of making it in to see this expedition were very slim indeed.

I got talking to some nice people in the queue and we waited for about thirty minutes as the queue moved at a snails pace. I asked one of the workers who was organising the queue if we were wasting our time stuck here near the back, or would we get in? "It will be close" she informed me. Well she was right, it was close, the person right in front of me got the very last ticket. FCUK!

The guy who I was talking to in the queue seemed pretty gutted for me, and he said loudly to the lady at the window "Hey, this guy is all the way from London England, please let him in". The guy pleaded for me, what a nice gesture. "Sorry sir" she replied, " we are completely sold out". She explained.

Then lady luck cuddled me yet again, as there was a man who had just collected a ticket right in front of us, and he must have heard my new friend mention me, so he came over and asked me if I wanted to buy his ticket from him. He said "I've been given this ticket by a friend and I'm not really bothered if I go in or not, do you want it?". "Yes please", I said.

This is where the fun started, as the ticket price was fifteen bucks and the guy had just arrogantly told me he got the ticket for free, and he wasn't particularly bothered about going in at all. "You can have it for twenty five bucks" he said. "What" I laughed, "You just told me you got the ticket for free and you don't really want to go in, and you wanna make a profit on it" I stated. "What the fcuk?" I sternly told him in my harshest cockney accent in from of loads of people.

"I'm not paying over the fifteen bucks the ticket costs mate, so you better go and enjoy the film" I insisted. Well this worked a treat as I got the ticket for fifteen dollars and I thanked my friend from the queue, as I got lucky purely because of him. But what a greedy bastard!

I entered the cinema and the place was packed solid, as you would have thought the Rolling Stones were in town as there was a real buzz about the place. Again I got lucky as most people were standing and I got a single seat next to a really nice guy in the front row of the area we were at.

The guy in question I sat next to, informed me he had done the very same expedition in which we were about to watch, a few years earlier, so he knew all about the river and what surprises it held.

The documentary was about an explorer back in the day,

who navigated his way through the Grand Canyon in a very basic boat, very little supplies, not enough food and no idea what was around every corner of the winding river. It was a very enjoyable documentary and one of the guys who was in it, was actually in the cinema and he was from Flagstaff. This was probably why the cinema was so packed, as a local celebrity was in town.

The group of people on the expedition had to go through so many incredibly dangerous rapids, it was an absolute miracle how they ever got to the end, but they did, but not all of them. A couple jumped ship (or boat) just a few days before the captain got through to the very end of the Grand Canyon, this was because they were on death's door with malnutrition.

Even with all the equipment of today, Dan Snow and his colleagues (incidently all so called experts in all different kinds of fields) re-enacting the early travellers footsteps or route, and struggled bigtime, making the initial trip of 1869 even more remarkable.

I loved this documentary and I had a great time with the guy next to me, as he explained a lot of the things I did not understand in the film. I felt like I had my very own personal tour guide.

So another good night was experienced and my Flagstaff chill out session was almost at an end, as tomorrow I was returning to Phoenix for the third and final time, this time just a short stop to catch a flight to my next stop, back to Denver.

I had another lucky break as an Aussie girl in my hostel named "Adele" (not the singer fortunately, as I would have not fitted into her small hire car!), was driving down to Phoenix the following day. We talked about a departure time in the morning, and we arranged to meet at breakfast and she would give me a lift back down to Phoenix. RESULT!

We arranged to go through the beautiful "Sedona", which I had already been to, but I wanted Adele to see it, as it was so beautiful, and a place not to be missed. There was also another quirky little town called "Jerome", we planned to drive through which I wanted to see, as I was told it was quite spooky, and I'm always up for spooky.

In the 1920's Jerome had over 10,000 inhabitants, in 2010, it had 444. It's been described as a ghost town now taken over by hippies, a very artistic place and a place I wanted to see.

So the plans were set. BUT! when I got up for breakfast, there was no sign of Adele. (absolute typical bird behaviour again) I had my breakfast, and then I heard from a few other guests that Adele had been out the previous night and had far too much to drink. When she finally did surface, Adele looked like shit warmed up, and she said I had to wait a few hours for her to sober up, as she was probably still over the limit. FCUKING GREAT!

So the beautiful Sedona and Jerome, which we had planned the night before, simply disappeared up Adele's ass. This really pissed me off as it was just another example of how some people's words mean absolutely nothing. I understand Adele has every right to go out and party, but we had plans,

and now we don't and yet again I'm the bloody loser.
BOLLOX!

I could have got the Greyhound bus, but her lift was
convenient for me, so I waited for her to sober up, and
eventually off we went back down the freeway to Phoenix.

Adele dropped me off, back at the HI Hostel where I
managed to get a room for the night before I flew to Denver
the next day. I thanked her for the lift, gave a her a few
dollars for petrol and off she went. NOOOOOOO!

As soon as she drove off, I remembered I had left my jacket
on the back seat of her hire car. What a fcuking wanker! It
was a jacket I loved which I bought in Whistler Canada,
when I was skiing with Bruce. SHIT!! I never had Adele's
number, but I guess I could track her down on Facebook,
but I could not remember her surname. FCCUUKKKK!

I knew Adele had stayed at the HI Hostel recently, but she
told me she had made a booking and never turned up, so she
did not want to be seen by the owner Keith as he may want
to charge her for the room she booked and swerved a few
days ago.

I signed into the hostel and I could see Adele's name on the
guest list of bookings, but I could not ask, as I would give
her game away and drop her in the brown stuff. I tried to
look for her surname and phone number, but the
handwriting was messy and I could not read it properly.
Then came a massive stoke of luck. I mentioned Adele to an
Italian guy who worked at the hostel, and the smile on my
face was as big as the Golden Gate Bridge, when he said

Adele was his facebook friend and he can give me her details. Oh boy, what a touch, I could have kissed him. I may as well, as I wasn't exactly kissing much during this barren period!!

I sent Adele a Facebook message, she returned, and I was reunited with my lovely jacket a few hours later, (a jacket I still have and more or less wear every day). She said as soon as she saw my jacket, she was always going to come back to the hostel and return it to me. What an angel, and a lovely girl. Thanks Adele.

The next morning I said goodbye to Keith for the third and final time, as well as my friend Josh who worked at the hostel, and I walked to the train station to catch a train to the airport, destination Denver.

I had a great four days relaxing in Flagstaff, I loved these small towns in America, as you can see and do almost everything in just a few days, something which is right up my boulevard.

I had seen the famous route 66, the incredible Grand Canyon and the beautiful Sedona. I had also met some very nice people and stayed at a lovely hostel, so I had a great time in the cold north of Arizona state. Thanks Flagstaff, you rock!

Play Off Game 3
AFC Championship
Mile High Stadium
New England Patriots @ Denver Broncos

I landed back into Denver and I did consider going back to
the "Funkhaus Hostel" that I had stayed at on my previous
visit, the place I called the "drugs den"!!, but I thought I
may bump into the elusive chick with the great rack, Ashley,
and this made me feel a little uncomfortable, especially
regarding the strange union between Ashley and Mark, the
owner of the Funkhaus, so I decided the swerve that place.

I had sent Ashley a few text messages saying I was
returning to Denver for a few days for the big championship
game, and as usual, the silence was deafening......until of
course.........after I left Denver. FFS, stupid cow!!!

I checked online for another hostel to stay at and I knew
about a place called "Hostel Fish", which was in the centre
of town, but at fifty dollars a night, this was very expensive
indeed for a dorm bed, (actually the most expensive of all
the hostels I stayed at across the country) as I had been
paying around half of that practically all over America.

I found the "Denver International Youth Hostel" online, and
it seemed perfect, the pictures looked OK, and the price was
right. I read the reviews, and to be honest I should have
taken a lot more notice as they were all terrible, but hey, he
who dares wins I thought, so I booked in for one night, with

the option of two more, as I was only staying in Denver for a few days.

I landed in Denver around 4pm, caught the bus from the airport to downtown, and I walked the rest of the way to my hostel, in an area called North Capital Hill. I called this place "Colfax" for some reason, probably because there was a busy road nearby I walked down a lot called Colfax, as I was so used to looking at this road on my map.

Anyway, this area was full of homeless people, a cardboard city of vagrants, drinkers and layabouts in every nook and cranny of all the buildings along the long street I walked down to get to my hostel. Again I never felt threatened by these people, as most of them were usually as pissed as farts/drunk, spaced out on planet cuckoo (remember Colorado is a legal state to smoke the funny fags) but it was never nice to see homeless people on such a huge scale.

God knows why there are so many homeless people in Denver, as it was absolutely freezing here, and it was now January, the middle of winter, at nightime especially, it really was bitterly cold.

I understood why, or how the streets of San Francisco had their homeless problems, as it was by far a much warmer temperature to beg, steal, borrow, drink and take drugs, but not here in the arctic conditions of Denver Colorado.

I found my hostel after a long walk, too long for my liking with my back breaking backpack, and I arrived at my new fixed abode a little early for the 6pm checking in time, as the hostel was closed for the afternoon, so I sat outside and waited for a while, and I got talking to a guy from California, and he let me inside as he was staying at the hostel and he had a key.

I knew as soon as I walked through the door, I had made a huge mistake booking into this shithole, as the acrid smell instantly hit me like a punch in the face, and I could feel my stomach muscles tighten immediately.

I thought the name "The Denver International Youth Hostel" sounded like a nice place to stay, and I perceived it to be like some kind of a university, with lots of younger people, pretty girls, handsome boys, kids on their gap years and all the usual things I had been used to over the past 3-4 months when staying in these hostels. HOW WRONG WAS I! It looked and smelt like a homeless shelter, and I was certainly in the right part of town for that.

I followed my new friend into the hostel and he took me down to the basement area for about ten minutes, where I chatted to a few of the other guests, before I went up to the reception area to check in.

These guys or guests (who looked to me more like "inmates" or even patients) I spoke to, were very surprised indeed that this very normal looking dude had chosen this particular venue to stay at. I explained to them I had booked it purely because it was cheap, as "Hostel Fish", the hostel up the road was over twice the price.

I talked with three random guys, and I sensed immediately they were all from the wrong side of the tracks, had all kinds of issues, as well as the blatantly obvious problems with drink and drugs. If this was a grocery store, then this was the section where all the "bad apples" were stored!

By this time it was starting to get dark, and very cold outside, I had had a long day of travelling and I was tired, so against my better judgement I checked into this dump for just one night. I met with the guy on reception, and my first impression of him was that he looked like a hippie who had not washed in months, a man who desperately needed a decent amount of quality time in the bathtub for a good old scrub up. What an introduction hey?

After all the niceties, I got my key and I went off to my room, which was on the third floor. I climbed the staircase up to my room and the smell was simply too much, it fcuking stank and was totally filthy. What on earth have I done?, I thought.

See when you book a room in a hostel online, you really are pissing in the wind, relying on honesty, decent photo's, real descriptions and basic truths, and my luck up until then had been perfect, without any major issues or dramas and nothing I could not put up with for a few nights. Until now.

I put my key in the door to my room, and what I saw next shocked me to my foundations. The room looked like it had been burgled/robbed, and trashed, there was clothing and personal items strewn all over ALL of the beds in the entire room, making it look like something from a disaster movie. But there was nobody home, in the eight bed dorm room, everybody was out.

I must have said out loud "WHAT THE FCUK?", and I

heard a voice shout "hey", coming from a small room off the main room I was standing in. I walked over to the small room, went in, and this was my introduction to a guy named "George".

George was a war photographer, an American and he lived in Ethiopia. Honest, how could I make this up?

George turned out to be my latest guardian angel, and if it was not for him, I would have walked out of this dump immediately and gone up the road to Hostel Fish, whatever the cost.

George encouraged me straight away that it would be better and safer for me to stay in the small room with him, as there was a spare bed, and the two other guys staying in this particular room, according to George were OK.

I dropped my stuff into this small dirty room that was no bigger or better than a tiny one man prison cell, and I hardly had room to put my backpack down on the ground, it really was that small and four of us would be sleeping in here. How? Fcuk knows.

George told me a story of a fight that happened just a few days ago in the bigger room next door, the room which I had just vacated and should have been staying in, where two of the guests were slogging it out over something pathetic or pointless. One of the guys in question had just been released from prison and he had one of those tags, thingamejig things around his leg. The other guy, or punchbag had just come out of drug rehab. GREAT! Nice roommates hey?

I learned immediately this was a million miles from the

tourist hostels I had been staying in all over America, in fact, this was nothing but a glorified homeless or rehab shelter, full of people with every social problem, disorder or disease the universe could throw at them.

These people were totally on the bottom link of the social food chain, as there were homeless, alcoholics, drug addicts, criminals and all kinds of people who had no money, jobs, and especially futures. George was the complete exception, except for me of course!! and I was completely staggered as to why on earth this nice and well groomed guy was staying here in this piss hole?

Like me, it was all down to the greenbacks/money and he had been here for two weeks. TWO WEEKS! I screamed, "how on earth can you do this"?

"Come on", I said, "Let's get out of this dump and go for a drink", and that's what we did, we found a nice pub called the "Cheeky Monkey", just around the corner from our homeless shelter........ I mean hostel!!

What a great guy George was, and is, he had some very interesting stories of times when he was working and taking pictures in the many war zones around the world he had covered. I kept saying to George, after he told me he was earning good money, I simply could not understand why he was staying in our terrible hostel, as it really was hell on earth, and a truly horrific place to stay. His answer was because it was cheap, and he wanted to save money. Fair play to him, but I will never understand how he managed to stay in this place for eventually over a month, maybe longer? as he stood out like dogs balls in comparison to practically all of the other guests.

After a few hours, a few beers and a bite to eat, we begrudgingly returned to our small and very smelly tiny box room. (well I did anyway, I don't know about George!) I needed a good few beers to help me sleep, as this was going to be one hell of an experience, as well as a complete test of my resolve and patience, and maybe one of my biggest challenges to date when it came to sleeping arrangements, as over the years I've stayed in some pretty shady places, but nothing quite like this place.

The bed I had, I never chose, it was the only one available and the mattress was very soft and it sank in the middle, fcuking brilliant I thought, as I got on it for the first time. "This is gonna kill my back", I thought, and yep.....it did. Then I went to the toilet, OMG!, you don't even wanna know how bad that was.

I remember thinking "how many scumbags over the years had used these facilities?", especially the toilet, (where I simply could not comprehend what activities had been performed in this filthy place) and more so in MY BED!!! These rediculous thoughts kept me awake as I struggled to switch off the lightbulb inside my spinning head.

I eventually met one of the other guys in my little room and he seemed quite normal compared to a lot of the characters I had bumped into next door and on the staircases, and this guy was going to be out all night, so that was good. Only one left!!! two including George, but he was cool.

George informed me that the guy sleeping below me was a

nice chap, he had been living here for months, (how? I will never know) and he was a chef, and he would not be home until the early hours, so I was praying I would be fast asleep by the time he came in, and I tried my best to, but I struggled to completely nod off under this kind of emotional pressure.

I did somehow temporarily dose off/fall asleep, god knows how as the bed was terrible, the bedsheets were full of stains, (god knows what kinds!) and it was just a complete nightmare situation to be in.

The bloke underneath me did eventually come in, in the very early hours of the night, waking me up of course, as when he laid down on his bed, he nearly catapulted me up onto the ceiling. He was a big boy, to put it politely, and he must have had a few beers as he fell onto his bed, almost sending me into orbit.

It wasn't long before my new friend below me was snoring like a bastard fcuking pig, and as you can tell, I was far from being a happy bunny. Looking back now as I write this section in my lovely clean surroundings, I can see the funny side, but at the time, I certainly was not laughing at all, it was pure torture on a major scale.

George mentioned to me he gets up very early every morning and he goes off to the local Starbucks and sits on his computer, where he talks to his wife who lives in Ethiopia. So when I awoke around 7am, after a terrible and very up and down night, George was gone, but I had his phone number so I could contact him if I wanted to.

I needed to use the toilet, so I got up, sat on the throne, and from this amazing vantage point, to my horror, I witnessed the incredible state of the bathroom for the first and only time from my front row seat. Oh boy, what a sight, the place was so disgusting, the floor totally filthy, the sink plug in the shower was full of matted hair, (and god knows what else?) as was the sink. That was the last straw for me, I could not stay here any longer and there was no way at all I was gonna take a shower or even brush my teeth in that place, it was hard enough just having a number two!

It took me all of ten minutes flat to be dressed, packed, (not washed) and out of that homeless shelter/rehabilitation centre like a bullet out of a gun. I walked through the bigger room next to my little prison cell of a room, and again it looked like the joint had just been trashed by a bunch of drug addicts looking for their next fix. What a hole that place was and a truly nightmare experience.

Please check out the feedback to this wonderful five star resort on Trip Advisor or Hostelworld, it's absolutely priceless!

I had made a lightening quick and spontaneous booking online at "Hostel Fish", (the fifty bucks a night hostel) about a thirty minutes walk away towards downtown Denver. I would have caught a bus, but I just wanted to get away from my scummy area as soon as possible, so I never even looked at a bus map.

It felt sooooo amazing to be out in the clean fresh air after twelve or so hours of breathing in that putrid stale and skanky smell, which was probably doing my lungs no favours at all, and severely irritating my gag reflex.

It was now Sunday morning, the day of the big AFC Championship game and it was bitterly cold at 7am as I walked past so many homeless people in doorways, as I made my way to my new fixed abode. Seeing these poor people made me realise my world was not so bad after all, as I had a choice to move on to pastures new, these unfortunate people never did. This was a real leveller to me and something which always highlighed to me how very lucky I really was.

I arrived into "Hostel Fish", and straight away I knew I had made the right decision. OK it cost fifty bucks a night, but after what I had to endure for twenty five bucks a night, it was a total no brainer.

"Hostel Fish" was a palace of a hostel, no wonder it was a little bit more expensive than the norm. The young girl working on the reception desk was gorgeous, a great start, no comparison at all to the unwashed hippy tramp who worked on the reception at the homeless shelter!

There was a great lounge area inside the hostel with a full bar in the middle, a big TV screen, good internet connection, and basically everything the homeless shelter never had. I honestly think this hostel was up there with one of the nicest, cleanest, trendiest hostels I have ever stayed in. Yep, probably even the best, and a universe apart from what I had just left. It was like getting out of a battered old van and into a Ferrari.

I checked into my dorm room and I had the choice of around

a dozen beds. I had the entire room to myself on my first night and the bed was as truly amazing, probably as comfortable as my lovely bed at home. Yes, I had to bite the bullet of fifty big ones/dollars, but trust me, from what I had experienced the night before, it was worth every cent.

Today was the big day, with both the AFC and NFC Championship games taking place, and I was attending the AFC game between the Denver Broncos and the New England Patriots. But before this massive game, I was going to another massive game, between Arsenal and Chelsea at the Denver branch of Arsenal America, in a bar with a fantastic name, "The Three Lions", the emblem to my lovely country's football team.

My day would not get off to the best of starts. See I hate Chelsea, with a passion, this team to me are the biggest cheats in the Premier League/EPL, they do everything that's bad in this game to win football matches. Some say it's a winning mentality, but I don't subscribe to this bullshit, to me is nothing more than downright cheating.

Diving, shirt pulling, feigning injury, screaming like babies when hardly touched, grappling at corners and basically trying to fool the ref at every opportunity are things that make my blood boil. I know it's a sign of the times, but please don't say to me these things are "all part of the game", because they are bloody well not. NO, these are the things which have ruined our game and I simply cannot state enough how much I hate this vile behaviour.

I used to be an Arsenal season ticket holder man and boy, for around 25-30 of my 49 years, I absolutely loved it with a passion. But now, I have another emotion towards the game, I hate it, all because of this terrible cheating, and Chelsea are the biggest culprits for this disgusting behaviour.

This was around my 10-15th different Arsenal America bar, and I still had not seen Arsenal lose a game. (Well kind of, except I did see Bayern Munich wallop us 5-1 in an AA bar in Cincinnati with my mate Billy, but there was only one other Arsenal fan in that bar, so I waived that one because it was not the Arsenal America experience that I'm used to) Sorry, my terms and conditions I'm afraid!

I arrived about fifthteen mins into the game as it started early, 4pm London time was about 9am Denver time, and I had been busy checking into "Hostel Fish", and checking out of hostel filth!

I found a seat at the bar of "The Three Lions", ordered breakfast, and before my food even arrived, the dreaded Chelsea fcukers scored, and what made it a whole lot worse for me, was that the goal was scored by the biggest scumbag in the team, the vile Diego Costa. This guy dives more often than Tom Daley (British Olympic diver), and to make things worse, our centre half Per Mertesacker gets himself sent off. BLOODY GREAT!

Half time comes and it's 1-0 to Chelsea. Bloody typical I thought, as Chelsea had been having a terrible season, something which made me very happy, but this bloody team always do well against my Arsenal.

As always, I met some great people in this Arsenal America bar, a few ex pat Brits now living and working in Denver, as well as a top bloke who told me he has been following me on Facebook as I zig zagged all across America. BRILLIANT! I was well pleased, I've actually got another fan!!!! That's two now, after my friend from the train in Jacksonville.

I took some pictures with these guys at half time outside the pub, met a few more fans, and then the second half started. Arsenal were now down to ten men and struggling bigtime, so we tried to get behind our boys by singing songs and chanting Come on Arsenal, come on Arsenal.

There was always lots of singing in these AA bars, I absolutely loved watching Arsenal games in these places as it was like a trip down memory lane, reminding me of the happy days from my youth of the many years I spent on the "North Bank" terraces at Highbury where I used to stand with my brother Paul and our many mates, singing, screaming and sometimes running from the fighting fans. Great times they were.

I was on the clock to get to the big AFC Championship game at the Mile High Stadium, as the game started at 1pm (I think it was) and I knew if I waited too long and watched the whole of this EPL game, I would probably get stuck in a lot of traffic, as I was catching the bus to the stadium and I certainly did not want to be late.

Arsenal were still losing 1-0 after sixty minutes when I finally left the pub to make my way to the Mile High and I was still constantly checking my phone for the hope of an equaliser while I was on the bus, but sadly for me Arsenal got beat by the scumbags 1-0, and my unbeaten run of around fifthteen games watched in Arsenal America bars around the country came to a very abrupt end. GUTTED! I suppose all good things must come to an end, but to lose this record to Chelsea, that bloody hurt.

The weather was much better in Denver than the last time I was here, especially when I was leaving, in a blizzard of snow. The sun was out, but it was still very cold, and I like these kind of days.

I was heading for the tailgate of Broncos SuperFan Robert "Woody" Woodworth, who amazingly offered me a ticket for this game for face value, which was his dad's, but for some reason he could not make it to the game. Good old Woody's dad!

I had been looking online all week and I could not find a ticket for anywhere near less than under 400 bucks. My face value ticket from Woody was 170 dollars and worth every single cent. Thanks a million Woody and please thank your old man for me.

I arrived at Woody's tailgate and as usual it took him all of ten seconds for a beer to hit my hand, followed closely by a plate full of his lovely BBQ. What a man Woody is, and it was great to see him again.

We spent a few hours chatting away, drinking beer and dreaming of Superbowl 50 for Woody's beloved Broncos. I had watched the Broncos beat the Pittsburgh Steelers the week before and I thought the Broncos looked very shaky in that game, and I expected a very easy win for Tom Brady and his Patriots, because they are a very good team. After watching all these games, by now you would actually think I knew just a fraction of what I was talking about, as yet again, this boy got it WRONG!

At the start of the season, I had a ten quid bet on the Patriots to win the Superbowl at 9-1, so I was hoping they would do the business for me. This was something I obviously kept to myself as I was surrounded by Broncos fans at the tailgate and inside the stadium, especially to Woody and his lovely wife who I sat next to watching the game. Sorry Woody, but sometimes I'm only loyal to my pocket I'm afraid, not just any old NFL team!!!!

It was a terrific atmosphere as Woody, his wife Lora and my good self entered the "Sports Authority Field" at the "Mile High Stadium". I now knew this was not the original "Mile High Stadium" I used to watch back in the 80's when Broncos legend John Elway was king, but a new one built practically next door from the old one. I was now over this small piece of minor detail, but not entirely to tell the truth!

I did love this stadium, it was probably in my top ten, maybe even five, and as we walked into a sea of orange, (the Broncos colours) I knew yet again I was a very very lucky boy to be here inside this stadium to witness such an important NFL game.

I have already mentioned I did a live radio interview while I was at this game, and I remember crouching down in a corner, screwing up my face, trying to hear what the people from Radio Five Live were asking me as I could hardly hear them because of the intense noise coming from the obvious excited fans.

It was a pleasure for me to talk to UK NFL journalist Nat Coombes and the legend that is Mike Carlson, but Mike doesn't let you get a word in edgeways, and before I knew it, the interview was over.

I returned to my seat and after all the usual pre game madness, the game started and I wished my friends Woody and Lora all the luck in the world (I never did tell them I was chearing for the Patriots!), as they were going to need it, or so I thought.

This game was billed as Peyton Manning verses Tom Brady, two of the finest quarterbacks ever to grace the NFL. My money was on Brady, but the Broncos started stronger and Manning threw a touchdown pass to take his team into the lead.

Tom Brady was looking a shadow of his normal awesome self, as he just could not get going, which is extremely unlike him. The Patriots did manage to get a running play touchdown to tie the game, or so I thought, but the Patriots normally super Mr Reliable kicker Steve Gostkowski missed the extra point, so after the first quarter the game was 7-6 to the Broncos.

The second quarter got even worse for Brady as he threw an early interception, which led to a second Broncos touchdown. Incredibly even more so when he threw a second interception, but the Patriots kicked a couple of field goals, meaning this game was still well and truly in the balance.

The third quarter was a lot closer and tougher with the only score in this period being a Broncos field goal, so going into the final quarter the Broncos were leading 17-12, and a one possession game was still on.

This game was not exactly one of the better games I had seen throughout the tour, but for drama, it was up there with the best I had seen, as it was very tense, dramatic, and full or errors from both sides. The crowd (90% Broncos fans) were still going absolutely wild, as their Broncos were definitely looking the stronger of the two teams and most likely to win the game and go onto Superbowl 50.

In the final quarter, at long last Tom Brady came to life and started to show some of his true amazing self. He threw a few nice passes to gain good field position for the first time in the entire game, but then with six minutes on the clock and a 4th and 1 play, the Patriots attempted to try to gain the first down, rather than kick an easy field goal from the Broncos 17 yard line. It was a risk that had to be taken........................ and it failed.

Sadly for the Patriots, they never made it, but after the next Broncos drive ended in a punt, the Patriots regained possession and made good field position, and with just over two minutes left on the clock, the Patriots yet again failed with a 4th down play. The Broncos team and their fan went ballistic as they thought the game was over, and so did I.

The same Broncos defense I thought were so poor against the Steelers last week were now playing like a strong and very tight unit, against the normally extremely impressive Patriots offensive line.

The Patriots somehow managed to get the ball back yet again, for the third time, and surely this was their final chance. This must have been utter torture to the 75 thousand Broncos fans inside the Mile High Stadium, as this game really should have been well and truly over, just like my first play off game in Cincinnati. How many lifelines did the Patriots need?

With 1.30 left on the clock and the Patriots on a 4th and 10, Brady finally came up trumps with a great throw down the middle to his main man and wide receiver Rob "Gronk" Gronkowski.

With 17 seconds left, the Patriots had their final chance. They needed a touchdown, followed by a two point conversion to take this fantastic AFC Championship game into overtime.

Brady took the snap, stepped back, and he finally got his rewards with a touchdown pass to his ever reliable best mate Gronk. The silence in the stadium was deafening!! What incredible drama, it was so tense, even for me! (remember I was thinking about my 100 quid winning bet!) I can't imagine how my friend Woody and Lora must have been feeling, but they looked completely sick and totally drained with all the ups and downs this game had to offer, and I can only guess what this did to their emotions and their nervous systems.

So now we have it, the conclusion and the very last play of the game, a two point conversion attempt, and if the Patriots score, we go into overtime. COME ON TOM!!

Even I was a nervous wreck by this time, as Brady took the final snap of regular time, he backed off, danced around inside the pocket, cocked his arm, and BAM! Brady's pass rocketed towards the brilliant "Julian Edelman" like a guided missile. Edelman is usually as reliable as anybody as to make this catch, and usually most peoples first choice, but the ball incredibly went right through his hands, gets tipped up into the air and caught by a Broncos defender. GAME OVER, what a finish!!

The stadium totally erupted as the Broncos had somehow held on. I turned to Woody and Lora and they were both going absolutely crazy, their beloved Broncos had done it against all odds and beaten the firm favourites the New England Patriots to make it to Superbowl 50.

Not for the first time, or last, I was wrong and my bloody bet had gone with it. FCUK! But what an ending, such incredible drama and yet again another brilliant occasion for me to experience.

Again I felt so lucky I had been at yet another fantastic football game. It was not the best of games, but because of what was at stake, the atmosphere, a championship game, with both teams at one point winning, then losing, near misses, great plays, just so much drama, it was totally compelling viewing. I felt drained. I had been so incredibly lucky to have been at the best three play off games of the season, not one, but three.

Later that evening the Carolina Panthers easily beat the Arizona Cardinals in the NFC Championship game to make Superbowl 50 the Carolina Panthers Vs The Denver

Broncos. That game was practically over by half time, at least my game went down to the very last play. The tension in the stadium was unbelievable and I felt so very blessed to have been there.

I have to say a huge thank you to Woody and his wife Lora, I was genuinely pleased for them their team had won and it really was a wonderful experience for me to spend the game with them, as I witnessed them both screaming, laughing, crying, cursing, praying and many more other emotions, all the way through this amazing game of football.

After eventually leaving the stadium, I said my goodbyes to Woody and Lora and I headed back to my luxury hostel in the downtown area of Denver. I had arranged to meet up with George at the same pub we had a drink at the previous evening, we had dinner, a few beers, and we watched the second half of the NFC Championship game together between the Panthers and the Cardinals.

One of the guys from the dump hostel I had stayed in turned up in the pub when I was with George, he was covered in tattoo's, including his face, had no money, dressed like a tramp, he seemed nervous and on edge, maybe he needed his fix?

He sat with us as he spotted and probably knew George, and he was actually not such a bad bloke, but I could see this guy had massive issues, and once he left, George informed me that he was the guy who had the fight a few nights ago in the next room to where we were staying.

After the game I said my final goodbye to George, he went

back to his homeless shelter, and I went back to my palace. I was completely exhausted as I had not slept much the previous night in the prison cell, and I was sooooo looking forward to my lovely soft bed in my very own twelve bed dorm, or private suite..........OH YES!

I really liked George, I'm hoping to see him again one day, as he completely saved my sanity in that horrible place, and I am so glad I met this very nice man. Cheers George. BUT?

A year later, and long after I had returned home to London, I got a very strange Facebook message from George, informing me of massive changes taking place in his life. I was completely gobsmacked when George informed me he was having surgery and changing his persona from "George" into "Georgina", and now he was calling himself the very strange and unusual name of "Miao Miao".

I know this must sound totally ridiculous and more than a little humourous, and obviously I laughed out loud when I was first told, as I thought it maybe an April fools joke!, but this is in fact true, and since my last correspondence with "Miao Miao", he/she continues to become more feminine.

George was so masculine and totally normal (whatever normal is) when we had met and I had absolutely no reason whatsoever to consider seeing a woman trying to break out of this tall handsome man's body. Just as I had no reason to see my Oakland Raiders friend at the time, Lee Matthews as a potential paedophile.

I did ask George/Miao Miao a few difficult questions over Facebook after he told me of his plans, and he did answer me truthfully, and I totally respect his new chosen lifestyle, whatever he does as I really enjoyed the company of this lovely person in the very short period of time we spent together in Denver. I wish him/her all the very best for the rest of his/her life, and I sincerly hope he finds his/her inner peace.

My final day in Denver after a great night sleep was to spend all morning in Starbucks on 16th street, which is the main drag of downtown Denver and where all the action is, as I was doing all my usual social media shit.

I had made arrangements to meet up with a lovely girl I had met in Tampa named "Bethany Walters", and she picked me up in the afternoon and we spent the evening together.

My inital plans for my last day were to go out to a place outside of Denver called "Boulder", where I was going to go for a hike in the mountains and hang out in this pretty little town. I had been told it was well worth the thirty minutes bus ride, and I was well up for that, but as I had woken up late, it was a bit chilly, and I was feeling a little lazy, I decided to settle for a day downtown instead in the nice warm environment of a coffee shop, for my signature dish of a coffee and a cake.

Beth was good company, we had a few drinks, reminisced about Tampa and we chatted away for a few hours before she dropped me back at my lovely hostel, my last night in Denver, as the next day I was flying off yet again, this time to see my good buddy and brother Jorge Gonzalez at his home, in the crazy place and beautiful sunshine that is Los Angeles California.

By the way, I never did manage to touch base, or especially touch the lovely rockets of my major ball breaker, timewaster and prick teaser Ashley, and boy did I try. This is something which will always be in my thoughts and my biggest regret whenever I think about the two visits I made to the beautiful city of Denver.

Oh what might have been??? I could honestly cry, as boy did I have some plans in store for that girl!

Los Angeles

I landed into LAX airport in Los Angeles and my good friend Jorge Gonzalez was waiting to pick me up, and take me back to his family home, where I would stay with him for the next few days.

I had visited Jorge two years earlier on a previous tour, but until then, I had not seen him for 23 years, after we met in Berlin Germany in 1992, which was my very first solo adventure, when we were both in our early 20's and backpacking around Europe.

Jorge is simply the greatest guy and my very good friend for life. He is so funny, always smiling and happy, he has a lovely wife, two beautiful little girls, a lovely house, and a nice car, basically eveything I would love to have......bastardo!!!!

Jorge is a big fan of the Pittsburgh Steelers, so he cannot have everything! So when he asked me what I wanted to do the following day, my immediate reply was "Please can you take me to the LA Colisseum?".

The LA Colisseum has a great history for sport, especially the Olympic games in 1984, where gold medals were won by the likes of Carl Lewis, Daley Thompson, Sebastian Coe, Steve Ovett and Tessa Sanderson, amongst many other brilliant sportsmen and women.

At the time, I knew this stadium would be the new home of the LA Rams for next season, but as I write this section of my book for the second time, another team will be in LA for

next season, the Los Angeles Chargers. Will these two
teams share this stadium?

It's funny how my NFL "circle of life" has indeed turned full
circle, as when I first started following the NFL way back in
the mid 80's, there were two LA teams, then for over twenty
years there were none. Now there are two again.

I wanted to go inside and see how it this stadium looked in
comparison to all the other stadiums I had been to. Jorge and
I wandered around the Colisseum for around thirty minutes
on a self guided tour. It was yet another great experience for
me to be in such an iconic stadium, but not in the history of
the NFL, this time the Olympic games, something I used to
also love watching as a youngster.

There was a great plaque on one of the walls with the lists of
names of all the competiters who won medals at these
Olympics, so many brilliant athletes, at a golden age in
Olympic history. (Before, in my opinion, like most thing in
these modern times, it became far too professional).

Next door to the LA Colisseum was the Space Museum,
which was obviously full of space related machinery,
equipment and crafts. There were so many amazing planes,
rockets, shuttles, lunar modules, capsules and other space
related things. I loved it, as I have always had a fascination
of all things connected to the subject of space.

Jorge drove me around downtown LA, where we saw a few
landmarks including the Staples Centre, where I saw the LA
Lakers play a few years earlier.

The following day, I went with Jorge and his wife Marlene

to watch their daughter (whose name is also Marlene) take part in a kids singing and dancing show at her school, to highlight the culture and foods of many countries from around the world. Marlene was in the group for Germany, she was in German national dress, and her little group of kids sang a song about Germany.

It was very entertaining and funny to see these very young kids in costumes from all over the globe, singing, dancing and having a great time with their teachers. Little Marlene and her sister Natalia are great kids, and very pretty little princesses, they must get it from their mum!!! Sorry Jorge.

This would have been something I would have been so very proud to have watched if I was a parent, so witnessing this made me feel a little sad as I know this is a day I will probably never get the chance to experience myself, as I now approach my 50th year.

There was also food from all over the world, including pizza from Italy, sausages from Germany, fish from Sweden, and the funniest thing I saw was on the Australian table was Australian English cake. I was wondering if the ingredients inside it were fish and chips!!!

I had a couple of days to chillout and relax at Jorge's place, and as I had been to LA two years earlier, I had done most of the things then I had wanted to do. But I did go back to Hollywood Boulevard to see the walk of fame, and the Chinese theatre, where all the hand and foot prints of the many famous actors and actresses of years gone by are all over the floor.

I had previously travelled on the LA subway quite a few times, and it was a long way from downtown LA to where Jorge lived in Orange County, which was in the south of LA. I had to pass through the notorious "Compton" on a few occasions, but I never had any problems, even though there were quite a few lets say, unusual looking dudes lurking about!

I really wanted to get out of the subway station and take a look around the very infamous and notorious Compton, but I knew this was not a good idea, as I didn't know the area at all and I could easily be in the wrong place at the wrong time. I could also be mistaken for a plain closed cop, something which could have caused big trouble for me, as this area has a big African America community, where guns were as easy to obtain as toothpaste.

Up until then I had been very lucky as not to get into any dodgy or dangerous situations over my entire tour, something which I could easily have done, as I was out late on my own many times, sometimes pissed up/drunk, in cities and areas where I knew I could be easy prey to many of the muggers, crazies, lowlifes and street people, but I was always streetwise and fully switched on, as I knew I was in a country were guns were everywhere.

I still had things to organise with regards to Superbowl 50, which was taking place in San Francisco in around ten days time and I did not want to be a burden to Jorge and Marlene and overstay my welcome. I also knew I would get bored in LA if I stayed for too long, as Jorge had to work and LA is not the easiest of places to get around without a car.

One option I considered, was to go and visit a good friend of both Jorge and mine, Daniel Nieto, who lived in Mexico City. Jorge is Mexican and originally from Mexico City, he knows Daniel after they met many years ago backpacking in Egypt, on the very same trip I met Jorge on way back in 1992.

So all three of us have the common ground as lovers of travel, and I was introduced to Daniel by Jorge and I stayed with him for a week or so two years ago in Mexico City.

Daniel is a fantastic guy, a university professor, very intelligent, loves a beer, loves a bird, and more importantly, he loves me!. And to be honest I love him too, as he treated me like a god when I stayed with him at his beautiful house in Texcoco, Mexico City.

I've met some wonderful Mexican people on my travels over the years, they are so friendly, generous and good people, so Daniel was an obvious choice for me to spend a few days relaxing in Mexico City.

A few weeks before I arrived into LA, completely out of the blue I got a text message from Daniel, saying "I love you". OK, I thought, that's nice, because we have told each other this on many occasions, as I do to my other boyfriend and one of my best friends from Italy Fabrizio Lombardo. Maybe this is a foreign/latin thing as I never say this to my English buddies. Fcuk that!

I'm cool with this, as I have no problem telling my friends I love them, but this was slightly different, as I got a long message from Daniel which was a shock, and it went something along the lines as this.

"Dennis my brother, I love you, last night I had a dream about you and your penis was in my mouth. Please don't tell anybody, but I really do admire you and love you very much". OMG!!!!!

I was in shock, I never saw this coming as Daniel has four kids with four different woman, and I know he loves chicks. I never considered that he may like dicks!

I sent him back a text saying "Wow, bro, I'm in shock, are you gay"? His reply was "Yes". To say I was surprised is the understatement of the century, as I never saw that one coming AT ALL!

After this conversation, how on earth could I go to Mexico City? The thought made me feel very uncomfortable indeed, so Mexico City was no longer an option or on the menu.

Then I thought, "Hang on a minute, how about I go to the Pro Bowl in Hawaii"?. I looked into the price of the flights, and they were almost on a par with Mexico City. Now I was super excited, Hawaii it is. I booked the flight, and I was set to leave LA in three days time, it really was as quick as that.

The very next day, I got another text message from my new lover in Mexico City, Daniel. This time, the message went along the lines of this.

"To my English brother, I am so sorry if I upset you with my last text message, a group of friends and I were playing a drinking game last night, and one of the forfeits to a challenge was I had to send a "gay message" to a close friend, and I'm sorry to say, it was you". PHEW!

My first emotion was total relief, but then I felt huge disappointment because I really wanted to go and see Daniel and my other friends Pavel and Eddie in Mexico City.

In the end the joke backfired on Daniel, as I know he would have loved me to have come back to visit him, but now I was off to Hawaii instead.

They say everything happens for a reason and I should really thank Daniel for his "gay message" as this pushed me into going to Hawaii, which to be honest, was never on my radar or in my thoughts.

Of course I forgave my good friend Daniel, as I do love him to pieces, and I would love to return to see him again in Mekiko City! but sometimes games and jokes can go wrong, as this one did for him, as I really was horrified when I received that message. But I'm so very happy indeed it was just a drunken prank by a bunch of crazy Mexican maricons!!!!

See I could never be gay, because getting rejected by guys as well as girls would be far too much for this boys ego to take!!!

The next few days were lazy, hanging around with Jorge and his lovely family. We had a few nights out in the bars, watching live music and hanging out at the house of Jorge's best friend, another top Mexican and another Jorge. How many Mexicans in LA are called Jorge!!

Jorge and Marlene really looked after me at their lovely

home, I had a nice big bed in my own room, the garden was nice to be lazy in, as well as playing with their little princesses Marlene and Natalia, who are two adorable kids.

My backpack was now as heavy as ever, so I asked Jorge if I could leave half of my stuff at his house and I would pick it up when I had finally finished my tour, which would probably be up the road in Las Vegas in about three weeks time.

Of course that was fine by Jorge and when I did leave for the airport to fly to Honolulu, it was a huge relief to me as my backpack was so much lighter to carry, and not putting the usual pressure onto my head from the muscles on my neck and shoulders that was taking the full force of the weight. Thank god for that!

I said a massive thanks to my bro Jorge, his lovely wife Marlene, and the girls, I took the subway to LAX airport, and I was ready for my next adventure injection, this time on the very beautiful island of Hawaii. Pro Bowl 50 here I come.

Hawaii-Pro Bowl Aloha Stadium

I said goodbye to my good friend Jorge Gonzalez as he dropped me off at Norwalk subway station in Orange County where he lives, south of Los Angeles.

I arrived at the international airport, known as LAX, in just a tee shirt and shorts, as it was around 90 degrees and higher outside. But inside the airport, it was like a fridge with the intense air conditioning and I was absolutely freezing.

After the usual check in that I had now become very accustomed to, I found myself looking for a place where the sun was shining through the windows and I ended up in a tiny pocket of a sunny area, far away in the corner of my departure gate and I stood on the window sill to try to catch some rays as I really was freezing my bollox off!!

After moving up and down the windows trying to keep warm in the sun, I eventually boarded my masssive 380 airbus plane, with beautifully painted flowers over it, which was the logo of Hawaiian Airways.

After a peaceful and stressfree six hours flight, I landed in Honolulu around 8pm.I was so happy to be here in Hawaii, because in my original plans for my tour, I never gave a thought to attending any play off games, let alone the Pro Bowl or the Superbowl. Actually by this stage, my tour should have been well and truly over, and maybe I would have now even been back home, perish the thought! but now it felt like I was on a proper holiday, a whole week in Hawaii, and you know what? I bloody deserved it after all I had been through.

I left the airport and caught a bus to the famous tourist area of "Waikiki", obviously known mainly for the beach. Just over a hour later, I arrived at my latest fixed abode, yet another cheap hostel, and as soon as I walked into my room, I knew this place was going to be a nightmare, as I was welcomed by the beautiful sound of two old fellas snoring in harmony. OH NO, NOT AGAIN!

The two guys in question were already in bed and it was only 10pm, so I dropped my very much lighter bag in my new dorm room and I headed straight out to see what the loose women of Waikiki were up to on this Friday night.

The only women I got close to were some old Doris/woman and her mate, at one of the beach bars called "Dukes". She was so pissed/drunk, she was probably looking at three of me! I had a few beers and a laugh with the ugly sisters, before I headed back to my new dump, at around 2am.

I did have a brief encounter or liaison with another woman on the way back to my hostel, sadly she was one of the local "women of the night", and she offered me her services of a massage with a "happy ending", which at the time I must admit was very tempting. After thinking about this for 30 minutes...only joking!), I decided to decline what was probably the best offer I had had in ages and I returned to my dorm, to hear my two new friends having a snoring competition.

The snoring never bothered me too much, and as I had had a long day, about five pints, and my ear plugs pushed as far down my lugholes/ears, as they could go, I slept like a baby. I probably snored louder than my two new room mates!!! I hope so anyway!

My first full day in Hawaii, I was determined to have a lazy day on Waikiki Beach, watching all the beautiful people parading themselves up and down this amazing place. I did not swim in the sea too much as the water was very rough, so I retreated into the pool area of a five star resort right on the beach, as you do!

I walked past the security guards like I owned the place, with my sunglasses and suntan, I grabbed a towel and I spent the next three hours on a nice and comfortable sun lounger, occasionally dipping myself in and out of a lovely swimming pool, surrounded by couples from all over the world. RESULT!

I pushed the boat out even further when I walked inside the hotel, and I followed signs to "The Spa". Again, as bold as brass, I go walking straight past pretty young girls on the reception desk, gave them a little wave of confidence and a big smile and off I went into a lovely jacuzzi, before disappearing into a steamroom.

Its amazing how much you can get away with if you just have the balls/confidence, or in my case, downright audacity! I tried lots of cheeky things on my tour, and most times I got what I wanted, but not always, as the following day I tried to get back into the same pool, but a member of staff saw me and I got kicked out. Ha! See, you can't win em all, but it never stopped me trying again. He who dares wins.... sometimes!!

The same day I wandered right into the bar area of another luxury five star hotel, and as I walked in, I found myself in the middle of a huge restaurant where the feast in front of me looked incredible. There were so many people getting stuck into the self service food, and the grub was absolutely everywhere, and I mean a proper feast of every meat, fish, deserts, and everything else in between, so it would have been very rude of me not to get stuck in. So I did.

I had sushi, steak, pork, loads of king prawns, and lots of other stuff that caught my eye, I even went back for a desert! What a cheek? I had what I call "a proper load up"!

This hotel was very plush indeed and the food was so yummy, I think if I would have had to pay what I ate, honestly, I would not have got much or any change from fifty bucks. NAUGHTY BOY!

I got sunburnt on my first day on Waikiki Beach, as before I made it to the flashy hotel, I had a lay down on the sand, and as the weather was quite overcast for a while, I never put any suntan lotion on. MISTAKE! I fell asleep on the beach, but only a catnap, then I wandered up and down the beach area, just so I knew what was there, as I would be here for almost a week and I wanted to familiarise myself with the area.

That night I tried a few new bars along Waikiki Beach, but I always found myself going back to the same one, "Dukes", mainly because that was where most of the action was, as well and some cracking looking women.

Dukes backed right onto the beach and there was an outdoor

area where people sat right next to the sea. It really was an amazing location to relax, have a few drinks and a bite to eat. But I was on my own, and most people in the bar were couples, and yet again, this was a time which made me feel very lonely, especially as on the previous time I was in Hawaii I had a beauitful young Australian chick hanging off my arm.

Sunday was the day of the "Pro Bowl", my very own personal "D-Mo Superbowl", as I had now labelled it, as I had to be honest with myself and admit defeat in the hope I would somehow manage to get myself a ticket to Superbowl 50.

For people who don't know, the "Pro Bowl" is an end of season game where the best performing players in that season from each NFL conference, play against each other. The game is between the AFC and the NFC divisions and is usually not played with the same passion as a regular season game, more like a friendly international soccer game.

I had never seen a Pro Bowl game on TV before, as it's not a game that ever really interested me, as it was usually played after the Superbowl each year, not a week before like this one.

I personally think this is a stupid time for the Pro Bowl to be played, simply because players from the two teams who made this year's Superbowl, The Carolina Panthers and The Denver Broncos, had no representation in this year's Pro Bowl.

The Pro Bowl is a very prestigious honour for a NFL player

to have on his CV, and I'm certain there would have been many players selected from both teams who made it to Superbowl 50, who would miss this game, understandably stopped by their prospective clubs, as they may get injured and miss the biggest game of their lives the following week. These players would have loved to have been selected to represent their conferences, its an honour, so why has the Pro Bowl been brought forward and played before the Superbowl?, only the NFL powers that be know and this is something which baffles me.

It was a very warm and humid morning as I headed to the "Aloha Stadium", the venue for the Pro Bowl, a 90 minutes bus ride from Waikiki. The bus was packed as we got half way to the stadium and I was so happy to be getting off when we did as I was cooking and sticky, as the bus was like an oven.

From the outside of the Aloha Stadium, my first impression was that it looked very old and run down, not like most of the flashy modern stadiums that I had been attending, all across America.

On this day, I arrived at the stadium without a ticket, I had been looking online and I was horrified to see that ticket prices were so much more than I expected, up to 400 dollars a pop. FCUK THAT! So I had yet another challenge on my hands, to try to get myself a ticket at the price I wanted to pay......which was as little as possible, but well achievable, as by now I was getting pretty good at this kind of thing, most of the time.

I tested the water with the usual sharks, the touts/scalpers, and I had some fun with them. I always tried to broker a deal with a smile on my face. They wanted 300 bucks for a ticket, far more than I ever wanted to pay. "How much"? I would say, "I can get three prostitutes for that!", I would joke. "How much"? I can buy your team a new quarterback for that"! After all the usual bartering, laughter and bullshit, the prices would start to drop.

See you have to be confident around these individuals, as they will rip off their own grandmothers to get as much money as they can for their tickets, but you have to bang heads with them, because the closer to game time you get, the cheaper the tickets get, and these charlatans start to panic and think they may get stuck with the tickets and end up with nothing. It's a game of patience, or sometimes like a Mexican stand off!

When trying to somehow get tickets at these games, you simply cannot be too shy, and you have to be prepared to just walk around and shout out "Has anybody got a spare ticket they want to sell"? I did this a lot over the course of my tour, and it never failed, just as on this occasion. BINGO!

I stood in an area where a lot of the people heading for the stadium had to cross a small bridge. I shouted out the usual message, in my strongest cockney accent, and it must have taken less than five minutes for a guy to come up to me and say "Hey buddy, I have a spare ticket for sale, would you like to sit with me and my friends"? "Sure, how much?" I replied. "thirty bucks" he said. "Deal" I said with a big smile on my face. It really was that easy. RESULT AGAIN!

Before I eventually attempted to go inside to watch the game, I had done the usual lap around the stadium, just to see what was going on and if I could blag my way onto a tailgate. I saw a guy in a Dallas Cowboys shirt, so I made a beeline for him, and I used my usual line of "Hey, I'm from England, and I'm a big Cowboys fan". Of course it worked, and I was drinking a cool beer and stuffing my face with some lovely grub in no time at all. Cowboys fans never let me down. Good old Cowboys!!

The queue outside the Aloha Stadium before the game started was probably the longest queue I had seen or been in all season. There was practically no security people monitoring the crowds, meaning most people were pushing in the queue, and where we were standing, we were going nowhere fast, and it was baking hot and very humid.

I must have queued for almost a hour with my new friends, and when we eventually got to the turnstiles, there were only just a few of them, with thousands of people trying to get in. I thought the organisation was terrible and very unneccessary, as the staff seemed to be so laid back and in no hurry at all as to get us in before the game started. In fact that's exactly what happened.

This would be my 35th and last game, and I got into the stadium after the game had started for the very first time on my tour.

But once we finally got into the Aloha Stadium, I was pleasantly surprised, as the stadium looked a damn sight better from the inside, than it did from the outside. The seats were painted in all different colours, and I noticed that one section was quite empty, probably because the baking hot sun was cooking the people in that section of the stadium, so they must have moved, as it was a very hot day.

I plotted up in a row of single seats that looked like they would be reserved for VIP's, disabled fans, or maybe even just very expensive seats, right on the 50 yard line. They were empty, so I sat down, nobody said a word or asked me to move, so I didn't.

I did this a lot over the tour, and it's amazing what you can get away with if you just have the balls to just go for it with a swagger of confidence. If you do get caught, and I did at times, I just pleaded ignorance and moved on. I'm very good at that too!!!

Pro Bowl 50 was between "Team Irvine" (Ex Cowboy Michael) and "Team Rice", (Ex San Francisco 49er Jerry) two old legends or dinosaurs from NFL past, and to be honest, I wasn't particularly bothered who won this game as you could see from how the players performed there was no real passion involved, and basically this was an exhibition game between a bunch of mates. It was still enjoyable, but not anywhere near the same excitement as all of the other games I attended were.

I watched a different quarter in a different part of the stadium, and as the fourth quarter approached, I found myself high up in the nose bleeds, my favourite part of the stadiums, and I now realised this would be for the very last time on my tour. I had finally come to the end of the road.

I watched the final quarter with very mixed emotions, as I

knew my NFL adventure was now coming to it's conclusion. Yes I would be going to "Santa Clara", just outside San Francisco for Superbowl 50, but I had to honest with myself, as I knew my chances of getting a ticket for the big game were slim to none, especially as I never have the funds to pay anywhere near big bucks, even if by the million to one chance I got the offer to buy a ticket, which I never did.

So I sat and reflected on what a sensational journey and experience I have had. I looked out across the horizon at the beautiful sunset going down, the red sky against the blue sea was an incredible background and the perfect setting to finish my tour, and I felt happy and extremely proud of myself as I had achieved what I had set out to do regarding the NFL, but sadly and as hard as I had tried, I never did get the lucky break I so deperately wanted, as to get my face splashed across everybody's TV screens. I got very little media coverage, and no interest in my music whatsoever. I felt terribly sad I had not made any progress at all in this area, I really was gutted and I felt like a complete failure after all the effort I had put in.

I had made an enormous gamble, to spend everything I had on this tour, all my eggs were in one basket, because I was that confident I would make some money on this journey as to keep me on the road, or at least make some excellent contacts, giving me the chance of a bright future. But by the time I eventually got to my final destination of Seoul in South Korea, after I left America, and also after three weeks of travelling around Japan, I had spent the lot. In fact I only returned home because the cupboards were empty, no petrol was left in the tank, or basically I was skint/broke.

My plans by this stage were to cross over to China, and take the "Trans Siberian Express" train through Russia to Moscow, or even the "Trans Mongolian Express" through Mongolia. I sooooooo regret this now, as you all must know by now how much I love trains, and adventure, and this was well and truly on my radar, but I simply ran out of dollars, and by now the train I was now on was only heading for one destination..... home.

Oh boy, I was distraught when I had to come home, I really was not ready, there were many more adventures this boy wanted to discover.

I will never never regret doing this tour... EVER. I had dreams of mass media coverage, "Wow, this crazy Englishman is going to all 31 NFL stadiums, let's have him on our show", is something I honestly expected to hear on a regular basis, and I'm still baffled as to why I never got this chance. I mean, this is not something people do all the time, right?

There was so much to organise and arrange on a massive tour like this, and most people cannot do without their home comforts, loved ones, jobs, friends, own bed, etc, but I gave all this up for my trip of a lifetime, and trust me, it wasn't easy at all.

Maybe I'm stupid, or just a dreamer, but I expected my song "Like a Touchdown" to get me some attention as I think it's a very good song which I thought would resonate with the NFL fans completely. I never got one single piece of interest in my song at all, and as a songwriter and musician this hurts, as nobody gave my song the time of day.

"Like a Touchdown" is about how you can compare the feeling you have when you are with your loved one, as to how you feel on that split second when your team scores a goal, home run, try, winning basket or a touchdown. It's in the first line of the song, "Like a Touchdown, your love is making me high". Have a listen on www.soundcloud.com/azboden it's a great track and potential future NFL anthem.

The final whistle came to end the 2016 Pro Bowl, and I sat looking out across Hawaii feeling numb and emotional that my tour was almost at an end. A big part of me was happy, but another part of me did not want this amazing journey to end.

The good thing for me now was that I could relax a lot more, as I never had to book anymore tickets, hostels, flights, trains, buses and so on. The down side was, where do I go next? I had about two grand left in the bank, and I was not going back to freezing cold England yet as I had no golf caddie work as it was out of season, so I looked at the world map in my minds eye, and I was already dreaming of a new adventure.

I eventually left the Aloha Stadium and I headed to the bus stop to catch the 90 minutes bus ride back to Waikiki, and my shitty hostel. The journey eventually took around two hours with the traffic being so bad, and as soon as I arrived back at the hostel, I decided I wanted to move out of this dump and into another hostel just up the road.

I had visited and checked out three different potential new hostels, and I chose the final one of the three, simply because it had a roof terrace, which is a great place to hang out and meet people. As soon as I saw there was a big TV screen to watch movies or sport on, that was the one for me.

As I checked into my new home, I met a nice German guy named "Matthaus" at the reception desk. He told me he had hired a car, and would I like to join him on a tour around the island? It took me all of one second to say yes, so off we went.

Our first stop was "Pearl Harbor", the infamous naval port bombed by the Japanese during the second world war. We had a wander around, went and had a look at "SS Arizona", one of the ships that was sunk and which is now a memorial and a permanent graveyard to many American sailors who sadly perished on that fateful day in history.

We watched a few short films about the events on that day, and it was very interesting viewing. I find it hard to believe that the nation who bombed Pearl Harbor, the Japanese, now practically own Hawaii. Sadly ironic hey?

We headed to the north to check out a beach and an area called "The Banzai Pipeline", where all the crazy surfers go to ride the massive waves. Sadly it was the wrong time of the day, or year to see the huge waves I had expected, and we only saw baby waves, but they still looked quite big to me, and I would definately not have gone swimming in them! We then stopped off at a pineapple farm, a bit of a tourist trap, YAWN, but at least we had a nice ice cream, pineapple flavour of course!

I asked Matthaus if he would mind driving me to the hotel

where all the NFL players who played in the Pro Bowl the previous day were staying. The hotel or resort is called "Turtle Bay", and it looked like an amazing place to stay, especially the beautiful looking golf course.

I got out of the car, took a few snaps of the golf course and the entrance to the hotel, which had a big NFL sign. Bloody tourists!!!

Next stop was lunch, and we had a nice local fish dish from "Romy's Prawns and Shrimp", before heading to see a small island off the coast called "Mokoi'i", but nicknamed "The Chinaman's Hat" by the locals.

The Chinaman's Hat was in a beautiful area surrounded by a huge cliff, extremely picturesque, and yet another very romantic place I was at, where a chick on my arm would have been the icing on the cake, certainly not a young German guy half my age!!!

We finished our circle around the island of "Oahu" by attempting to watch the sun go down from the top of "Diamond Head", a lookout point at the top of a tall hill looking down on Waikik Beach and all across Honolulu.

Matthaus took the wrong turning at a junction, and we found ourselves on the main motorway/freeway of Oahu, as we were trying to take the coastal road to the east side of the island. We probably wasted around a hour in heavy traffic by the time we eventually got to Diamond Head, which was a huge kick in the nuts because just as we arrived, Diamond Head was closing. TYPICAL!

I soooo wanted to see the sun go down from this amazing

view across Honolulu and Waikiki Beach, and we had missed it. But did we? The security guy informed us that Diamond Head closed at the same time every day, and the sun had not quite gone down yet. So how can people see the sun go down on Diamond Head? The answer is, they can't. This made me feel a whole lot better and that I had not missed out on anything spectacular.

We headed east on our way to a place called "Hanauma Bay", as there was a nature reserve there, but it was now getting dark, so we stopped off at a lovely beach called "Aina Haina", where we watched a very beautiful sunset go down behind Diamond Head.

What an amazing sunset and incredible views at a perfect peaceful and tranquil place, again a lovers paradise and yet again no lover around for this boy, so sadness fills my heart for the 500th time on the tour!

After around thirty minutes of pondering over life at this lovely setting, Matthaus and I returned to our hostel, before deciding to go to a local bar for a well earned couple of tropical beers!

We walked into a bar close to our hostel with a terrace overlooking the road, which was a place I had chosen, as it looked like a nice place to chill and people watch. I did smell a rat as soon as we walked in, due to the noticable absence of the female species and the abundance of men, mostly in pairs. Combine this with the whole bar looking at these two fine young, (well one not so young), looking specimens, cruising across the room like a couple of new pieces of fresh or tender meat! It soon became quite obvious we were in a "Blue Oyster Bar", so we did a rapid 360 and we were out of that place like a couple of ferets down a rabbit hole.

On the way out I said to the chubby guy on the reception desk, "Excuse me, but is this a gay bar"? "Sure is" he replied with the biggest smile in Hawaii and looking at me like I was the sweetest cream bun in the bakery! I said bun!

I had a really nice day with Matthaus, he was great company and a very nice guy, sadly I was only with him for about eight hours in total, and it was hard to say goodbye to him, as he was leaving early the next morning and it would have been nice to have spent a few more days with him.

I met so many lovely people for the odd day or two on my trip, and I hate saying goodbye to people I don't want to go, as I had so many of these sad moments. Maybe I just get too attached to nice people? Maybe I'm even nice myself, who knows?

I had a couple more days left in Hawaii before I headed back to San Francisco for Superbowl 50, and on my radar was a very dangerous but exciting hike called "The Haiku Stairs" or "The Stairway to Heaven".

I had watched a video on YouTube of a guy climbing this incredible looking staircase up to the top of a hill, mountain, volcano, whatever you wanna call it.

I spoke with a few people about it and I was advised not to do it, for a number of reasons. The first reason was that many people have died trying to climb this staircase, mainly from trying to take stupid selfies (now would I do that?) and falling like a stone, but my reason for eventually not doing this "death climb" was because it is officially illegal, but there is a guard at the entrance who does let tourists go up, if you cross his palm with silver, if you know what I mean?

Apparently if you do get caught by the fuzz/police, there is a chance they will cart you off to the local nick/prison. I know it sounds silly that death does not scare me but prison does, well I usually take risks, and if I think its not worth the risk, I will simply abort the mission. Prison?, well that's a whole new ball game, as I love the current shape of my bum hole thank you very much!!

Check out the "Stairway to Heaven Hawaii" on Youtube, it's very impressive, and bloody scary. But I wish I did it!!!!!!

The following day, my last in Hawaii, I returned to climb up "Diamond Head" to see the amazing views across Waikik Beach. There were four chicks in my hostel who were going up to see the sunrise and as much as I wanted to go with them, they were going at stupid o'clock, far too early for this old boy, and they had bonded pretty well and they didn't need this old cradle snatcher cramping their style and perving all over them!

I had a lay in, had breakfast and I headed up to Diamond Head, which took around two hours to get from my hostel to the very top. It was a hot day, but very clear, so I took my time to get to the summit, which was well worth the effort as the views were breathtaking. I got some greats pictures, some taken by another English guy I met at the top, who was working in Hawaii.

Waikiki Beach looked fantastic from the top of Diamond Head and I must have spent a hour just gazing into space, mesmorized at the beautiful surroundings. I sat and daydreamed what might have happened had my song been played on the radio and America became my oyster, rather than being more like my ostrich, with its head firmly planted up its own ass! I dreamed that I could have bought a house here in Hawaii, I could have had the fame, the fortune, and all the groupies I would have been fighting off with the proverbial stick, but letting a few dozen or so through my incredibly badly sewn safety net!

To say I was, and still am gutted is the understatement of the century. So what am I now going to do with myself after America?

I had a seed planted in my mind that Japan was definately on the menu, but not Tokyo, as it's far too busy, commercial, western, crazy, touristy and expensive for my liking, everything I wanted to get away from. Plus I had already been there for the soccer world cup in 2002, and I wanted to explore what I perceive as the real Japan, far away from most of the obvious places or tourist traps.

By this time, I had now decided my new adventure would start in the south of Japan, a place called "Beppu", mainly because it was an area full of natural springs, spas, or onsens (Japanese bath's) as they are known as in Japan, and I wanted to relax and be lazy for a few weeks as by this time I was kind of running on empty and I needed to recharge my batteries.

I would then head north and go no further than Kyoto, check

out all the beautiful temples and gardens, go and watch some "Sumo" wrestling in Osaka, then return to the south on the Shinkensen/bullet train via Hiroshima, and visit a few other places I have never been to.

I would then finish in Fukuoka, returning full circle on my Japanese adventure, as this was where I would fly into from LA, before catching the ferry across to Busan in South Korea, onto Seoul, head to Vladivostok in China to catch the Trans Siberian Express back through Russia, with a brief stop off to have a little look around Mongolia. Sounds like a plan, and a plan in which I never quite made to the very end, but almost.

After my daydreaming, I eventually left Diamond head, and I returned to my hostel for my final night in the beautiful Honolulu, before I returned to mainland America the next afternoon.

There was another guy at my hostel, I wish I could remember his name, but all I can say is that he was Russian and he worked there. This guy was one of the funniest guys I have ever met, as no matter what he said, I laughed. He could have been telling me the time, or reading me a chinese takeaway menu, I would still laugh. It was mainly HIS laugh, and he constantly laughed all the time he talked to me, whatever he was saying. This crazy fruitcake was such a hilarious human being, I loved this guy.

I spent a few days around this top man, and when I finally said goodbye to him as I left the hostel, he said two things to me which made me laugh to the point of crying, and smile to the point of crying, in a very touching way.

The funny thing he said to me was, "You remind me of that famous Englishman". "Who", I laughed, "David Beckham"? "Nooooo" he replied. "Daniel Craig"? I joked. "Nooooo" he chuckled, "Who then" I wondered with anticipation. "Meester Bean", he said in his funny Russian accent. Well, we both laughed and laughed until our bellies ached. Mr Bloody Bean, what a compliment that was!!! Oh it was so funny, you just had to be there, we were both crying our eyes out.

But then once we calmed down, he said something which really touched me in a deep way, or place. He said, "Every English person should be like you". It was the way he said it, I could see and feel that he really meant it. This was such a nice thing to say and his words completely pulled on my heart strings. Of course all human beings love nice compliments, but the way he told me he thought I was a pretty decent guy, really hit my internal soft spot and I felt like a plate of jelly.

Again I wished I had more time to spend with my Russian friend as he was such great company. Maybe he had some bad experiences with other English people, so it was nice for him to see that not all English people are assholes, but sadly, a lot of them really are when they are on holiday/vacation, usually fueled by copious amounts of "liquid dymanite" or the "devils water"....alcohol.

I've always tried my best to behave in a respectful manner on all my adventures over the many years of travelling I have been lucky enough to have done in my lifetime. I see myself as a kind of ambassador of my country, I am representing England, so I want the world to see that not all

English people are noisy drunken yobbo's, just most of them!!

I see the same problem with the perception of the English towards the Americans, being typecast as loud, brash and aggressive. I love American's, well most, as a massive percentage of the Americas I have met were the nicest people anybody could possibly meet. Obviously not all, as there are always bad eggs in all walks of life or nationalities.

Us English seem to be typecast as thugs, arrogant and basicially thinking we are the best in the world, which of course we are!! I have met so many great people from so many countries all over the planet who have been so kind, as well as a lot of English people whom I have found to be repulsive, whose behaviour has been shocking and embarrassing, especially after a few drinks. So for my Russian friend to pay me this ultimate compliment made me feel good about myself, and that maybe I have been doing something right and making a good impression of not only me, but of my country, and this is something which is very important to me and I am so very proud of.

I thoroughly enjoyed my week "holiday" in Hawaii, it's such a beautiful place, which I recommend to anybody, especilly lovers as this is truly a wonderful and romantic island. My batteries were now fully charged as I entered the home straight on my NFL adventure.

The following morning I had breakfast, said goodbye to my funny Russian friend, and I took off to catch the bus to Honolulu airport, returning to San Francisco for the third and final time, and more importantly, the big one, the finale,

and the final stop on my " The Wrong Shaped Balls Tour".
Superbowl 50.

Superbowl 50
Levi Stadium San Francisco
Carolina Panthers Vs Denver Broncos

I landed back into San Francisco for my third and final visit to this beautiful city, and I headed back to the same Adelaide hostel I had stayed in on my previous visits, as it was in a good location. The price had gone up a little since my last visit, simply to rinse the people here for the Superbowl, which to be honest, is understandable as everybody here in San Fran was on the gravy train and doing it.

I had a few days until the day of Superbowl 50, so my intentions were to indulge into the swing of things and atmosphere of all things Superbowl. There was a NFL fans dream exhibition named "Fan City", an area near Fisherman's Wharf dedicated to the Superbowl. Then there was the Moscone Media Centre, where all the world's media would be hanging out and doing all kinds of interviews, including many ex NFL players and legends of the good old days of NFL past, and some of the stars of today.

Thursday was my first day back in San Fran, so off I went to check out Fan City. It was a beautiful sunny day and you could feel the excitement in the air, and that we were building up to something special as the huge crowds of people queued up to get into Fan City.

Once inside, it was a NFL fan's heaven, lots of interactive stuff going on, exhibitions, competitions, music, videos, stage performances and the chance to meet some NFL players.

I met the San Francisco 49ers quarterback Blaine Gabbert and a current player from the Oakland Raiders, whose name I can't remember, but he must have been a defensive player as he was absolutely huge.

I wandered around Fan City for a few hours, and it was great to be in San Francisco on this very special occasion. I felt blessed and very lucky to be here, the climax of an amazing NFL tour.

Mosconi Media Centre was next, and my quest was to try to get an interview or three from anybody who maybe interested in me and my tour. HA!

Before I entered the centre, I bumped into Shawn Gayle, the ex Chicago Bears and San Diego Chargers player, whom I had previously met at the Hippodrome Casino in London, as well as in the street in Teddington with Kevin Cadle, when I gave Kevin a CD of my song "Like a Touchdown".

Shawn knew all about my tour, and it was nice he actually recognised me. I asked him where the UK NFL guys were, and he told me inside the centre. So my quest was to find them.

The Mosconi Media Centre was the place where all of the worlds media were sending back all kinds of news to their respective countries, interviews with many ex players, news, gossip and all things NFL.

I saw a few people I recognised, like Jerry Rice, the ex 49ers wide receiver, probably one of the best of all time. I saw current Oakland Raiders quarterback Derek Carr, and another one of the old all time greats, Joe Namath. He was surrounded by guards and kept away from the crowds as he is now a very fragile old man. Seeing Joe in the flesh was special, as this guy really was a legend back in his day.

The Mosconi media centre was manic, with people being interviewed all over the place, by many different nationalities of journalists, and it was exciting for me to see this side of the game.

I eventually found the Sky Sports team from the UK, and I waited patiently as they were doing a live TV link as I arrived at their section of the media centre.

I stood watching Neil Reynolds, Jeff Reinebold and a couple of other people I did not know, giving their opinions on all kinds of football related items. Once they had finished, I found myself standing next to Neil Reynolds.

"Hello Neil", I said, "I'm the English guy who has been to all 31 NFL stadiums this season on my "The Wrong Shaped Balls Tour", and I've been trying to contact you on Twitter all season".

Now call me "fcuking stupid", but I expected not only for Neil to know exactly who I was, (how could he not?, as I had been blitzing every NFL social media forum for over a year) I expected him to at least show me some kind of friendly welcome or appreciation. His reply to me was, "Oh I don't respond to people on social media", in a very stroppy and arrogant way.

I tried to tell him about my tour, and I hoped to get ANY kind of interest, feedback or help from him or the Sky Sports team in the ten seconds of airtime he allowed me in his presence. He responded, "It's not a story that interests us as your tour has been done before".

He was so dismissive and arrogant, he showed absolutely NO INTEREST AT ALL, in my incredible journey. My blood was fcuking boiling and I wanted to punch this smug prick right in the face.

Reynolds had ignored ALL of the many of my messages for help and support over the entire NFL season, and when I eventually met him, I at least expected him to show a fraction of interest in what I thought was a fantastic achievement from a boy from the UK. NOPE. This horrible individual never gave me the bloody time of day. I spoke to him for only about a minute, and he really made me feel like he could not give a shit, he never said a word of well done, amazing, how was it?, have you had a good time?, any problems????? Not a sausage/NOTHING!

An English guy named Adam Goldstein had done a similar trip a few years before, but he never got much, or any media coverage from SKY TV as far as I know, so how had this been done before if SKY had nothing to do with it? Why was this not a good story, especially as this is the perfect advert for the NFL in the UK? I simply cannot tell you how totally amazed I still am to this very day that NOBODY from ANY of the UK NFL industry, took a single shread of interest when there will now be four NFL games played in London each year and the NFL in the UK is growing bigger and bigger each season. I'M COMPLETELY

BAFFLED!!!!!!!

This was a very low moment and a major kick in the bollocks for me. These are people (Reynolds, Reinebold, Cadle) I would watch each week on TV, and I stupidly thought these guys would follow me all across America, maybe interview me, or at least highlight my tour on their show? Surely this would be in the interest of every follower of the NFL in the UK, to keep tabs on this crazy Englishman living HIS, and everybody elses dream of going to every stadium in the country??? NO, NO, NO, NO and NO. I just don't understand why not?

I always thought that if this tour would have been attempted by some random reality TV star or Z list celebrity, or maybe some dopey ex player, the TV networks would be all over this like a virus. I'm just so gutted I never got the chance to show the world's media that I'm actually not a bad broadcaster and live speaker. I can be very funny, interesting or spontaneous on TV, when the moment catches me. Trust me, it would have been compelling viewing, but I simply never got the chance.

Another media guy who offered the hand of friendship and assistance before I left home was a guy from Talksport named Olly Hunter. Later renamed by me as something a little more cockney rhyming slang! I will never understand as long as I have a hole in my ass, as to why a decent human being offers to help you, then simply disappears and ignores all attempts to be contacted, then appears out of nowhere to slag you off on social media. That's exactly what Olly did to me.

Olly was in San Francisco to cover the Superbowl, and yet again I just cannot understand why he would not want me on his show talking about my tour. Only he knows?

Olly called me "crass", (a word I never even knew the meaning of, until I went online and looked up) purely because of a comment I made to a Tweet from ex Arsenal football player Ray Parlour, regarding the untimely death of TV and Radio legend Terry Wogan.

I responded to Ray Parlour's tweet, by saying something like, "RIP Terry Wogan, you were a legend, especially your commentary on the Eurovision song contest".

So, no harm there, but then I tweeted Ray, asking him to follow me on my trip around America, something I had done to soooooooooo many other groups, people, footballers, etc etc etc. I honestly did not feel like I was bombing his tweet or being disrespectful to Ray's post or Terry Wogan, actually I thought I had sent him a personal message, but Olly took umbridge to this, and he miraculously resurfaced from months of hibernation, or deafening silence to abuse me and call me crass.

I had a little tweeting war with Olly, but not ONCE did he EVER ask me how my tour was going, he just wanted to punch me in the ribs, I was so upset and ABSOLUTELY FUMING.

Olly surfaced once again to respond to something I said on Facebook. Again, this little rat could not wait to put the boot into me. WHY? All I ever wanted was his support. I wanted to be his friend, not his enemy. The facts were, he

OFFERED to help ME before I left London, he ignored ALL my emails and tweets, disappeared for months, then resurfaced only to slag me off and run me down. Only Olly knows why. I would love to know Olly, so over to you. Maybe we can talk about it on your show? Email me.

Olly really messed me about and frustrated the fcuking life out of me, as when someone of influence offers the hand of friendship, then slaps your face with the very same hand, that fcuking hurts.

I met Olly's partner, some fat guy whose name I cannot even remember and I know he knew exactly who I was and what I had acheived. I had a chat with him, and he seemed like a nice fella, and I gave him ample chance to show any kind of interest in my tour, and sadly he never did. Again I felt so gutted. Why are these people just not interested in getting me on their shows? It would have been great radio, not just for me, but for THEM.

I left the Mosconi centre totally deflated and with the raving hump/pissed off. All the people I had vertually begged for help, guidance, assistance etc over the past year, were all in THAT centre, and every single one of them had ignored my pleas, or basically spoke to me like I never existed. I really was gutted, and also very angry. These people were the heartbeat of the NFL in the UK, and not one of them gave me or my amazing achievements the time of day. These people could have helped me so so much, and being rejected by ALL OF THEM was just so hard for me to take. I wanted to cry. I felt like I was just nothing to these people, which is exactly what I was.

I think the NFL media in the UK missed out on an enormous opportunity by ingoring me and my tour. It's estimated that well over 2 million people regularly follow the NFL each week in the UK, and I believe that every single one of them would have loved to have watched my adventures unfold, and seen me reporting back from each town I visited in the US, over the 5 months of my tour.

I could have been a kind of "salesman", selling, promoting, raising awareness and telling my story from the perspective or angle of a member of the UK audience. But no, I was just seen as irrelevant and ignored by all.

The night before the Superbowl, one of my favourite bands, Metallica were playing a concert at the San Francisco Giants AT&T Stadium (great name!). The Giants are the big Baseball team of San Fran, and their stadium was a short walk from the Mosconi Centre, so off I went to have a look at it, tried to buy a ticket and basically see its location for when I attended their concert in a couple of days time.

The Stadium is right on the sea front, and just as I arrived, the ticket office closed, GREAT!, so I had no idea how much, or if in fact there were any tickets left for the concert. I had looked online, and the prices were sky high, so my intention was to go on the night and do my usual things to try to get a ticket. Remember I am the "master of tickets" (not Puppets!......one of my favourite Metallica songs). Well most of the time I was!!

After my usual lap around the stadium, I wandered off home, back to my Adelaide Hostel. It had been a long day, lots of walking, and I was knackered and ready for an early night.

I was feeling pretty sorry for myself as my tour was almost over, and I had made absolutely no progress at all to break America with my music, or get any help from any of the people from the UK who could have opened doors for me, but chose to ignore me. So I ended up going to bed feeling terribly low and needing a friend, or just someone to show me some compassion or love.

It was now Friday, and just 48 hours away from Superbowl 50. The atmosphere in town was great, the sun was shining as usual, and there was lots going on for the fans.

I spent the next day up and down town on the famous San Francisco trams, and I eventually turned up back at the baseball stadium, where Metallica were playing the following night.

I noticed there were a few people hanging around ouside the stadium, so I asked a couple of fans what was going on. One of them told me Metallica were doing a soundcheck in front of only 300 fans, these fans were winners of an online competition that was held on their website. I was told you had to answer a few Metallica related questions, and the 300 winners won the chance to see Metallica soundcheck in front of an audience for the very first time in their careers.

There were a few women who must have worked for the organisers or record company, handing out black wristbands to the winners, who went up to them with their I.D's, to confirm who they were, and that they were in fact one of the 300 winners.

I went up to one of the woman and I asked, "Is there any chance of me getting in to see the soundcheck?". "Sorry, but no, this is only for the competition winners I'm afraid". The lady replied.

I could see a part of the stage through some bars at the entrance to the stadium, so I thought I would stick around for a while, and watch, or at least listen to the soundcheck from outside. I walked around the whole stadium, just to see if there was any back doors, or secret entrances I could wander into, as I'm usually good at finding a way to get in through an unlocked door!

There was an area on the other side of the stadium where I could see the entire stage, and I could see a couple of the members of Metallica were talking. After seeing them, I knew I had to get in to see this. There was a lot of security, and I knew it would be hard to get into this area, where there were lots of roadies and other people constantly going in and out of this section.

I remember thinking that if I grabbed some random piece of equipment, which was all around me, I could pick it up and walk straight in, as bold as brass like I was one of the roadies. I very nearly did, but if I got caught, I could have been in big trouble with the security people, so I bottled it/decided against my better judgement.

I returned to the area where I had started, and by now all the competition winners were queuing up and looking as excited as kids at christmas. Watching them getting their wristbands and going into the stadium, I felt as jealous as hell.

I could see an area through the bars, where some guys were getting tee shirts ready to sell at the concert the following night. I asked the guys through the bars if I could buy a tee shirt now, because I never had a ticket for the show. They said yes, and I purchased two shirts for 40 bucks each. I think I was probably the first person to get those tee shirts before any other Metallica fans. ROCK N ROLL!!

I put one on straight away, and within 5 minutes, over 4-5 people had asked me where I got the shirt from. "Up there, through the bars" I pointed.

On the back of one of the tee shirts it said "Too heavy for halftime". This meant the half time slot at the Superbowl, as Metallica were apparently too "heavy" for it, and this statement was basically taking the piss.

I personally think Metallica would be a great choice for the Superbowl and I'm surprised they had not already done one, especially as you hear their songs played by the stadiums sound man in practically every NFL stadium in the country, every single week. That makes no sense to me at all.

I went back to the lady who had told me earlier I would not be going in and I cheekily said to her, "I've been waiting here for a couple of hours now and if there is absolutely no chance of me getting in, I'm going home". Her reply to me was short and sweet, "Don't go home", she said.

There must have been around 25 of us all hanging around and hoping for a miracle and to our amazement the lady came over to us and she said, "Right you lot, line up and hold out your wrists". RESULT!!!!!!!!! Oh boy, I was

soooooo excited, elated, over the moon,
METALLLIIIICCAAAAAA!!!!!!!!!!

We entered the stadium and I joined up with the 300
competition winners and we were finally led into this
massive but completely empty AT+ T Stadium, which on
the following night would be full to the tune of around 60
thousand screaming fans, but tonight, I was one of the
extremely lucky 300 or so. I was in dreamland.
YYEESSSSSS!

As soon as we walked in, Metallica were already playing
and they started with one of my favourite Metallica songs,
called "For whom the bell tolls". Dun, dun, dun dunnnnn,
dun, dun dun dunnnnn, dun, dun, dun dunnnnn, dun dun
dun!!!

It was SOOOOOO loud, and absolutely fcuking brilliant.
The stage was massive and so were the screens behind the
band. I walked right to the front and I saw the four members
of the band right in front of my face, just feet away, it was
just too awesome for words.

This was simply a once in a lifetime experience I would
never ever ever see again, and I enjoyed every single second
of the 6-8 songs Metallica played, as much as I could. I took
loads of pictures and videos, and I had to pinch myself, as I
was so close to my heroes, it really was one of the best
nights of my life and one of the biggest highlights of my
tour by far.

On one of the songs they played, bass player Rob Trujillo,
was right in front of me, If I would have streached my arm

out, I could have touched the strings to his bass guitar, I was that close to him. I was so happy to be here, but also very very jealous as I always so wanted to be a rockstar and play on big stages like Metallica do. I wanted to laugh and cry at the same time!

On the stage with the band was a guy I had met many years ago when I was a teenager, and working in a photographic shop in London. His name is Ross Halfin and he is the official photographer for Metallica. Ross got me and a friend on the guest list at an Iron Maiden concert in Edinburgh many years ago, as he is also their official photographer.

Ross was taking pictures of the band as they played and I tried to get his attention at the end as I would have loved to have said hello to him. I took a great picture of Ross taking a picture of the bass player Rob and I posted it to him on Facebook. Ross replied "great shot" and this made my day. Thanks Ross.

The soundcheck was totally amazing and watching a band so relaxed, in normal clothing, talking to each other, as well as the sound engineers, interacting with the fans, was just a brilliant brilliant experience to witness. 100 times better than a staged concert.

After the soundcheck, I floated out of the stadium on the crest of a wave, realising I had experienced something very special indeed. I felt so lucky to have witnessed what millions of Metallica fans would have paid a fortune to see, and I got it for free. Sometimes you win some, and this time, I won bigtime!

Check out this link, and you will see what I saw on that brilliant night. If you look closely, you may see me at the front taking pictures and videos!!

https://www.youtube.com/watch?v=gvCZZHpMPoU

As I walked home back to my hostel, I was on a natural high, I just had one of the best nights of my life, and it was now all down hill from this point onwards!

Saturday I was meeting up with some of my friends who were coming in from Seattle for the Superbowl festivities. Cannonball, my Seahawks Superfan friend, Jimbo Sabado, a few of their friends and partners, King Kirk the Oakland Raiders Superfan, and a few others, all congregated inside "Fan City", to check out what was going on, and to have a few beers.

It was great to see these guys again, as when we met in Seattle, we never had much time together as I was on the clock, and I only stayed for a short period of time. I loved being in the company of these guys, they made me feel so welcome and I felt like I had known them all for years.

I had yet another result when one of the guys, Raider Kirk had a spare ticket for the Metallica concert that evening. This was great news as I did not have to try the usual bullshit and I could now relax in the knowledge I had a ticket for the big concert, all thanks to Kirk.

We stayed in Fan City for a few hours, and as I had already been there a few days earlier, I followed the gang around, and I was just happy to be in their company.

I did the same as we headed for the Mosconi Media Centre where we spent some time, before we headed to a resturant for a nice dinner, then I headed off to the Metallica concert with Kirk. A big thanks to my Seahawks family for a wonderful day.

I was really looking forward to the concert, but how could it possibly beat what I had experienced the night before? It was simply not possible.

Our seats were right at the back underneath one of the upper sections of the stadium. Yesterday I was in the front row, now I was around 200 yards back, and when Metallica were on the stage, they looked as small as ants!

But it was still a great concert, they played all the hits and most of my favourite Metallica songs. The light show with all the lasers was incredible, especially when they played their songs "One" and "Master of Puppets", two of my favourite Metallica tracks.

I had seen Metallica from both ends, with 300 people and now with 60 thousand. I looked upon this occasion as the highlight of my tour, a special treat to myself for my achievement, and the pleasure I got from these two nights was probably more than every one of the 35 NFL games I saw over the past 6 months put together. That's how much music means to me, but don't get me wrong, I love the NFL, I just love music a little bit more.

The following day was THE big day, Superbowl 50, the final day of almost 6 months of zig zagging across America, to watch the game I love in every NFL stadium in the country.

As I had been to the Levi Stadium before, on my 31st and last regular season game, I knew it was not an easy place to get to, and I expected many more fans to be packing into the trains heading for Santa Clara than last time.

I got to the train station extra early to try to beat the rush and I was surprised by how few fans were there waiting for the train as I arrived, I thought it would be packed. It was also a surprise to me there were no extra trains laid on for the many fans attending this massive event, and I was lucky to walk straight on and get a seat on a half empty train. I could'nt believe it. Where was everybody?

Of course the ticket prices were different from the last time I boarded this train, almost double from what I could remember, another kick in the teeth for the football fans and yet another way to bleed the public by the powers that be.

I had been told by a friend of mine to be careful when I boarding the train out of San Francisco, as I would be asked to show my Superbowl ticket as proof I was attending the game, as to be allowed to get on the train. So I was a little apprehensive as I approached the train guard at the barriers, but he looked at my ticket, waived me through, so off we went with no problem at all. PHEW!

I was a bit relieved to be on board the train and I was looking forward to a brilliant climax to my tour. So much for the words of warning. HA! or so I thought.

After a hour of so, we had to change trains, so off we all got and headed for the second platform. As I approached the barriers, there were many ticket guards, and to my horror, they were asking to see peoples tickets for the game, as to let people board this train. NOOOOO.....

So my friend was right, FCUK! I had to show a ticket to get past these guards, so I stood back for a moment, took a deep breath and I thought "he who dares wins", so I confidently walked towards the guards and to my horror, one of them asked to see my ticket. FCUK!

I showed him my train ticket and I quickly carried on walking. "Can I see your game ticket sir?", he shouted to me as I ignored him and continued to walk.

I got stopped by another guard, so now I had a real dilemma on my hands and I had to think quick on my feet with some instant random bullshit to try to get me on the train. "I work for the English BBC, and my ticket is at the stadium", I told the guard in my poshest upper class English accent. "You aint getting on this train without your game ticket buddy", was his response. "But I have to collect it at the stadium", I lied. "No ticket, no train", was his abrupt message. "So how am I going to get to the stadium", I asked. "There are buses parked 100 yards up the street, they will take you to the Levi Stadium".

After my inital shock that I was not getting anywhere near the stadium, which would have been a complete and utter disaster, I was as happy as Larry I now had my "get out of jail card" and a way of getting to my destination. I found the buses, and in no time, I was back on the road to the Levi Stadium. PHEW!!!!!

To be honest, I would have walked to the Levi Stadium if I had to, there was no way I was missing out on my final game of the tour. No chance whatsoever.

It was little blips or mishaps like this, that made my adventure what it was, an adventure. As you have probably already read, things didn't always go to plan, and sometimes things went against me, but I expected them to, sometimes I got lucky, and most of the time I made my own luck. But I did get a lot of help, and this was something I was always so very grateful for, as most of the time, boy did I need it!

I never felt too down when I could not get my way, I actually saw this as a challenge. You win some, you lose some was always my motto and looking back, I won far more times than I lost, so when I lost, I just accepted it and I moved on to the next adventure.

The bus arrived at the Levi about a hour later, so now I found myself walking to the Stadium for Superbowl 50, with a huge smile, as this was an absolute dream come true for this boy.

I have been watching this amazing event since way back in the 80's, when the NFL was first shown on English TV, and now I was here, something I never thought would ever happen. I was walking on air.

Now I'm going to explain something to you, which many of you may not understand.   I do think all my Superfan family and most passionate NFL football fans will empathise with my reasoning, although most people will simply think I am just plain stupid.

I never had any intention of even trying to attend the Superbowl before I left home 6 months ago, and that never changed for one single second on my entire tour.

Of course I would have loved to have got a ticket for this game, but in my mind, I always knew this was never going to happen, as 60% of Superbowl tickets are corporate, so the chances of me getting a face value ticket was totally more than impossible, leaving the only option of a scamming tout, and anyway, I just could not afford it, as George Washington was now questioning our relationship and very close to divorcing me, if you know what I mean, as by now, basically I was skint/broke.

I was hoping by the time I got to the Superbowl 50, I would get an invite from one of the many contacts, sponsors, corporations, TV networks, NFL teams, NFLUK, etc I had touched base with or met along the way. HA! WHAT A BLOODY STUPID IDIOT I AM. In fact, I ended up with no contacts at all, not ONE, to even buy me a hotdog let alone a ticket for the game.

I even sent an email to the PA of Shad Khan, the owner of the Jacksonville Jaguars, who so very kindly invited me to watch a game with him in Jacksonville, but she said all the tickets were for clients and sponsors. So that door closed before it even slightly opened. But I expected that, but you can't blame a boy for driving down "Every Avenue"!! Sorry, my jokes are getting worse!

So why am I here, at Superbowl 50?, I hear you cry. Well, of course I had to be, how could I not after all I had already acheived. I just wanted to be around the stadium for this monumental occasion and to take in the atmosphere, tailgate, watch the game with thousands of Panthers and Broncos fans, eat, drink, party and have an excellent lifetime experience and a special day to remember on the final game of my NFL tour.

Of course I was going to try to get in to see the game, but I was never going to pay the 3-4 thousand bucks tickets were selling for outside the stadium by these sharks or scalpers/touts, where some tickets were obviously fake (like I had experienced twice on my tour). I made sure this was not going to happen to me a third time, so I deliberately only took a few hundred dollars with me, as I simply could not afford these crazy prices, and I was adamant this was simply not an option and was not in my plans.

My plan was to bunk in, climb over, or under a fence, over a wall, through a gate, slip 100 bucks to a guard etc etc, anything to try to blag my way in. In fact I actually got past the first line of security with a quick movement of my feet while the guard was looking at another person's ticket, but there was a second and a third hurdle to jump, or checkpoint to pass, so I knew immediately I had no chance at all getting in this way.

There had been rumours of a terrorist attack at the Superbowl, so security was as tight as a bulls ass, more than normal if that's possible, so I gave up on the idea of getting in, as if I got caught trying, I would have been arrested, or even shot if they thought I was a danger to the thousands of other people inside the stadium.

I met a group of cheeky chappies/guys outside the main

entrance to the stadium, holding up a big sign, asking if anybody had a spare ticket for free! but of course none of them got one, but they were a nice bunch of lads, and we did have a laugh trying.

But what was to come, was the biggest disappointment of my NFL tour bar none. The whole football experience on gameday that I was now so very used to, did not take place at all at Superbowl 50. As I have mentioned, I came here for the party and atmosphere, to immerse myself in all the festivities surrounding the biggest game of the season, and maybe the biggest sporting event in my lifetime.

I was completely shocked when I noticed there was not one single tailgate, not a single outlet selling beer, and the only person selling food was a little old man with a hot dog table, probably a chancer taking an opportuity to make a few bucks off the back of the total lack of, or no competition outside the Levi Stadium.

But the worse thing for me was the total absence of people selling official merchadise. WHAT? I sooooooo wanted to buy an official Superbowl 50 tee shirt, which would have been a great momento for me to remember this monumental occasion, or even a game programme, a cap, or even a bloody fridge magnet, there was absolutely nothing. I kept thinking how much money the NFL must be losing in revenue, as these items would have sold like hot cakes.

There were many shops in the centre of San Francisco selling this kind of stuff, but it didn't feel the same, or as special as buying something in the moment and at the venue of the game.

It got far worse, as there was not a single TV screen showing the game. OH FFS? I came to Superbowl 50 for the occasion of occasions and I cannot even watch the game with the fans on the telly? FCUKING HELL!!!!

I could not believe it, so I walked all around the stadium looking for a TV screen to watch the game. There were some screens, but none of them were showing the game, just pre recorded shit to the build up to the game. I cannot begin to tell you how fcuking gutted I was.

I returned to the main entrance, where I had spent most of the time, just to see if any of the other people I had met, who like me did not have a ticket, were having any luck getting in. There was a young lad hanging around, and I was told by somebody he had just been scammed for 3000 bucks for a ticket which was a fake as he tried to go into the stadium. I felt so sorry for him.

The scalpers were so aggressive towards the buyers and there were some people opening their fat wallets and paying big money for tickets, probably their only games of the season, something that makes me sick. Where were these so called "fans" on a cold and wet Monday night game in December? Glory hunters, I hate them!!!

So I digress, everybody knows that most cup finals in any sporting events around the world, are games that are never aimed at, or fair for the fans who have supported their teams all season. It is all to do with the one and most disgusting reason and a reason that makes my stomach turn and blood boil. MONEY.

The NFL make an absolute fortune all season from the millions of loyal NFL fans who follow and attend the games of their beloved teams, only for these fanatical fans to have almost no chance of getting a ticket for the game of their lives. This is something that disgusts me and the whole reason why I never wanted to go into the Levi Stadium for Superbowl 50. I did not want to take away the chance of a loyal NFL fan, who had probably watched their team at all 8 home games, and probably a few away games, with me getting in, and them not. I just felt these guys are more worthy of the ticket than me.

HOWEVER. If I had been given the chance to have gone in, would I have? Of course I would, but let me clarify the situation before I am accused of being a hypocrite.

I never expected to get in, so my emotions were well and truly switched off. I never once tried to buy a ticket. I deliberatly only took enough money to buy food, drink and a few momentoes as I never wanted the temptation to even try to waste my time looking for a ticket.

But if someone I had met from say, an NFL team, a player, a TV channel, a radio station, a rich man who knew my story, or even NFLUK, would I have offered me a free ride with all the trimmings, of course I would have snapped it up, who wouldn't. I saw this avenue as a way of getting in without taking away the chance of a true fan getting a face value ticket. I hope this makes sense.

The vast majority of tickets for the Superbowl go to the corporate world, and I understand this to a degree, as these companies invest a lot of money into this game. But the two teams fans who get to the superbowl, get 20% each of the cut of the tickets, with 60% going to the corporate world. And those ticket prices are so overpriced, even at face value, and to me, this is purely exploitation and I hate it.

I saw things outside the Levi Stadium that made me sooooooo mad, it made me feel sick. There were people going into the game who probably didn't even know which two teams were playing, or even what the shape of a NFL football is.

I saw a woman who looked like a prostitute, or she had just been pole dancing in a nightclub, wearing a dress that was ripped to shreads, with everything hanging out. She did look amazing I have to be honest, and as she walked right past me into the stadium, on the arm of an old guy who could quite easily had been her dad, I shouted to her, "Hey, any chance of a picture with you honey". She instantly replied "Five dollars!". I had to laugh, as it was a great and very quick answer, but this summed up Superbowl 50 for me, it's just about the MONEY. I bet that bitch does not even know who Cam Newton is?

The time had arrived and the big game started, and all of us people standing outside the stadium could not even hear any announcements from the loud speakers, only the odd muted cheer of the crowd.

I got talking to a guy who was watching the game on his cellphone, he was waiting for a scalper/tout to come back to him with a ticket they had just agreed on a price of two grand for. The guy said he knew he was taking a huge risk buying a ticket from this extremely unreliable and dodgy source, but he just wanted to see a Superbowl, and he had no other choice. I stood chatting with this guy until around half time, but the scalper never returned. No question the ticket was a fake.

As I stood outside the main entrance to the stadium, more and more people were still entering, well after the start of the game. It was almost half time and I witnessed yet another old man with a blonde bimbo on EACH ARM (greedy b@stard!), walking in and missing the whole of the first quarter and even most of the second. This was absolute torture for a fan like me to witness and I was just steaming with anger, because if that was me, I would have been inside the stadium two hours before the game even started, not at bloody half time.

For me this was a slap in the face for every NFL fan who would have loved to have been at this game and an insult to the game and occasion itself, that some people have no respect for it by turning up at half time. This is just one of the many reasons why I saw this game as nothing but a huge joke.

By now I had long given up at getting into see the game and after what I had witnessed outside the stadium, I would have not paid a single dollar to get in. (that's a bit of an exageration as I would have!!), but I was seeing a side of this wonderful game I really did not like AT ALL.

I had hardly seen a single play of the entire first half, except for the very few I saw on the screen of some guys tiny cellphone and with half time approaching, I had no idea what the score was, something I never dreamed or envisaged would be happening to me on the climax and my Superbowl 50 adventure.

At least I had something exciting to look forward to, the half time entertainment, which this year, was provided by Coldplay and Beyonce, and as I am a big fan of both these brilliant artists, I waited in anticipation. WRONG YET AGAIN!

As half time came, the entertainment started inside the stadium, but outside the stadium we were still waiting to hear what songs our heroes would be playing. We waited, and waited, until we all realised it had in fact already started, but........WE COULD NOT HEAR A FCUKING THING.

This was the very last kick in the bollocks for me, on what should have been a day to remember, a day of immense celebration, the final stop on my tour, and a finale or highlight, to end on a massive high, not a day in which nothing went to plan in the slightest. I really wanted to hear the music, just to have something to remind me of this special day. I don't know how the organisers managed to stifle or mute the sound, maybe they never did? but all of us standing outside the stadium heard nothing and we were standing right outside the main entrance.

This summed up my day completely, I was at the party, but I had no drink. I was at the brothel, but I couldn't join in as I never had a condom!!! That's how I felt, pushed to the side, not allowed to take part in any of the festivities, simply irrelevant, not even allowed to hear the music. TOTAL BULLSHIT.

The lucky ones were inside, getting the full treatment, absolutely everything, and rightly so, as they have paid for it, but the ones outside were given absolutely nothing, we were invisible, ignored, not worthy, without a single TV screen to just see the game, or even watch the half time show that everybody across America was watching. It was purely a case of us and them, the have's and the have not's. Well that's how it felt for me anyway.

The half time entertainment finished and to my total amazement, lots of people were leaving the stadium and going home. Many people standing outside the stadium exits were asking the people leaving, if that could buy their tickets to try to gain re entry, but this was not going to happen as we were told by security before the game started that re entry is simply not an option, so that plan was crushed before it started.

What happened next was the final straw for me. I had asked at least five different groups of people who were leaving the stadium as the third quarter was about to start, "What is the score of the game", as I honestly had no idea, how could I? unless I asked somebody who was online. To my total disbelief the same answer came back at my everytime, "I don't know", was the response.

How could these fcuking wankers not know the score of the Superbowl at half time? What the fcuk were they doing inside the stadium? Obviously not watching the game. Probably riding on the corporate gravy train, eating, drinking and doing business, probably making even more money, everything other than watching the game.

This probably annoyed me more than anything else on that fateful day and what a complete lack of respect for this occasion. This sums up how I felt about this event because Superbowl is not for genuine fans, it's for the privileged, the vile super rich, the establishment, celebrities and basicially people with far too much MONEY. It fcuking stinks!! After all of this bullshit, I was so happy I never got into the stadium and be a part of this media circus.

The third quarter was coming to an end and people were leaving in their hundreds, making my blood pressure rise more and more.

Outside the stadium I got talking to a top bloke named "Big Beefy", by the main entrance area where people were leaving early, and he was trying to buy a golden Superbowl ticket stub from the early leavers as a momento.

Big beefy is his nickname, born in Wales, now living in Australia, Beefy was on a tour of his own, to do as many different sports as he could in 365 days, so we had quite a lot in common and to talk about.

There were about a dozen people trying to get these golden Superbowl 50 ticket stubs from the early leavers, and some of these idiots were annoying me, one guy in particular who had already managed to get around 4-5 of these golden tickets from the people exiting the stadium, obviously who had no interest in keeping this momento for themselves. This annoying prick was obviously getting these ticket stubs and selling them, (he actually assured me he was not....fcuking liar) and he got a few stubs from people as I watched, purely because he was being a little more forthcoming or forward than Big Beefy in his approach to the leavers, unlike the rest of the, shall I say, more polite people who were looking for these golden ticket stubs.

Now this is right up my boulevard, I'm sure you must know me by now! I have no shame in situations like this in asking for anything. Enter D-Mo.

I liked Big Beefy, so when I saw a group of people coming out, one guy was up for selling his ticket stub for twenty bucks. So I barged the "prick" (who already had a few golden tickets), out of the way and I said in my most arrogant and confident East End way, "this fcuker already has five tickets and he's selling them, I just want a momento of Superbowl 50". I practically snatched the ticket from this assholes's grasp, gave twenty dollars to the guy, and the ticket was mine. WALLOP!

The prick in question didn't like this, but honestly, I was so pissed off with how Superbowl 50 had panned out, I was ready to fight him, and he could see this and he backed off immediately. So I got a Superbowl 50 golden ticket stub, walked straight over to Big Beefy, and I gave it to him, for 20 bucks of course.

Looking back now, I have to laugh, especially as some guy offered Big Beefy 100 dollars for that ticket stub, two minutes after I got it for him. I would have gone mad if he sold it after what I had done for him, but I could see how much it meant to Beefy and as he had been trying for while, I was happy to part with it. To me it was just another game or challenge.

Thinking about it now, it would have been a nice souvenir to have kept, but at the time, I thought it was the right thing to do, a favour for a nice guy and a new friend.

The game was now almost at it's finale and I was thinking about how difficult it would be for me to get back home to San Francisco with all of those fans coming out of the stadium together at the end, if I stayed until the final second.

At this point I still had no idea what the score of the game was, and by this time, I didn't really care anymore, as the game was coming to an end, I had seen fcuk all, heard no music, had no real fun, no tailgate, no food, drink, or atmosphere, but I had had another exciting experience, if that what you wanna call it. Lets just say an experience.

Superbowl 50 did not exactly go according to plan, far from it, as it turned out to be a day of complete fcuk ups, and it is a day I look back on and laugh, as everything that could have gone wrong....did.

I said goodbye to my new friend Big Beefy (whom I am still in touch with), as I decided is was the right time to board the first train out of Santa Clara, just before Superbowl 50 ended.

The Denver Broncos eventually beat the Carolina Panthers to become the world champions of the season 2015-16, well that's what they are called, even though this game is only played in America. I was hoping for a Carolina Panthers win, as I wanted a team who had not won a Superbowl before, to win on the year of my tour. Sadly, this did not happen as the Panthers simply did not perform on the day, especially the normally brilliant Panthers main man Cam Newton.

Its funny how I say that the Panthers didn't really perform, commenting like I actually saw the game, and knew exactly what had happened, when in actual fact, to this day, I have only seen a few of the plays over the entire game, and as a climax to my incredible tour and adventure, it was not exactly the way I wanted this experience to end.

It was a very sad, sombre, lonely, tired, and emotionally draining train ride back into San Francisco for me after Superbowl 50 ended. This was it, full time, the final whistle, the last stop, the end of the game, end of the story, and the end of my tour. I felt incredibly relieved it was now finally over, but I also felt incredibly sad it was in fact all over.

I remember reminiscing at the time and thinking, "would I ever do anything like this ever again?", my immediate answer was "absolutely fcuking not in a million years", or " not as long as I have a hole in my ass!". But ask me the very same question today and my immediate answer would now be, " I would do it all over again tomorrow".

That night in my Adelaide Hostel in San Francisco, I raised a glass, or beer can, and I toasted myself, for my amazing feat of human endurance, something I never even knew I had, my stubborn never say die attitude, drive and determination, which got me through six months of so many ups and downs on my incredible journey, and something I am so very proud to say...............................I did it!!!

I had the most amazing time anybody could possibly have

had, living out my dreams of going to every NFL stadium in the country and indulging in one of my passions in life, American Football.

I really did live the dream and I will never forget for a second how lucky I was, to have been given the opportunity, which was funded by the sad death of my uncle Mick.

I met some of the most kind, generous, lovely, crazy, passionate, wonderful, and loving people, who will be my friends for life, and without these amazing people, my tour would have never been anywhere near as incredible as it was.

You guys were a massive part of the overall jigsaw puzzle on my "The Wrong Shaped Balls Tour". There really are no words I can write to express how grateful I will always be to you, for the love you gave to me, when you never even knew who I was until I arrived into your cities or even your tailgates. You all made me feel sooooooooooo welcome, and for this I would like to say the biggest THANK YOU in the history of thank yous, for making me feel a part of your very special family of football fans, all across America.

I dedicate this book, to all my Superfan buddies and their friends who I met along the way, who were so very kind to me and opened so many doors, doors that I could have never opened without your help, making this tour, one of the highlights of my life.

I cannot thank you special guys and girls enough, because without your kindness, I could have NEVER done it without you.

After the party was over

I arrived back to my hostel in San Francisco and I pondered over where I would be off to next for a new adventure. There was a celebrity golf tournament at the beautiful "Pebble Beach" golf club in Monterey, just a few hours up the road from San Francisco, and after this short pitstop, I was meeting my friend Mike McCarron in Las Vegas a week later. So what better way to spend time, hanging out on one of the world's most iconic and spectacular golf courses.

I said my third and final goodbye to the beautiful city of San Francisco and I headed to Monterey on a three hours ride on the Greyhound bus. I checked into the only hostel in Monterey and once I arrived, I immediately got a very lucky break.

I was looking for a plug to charge my phone, and I asked a random lady if it would be OK for me to plug into a socket next to where she was sitting and working on her laptop. We got chatting and she told me she was working as a marshall at the "AT+ T" (great name again!) golf tournament at Pebble Beach. I told her that was the reason why I was here. "I have a spare ticket if you would like to come with me", she said. "Let me think about it, OK", I replied in a heartbeat. RESULT!

The next two days, I spent walking around the most amazing golf club I have ever had the pleasure to experience, and I have been to, and worked on a fair few cracking ones over the past ten years.

The weather was beautiful and the surroundings and views right on the coastline of Northern California were absolutely breathtaking.

This tournament was organised by the legend and actor Clint Eastwood, and seeing him in the flesh was another memorable experience. I knew this tournament was full of top golfing professionals and celebrities, including a few NFL players, so I was well up for meeting a few of these guys.

I knew Aaron Rodgers (Green Bay Packers Quarterback) was playing, but this tournament was being played on three different courses, all in close proximity to each other, but not close enough for me to get from one to another, unless I hopped on a shuttle bus.

So off I went on a mission to locate Mr Rodgers, but I could not find him at all. I wandered around the course for a few hours, eventually giving up, and I said hello to a few pro golfers I had met before in my job as a golf caddie.

I chatted to Ian Poulter, tried to talk to the very rude and arrogant Padraig Harrington, met some great and friendly celebrities like Andy Garcia, and a very famous country singer named Jake Owen, who at the time, I had no idea who he was, until somebody told me.

Jake was walking down the fairway and I called out "Jake". He walked over, and I said, "I'm a songwiter from England and I have recorded in Nashville, I just want to say hello".

He was really friendly and a lovely guy. I never knew exactly how big he was until I googled him later that evening, and guess what? he's now following ME on Twitter. What a top man!

I heard there was a million dollar hole in one competition on the famous par 3 7th hole at Pebble Beach, so I headed off to see a piece of the action.

As I got about 150 yards, or a 7 iron from the stands where all the action was to take place, there was a bit of a commotion from the crowd as a flashy car pulled up. Who could this be I thought?

So I made a conscious effort as to stand right by the door, and when it opened, who gets out? Aaron the legend Rodgers. YYEESSSSSSSSSSSSSSSSS! I found him.

I walked straight up to him, pushed past loads of people and said "Hi Aaron, I've just finished a tour of all 31 NFL stadiums in one season and I was at both of the games that you threw the "Hail Mary" passes at".

He was very impressed and a lovely guy. I got a selfie with him, shook his hand, and he even signed my The "Wrong Shaped Balls" hoodie (which incidently I am wearing right now as I type away these words on my laptop).

Meeting Aaron was so special to me, it felt like a piece of "karma" had touched me, and after what I had been through, I bloody deserved it! Green Bay are the second team I follow behind my Dallas Cowboys and Rodgers is just such a legend. I was soooooooooo happy I got the chance to meet him.

The hole in one challenge started and all the celebs had three shots to score the big prize for their respective charities. I watched as many of the planet's best or high profile sporting greats, film stars and TV personalities past and present, gave it their best shots.

There was Ice Hockey legend Wayne Gretsky, the crazy Bill Murray, NFL stars Aaron Rodgers and Kansas Chiefs QB Alex Smith, Justin Timberlake, and of course Clint Eastwood, amongst many other big stars on show.

When this was finished, I attempted to say hello to Justin Timberlake. Of course all the chicks were following and screaming at him, but at one point I got very close to him, but he didn't stop to sign any autographs. So I flippantly shouted to him, "Hey Justin, don't be so quick to walk away", which if you are a fan, you will know this is a line from one of his songs. I actually thought it was quite funny, but he just walked on, nobody laughed, and it went down like a french kiss at a funeral! HA, you have to try, right?

Another guy I wanted to meet was Arizona Cardinals wide receiver Larry Fitzgerald, the guy who almost scored what would have been the best touchdown of all time in the play off game I attended in Phoenix, incidently the same game where Aaron Rodgers threw his second Hail Mary pass in.

I knew which hole Larry was on, so I waited. Then I found out he had played badly and walked off the course with the raving hump/upset, two holes from where I was waiting. BOLLOX!! Nice one Larry. Who the hell walks off Pebble Beach? Is he mad!

I bumped into a mate of mine who caddies for Justin Rose, Mark "Fooch" Fulcher, and I walked down a few holes chatting away to them both, having a laugh and not a care in the world. I told Justin I had just walked up to Clint Eastwood and I said to him, "Hey Clint, what do you call a cowboy with no money?", "What" he replied. "Skint Eastwood" I chuckled. Justin laughed, but I never really said it to Clint as he would have probably pulled out a colt 45 and told me to make his day!!! It was just one of my many terrible jokes!

I also walked three holes with two very rich Irishman, Dermot Desmond, who owns Celtic Football club in Scotland, and JP McManus, whom I have met many times at Wentworth golf club and at various racehorse meetings around the UK, as his horses usually run (and win) against my baby Vibrato Valtat.

Pebble Beach was a great two days of relaxation for my old aching bones, checking out celebs, and the amazing golf course. Hopefully the next time I am there I can actually play on the damn thing!!!

My next stop was Las Vegas, but from Monterey it was a very long Greyhound bus ride, all of twenty hours via Silicon Valley, San Jose and LA. A piece of piss/easy, for this boy, who is now the king of long bus rides!

I arrived into Las Vegas at 5am, and I headed straight for the "Mirage Hotel" where I was staying. My friend Mike was not arriving until lunchtime, so I found a quiet spot in the sportsbook area and tried to sleep until he arrived. This was not possible as the security people told me to move on, after they probably heard me snoring!

I stayed with Mike for six nights in Vegas, we did the usual few rounds of golf, watched Champions League soccer in the sports bars, but spent most of the time on the blackjack tables having a good old gamble. PARADISE.

I absolutely love Las Vegas, I've been there many times, and I'm planning on going back again next February/March. It's not just about the gambling why I love Vegas so much, it's got great golf courses, shows, bars, iconic hotels that are like shopping centres, and so much more. It's like an adults toy shop, a fun factory where you can basically buy anything you want. Yep anything! Everybody has to experience Las Vegas once before they finally go upstairs and meet their makers, me thinks.

The very last stop on my six months American adventure was to return to LA, to visit my good friend Jorge Gonzalez and his family.

My return ticket departed from LA, but I was far from ready to return home, as I was now absolutely craving for a brand new adventure and another exciting but completely different chapter in my life. So I had a few days to think of somewhere interesting I would head off to next before I finally went back home to London, but only after I had spent every single penny I had left in my pocket or bank account, because if I had unlimited funds, I would never have came home.

It was great to see my good buddy Jorge again, I love that man, just such a lovely human being, so we spent a few days relaxing, hanging out and enjoying my final few days in America.

I finally decided Japan and South Korea would be my next adventures, closely beating Cuba, Jamaica and Mexico, so I gave up my return flight to London and I took the fourteen hours flight to Fukuoka in the far south of Japan.

I headed straight to a spa area and town called "Beppu", and for the next three days I spent as much time in hot Japanese onsens/baths as I could, as boy did I deserve it!

Over the next few weeks, I reflected on what was an amazing achievement and a wonderful life changing experience I had on my incredible journey and NFL adventure in the good ole US of A.

Conclusion

A book was never something that entered my mind, as I planned and travelled the six months across America having the time of my life. It was only when people I had met along the way asked me if I was indeed going to tell my story, that a seed was planted, and I'm incredible happy it was, because writing these words and reminiscing about the so many amazing events I encountered on my incredible journey has brought back some wonderful memories, most of which would have certainly been lost, somewhere in the back of my memory banks and completely forgotten.

God knows how I have remembered so much of the finer details to so many of these stories, which I somehow managed to find in the corners of my mind, great memories of all the ups and downs, incredible excitement, total despair and the fcuk ups I had on my tour.

Looking back on my website and the pictures I posted on social media over the length of time on my tour, has been an invaluable help as to jog my memory.

I laugh out load to myself when I wrote about some of the funny things I did, especially the stupid, but I also cringe at some of the hardships I had to endure, and boy there really were so many. I smile, get a shudder and feel a tear developing in my eyes when I remember the so many wonderful people I met along the way, who were sooooo kind to me, full of support and encouragement, something that kept me going through the very difficult times, when coming home really would have been so very very easy to do.

I needed that support and the love I received from these beautiful people so much, to give me the strength and drive to overcome some extremely difficult times and obstacles.

I also feel intense anger towards the many people who offered their services, hands of friendship or support to me before I left home, then basically slapped my face, ignoring and deserting me in a time when I desperately needed their help as to achieve the goals I had set myself.

The amount of messages I sent to these people, mostly NFL and media based, which were never returned is countless, and this pattern continues to this very day. I just want to know WHY people do this? These very same people know exactly what I did on my tour, as they were probably watching me the whole way via social media, as sometimes these very same people would jump into one of my posts from nowhere and to kick me in the bollox, even when they had ingored my pleas for help for months on end.

Silence hurts me a damn sight more than NO ever will. I can easily live with NO.

On reflection, over a year since my tour ended, I now look back on the whole adventure with so much pride and feel I had the most amazing time I could have possibly had, living out my dreams of going to every NFL stadium in the country and indulging in one of my passions in life, American Football.

My tour was not just about American Football, far from it, as I made the effort EVERY SINGLE DAY, to explore and experience as much of every place I visited to the max, checking out as many of the places of interest and sights as possible, ate the local foods, and of course drank the local beers. The only thing I never did was shag the local women, but boy did I bloody try!!!

I went to watch basketball games, baseball, hockey, a college football game, many Arsenal games in Arsenal America bars all over the country, as well as going to many museums, to learn about all things local to where I was at the time.

I attended as many music events as I could, watching local bands, going to music museums or places of interest I could without a car, I played guitar in as many places as I could, singing to anyone who would listen, mainly in hostels, as well as watching the most amazing soundcheck to a concert ever.....Metallica, in San Francisco, the night before Superbowl 50, which was definitely one of the highlights of my entire tour.

I really did live the dream, even though the beginning was so terribly difficult for me, as I felt so ill, anxious and tired after all the research and attempts to make connections into the world of so many sectors, I was completely burnt out, even before I saw my very first game, a game in which I so very nearly missed.

But slowly I recovered, became strong, focused and driven, as well as very very excited. Every new day brought a new adventure, challenge or obstacle, which I always overcame in the end with pure bloody mindedness and determination. In all of the six months I was in the US, even in my darkest hours, I was never going to fail and come home. To me, this was simply not an option, NEVER!

I met so many kind, generous, lovely, crazy, passionate, wonderful, and loving people along the way, people who will be my friends for life, and without these amazing people, my tour would have never been anywhere near as incredible as it was.

You guys were and will always be so many important pieces of the huge overall jigsaw puzzle that my "The Wrong Shaped Balls Tour" was. There really are no words I can write to express how grateful I will always be to you guys, for the love you showered upon me, even though most of you never knew who I was until I arrived into your cities or even at your tailgates. You all made me feel soooooooooo welcome, and for this I would like to say the biggest THANK YOU in the history of thank you's, for making me feel a part of your very special family of football fans, all across America.

I dedicate this book to all my Superfan buddies, especially the guy who started the snowball effect, the amazing Tampa Bay Buccaneers madman Tim "The Captain" Young, and all of their friends whom I met along the way, who were so very kind, courteous and generous to me.

You guys opened so many doors I could have never opened without your help, giving me lifelong friends, wonderful memories and experiences, making this tour, one of the highlights of my life.

To all the people I have slated/slagged off in this book, I'm not gonna apologise to a single one of you, even if you feel I have been a little harsh to you (that's if you even bothered to read it). I can only write what I felt at the time, and what really DID HAPPEN on my travels, as there are no lies, no gossip, just facts. You guys were in positions to have helped me BIGTIME, but for your own reasons, you chose not to. You ignored my pleas for help, and you did nothing, in times where I so desperately needed a contact in a influential place, encouragement, a lucky break, or even just a friendly face or stranger, someone who would give me the platform or forum, to let the NFL world know that I even existed.

This is something I simply cannot forgive you for, as your silence and broken promises really did make my journey so much more difficult than it could, and should have been. When all you people holding the cards could have very easily called in a marker, a favour or two and place me in a favourable position or situation, or even just believed in what I was attempting and supported me, just like YOU said YOU would before I left home, then leaving me high and dry, up shit creek without a paddle, and sometimes in a place, or a situation when I did not really know what my next step was going to be. I had more than a few sleepless nights because of my huge disappointment which manifested from these broken promises.

Now over a year later, I reflect on what might have been, if only just ONE of you, believed in me, a fraction as much as I believed in myself, and my ability to break America with my music, just showing a fraction of interest, maybe made the one call, email or tweet to open up a door of possibility, then maybe I would not be walking round a golf course today, carrying other people's golf clubs, I would be playing at the clubs like Pebble Beach and have a caddie of my own!!!

Or maybe I would be where I should be, playing my guitar on my latest world tour with my band AZBO, or writing catchy pop songs for some latest in vogue boy/girl bands.

I will NEVER NEVER NEVER understand how this crazy or stupid Englishman, living every single NFL fan around the world's dreams of going to every stadium to watch a game in one season, got completely and utterly ignored by EVERYONE connected to the NFL in the UK, and I mean EVERYONE. Talksport were the only ones who gave me any airtime, but they are not exactly NFL connected. I will always be very grateful to them for the brief 4-5 live chats we did, but if only I was just given the platform to have shown the world what I was doing, it really would have been TV gold.

NFLUK had a humongous opportunity to use me as a kind of ambassador, to help spread the word across the pond as to demonstrate exactly how big the NFL has become in the UK, as well as in Europe. They had me BIGTIME, AND FOR FREE. They all knew at NFLUK I would be watching a game at the invitation of Shad Khan, the owner of the Jacksonville Jaguars and the main man behind the biggest potential team (probably in London, my home town) to be the first non American franchise in NFL history, and I was promised much support by NFLUK after my meeting with them before I left for my tour, and they TOTALLY AND UTTERLY IGNORED ME, AND STILL DO TO THIS

DAY. I simply do not understand WHY?

That's why I wanted to write this book, warts and all, and try my very best to tell the whole story of exactly what I endured over six months in my quest for fame, fortune, and fun, as well as trying to be somebody.

I really did give this tour my very best shot, I could not possibly have done anymore with the very limited tools or resources I had in my armoury. All I could do and be, was to be ME, and I sincerely hope that my personality and honestly shines through in this book.

I also hope all the people I touched base with, or crossed paths with all across America, enjoyed my company just a fraction as much as I enjoyed being in theirs.

In the words of a very famous and well respected man, I had a dream, to "Break America", but America nearly broke me, and from the deepest depths of my heart, soul, and mind, it absolutely devastates me to say, that in what I was looking to try to acheive on a professional level.......... I failed miserably.

But on a personal level, I achieved absolutely EVERYTHING. And boy did I have a lot of fun trying!!!!!!

Lets hope this book can maybe reignite the flame, as the world has not seen the last of D-MO. No sir, as I can feel a new adventure coming soon. Watch this space.

Printed in Poland
by Amazon Fulfillment
Poland Sp. z o.o., Wrocław